Nonfiction Classics
for Students

Presenting Analysis, Context, and Criticism on Nonfiction Works

Volume 5

David Galens, Project Editor

GALE®

THOMSON

GALE

Detroit • New York • San Diego • San Francisco • Cleveland • New Haven, Conn. • Waterville, Maine • London • Munich

Nonfiction Classics for Students, Volume 5

Project Editor
David Galens

Editorial
Sara Constantakis, Anne Marie Hacht, Ira Mark Milne, Pam Revitzer, Kathy Sauer, Timothy J. Sisler, Jennifer Smith, Carol Ullmann

Research
Michelle Campbell, Sarah Genik, Tamara Nott

Permissions
Lori Hines

Manufacturing
Stacy Melson

Imaging and Multimedia
Lezlie Light, Daniel William Newell, David G. Oblender, Kelly A. Quin

Product Design
Pamela A. E. Galbreath

ISBN 0-7876-6034-5
ISSN 1533-7561

Printed in the United States of America
10 9 8 7 6 5 4 3 2 1

Table of Contents

Literature: Conversation, Communication, Idea, Emotion

The so-called information age of which we are all a part has given birth to the internet, and so literature—the written word in its many forms—now has vaster, faster avenues in which to circulate. The internet is the latest revolutionary development in communication media. Before the internet, the development of the printing press and the advent of radio and television were equally astonishing events. This great network of circulating words and images amongst persons and populations can be thought of as a vast human conversation.

In conversation, speech arises from the desire to communicate an idea or a feeling or else it follows from an address and is a reply of sorts. How quickly one can formulate a communication or a reply depends upon the nature of the problem or of the address. Does one wish to communicate something simple, such as a command? Or does one wish to meditate on a significant problem or issue in one's personal life? Or in history or science? Is the address a greeting, an email, a painting, a letter, or a novel? Nonfiction works, the subject of *Nonfiction Classics for Students*, are written literary communications of a sustained nature, unlike ephemeral written communications such as emails or memos which are concerned with the immediately occurring events of the day. The length and breadth of the novel form follows from the amount of learning and experience that goes into the making of each novel, and from the amount of information it can convey. Nonfiction works that have become

classics are those which have been particularly moving or influential, or both. These works have changed the way people live, think, and see.

Influential and admired nonfiction works can be thought of as significant events in the traditions in which they are working or to which they are related, traditions such as autobiography, biography, history, science, the essay, and so forth. For example, published diaries such as *Anne Frank: The Diary of a Young Girl* are related to the traditions of autobiography and history. If the diary of this child is so valued by readers it is because, besides being engagingly written, it vividly brings forth an era and a set of world-effecting political disasters and events. Through the words of Anne Frank, the reader enters the world of a bright, hopeful teenager who is, nevertheless, haunted by the fear of her imminent death as the world around her crumbles. To know that this child eventually was captured and died in a concentration camp moves us to be more assiduous and vigilant in our protection of innocents, and we lament this terrible suffering and senseless waste of life.

Yet, if we wish to learn how it was that World War II came about, or who Europe's leaders were and what these leaders' beliefs and ideologies were, then we must turn to the written works which are histories and not autobiographies, works whose subject is not the history of a single person but rather the reconstruction of the social, cultural, and political panorama of the period or age under study. Histories, in turn, are related to the traditions of political and social science. The more polemical or argumentative the history book, the more it is a work of political theory, where facts are important—though not as critical as ideas about how human society works or can be arranged. Through the written word, social and political thinkers and philosophers make their arguments, and societies, cultures, and ways of governing rise and fall.

In the form of nonfiction, scientists make their arguments and present their formulae and technology, and medical and psychological treatments are changed. It is because of the printed, widely disseminated word that women and other minorities win equal opportunity in the world. Ideas change the world, they are a part of our history. Students of literature enter into this vast human conversation and have the opportunity to contribute to it. *Nonfiction Classics for Students* prepares and equips these students so that his or her entry into this conversation is meaningful.

Nonfiction Classics for Students also presents relevant information and discussion about major figures and ideas. As for what makes a particular autobiography or diary stand out, it is often because the story of the single person seems to speak for many or because it is powerfully and beautifully written. While we do not necessarily demand high artistry from some writers of nonfiction prose, we do expect some degree of fluency from those writers practicing the art of the essay, autobiography, or biography. The various reasons why a particular work has been or is admired and its reputation past and current are also discussed in the pages of *Nonfiction Classics for Students*. In presenting students with discussions of a work's artistry and reputation as well as of relevant, related traditions, theories, and ideas, *Nonfiction Classics for Students* models a process of reading and systematic study that a student can apply to any work he or she reads.

What this study of and engagement with a work of literature can produce is either a research paper, which is a presentation of what has been learned, or else it can give rise to a reply, a counter-communication. In composing writing in response to a work, a student participates in and contributes to the vast human conversation. The entries in *Nonfiction Classics for Students* suggest relevant topics for classroom discussion. *Nonfiction Classics for Students* is an aid to students who set out to inform themselves responsibly about a particular nonfiction work. This series equips students to contribute meaningfully to the vast human conversation. Are a writer's ideas productive and useful? Does the book teach us important lessons or move us? Do we detect the circulation of heinous ideologies in our present times that remind us of destructive ideologies and beliefs from the past? In reading and learning and communicating, we engage with history; to the extent that we live by what we learn, we make history when we respond to and act on what we have read.

Carol Dell'Amico
Santa Monica College, Santa Monica, California

Introduction

Purpose of the Book

The purpose of *Nonfiction Classics for Students* (*NCfS*) is to provide readers with a guide to understanding, enjoying, and studying nonfiction works by giving them easy access to information about the work. Part of Gale's "For Students" literature line, *NCfS* is specifically designed to meet the curricular needs of high school and undergraduate college students and their teachers, as well as the interests of general readers and researchers considering specific works. While each volume contains entries on "classic" works frequently studied in classrooms, there are also entries containing hard-to-find information on contemporary pieces, including works by multicultural, international, and women authors.

The information covered in each entry includes an introduction to the work and the work's author; a summary, to help readers unravel and understand the events in a work; descriptions of key figures, including explanation of a given figure's role in the work as well as discussion about that figure's relationship to other figures in the work; analysis of important themes in the work; and an explanation of important literary techniques and movements as they are demonstrated in the work.

In addition to this material, which helps the readers analyze the work itself, students are also provided with important information on the literary and historical background informing each work. This includes a historical context essay, a box comparing the time or place the work was written to modern Western culture, a critical essay, and excerpts from critical essays on the work, when available. A unique feature of *NCfS* is a specially commissioned critical essay on each work, targeted toward the student reader.

To further aid the student in studying and enjoying each work, information on media adaptations is provided, as well as reading suggestions for works of fiction and nonfiction on similar themes and topics. Classroom aids include ideas for research papers and lists of critical sources that provide additional material on each work.

Selection Criteria

The titles for each volume of *NCfS* were selected by surveying numerous sources on teaching literature and analyzing course curricula for various school districts. Some of the sources surveyed included: literature anthologies; *Reading Lists for College-Bound Students: The Books Most Recommended by America's Top Colleges;* a College Board survey of works commonly studied in high schools; a National Council of Teachers of English (NCTE) survey of works commonly studied in high schools; Arthur Applebee's 1993 study *Literature in the Secondary School: Studies of Curriculum and Instruction in the United States;* and the *Modern Library*'s list of the one hundred best nonfiction works of the century.

Input was also solicited from our expert advisory board, as well as educators from various areas. From these discussions, it was determined that each volume should have a mix of "classic" works (those works commonly taught in literature classes) and contemporary works for which information is often hard to find. Because of the interest in expanding the canon of literature, an emphasis was also placed on including works by international, multicultural, and women authors. Our advisory board members—educational professionals—helped pare down the list for each volume. If a work was not selected for the present volume, it was often noted as a possibility for a future volume. As always, the editor welcomes suggestions for titles to be included in future volumes.

How Each Entry Is Organized

Each entry, or chapter, in *NCfS* focuses on one work. Each entry heading lists the full name of the work, the author's name, and the date of the work's publication. The following elements are contained in each entry:

- **Introduction:** a brief overview of the work which provides information about its initial publication, its literary standing, any controversies surrounding the work, and major conflicts or themes within the work.

- **Author Biography:** this section includes basic facts about the author's life and focuses on events and times in the author's life that inspired the work in question.

- **Summary:** a description of the major events in the work. Subheads demarcate the work's various chapters or sections.

- **Key Figures:** an alphabetical listing of major figures in the work. Each name is followed by a brief to an extensive description of the person's role in the works, as well as discussion of the figure's actions, relationships, and possible motivation.

  Figures are listed alphabetically by last name. If a figure is unnamed—for instance, the narrator in *Pilgrim at Tinker Creek*—the figure is listed as "The Narrator" and alphabetized as "Narrator." If a person's first name is the only one given, the name will appear alphabetically by the name. Variant names are also included for each person. Thus, the full name "Richard Monckton Milnes" would head the listing for a figure in *The Education of Henry Adams,* but

listed in a separate cross-reference would be his more formal name "Lord Houghton."

- **Themes:** a thorough overview of how the major topics, themes, and issues are addressed within the work. Each theme discussed appears in a separate subhead, and is easily accessed through the boldface entries in the Subject/Theme Index.

- **Style:** this section addresses important style elements of the work, such as setting, point of view, and narration; important literary devices used, such as imagery, foreshadowing, symbolism; and, if applicable, genres to which the work might have belonged, such as Gothicism or Romanticism. Literary terms are explained within the entry but can also be found in the Glossary.

- **Historical Context:** This section outlines the social, political, and cultural climate *in which the author lived and the work was created.* This section may include descriptions of related historical events, pertinent aspects of daily life in the culture, and the artistic and literary sensibilities of the time in which the work was written. If the piece is a historical work, information regarding the time in which the work is set is also included. Each section is broken down with helpful subheads.

- **Critical Overview:** this section provides background on the critical reputation of the work, including bannings or any other public controversies surrounding the work. For older works, this section includes a history of how the work was first received and how perceptions of it may have changed over the years; for more recent works, direct quotes from early reviews may also be included.

- **Criticism:** an essay commissioned by *NCfS* which specifically deals with the work and is written specifically for the student audience, as well as excerpts from previously published criticism on the work, when available.

- **Sources:** an alphabetical list of critical material used in the compilation of the entry, with full bibliographical information.

- **Further Reading:** an alphabetical list of other critical sources that may prove useful for the student. It includes full bibliographical information and a brief annotation.

  In addition, each entry contains the following highlighted sections, set separate from the main text:

- **Media Adaptations:** a list of important film and television adaptations of the work, including source information. The list may also include such variations on the work as audio recordings, musical adaptations, and other stage interpretations.

- **Topics for Further Study:** a list of potential study questions or research topics dealing with the work. This section includes questions related to other disciplines the student may be studying, such as American history, world history, science, math, government, business, geography, economics, psychology, etc.

- **Compare and Contrast:** an "at-a-glance" comparison of the cultural and historical differences between the author's time and culture and late twentieth-century/early twenty-first century Western culture. This box includes pertinent parallels between the major scientific, political, and cultural movements of the time or place the work was written, the time or place the work was set (if a historical work), and modern Western culture. Works written after 1990 may not have this box.

- **What Do I Read Next?:** a list of works that might complement the featured work or serve as a contrast to it. This includes works by the same author and others, works of fiction and nonfiction, and works from various genres, cultures, and eras.

Other Features

NCfS includes "Literature: Conversation, Communication, Idea, Emotion," a foreword by Carol Dell'Amico, an educator and author. This essay examines nonfiction as a lasting way for authors to communicate as well as the influence these works can have. Dell'Amico also discusses how *Nonfiction Classics for Students* can help teachers show students how to enrich their own reading experiences and how the series is designed to aid students in their study of particular works.

A Cumulative Author/Title Index lists the authors and titles covered in each volume of the *NCfS* series.

A Cumulative Nationality/Ethnicity Index breaks down the authors and titles covered in each volume of the *NCfS* series by nationality and ethnicity.

A Subject/Theme Index, specific to each volume, provides easy reference for users who may be

studying a particular subject or theme rather than a single work. Significant subjects from events to broad themes are included, and the entries pointing to the specific theme discussions in each entry are indicated in **boldface.**

Entries may include illustrations, including photos of the author, stills from stage productions, and stills from film adaptations.

Citing Nonfiction Classics for Students

When writing papers, students who quote directly from any volume of *Nonfiction Classics for Students* may use the following general forms. These examples are based on MLA style; teachers may request that students adhere to a different style, so the following examples may be adapted as needed.

When citing text from *NCfS* that is not attributed to a particular author (for example, the Themes, Style, Historical Context sections, etc.), the following format should be used in the bibliography section:

> "The Journalist and the Murderer." *Nonfiction Classics for Students*. Ed. Elizabeth Thomason. Vol. 1. Farmington Hills, MI: The Gale Group, 2001, pp. 153–56.

When quoting the specially commissioned essay from *NCfS* (usually the first piece under the "Criticism" subhead), the following format should be used:

> Hart, Joyce. Critical Essay on "Silent Spring." *Nonfiction Classics for Students*. Ed. Elizabeth Thomason. Vol. 1. Farmington Hills, MI: The Gale Group, 2001, pp. 316–19.

When quoting a journal or newspaper essay that is reprinted in a volume of *NCfS*, the following form may be used:

> Limon, John. "*The Double Helix* as Literature." *Raritan* Vol. 5, No. 3 (Winter 1986), pp. 26–47; excerpted and reprinted in *Nonfiction Classics for Students*, Vol. 2, ed. Elizabeth Thomason (Farmington Hills, MI: The Gale Group, 2001), pp. 84–95.

When quoting material reprinted from a book that appears in a volume of *NCfS*, the following form may be used:

> Gunnars, Kristjana. "Life as Fiction: Narrative Appropriation in Isak Dinesen's *Out of Africa*," in *Isak Dinesen and Narrativity*, ed. Gurli A. Woods, (Carleton University Press, 1990), pp. 25–34; excerpted and reprinted in *Nonfiction Classics for Students*, Vol. 2, ed. Elizabeth Thomason (Farmington Hills, MI: The Gale Group, 2001), pp. 281–86.

We Welcome Your Suggestions

The editor of *Nonfiction Classics for Students* welcomes your comments and ideas. Readers who wish to suggest works to appear in future volumes or who have other suggestions are cordially invited to contact the editor. You may contact the editor via E-mail at: **ForStudentsEditors@gale.com.** Or write to the editor at:

Editor, *Nonfiction Classics for Students*
The Gale Group
27500 Drake Rd.
Farmington Hills, MI 48331–3535

Literary Chronology

1842: William James is born on January 11 in New York City.

1854: Sir James Frazer is born James George Frazer on January 1 in Glasgow, Scotland.

1869: William Strunk, Jr. is born on July 1 in Cincinnati, Ohio.

1877: G. H. (Godfrey Harold) Hardy is born on February 7 in Cranleigh, Surrey, England.

1888: T. S. (Thomas Stearns) Eliot is born on September 26 in St. Louis, Missouri.

1890: James Frazer's *The Golden Bough* is published.

1899: E. B. White is born on July 11 in Mount Vernon, New York.

1902: William James's *The Varieties of Religious Experience* is published.

1908: Dee Alexander Brown is born on February 28 in Alberta, Louisiana.

1909: E. H. (Ernst Hans Josef) Gombrich is born on March 30 in Vienna, Austria.

1910: William James dies on August 26 in New Hampshire.

1921: Betty Friedan is born on February 4 in Peoria, Illinois.

1930: Kappa Senoh is born in Kobe, Japan, in 1930.

1932: T. S. Eliot's *Selected Essays, 1917–1932* is published.

1936: Abbie Hoffman is born on November 30 in Worchester, Massachusetts.

1940: G. H. Hardy's *A Mathematician's Apology* is published.

1940: Annie Ernaux is born on September 1 in Lillebonne, France.

1941: Sir James Frazer dies in Cambridge, England.

1946: William Strunk, Jr. dies on September 26 in Ithaca, New York.

1947: G. H. Hardy dies on December 1.

1951: Jim Carroll is born on August 1 in New York City.

1955: Mary Karr is born.

1959: William Strunk, Jr. and E. B. White's *The Elements of Style* is published.

1960: E. H. Gombrich's *Art and Illusion: A Study in the Psychology of Pictorial Representation* is published.

1963: Betty Friedan's *The Feminine Mystique* is published.

1965: T. S. Eliot dies in London on January 4.

1970: Dee Brown's *Bury My Heart at Wounded Knee* is published.

1971: Abbie Hoffman's *Steal This Book* is published.

1978: Jim Carroll's *The Basketball Diaries* is published.

1978: E. B. White is awarded a special Pulitzer Prize for his body of work.

1985: E. B. White dies on October 1 in Brooklin, Maine.

1989: Abbie Hoffman commits suicide with a barbiturate overdose on April 12.

1995: Mary Karr's *The Liars' Club* is published.

1997: Kappa Senoh's *A Boy Called H* is published.

1997: Annie Ernaux's *Shame* is published.

2000: Karin Evans's *The Lost Daughters of China* is published.

2001: E. H. Gombrich dies on November 3 in London, England.

Acknowledgments

The editors wish to thank the copyright holders of the excerpted criticism included in this volume and the permissions managers of many book and magazine publishing companies for assisting us in securing reproduction rights. We are also grateful to the staffs of the Detroit Public Library, the Library of Congress, the University of Detroit Mercy Library, Wayne State University Purdy/Kresge Library Complex, and the University of Michigan Libraries for making their resources available to us. Following is a list of the copyright holders who have granted us permission to reproduce material in this volume of *Nonfiction Classics for Students (NCfS)*. Every effort has been made to trace copyright, but if omissions have been made, please let us know.

COPYRIGHTED MATERIALS IN *NCfS*, VOLUME 5, WERE REPRODUCED FROM THE FOLLOWING PERIODICALS:

Arethusa, v. 17, Fall 1984. © The Johns Hopkins University Press. Reproduced by permission.—*Commonweal*, v. CXXIX, March 8, 2002. Copyright © 2002 Commonweal Publishing Co., Inc. Reproduced by permission of Commonweal Foundation.—*Feminist Review*, n. 27, Autumn 1987. Reproduced by permission of the publisher and the author.—*Japan Quarterly*, v. 47, April-June 2000. Reproduced by permission.—*Journal of the West*, v. 39, January 2000. Copyright © 2000 by Journal of the West, Inc. Reproduced by permission of Journal of the West, 1531 Yuma, Manhattan, KS 66502, USA.—*New York Magazine*, v. 28, April 24, 1995, Copyright © 1995 PRIMEDIA Magazine Corporation. All rights reserved. Reproduced with the permission of New York Magazine.—*Nineteenth-Century Prose*, v. 19, Summer 1992. Reproduced by permission.—*Southern Review*, v. 33, Winter 1997. Reproduced by permission of the author.—*The Writer*, v. 114, August 2001. Reproduced by permission of the author.—*Yale Journal of Criticism*, v. 39, Fall 1989. © The Johns Hopkins University Press. Reproduced by permission.

COPYRIGHTED MATERIALS IN *NCfS*, VOLUME 5, WERE REPRODUCED FROM THE FOLLOWING BOOKS:

Horowitz, Daniel. From "The Development of *The Feminine Mystique*, 1957–63," in *Betty Friedan and the Making of "The Feminine Mystique": The American Left, The Cold War, and Modern Feminism*. Edited by Christian G. Appy. Amherst: The University of Massachusetts Press, 1998. Copyright © 1998 by Daniel Horowitz. Reproduced by permission.—Smith, John E. From "Introduction," in *The Varieties of Religious Experience*, by William James. Frederick Burkhardt, general editor; Fredson Bowers, textual editor. Harvard University Press; Cambridge, Mass, 1985. Copyright © 1985 by the President and Fellows of Harvard College. All rights reserved. Reproduced by permission Harvard University Press.—Weinblatt, Alan. From "Adequation as Myth in the Design of Selected

Essays," in *T. S. Eliot and the Myth of Adequation*. UMI Research Press, 1984. Edited by A. Walton Litz. Copyright © 1984 Alan Weinblatt. Reproduced by permission of the author.

PHOTOGRAPHS AND ILLUSTRATIONS APPEARING IN *NCfS*, VOLUME 5, WERE RECEIVED FROM THE FOLLOWING SOURCES:

Aerial view of a village in Normandy, France, photograph. © Roger Ressmeyer/Corbis. Reproduced by permission.—Alighieri, Dante, photograph.—Baudelaire, Charles, illustration. The Library of Congress.—Brown, Dee, photograph by Dee Brown. Reproduced by permission of Dee Brown.—Carroll, Jim, photograph. © Roger Ressmeyer/Corbis. Reproduced by permission.—Constable, John, "The Haywain." 1821. Oil on canvas. National Gallery, London, England. The Art Archive. Reproduced by permission.—DiCaprio, Leonardo, in scene from the 1995 film *The Basketball Diaries*, directed by Scott Kalvert, based on the novel by Jim Carroll, photograph. The Kobal Collection/Island Pictures. Reproduced by permission.—Edwards, Jonathan, engraving. The Library of Congress.—Eliot, T. S., photograph. International Portrait Gallery. Reproduced by permission.—Ernaux, Annie, photograph. © Bassouls Sophie/Corbis Sygma. Reproduced by permission.—Friedan, Betty, photograph. The Library of Congress.—Froines, John, Weiner, Lee, Hoffman, Abbie, Dellinger, David, Davis Rennie, Hayden, Tom and Rubin, Jerry, photograph. AP/Wide World Photos. Reproduced by permission.—General Douglas MacArthur (left) and Japanese Emperor Hirohito standing together during their first meeting at the U.S. Embassy in Tokyo, Japan, photograph. AP/Wide World Photos. Reproduced by permission.—Hirohito, touring bombed area of Tokyo, photograph. Hulton Getty/Liaison Agency. Reproduced by permission.—Hoffman, Abbie, photograph. AP/Wide World Photos. Reproduced by permission.—Hoffman, Abbie, photograph. NY Times collection, © Archive Photos, Inc. Reproduced by permission.—James, William, photograph. The Library of Congress.—Mead, Margaret, photograph. © Bettmann/Corbis. Reproduced by permission.—Sitting Bull, Chief of the Oglala Sioux, photograph. The Library of Congress.—St. John of the Cross.—Suburban housewife sitting on front step, photograph. © H. Armstrong Roberts/Corbis. Reproduced by permission.—Tilley, Eustace, photograph. Originally appeared on the cover of the February 19, 1955, issue of *The New Yorker*. Artwork by Rea Irvin. Copyright © 1955 *The New Yorker Magazine*, Inc. Reprinted by permission. All Rights Reserved.—White, E. B., photograph. AP/Wide World Photos. Reproduced by permission.—Wikes, John (seated, holding "LIBERTY"), engraving by James Moore after a drawing by William Hogarth. Archive Photos, Inc. Reproduced by permission.

Contributors

Bryan Aubrey: Aubrey holds a Ph.D. in English and has published many articles on twentieth century literature. Entries on *A Boy Called H: A Childhood in Wartime Japan*, *The Liars' Club*, and *The Lost Daughters of China: Abandoned Girls, Their Journey to America, and the Search for a Missing Past*. Original essays on *A Boy Called H: A Childhood in Wartime Japan*, *The Liars' Club*, and *The Lost Daughters of China: Abandoned Girls, Their Journey to America, and the Search for a Missing Past*.

Adrian Blevins: Blevins is a poet and essayist who has taught at Hollins University, Sweet Briar College, and in the Virginia Community College system; Blevins's first full-length collection of poems, *The Brass Girl Brouhaha*, is forthcoming from Ausable Press in September of 2003. Original essays on *The Elements of Style* and *The Liars' Club*.

Allison DeFrees: DeFrees has a bachelor's degree in English from the University of Virginia and a law degree from the University of Texas, and is a published writer and an editor. Original essays on *The Elements of Style*, *The Lost Daughters of China: Abandoned Girls, Their Journey to America, and the Search for a Missing Past*, and *Shame*.

Douglas Dupler: Dupler has published numerous essays and has taught college English. Origi-nal essays on *The Basketball Diaries* and *Bury My Heart at Wounded Knee*.

Erik France: France holds an M.S.L.S. from the University of North Carolina at Chapel Hill and a Ph.D. in history from Temple University. He is a librarian, college counselor, and teacher at University Liggett School and teaches writing at Macomb Community College near Detroit, Michigan. Original essay on *The Basketball Diaries*.

Joyce Hart: Hart, with degrees in English literature and creative writing, focuses her published works on literary themes. Entries on *Shame* and *The Varieties of Religious Experience*. Original essays on *The Feminine Mystique*, *Shame*, and *The Varieties of Religious Experience*.

Diane Andrews Henningfeld: Henningfeld is a professor of English at Adrian College and has written widely on contemporary literature for reference and educational publishers. Entry on *Art and Illusion: A Study in the Psychology of Pictorial Representation*. Original essay on *Art and Illusion: A Study in the Psychology of Pictorial Representation*.

Catherine Dybiec Holm: Holm is a freelance writer with speculative fiction and nonfiction publications. Original essays on *A Boy Called H: A Childhood in Wartime Japan*, *A Mathematician's Apology*, and *Shame*.

David Kelly: Kelly is an instructor of creative writing and literature at College of Lake County. Entries on *The Golden Bough* and *Steal This Book*. Original essays on *The Golden Bough* and *Steal This Book*.

Candyce Norvell: Norvell is an independent educational writer who specializes in English and literature and who has done graduate work in religion. Entry on *The Elements of Style*. Original essays on *The Elements of Style* and *The Varieties of Religious Experience*.

Josh Ozersky: Ozersky is a critic and historian. Original essays on *The Liars' Club* and *Steal This Book*.

David Partikian: Partikian is a freelance writer, editor, and English instructor. Entry on *A Mathematician's Apology*. Original essay on *A Mathematician's Apology*.

Ryan D. Poquette: Poquette has a bachelor's degree in English and specializes in writing about literature. Entries on *The Basketball Diaries*, *Bury My Heart at Wounded Knee*, and *The Feminine Mystique*. Original essays on *The Basketball Diaries*, *Bury My Heart at Wounded Knee*, and *The Feminine Mystique*.

Michelle Prebilic: Prebilic writes children's books, analytical essays, and technical publications, and assists students in San Ramon, California, with language and reading skills. Original essay on *The Lost Daughters of China: Abandoned Girls, Their Journey to America, and the Search for a Missing Past*.

Chris Semansky: Semansky is an instructor of literature and writes on literature and culture for various publications. Original essay on *Steal This Book*.

Scott Trudell: Trudell is a freelance writer with a bachelor's degree in English literature. Entry on *Selected Essays, 1917–1932*. Original essay on *Selected Essays, 1917–1932*.

Art and Illusion: A Study in the Psychology of Pictorial Representation

E. H. Gombrich

1960

Art and Illusion: A Study in the Psychology of Pictorial Representation, published in 1960, is one of the most influential books written during the twentieth century on the subject of art. Following the publication in 1950 of his incredibly popular book, *The Story of Art*, Ernst Hans Josef Gombrich consented to give the A. W. Mellon Lectures in the Fine Arts at the National Gallery of Art in Washington, D.C., in 1956. Those lectures became the book *Art and Illusion*. Critics generally agree that this volume, among Gombrich's myriad publications, is his most far-reaching and influential work. Gombrich continued to advocate many of the ideas put forth in this book throughout his life. Indeed, he not only revised the text and wrote a new preface for the second edition of the book published in 1961, he also wrote a new preface for the ''Millennium Edition'' published in 2000, in his ninety-first year.

In *Art and Illusion*, Gombrich poses this essential question: ''Why is it that different ages and different nations have represented the visible world in such different ways?'' Throughout the pages of the book, Gombrich attempts to address this question using science, psychology, and philosophy to help formulate his answer. At the heart of his theory is the notion of ''schemata,'' that is, the idea that the artist ''begins not with his visual impression but with his idea or concept'' and that the artist adjusts this idea to fit, as well as it can, the object, landscape, or person before him or her. Gombrich calls this theory ''making and matching.''

While art critics and historians have developed new ideas about representation since the first publication of *Art and Illusion*, Gombrich and his ideas continue to be a mighty force. Thus, serious students of art and art history find *Art and Illusion* an important and necessary part of their education.

Author Biography

Ernst Hans Josef Gombrich was born in Vienna, Austria, on March 30, 1909, to Karl B. Gombrich, a lawyer, and Leonie Hock Gombrich, a pianist. Gombrich credits his intellectual development to the music in his home. Indeed, Adolf Busch, the leader of the Busch Quartet, was a frequent visitor to the Gombrich home. Leonie Gombrich was also well-acquainted with the great modernist composer Arnold Schoenberg and Sigmund Freud, the father of psychoanalysis.

Although the atmosphere in his home led to his development as a thinker, Gombrich did not follow his mother's footsteps into music but chose rather to study art history at Vienna University. Gombrich said that he made his decision because "art was a marvelous key to the past" (*The Essential Gombrich*). At the university, he studied with the great art historian, Julius von Schlosser. Another important influence in the life of young Gombrich was Ernst Kris, who asked Gombrich to help him write a book on caricature which incorporated the work of Freud.

The rise of Nazism in Germany, however, interrupted the project, and Kris encouraged his Jewish assistant to leave Austria. It was largely due to Kris's urging and his recommendation of Gombrich to the director of the Warburg Institute that Gombrich moved to London in 1936.

When World War II began, Gombrich served as a "radio monitor," working for the British Broadcasting Corporation as part of the war effort. His duty was to listen to and translate German radio broadcasts for the use of the military. With the end of the war, Gombrich returned to the Warburg Institute, becoming its director in 1959.

During the 1950s, Gombrich wrote prolifically and lectured widely. His introduction to Western art, *The Story of Art*, was published in 1950. Since that time over six million copies of that volume have been sold. In 1956, Gombrich gave a series of Mellon lectures in Washington, D.C., choosing as

his subject "Art and Illusion." These lectures were later collected into the book *Art and Illusion: A Study in the Psychology of Pictorial Representation* (1960). Many critics consider this book to be the most influential of Gombrich's works.

Over the next forty-two years, Gombrich published more than twenty books and hundreds of journal articles. Indeed, J. B. Trapp compiled a book-length bibliography of Gombrich's work in 2000, and the list of publications filled more than one hundred pages. His last full-length book, *The Preference for the Primitive*, was published in August 2002.

During his lifetime, Gombrich received many honors and awards. Most notably, he was named a Commander of the Order of the British Empire in 1966, and he was knighted in 1972. Gombrich died in London on November 3, 2001, at the age of 92. He is generally acknowledged to be one of the most influential art historians of all time.

Plot Summary

Part 1: The Limits of Likeness

In the introduction to *Art and Illusion*, Gombrich asks the question, "Why is it that different ages and different nations have represented the visible world in such different ways?" This is the question he attempts to answer in his book. First, however, he provides the reader with a critical account of the history of style and the psychology of representation. That accomplished, he turns to Chapter One, "From Light into Paint." In this chapter, Gombrich notes that the English painter, John Constable said, "Painting is a science." Like Constable, Gombrich believes that science is involved in both the creation and the appreciation of art. He explains the many ways that artists through the years have learned how to represent light in their paintings.

Chapter Two, "Truth and Stereotype," begins with a discussion of how a picture can be neither true nor false. By contrast, the caption of the picture can be so judged. Further, when artists undertake to paint pictures, they start not with what they see, but rather with an idea or concept, what Gombrich calls a "schema." The schema, Gombrich argues, is "the first approximate, loose category which is gradually tightened to fit the form it is to reproduce.'' Thus, in portraying a person, animal, landscape, or thing in art, the artist must have a starting point, for, as Gombrich states, ''you cannot create a faithful image out of nothing.'' Furthermore, an artist will tend to look for ''certain aspects in the scene around him that he can render. Painting is an activity and the artist will therefore tend to see what he paints rather than paint what he sees.''

Part 2: Function and Form

The first chapter, ''Pygmalion's Power,'' covers the connection between the artist and creation. It is not, Gombrich argues, the artist's aim to make a likeness, but rather to create something real. In so doing, the artist particularizes, starting with an idea, say, of chairness, and particularizing this idea until it represents the chair that is the subject being painted.

The section continues with a description of how Greek art moves from a stiff rendering to more ''lifelike'' rendering. Gombrich asserts that this is a perfect illustration of the theory that making always occurs before matching. That is, an artist (or culture) begins with a schemata, which the artist then adjusts and corrects to make it ever closer to the appearance the artist wants the creation to have. Gombrich then moves to an exploration of ''the basic geometric relationships that the artists must know for the construction to be a plausible figure.'' In so doing, he considers the Medieval and Renaissance ''drawing books'' which used geometric shapes as formulas for teaching drawing. These books, according to Gombrich, ''form a reservoir of formulas or schemata which spread throughout Europe.'' He compares these books with basic vocabularies; in a very real sense, they provided artists with the building blocks of the language of art. For Gombrich, however, ''effective portrayal'' is only possible when the artist goes beyond the formulas and demonstrates a willingness ''to correct and revise.''

Part 3: The Beholder's Share

The chapters of this section focus primarily on the role of the viewer in the reading of an artist's image. Gombrich relates this tendency to what psychologists call ''projection,'' wherein a person projects onto another person his own desires and personality. A beholder of art will likewise project his or her catalog of classifications onto the images created by artists. In this case, the artist creates and the beholder projects; both are necessary ingredients in the making of meaning.

In an important section of Part Three, Gombrich turns to ''the perception of symbolic material,'' using his experience as a British Broadcasting Corporation monitor during World War II. He discusses how our knowledge and expectations contribute to what we actually see or hear. The greater the likelihood a given word will occur, the less likely we are to listen. In Gombrich's own words, ''Where we can anticipate we need not listen. It is in this context that projection will do for perception.'' The beholder, in other words, closes the gaps through projection, the act of projecting the image he or she expects into ''an empty or ill-defined area.''

Likewise, incomplete visual images push the beholder into completing the image: artists provide the hints that the viewer must use to complete the image. Artists cannot represent every detail of reality, no matter how painstakingly they work. It is the creation of an illusion that allows the beholder to fill in the details. Gombrich asserts, ''I believe that this illusion is assisted by what might be called the 'etc. principle,' the assumption we tend to make that to see a few members of a series is to see them all.'' Furthermore, the expectation of the viewer as well as the context of the image affect the meaning the viewer assigns to an image.

In Chapter 8, ''Ambiguities of the Third Dimension,'' Gombrich tackles perspective and the ''rendering of space in art.'' The problem, of course, is how one renders the illusion of three dimensions in a two-dimensional medium such as painting. A painting clearly has only two dimensions, height and width. In order for the painting to have depth, however, the painter must engage in the art of perspective. As Gombrich argues, ''One cannot insist enough that the art of perspective aims at a correct equation: it wants the image to appear like the object and the object like the image.'' He further asserts that perspective depends on certain expectations of the beholder, most notably on the size-distance ambiguity. That is, a viewer estimates the distance of an object by how large or small it appears. Image makers take advantage of this assumption. In opposition to Gestalt psychologists, Gombrich asserts that interpreting perspective in a flat image is a learned behavior rather than an innate skill. In this, he draws on the work of philosopher Sir Karl R. Popper. Painting, then, that accounts for perspective is illusionist painting, meant to be viewed by a beholder who "willingly suspends disbelief" and sees what he or she expects to see, not what is really in the painting. Gombrich credits the rise of cubism, by contrast, to a "radical attempt to stamp out ambiguity and to enforce one reading of the picture—that of a man-made construction, a colored canvas."

Part 4: Invention and Discovery

After recapitulating his stance on the power of interpretation, Gombrich next offers a brief history of perception, referring to Bishop Berkeley, John Ruskin, and Roger Fry. Gombrich argues that "all thinking is sorting, classifying." Further, after summarizing Ruskin's position, he rejects Ruskin's notion of "the innocent eye." For Gombrich, this term is impossible, for no human eye can be "innocent," that is, unaffected by experience and attitude. The eye is connected to the brain and the experience of the viewer, and the perception of any viewer will make meaning using that connection. For the painter, this process is deeply affected by his or her ability to view his or her subject in terms of the traditions of painting. Gombrich writes, "A painting, as Wölfflin said, owes more to other paintings than they owe to direct observation."

In this section, Gombrich also touches on the importance of experimentation. With Constable, who viewed art as natural philosophy (or science), Gombrich agrees that "only experimentation can show the artist a way out of the prison of style toward a greater truth. Only through trying out new effects never seen before in paint could he learn about nature. Making still comes before matching."

Gombrich differentiates himself from nineteenth-century models of both art and science, however, models that believed in the possibility of neutral observations, or what is known as the belief in induction. Gombrich argues that "pure observation" is impossible in either science or art. Rather, all observation is predicated by hypotheses, which in turn, create expectations. Only through testing hypotheses do scientists and artists amend their already perceived picture of reality.

In one of the most interesting chapters of the book, Gombrich turns to a discussion of caricature, drawing on his earlier work with Ernst Kris. He uses the work of Freud and other psychologists in the exploration of the "minimum clues of expression," those features that allow a viewer to see a face in

only a few lines. Finally, Gombrich closes this section and the book with a discussion of the similarities between "the language of words and visual representation," concluding "the true miracle of the language of art is not that it enables the artist to create the illusion of reality. It is that under the hands of a great master the image becomes translucent."

Key Figures

Gertrud Bing

Gertrud Bing was Fritz Saxl's assistant and a close associate of Gombrich. She is noted for writing the introduction to the Italian translation of Aby Warburg's papers.

Karl Bühler

Gombrich recalls in autobiographical writing that the work of Karl Bühler was an important influence on his own thinking, especially in *Art and Illusion*. Bühler was a professor of psychology in Vienna during the 1920s and 1930s. In addition, he was an early writer on the Gestalt theory of thinking, which worked its way into the theory of art through Rudolf Arnheim. Perhaps most important for Gombrich was Bühler's model of communication and his theory of language.

John Constable

John Constable, an early nineteenth-century English landscape painter, was one of the first painters to consider science and observation in his understanding of painting. Gombrich devotes a chapter of *Art and Illusion* to Constable and his experiments with paint and light, noting that Constable remarked, "Painting is a science and should be pursued as in inquiry into the laws of nature. Why, then, may not landscape painting be considered as a branch of natural philosophy, of which pictures are but the experiments?" Constable's "experiments" were an attempt to render paintings that ever more closely resembled the appearance of the scene in front of him. Gombrich suggests that it is only through experiments like Constable's that a painter can make his or her "way out of the prison of style toward a greater truth." Constable's work provides for Gombrich an easily understood illustration of some of the theories he propounds in *Art and Illusion*.

Sigmund Freud

Sigmund Freud, the great Viennese psychologist and the founder of modern psychiatry, attempted to chart in a scientific manner the mysterious regions of the human psyche. Gombrich's interest in psychology and perception necessarily led him to both intersect and interact with Freud's theories. Gombrich specifically cites Freud's study of the work of Leonardo da Vinci.

Roger Fry

Roger Fry was an English art critic and painter whose work became important for Gombrich as he wrote *Art and Illusion*. According to Gombrich, Fry hailed "impressionism as the final discovery of appearances." For Fry, the difficulty in painting was in the "difficulty of finding out what things looked like to an unbiased eye." Furthermore, the only way an artist can represent reality is through, ironically, the "suppression of conceptual knowledge." An important theorist for the history of art, Fry died in 1939 while delivering a series of lectures on art history.

William Hogarth

Gombrich states that William Hogarth was one of the most interesting of eighteenth-century artists. Hogarth produced a series of prints called *Characters and Caricatures*. According to Gombrich, Hogarth believed that "caricature rests on comic comparison" while character "rests on the knowledge of the human frame and heart." Gombrich includes many of Hogarth's drawings to illustrate his understanding of caricature.

Ernst Kris

Ernst Kris, a close friend of Gombrich, worked as keeper of the Department of Applied Art in the Kunsthistorisches Museum. Kris was part of Sigmund Freud's inner circle, and he taught Gombrich about psychology. Together, Kris and Gombrich worked on a book on caricature, using Freud's theories. Kris was acutely aware of the rise of the Nazi Party, and he urged Gombrich to leave Austria to find work. Kris recommended Gombrich to Fritz Saxl who was the director of the Warburg Institute in London.

Gombrich credits Kris for both his fortuitous move from Austria and his first job.

Karl R. Popper

Karl Popper was a highly influential philosopher. Born in Vienna like Gombrich, Popper also immigrated to London. The two men became close friends, and Gombrich openly acknowledged his indebtedness to Popper's thinking. Most notably, Popper rejected what he called the "bucket theory of mind." That theory suggests that the human mind is an empty container, like a bucket, waiting to be filled up with sensory data. This theory defines the mind as a passive recipient. Popper opposed his own "searchlight theory" of mind to the bucket theory. He hypothesized that gathering information about the world is an active proposition, one that requires the mind to match internal schemata with sensory information from the world. Most importantly for Popper and for Gombrich is the notion of "activity." The beholder is an active participant in meaning making.

John Ruskin

John Ruskin was a prominent Victorian art and literary critic as well as a social reformer. Born in 1819, Ruskin became interested as a child in art and architecture. Ruskin is perhaps most famous for his multi-volume work *Modern Painters*. This book exerted tremendous influence on nineteenth-century artists, critics, and viewers. Ruskin championed the work of artist J. M. W. Turner as well as the Pre-Raphaelites. Although Gombrich shows Ruskin a great deal of respect throughout *Art and Illusion*, he also clearly rejects many of Ruskin's ideas about art, most notably, that an artist should look at nature with an "innocent eye" in order to best represent nature in art.

Fritz Saxl

Fritz Saxl was the director of the Warburg Institute in London. He hired Gombrich in 1936 in order to help him publish the papers and letters of Aby Warburg.

Julius von Schlosser

Julius von Schlosser, Gombrich's art history teacher at the University of Vienna, was the author of an important text *Die Kunstliteratur*. Although Gombrich recalls that he was not a good lecturer,

Schlosser influenced the young student, particularly in the seminars he held in the Vienna Museum's Department of Applied Arts. In these seminars, Schlosser would ask his students to talk about artifacts contained in the museum. In addition, he also gave seminars in problems, in which he would ask his students to consider a problem in art history. For example, he asked Gombrich to discuss hand gestures represented in a medieval law manuscript. Gombrich dedicates *Art and Illusion* in part to Schlosser's memory as his teacher.

Aby Warburg

Aby Warburg was the founder of the Warburg Institute in London, which housed his books, papers, and letters after he was forced to move from Hamburg with the rise of Nazism. The Institute's main focus was the study of cultural history, particularly of the Italian Renaissance. Warburg collected everything he could find that would help contemporary scholars understand the social milieu of the Renaissance in Italy. His interest in art was not for art's sake but rather for what it could reveal of the times in which it was created. Gombrich wrote the definitive biography of Aby Warburg in 1970.

Themes

Perception

One of Gombrich's most important themes in *Art and Illusion* is that of perception. Technically, perception is the process through which a human being gains sensory information about the physical world. Twentieth-century scientists and philosophers have been intrigued by perception and by the way the brain takes sensory information and transforms it into a meaningful picture of the world. For example, how is it that humans have depth perception? How does the brain translate the images on the retina of the eye into a three-dimensional picture of the world? Those who study perception debate whether interpretation of sensory data is innate or learned. In other words, they explore whether people are born with the ability to understand sensory information or must learn how to interpret sensory information through trial and error.

Gombrich, with his close attention to science and philosophy, is intrigued by questions of perception. He writes:

The question of what is involved in "looking at nature"—what we today call the psychology of perception—first entered into the discussion style as a practical problem in art teaching. The academic teacher bent on accuracy of representation found, as he still will find, that his pupils' difficulties were due not only to an inability to copy nature but also an inability to see it.

For Gombrich, then, perception is more than merely a physiological response to light and dark or patterns and background. Perception and the ability to "see" nature depend not only on the correctly functioning eyes, retinas, and brains but also on the viewers' experiences and training. This point is important for both the artists and the beholders, since they all must use their powers of perception to derive meaning from the work of art.

Illusion

Illusion is one of the most puzzling phenomena in the study of perception and by extension, the study of representational art. In the case of an illusion, perception is not dependent on how the receptors in the eye and brain react, nor is it dependent on the object being perceived. That is, a human being is able to make meaning from an image independent of the physiology of either the eye or the image. For example, when children see a picture of a duck in a book and are asked what they see, they will answer, "A duck." Now, the light receptors in the children's retinas do not fire in an identical way when the children see a real duck outside in a pond and when they see a picture of a duck. Likewise, the picture does not resemble in any real way the duck in the real world. The picture, therefore, is illusory; it is paint on paper. Yet the human mind is capable of perceiving the paint on paper as a duck. Gombrich uses the following example to illustrate the ways that human beings confront illusions each day and still make sense of the world:

If the reader finds this assertion a little puzzling, there is always an instrument of illusion close at hand to verify it: the bathroom mirror. I specify the bathroom because the experiment I urge the reader to make succeeds best if the mirror is a little clouded by steam. It is a fascinating exercise in illusionist representation to trace one's own head on the surface of the mirror and to clear the area enclosed by the outline. For when we have actually done this do we realize how small the image is which gives us the illusion of seeing ourselves "face to face." To be exact, it must be precisely half the size of our head.

Clearly, the perception of representational art requires the use of illusion. It is only through illusion that the viewer recognizes the landscape in the painting to be the landscape out the window. One of Gombrich's main purposes, then, in *Art and Illusion* is to investigate how artists, across time, have developed the particular illusions that they have in order to render their paintings ever closer to the perception of "reality."

Style

Narration

Narration is the telling of a series of events, often in chronological order, and generally in a way that creates a story. Certainly, in his *Story of Art*, Gombrich creates a narrative that gives a sense of unity to the history of art. Likewise, in *Art and Illusion*, Gombrich's stated purpose is to "explain why art has a history." Although he begins with the nineteenth-century painter John Constable, Gombrich soon jumps back to early Greek art to begin his story of "making and matching." Gombrich's narration is one that traces the way artists attempting to represent reality employ tradition and experimentation in their art. Furthermore, Gombrich includes in his narration both the changes artists make and the changes viewers must make as they are confronted with new ways in which art represents reality. Because Gombrich chooses to use a narrative style, the book itself, while long and at times technical in vocabulary, is nonetheless accessible to a general audience.

Metaphor

A metaphor is a figure of speech that expresses an idea through a comparison between two objects or ideas. In *Art and Illusion*, Gombrich uses language as a metaphor for art. That is, he suggests that artists develop a "vocabulary" of artistic schemata that allow them to build their images. But the schemata available in any historic period can constitute a limitation within which artists tend to work. He likens the schemata to a writer's vocabulary that both builds and limits the work the writer creates. Indeed, through his use of the words "language of representation," "reading," "grammar," and "articulation," for example, Gombrich further builds the metaphor that art and language are comparable forms of human communication and representation.

Topics for Further Study

- Find several of John Constable's paintings. Demonstrate your understanding of Gombrich's analysis by applying his theories to the paintings you find. Write a short paper detailing what you note.

- Research Sir Karl R. Popper's "searchlight theory." How does this theory coincide with Gombrich's approach to art?

- Find examples of several optical illusions. Using Gombrich's theories, explain why the illusions deceive the eye. What accounts for our "reading" of the image in the way we do?

- Read "Illusion and Reality," the first chapter of Leonard Shlain's *Art and Physics* (1991). Compare and contrast the ideas you find in this chapter with the ideas you find in *Art and Illusion*.

Historical Context

Gombrich and World War II

Although Gombrich did not publish *Art and Illusion* until 1960, many of the ideas contained in the book had root in Gombrich's experiences in London during World War II. Critics and biographers alike note this fact, as does Gombrich himself in Part Three of the book. Gombrich developed many of his ideas about perception while working for the British Broadcasting Corporation in their Monitoring Services division. His job was to listen to and translate all radio transmissions coming out of Germany for the six years of the war. Through this surveillance, the British government hoped to gain information about what the Germans had planned. However, often the transmissions were faint or garbled. As a result, Gombrich became skilled at "filling in the gaps," so to speak. As he notes in *Art and Illusion*,

> Some of the transmissions which interested us most were often barely audible, and it became quite an art, or even a sport, to interpret the few whiffs of speech sounds. . . . It was then we learned to what an extent

Compare & Contrast

- **1950s:** Post–World War II Europe is still recovering from the uncertainties and devastation of the war years. The growth of the Soviet Union and ongoing hostilities between Eastern Bloc countries and NATO lead to the Cold War.

  1990s: Although the Cold War ends with the breakup of the Soviet Union in the 1980s, fear and uncertainty continue to dominate the international political scene.

- **1950s:** Growth of technology as well as the ''miracles'' of science lead to a general belief in the application of the scientific method to all fields of endeavor, including art criticism and history.

  1990s: While technology continues to grow at unprecedented rates, there is evidence of some distrust of science, most notable in the critiques of science offered by scholars such as Bruno Latour.

- **1950s:** Gombrich's theories are set forth in the 1956 Mellon lectures, appearing in 1960 as the book *Art and Illusion*. Its influence on the field of aesthetics is formidable, according to Dieter Peetz.

  1990s: Dieter Peetz identifies Nicholas Wolterstorff's *Works and Worlds of Arts* (1980) as having ''innovative power and imaginative sweep'' for those involved in philosophical aesthetics at the close of the twentieth century.

- **1950s:** Literary critics known as the ''New Critics'' identify the quality of a text by its ''universal significance.'' That is, this theoretical school posits that meaning and value of a text is contained within the text, is true across cultures and eras, and thus does not depend on context.

  1990s: Reader response critics, basing their analysis on the seminal work of the 1970s and 1980s of theorist Stanley Fish, among others, argue that there is no innocent reader and that the meaning of a text is created by a collaborative effort between writer and reader.

---

our knowledge and expectations influence our hearing. You had to know what might be said in order to hear what was said.

For Gombrich, making sense of what he heard required that he match what he heard to his internal catalogue of possible German word combinations. The difficult part of this process, of course, was that he could not let his expectations lead him to fabricate illusions about what he heard. He needed to use both his knowledge of possibilities and his critical faculties. As the receiver of auditory information, Gombrich needed to consider both the words and their contexts while keeping in mind his own expectations.

Without this wartime experience of listening and translating, Gombrich may not have considered how expectations affect recipients of sensory input and he may not have considered the importance of the psychology of perception for the understanding of art. Viewers of art fill the gaps of what they see based on their internal catalogues of what is possible. Moreover, according to Gombrich, ''the context of action creates conditions of illusions.'' Context and expectation shape the meaning viewers impart to works of art, just as Gombrich and his colleagues used context and expectation to interpret German messages.

The Significance of Art and Illusion

Critics are nearly unanimous in their assessment of *Art and Illusion*: they consider it to be the most influential work of Gombrich's life, and they consider Gombrich to be the most influential art historian of the twentieth century. Indeed, it is difficult to overestimate the significance of this work. Perhaps most important is its attempt to connect the appreciation of artistic creation with the scientific study of perception. Gombrich carefully builds a case that the meaning of a work of art resides in a collaborative communication between individual artists and viewers. He rejects the notion of a transcendent *zeitgeist,* or spirit of the times, that creates artistic representation. Furthermore, he destroys Ruskin's nineteenth-century notion that one could view a piece of art with "an innocent eye." For Gombrich, the innocent eye was an impossible abstraction. What the artist sees and what the beholder sees are both inextricably shaped by cultural and historical contexts. That this notion seems so patently obvious in the early twenty-first century is an indication of how thoroughly Gombrich's work has been assimilated by all studies of art history.

Critical Overview

When *Art and Illusion* was published in 1960, it was immediately hailed as a masterpiece. In an obituary appearing in *Art in American* shortly after Gombrich's death in 2001, critics Stephanie Cash and David Ebony provide a retrospective of Gombrich's work. They hail *Art and Illusion* as Gombrich's "most influential volume." They also note that Gombrich "rejected the notion that artistic change was the result of a collective mind or 'spirit of the age.' Instead Gombrich preferred to focus on how individual artists dealt with specific technical problems."

The importance of a book can often be determined by the amount of critical response it generates over the years, and by this standard, *Art and Illusion* has demonstrated its ongoing influence from the time of its publication to the present day. Moreover, the intellectual heft of those scholars who respond to a book also increases a book's prestige. In the case of *Art and Illusion*, some of the most respected philosophers of the era respond to and use Gombrich's work.

For example, Nelson Goodman, an important theorist in the area of perception, refers to Gombrich in his classic *Languages of Art* (1968). Although Goodman and Gombrich had what has been described by Malcolm Bull as an "uneasy relationship," Goodman nonetheless acknowledges Gombrich's accomplishments in *Art and Illusion*: "Gombrich . . . has amassed overwhelming evidence to show how the way we see and depict depends upon and varies with experience, practice, interests, and attitudes."

The longevity of Gombrich's work is also impressive, and a number of late twentieth-century

scholars continue to engage *Art and Illusion*. Bull, for example, in "Scheming Schemata," an article published in the July 1994 issue of *The British Journal of Aesthetics,* is interested in using the work of both Gombrich and Goodman to develop a new theory of pictorial representation.

In another important article appearing in the Winter 1998 issue of the *The Journal of Aesthetic Education,* Leslie Cunliffe links Gombrich's theories and social constructivism. He argues, "In *Art and Illusion*, Gombrich convincingly demonstrates that it is the symbolic representations embedded in a given culture that give rational purpose to the work of artists, providing the necessary direction, visual codes, strategies, and critical feedback mechanisms that enable them to create art."

Norman Turner in the Spring 1992 issue of *The Journal of Aesthetics and Art Criticism* starts with Gombrich's assertions about perspective in *Art and Illusion* and suggests questions that still need to be addressed. He writes: "The purpose of this essay is to take up these questions. In elaborating them, what stands forth is that perspective operates, like other schema of representation, not to literally replicate the actual world, but as what might well be called a species of visual trope."

Perhaps no other scholar has done more investigation of Gombrich's work than Richard Woodfield. The writer of many articles on Gombrich and the editor of many important collections of Gombrich's work, Woodfield summarizes Gombrich's arguments in *Art and Illusion* and identifies succinctly many of the critical approaches to *Art and Illusion* in his introduction to a collection of essays, *Gombrich on Art and Psychology* (1996). He concludes the chapter by asserting, "the area between psychology and linguistics, whose subject is the visual image, needs something better than contemporary popular semiotics to deal with it. Gombrich's use of Bühler has resulted in great gains, but, as he has frequently said, it is not method which offers a way forward, but a sense of the problems which need to be solved."

Criticism

Diane Andrews Henningfeld

Henningfeld is a professor of English at Adrian College and has written widely on contemporary

"The Haywain," 1821 oil by John Constable, whose treatment of painting is discussed by Gombrich

literature for reference and educational publishers. In this essay, Henningfeld compares the role of the beholder in the theories of E. H. Gombrich with the role of the reader in the theories of reader response literary critics.

Throughout his book *Art and Illusion: A Study in the Psychology of Pictorial Representation*, writer E. H. Gombrich compares painting to language. The comparison offers him a useful metaphor: he is able to speak of an artist's vocabulary, the grammar of art, and the syntax of painting. Gombrich's primary argument is that an artist builds his or her representation of reality through the use of schemata, or formulas, which function in much the same way that vocabulary functions in the verbal representation of reality. Furthermore, he suggests that only certain combinations of schemata are available to an artist at any particular time, just as there are only certain combinations of English words that can work together in an intelligible English sentence.

While Gombrich's argument is persuasive, not all scholars agree with this analysis. For example, Svetlana Alpers in her essay "No Telling, with Tiepo," published in the collection *Sight and Insight,* (1994) states bluntly, "It is a matter of common sense that image is different from a text, that painting is not language." She goes on to discuss the role of narrative in painting and the ways story telling and painting differ.

Alpers' essay notwithstanding, there are striking similarities between Gombrich's theory of "reading" a painting and the theory of reading a text developed by reader response theorist Stanley Fish. The starting point for exploring these similarities is to return to Gombrich's experiences during World War II and to Part Three of *Art and Illusion*, "The Beholder's Share."

Gombrich reports that his experience as a radio monitor during World War II, working for military intelligence by listening to and translating German broadcasts, greatly affected his understanding of perception. Often, the broadcasts he listened to were faint and difficult to understand. However, Gombrich and his associates became skilled at "filling in the gaps." That is, because Gombrich had particular experiences and understood the context of the broadcast and the language, he was able to fill in the spaces where he could not clearly hear the words. There are, he argues, only certain words and ideas that are possible given the contexts.

What Do I Read Next?

- Gombrich's *The Story of Art,* published in 1950, remains the best selling work of art history ever written, with over six million copies sold by 2002. Gombrich masterfully shapes the history of art into a clear, chronological narrative.

- *The Essential Gombrich* (1996), edited by Richard Woodfield, is a treasure trove of Gombrich's best writing. It includes excerpts from Gombrich's major works, interviews, journal articles, and musings. Woodfield provides cogent introductions as well as a valuable list of books of interest for each selection. This compilation is a must-read collection for every student interested in Gombrich's work.

- French intellectual Didier Eribon and Ernst Gombrich collaborated on the book *Looking for Answers: Conversations on Art and Science* (1991). The book includes extended interviews and conversations between the two men.

- Leonard Shlain's *Art and Physics: Parallel Visions in Space, Time, and Light* (1991) is a highly readable alternate vision of art. Shlain, a surgeon, pairs breakthroughs in art with breakthroughs in physics.

Likewise, when he discusses the beholder's role in the reading of an image, he argues that the beholder brings with him or her a certain range of experiences and knowledge that allow him or her to understand a painting. In addition, Gombrich discusses the way that a painter can leave out portions of a painting and merely provide hints at what actually belongs there. The viewer completes the painting by seeing what is not there. An example of this phenomenon occurs when an artist paints part of a tree at the edge of a painting. While only part of the tree actually appears on the canvas, the beholder will see the entire tree because of his or her horizon of expectation and the hints left by the painter.

Likewise, for Stanley Fish and reader response critics, the reader of a text fills in the gaps left by the writer. How the reader fills in these gaps is largely dependent on the reader's background, experience, horizon of expectation, and context, as well as the hints the writer puts into the text. For reader response critics, readers do not so much interpret texts as create them; making meaning is a collaborative effort between the reader and the writer. An unread text, necessarily, is a meaningless text. Further, just as a beholder of a painting will finish incomplete images in a painting, a reader of a text will finish incomplete thoughts or development in a text.

Second, Gombrich suggests that in order for a beholder to understand a painting, he or she must share some of the traditions and cultural background of the artist. That is, the artist and the viewer must share some common language. Gombrich famously rejects Ruskin's notion of the "innocent eye," the notion that one can observe a painting from a completely objective and neutral stance. Rather, Gombrich argues that there is no innocent viewing of a work of art. A reader's background and learning will largely determine how much meaning the reader derives from the art.

Fish would agree with this position. Reader response critics argue there are many possible readings for a given text, and any reading is dependent on the reader's background and experience. Consequently, there are some things a text simply cannot mean at a given time or place, simply because the context and vocabulary do not exist to make such a reading possible. For example, prior to World War II, critics could not read Shakespeare's *The Merchant of Venice* with knowledge of the Holocaust. Similarly, critics cannot now read *The Merchant of Venice* without knowledge of the Holocaust. Another instance might be the common Oedipal reading of *Hamlet,* a reading that would have been impossible before Sigmund Freud developed the vocabulary necessary to create the reading.

Caricature of John Wilkes by William Hogarth referred to by Gombrich in the section on caricatures

Another point of comparison between Gombrich and reader response theorists is their objection to formalism. A formalist approach to art and literature argues that all meaning inheres in the work of art or text itself, regardless of the artist or the viewer. For the formalist critic, the text is complete unto itself; its meaning, when the "true" meaning is derived, will be true for all people in all times. Gombrich's notion of "making and matching" is in clear opposition to a formalist approach. He argues that both the artist and the beholder use schemata to help them understand both reality and art. The meaning of a work of art does not begin with the paint on the canvas but rather with an idea in the artist's mind. Likewise, the beholder of the work of art must draw on categories and expectations within his or her mind to make sense of the art. In a similar manner, a reader of a text will draw on his or her own understanding of literary conventions and cultural backgrounds to make sense of a text.

Reader response theorists and Gombrich would also agree on the pleasure derived in the reading of a text or the viewing of a work of art. Gombrich describes one such pleasure: "what we enjoy is not so much seeing these works from a distance as the very act of stepping back, as it were, and watching our imagination come into play, transforming the medley of color into a finished image." Likewise, as one reads a text, the individual details, through the imaginative response of the reader, form themselves into a coherent whole. The pleasure for the reader, then, is derived from watching the text come into focus.

Finally, Gombrich and reader response critics would find themselves in agreement with what they imagine happens when a beholder encounters an image or text for a second time. Both would agree that one can never recover the initial encounter with an image or text and that all subsequent encounters will be informed by the first. Thus, a reader who knows that both Romeo and Juliet die at the end of their famous play will read the play differently from a naive reader who has not yet encountered this information. In the same way, once a beholder sees particular details of a painting, he or she cannot go back to the time when he or she did not notice these details. Subsequent readings are always built on earlier ones, and the meaning of the image or text changes with the reading.

For students in the early twenty-first century, such privileging of the reader or the beholder might seem intuitively commonsensical. That this is true suggests the great power that both Gombrich's and Fish's ideas have had on meaning making. For both, an encounter with a work of art, whether it is a visual image or a text, requires active participation on the part of the beholder, not passive appreciation. As Gombrich writes, "What we called the 'mental set' may be precisely that state of readiness to start projecting, to thrust out the tentacles of phantom colors and phantom images which always flicker around our perception." Meaning making is hard work, but it is in the work that the art becomes art.

Source: Diane Andrews Henningfeld, Critical Essay on *Art and Illusion: A Study in the Psychology of Pictorial Representation,* in *Nonfiction Classics for Students,* Gale, 2003.

Sources

Alpers, Svetlana, "No Telling, with Tiepolo," in *Sight and Insight,* edited by John Onians, Phaidon, 1994.

Bull, Malcolm, "Scheming Schemata: Pictorial Representation in Theories of E. H. Gombrich and Nelson Goodman," in the *British Journal of Aesthetics,* Vol. 34, No. 3, July 1994, pp. 207–18.

Cash, Stephanie, and David Ebony, Obituary for E. H. Gombrich, in *Art in America,* Vol. 90, No. 1, January 2002, p. 134.

Cunliffe, Leslie, "Gombrich on Art: A Social-Constructivist Interpretation of His Work and Its Relevance to Education," in *Journal of Aesthetic Education,* Vol. 32, No. 4, Winter 1998, pp. 61–77.

Fish, Stanley, *Is There a Text in This Class? The Authority of Interpretive Communities,* Harvard University Press, 1980.

Gombrich, E. H., *Art and Illusion: A Study in the Psychology of Pictorial Representation,* The A. W. Mellon Lectures in the Fine Arts, Vol. 5, 2d ed., Princeton University Press, 2000.

———, "The Mask and the Face: The Perception of Physiognomic Likeness in Life and Art," in *Art, Perception, and Reality,* by Julian Hochberg, Max Black, and E. H. Gombrich, Johns Hopkins University Press, 1972.

Goodman, Nelson, *Languages of Art: An Approach to a Theory of Symbols,* Bobbs-Merrill Company, 1968, p. 10.

Turner, Norman, "Some Questions about E. H. Gombrich on Perspective," in the *Journal of Aesthetics and Art Criticism,* Vol. 50, No. 2, Spring 1992, pp. 139–50.

Woodfield, Richard, ed., *The Essential Gombrich,* Phaidon Press, 1996, pp. 28–36.

———, *Gombrich on Art and Psychology,* Manchester University Press, 1996, p. 19.

Further Reading

Gombrich, E. H., *The Image and the Eye: Further Studies in the Psychology of Pictorial Representation,* Cornell University Press, 1982.

In a companion volume to *Art and Illusion,* Gombrich takes as his subject "the perceptual basis of art, psychology, and visual phenomena." In this book, he further refines his theories.

———, *Meditations on a Hobby Horse,* 4th ed., Phaidon, 1985.

In this collection, Gombrich considers how the activity to which an image or object is put informs the meaning a person derives from the image or object. Thus, a broom in a corner is just a broom until a child chooses to use it as a horse.

Preziosi, Donald, ed., *The Art of Art History,* Oxford University Press, 1998.

Preziosi has collected the essential theoretical texts of art history as a discipline. In addition, he has included helpful introductory chapters for each section of his text.

The Basketball Diaries

Jim Carroll

1978

The publication of Jim Carroll's diary, entitled *The Basketball Diaries: Age Twelve to Fifteen* (1978), had been eagerly awaited. The book, which is generally referred to by its main title alone, had started appearing in excerpt form throughout the late 1960s and early 1970s in various literary publications. Carroll claimed that the diaries were written at the time in which the events related took place. However, some critics wondered how much the diaries were edited before publication, especially since the book includes many outrageous incidents. Regardless of its authenticity, the book made a statement when it was published. Some people at that time were glorifying the image of life in the 1960s urban counterculture. Carroll's gritty diary was explicit; it took readers inside the real world of drug addiction, male prostitution, and crime in 1960s New York.

The book also discussed what life was like for war babies—people who grew up under the constant fear of nuclear annihilation during the Cold War—and the difficulty in remaining neutral in the 1960s antiwar debate. *The Basketball Diaries* has become Carroll's best-known work, especially after the release of a 1995 film adaptation starring Leonardo DiCaprio. In 1987, Carroll published a sequel, *Forced Entries: The Downtown Diaries, 1971–73.*

Nonfiction Classics
for Students

National Advisory Board

Author Biography

Jim Carroll was born in New York City on August 1, 1951. When he was growing up on the tough streets of Manhattan, Carroll pursued careers as a basketball player and writer. While Carroll's massive drug use as a teenager extinguished any hope of his becoming a basketball star, his poetry about these drug experiences put him on the road to literary stardom. After the publication of his first two poetry collections, *Organic Trains* (1967) and *Four Ups and One Down* (1970), Carroll's poetry was relatively unknown outside underground circles. That changed with the publication of his third poetry collection, *Living at the Movies* (1973). By this time, Carroll was also making a name for himself with his autobiographical prose writing, which had begun appearing in various literary magazines in the late 1960s and early 1970s.

In 1978, these disjointed prose writings were collected in one limited-edition volume, entitled *The Basketball Diaries*, which was reprinted in larger numbers in 1980. The book established Carroll's literary career and gave him name recognition that he translated to success in other areas. The most notable of these was Carroll's music career. Patti Smith, one of Carroll's former girlfriends, encouraged him to make the transition from poet to rock musician, as she had done. In 1980, the same year that *The Basketball Diaries* went into wide distribution, the Jim Carroll Band released its first album, *Catholic Boy*, which featured the hit single, "People Who Died." The song, which lists Carroll's many friends who died from murder, suicide, drug overdose, and other unnatural causes, is generally acknowledged as the high point of Carroll's musical career. In 1995, "People Who Died"—along with several other songs by Carroll or his band—was included on the soundtrack of the film adaptation of *The Basketball Diaries*.

During the 1980s, Carroll released another poetry collection, *The Book of Nods* (1986), and his second collection of diaries, *Forced Entries: The Downtown Diaries* (1987). Neither of these books was as successful as *The Basketball Diaries*, which continued to be Carroll's best-known work. In 1992, Carroll released a spoken-word musical recording entitled *Praying Mantis*, and in 1999 he published a nonfiction book entitled *Permissive Bargaining and Congressional Intent: A Special Report*.

Besides these two works, most of Carroll's publications after the 1980s were poetry collec-

Jim Carroll

tions. These include *Fear of Dreaming: The Selected Poems of Jim Carroll* (1993) and *Void of Course: Poems 1994–1997* (1998). Carroll lives and works in New York City, where, as of 2002, he is working on his first novel.

Plot Summary

Fall 1963

In the first entry of *The Basketball Diaries*, a thirteen-year-old Carroll uses a fake birth certificate from his coach, Lefty, to get into a twelve-and-under basketball league. Carroll and his friends sniff cleaning fluid to get high, steal purses, and steal from another basketball team. On Halloween, they attack the neighborhood girls with flour-filled socks then get drunk and use rock-filled socks to break windows. Lefty catches some of his players sniffing glue, but Carroll dumps his before getting caught. Carroll and his family move into their new apartment in the tip of Manhattan. Carroll and the gang get drunk, but one of them drinks too much and has to get his stomach pumped.

Winter 1964

Carroll, a non-Catholic, is forced to go to confession at his new Catholic school. He attends a funeral for one of his friends who dies in a glue-sniffing accident. Carroll scores high on a test but is punished for lack of effort. He describes his first experience with heroin, which he believes is nonaddictive. He steals clothes from a department store and smokes marijuana with one of the older guys in his new neighborhood. A priest in Carroll's school spanks a student's naked buttocks behind closed doors and is sent away after the student's brother labels the priest a homosexual. Carroll's mother finds and destroys a bag of Carroll's marijuana.

Spring & Summer 1964

Carroll talks about the caves near his new apartment building, where he goes to smoke marijuana. He describes the rush he gets late at night while masturbating naked on the roof of his building. Carroll and his friends have a huge party in the woods, jump off a cliff into the Harlem River, and steal basketballs from the park house. Carroll loses his job as a seller at Yankee Stadium as a result of his drug use. Carroll and his friends steal liquor from their school that is intended for an American Legion party. He describes a sexual encounter with a girl at his friend's house.

Fall 1964

Carroll has trouble adjusting to the strict etiquette at the new private school that he is attending on a basketball scholarship, but he impresses his classmates with his confidence and athletic ability. During a routine trip with his gym class to Central Park, Carroll almost gets caught smoking marijuana. He notes the futility of the school's symbolic Thanksgiving fast for hunger. He describes a sexual encounter with a communist girl.

Winter 1965

Carroll accidentally exposes himself during a basketball game. He starts hanging around Headquarters, an apartment that hosts all of the local drug users. He drinks codeine cough syrup to get high. He describes his recurring fantasy about shooting a machine gun in class. He goes to a Communist Party meeting but is not impressed. He steals money from the wrestling team. Carroll and some of his team members take drugs that severely affect their game performance.

Spring 1965

Carroll gets picked up by a person who turns out to be a male transvestite. He talks about a kleptomaniac friend, Bobby Blake, who gets high and breaks into a closed ice cream parlor. Carroll's mother receives a notice from his principal about Carroll's bad grades and behavior problem. Blake gets high again, and this time he breaks into a clothes store and starts handing out free clothes to passersby, including the police who take him away. Carroll and a friend skip class to shoot up heroin in a basement, and they nearly get caught by the police. A little girl talks with Carroll about his antiwar views.

Summer 1965

Carroll describes how he hustles homosexuals for money, and he says that his hustles have gotten weird lately. He and several friends find a half-dead, naked woman who has committed suicide by jumping out of a window. Carroll describes the bathroom at Grand Central Terminal, where men from all walks of life go to look at other men and masturbate. He recalls the first time he saw transvestites naked, when he was about nine years old. He talks about his fear of atomic war. Carroll and his friends get high and steal food from a restaurant. He gets high on a train and becomes paranoid that the other passengers are going to throw him off. He gets a case of gonorrhea, a sexually transmitted disease, and goes to an underground doctor in Harlem to get a shot and some pills. He realizes that he is not in control of his growing heroin addiction, but he says that he better get in control if he wants to do well in school and basketball.

Fall 1965

Carroll describes what it is like growing up as a war baby, living in constant fear of nuclear war. He says that getting high at Headquarters is the only way he can avoid getting involved in war politics. He notes that narcotics police steal most of dealers' drugs for themselves. He takes some LSD, a hallucinogenic drug also known as acid. The police raid Headquarters after a noise complaint. Carroll takes more acid and watches a moon eclipse. He describes his experiences during a massive electrical blackout. Carroll gets high and has sex with his latest rich girlfriend. He says heroin is so addictive that addicts will risk using a filthy needle in order to shoot up. Carroll talks about his parents, saying that they try to draw him into arguments and political debates. He gets frustrated with the ineffectiveness of peace marches.

Winter 1966

Carroll has another classroom-shooting fantasy. He says his fear of atomic warfare has lessened but that he is still paranoid. He talks about his experiences during the National High School All Star Basketball Game, when he is groped by Benny Greenbaum, a homosexual college scout. Carroll explains his passion for writing about New York. Carroll describes what it is like shooting up and says that it is getting hard to concentrate on his writing. Carroll's drug habit continues to affect his basketball performance. He talks about an older woman with whom he has been having an affair; the rich divorcée pays for his drug habit and in return she makes him engage in abnormal sexual acts. Carroll talks about a junkie friend who is in prison for two years. Carroll and a friend get swindled by a drug dealer. Carroll buys heroin from a new dealer and begins to like the vomiting that comes as a side effect. He finds out that one of his old friends is in prison for a drug-related murder. Carroll gets sent to Riker's Island Juvenile Reformatory for three months for heroin possession.

Spring & Summer 1966

Carroll's headmaster intervenes and Carroll gets out of Riker's after one month. A friend offers him a shot of heroin, and Carroll is unable to refuse. Carroll has a bad acid trip and decides to stick to heroin. Since most heroin dealers have been arrested, he buys some methadone instead; while he is waiting for it to take effect, he notes that he is not in control of his addiction. Carroll hustles a homosexual. He defines the three types of junkies. Carroll and a group of friends steal a Porsche, but it gets towed before they can return with a buyer. Carroll and a friend steal raffle books from the American Legion then sell them door to door. In the process, they run across an older woman who has sex with them. They use their earnings to buy a spoon of cocaine. Carroll and a friend eat peyote, another hallucinogenic drug.

Carroll tries to give up heroin abruptly and describes his withdrawal symptoms in detail. Carroll steals some heroin from a friend and starts shooting up again. He goes to a drug-therapy session but soon returns to using heroin. Carroll talks to a junkie friend who has also been trying—and failing—to quit. Carroll and a friend go to New York's Chinatown to get heroin. In the last diary entry of the book, Carroll surfaces from a four-day high, realizing that he wants to be pure.

Media Adaptations

- In 1994, *The Basketball Diaries* was adapted as an abridged audiobook by Audio Literature. The audio diaries are read by the author. The same audiobook is also available as an audio download from audible.com, an on-line audiobook retailer.

- *The Basketball Diaries* was also adapted as a film in 1995 by Island Pictures and New Line Cinema. Directed by Scott Kalvert, the film featured Leonardo DiCaprio as Carroll. It also featured Lorraine Bracco, Mark Wahlberg, Juliette Lewis, Ernie Hudson, and a small role for Carroll himself. The film, which is set in the 1990s, retains much of the book's 1960s language and slang, giving the film an anachronistic feel. It is available on DVD from Ryko Distribution and contains many special features, including interviews with several cast members and an anti-drug trailer.

Key Figures

Bobby Blake

Bobby Blake is one of Carroll's junkie friends who gets high and performs ridiculous, illegal acts.

Mr. Bluster

Mr. Bluster is the principal at the Catholic private school Carroll attends on scholarship. Bluster gets Carroll released early from Riker's juvenile prison.

Brian Browning

Brian Browning is one of Carroll's junkie friends and is one of two men who rent the apartment that serves as Headquarters—the local junkie hangout. When Carroll is strung out and needing a heroin fix, Browning goes to get it for him while Jim waits with his older lover. Browning notes that junkies curl up into fetal positions because they are trying to get back to the womb.

Jim Carroll

Carroll is the author and narrator of *The Basketball Diaries*, an autobiographical account of Carroll's coming of age on New York's tough streets. In the first entries, Carroll is a thirteen-year-old who has had limited experience with sex, drugs, and crime. Carroll is also a novice basketball player in his first organized league. All of these aspects of his life change rapidly. He becomes a star basketball player, winning a scholarship to a rich private school. He has many heterosexual experiences and starts using increasingly harder drugs. His heroin addiction starts out small, and he lies to himself about being able to control it. However, as his addiction grows, it changes the quality of every other aspect of his life. He starts committing more crimes, including stealing cars, in order to finance his drug habit. In addition, he makes money by selling his body to homosexuals and older women. As his use of heroin and other drugs grows to include cough syrup, various kinds of pills, methadone, cocaine, and LSD, drugs become the central focus of his life, replacing even his love of basketball. In fact, his massive drug use destroys his dream of playing professional basketball and eventually lands him in juvenile prison. At the end of the diaries, Carroll surfaces from a four-day heroin high and laments about how low he has sunk in life. He says that he only wants to be pure.

Over the course of the diaries, Carroll is exposed to several cultural and political issues. He makes scathing attacks on hypocrisy. He condemns the U.S. use of the communist scare as a justification for building more nuclear weapons and engaging in the Vietnam War. He notes that poor junkies like him do not have the same treatment programs or escape options as middle-class or rich junkies have. He exposes the hypocrisy of narcotics police, who keep most confiscated drugs for themselves—to sell it on the streets. Ultimately, he predicts the publication of *The Basketball Diaries*, in which he intends to expose these views and facts.

Carroll's Father

Carroll's father is largely absent in the diaries. Even when he and his father talk, the conversation generally ends badly. Carroll is against the Vietnam War, while his father is for it. Also, Carroll wears his hair long like other members of the counterculture, something that bothers his father and his father's friends, who goad Carroll's father into picking fights with his son.

Carroll's Mother

Carroll's mother is largely absent in the diaries. She finds a bag of her son's marijuana, but Carroll fools her into thinking that he does not have a drug problem. When he is in Riker's juvenile prison, she does not come to see him.

Carroll's Older Lover

Carroll describes an affair he has with an older woman, a rich divorcée who makes Carroll engage in bizarre sex acts in exchange for paying for his drug habit. However, when she tries to force a strung-out Carroll to have sex with her, he breaks off the affair.

Marc Clutcher

The junkie Marc Clutcher is one of Carroll's basketball teammates. Along with Carroll and Anton Neutron, Clutcher performs poorly on the team because of his drug use. With others, Clutcher witnesses the woman who tries to commit suicide by jumping out of a window. He also smuggles peyote back from Mexico.

Deborah Duckster

Deborah Duckster, one of Carroll's neighborhood friends, is a model. When Willie gets too drunk one night, he lunges for her, and she kicks him in the groin, knocking him out. Duckster witnesses the woman who tries to commit suicide by jumping out of a window.

Benny Greenbaum

Benny Greenbaum is a homosexual college scout who travels with Carroll's high school team to some games. Greenbaum pays one of the team members to perform oral sex and gropes Carroll in his hotel room—under the pretense of fitting Carroll for a college uniform.

Lefty

Lefty is Carroll's basketball coach in the Biddy League; Carroll suspects that Lefty is a homosexual, since Lefty gropes his players.

Jimmy Mancole

Jimmy Mancole is one of Carroll's junkie friends. When the police raid Headquarters after a noise complaint, Mancole retaliates against the woman next door, whom he assumes made the complaint. Mancole and Carroll almost get caught shooting up in the park, and then they are swindled by a Mexican drug dealer. Mancole gives Carroll his first heroin shot when Carroll gets out of Riker's and helps Carroll mug people in the park.

Anton Neutron

The junkie Anton Neutron is one of Carroll's basketball teammates. Along with Carroll and Marc Clutcher, Neutron allows drug use to affect his performance on the team.

Willie

The junkie Willie is one of Carroll's old basketball teammates. Willie is the first person who smokes marijuana with Carroll at school. Willie gets so drunk one night that he is rushed to the hospital to get his stomach pumped. Willie gets revenge on an assailant by spiking the person's soda with a dangerously large amount of crystal amphetamine.

Themes

Escape

From a very early age, Carroll tries to escape his tough existence on the streets of New York by pursuing other activities that bring him enjoyment. At thirteen, he begins playing basketball in the Biddy league, his first organized league. Give that he has natural athletic ability, basketball quickly becomes a lifestyle for him, which leads to minor fame and a basketball scholarship to a rich, private school. However, in the process, he also engages in self-destructive activities, such as stealing, drinking, and doing drugs. On one occasion, Carroll and some of his teammates take pills that they think will improve their performance, but the pills do the opposite. Says Carroll: ''My legs began to get the feeling someone slit a nice little hole at the top of my thighs and poured in a few gallons of liquid lead.'' Carroll and his fellow drug-using teammates get kicked out of the game, an occurrence that happens more frequently as Carroll's addiction worsens.

Ultimately, the physical side effects of massive drug use, coupled with Carroll's arrest for drug possession, destroy his dream of playing professional basketball—one of his few chances of escape from his street existence. Carroll notes that street users like him find it hard to escape a heroin addiction; they do not have the support networks or financial means of rich users, who can ''take off to the Riviera'' if they feel their addictions are getting too strong. Carroll has a conversation with a friend and notes that a junkie on a high often curls up like a fetus. Carroll's friend thinks this is an indication of heroin's power to give junkies a sense that they can escape to the ultimate comfortable, secure place. ''That's what it's all about, man, back to the womb.''

Addiction

Carroll's heroin habit starts out small, what he calls a '''Pepsi-Cola''' habit, but his addiction eventually gets out of control—a fact that he recognizes when he tries to stop using heroin and finds that he cannot. He is physically ill from his addiction, but the hardest part is trying to avoid the little voice in his head that keeps telling him to have just one more hit of heroin. ''I got to do something to off that little voice, I can gladly take sore muscles but my mind can't handle the monkey back there.'' Unfortunately, the monkey, the voice of Carroll's addiction, is so strong that he continues his habit. This is so even when he has to use dirty needles to shoot up. He notes a certain needle, stashed in a park, that many local junkies share. Says Carroll, ''it's the filthiest spike you ever could see.'' However, despite this fact, ''there is not one bit of hesitation in drawing your shot into that harpoon and shoving it into your mainline.'' Even unpleasant side effects like vomiting—a side effect of a certain brand of heroin he gets—become part of the experience, and he grows to like it. ''I puke four times a day and I love it now. Puking's the newest thing on the junk scene.''

Sexuality

Carroll's diaries offer several examples of his potent and varied sexual experiences. When he is around nine years old, he has his first transvestite experience. At thirteen, he gets into the habit of masturbating while watching the stars from the roof of his apartment building. He is excited by ''the possibility of being caught in a situation where there is no possibility of explaining yourself.'' At thirteen, he notes how his coach tends to fondle him and his teammates. ''I'm too young to understand about homosexuals but I think Lefty is one.'' This igno-

Topics for Further Study

- On an enlarged map of Manhattan, plot the approximate dates and locations for the major events in the book. Research the history of these areas and try to find other, highly publicized events that took place in these areas. Plot these dates and descriptions as well.

- Watch the film adaptation of *The Basketball Diaries* and compare it to the book.

- Find another region in the 1960s that experienced as much drug use, prostitution, and crime as New York. Write a two-page portrait of what

life was like for individuals who grew up in this area during this time.

- Research the current drug problem in the United States, and compare it to the drug problem in the 1960s. What methods of enforcement have been used in each time period to slow or stop the sale and use of drugs? What has been the economic impact of the drug problem in each era?

- Choose a professional athlete, from any point in history, who has been caught using drugs. Write a biography about this person, including whether the athlete used drugs as a teenager and what happened to this person when he or she was caught.

---

rance does not last long. Carroll initially pursues heterosexual encounters for pleasure and avoids homosexuals. However, once Carroll becomes hooked on heroin, his addiction is so strong that he starts selling his body to homosexuals for drug money. With the exception of one case in the diaries, in which he gets a ''strange pleasure [from] . . . this naughty act of perversion for profit,'' Carroll is disgusted by these encounters.

Also, in the beginning of the diaries, Carroll does not mind getting rid of a drug high to have sex. For example, before he goes to one party, he drinks some codeine cough syrup. However, when he meets a girl there, he perceives ''sexual overtones creeping about, so I figured I better go into the bathroom and throw up the medicine to bring me down a bit, in order to get it up a lot.'' However, as Carroll's heroin addiction gets worse, getting heroin becomes more important than anything else, including sex. On one occasion, Carroll breaks up with his older lover when she tries to initiate sex with him while he is strung out from a heroin withdrawal and waiting for a friend to bring him his fix. ''I told her she had no idea how I felt and to just let me lie down and sweat out the wait. Her slightest touch set little stinging grenades off in my head.''

Style

Diary

A diary details the events in one's life as a series of periodic entries. *The Basketball Diaries* is composed of ten sections, one for each season—in some cases two seasons—from Fall 1963 to Summer 1966. Each section is composed of five to twenty-six separate entries. Most diaries are kept for personal reasons and are not intended for publication. As a result, the diarist may jump around and discuss many topics, instead of developing one major plot, as other kinds of storytellers do. At first glance, *The Basketball Diaries* appears to follow this episodic format, since each short entry describes a separate event. However, collectively, these entries describe Carroll's coming-of-age transformation—from a healthy, relatively naïve juvenile delinquent into a strung-out, culturally aware, heroin-addicted criminal.

Setting

The events take place in the 1960s in New York City, primarily Manhattan, a small island that contains within its small area some of the world's richest and poorest people. Carroll, a boy from the poor section of New York, is able to use his basketball talent to get into a local, rich private school. He also dates rich young girls, something that he says his friends from the poor part of the city would not believe. "I'm gonna bring all the dirt heads from old Madison Square Boy's Club up here some night: they'll freak out in one second." If he were living in some other U.S. cities, where the physical distance between rich and poor is often greater, it would be harder for him to do this. In addition, New York is notorious for its high crime rate and its drug abusers. In fact, as Carroll notes, his diaries "have the greatest hero a writer needs, this crazy . . . New York." Finally, as the largest American city and one which contained a significant number of landmarks and economic centers, New York—especially Manhattan—was thought to be a prime target for a nuclear warhead during the Cold War, a fear that Carroll expresses on several occasions.

Language

The Basketball Diaries is conspicuous for its graphic profanity. Many entries include at least one profane word, and in some cases, Carroll uses several. These profane words are used to describe sexual acts—in which case he uses many—and are often used for emphasis, even when describing relatively normal events. Carroll also includes a lot of slang—a type of language used in everyday life by common men and women, typically those in the lower or working classes. Slang words are often established words that have been given different meanings. For example, in the English language, a "spade" is a gardening tool. However, in street slang, a spade is an African American. This term is derogatory, which is another common characteristic of slang words. Sex, drugs, and alcohol are three areas in which slang is often used. For example, Carroll refers to sexual intercourse as "nooky," calls condoms "scumbags," and refers to breasts as "knocks." Marijuana is "weed" or "grass," while heroin is "scag." A "spiller" is someone who acts like he has drunk more than he has, and someone who is drunk is "smashed." These are just some of the countless examples of slang in the book.

Imagery

The imagery in the diaries is also graphic. For example, Carroll and his friends come across a woman who has committed suicide by jumping out of a window. Says Carroll: "I spot a long deep gorge in her ankle and it's oozing blood in slowmotion spurts." Besides violent images, Carroll also uses graphic imagery to describe his sexual experiences. For example, as he is about to say goodbye to his girlfriend before basketball practice one day, he states that she "socks her tongue in my mouth and grinds her sweet bottom up against me." Since Carroll has forgotten to wear a jock strap that day, his resulting erection makes it look "like [he] was shoplifting bananas." Drug imagery is also graphic, particularly the images associated with shooting up heroin. On one occasion, Carroll describes what it looks like when he shoots up: "Just such a pleasure to tie up above that mainline with a woman's silk stocking and hit the mark and watch the blood rise into the dropper like a certain desert lily."

Historical Context

The Cold War

The U.S. use of atomic bombs on Japan ended World War II in 1945, and ushered in the atomic age. After these demonstrations, several countries, including the Soviet Union, rushed to create and test their own atomic bombs. As tensions between the communist Soviet Union and the democratic United States increased, the U.S. government began a policy of backing smaller foreign countries that were in danger of being overthrown by Soviet-backed groups. The resulting tension between the Soviet Union and the United States—and between communism and democracy in general—was labeled the Cold War, and for good reason. Although much of the period was technically spent in peace, the pervasive feeling of suspicion and paranoia that was generated by this clash of superpowers made many feel that they were fighting a war. In the United States, the public was well aware that one mistake on either side could inadvertently trigger World War III. In the diaries, Carroll describes on many occasions what it was like growing up as a "war baby" in a major city during the Cold War, living in constant fear that he was going to die in a nuclear attack:

> It's always been the same, growing up in Manhattan. . . . the idea of living within a giant archer's target . . . for use by the bad Russia bowman with the atomic arrows.

Vietnam and the Antiwar Movement

Although the peak years of the Cold War were over by the 1960s, the U.S. fight against communism in foreign countries continued. The United

Compare & Contrast

- **1960s:** Young American men are sent, often through the draft and against their will, to fight in the Vietnam War. Some seek to escape the horrors of guerilla war by using illicit drugs like marijuana and heroin—the latter of which is cheap and readily available in Southeast Asia.

  Today: Following terrorist attacks in New York and Washington, D.C., the United States engages in a war against terrorism, including military engagements in the Middle East. The terrorist attacks spark a patriotic response, and many young men and women choose to enlist in the armed forces.

- **1960s:** The use of illicit drugs spreads into the mainstream United States. The counterculture movement of the 1960s and 1970s helps to promote this increased use of drugs, especially marijuana and LSD. Heroin, which is used by junkies (drug addicts), is often avoided by hippies.

  Today: The heroin-related deaths of River Phoenix, Kurt Cobain, and other prominent celebrities spark a national awareness of heroin abuse. Although the use of illicit drugs is still a problem in the United States, drug use has dropped by nearly 45 percent since its peak in the late 1970s.

- **1960s:** Sexual freedom becomes a hallmark of the decade. Pregnancy is less a concern with the increased use of birth-control pills. Likewise, some sexually transmitted diseases, like gonorrhea, can often be treated by easily obtained prescription antibiotics.

  Today: Although U.S. youth still engage widely in sexual activity, the risks today are much greater as a result of Acquired Immune Deficiency Syndrome (AIDS), a disease that is generally transmitted through unprotected sex, the sharing of drug needles, and blood transfusions.

States had been supporting South Vietnam for decades in its conflict against Ho Chi Minh's communist forces in North Vietnam. Most Americans were unaware of this involvement, since U.S. soldiers in Vietnam were disguised as advisors. However, in 1965, the United States escalated its involvement, adding fifty thousand new ground troops to the twenty-three thousand already stationed in Vietnam. At this point, the U.S. public was more informed about what was going on, and a massive antiwar movement began. Many people, like Carroll, were forced to take a side in this conflict.

The Counterculture in the 1960s

Carroll, like many other members of the counterculture—a group of people who rebelled against the U.S. capitalist establishment—was against the war. The counterculture grew as many people, especially American youth, became hippies or junkies. Hippies wore their hair long, dressed in deliberately shabby clothes, and believed in nonviolent forms of antiwar protest such as sit-ins and peace marches. Hippies tended to use recreational drugs, particularly marijuana and LSD; they believed these drugs freed their minds and gave them better understanding about the human condition. Junkies shared many characteristics with hippies, however, junkies like Carroll were mainly interested in getting high, and were not opposed to violence and crime. In fact, as Martin Gilbert notes in his book, *A History of the Twentieth Century, Volume Three: 1952–1999:* ''The need to supply and finance the drug habit, if necessary by theft and violence, undermined the moral outlook of many individuals.''

Critical Overview

By the time *The Basketball Diaries* was published in a limited-edition book in 1978, and again in wider distribution in 1980, it was already a hit with underground readers. Literary critics soon followed suit. Many of them, such as Jamie James in his 1980 review of the book for *American Book Review,* discuss the gritty nature of the book. As James notes, it is "a blow-by-blow account of a season in Hell." James, like many other critics, was impressed by the literary skill of the young Carroll. Says James of the book, it "is a literary miracle; a description of the formation of an artistic sensibility written by the artist, not in retrospect, but in the process." Several other critics also note Carroll's talent. Says Barbara Graustark of Carroll in her 1980 review of the book for *Newsweek:* "His terse wit, with its archly contrived naïveté, transformed a tale of teen-age rebellion into a contemporary classic."

The Basketball Diaries received additional notice when the Jim Carroll Band released its first album, *Catholic Boy,* in 1980. The album's lyrics were rough and dark, like his diaries, and several music critics commented on the book in the course of reviewing the album. In his 1981 review of the album for *Stereo Review Magazine,* Steven Simels calls the book "a scary, mordantly funny odyssey along the dark underbelly of the Sixties, a virtuoso performance that ought to be must reading for those who still tend to romanticize the counterculture."

The Basketball Diaries also received favorable critical attention in 1987, when it was reprinted to coincide with the publication of its sequel, *Forced Entries.* The same was true in 1995, when the book was reprinted to coincide with the film adaptation of the book. This time around, with the help of a tie-in cover featuring actor Leonardo DiCaprio, the book landed on the bestseller list. Some critics, like Lewis MacAdams in his 1995 profile of Carroll for *Entertainment Weekly,* praised the book again. MacAdams notes "the miracle of Jim Carroll," a boy who "wrote like an angel, creating a transcendent autobiography." Others, like Wayne Jebian, in his review of the book for the *Columbia Journal of American Studies,* note how the book's graphic language did not turn off many readers, as one suspected it might. Says Jebian: "Words that might bore or disgust if spouted by a dirty old man sitting on your couch instead shock and amaze when uttered by a tender-aged youth in a pre-political correctness era." For Cassie Carter, the graphic quality of Carroll's life is what leads to his genius and his literary success. In her 1996 article for *Dionysos: Literature and Addiction Quarterly,* Carter notes that *The Basketball Diaries* "performs an amazing feat of alchemy, transforming the waste of Carroll's adolescence into a victory."

Still, despite its legendary status with both reviewers and popular readers, the book is not without its critics. Most of the negative criticism has centered on the book's graphic depictions of sex, violence, and drug use, and the book has been banned in certain areas as a result. In addition, in 1997, following Michael Carneal's killing spree in West Paducah, Kentucky, the film version of *The Basketball Diaries* came under fire. Carneal claimed that a scene depicting one of Carroll's classroom-shooting fantasies from the book had encouraged him to kill his classmates.

Criticism

Ryan D. Poquette

Poquette has a bachelor's degree in English and specializes in writing about literature. In the following essay, Poquette discusses Carroll's use of extremes in The Basketball Diaries.

Jim Carroll fills his autobiographical diaries with graphic language and imagery and includes situations that take the reader from one extreme emotion to another. Says Jamie James, in his 1980 review of the book for *American Book Review,* "When it is funny it is hilarious, reminiscent of Lenny Bruce at his best. When it hits a blue note, it is harrowing."

An example of a hilarious incident is Carroll's observation of the melodrama during a going-away party for Gums, a local military recruit. Gums's family makes a big fuss about his potentially dangerous involvement in the Vietnam War, but Carroll finds out that the boy is really only going to serve six months in a local reserve unit. As Carroll notes, "from the scene here you'd think old Gums had to assassinate Chairman Mao with a water pistol." On another occasion, Carroll talks about a kleptomaniac friend, Bobby Blake, who gets high, breaks into a closed ice cream parlor to steal the cash register, and ends up making himself an ice cream soda instead. He is still drinking it when two police arrive, "not believing for sure anything they see, Bobby not budging but biting away, cash register wrecked on the floor and the grilled cheese sandwich which Bobby forgot about burning to a crisp."

Carroll also describes some extremely gut-wrenching episodes, such as the various sex acts he has to engage in to support his drug habit, which lately have involved "handcuffs, masks, snakes

Leonardo DiCaprio as Jim in the 1995 film version of the work

(yeah, that's right, real ones), chains, whips, last week a guy had a pet parrot that he had eat grapes out of my pubic hair.'' One of his heterosexual encounters leads to getting a case of gonorrhea, which he describes in excruciating detail: ''it's quite a bringdown waking up with your underwear a mass of red-brown blotches, all stiff as cardboard except where the gooey fresh blobs are.'' Some of the most harrowing descriptions in the diaries are associated with Carroll's heroin use. When he resurfaces after a four-day high, he notices two sets of needles next to him ''in the slightly bloody water in the plastic cup on the crusty linoleum, probably used by every case of hepatitis in upper Manhattan by now.'' When Carroll goes through heroin withdrawal, his descriptions get even more disturbing. On one occasion when he is strung out, he waits the hour that it will take for a dose of methadone—a slower-acting drug—to take effect. ''You bet that's a long hour too, with them cold flashes shooting up from your crotch right out your skull and your muscles feeling like wood and your energy to a sad eyed drip.''

Besides the funny or disturbing descriptions, the situations themselves are often extreme. Even ordinary situations, like the many basketball games that Carroll plays, fall into one of two extremes—he either plays well or he takes drugs and plays horribly. In the beginning of the diaries, Carroll is a basketball star. The diaries are filled with several accounts of Carroll and his team dominating lesser teams. For example, at one point, Carroll's team is shorthanded while playing another team, but ''it was the lamest bunch of saps ever put on a court, this other team, and we wiped them out by at least forty points.'' On another occasion, Carroll's team is ''ahead by 23 points'' by the end of the first four minutes of the game. As for Carroll himself, he easily impresses girls at his games. For example, he describes one game, during which the girls in the stands open their legs wider and wider as they let out ''oohs'' and ''ahhs'' to show their amazement at Carroll's athletic ability. This phenomenon increases ''in direct proportion to each 'ooh' that by the time I dunked one backwards I could almost distinguish what color panties each chick sitting there was wearing.''

At the other extreme, Carroll plays badly in games in which he takes drugs, such as when he takes some pills that he mistakenly thinks will make him faster. In reality, they drag him down. ''The other team's dude who I normally leave looking at my shoelaces sailed over me and easily laid it in.'' Later in the diaries, Carroll notes that the massive

What Do I Read Next?

- Although many today only know Carroll's prose writings, he made his start in the literary world as a poet. *Fear of Dreaming: The Selected Poems of Jim Carroll* (1993) includes poems from *Living at the Movies* (1973) and *The Book of Nods* (1986) as well as several more recent poems. This collection gives a portrait of Carroll as an artist in various stages of his writing career.

- Carroll's *Forced Entries* (1987) continues the autobiographical story of the author's drug addiction, starting five years after the last entry in *The Basketball Diaries.* However, in his first diary collection, Carroll detailed how he became a heroin addict. In this one, he describes his fight to overcome his addiction.

- In 1954, Aldous Huxley, a well-known author, published *The Doors of Perception,* a small, journalistic book detailing his experiences while under the influence of mescaline, a hallucinogenic drug. First-person accounts of drug use from later journalists like Hunter S. Thompson and Tom Wolfe have since overshadowed Huxley's book, which was very controversial in its time.

- Hunter S. Thompson is infamous for the massive amounts of drugs that he uses in the course of writing his provocative journalistic pieces. *Fear and Loathing in Las Vegas: A Savage Journey to the Heart of the American Dream* (1972), his best-known work, documents the journey of Thompson and a friend through Las Vegas. Over the course of the journey, the two men consume large amounts of alcohol, marijuana, mescaline, acid, cocaine, and various other drugs, while seeking the elusive American Dream.

- Irvine Welsh's first novel, *Trainspotting* (1993), offers a gritty portrait of heroin addiction among teenagers in modern Edinburgh, Scotland. The main character, Mark Renton, like Carroll in *The Basketball Diaries,* spends most of his time on the street with a gang of delinquents who do whatever it takes—including committing a variety of crimes—to get their next heroin fix.

---

drug habits of his and two of his teammates are affecting the team's performance. "It is common knowledge around the entire school that Marc Clutcher, Anton Neutron and myself are f—ing up our basketball team by taking every drug we can get our hands on before games."

Carroll's experiences with drugs are also extreme. At thirteen, Carroll is sniffing cleaning fluid. On another occasion, he is able to drink an enormous amount—two bottles—of codeine cough syrup before a party. When he first starts using heroin, he mainlines it, meaning that he injects it directly into a vein as opposed to injecting it into his skin or sniffing the dry powder. Novice heroin users usually avoid mainlining, since the high is so strong and it is easier to overdose. Says Carroll, "Tony said I might as well skin pop it. I said OK. Then Pudgy says, 'Well, if you're gonna put a needle in, you might as well mainline it.'" On another occasion, Carroll's friend, Willie, was beaten up by mistake; the attackers try to make up with Willie by letting him wash his bloody mouth out with soda. "Willie took one sip of the soda, slipped in (and this is true) 200 mgs. of pure crystal amphetamine, and gave it back to the prick, who drank the rest."

Carroll's deliberate statement that this incident is true highlights its extreme nature. In fact, after another extreme episode, Carroll notes: "You probably figure I made this one up, but I swear every word is true." In fact, the many outrageous episodes in the book have caused some critics to question its authenticity. In his 1981 review for *Creem,* Richard Riegel calls *The Basketball Diaries* "a disturbingly seamless mixture of fact and fiction." Likewise, in his 1987 *New York Times* review of *The Basketball Diaries* and its sequel, *Forced Entries,* Christopher

> **However, in the end, the diaries are true, even if Carroll did make some of it up. They offer an accurate reflection of what life was like for kids like Carroll, growing up on the tough streets of New York in the 1960s."**

Lehmann-Haupt notes that *The Basketball Diaries* was "filled with a kind of vitality, though clearly exaggerated in its boastful accounts of drinking, drugs, sex and every sort of crime from stealing cars to hustling homosexuals in Times Square." As James notes, "It suffers from all the faults of the genre," including the fact that "some of the stories sound made up." However, as Peter Delacorte notes of *The Basketball Diaries* in his 1987 *San Francisco Chronicle* review of *Forced Entries*, ultimately, the speculation over the work's authenticity does not matter. Says Delacorte: "Of course, from the author's point of view the reader's confusion on such a point is absolutely irrelevant, as long as the reader stays interested."

In fact, Carroll himself is aware that normal situations make uninteresting diaries. At the end of one of the rare entries that does not include an outrageous situation, Carroll notes that this particular entry is boring. "I just couldn't think of anything else to write about anyway, no dope, no nooky, no queers following me today, I guess you start writing lame diaries like this." With this statement, Carroll hits on a well-known belief. Most people's lives are not that interesting. Despite the popular demand for biographies of interesting people, on a day-to-day basis most people—even celebrities—lead normal, and even boring, lives. Not Carroll, however. In his life, as depicted by *The Basketball Diaries*, there little boredom; readers are treated to a continuous, exciting variety of extreme dialogue, imagery, situations, and characters.

However, in the end, the diaries are true, even if Carroll did make some of it up. They offer an accurate reflection of what life was like for kids like Carroll, growing up on the tough streets of New York in the 1960s. At one point in his diaries,

Carroll says that most people are unaware of what life is like in the city. He says that he will soon let people "know what's really going down in the blind alley out there in the pretty streets with double garages. I got a tap on all your wires, folks. I'm just really a wise ass kid getting wiser." Carroll's main purpose in writing his diaries is not to provide a completely accurate account of his own life but to represent his life and the lives of all those like him. His is the voice of criminals, junkies, prostitutes, and other urban characters who, like him, have struggled against their disadvantaged surroundings and who have failed to "become pure."

Source: Ryan D. Poquette, Critical Essay on *The Basketball Diaries,* in *Nonfiction Classics for Students,* Gale, 2003.

Erik France

France holds an M.S.L.S. from the University of North Carolina at Chapel Hill and a Ph.D. in history from Temple University. He is a librarian, college counselor, and teacher at University Liggett School and teaches writing at Macomb Community College near Detroit, Michigan. In the following essay, France discusses both historical context and the tradition of the poet as rebel in The Basketball Diaries.

The primary value of Jim Carroll's *The Basketball Diaries* is its contextual vision of time (from the fall of 1963 to the summer of 1966) and place (New York City and its environs) and its carrying onward of a dramatic cultural strand that presents the (in this case young) artist as incorrigible rebel. The importance of the historical content highlighted in the published text is heightened by comparison with the financially successful movie adaptation, starring actor Leonardo Di Caprio that was released in 1995. In the latter version, all references to the 1960s are excised; the setting in the movie version is still New York City, but it is a very different, much more affluent and much more apolitical version of the city apparently of early- to mid-1990s vintage. Indeed, even though the movie quotes extensively from the printed version, it loses much of the charm and background tension and interest rendered in the book. The original diarist makes much of the atomic jitters caused by the Cold War, the Vietnam War, and ferment caused by class and racial friction, indirectly (and at times directly) using his and societal fears as justifications for his rebellious attitude, drug-use, and generally antisocial, at times violently sociopathic behavior.

In his "Author's Note" to *Forced Entries: The Downtown Diaries, 1971–1973,* Jim Carroll writes: "This diary is not the literal truth and is not meant to be a historical recounting of the period. The entries were consciously embellished and fictionalized to some extent. My purpose was simply to convey the texture of my experience and feelings for that period." The same probably holds true for *The Basketball Diaries.* What the reader can gain from the early diaries is a sense of what life was like in New York City during a three-year period for a precocious adolescent and teenager who was a good basketball player, drug addict, and neophyte poet. From his wry observations, often dangerous preoccupation and conflicts, one can also learn much about attitudes that oppose his, the prevailing norms, and generally what was going on culturally. Simply put, Jim Carroll's rebelliousness tapped into a relatively small but growing societal discontent that was building momentum for the entire duration of that historical period.

One of Jim Carroll's heroes throughout the diaries is singer-songwriter Bob Dylan, an important cultural rebel and icon of the period and ever since. A Summer 64 diary entry observes: "I spent most of the time just drinking beer in the corner and listening to Dylan on the jukebox." At a time when bands such as the Rolling Stones and the Beatles were spearheading the famous musical upheaval dubbed the British Invasion, Carroll chose to focus most of his musical attention on Minnesota-born, New York veteran Bob Dylan (he mentions charismatic soul singer James Brown in one incident). This makes perfect sense in that Dylan defined himself as rebel-poet, the very thing Jim Carroll wanted to become in full. Bob Dylan could fuse the power and possibilities of poetry with music, passionately rail against the things in society he didn't like, and become rich and famous all at the same time. Technically, he couldn't even sing very well, an evident fact that inspired all sorts of aspiring poets and singers. Indeed, Jim Carroll himself eventually (in the late 1970s) formed a rock band and sang his own poems and lyrics just like his hero, including "People Who Died," a very memorable song on the album *Catholic Boy* that chronicles the deaths of friends and acquaintances, many of whom appear and whose deaths are mentioned or similarly described in entries of *The Basketball Diaries.* This song also appears in the movie version, tying four art forms (written diary, poetry, music, and cinema) together. Carroll's interest in Bob Dylan persists throughout *The Basketball Diaries.* It is worth not-

> **One of Jim Carroll's heroes throughout the diaries is singer-songwriter Bob Dylan, an important cultural rebel and icon of the period and ever since."**

ing that Carroll's voice has an imprint that is almost equally affected and unique as Dylan's. For Carroll as a boy, as with heroin, once hooked, it would have been difficult to avoid his interest in Dylan, for during the approximate period covered by the diaries, Dylan released no fewer than six very influential albums; indeed, halfway through the period he caused a ruckus among folk music "purists" by changing from acoustic to electric guitar. Carroll, in a Winter 1966 entry, describing an incident shooting up heroin, notes: "Bob Dylan, he's in the radio. He glows in the dark and my fingers are just light feathers falling and fading down. . ." Carroll was sensitive enough to discover that Dylan did not and does not carry his appeal to everyone, in one case to an African-American friend. In the spring of 1966, after the electric album *Highway 61 Revisited* had climbed the predominantly white popular music charts, Carroll noted in his diary: "I tell my friend play Dylan . . . 'Who he?'"

The Basketball Diaries also taps into one of Bob Dylan's major literary influences, the Beat Generation. This loosely defined group of poets and writers included novelist Jack Kerouac, author of *On the Road* (1957), poet Allen Ginsberg, author of "Howl" (1956), and writer William S. Burroughs. Carroll does not inform the reader whether these are important influences on him at the time as well, but their impact and his meetings with some of the Beat figures is definitively mentioned in *Forced Entries: The Downtown Diaries, 1971–1973.* As with his fondness for Dylan, this again make sense, for Carroll shares many of the same values and interests as the Beats. In fact, Carroll's preoccupation with drug addictions, especially with heroin, parallels Burroughs' recounting of his own addictions in the memoir, *Junky.* All three of these key Beat Generation figures spent formative college years in New York City during the World War II barely twenty years before the events and musings of *The Basket-*

ball Diaries, so he shared the same geographical space, the same sense of rebelliousness, a common exposure to drugs, numerous (including sometimes bizarre) sexual encounters, and at times criminal behavior. With Ginsberg he shared a love of poetry and a sense that prevailing society must be questioned and challenged because of its at best apathetic and at worst reactionary politics. They all enjoyed bucking the status quo, a hallmark of and now a stereotyped way of viewing the 1960s.

In *The Basketball Diaries,* Jim Carroll frequently argues with his father over societal and political issues that raged during the period. In the movie version, it is worth noting, Carroll's father is edited out along with the 1960s. Carroll's father, in the book version, sides with the status quo along with most of white Americans at the time: to show one's patriotism, one should trust and not criticize the government or religious institutions. But Jim Carroll distrusted, and he criticized vociferously. Like Dylan and Ginsberg, he had specific reasons to feel distrust and anxiety and to show opposition. One was fear of incineration by nuclear weapons as a by-product of the Cold War between the Americans and the Soviet bloc. Just prior to the period covered by *The Basketball Diaries,* a third world war had nearly broken out during the Cuban Missile Crisis (1962); not mentioned but clearly felt by Carroll and most New Yorkers at the time, President John F. Kennedy was assassinated on November 22, 1963; and in 1964 United States began escalating its involvement in the Vietnam War (1964–1972). Intermittently throughout *The Basketball Diaries* Carroll addresses his pervasive fear of nuclear holocaust. He describes feelings of being stuck at ''ground zero in one fireball Island'' in a Summer 65 diary entry devoted to atomic jitters and the psychic trauma it inflicts. ''After all these years of worry and nightmares over it,'' the entry continues, ''(I remember my brother enticing me on to panic during the Cuban crisis saying they were coming any minute) I think by now I'd feel very left out if they dropped the bomb and it didn't get me.'' When a power outage shut down much of New York City and the east coast in the fall of 1965, Carroll was caught in a subway train and thought the end had come, later noting to his diary, ''the fact there were no tunnel lights on either made for more A-bomb paranoia.'' Carroll's diaries also intermittently mention his dread of Vietnam, for after high school he might be drafted into military service there, mixed with the recurrent fear of nuclear war. In a Winter 1966 diary entry, things have gotten so bad that he

thinks of his whole life as a reprieve from the inevitable. ''It's just gotten bigger now . . . will I have time to finish the poems breaking loose in my head? Time to find out if I'm the writer I know I can be? How about these diaries? Or will Vietnam beat me to the button? Because it's poetry now . . . and the button is still there, waiting . . .''

The movie version of *The Basketball Diaries* was made and released in a rare bubble of time. The Cold War had ended, and so had some of the decades-old fears of nuclear war between the United States and the Soviet Union. The American economy boomed at the time, so there probably seemed no reason to set the film back during the tumultuous 1960s. At the time, who would have cared? The relevance and acuteness of Jim Carroll's awareness and fears of New York City as a target of sudden attack feels far more visceral and immediate since the events of September 11, 2001, a sad and tragic fact that nonetheless helps the text version of *The Basketball Diaries* to resonate again in time and place, both as a recapturing of the past and prophesying for the future. Artists and poets may seem paranoid at times, but this does not mean that something like what they fear does not sometimes really come to pass.

Source: Erik France, Critical Essay on *The Basketball Diaries,* in *Nonfiction Classics for Students,* Gale, 2003.

Douglas Dupler

Dupler has published numerous essays and has taught college English. In this essay, Dupler analyzes the destructive rift between an adolescent young man and the adult society around him.

A picaresque novel differs from a conventional novel in that the picaresque form usually revolves around a main character who travels loosely from scene to scene, encountering other characters and situations in a random fashion, gathering whatever seeds of wisdom that present themselves. The conventional novel, on the other hand, typically involves characters whose actions and conflicts form a plot, which leads to some sort of resolution in the end. Miguel de Cervantes's (1547–1616) *Don Quixote* was the original picaresque novel, from which a long tradition of storytelling has evolved. Don Quixote was a knight whose travels have been viewed by critics as a spiritual quest, a journey undertaken for self-knowledge. The main character in *The Basketball Diaries* might be considered, in a stretch, a modern-day teenage knight, whose battles are on the basketball courts and on the streets, and who also is on a quest, when he states that he just wants "to be pure." But this is the only similarity between these distant stories that somewhat share a form. Knights in Don Quixote's day had very strict societal codes of conduct (chivalry), while the main character in this book is an unformed young man who is either lacking in reliable codes of conduct, or whose main mission seems to be to challenge and test codes and ethics.

Carroll portrays his main character and his street-wise life with a palette of decadence. The protagonist's reality is a downward spiral of drug abuse, theft, violence, altercations with police and other authority figures, sexual abuse, and prostitution, often described with crude and profane language. Indeed, the repetition of these sordid scenes and the protagonist's capacity for self-destruction and wayward behavior would be tiresome if not for the Tom Sawyer-ish charm the protagonist manages to maintain throughout the story. The reader can be attracted to this character despite his trouble-making and his tough-guy posturing because the story plays upon sympathy; the reader knows that this young man has been dealt a harsh reality by fate, lacking in teachers, mentors, and caring parents. The young man, as evidenced by his striving on the basketball courts, also wants to rise above it all and occasionally does, and records these efforts poetically and intelligently at times. The reader feels for him when the protagonist becomes mired in addiction and the troubles of street life.

The protagonist of *The Basketball Diaries* is curiously without any deep relationships throughout the story. His friends of his own age are partners in petty crime, but none of these adolescents are described with any conviction and remain vague for the reader. No characters in the protagonist's life are memorable and these characters only briefly appear and disappear in the narrative. The protagonist does not even give his own name; perhaps the author wants the reader to believe that it actually is a diary. A policeman refers to the main character as "Jim," keeping with the diary form. However, this omission of a proper name also has the effect of making the protagonist seem young, unformed, and very isolated; the story is told from a vague first-person perspective. The protagonist comments on his isolation when he describes a feeling he has while standing on a rooftop, looking down at the city: "It's just me and my own naked self and the stars breathing down. And it's beautiful." This is a revealing scene; the young man wants to soar above

Leonardo DiCaprio in the leading role of the 1995 film adaptation of The Basketball Diaries

the troubles of the street, but he can only do so by himself, as other people seem so dangerous and distant to him. At the same time, he discloses later in his narrative that it is not really beautiful to be isolated; he has a dream in which he longs for "an incredible love somewhere in my world," and near the end of the story, he has a horrifying drug experience in which he realizes, with emphasis, that "I AM ALONE." His isolation ends in increasing self-destruction and addiction without anyone to help him.

Of all the brief relationships described in the narrative, the protagonist's relationship with authority might go the deepest in giving insights into his character and his troubles. Like Tom Sawyer, he finds the adult world alien and to be avoided. Adults in these diary entries have few redeeming features and give reasons for profound distrust. On the first page of the book, the basketball coach (a classic mentor figure for young people) is revealed with undertones of potential sexual abuse, and later in the book priests, teachers, and a basketball scout are all portrayed as sexual predators. Adults are also shown as helpless addicts, such as the alcoholics that single out the protagonist on trains, or as desperate prostitutes. The protagonist sees a woman commit suicide

> In the end, the protagonist of *The Basketball Diaries* uses drug addiction to fill the void created by a lack of positive authority and genuine mentors."

as though it is a common occurrence in the adult world, and he can only turn to heroin to dull his shock. The protagonist and his friends are in a constant struggle with police, the symbol of society's authority. However, these authorities are also untrustworthy; a policeman, for instance, unjustly strikes the protagonist. When the protagonist's basketball talents gain him a scholarship to a prestigious school, he recoils against the school and remarks, "I feel like . . . blowing up the 257 years of fine tradition of this place."

Tradition is not the only thing the protagonist wants to blow up. He is alarmed by the violent thoughts that fill his mind; he sits in class and fantasizes about taking "a machine gun and . . . firing like mad" to "release some tension." It seems that there are areas in this young man's psyche that haunt him and that he is unable to confront, and he has no trustworthy adults who can guide him to deeper self-knowledge, or with whom he can even share his troubles.

The protagonist's parents are no help to him. His father accosts him with anger, and the young man describes that relationship as "an unending rift." At one point the young man swears on his "mom's grave," then quickly notes that his mother is not really dead, although she only pops up in his narrative when she finds drugs and lectures him on the matter, or when she unreasonably attacks his beliefs. He describes his home as "a screaming maniac nut house," and hints that his parents are angry racists, although at the same time he clearly needs his parents' love. He tries to escape his family strife through heroin, writing how his "veins are sore," yet he still loves his parents "somehow more" through the pain and addiction. Near the end of the diaries, when he is in a juvenile reformatory and his mother refuses to visit him, he wishes he has godparents.

The narrator does give hints that he may recognize that he has a problem with authority, and perhaps justifiably so. This is a young man who lives in a period and culture haunted by war; in his fantasies of violence, he dreams of fighting the Germans of World War II. He describes his boss at Yankee Stadium as a man who could be a "commander in any of Hitler's war camps." Furthermore, the Cold War atmosphere in which he exists haunts him deeply. Several times he notes his fear of a nuclear bombing, remarking on his "A-bomb paranoia" and the specter of the "Russians" with their "atomic arrows." He describes his state of mind as "hideous fear" brought on by "constant drills in schools and TV flashes." His fear and fatalism concerning nuclear annihilation have been with him for so long that he says, "I'd feel very left out if they dropped the bomb and it didn't get me."

The political atmosphere in which the protagonist lives gives him a sense of hopelessness and powerlessness. For instance, when his school arranges a traditional Thanksgiving fast to support the poor and hungry, the protagonist can not believe that such a gesture could be beneficial and calls it a "farce." At a peace march, he comments, "Who needs leaders?" He concludes that violence is a better means to solve problems than peaceful demonstration, and there are no wise people or leaders present who can guide him and share ideas. At the same time, the protagonist is sensitive enough to ask a little girl if "Christ would fight in the war?" Rather than finding a meaningful way to express and sort out his beliefs, the protagonist turns again to drugs and denial, so that he will not feel "guilty about not fighting a war" and as a means to escape the "scheming governments of death."

Finally, as meaningful relationships with other people and with authority figures are lacking in these diaries, the protagonist develops his addictive relationship with drugs. In the beginning of the story, the reader is told about the young man's first heroin experience, as well as his experiences with marijuana and psychedelic substances. At first, the protagonist seems to approach drugs with a sense of adventure, recalling the French poet Rimbaud's (1854–1891) famous quote that a poet must use any means available to cause a 'derangement of the senses,' in order to enhance poetic and visionary experience. However, when the reader becomes familiar with the young man's pains and troubles, it becomes clear that his drug experiences are far from positive and visionary. A flirtation with drugs leads to destructive addiction. Although the narrator describes an experience with the Native-American ritual plant peyote as ''incredible,'' the reader still grasps the escapist motive when the young man writes that his mind went ''somewhere'' the ''bald headed generals and wheelchair senators could never imagine.'' Unlike the Native-American vision-seekers, who have had organized rituals and elder guides for excursions into their experimental realms, the protagonist only has a casual friend to accompany him. His experience becomes one of escape from the world and from his own society's elders, with no life-changing wisdom or visions following it.

In the end, the protagonist of *The Basketball Diaries* uses drug addiction to fill the void created by a lack of positive authority and genuine mentors. The young man, although once a star on the basketball court, cannot shine by himself in the world. In his final diary entries, he goes through cycles of addiction and withdrawal, and seems to hope that the police catch him, a desperate plea for attention from authority. He blames impersonal ''big business'' men and ''white haired old men in smoking jacket armchairs'' for the troubles in the world. In his last diary entry, he describes ''four days of temporary death.'' Lacking any true adult guides in life, and too young and inexperienced to guide himself, he remains an unformed ''foetus'' longing to go ''back to the womb,'' rather than a young man with great potential springing forward into the adult world.

Source: Douglas Dupler, Critical Essay on *The Basketball Diaries,* in *Nonfiction Classics for Students,* Gale, 2003.

Alex Williams

In the following interview-essay, Williams offers background on Carroll's life and career with comments from Carroll on the occasion of the film release of The Basketball Diaries.

''I could get my shooting eye back,'' says Jim Carroll in a voice from the Borough of Lost Souls. ''But that first step, man, that's the first thing to go.'' Carroll, at 44, still has the wounded-fawn cheekbones and red hair of the immortal adolescent. Thirty years ago, he was already a god in his small New York universe, a basketball star, literary prodigy, and fledgling heroin addict. That boy has been mummified in celluloid in the film version of his memoir, *The Basketball Diaries*, with Leonardo Di Caprio playing the stoned angel in a blazer and rep tie.

The actual Jim sits today in a Madison Avenue coffee shop, over rice pudding and apple-cinnamon

> **" The actual Jim sits today in a Madison Avenue coffee shop, over rice pudding and apple-cinnamon tea, and looks back on his glory days with toneless eyes of battleship gray, eyes that look like they have seen three lifetimes."**

tea, and looks back on his glory days with toneless eyes of battleship gray, eyes that look like they have seen three lifetimes.

''I was always such a f—n' gunner,'' he says. ''Y'know, if they had a three-point line back then, I woulda scored, like, seven more points a game. But see, I wasn't a natural one-step leaper. I didn't have spring. But I worked really hard with, like, weighted spats and stuff. So by my sophomore year, I could dunk a ball, like, backwards, take off from the foul line. After a while, they'd have a guy just sitting there for me. Y'know?

That was in 1966. Carroll was an all-city guard for Trinity, sparring with legends like Vaughan Harper—the Felipe Lopez of his day—and ''the Goat,'' Earl Manigault, on the playgrounds of Harlem. By night, he was traversing the city in a hormonal search for significance, pulling off wild stunts and minor crimes with pals like Pedro and Herbie, and using his basketball-star status to score with girls from Park Avenue to the Grand Concourse. And, amazingly, he was getting it all down on paper. Jack Kerouac said that at 13, he wrote better prose than 89 percent of the novelists in America (''I'm so sick of that f—n' quote, man,'' says Carroll). It was a world without gravity.

Carroll is on his second coffee shop and it's only 10 A.M. He's just met with a few friends from Drugs Anonymous and is stopping off before continuing an epic walk to the Fifth Avenue office of his lawyer, ex-wife, and friend Rosemary Carroll. A few minutes ago, he was walking down Lexington Avenue when a guy in Chuck Taylors, maybe 25, stalked him for a block before interrupting, reverentially: ''You're Jim Carroll! I just heard this *voice. . . .''*

''It's, like, I call up stores, and the person on the other end of the line says, '*Is this Jim Carroll?*''' Carroll says in his characteristic pinched whine, equal parts Edith Bunker and William Burroughs.

He wears a denim work shirt, blue watch cap, and black sunglasses. Flecks of gray have pushed into his thin, incongruous beard. Tiny folds of skin gather under the eyes, though no one can see past his black-framed sunglasses. And he's talking incessantly, allowing each story the freedom to ramble.

Carroll is talking ball again, wagging his wrist in a dribble motion. ''So it was the day we were auditioning Patrick [McGaw], who plays Neutron in the film, and they were short a guy for three-on-three. It was freezing, y'know, down on Thompson Street, with ice all over the side of the court, like where your hands get all cracked, like, when you're a kid, playin' outdoors in winter? It was me and Marky [Wahlberg] and James Madio versus Patrick, Leo [Di Caprio], and Bryan [Goluboff], the screenwriter. And *I was pa-thet-ic.* I go up for this little jump shot, with Leo guarding me, and he's got no leaps at all, and he comes in and *blocks my shot!*'' He shakes his head. ''I hate them for making me do that.''

''That's the thing about this project, the biggest downer,'' Carroll says. ''I had that moment. I'm not going back to try to recapture it. I had that one chance. . . . ''

A world without gravity. Twenty-five years ago, *The Paris Review* published his teenage diaries over his strong reservations; he saw himself as a poet. But the diaries themselves are poetry of a sort: *He's down dealing on the hottest corner in the city, like a furnace that street, can feel narco heat waves through your sneakers.*

''I think they saw the diaries in *The World* magazine, published by the Poetry Project. They told me Plimpton wanted to see them,'' Carroll says. He says that Truman Capote's editor at Random House, Joe Fox, wanted to publish the diaries as a book, but Carroll was adamant about doing a poetry collection. He finally sold the rights to Bantam in 1979, insisting on paperbacks only. ''It was the perfect book for the time, the punk scene, but I thought it would be out-to-lunch to publish it as this $19.95 hardcover.'' Carroll estimates the book has sold around 500,000 copies, and Bantam did a study that showed six people read it for every one who bought it.

The Basketball Diaries, which Carroll wrote between the ages of 13 and 15, is a panorama of winos, preppies, hustlers, and fools. It's New York picaresque—Oliver Twist with a habit. Carroll published poems in *Poetry* when he was still shooting jumpers against Riverdale High. In the seventies and early eighties, he played rock and roll and almost made it big.

Now, with the arrival of the long-awaited film, comes Carroll's unsolicited midlife retrospective. Carroll sighs, a little weary: ''With the records and everything, I've *had* my time above-ground. Y'know?''

Jim Carroll was an idea fifteen years in the making for his parents, Tom and Agnes Carroll. They had tried to have kids well before Tom's wartime tours of Iwo Jima and Saipan. They'd given up when Thomas Joseph Jr. was born in 1949; James Dennis (''from Dionysius'') followed a year later.

Carroll spent his early years in the East Twenties, a tough neighborhood at the time; at 13, his family moved to the more middle-class Irish enclave of Inwood in upper Manhattan. That was the first year he shot up. ''I think the main reason I started using heroin was that everyone else was always going out drinking, and I hated drinking,'' he says innocently. He hated Catholic school, though, and as a freshman used basketball and good grades as a ticket to the affluent Trinity School on the Upper West Side.

His father was a hard-assed war vet whose own father had run a Harlem speakeasy for Dutch Schultz. ''My old man would listen to the music I was playing, Phil Ochs, and say, 'What the f— is this *Phil Ouches* guy? What is this goddamned Communist s—t I'm hearing?''' Carroll says. ''Y'know, his bar was this real cops-and-construction-workers redneck bar, and he'd have to listen to them go, 'What the hell is with your son with his long hair? You know, I used to read about him in the sports pages, scored 40 points; now he's got hair down to here.' And then Smitty, the postman from our building, the loudmouthed bastard, starts saying, y'know, 'Your son gets all this poetry stuff in the mail; I mean, what in the hell is that?' Because that's the take in any neighborhood, in the Jimmy Breslin sense. Poetry is sissy stuff. Anybody who writes poetry is a fag.'' Carroll laughs. ''Which I found out is absolutely true when I got out on the scene.''

By the time he was a junior in high school, Carroll was traveling down to open poetry readings at St. Mark's Church, swallowing his fear, and turning heads. He impressed poet Ted Berrigun as well as influential literary editors.

He tried college, attending Wagner in Staten Island "for a year, as far as the draft was concerned." He adds, with disbelief, "My dorm roommates, like, they thought the biggest thrill was to go down and see the Johnny Carson show." He was gone within weeks, and spent even less time at his next school, Columbia.

In 1973, Carroll published his first poetry collection, *Living at the Movies*, and moved to San Francisco with a girlfriend and his methadone. From there it was up the coast to the art colony of Bolinas, where he met Rosemary. "I learned to like being by myself. Maybe too much. But that was the first time I discovered a writing routine."

He might have stayed on that path had it not been for a night in San Diego in 1978. Jim was hanging out with Patti Smith, an old girlfriend, before a gig. There was a scuffle involving roadies, and Smith booted the opening act from the bill. In a pinch, she suggested Jim open the show, just get up and speak-sing some poems, as he had done for her before. Her band would back him, just riff. "I was like, 'Uhhh...'" says Carroll, eyes wide with mock terror. "I didn't even like rock and roll that much." The gig lasted seven minutes. But the Jim Carroll Band was born.

"When I came back to New York, it was such a joke, because I was always referred to as the pure young poet who wasn't in it for what he could get out of it; and all of a sudden, the pure young poet comes back, and I've got this deal for the paperback of *The Basketball Diaries*, and I'm *hanging out with the Rolling Stones*."

The single "People Who Died" was his rock-and-roll master work, a Ramones-style guitar grind molded around a terse catalogue of the victims he knew in his New York adolescence. "There was that line, *G-berg and Georgie let the gimmicks, go rotten/died of hepatitis in upper Manhattan*. It was actually five of us that shared that needle, and three of us died from it. I just say 'G-berg and Georgie' because of the scan," he says. "G-berg, yeah, like Goldberg. The guy's name wasn't Goldberg; he was a Puerto Rican guy, but everyone said he looked Jewish."

Carroll's album *Catholic Boy*, which came out in 1980, put him on the commercial radar. Within two years, Carroll's group was opening for the J. Geils Band in hockey arenas. "There were always these girls pushing to the front to sock their tongues into your mouth," he recalls.

The fact that the next two records didn't move was no great tragedy. "These guys were always saying, 'The minute you get onstage, it's great, no matter how much you're hurting.' But that didn't work for me. There were some nights I did *not* want to get out there," he says.

He moved back to New York in 1986, and split amicably with Rosemary (two years later, she married Danny Goldberg, who is now chairman of Warner Bros. Records). He published a collection of poems, *The Book of Nods*, which even Carroll admits wasn't totally successful. "Rock and roll kind of screwed up my voice, poetically. I found myself having this 'Beat' voice in my poems. It was like this self-fulfilled prophecy, because everybody was calling me this rock poet, this Beat poet."

Carroll moved back to Inwood, two blocks from his old building. His mother had died, and he had made peace with his father, who was reduced to visiting her grave every day. He also wrote a sequel to *The Basketball Diaries*, which he called *Forced Entries*. The book was a journal of tawdry, Warholian downtown New York in the early seventies.

Carroll arrives at Rosemary's office. He's there to view a short film by a worshipful NYU student based on the final, cathartic passage of *Forced Entries*. Carroll's got a headache, so he asks a secretary for some Tylenol. He takes four, then wanders into a nearby conference room.

Cyril Connolly once said, "Whom the gods wish to destroy, they first call promising." Carroll sums it up a little differently: "I was always the young guy. And when you're successful when you're young, it leads to an arrested adolescence or something, y'know. And there's that ecstasy period in your life as an artist. Every artist goes through this. I tried to get it back at first with music, and got, y'know, that adrenaline. But," he says cautiously, "there's a time when you switch into a more sober period."

Carroll knows that after the film hype fades, he'll finally have time to work on two novels that he says "just came to me three or four years ago. Like a gift." One is about a miracle, two priests, and an investigation by the Vatican. (He's been brushing

up on the Gnostics.) The other is about a young star
painter who walks away from art in a spiritual crisis.
There are no drugs, and the painter is a virgin.
"These are straight, linear novels in the third person. My editor was shocked. He was like, 'Jim!
These are money books.' But if I don't get to work
on these things, boy, I am betraying a gift; I mean,
that's what *I* would define as a sin."

It helps that Carroll has finally achieved a quiet
writer's ritual. "It's like I've been so jubilant, I just
eliminated that need." Carroll rises every morning
around 4:30 A.M., when he does his best writing.
And he's shaken a nasty TV habit: "After that
afternoon nap, it was always *Oprah* time. . . . So I
got rid of cable and my VCR, but I found I was
watching, like, infomercials instead of movies. But
these days—" He pauses, indignant. "To me, late-
night movies are old black-and-white movies with
Cagney and Bogart, but today, old movies are like
The Sting II with Jackie Gleason."

During the summer, he often teaches at Allen
Ginsberg's Naropa Institute. He lectures and reads
at colleges, maintaining little contact with the downtown New York he helped define, although he
recently went to a viewing of *Diaries* at Rosemary's
place with Lou Reed and Sonic Youth's Thurston
Moore and Kim Gordon. "It moves well," he says.
"It's hard for me to really register on it because of
the personal attachment."

Carroll has been clean of heroin since the early
seventies. He still has an occasional margarita,
although he has never liked drinking. "I can't go for
that complete-abstinence thing. I mean, I obviously
have an addictive personality, especially for heroin.
But I haven't smoked grass in like eight or nine
years. I mean, I *wish* I could still smoke grass. But
New York is just so speedy, it's so fast-paced. I
mean, the phone's going to ring any minute and
someone's going to lay a big trip on me, and I'll
spend the first hour paranoid."

Source: Alex Williams, "Lord Jim," in *New York*, Vol. 28,
No. 17, April 24, 1995, pp. 64–66.

Sources

Carroll, Jim, *The Basketball Diaries,* Tombouctou Books,
1978, reprint, Penguin Books, 1995.

———, *Catholic Boy,* Atco, 1980.

———, *Forced Entries: The Downtown Diaries, 1971–1973,*
Penguin Books, 1987, p. vi.

Carter, Cassie, "'A Sickness That Takes Years to Perfect':
Jim Carroll's Alchemical Vision," in *Dionysos: Literature
and Addiction Quarterly,* Vol. 6, No. 1, Winter 1996, pp.
6–19.

Delacorte, Peter, "A Follow-Through beyond the Hoop," in
the *San Francisco Chronicle,* July 12, 1987, p. 3.

Gilbert, Martin, *A History of the Twentieth Century,* Vol. 3,
1952–1999, Perennial, 2000, p. 307.

Graustark, Barbara, "Mean Streets," in *Newsweek,* Vol. 96,
No. 10, September 8, 1980, pp. 80–81.

James, Jamie, Review of *The Basketball Diaries,* in *American Book Review,* Vol. 2, No. 2, February 1980, p. 9.

Jebian, Wayne, "Diaries of the Damned," in the *Columbia
Journal of American Studies,* Vol. 1, No. 1, 1995.

Lehmann-Haupt, Christopher, Review of *The Basketball
Diaries* and *Forced Entries,* in the *New York Times,* July 9,
1987, p. C23.

MacAdams, Lewis, "Jim Carroll," in *Entertainment Weekly,*
No. 281–282, June 30, 1995, pp. 50–51.

Riegel, Richard, Review of *Catholic Boy,* in *Creem,* Vol. 12,
No. 9, February 1981, p. 44.

Simels, Steven, "Jim Carroll," in *Stereo Review Magazine,*
Vol. 46, No. 2, February 1981, p. 40.

Further Reading

Baum, Dan, *Smoke and Mirrors: The War on Drugs and the
Politics of Failure,* Little, Brown, 1997.
   This retrospective look at the United States' war on
   drugs deviates from other books in this genre that tend
   to use anecdotes to depict the government as deliberate participants in the spread of drugs. Instead, Baum,
   a journalist, provides balanced criticism about why
   the war on drugs has failed, using facts to back up his
   assertions.

Braunstein, Peter, and Michael William Doyle, eds., *Imagine
Nation: The American Counterculture of the 1960s and '70s,*
Routledge, 2001.
   This collection of essays offers a thorough examination of the major cultural issues in the 1960s and
   1970s. Topics include Drugs in the Sixties Counterculture, Insurgent Youth and the Sixties Culture of
   Rejuvenation, Film and the Counterculture, and Media
   and Pop Culture.

Holmes, Ann, *The Mental Effects of Heroin,* The Encyclopedia of Psychological Disorders, Little, Brown, 1997.
   Holmes reviews the history of heroin use, discusses
   the physical and psychological effects of using heroin, and talks about the causes of and various treatments for heroin addiction. The book also includes
   several appendices, including contact information for
   substance-abuse agencies, heroin-related statistical
   tables, a bibliography, and a glossary of drug-related
   terms.

Unger, Irwin, and Debi Unger, eds., *The Times Were a Changin': The Sixties Reader,* Three Rivers Press, 1998.

In this book, the Ungers present an extensive anthology of speeches, articles, court decisions, and other documents that defined the 1960s. Organized in twelve categories, the book's sections feature an introduction from the editors as well as specific commentary on the documents.

A Boy Called H

Kappa Senoh

1997

A Boy Called H: A Childhood in Wartime Japan (Japanese, 1997; English, 1999), by Kappa Senoh, is an autobiographical novel. Senoh describes his life growing up in the port city of Kobe, Japan, from the 1930s until a few years after the end of World War II. In fifty short chapters, each focusing on a few incidents, some minor and amusing, others tragic and moving, the novel gives a remarkable picture, through the eyes of a young boy, of a society at war. H describes how life in Kobe gradually changes as the war with China, and later with the United States, drags on. There is an increasingly authoritarian atmosphere, marked by excessive nationalism that no one dares to question openly. H learns there is a difference between official versions of events, as reported in the newspapers, and what is really happening. He also goes through some harrowing experiences. In a massive air raid by American B-29 bombers, his home is destroyed. On another occasion he narrowly escapes being killed by machine gun fire from an American fighter plane. These experiences force H to grow up quickly, and the novel is really a coming-of-age story. As he reaches adolescence, H quarrels with his parents and moves out of the family home. The story ends during the post-war U.S. occupation of Japan, as H trains to be an artist.

Author Biography

Kappa Senoh was born in Kobe, Japan, in 1930. His given name was Hajime, which he later changed to Kappa. His father was a tailor, and both his parents were Christians, a minority faith in Japan. As a boy, Senoh demonstrated a talent for drawing, and on leaving school a few years after the end of World War II, he worked as a graphic designer. When he was in his twenties, he became a stage designer. He has since been the set designer for numerous operas, theater productions, and musicals and is recognized as one of Japan's leading designers. He has won many awards for his work.

Senoh is also a best-selling essayist and illustrator in Japan. He is particularly well-known for his travel book series *Kappa Takes a Look at . . .* , which describes various parts of the world and is notable for Senoh's detailed drawings.

In 1997, Senoh published his autobiographical novel *A Boy Called H: A Childhood in Wartime Japan*. This work was his first venture into full-length book form. The novel was a best-seller in Japan and other countries in Asia, selling over two million copies. It was adapted for the stage, and a television dramatization was made in 1999. The novel was translated into English in 1999.

Plot Summary

A Boy Called H begins in 1937. H (short for Hajime) lives in Kobe with his father, mother, and younger sister. H is about seven years old. Japan is at war with China, and this conflict forms the background for the early part of the novel. It can be seen when H befriends a young man who works at the noodle shop and is shocked when his friend is arrested by the police as a communist and made to join the army. Another of H's friends, the projectionist at the movie theater, hangs himself rather than be drafted into the army.

In "Tambourine," H tells of his parents' backgrounds. His father, Morio, came to Kobe in 1918 to become a tailor's apprentice; his mother, Toshiko, came to Kobe to marry Morio. She also became a devoted Christian, but H hates the sound of the tambourine she plays as the Christians preach in the street. Toshiko likes to ape Western customs and insists that her family eat with knives and forks rather than chopsticks.

H's father takes him to a restaurant, and H is allowed into the adjoining movie theater for his first taste of a film. Not long after this experience, H gets a chance to make money of his own through an ingenious arrangement. He resells the paste that his father uses in his tailoring business to his school friends for use in their handicraft classes.

But H's life has its troubles. "Maps and Eggs" describes the futile efforts H and his parents make to curb his bed-wetting. And in "Love," H learns to his embarrassment that the word love can have many different connotations. In "A Boy and a Sea," he and his friends row a dinghy too far from the shore and endanger themselves. Then torrential rains drench Kobe for days and lead to a serious flood. In his borrowed book *The Three Treasures,* H secretly reads children's stories in a book he borrows from a friend, even though his mother disapproves of his reading fiction.

In "The Living God," H asks his schoolmasters awkward questions about the emperor, who is regarded as a god. He soon asks more awkward questions about the global political situation, which he learns about from his father. Japan allies itself with Germany and Italy, but Morio thinks this will damage Japanese relations with the United States. H decides that Germany is not to be trusted.

World War II begins. In Japan, the state controls more and more aspects of individuals' lives and decrees that everyone should wear a new national dress, unlike Western clothes. This edict badly affects Morio's business, since he makes Western-style suits.

In "Military Secrets," H learns about the restrictions on his hobby of drawing. Instead of sketching ships, he goes into business exchanging photos of sumo wrestlers. "The Founding of the Nation" describes the five-day celebration, in 1940, of the 2,600th anniversary of the founding of the Japanese nation. Studies at H's school become more patriotic. Japan signs a non-aggression pact with the Soviet Union, which displeases Morio since it will further irritate the United States.

War with the United States breaks out after the attack on Pearl Harbor in December, 1941. Morio is skeptical of the official versions that explain why Japan went to war, and he tells H he must form his own opinions and not accept everything he hears. Christianity in Japan comes under attack because it is also the religion of Great Britain and the United

States. H is taunted at school for coming from a family of Christians.

Toshiko becomes head of the newly formed neighborhood association, and H learns air raid drills. The radio reports a continuing stream of Japanese military victories, but Morio remains skeptical because the Americans have far greater resources.

The first incendiary bombs fall on Kobe, and the residents are issued gas masks. In a spy scare, Morio is detained by the authorities because he has foreign clients for his tailoring business.

For their summer holidays, H and his sister visit their mother's relatives in the countryside near Hiroshima. When they return to Kobe, there are more changes: American and British films are banned, and people are urged to give up all their metal goods for use in the war. H passes his Second Middle exam by mouthing the patriotic slogans he has read in the newspaper, knowing his examiners want to hear them.

At his new school, H joins the riding club and learns how to ride a difficult horse called Kamikeru. But he runs foul of Inspector Tamori, who is in charge of military training. Tamori is furious when he discovers in H's notebook a drawing of a nude woman, copied from a painting by Manet. To escape Tamori, H joins the rifle club, where he learns military drills and target practice. This training culminates in an arduous night march.

The military exercises continue. H fires live ammunition for the first time and discovers that he is a good shot. Another military exercise involves students simulating leaping up from a hiding place in the ground and throwing a grenade at an enemy tank.

During 1944, after Paris has fallen, air raids on Kobe increase. A dead Japanese fighter pilot is laid out in the school reception area, and the first Middle school student is killed. The big raid comes in March 1945. H's family home is destroyed and fires rage throughout the city. H and his mother escape and obtain lodgings in a church. H and his father, who works at the fire station during the raid, retrieve his damaged sewing machine. Wandering around Kobe, H is astonished at the extent of the damage and is relieved to find that his friends are safe. But another adventure is soon upon him: he is strafed by machine gun fire from an enemy plane and narrowly escapes being hit.

H goes to stay with his Uncle Hadano, but he cannot settle there and returns to Kobe. At the Second Middle school he works in the school factory, assembling motors. In another adventure, he is summoned by a military policeman to assist in the capture of an American pilot who has been shot down over Kobe.

Germany surrenders, and H realizes that Japan will lose the war. Meanwhile, in the school factory, workers are urged to increase production. The government publishes a manual teaching people how to resist in hand-to-hand combat. Shortly after, H hears that the United States has dropped the atom bomb on Hiroshima, although the authorities minimize the damage it causes.

The students gather at school to hear the emperor's radio broadcast, accepting the terms of the Potsdam Declaration. No one mentions directly that this event involves Japan's unconditional surrender.

After the war, H continues to resent the lies the government told. When occupation forces arrive in Kobe, he marvels at the superiority of their vehicles and weapons. An American serviceman allows him to sketch an M1 carbine, and H gets a favorable impression of U.S. soldiers. He also finds out the purpose of the occupation is to eradicate militarism and instill a democratic spirit. He is irritated by the fact that some of the teachers who were ardent militarists now become ardent democrats.

Living in a temporary dwelling with his family, H gets angry about everything he does not like. Under emotional strain, he quarrels with his parents and leaves home. He intends to commit suicide by lying under a train but pulls back at the last minute. For a while he lives in secret in a building at the school. Unsure of whether he will be allowed to graduate, he decides to study art. He seeks out a well-known artist, who allows him to work at his studio. The novel ends with H working as a sign painter during the day and studying at night with fellow artists at a studio.

Key Figures

Don-chan
See Haruo Ota

Joji Fujita

Joji Fujita, whose nickname is George, is a year older than H, but the two boys become friends when they work together in the same school factory. They have a lot in common. They both come from a family of Christians, but both are atheists. George speaks excellent English and always knows a lot about the war because he listens to the American radio broadcasts.

Fukushima

Fukushima is a friend of H in Second Middle School.

Furuta

Furuta is one of the members of the Second Middle School rifle club, and he encourages H to join.

George

See Joji Fujita

H

See Hajime Senoh

Uncle Hadano

Uncle Hadano is a civil engineer. He is a close friend of the Senoh family, and that is why H calls him uncle, although he is not a blood relative. H is fond of him and regards him as another father. The affection is mutual. H stays with Uncle Hadano for a while towards the end of the war. Uncle Hadano gets sick with cancer and dies shortly afterwards.

Iwao Hayashi

Iwao Hayashi is a friend of H. They are in the same grade at primary school. Hayashi is a champion wrestler; he is also intelligent and like H is good at drawing.

Instructor Hisakado

Instructor Hisakado, a teacher at Second Middle School, is in charge of the rifle club. He was formerly a watchmaker, and he is interested in art and music. He is a decent man and the students trust him. He teaches them that the true warrior is not one who does not fear death but one who has the skills necessary to protect himself.

Itchan

Itchan is a close friend of H at primary (or national) school. H confides in him that he owns a postcard from New York and talks to Itchan about the United States. Itchan passes this information on to another boy, who writes ''spy'' on H's desk in chalk. However, H and Itchan are soon reconciled.

Ryohei Koiso

Ryohei Koiso, a well-known artist, helps H in his studies after he graduates from Second Middle School.

Mr. Matsumoto

Mr. Matsumoto is the teacher of English at Second Middle School. H likes him because he says he will continue to teach them English, even though it is the language of the enemy, as long as he is able.

Mr. Nakata

Mr. Nakata is H's physics and chemistry teacher. He and H dislike each other.

Nishioka

Nishioka is a friend of H in Second Middle School.

Muneo Ogura

Muneo Ogura is a close friend of H toward the end of his time at Second Middle School.

Okubo

Okubo is a friend of H in Second Middle School. Like H, Okubo does not believe the official versions of the war.

Haruo Ota

Haruo Ota is one of H's classmates and the head boy. Haruo is known as ''blackpatch'' because of a birthmark on his head. H calls him ''Donchan.'' Haruo lends H a book called *The Three Treasures* from his father's collection.

Red Horse

See Instructor Tamiyama

Hajime Senoh

Also called H, Hajime Senoh is the son of Morio and Toshika Senoh. As a young boy in primary school he is intelligent and mischievous. According to his father, Hajime has a habit of saying the first thing that comes into his head. Hajime learns ways of getting what he wants even if he has to be devious. When he has no money but wants to see a ''puppet peepshow'' at a fairground, he tries to scare off the adults who are watching it by telling them they can contract an eye disease by touching the lens. Significantly, his favorite god in Japanese myth is Susanowo, who has a reputation for behaving badly.

Others tend to see H as an odd boy, although he has plenty of friends at school. But he is always questioning authority and asking awkward questions about why things are as they are. He is puzzled by the adults who say that everything that happens in the war is the will of the emperor, since H cannot see how the emperor can possibly be aware of all the things being done in his name. H's instincts are pacifistic, and he does not want to join the rifle club because he feels it is too warlike. He makes up his own version of a patriotic jingle, neatly reversing its meaning. He becomes exasperated when he realizes that the newspapers are not telling the truth about the war.

H rebels against what is expected of him in many ways. He skips classes when he is supposed to be studying for examinations. In response to the drive to collect scrap metal, he refuses to give up his precious collection of metal buttons. Rather than hand them over as a contribution to the war effort, he digs a hole and buries them. H also has a habit of turning in an exam paper with nothing written on it except his name and sometimes a sketch of his own hand on the back. He reserves this treatment for teachers who have a reputation for hitting their pupils. H is also impatient with what he sees as hypocrisy. After the war, if a teacher he dislikes comes into the classroom, he simply bows and walks out.

H does not want to be a tailor like his father. Instead, his greatest talent is drawing, and at the age of sixteen he resolves to become an artist.

Morio Senoh

Morio Senoh, H's father, is a kind, mild-mannered man, a tailor by profession. He moved to Kobe when he was fifteen years old to do his apprenticeship. After he married Toshika, he too became a Christian, although he is less enthusiastic about the religion than his wife is.

Morio's tailoring business suffers when all citizens are encouraged to wear national dress rather than the Western suits that he makes. Then when he joins the fire brigade during the war, he only has time to practice tailoring part-time. During his fire service, he distinguishes himself with his courage in saving lives.

Morio has a lot of common sense, and he is skeptical of the official claims that Japan is winning the war. He always suspects that the United States will eventually win. Since as a tailor he has many foreign clients, he is more cosmopolitan than the average resident of Kobe.

Morio is unfailingly kind and attentive to H, always ready to give him sound advice. Even when H throws a rice pot lid at him and walks out of the house, Morio does not blame him and welcomes him back with warmth.

Toshika Senoh

Toshika Senoh, H's mother, came originally from Hiroshima but moved to Kobe when she was eighteen and her family arranged her marriage to Morio. Toshika enthusiastically embraces whatever new ideas come along, and in Kobe she converted to Christianity, even though her birth family were Buddhists. Toshika is zealous for her religion, playing the tambourine on the streets with a group of Christians. She also tries to bring up her children in the Christian faith and does not let them read anything other than the Bible. Her habit of trying to express Christian love for everyone and everything irritates H. He often reacts negatively to her emotional and impulsive nature. During the war, Toshika becomes head of the neighborhood association and performs her duties well.

Yoshiko Senoh

Yoshiko Senoh, H's sister, is two years younger than H. She likes to cling to her older brother, and H finds this attachment a nuisance. But in one incident Yoshiko shows him kindness and he thinks better of her. This event occurs when she insists on eating with the fork that has one prong missing, even though it was H who broke the fork. Yoshiko is evacuated to the countryside when the air raids start.

Sumiyama

Sumiyama, a friend of H in Second Middle School, is kind to H when H's house is burned down. Sumiyama also enthusiastically practices how to fight and kill enemy soldiers if they should land in Japan.

Instructor Tamiyama

Instructor Tamiyama is a military instructor at the Second Middle School. He is nicknamed ''Red Horse'' because of his long face and red complexion. He is popular with the students. He volunteers to go to the battlefront.

Lieutenant Tamori

Lieutenant Tamori is the teacher in charge of military training at H's Second Middle School. All the students fear him. He is known as "His Lechery" because not only does he cultivate an imperious manner, he also makes inappropriate inquiries about the boys' sisters. Tamori takes a dislike to H when he finds H's sketch of a female nude in his notebook. In another incident, Tamori hits H for what he regards as an insolent remark. H joins the rifle club to escape him. Later he hears a rumor that some years earlier, Tamori's wife ran off with another man. This information makes H believe that Tamori must be lonely, and he feels compassion for him.

Mr. Tan Watanabe

Mr. Tan Watanabe is a teacher of English grammar at Second Middle who makes fun of Lieutenant Tamori.

Yokota

Yokota is a friend of H, and H considers him to be worldly-wise. Yokota is one of the students who participates with H on the arduous night march and other military drills. He and H go on a secret riding excursion together and are consequently expelled from the riding club. Yokota's family home is burned down following the big air raid on Kobe in 1945. Not long after this event, his father is killed in action in the South Pacific.

Themes

Militarism

Lurking behind the day-to-day experiences of the growing boy is the specter of the imperialism and militarism that characterized Japanese society in the 1930s and continued until the Japanese defeat in 1945. Imperialism and militarism are apparent almost from the beginning, in the passing reference to the neighborhood celebrations that followed the fall of Nanking, China, to invading Japanese forces

Topics for Further Study

- Based on your reading of the novel, why were so many ordinary Japanese people caught up in militarism and war fever during the 1930s and 1940s?

- Is there ever a justification for press censorship during times of war, or should the press always be free?

- Research the U.S. dropping of the first atomic bomb on Hiroshima in 1945. Why did the United States drop the bomb? Was the decision to use the bomb justified?

- Research the American Occupation of Japan after World War II. How did the American authorities go about eradicating militarism and instilling a democratic spirit?

- In what ways has the novel given you a better understanding of World War II?

- By the end of the novel, does H still seem like a boy from a foreign culture, or does he seem more like teenagers in other places? Is he very different from an American or not?

in 1937. H is affected by the war when he is only seven years old, when two of his friends are called up to the army. One of them commits suicide rather than enlist.

In the schools, boys are indoctrinated with the belief that their highest duty is to sacrifice themselves for the emperor, to die for the nation. No one except H seems to question this view, and as the years go by, militarization gets more pronounced. When H is about nine, the boys have a swimming class and are taught the "navy's way of swimming," which means to swim slowly and not splash much. "If your ship sinks, whether you survive or not will depend on this," the students are told.

In Japanese wartime society, everyone must be careful about what they say. No one dares to voice sentiments that might be considered un-Japanese.

Everything is secretive. Even the weather forecast is removed from the newspapers, on the grounds that it might give information to the enemy. A telling incident occurs when H is about eleven years old and takes a trip to the country by train. When the seacoast comes into view, the passengers automatically, without anyone saying anything, pull down their window blinds because the government has made it clear that no one is allowed to look out to sea. Warships may be visible, and that must be kept secret.

H always questions the need for such extreme secrecy, and at the end of the war he believes that the constant indoctrination of such ideas as dying for the emperor has made people unable to make mature judgments about how to behave and what to believe.

Coming-of-age

The narrative begins when H is about seven years old and ends when he is seventeen. During the war years he is forced to mature quickly. He learns to think for himself, to take charge in moments of crisis, and to discover his own identity.

H's transition from childhood to early adulthood is apparent in several major episodes. Firing live ammunition with the school rifle club for the first time is a significant moment, for example. So are the many times when he questions the validity of reports he reads in the newspapers about the progress of war. But the most important episode is when the family home is set on fire following an American air raid with incendiary bombs. Fifteen-year-old H immediately takes charge, giving his mother instructions about what to do and dousing a quilt in water so that they can put it over their heads as they flee. When his mother stops to pray, he tells her they must keep moving. In fact, she has fainted, and H's slaps get her conscious again. Then they come upon a woman whose son is badly injured. H almost faints at the sight of the blood, but he regains control of himself and offers the woman his flask of water, which she gives to the boy. But this is not enough to save him. For the first time H witnesses death, and H feels compassion for the dead boy—at least he is no longer in pain.

A short while later, he again takes the lead when he returns with his father to their ruined house. He is mature enough to ask his father whether he wishes to see the badly damaged sewing ma-chine, since he knows that his father's livelihood depends on the machine and fears he may be upset by its ruined condition.

A few days after the bombing, H observes the area around Hyogo Station, which is completely leveled. Dead bodies yet to be cremated are visible in the area. It is a sobering moment for H, who as a result of the air raid has been forced to lose any childhood innocence he may have had left: "'So this is war,' he thought as he gazed over the seemingly endless sea of destruction."

In the coming-of-age process, it is common for a teenager to get into conflict with his parents, and H is no exception. He becomes impatient with what he sees as his father's apathy after the war, and his mother's brand of pious and missionary Christianity annoys him more and more. When he throws the heavy lid of a rice pot directly at his father, he knows it is time to move out. He then tries to commit suicide but thinks better of it at the last minute. This experience is all part of the maturing process. H has to find out who he is and what his vocation in life is, independently of his family. By the end of the novel it appears that he has succeeded, since he is set for a career as an artist.

Style

Point of View and Language

Although *A Boy Called H* is an autobiographical novel, the story is told in the third rather than the first person. In this case, the point of view—the consciousness through which the story is told—is limited to H. Other characters, and all situations and events, are seen through his eyes. And since H is a young boy, the style employed to convey his point of view is for the most part quite simple. The sentence structure is simple, and the vocabulary is appropriate for a boy of H's age. Also, the story is told in a straightforward, chronological manner. There are no flashbacks (except in chapter 2, when H tells of his parents' backgrounds) or other more sophisticated literary devices.

The diction includes both informal and colloquial elements, as well as a fair amount of slang. (Of course, the translator has had to find English equivalents for the Japanese slang expressions.) The effect of this choice of diction is an unpretentious style. The narrative is not weighed down with deep thoughts or reflections, only such as arise in the immediate context of events, and even these are not dwelt upon excessively. The result is a somewhat detached, objective style, which gives the impression that H is a good, steady observer of life, rather than someone who gets too emotionally caught up in things, although that steadiness is sometimes belied by his rebellious behavior. It therefore comes as a surprise when late in the novel H comes close to mental breakdown and suicide. It suggests that the rather flat, even tone of the narration hides a depth of emotional turbulence which eventually finds its way to the surface.

Although the manner of narration is generally matter-of-fact and literal, occasionally the author uses poetic, figurative language to striking effect. A notable example is after the air raid on Kobe. When H sees the unburned pages of his books caught up in the wind and swirling in the air, he at first mistakes them for white butterflies: ''The scene, with white cabbage butterflies dancing round and round over the overall black of the ruins, was dreamlike, fantastic.'' He feels that the white flakes are ''the very souls . . . of the books.''

Historical Context

Japan in the 1930s and 1940s

Like the rest of the world, Japan suffered from the great economic depression of 1929 to 1931. As other countries introduced import tariffs on Japanese exports, the Japanese economic situation rapidly deteriorated. Needing new markets and raw materials, Japan turned its attention to China, knowing that a military conquest of China would give it exclusive control of a large economic area, including markets and raw materials. In 1931, Japan occupied Manchuria and set up the puppet state of Manchukuo to the south. China was militarily weak and could not stem the Japanese advance. By 1933, the Japanese had reached the Great Wall of China.

Japanese expansion into China created friction with the United States and Britain, both of whom had interests in the Far East. The League of Nations condemned the Japanese invasion, and in 1933 Japan withdrew from the League. After this decision, Japan began to look to Germany for support.

In 1937, Japan, Germany, and Italy signed a tripartite pact against Russia. With the United States still neutral, Japan launched on a major war of conquest. In the first few years, Japan met with

unbroken success. Most of Northern China was under its control. It had seized the chief ports, and it controlled the railroads and all lines of communication. The Japanese navy controlled the seas. Although out-fought, China continued to resist as well as it could.

In 1940, after the outbreak of World War II, the signatories of the tripartite pact mutually acknowledged German and Italian leadership of Europe, and Japanese leadership in East Asia. Britain, fighting in Europe against Nazi Germany, had few resources to spare for protecting its far eastern outposts or countering Japanese expansion.

Relations between Japan and the United States were tense. In the 1930s the isolationist United States took no steps to curb Japanese expansion other than to affirm the principle of Chinese integrity. But hostility to Japan was growing, particularly after 1937, when Japan stepped up its assault on China. The United States began to build up its Pacific navy, banned oil and other exports to Japan, impounded Japanese assets in the United States, and closed the Panama Canal to Japanese ships.

Negotiations between the two countries continued throughout 1941, but in December, without warning or a declaration of war, the Japanese attacked the U.S. fleet at Pearl Harbor. This event brought the United States into World War II, with Germany and Italy declaring war on the United States.

For the first six months following Pearl Harbor, Japanese forces put together a string of spectacular victories. Hong Kong, Sarawak, and the Malay Peninsula fell. In February 1942, the British naval fortress of Singapore, previously considered impregnable, surrendered. By March, Japanese gains were such that even Australia was threatened with invasion. By May 1942, the Japanese controlled Burma, and the whole of southeast Asia and the Western Pacific were in Japanese hands. The British and the Americans had been expelled.

But Japan's resources were stretched too wide, and the tide began to turn. In June 1942, the United States defeated the Japanese navy at the battle of Midway. American air power also soon began to tell. In 1943, from new bases in the Pacific, U.S. forces were destroying Japanese positions in the empire and in Japan itself. The first raid on Tokyo was in the spring of 1942.

Little by little, the Japanese were pushed back, in spite of their dogged resistance. By the spring of 1945, it was clear that Japan had lost the war. Its

Compare & Contrast

- **1930s–1945:** Increasing tensions between Japan and the United States lead to war. The United States is victorious after nearly four years of conflict.

  Today: The United States and Japan are allies, and their alliance ensures political stability in East Asia.

- **1930s–1945:** Japan is an authoritarian society in the grip of an imperialistic, militaristic way of thinking that glorifies war.

Today: Japan is a democracy based on Western-style political institutions.

- **1930s–1945:** The Japanese emperor is considered divine. Emperor Hirohito reigns over his people as a distant, god-like figure, often pictured on a white horse.

  Today: Japan retains its imperial family. But like surviving European monarchies, Prince Akihito, the son of Hirohito, is a figurehead and does not wield real political power.

---

navy had been completely destroyed, and American aerial bombardment was wiping out whole Japanese cities. H's home city of Kobe was not spared; it suffered devastating air raids in March and June 1945.

In July 1945, the three great powers, the United States, Britain and Russia, called on Japan to surrender or face utter destruction. On August 6, 1945, the United States dropped the first atomic bomb on the city of Hiroshima. About one hundred thousand people were killed in the first ten seconds. Three days later the United States dropped a second atomic bomb, this time on the city of Nagasaki. On August 14, Japan surrendered unconditionally.

By the end of the war, Japan had lost all the territories it had conquered, including Manchuria, and submitted to an American occupation. The Allies conducted trials of those it charged as war criminals, and Japan was given a new, democratic constitution.

Critical Overview

When first published in Japan in 1997, *A Boy Called H* quickly became a best-seller. Over two million copies were sold, and critics hailed the book as an outstanding example of literature about World War

II, although there was also a feeling that the book was not absolutely reliable in its historical details. Most of these details were minor. For example, in an incident that takes place in the book in the summer of 1942, H's sister sings a patriotic song that was not published until 1945.

When the book was translated into English and published in the United States in 1999, the critical response was enthusiastic. For Steven I. Levine, in *Library Journal,* the book provided "an accessible, unforgettable, and intimate introduction to the effects of the war upon Japanese family life, friendships, school, and society." Levine argued that the book belonged "with a handful of classics about children in wartime."

Hazel Rochman, in *Booklist,* commenting on how World War II becomes increasingly real for H, noted that "The writing is quiet, almost detached at times, until you come to realize that the young boy is fighting emotional breakdown."

The reviewer for *Publishers Weekly* described the book as "refreshing in the honesty with which it faces some ugly realities in Japan before and during WWII." The reviewer commented that one of the most shocking aspects of the novel was the way in which H, although he held many private doubts about the war, nonetheless in public was openly zealous about it and always supported the propaganda of the authorities.

Japan's Emperor Hirohito tours an area of Tokyo after a U.S. bombing during World War II

Criticism

Bryan Aubrey

Aubrey holds a Ph.D. in English and has published many articles on twentieth century literature. In this essay, Aubrey discusses the issue of press censorship in wartime, from Japan in World War II to today's United States.

A recurring theme in *A Boy Called H* is the extent to which the Japanese newspapers during wartime did not report the truth. H gets frustrated with what he reads about the war because he senses, as does his father, that they are not getting the whole story. When the first air raids are made on Kobe, the newspaper headlines read, "The Neighborhood Association Spirit Beats the Raiders." This puzzles H because he knows that, in fact, the air raid had taken the Neighborhood Association by surprise and that, in practice, the hazards of putting out fires were nothing like the smooth drills they had been regularly practicing. Also, someone is killed in that first raid, but the newspapers fail to report it. H decides that the newspapers "are just a pack of lies!" and he does not change his opinion from then on.

On the overseas battle front, the Japanese press enthusiastically reports Japanese victories but engages in subterfuge whenever there is a Japanese setback or defeat. One example in particular is quite amusing, illustrating as it does the extent to which language can be manipulated to disguise meaning. In 1943, Japanese forces were facing stiff opposition in the islands of the South Pacific. One morning the newspapers report the following:

> Our forces operating on Buna Island in New Guinea and Guadalcanal Island in the Solomons, which had been smashing persistent enemy counterattacks despite a shortage of manpower, have now achieved their objects and in early February were withdrawn from the islands and ordered to advance in another direction.

Behind the welter of difficult words, H concludes that this means Japan is losing in that area of the war. He asks his father, "Does 'advancing in another direction' mean retreating?" His father does not give him a satisfactory answer.

As H and his father guess, the newspapers in Japan during World War II were indeed subject to government and military censorship. This pattern was a matter of some importance, since Japan was (and still is) a nation of newspaper readers. Before

What Do I Read Next?

- Peter Wuden's *Day One: Before Hiroshima and After* (1984) tells the story of the making of the atomic bomb, the decision by President Harry Truman to use it in 1945, and the effects the bomb had on Hiroshima. The book includes maps and photographs.

- *Rising Sun: The Decline and Fall of the Japanese Empire, 1936–1945* (1970), by John Toland, is a history of Japan and its wars during the years covered by *A Boy Called H.* Toland views the events largely from the Japanese perspective.

- *Diary of Darkness: The Wartime Diary of Kiyosawa Kiyoshi,* translated by Eugene Soviak and Kamiyama Tamie (1998), is a diary kept by a liberal journalist in Japan from 1942 to 1945. He records his opposition, which he could not express openly, to the rampant Japanese nationalism and bureaucratic control of every aspect of life. He also notes Japan's descent into poverty and crime as the inevitability of defeat loomed.

- Anne Ipsen's *A Child's Tapestry of War* (1998) is a memoir about Ipsen's Danish childhood, which included the Nazi occupation of Denmark during World War II. Although born into a privileged family, Ipsen is touched by the horrors of war, as when her elderly half-Jewish cousin is sent to a concentration camp; a school is accidentally destroyed by bombs; and she hears her father's account of a mission to help concentration camp survivors.

Japan went to war against the United States in 1941, daily circulation of newspapers was about nineteen million, which was more than one newspaper per household. Newspapers were not controlled by the government, and they were free to criticize politicians, although even before the war they tended to be supportive of the government's foreign policies.

After the war began with China, the government expected the press to be loyal to the Japanese cause, and restrictions were placed on it. Any news regarding the economy or foreign events was considered to be a state secret and could not be published without permission. (In *A Boy Called H*, H frequently expresses annoyance and frustration at the number of things that are declared state secrets.) Further regulations made it a punishable offense to deviate from official guidelines or to reveal any information considered helpful to the enemy.

In *Politics and Culture in Wartime Japan,* Ben-Ami Shillony states that as long as Japan was successful, press reports of the progress of the war were largely accurate. But when the tide turned and Japan experienced defeat after defeat, official bulletins printed in the newspapers were glaringly false. Shillony uses the decisive battle of Midway in June 1942 as an example. In that battle, Japan lost more than twice as many ships and planes as the United States and nearly twelve times the number of men. But the Japanese press was obliged to present Midway as a victory for Japan, denouncing any other view as enemy propaganda.

The defeat on Guadalcanal was also initially reported as a success, until, as H found out, it was conceded that Japanese forces had made a "sideward advance" (which as Shillony shows is a translation of the Japanese word *tenshin* and is the equivalent of the phrase "advancing in another direction" that H reads about).

Although H frequently bemoans the fact, censorship of the press in wartime is a common phenomenon, not only in Japan but elsewhere. Governments usually assume that keeping up public morale in difficult times is more important than allowing the press to report the unvarnished truth. In the United States during World War II, the press censorship was voluntary. It was supervised by the Office of Censorship, which was a civilian, not a military, body. In January 1942, guidelines for news reporting were sent out to all U.S. newspapers, magazines, and radio stations. During the course of the war, not a single print journalist and only one radio journalist deliberately flouted the censorship guidelines. This compliance was in part because the war was generally supported by the American public, and journalists were no different. Along with most Americans, they felt that the war against Hitler's Germany and Imperial Japan was justified and were more than willing to support the government. Of course, had results on the battlefield not, after mid-1942, begun to favor the United States, the censorship guidelines might have come under strain, as they did in Japan. It is much easier to report the truth when one's own side is winning.

After the war, the U.S. occupation forces maintained extensive censorship of Japanese newspapers, as H finds out when the newspaper he reads, the *Asahi Shimbun,* has to suspend publication for two days at the order of the U.S. commander, General Douglas MacArthur. As William J. Coughlin explains in *Conquered Press,* the censorship code was designed to prevent the publication of false stories and any story that was likely to arouse ill-feeling towards the Occupation forces. Nothing could be printed that put the United States in a bad light. Much international news was censored, including the deteriorating relations between the United States and the Soviet Union. Anything that encouraged the reemergence of militarism was also banned. Some Japanese complained that there was less freedom of thought and speech in U.S.-occupied Japan than there had been during the war.

H, however, prefers American censorship to the Japanese version, and he explains why in the chapter, "Homes for Air Raid Victims." In his experience, it was easier to find out the reason why a certain article had been banned or had displeased the censors than it had been under Japanese censorship, when no reasons were ever given.

Press censorship in Japan was eased in 1948, when it was made voluntary. It was assumed that the Japanese editors had absorbed the censorship code and would observe it voluntarily. In most cases this was true, but there were many instances of Japanese newspapers being fined or reprimanded for stepping out of line.

Since World War II, the subject of the freedom of the press in wartime has not come up again in Japan, since the nation's postwar constitution forbids it to engage in war. However, the same subject has been a thorny issue in the United States. Rela-

> **"** In a democratic society, there is an inherent tension between the government, which likes to 'manage' the news, and the press, whose job it is to seek it out and report it objectively."

tions between the government and the press during the Korean War, which lasted from 1950 to 1953, were sometimes strained. U.S. war correspondents were critical of military strategy, and the U.S. Army command accused them of giving aid and comfort to the enemy.

The Vietnam war provides another example. As the war, which began in the early 1960s, dragged on into the late sixties, with no end in sight, the press became increasingly critical of U.S. war policies. In one devastating episode, in 1971, the *New York Times* published what became known as the Pentagon Papers. Drawn from seven thousand pages of secret documents, the Pentagon Papers exposed many of the shortcomings of U.S. policy in Vietnam. Such a bombshell dropped by the press would have been unthinkable in World War II. The difference was that World War II was a popular war, a "good" war, whereas the Vietnam war, certainly by its later stages, was an unpopular war that many Americans believed should not have been fought.

Press freedom in wartime continued to be an issue after Vietnam. In 1983, for example, journalists were banned from directly covering the U.S. invasion of Grenada. They were only allowed into the country after U.S. forces had the situation under control. The same rules were applied to the U.S. invasion of Panama in 1989. The U.S. military believed that it could not rely on journalistic discretion or self-censorship in reporting the military clashes. The U.S. actions in both Grenada and Panama were widely supported by the American public, but later investigations suggested that the operations had not gone as smoothly as was at first believed.

None of this should be surprising. In a democratic society, there is an inherent tension between the government, which likes to "manage" the news, and the press, whose job it is to seek it out and report it objectively. In wartime, this tension may increase, since the government usually feels the need to prevent public confidence in its policies from being undermined by an inquisitive or critical press. On the other hand, at times when the nation is united in war, tensions between government and press may abate. A case in point is the aftermath of the terrorist attacks in New York and Washington, D.C., on September 11, 2001. After President George W. Bush's declaration that the nation was at war with terrorism, the press rallied around the president. No one wanted to appear unpatriotic in a time of need. Only gradually over the course of the following year did some muted criticism of government strategy in the "war on terror" begin to emerge in the main-stream press.

As young H found out in wartime Japan, the relationship between the government and the press is not always ideal. H relied on his common sense and his independence of mind in order to not be fooled by the official line of the Japanese government, especially when it contradicted his own experience. Although we may suspect that the author exaggerates the extent to which H was able, with his limited sources of information, to reach skeptical conclusions about the information he read in the newspapers, it is as well to be reminded of the fact that the words of those who claim to be defending the national interest should not always be taken at face value.

Source: Bryan Aubrey, Critical Essay on *A Boy Called H: A Childhood in Wartime Japan*, in *Nonfiction Classics for Students,* Gale, 2003.

Catherine Dybiec Holm

Holm is a freelance writer with speculative fiction and nonfiction publications. In this essay, Holm looks at how Senoh captures the insidious effects of war in a young boy's daily life.

For those of us in a country that has never seen traditional warfare on its soil, it can be difficult to imagine the day-to-day realities of living in a nation under attack. Even news coverage cannot come close to capturing the insidious ways that war can affect individual lives. Kappa Senoh's fictionalized autobiography, *A Boy Called H: A Childhood in Wartime Japan*, does a fantastic job of capturing the process of war and its increasing presence in the life of H and others. The book's precocious protagonist does not flinch from making his views about war

known to the reader, even though H feels he must keep his opinions to himself in many public situations.

Right away, we are given a hint of the public paranoia that will increase over time. So early in the book, this instance of subtle public fear is an almost unnoticed foreshadowing of events to come, since it is combined with other apparently pleasant details of everyday life. H becomes friendly with a man from the noodle shop. When Noodles (as H calls him) invites H up to his apartment to listen to records, H is so taken with the music that he calls Noodles "Red Label," after the labels on the record collection.

> H found himself liking the delivery boy more and more and decided that as a mark of respect he'd give him the nickname "Red Label." The next time he went to visit, he told him about it. To his surprise, the smile was wiped off his face in a flash. "No, thank you!" he said in a loud voice, "You stick to 'Noodles'—I don't want any 'Red Label.'"

Later it turns out that Noodles is captured right in H's neighborhood; and that Noodles is thought to be a Communist informant. But when H hears the neighbors talking about the incident and tries to decipher their meaning, he is brushed aside. "'What're dangerous thoughts? Who're the secret police?' H asked them anxiously, but the grown-ups suddenly clammed up. 'Keep your voice down,' he was told with a look of fierce disapproval."

H notes that the paper never reports on the incident. Throughout the book, he'll continually notice discrepancies between reality and what the news reports, especially as the war accelerates. And possibly, for the first time in his life, the concept of being an informant is really understood by the boy. He begins to fear that Noodles will think H informed on him.

Even though Japan is not at war in the beginning of this book, the stage is being set as the author skillfully accents aspects of H's life that will later prove to have a direct relationship, in some way, to war. Early on, H's mother is described as an ardent Christian. The practice of Christianity is not the norm during this period in Japan. H's mother came from a family of Buddhists, and "no one had dreamed for a moment that she might become Christian, and it caused quite a stir in the village." Later, H's family is suspect in a general way, as wartime propaganda paints a picture of Christianity as the religion of the "British and American fiends." H's family is considered unusual in the community of Kobe, since H's father is a tailor and has customers of all nationalities (Kobe has an international population). As the wartime situation becomes more tense, H's family needs to consider how openly they can practice their religion. H's father wonders if he'll still have international customers and how his business will fare.

In the fourth grade, H experiences another side to the war besides the patriotism that is touted by the government and, increasingly, by the press. Girly Boy, a young man in the community that H is friendly with, gets his call-up papers. Three days after Girly Boy leaves, the military police come to Kobe looking for him; apparently Girly Boy has deserted. When H and some friends are playing, H discovers Girly Boy in an old shack. Horrified, H realizes that Girly Boy hanged himself to avoid serving in the war.

H is indeed horrified, even if the tone of the narrative is relatively subdued. In fact, throughout the book, H seems to process many horrifying experiences in a subdued, almost clinical way. It is difficult to tell whether this is part of the author's style or whether the protagonist, as reviewer Hazel Rochman suggests in *Booklist,* sounds detached because "the young boy is fighting emotional breakdown."

It is immediately after the Girly Boy incident that H's true feelings about war begin to become clear. H begins to have the courage to process such thoughts internally, even though they run counter to what the government would have the public believe about the war. With surprising clarity for a young child, and an unusual lack of fear at the circumstances, H reflects on the situation. "His friend hadn't wanted to be a soldier, he thought to himself: suicide was the only alternative. He wondered if hanging himself had seemed better than being killed by a bullet on the battlefield."

Throughout *A Boy Called H: A Childhood in Wartime Japan*, H continues to have troubling thoughts that explore the ethics of war. His musings are mature for a person his age, probably in part because his parents are thoughtful and deviate from the norm. Keeping his thoughts to himself, or occasionally confiding to a few like-minded adults (including his father), H questions the official party line and finds discrepancies in news coverage of the war. In some cases, H realizes that his views differ from those of his friends or his teachers. In riskier instances, he is silent, as when he is interviewing for a slot in school and is asked about his opinion on the

> Senoh seems to be asking us—Who can make sense of the insanity of war?—even though each person may hold a different opinion or have suffered different losses during wartime."

war. A reviewer in *Publishers Weekly* suggests that this discrepancy

> . . . leaves a gaping hole in the center of the narrative. Senoh seems more comfortable hinting at, rather than directly confronting, big questions about personal responsibility and collective guilt. Maybe these questions remain too painful, both for himself and the entire Japanese nation.

While this reviewer might find that these "big questions" would have been dealt with more directly had H voiced them aloud, H does, on many occasions, struggle with the questions internally, giving the reader a good argument regarding the ethics of war.

It is understandable that H would be cautious, even paranoid, about voicing his true feelings during the tense social climate of wartime. Senoh makes it clear that Japanese felt the need to modify their behavior during these times, and hide or draw attention away from certain pursuits that used to be undertaken without a worry. Thus, H's Christian parents worry about practicing their religion too visibly, since Christianity is now associated with western nations and the "British and American fiends." Passengers riding a commuter train automatically draw the shades down when the train passes the ocean, so no one will see the ocean that the train is passing—and possibly witness a "military secret." Such paranoid and necessary behaviors become a part of everyday life for the Japanese, until the populace can barely remember living any differently. Senoh makes the experience ultimately knowable for the reader, since anyone can imagine being in these everyday, real yet surreal, situations.

But H has been struggling with his conscience even before the acceleration of war. These internal ethical struggles are ones that readers can identify with. How many people, for example, have experienced modifying what they truly wish to say, for fear of reprisal? H recalls how he was singled out as a first grader, because of his family's religious practice:

> He'd been surrounded by other boys who said to him, "Your family are Amens, aren't they? You people are supposed to love your enemies, right? So you love Chinks, do you?"
>
> Frightened, H was so keen to get away that he blurted out tearfully, "I'm not a Chink-lover. I don't love them. I *hate* Chinks!"
>
> The incident continued to bother his conscience long after that.

H fights with his conscience through much of the book. In showing this, Senoh has made the book completely readable, since H is confronting aspects of the human condition others can relate to.

War continues to make its presence known in everyday life, often in surprising and detailed ways. H and his classmates are taught specific ways to swim and remain afloat in a survival situation. When air raids become common, schoolchildren are given detailed instructions on how to take shelter on the floor under desks, and to open their mouths and cover their ears and eyes so that their ears and eyes stay intact during an explosion. When food shortages increase, residents receive information on how to use parts of the rice plant (such as rice grass) that were previously considered inedible. In Senoh's unsurprised, detailed narrative, the already surreal events become even more surreal to the reader. These changes become commonplace and accepted as an everyday part of life, much like the words "terrorism" and "anthrax" became a more commonplace part of American reality and language after the terrorist attacks against the United States in September 2001.

With a true nonconformist's mentality, H makes it clear early on that he respects people who stand for their principles. Though his mother has forbidden him to read anything but the Bible and textbooks, she finds that he is secretly reading *The Three Treasures* (H loves books and movies). When she confronts an unsuspecting teacher about this, the teacher covers for H, saying that reading such books was good for H, and reading only the Bible "wasn't likely to do [children] much good." H admires the pragmatism and forthright nature of the teacher. Given such glimpses at H's parents, it is easy to see how such a young protagonist developed such a questioning and intelligent nature. Although

his mother is an evangelist, she is at least willing to change her stance regarding H's reading material after meeting with the teacher. H's father also has a number of interesting discussions with H on the subjects of war, tolerance for other religions and cultures, and ethics. At one point, H's father tells the boy, "If you're going to call religions that other people believe in 'heathen,' you can't complain if other people refer to Christianity as heathen."

From early on, H has been taught by his parents to consider both sides of any issue. But perhaps his reluctance to voice his opinion begins with friends at the beach in the winter of 1940.

> "Say what you like, Japan's got a strong navy!" cried Shogo in a shrill voice.
>
> "If it was a real war, though," said H, even though he was just as excited, "the enemy wouldn't just sit still, they'd fire back."
>
> This prompted an immediate barrage of cries along the lines of "Whose side are *you* on anyway?" from the others, so H decided he better be careful about this habit of putting forward the other side of things.

This is an intensely real, human reaction—one that any reader who has taken a risk (or considered taking a risk) in voicing a dissenting opinion will recognize.

In an interesting scene toward the end of the book, H expresses sudden joy that the war is over. His friend is upset with H's reaction and joy, since the friend's family members are potentially dead or injured because of the war. The friend smacks H in anger, and H experiences a sudden catharsis. "Suddenly, the tear spilled from H's eyes too—not from regret at the defeat, but out of sheer, frustrated puzzlement as to what the war had been all about."

This is also a completely human reaction. Senoh seems to be asking us—Who can make sense of the insanity of war?—even though each person may hold a different opinion or have suffered different losses during wartime.

H is a nonconformist and a pragmatist. He is also a survivor. It's no surprise, therefore, when H begins to pursue a career as an artist toward the end of the book. Many artists, through their work, pursue an ideal of telling the truth, of speaking the truth and letting it be known. Although the character H may hesitate, out of necessity, to voice his opinions, the author has used effective honesty in giving us a look at the difficult ethics and the surrealistic everyday life in wartime Japan.

Source: Catherine Dybiec Holm, Critical Essay on *A Boy Called H: A Childhood in Wartime Japan,* in *Nonfiction Classics for Students,* Gale, 2003.

Mary Goebel Noguchi

In the following review, Noguchi praises A Boy Called H *for its "gradual development of understanding on the part of the narrator" but questions the accuracy of the story.*

Senoh Kappa's *A Boy Called H*, the English translation of *Shônen H*, is the story of a bright, curious boy growing up in an unconventional family in Kobe during Japan's "15-year war." It is a tale of loss of innocence, as the boy's penchant for questioning everything is subject to the tightening constraints of the social, educational and political systems of a country increasingly entrenched in war and insistent that its entire population devote itself to ultimate victory.

The hero is dubbed "H" by his friends because his mother, inspired by a photograph she received from a foreign missionary friend, has knit the first letter of the boy's name, Hajime, into a sweater that he often wears. Both of his parents are devout Christians with many contacts in the foreign community of Kobe, and both strive to live according to their principles, especially by showing brotherly love to all people.

The book begins when H is an elementary school student in the late 1930s and follows him through World War II, the fire bombings of Kobe and destruction of his family home, and on through Japan's surrender, when all the contradictions in the society around him drive H to attempt suicide. It ends in 1948 when the youth has finally been able to pick up the pieces of his shattered life and find a useful outlet for his artistic talents. Working for the Phoenix Studio, a sign-maker's shop, he sees his country rising from the ashes of war like the immortal bird in the company name.

A Boy Called H is carefully constructed to recreate the boy's development. The first chapters artfully illustrate his early innocence, curiosity and exuberance with a series of anecdotes reminiscent of the adventures of Tom Sawyer and Huckleberry Finn. Like Mark Twain, Senoh Kappa narrates the story from the perspective of the youth, so that we see all his questions and confusion about the complex social issues in the world around him, but in a

U.S. General Douglas MacArthur and Emperor Hirohito during their first meeting at the U.S. embassy in Tokyo

way that allows the more informed adult reader to laugh gently at his foibles.

Although the dark side of Japanese pre-war society is apparent from the start, when a local noodle delivery boy is arrested by the Secret Police because of his "dangerous ideas," H's life during the first quarter of the book seems almost idyllic. He pours his energies into sneaking into movies and peepshows, earning pocket money by selling paste and trading pictures of sumo wrestlers, and spending long days at the seaside learning to row and trying to make salt from seawater.

However, as the military increasingly controls every facet of daily life, H has to come to grips with emperor worship, deprivation, war slogans, fear of the Secret Police, and worst of all, the transformation of schools into factories and military training institutes. With his rationality and Christian principles, H has great difficulty accepting the changes in the society around him. He asks many of the same questions a Westerner or a Japanese youth today might ask: Why does everyone put up with the shortages? Why do they go along with all of the propaganda and the unreasonable demands of the military? Why don't the adults say that the country

"... any astute reader should see A Boy Called H as a literary work. Each chapter is neatly constructed to make a single point and could stand alone as a short story, complete with beginning, middle and end."

is on the wrong course? Why don't the newspapers print the truth?

With great compassion, Senoh shows us why. In many cases, H himself is drawn in by goodies distributed to quell the people's anxieties and doubts. When special rations of sake, sweets and rubber balls are to be handed out to mark the fall of Singapore, for example, we find, "For all H's avowed dislike of war, the enticement of such special rations convinced him that victory in war wasn't a bad thing after all."

H's father Morio also helps the boy understand other people's reactions. When H asks Morio why the usually soft-spoken young man at a local shop bellowed out a speech welcoming his draft notice, Morio points out that "he probably has this basic idea that it's a man's duty to give up his life for his country," and even though his "mother and the others in his family don't want to lose him," he "may well have wanted to declare to himself and everyone else that [he] . . . was a real man now." H also sees Morio himself slowly becoming more circumspect, even in his conversations with his son, since the child's bragging that his father has a picture postcard of a tall building in America is enough to get Morio dragged into the police station for questioning.

Gradually, H comes to be more accepting of those around him who seem to be blindly devoted to the war effort. Although he initially rebels against a fanatical military instructor at his middle school, he eventually finds that "the strong resentment he'd once felt had given way to a feeling that the man was a lonely, pitiful figure. Possibly, as the war situation grew increasingly critical, he was desperately feel-

ing that he should do something, without knowing what that something was."

This gradual development of understanding on the part of the narrator makes this a valuable work. Not only does the original *Shônen H* explain to young Japanese today why the nation was led so badly astray a half-century ago, but the English translation also helps make the Japanese of that period appear far more human to Westerners, with their cultural tendency to stick to principles and strive for consistency in their own lives. For this reason, *Shônen H* was highly acclaimed in Japan by a number of critics and authors who had lived through the war. The pocketbook (*bunkobon*) edition of the work includes a short essay by renowned author Inoue Hisashi praising Senoh for explaining a period in the nation's history which, to anyone who did not live through it, can only be viewed as a time of sheer craziness.

Published in January 1997, *Shônen H* became an instant bestseller. The story was adapted for the stage, and a TV dramatization was broadcast in the fall of 1999. Moreover, because Senoh wrote the work in a style that would be accessible to children and insisted that the readings of most Chinese characters be provided, many junior high school teachers have added it to their recommended reading list or used excerpts in history classes.

The English translation masterfully captures the spirit of the original. Veteran translator John Bester conveys just the right combination of naivete and humor in the early chapters and then gradually darkens the tone to set the mood for the hero's descent into the hell of war. He has taken great pains to accurately render the many place names and dated technical terms that fill the work's 528 pages.

Nonetheless, a fair number of awkward sentences, dangling modifiers and small mistakes give the impression that the translation was rushed into publication without the benefit of a careful re-reading by translator and editor. However, these are minor quibbles with a basically solid translation.

A more serious problem arises when we try to classify this work in order to understand how to read it. Only at the end of the original *Shônen H* do we find the label *shôsetsu* to suggest, that it is fiction. The author has claimed on TV talk shows that the work is an accurate account of his childhood (Hajime being his given name and Kappa his pen name. He has since had his name legally changed to Kappa on his family register). Senoh says he consulted chronological tables and other historical sources to make the work as accurate as possible. He also sent chapters to several people his age to check on the historical veracity of his work and confirmed other facts and figures with people who appear in the story. The personal names in the book are the real names of people in his life, and the Japanese edition includes photographs of Senoh's teachers and classmates as well as those of friends who feature prominently in the story. Maps of his neighborhood in Kobe are also provided to help the reader visualize the locations in the narrative.

Yet one has to wonder about the accuracy of this "autobiographical novel" (as the translator calls it). Do we read it as "The Truth" or as historical fiction? Differing answers to this question have led to controversy over the book in Japan. Early media accounts praised the remarkable accuracy and detail of Senoh's memory. However, by late 1997, the selection committees for two awards for juvenile literature were embroiled in debate over historical inaccuracies in the work. In the end, *Shônen H* received neither the Shôgakukan Jidô Shuppan Bunka-Shô nor the Noma Jidô Bungei-Shô, even though it had been the front-running nominee for both prizes.

The most vociferous critic of the work has been Yamanaka Hisashi, an author of historical books for children and a member of that year's selection committee for both awards. Yamanaka was so incensed by the uncritical acclaim Senoh's book received that he and his wife, Yamanaka Noriko, wrote an 845-page critique titled *Machigai Darake no Shônen H* (Shônen H: A Book Full of Mistakes). Yamanaka's tome points out three major flaws in Senoh's book. First, he claims the work is riddled with mistakes in historical fact. For example, in a chapter that takes place during the summer of 1942, Senoh's sister sings a patriotic song that was published and performed for the first time in 1945. In another chapter, a postman delivers a draft notice, even though these papers were actually delivered by special military personnel.

Second, Yamanaka feels that characters in the book, especially Morio, know things and make predictions of the course of the war in a way that was not possible at the time because of media censorship. Yamanaka, who is only a year younger than Senoh, asserts that people in Japan at the time were completely fooled by the government and that there is no way that anyone could have entertained the kind of doubts that a number of the characters in

Shônen H expressed. Finally, Yamanaka doubts whether H (Senoh) himself really questioned the war at the time as much as he does in the book.

Senoh apparently recognized the validity of a number of Yamanaka's claims about historical inaccuracies and revised later editions of *Shônen H*, although the latter two concerns were not addressed by the author. *A Boy Called H*, based on the 18th printing published in September 1997, reflects only some of the changes. As of February this year, the 29th printing was issued.

I also wondered whether Senoh had added many of the questions H asks and his attacks on the government after the fact. Other historical accounts of this period indicate that most Japanese supported the war. For years, it was impossible in Japan to bring up the question of the emperor's responsibility for the war. As recently as 1990, the mayor of Nagasaki, Motoshima Hitoshi, was shot by a rightist for daring to publicly state that the emperor bore at least some responsibility. Thus it is hard not to conclude that Senoh's recollection of his youth must be tinged by insights gained as an adult.

Yet any astute reader should see *A Boy Called H* as a literary work. Each chapter is neatly constructed to make a single point and could stand alone as a short story, complete with beginning, middle and end. Senoh said on a TV talk show that the chapters were written so that they would not have to be read in any particular order. Indeed, the author often explains characters and H's current situation in a way that appears redundant to someone who is reading the book straight through.

If taken as an artistic attempt to explain why Japan continued along the path to what in retrospect can only be seen as its inevitable self-destruction, then *A Boy Called H* serves as a valuable aid for those who did not live through that process to be more compassionate with those who did. As such, it is well worth reading.

Source: Mary Goebel Noguchi, "Compassionate Look at a Nation Co-opted," in *Japan Quarterly,* Vol. 47, No. 2, April–June 2000, pp. 98–101.

Sources

Coughlin, William J., *Conquered Press: The MacArthur Era in Japanese Journalism,* Pacific Books, 1952, pp. 46–58.

Levine, Steven I., Review of *A Boy Called H,* in *Library Journal,* Vol. 125, No. 6, April 1, 2000, p. 113.

Review of *A Boy Called H,* in *Publishers Weekly,* Vol. 247, No. 7, February 14, 2000, p. 182.

Rochman, Hazel, Review of *A Boy Called H,* in *Booklist,* Vol. 96, No. 12, February 15, 2000, p. 1084.

Shillony, Ben-Ami, *Politics and Culture in Wartime Japan,* Clarendon Press, 1981, pp. 91–97.

Sweeney, Michael S., *Secrets of Victory: The Office of Censorship and the American Press and Radio in World War II,* University of North Carolina Press, 2001.

Further Reading

Cook, Haruko Taya, and Theodore F. Cook, *Japan at War: An Oral History,* New Press, 1993.

> This work of oral history captures in the words of ordinary people exactly what it was like to live in Japan during the time of Japan's war with China and the United States. As in *A Boy Called H,* many Japanese express a view of the war that is very different from the official versions.

Nimura, Janice P., Review of *A Boy Called H,* in *Washington Post,* August 6, 2000.

> Nimura comments admiringly on Senoh's prose that seems so artless but manages to convey an entire social world.

Siegenthaler, Peter, Review of *A Boy Called H,* in *Persimmon: Asian Literature, Arts, and Culture,* Vol. 1, No. 2, Summer 2000. Available on the Internet at http://www.persimmon-mag.com/summer2000/bre_sum2000_3.htm (last accessed December 23, 2002).

> Siegenthaler regards one of the strengths of the book to be how it shows many ordinary Japanese doubting the official versions of how the war was progressing but lacking the ability to give voice to their doubts in any public forum.

Bury My Heart at Wounded Knee

Dee Brown

1970

Dee Brown's *Bury My Heart at Wounded Knee* was first published in the United States in 1970. This landmark book—which incorporated a number of eyewitness accounts and official records—offered a scathing indictment of the U.S. politicians, soldiers, and citizens who colonized the American West. Focusing mainly on the thirty-year span from 1860 to 1890, the book was the first account of the time period told from the Native-American point of view. It demonstrated that whites instigated the great majority of the conflicts between Native Americans and themselves. Brown began searching for the facts about Native Americans after he met several as a child and had a hard time believing the myths about their savagery that were popular among white people. Brown published his book a century after the events took place, but it was a timely publication, since many U.S. citizens were already feeling guilty about their country's involvement in the Vietnam War. Brown's book depicted, in detail, the U.S. government's attempt to acquire Native Americans' land by using a mix of threats, deception, and murder. In addition, the book showed the attempts to crush Native-American beliefs and practices. These acts were justified by the theory of Manifest Destiny, which stated that European descendents acting for the U.S. government had a God-given right to take land from the Native Americans. *Bury My Heart at Wounded Knee* is Brown's best-known work and has since overshadowed all of his other books.

Author Biography

Dee Brown was born on February 28, 1908, in Alberta, Louisiana. He grew up in Arkansas, where he met many Native Americans. He found it hard to believe the myths of Native-American savagery and read everything he could find about the real history of the American West. Since he was pursuing a career as a librarian at the same time, he frequently had access to the materials he needed. At George Washington University, he studied library science and worked as a library assistant for the United States Department of Agriculture. After receiving his bachelor's degree in library science in 1937, Brown held his first librarian position, at the Beltsville Research Center (1940–1942).

In 1942, he published his first novel, *Wave High the Banner*, a historical novel based on the life and adventures of Davy Crockett, the legendary frontiersman. Over the next few decades, Brown wrote several more novels and nonfiction books about the American West and earned his master's degree from the University of Illinois (1952). He also worked as a librarian for the United States War Department and the University of Illinois, ultimately becoming a professor of library science at the university from 1962 to 1975.

However, despite all of these accomplishments, it was Brown's 1970 publication of *Bury My Heart at Wounded Knee* that made him a household name. After that, Brown published several works, including a nonfiction book, *Wondrous Times on the Frontier* (1993); a collection of autobiographical writings, *When the Century Was Young: A Writer's Notebook* (1993); and a novel, *The Way to Bright Star* (1998). However, none of these works received the attention or praise of *Bury My Heart at Wounded Knee*, which is still Brown's best-known work. Brown lives and works in Little Rock, Arkansas.

Plot Summary

Chapter 1: "Their Manners are Decorous and Praiseworthy"

Bury My Heart at Wounded Knee begins with an overview of the relations between Native Americans and white settlers from the late-1400s to the mid-1800s. Initially peaceful, these relations become more tense as white emigration from Europe to the United States increases.

Chapter 2: The Long Walk of the Navahos

The government wants Navaho land for settlements and mining, so the U.S. Army kills or displaces all Mescalero Apaches and Navahos in the region. Many Navahos die when they are forced to live at the Bosque Redondo reservation. Ultimately, the Navahos sign a peace treaty and are allowed to return to what is left of their land.

Chapter 3: Little Crow's War

Manipulated by deceptive treaties, the Santee Sioux surrender most of their land for money and provisions they mostly do not receive. Little Crow does not want to fight the military might of the United States but has no choice when some of his men kill white settlers. The Santees are ultimately overpowered by the Army and by a Santee traitor.

Chapter 4: War Comes to the Cheyennes

White settlers ignore a treaty and begin settling on Native-American territory. After Cheyennes and Arapahos meet with the Colorado governor to try to maintain peace, many Cheyennes are mutilated or massacred in their Sand Creek village. The Cheyennes split, some going north to join the Northern Cheyennes and the Teton Sioux in Powder River country, while others go south, below the Arkansas River, where they are coerced into signing away their land in Colorado.

Chapter 5: Powder River Invasion

The Cheyennes learn that soldiers are building a fort in the Powder River country. A Cheyenne warrior tries to warn some Arapahos of coming soldiers, but they do not believe him, and their village is destroyed by one military column. A group of Sioux chase the half-starved, frozen soldiers of two other military columns and attempt to beat them in battle but are overpowered.

Chapter 6: Red Cloud's War

The government says it wants to buy transportation rights in the Powder River country, but it deploys soldiers even before a treaty is discussed. Angry at this deception, the Sioux fight a successful guerrilla war, cutting off the soldiers' supply lines, trapping soldiers in isolated battles, and derailing a train. Ultimately, the government withdraws its troops and settles for a peace treaty.

Chapter 7: "The Only Good Indian Is a Dead Indian"

Some of the exiled Southern Cheyennes and Arapahos, encouraged by the Sioux's successes, try to return to their old tribal lands. This action results in a war between the Army and several Native-American tribes, including the Cheyennes, the Arapahos, the Comanches, and the Kiowas. At the end of the fighting, all tribes except the Kiowas surrender and go to reservations.

Chapter 8: The Rise and Fall of Donehogawa

Red Cloud finds out that the peace treaty he signed included items he did not know about. Donehogawa, an educated Native American, is Commissioner of Indian Affairs at the time. He invites Red Cloud and several other Sioux to state their case to President Grant in Washington, D.C. Red Cloud is successful, but Donehogawa loses his influence due to political pressure and resigns.

Chapter 9: Cochise and the Apache Guerrillas

Several Apaches refuse to live on a reservation and instead they engage in a guerrilla war. Settlers massacre a peaceful band of Apaches at Camp Grant, prompting President Grant to send out a commission to talk to the Apache chiefs. After much fighting, most of the Apaches settle on reservations or live in exile in Mexico.

Chapter 10: The Ordeal of Captain Jack

The Modocs do not receive treaty provisions from the government and return to their old lands, the U.S. military comes to remove them, and Captain Jack takes his people to a stronghold. Hooker Jim's band kills some settlers in revenge then forces Captain Jack into killing General Canby, which instigates a war. Hooker Jim and his men surrender to the soldiers, then track down Captain Jack, who is hanged.

Chapter 11: The War to Save the Buffalo

The Kiowas are forced to go to a reservation. They resolve to leave the reservation to fight the white hunters who are destroying the buffalo but are overpowered. Some tribes choose to go back to the reservation, while others hunt buffalo at Palo Duro Canyon, the last remaining range. The Army destroys their village and forces the Kiowas to surrender.

Dee Brown

Chapter 12: The War for the Black Hills

A force of several thousand Native Americans fights to save the sacred Black Hills. They win a major battle by destroying General Custer's army at the Little Bighorn, but the government uses the battle as justification for taking the Black Hills. They also send more troops to make most of the Native Americans surrender. Sitting Bull and some of his people escape to Canada.

Chapter 13: The Flight of the Nez Percés

The Nez Percés are told to give up their land and report to a reservation. Young Joseph advocates peace but is forced to fight when some of his men kill white settlers. The Nez Percés try to flee to Canada to join Sitting Bull, and some make it. However, after a surprise attack by the Army, most of Chief Joseph's people surrender and are sent to Indian Territory.

Chapter 14: Cheyenne Exodus

The Northern Cheyennes at Fort Robinson are transferred to Indian Territory, where many die. Some stay, while others attempt to return to their old lands. Soldiers chase the latter, killing several Cheyennes in the process. The Northern Cheyennes split again. Some are captured and sent back to Fort Robinson, where most are killed in an escape attempt. Others spend the winter in hiding, then surrender.

Chapter 15: Standing Bear Becomes a Person

The peaceful Poncas are sent to Indian Territory with other hostile Native-American tribes. Several die, including the son of Standing Bear, who tries to take the body to their old burial grounds. General Crook captures them but intervenes on their behalf, helping Standing Bear win a court case that gives him the right to stay on his land. Other Poncas try and fail to enforce this new right to return to their land.

Chapter 16: "The Utes Must Go!"

Through the skills of a chief, Ouray the Arrow, the Utes successfully retain one rich portion of their land as a reservation. A new agent, Nathan C. Meeker, tries to convert the Utes to his religion. His efforts instigate a battle between the Utes and the Army. The local government uses the incident as justification for taking the rest of the Ute land.

Chapter 17: The Last of the Apache Chiefs

Order breaks down following the departure of an agent who has established peace on the White Mountain reservation. Many Apaches leave the reservation and engage in raids. General Crook is sent to establish order. He gets Geronimo to surrender, but Geronimo leaves the reservation again when he thinks he is about to be arrested. Another general and several thousand men are enlisted to hunt down Geronimo and his twenty-four warriors. Geronimo surrenders.

Chapter 18: Dance of the Ghosts

The government lures Sitting Bull back to the 'ed States under false promises of amnesty. ' Sioux agree to sell their land, under the threat ing it taken away from them by force. The s Ghost Dance becomes the craze among mericans on reservations, and the govern- to suppress it. The government chooses to g Bull, who gets killed in the process.

· Wounded Knee

Sitting Bull's death at Standing Rock y Native Americans there attempt

to flee to Red Cloud's Pine Ridge reservation. The Army intercepts them and attempts to disarm them. After a shot is fired, the armed soldiers open fire with heavy artillery on the mainly unarmed Native Americans, killing most of them.

Key Figures

Big Foot

Big Foot is a Minneconjou chief who surrenders his people when the military starts killing indiscriminately in revenge for the death of Custer. After he is identified as an instigator of the Ghost Dance, Big Foot tries to take his people to Red Cloud's Agency at Pine Ridge. The Army captures and tries to disarm them. In the process, a Minneconjou fires a shot and the military reacts, killing Big Foot and most of the Minneconjous.

Black Kettle

Black Kettle is a Cheyenne chief who goes to great lengths to keep peace with white people. He assures his people at Sand Creek that they have protection from the Army, who slaughters the village. He escapes, but is tricked once again at a later date, and dies while trying to make peace with the soldiers. General Sheridan lies about Black Kettle's death, saying that he was offered peace but chose to make war.

Captain Jack

Captain Jack is the chief of the Modocs; he tries to make peace with white people, even after some Modocs are killed. However, when Hooker Jim's band of Modocs kill some settlers, Captain Jack agrees not to turn them in. He kills General Canby under pressure from this band who then betrays Captain Jack by helping the Army find him. Captain Jack is hanged.

Cochise

Cochise is an Apache chief who fights many battles with the American military, escapes capture on several occasions, and helps lead raids against white settlers. When American soldiers shoot his father-in-law, Mangas, Cochise rides to Mexico and forces a Mexican surgeon to save Mangas's life. Cochise is able to secure a reservation that encompasses part of the Apaches' land.

Crazy Horse

Crazy Horse is a Sioux chief who refuses to live on a reservation. As a young man, Crazy Horse distinguishes himself in Red Cloud's War. He is one of the many chiefs who oppose selling the Black Hills to the government, and he helps lead several battles in this war, including the Battle of the Little Bighorn, in which General Custer is killed. When the military comes in overwhelming force to avenge Custer's death, Crazy Horse attempts to fight them, but ultimately he surrenders. When several of his people enlist with the military to help fight other Native Americans, Crazy Horse tries to take the rest of his people and return to his land. He is captured and is fatally stabbed while trying to escape. Crazy Horse's parents bury his heart and bones near Wounded Knee Creek.

General George Crook

General Crook leads several campaigns against the Apaches—who call him Gray Wolf—and the Plains Native Americans—who call him Three Stars. Over the course of a decade, Crook's cold attitude towards Native Americans changes to one of respect and sympathy. He helps the runaway Poncas win their freedom in court, uses diplomacy instead of force to get Geronimo to surrender, and condemns local newspapers for spreading lies about the Apaches. He resigns when the War Department does not recognize Crook's surrender terms with Geronimo. The government later dupes Crook into convincing the Sioux that the government will take their lands by force if the Sioux do not sell them.

General George Armstrong Custer

General Custer participates in several campaigns against the Plains Native Americans—who call him either Hard Backsides or Long Hair. Custer reports that the Black Hills are filled with gold, which attracts many gold seekers to the region. During the resulting War for the Black Hills, at the Battle of the Little Bighorn, Sioux and Cheyenne warriors kill Custer and all of his men—the greatest defeat suffered by the United States Army in the conflicts with Native Americans. The government's massive retaliation for this defeat ultimately leads to the end of freedom for all Plains Native Americans.

Donehogawa

Donehogawa, an Iroquois who takes the American name of Ely Samuel Parker, has an unusual

Media Adaptations

- *Bury My Heart at Wounded Knee* was adapted as an audio book in 1970 by Books on Tape.

amount of success in the world of white people. He learns English and goes to law school but is refused the right to take the bar exam. He becomes a civil engineer and serves with General Grant during the Civil War. When General Lee surrenders at Appomattox, Parker writes out the terms of surrender. When Grant is elected president, he makes Parker his Commissioner of Indian Affairs. However, a strong political group opposed to any Native American in government eventually harasses Parker until he resigns.

Dull Knife

Dull Knife is a Northern-Cheyenne chief who helps lead a number of battles. Following Custer's defeat at the Little Bighorn, the military attacks and destroys Dull Knife's village. The Northern Cheyennes are transferred to a Cheyenne reservation in Indian Territory, where many die from hunger and disease. Dull Knife and several Cheyennes seek sanctuary with Red Cloud but are captured. They escape, but only Dull Knife and a small band of Cheyennes make it to Red Cloud's agency, where they become prisoners.

Geronimo

Geronimo is an Apache chief who leads many raids into Mexico. When the government places soldiers near his reservation, Geronimo thinks he is in danger. He and others escape to their Mexican stronghold and build a small army. Geronimo surrenders to General Crook but leaves the reservation again when he hears rumors he is going to be arrested. The Army sends a force of several thousand against Geronimo's twenty-four men. Geronimo surrenders and is sent to prison in Florida. He dies on a reservation as a prisoner of war.

The Gray Wolf
See General George Crook

The Great Warrior Sherman
See General William T. Sherman

Hard Backsides
See General George Armstrong Custer

Kicking Bird
Kicking Bird is a Kiowa chief who refuses to engage in or support aggressive acts against the Army. Because of this allegiance, the government forces Kicking Bird to choose several Kiowas to answer for the tribe's part in their battles. Kicking Bird dies mysteriously after drinking a cup of coffee, two days after his life was threatened by a medicine man.

Little Crow
Little Crow is a chief of the Santee Sioux, who are repeatedly swindled out of their treaty provisions. Little Crow does not want to fight the powerful U.S. military, but he has no choice when some of the Santee Sioux young men kill settlers. The Santees win some battles but lose the war when their major ambush fails and when Little Crow is betrayed by another Santee. Little Crow is shot and killed by a white settler.

Little Wolf
Little Wolf is a Northern-Cheyenne chief who helps lead a number of battles. The Northern Cheyennes are transferred to a Cheyenne reservation in Indian Territory, where many die from hunger and disease. Little Wolf and several other Cheyennes flee north towards their old territory but surrender after spending a winter hiding from soldiers. Little Wolf is one of many Native Americans who is destroyed by alcohol.

Lone Wolf
Lone Wolf is a Kiowa chief who arranges for the parole of Satanta and another chief. He argues with Kicking Bird's peaceful ways. Lone Wolf joins with the Comanches and participates in several battles with white soldiers and hunters, in an attempt to drive them out of the region and save the buffalo. When his son dies in one of these battles, Lone Wolf strengthens his resolve. Lone Wolf is one of the last Kiowas to surrender and is one of the people chosen by Kicking Bird to be imprisoned.

Long Hair
See General George Armstrong Custer

Manuelito
Manuelito is a Navaho chief who tries to maintain peace with the United States through treaties. However, after U.S. soldiers cheat during a friendly horse race—and shoot Navahos who try to protest—the Navahos go to war with the soldiers. Manuelito is the last chief to surrender. He and the others live in squalor for two years at the Bosque Redondo reservation, before the government allows them to return to a small portion of their old land.

Ouray the Arrow
Ouray is a Ute chief who is fluent in English. He uses these skills to retain a large chunk of Ute land. When a new agent comes to the White River Agency and attempts to convert Ouray and the Utes to his religion and ways of life, the agent instigates a battle. The government uses the incident as justification to take the Ute land.

Ely Samuel Parker
See Donehogawa

Red Cloud
Red Cloud is a Sioux chief who wins many battles against the U.S. government. He engages in a successful guerrilla war that causes the government to withdraw the Army from the region. When Red Cloud finds out later that the peace treaty he signed had unknown items in it, he successfully presents his case to President Grant and Donehogawa. He also wins over a crowd of New Yorkers with his impassioned speech about the false treaty. Ultimately, however, Red Cloud loses all that he has gained when he is forced to sign a treaty giving away his lands and move his people to a reservation.

Roman Nose
Roman Nose is a Southern-Cheyenne warrior. Although he is not a chief, he commands the alle-

giance of the Dog Soldier Society, a powerful group of Cheyenne warriors. He leads a successful attack against soldiers in the Powder River country and unifies the Southern Cheyennes and Arapahos to fight for their own country. The government knows that Roman Nose is the key to a lasting peace in the area, but he refuses to attend a peace commission. Instead, he leads several raids against settlers and dies while fighting a small band of Army scouts.

Satanta

Satanta is a Kiowa chief who is captured and imprisoned. Eventually, Lone Wolf arranges for his parole. Satanta and his warriors are unsuccessful in their fight to drive away the white buffalo hunters. Satanta is eventually given life in prison, where he commits suicide.

General Philip Sheridan

General Sheridan leads several campaigns against the Plains Native Americans. He lies about the massacre at Black Kettle's village, saying that he had offered the chief sanctuary. Sheridan makes a comment that in being quoted eventually evolves into the hate statement: ''The only good Indian is a dead Indian.'' Sheridan believes that killing all of the buffalo is the best way to get Native Americans to adopt white culture.

General William T. Sherman

General Sherman, a Civil War hero known as the Great Warrior Sherman by most Native Americans, oversees American forces through many of the Native-American wars. He attends several peace commissions with various Native-American tribes. Following Custer's defeat, Sherman assumes military control of all reservations. After Standing Bear wins his court case and freedom, Sherman defies the new law by giving General Sheridan military authority to apprehend other Poncas.

Sitting Bull

Sitting Bull is the Sioux's most powerful chief, and on some occasions he commands allegiance from other Native-American tribes as well. He fights many battles with U.S. soldiers to preserve his freedom and the Sioux ownership of the Black Hills. He and Crazy Horse defeat Custer's forces at the Battle of the Little Bighorn. When the military comes in overwhelming force to avenge Custer's death, Sitting Bull and some of his followers move into Canada. However, he becomes a military prisoner after he returns to the United States under a false promise of amnesty. Many chiefs, newspaper reporters, and others come to visit him, and Sitting Bull soon becomes a celebrity. He even receives permission to go on tour around the country. The government incorrectly believes that Sitting Bull is responsible for the spread of the Ghost Dance and tries to arrest him. He is killed in the process by two Sioux policemen.

Standing Bear

Standing Bear is a Ponca chief. Standing Bear's people are tricked into being transferred to Indian Territory, where many of them die, including his last son. He and a group of Poncas are captured while trying to return to Poncas land to bury him. General Crook, two lawyers, and a sympathetic judge intervene, and Standing Bear successfully wins freedom for him and his escort party but not for the rest of his people.

Three Stars

See General George Crook

Young Joseph

Young Joseph, generally known as Chief Joseph, is a Nez-Percé chief. When miners pressure the government to move the Nez Percés to a reservation, Chief Joseph tries to go peacefully but resolves to fight after some of his warriors kill settlers. He leads his noted marksmen to several victories against superior forces, but the military ultimately overpowers him and he surrenders. He and most of the others are sent to Indian Territory, where he dies of a broken heart—according to the agency physician.

Themes

Manifest Destiny

Much of the mistreatment of Native Americans in the nineteenth century can be attributed to a concept known as Manifest Destiny. This theory stated that European descendents in the United States were destined to spread over the North Ameri-

Topics for Further Study

- On a current map of the United States, plot all of the existing Native-American reservations. For each one, include a brief description of when and how it was created, what tribes live there, and the population size at the time it was founded and at the time of the 2000 Census.

- Research the various ways that Native-American language and culture have been incorporated into American language and culture since the 1860s. Find one area of the United States that has been particularly influenced by Native Americans, and write a short, modern-day profile of this region and its people.

- Research the prehistory of the Americas, and discuss how Native Americans first came to North America. Imagine that you are one of these early Native Americans. Write a journal entry that describes your typical day in these prehistoric times, using your research to support your writing.

- Research what life is like on a Native-American reservation today. Outline the current problems faced by Native Americans on reservations, research any potential courses of action that are being taken, and propose your own solutions to these problems.

can continent and that they were justified in doing so. As a result, many politicians, military personnel, and settlers felt it was their God-given right to take land from whoever stood in their way. As Brown notes, the concept of Manifest Destiny simply "lifted land hunger to a lofty plane." Says Brown: "Only the New Englanders, who had destroyed or driven out all their Indians, spoke against Manifest Destiny."

Deception

Manifest Destiny provided the justification for many deceptions, the most notable form of which was broken treaties. When white settlers first began their relations with Native-American tribes, they made treaties—paper contracts that ceded Native-American land to the United States, often in exchange for money or provisions. However, in many cases, the systems set in place to monitor these transactions became corrupted by white middlemen who profited at the Native Americans's expense. For example, Dee Brown states: "Of the $475,000 promised the Santees in their first treaty, Long Trader Sibley had claimed $145,000 for his American Fur Company as money due for overpayment to the Santees." In other cases, Native Americans were deceived into signing false treaties. Most Native Americans could not read or write English. As a

result, they often had no way of verifying that the paper they signed included the correct terms of their agreement and were surprised when they found out later that the treaty included additional terms.

When the government could not get the desired land by diplomacy, it often ignored past treaties and took the land by force. For example, at one point, a number of Native-American tribes came to a council with U.S. commissioners to talk about building additional transportation routes through tribal lands. However, during this council, a regiment of Army infantry arrives, and the Native-American assembly realizes "that the United States government intended to open a road through the Powder River country regardless of the treaty." Brown reports that Red Cloud stated in the council: "Great Father sends us presents and wants new road. But White Chief goes with soldiers to steal road before Indian says yes or no!"

In addition to treaty violations, Americans also made false promises, such as agreeing to keep the peace when they had no intention of doing so. One of the best examples of this deception is the massacre of Cheyennes at Sand Creek. Major Scott J. Anthony tells the Cheyennes that if they return to their village at Sand Creek, they will be safe. Anthony arranges it so that two additional men, known to be peaceful, go to the village, in an attempt to "lull the Indians into a sense of security and keep them camped where they were." In the meantime, Anthony receives reinforcements. His plan works, and the Cheyennes are totally unprepared when Anthony attacks and destroys the village with his large force.

Perhaps the worst deception is the betrayal of Native Americans by their own. For example, the Modoc known as Captain Jack refuses to turn in Hooker Jim and others who have murdered white settlers. In the end, however, these same men who he risked his life to save end up betraying him to save their own lives. Says Brown, "Hooker Jim's band surrendered to the soldiers and offered to help them track down Captain Jack in exchange for amnesty."

Murder

Bury My Heart at Wounded Knee is saturated with examples of indiscriminate and often premeditated killing. Many of the murderous acts become genocidal when they are performed by Army officers and others who are determined to kill all Native Americans. One of the most chilling examples of genocide happens at Sand Creek. Although a few officers disagree with Colonel Chivington's plan to murder all Native Americans at Sand Creek, Chivington threatens them with a court-martial if they do not join the expedition. Brown quotes Chivington as saying: "I have come to kill Indians, and believe it is right and honorable to use any means under God's heaven to kill Indians." This attitude was shared by other Americans, particularly frontier settlers, some of whom engaged in or supported the murder of Native Americans wherever they were found.

Style

Setting

The setting is extremely important in this book. The action takes place in the mid to late 1800s, when a large number of white settlers emigrated to the frontier American West seeking property, gold, or both. Some Native Americans moved to other areas, thinking that there was room enough for both races.

However, the land, which had been large enough to accommodate countless tribes, was quickly overrun by white settlers and military troops. Some, like Sitting Bull, tried to leave America for a new setting. Brown states: "He decided there was no longer room enough for white men and the Sioux to live together in the Great Father's country. He would take his people to Canada." The setting is also important for military strategy. Many battles in the book are determined by the location and terrain on which the battle is fought. Native Americans are often able to beat much larger forces because they know how to use the Western terrain to set effective ambushes, to hide, or to defend themselves.

Point of View

The book is written mainly in the third-person omniscient viewpoint. This broad viewpoint gives the author unlimited power to move through time and space and in and out of characters' minds as necessary. For example, Brown notes during the description of one battle that "Roman Nose was wearing his medicine bonnet and shield, and he knew that no bullets could strike him." Like many such descriptions in the book, Brown combines historical facts with his own assumptions about Roman Nose's thoughts and motivations to bring the historical figure to life. Interspersed with these descriptions, Brown also includes first-person, eye-witness accounts such as speeches, proclamations, and official records. For example, one Native American notes, "From a distance we saw the destruction of our village. . . . Our tepees were burned with everything in them. . . . I had nothing left but the clothing I had on." These intimate accounts—from both Native Americans and white people—lend credibility to Brown's descriptions, but they also help the reader to understand what it was like to be involved in this conflict.

Imagery

Brown includes powerful and violent imagery in his book, which is to be expected in a book that details several wars. Though many cultures adhere to war rules that forbid certain actions, such as killing women and children or mutilating bodies, during the battles to win the West, U.S. soldiers engaged in certain acts, which were even then considered war crimes. For example, as Captain Nicholas Hodt notes of a spontaneous massacre of Navahos, he saw a soldier killing "two little children and a woman. I hallooed immediately to the soldier to stop. He looked up, but did not obey my order.'' Hodt orders the man to turn himself in as a prisoner but notes that even some of his superiors engage in the slaughter. Another eyewitness, Lieutenant James Connor, this time at Sand Creek, overheard ''one man say that he had cut out a woman's private parts and had them for exhibition on a stick.'' These and countless other chilling images of mutilation, murder, and desecration help to underscore the great injustice and cruelty perpetrated upon Native Americans.

Historical Context

Vietnam and the My Lai Massacre

When Brown first published *Bury My Heart at Wounded Knee* in 1970, the United States was engaged in an undeclared war in Vietnam, and the U.S. public was inclined to revisit the country's guilt over the past treatment of Native Americans. The parallels between the United States-sponsored massacre of Native Americans in the 1800s and the United States' actions in Vietnam in the late 1960s and early 1970s were not lost on readers of Brown's book. This insight was especially available in 1970, when twenty-five U.S. Army officers and enlisted men were indicted for the 1968 massacre of hundreds of civilians in the South Vietnamese village of My Lai. Despite Army efforts to cover up the incident, a few concerned soldiers who were either at or near My Lai helped bring it to light, and the story was quickly picked up by the national media. Only a few men were actually tried for their part in the massacre, and only one—Lieutenant William Calley—was found guilty. Calley was sentenced to a lifetime of hard labor. However, three years later, President Nixon intervened and secured Calley's parole. Shortly after this incident, polls indicated that, for the first time since the war began, a majority of Americans opposed the United States involvement in Vietnam.

American Indian Movement (AIM)

At the same time, Native Americans in both Canada and the United States began to organize and protest in many isolated regional events. In 1968, four men established the American Indian Movement (AIM). The group wanted to host a demonstration to help promote Native-American issues and at the same time help to unify the various separate Native-American groups. In 1969, AIM received its opportunity. Following a convention in San Francisco to discuss Native-American issues, the Indian Center that was hosting the convention caught fire and burned to the ground. Realizing that there were no government funds to build a new Indian Center, a group of Native Americans, supported by AIM and calling themselves the Indians of All Tribes, seized Alcatraz, the famous island-based prison that had lain empty since 1964. Citing treaty rights that stated Native American rights to surplus government land, the group demanded that the government let its members turn the defunct prison into a cultural-educational center. Individuals occupied Alcatraz peacefully for twenty months until they were removed by federal marshals. With nationally recognized protests like the one staged on Alcatraz, AIM became more visible.

Critical Overview

Brown's 1970 publication of *Bury My Heart at Wounded Knee* marked the first time a white author had written a book about the colonization of the American West from the point of view of Native Americans. As a result of this unique perspective, the book was received very well by critics and popular readers, who made it a best-seller. In her 1971 review of the book for the *New Statesman*, Helen McNeil notes that ''the new perspective is startling.'' McNeil also says that one of the most powerful aspects of this ''Indian historical viewpoint lies in its contrast to the vulgarity of the 'Turner thesis.''' McNeil is referring to Frederick Jackson Turner's 1893 proclamation, which claimed that it was the settling of the frontier lands that gave modern Americans their distinct character, because they had to work hard in the new, unfamiliar land. As McNeil notes, Turner's thesis considered the frontier to be ''empty land'' and did not take into account the Native Americans who were killed or displaced. McNeil compares this type of imperialistic thinking to that found in the Nixon White House; she states that *Bury My Heart at Wounded Knee*—which was published at the height of the Vietnam War—is very timely. Says McNeil:

> Now that Vietnam has brought the United States to the point of accepting national guilt for the first time, this scholarly and passionate chronicle . . . has attained

Compare & Contrast

- **1860–1890:** U.S. soldiers engage in several wars in the American West, in an attempt to acquire the lands of the Western frontier from the Native Americans who live there.

  Late 1960s–Early 1970s: U.S. soldiers engage in an undeclared war in Vietnam, purportedly in an attempt to stop the spread of communism in Southeast Asia.

  Today: An increasing number of U.S. soldiers occupy several parts of the globe, as part of the U.S. war on terrorism.

- **1860–1890:** The United States government attempts to destroy Native-American culture.

  Late 1960s–Early 1970s: The American counterculture movement rebels against the ways of the wealthy corporate establishment, and many hippies dress like Native Americans and adopt their close-to-nature ways of life.

  Today: On September 11, 2001, terrorists destroy one of the most prominent symbols of U.S. wealth and international power—the twin towers of the World Trade Center in New York City.

- **1860–1890:** The plight of Native Americans is rarely represented accurately in U.S. newspapers and books. In addition, many Native Americans cannot write in English, and so they are generally unable to inform the white public of the injustices they face.

  Late 1960s–Early 1970s: N. Scott Momaday, a Native-American author, wins the Pulitzer Prize for fiction in 1969 for his novel *House Made of Dawn*. The novel depicts the difficulties Native Americans face when trying to fit in among other Americans, and it helps to spark an increase in writing by and about Native Americans.

  Today: Many Native-American authors, such as Sherman Alexie, Louise Erdrich, and Leslie Marmon Silko, have earned critical and popular success with works that depict the plight of contemporary Native Americans.

US bestsellerdom by fixing the image of the nation's greatest collective wrong: the extermination of the American Indian.

Other critics notice the similarities to the situation in Vietnam. In his 1971 review for the *New York Times Book Review,* N. Scott Momaday, a prominent Native-American author, refers to the American ''morality which informs and fuses events so far apart in time and space as the massacres at Wounded Knee and My Lai.'' Momaday also praises the book as ''a story, a whole narrative of singular integrity and precise continuity; that is what makes the book so hard to put aside, even when one has come to the end.''

A decade later, upon the publication of Brown's Native-American novel *Creek Mary's Blood* (1980), some critics used the opportunity to discuss how they liked it much less than *Bury My Heart at Wounded Knee.* Says Joshua Gilder, in his review of the novel for *New York Magazine: Bury My Heart at Wounded Knee* ''had a sweep and an authenticity due in large measure to his letting the Indians speak for themselves.'' Gilder finds this quality missing in *Creek Mary's Blood.* Likewise, in her 1980 review of the novel, Leslie Marmon Silko, another prominent Native-American author, notes that *Bury My Heart at Wounded Knee* was brought alive through ''the strength and conviction of Dee Brown's view of this history.''

Not all critics compare Brown's later novels with *Bury My Heart on Wounded Knee.* In his review of *Killdeer Mountain* (1983) in the *Los Angeles Times Book Review,* John Rechy acknowledges *Bury My Heart at Wounded Knee* as ''a moving, resonant book.'' However, Rechy says that one must also ''ignore the expectations aroused by'' this book, when critiquing Brown's later works. Rechy is the rare critic that does this. Even today,

---

Brown's reputation rests primarily on *Bury My Heart at Wounded Knee*, even though he has also written many novels and children's books.

Criticism

Ryan D. Poquette

Poquette has a bachelor's degree in English and specializes in writing about literature. In the following essay, Poquette discusses the techniques that Brown uses in Bury My Heart at Wounded Knee *to make his readers see through the common misconceptions about Native Americans.*

In *Bury My Heart at Wounded Knee*, Dee Brown relies on many harrowing eyewitness accounts from Native Americans, letting them tell their side of how the West was won. Several reviewers consider these eyewitness accounts the most important part of the book. For example, in her *New Statesman* review, Helen McNeil says that the book "awakens a more authentic sense of . . . grandeur with the moving speeches of the great chiefs." In fact, Brown's later Native-American books that do not include these eyewitness accounts have often been panned because Brown does the talking. For example, in his *New York Magazine* review of Brown's Native-American novel *Creek Mary's Blood* (1980), Joshua Gilder says it lacks the "sweep and . . . authenticity" of Brown's *Bury My Heart at Wounded Knee*, which was "due in large measure to his letting the Indians speak for themselves."

Despite the popularity of the eyewitness accounts, Brown is not an absentee narrator. Like one of the military leaders in the book, Brown serves as a general, deploying his two main forces—the techniques of language and plot—in a calculated manner to give the eyewitness accounts as much impact as possible. In the process, he attempts to defeat his enemy: the misconceptions and falsehoods that have plagued Native-Americans and their reputation among non-Natives.

Brown's first weapon is language. His book differs from previous books about Native Americans in this time period, because he uses many Native-American interpretations. For example, the Sioux and Cheyennes frequently see trains pass through their land in the Powder River country.

Says Brown: "Sometimes they saw Iron Horses dragging wooden houses on wheels at great speed along the tracks. They puzzled over what could be inside the houses." Brown uses the terms "Iron Horses" and "wooden houses" to describe trains and train cars as a Native-American at this time would have perceived them. Brown also uses the Native-American designations for U.S. military ranks in his descriptions. For example, to a Native American at this time, a general was known as a "Star Chief" and a colonel was an "Eagle Chief."

In addition, Brown refers to prominent American historical figures by their Native-American names. For example, many Native Americans called General George Armstrong Custer "Hard Backsides," "because he chased them over long distances for many hours without leaving his saddle." Brown also uses Native-American naming systems for natural processes like time. White people divide the year into twelve months and refer to these time periods by cryptic names like May and June. However, Native Americans referred to these time periods by their actual, perceivable correlation to nature. So, in Brown's book, May is "the Moon When the Ponies Shed" and June is "the Strawberry Moon." By using distinctly Native-American interpretations like these in his narration, Brown takes his readers deep into the Native-American experience. In the process, the reader begins to identify with the Native Americans.

When readers identify with characters, they tend to feel sympathy for them. Through his second weapon, plot, Brown organizes his story to maximize his readers' sympathetic emotions. With any historical book, the author has to make choices about what events to include and how to organize them. As McNeil notes, Brown does not choose to make many distinctions among the various tribes: "One isn't reminded that the Navahoes were settled, the Apaches predatory, the Poncas gentle or the Utes lazy, since in any case the same fate awaited them all." Brown establishes a three-part structure for most chapters, which demonstrates again and again that Native Americans lost no matter what they did. Typically, the chapter begins with a discussion of a chief or tribe who has lost something—generally a piece of their land—and still has more to lose. For example, in the beginning of the second chapter, Brown notes: "As the result of two deceptive treaties, the woodland Sioux surrendered nine-tenths of their land and were crowded into a narrow strip of territory along the Minnesota River."

What Do I Read Next?

- Brown's sixth novel, *Creek Mary's Blood* (1980), takes place in the nineteenth century during the westward expansion that pushed Native Americans off most of their land. The story combines historical and fictional elements in order to tell the various stories of Creek Mary and her family as they constantly move westward.

- *In the Absence of the Sacred: The Failure of Technology and the Survival of the Indian Nations* (1992), by Jerry Mander, examines the effects that increasing technology has had on society and advocates a return to a Native-American way of life. In addition, Mander discusses how some Native Americans who try to maintain their way of life in modern times have clashed with the corporate world.

- *Native American Testimony: A Chronicle of Indian-White Relations from Prophecy to the Present, 1492–1992* (2 volumes, 1978–1988), edited by Peter Nabokov, also gives the Native-American side of the colonization story. Like Brown's work, this book relies on original documents and stories from Native Americans. However, this book takes a longer view, examining the entire five-hundred-year history of colonization.

- Native-American storytelling has a long history, rooted in oral tradition. In *Coming to Light: Contemporary Translations of the Native Literatures of North America* (1996), published by Vintage Books, editor Brian Swann assembles many of these oral stories, songs, prayers, and orations, which collectively represent more than thirty Native-American cultures. Each of the pieces in this anthology is accompanied by an introduction from the translator, which explains the meaning behind the selection, as well as how it was spoken or sung in its time.

Following the discussion of what has been already lost, Brown introduces the second part of his three-part structure, the struggle. For Native Americans in the nineteenth century, the struggles were many, whether they decided to go to war or did not. Many tribes in the book do choose to fight to retain their remaining land and freedom. In most cases, the tribes win some battles but end up losing the war. The U.S. soldiers are too advanced and numerous to be defeated, something that the Native Americans begin to realize. For example, Little Crow is leery about fighting at first, because "he had been to the East and seen the power of the Americans. They were everywhere like locusts and destroyed their enemies with great thundering cannon." Even when the Native Americans outnumber the whites, the latter's military technology can be the decisive factor in the victory. As many Native Americans learn: "Bravery, numbers, massive charges—they all meant nothing if the warriors were armed only with bows, lances, clubs, and old trade guns of the fur-trapper days."

In cases where the Native Americans try to remain peaceful, Brown shows many ways that they are provoked into war. In several cases, settlers or miners hungry for the Native Americans' remaining land spread incriminating lies in an effort to get the government to take their land. During the Civil War, Native Americans were sometimes provoked into fighting because it was the safer of two options for white, male citizens. Says Brown about the Cheyenne wars in Colorado: "There was political pressure on Evans from Coloradans who wanted to avoid the military draft of 1864 by serving in uniform against a few poorly armed Indians rather than against the Confederates farther east." Even after the Civil War, when the draft was no longer an issue, some settlers used lies to provoke Native Americans and and kill them because peace was not profitable for the settlers. Brown notes that Tucson citizens in 1871 "were opposed to agencies where Apaches worked for a living and were peaceful; such conditions led to reductions in military forces and a slackening of war prosperity."

> " Brown has gotten his readers to root for the underdogs by using eyewitness accounts and language to draw readers into the Native-American experience. Yet, in each chapter Brown steadily crushes any hope that the reader might have for the Native Americans winning much of anything."

The final part of Brown's three-part plot structure in most chapters is the bitter ending. Due to the massive struggles that Native Americans faced whether or not they chose to remain peaceful, most chapters end badly. The chiefs, who are often depicted as strong in the beginning and middle of the chapters when they are fighting for their land and people, end up dead, in prison, in exile, or on a reservation with the rest of their people. Even the exceptions to this rule, such as the chapter depicting Red Cloud's successful war, ultimately end negatively. In a later chapter, Red Cloud is forced to sign away his beloved Powder River country and live on a reservation. Red Cloud's plight highlights the overall plot structure of the book, which mimics the three-part structure of the individual chapters. The book starts out with many Native Americans living free and retaining parcels of their land. As the story progresses and the trickle of white emigration turns into a flood, ever-larger armies and groups of land-hungry white settlers cut down the various tribes. By the end of the book, the noose of white emigration has tightened around so much of the country that most Native Americans are dead, in prison, or on scattered reservations.

The effect on the reader is profound. Brown has gotten his readers to root for the underdogs by using eyewitness accounts and language to draw readers into the Native-American experience. Yet, in each chapter Brown steadily crushes any hope that the reader might have for the Native Americans winning much of anything. By using these strategies, Brown makes his readers more receptive to the most important aspect of his book—his anger. Brown's

tone, or attitude towards his subject matter, is one of barely restrained outrage, and he wants readers to get angry, too. To this end, he fills his book with sarcastic and scathing comments that further underline the savagery of whites in the late nineteenth century. For example, at the end of one chapter, Brown describes how three major Cheyenne leaders were killed, and in the process he mimics the infamous saying: "The only good Indian is a dead Indian." Says Brown: "Roman Nose was dead; Black Kettle was dead; Tall Bull was dead. Now they were all good Indians."

Source: Ryan D. Poquette, Critical Essay on *Bury My Heart at Wounded Knee*, in *Nonfiction Classics for Students*, Gale, 2003.

Douglas Dupler

Dupler has published numerous essays and has taught college English. In this essay, Dupler examines the effectiveness of the technique used by an historian to record an alternative history of North America.

Bury My Heart at Wounded Knee, written by the eminent historian Dee Brown, is an epic history of the invasion of Native America by the white Europeans. Many histories that deal with this time period are written from the point of view of the white conquerors and tend to ignore or de-emphasize the violence and deceit perpetrated by the United States government and the European settlers upon Native America. Brown shows that the "westward expansion" of white history was much more complicated when viewed from another angle. Brown's powerful history is told from the point of view of the victims of the invasion themselves. In his history, he tells the compelling and heartrending story of the Native Americans beset by a vastly more powerful enemy, and shows their attempts to heroically defend themselves against their tragic fate. Using an array of sources and quoting from the Native Americans of that era, Brown's history is a graphic account of the broken treaties and the genocide that the United States government and its citizens inflicted upon the indigenous peoples of the continental United States.

The United Nations Convention on the Prevention and Punishment of the Crime of Genocide describes genocide as actions done with the intention of destroying a particular group of people. The convention declares that genocide is a crime whether committed during war or peacetime. It bans killing or causing serious injury, either mental or physical, to an individual because of his or her group identity. It bans destroying a people's means of survival. It bans taking children away from a people and giving them into the care of people of another group. In *Bury My Heart at Wounded Knee*, Brown demonstrates, in retrospect, that the United States government, in its relationship with the Native Americans, committed these acts. Using old records as well as the words of Native Americans, Brown recounts in detail how the United States military, often aided by white civilians, repeatedly attacked peaceful Native-American camps without provocation. Native Americans were often shot and killed by soldiers as well as civilians because of their racial identity. These murderous deeds were often justified by such sayings as, ''The only good Indian is a dead Indian.'' At the time, the term ''genocide'' was not used. That seems to be a point that Brown is making in his history; the conquerors, acting with such simple and shallow directives, were able to perpetrate deeds that their own value systems deemed immoral and unlawful.

Brown's technique is so effective because it takes the common history of events and brings it to life. Brown is a conventional historian when he recounts the timeline of history on the North American continent, beginning with the Arawak, the natives of San Salvador where Columbus had first landed. He goes on to show the conquest of the entire continental United States, stretching from the East Coast, where the English first landed in 1607, to the West Coast where gold was discovered in California in 1848. Brown also utilizes novelistic technique in his history, which adds a powerful dimension. Drawing on a broad array of sources, he brings his history and the individual characters involved alive with this writing technique. This history uses dialogue to give characters in the struggle real voices, from both sides of the conflict, as well as photographs of many of the Native-American warriors who tried to help their people survive the white onslaught. Brown even includes old Indian songs. The Native Americans are seen to have been real people, happy with their way of life, and even willing to share the bounty of their land. Bringing history to the personal level, Brown's book gives a different and disturbing view of the discovery and conquest of North America. For instance, Mangas Colorado of the Apaches, Big Snake of the Poncas, Crazy Horse of the Lakota Sioux, and many others were all murdered while in the custody of the United States Army. The reader feels these tragic deaths

> **By so intricately researching and assembling his history, Brown is able to show how the forces of cultural imperialism were so devastating, and brings the individuals and tragedy in this history alive for the reader.''**

when the human voices and faces are included vividly in the text.

By so intricately researching and assembling his history, Brown is able to show how the forces of cultural imperialism were so devastating, and brings the individuals and tragedy in this history alive for the reader. There are white conquerors and Native-American resistors in this history. The complexities of the history are also revealed when Brown shows sympathetic whites and honest settlers, as well as Native-American mercenaries who helped to devastate their own people. Brown's history also shows the insidious nature of the violence. The aggressive soldiers are displayed as men taking orders from a distant political bureaucracy, carrying out impersonal directives that become extremely violent on the ground level. Brown shows how the whites justified to themselves their broken treaties, their wanton killings, and their destruction of a culture as they followed the policy of Manifest Destiny, the belief that God had given them the rights to the land.

Brown's history connects the relationship between cultural imperialism and religious and economic beliefs. The European settlers believed that the Native-American religions were not valid. The government often gave Native-American leaders the choice between accepting the European religion and way of life, or perishing. Brown reveals that many Native-American chiefs were aware of this choice, and heroically chose death before the destruction of their cherished beliefs. Thus, Brown makes the reader aware of the tragic loss of an entire culture, tragic because its people defended it valiantly.

Brown gives many instances of how the Native Americans and their culture were continually reviled. The whites in this history, with deeply imbedded racism, saw the Native Americans as savages who did not deserve civilized treatment. In spite of Judge Dundy's legal decision in 1879, they were not considered persons under the law. A main thrust of Brown's history is the contention that the United States government and its citizens justified their genocide by falsely declaring that the Native Americans and their various cultures were inferior to their own. This was so strongly ingrained within the white culture that any white person who dared to be friendly to the Native Americans was called an ''Indian lover'' and was usually met with great disfavor, often of a violent nature, from the rest of the white populace. When Brown uses quotes by Native-American leaders speaking in English, it reveals the eloquence and intelligence of the human beings on the losing side of the war.

The ordinary white settler, from Brown's point of view, seemed unwilling to look closely at the genocide perpetrated by their government on their behalf. The average settler just wanted land, a place of his or her own, and many were willing to kill (or let the army kill) the former inhabitants to get it. Brown uses the details of white history to show how the land was taken. For instance, in Colorado in the early 1850s, Governor Evans, in collusion with Colonel John M. Chivington—head of the Colorado Volunteers—and the Indian Agent Samuel G. Colby, schemed to drive all of the Native Americans out of Colorado. They wanted the land for themselves and their friends. In particular, Denver had been built upon Arapaho land, and unless the Native Americans were completely driven out of the state, they would have a claim upon the city. To achieve this end, Governor Evans ordered all the Cheyennes and Arapahos to report to the reservation at Fort Lyons. He then issued a proclamation giving all citizens of Colorado the right to pursue and kill any Indians found living out on the plains. Soon there were no free Cheyennes or Arapahos in Colorado, and Brown's history clearly shows the violent mechanism of white land acquisition.

Writing his history from the point of view of the victims rather than the conquerors, Brown shocks the reader by recounting deadly brutality. He details instances when the United States military, often aided by white settlers, attacked and destroyed entire Native-American villages, killing men, women, and children indiscriminately, burning the tipis, clothing and other means of survival. Often they would kill or steal the Native-Americans' horses, leaving the survivors on foot and without adequate food, clothing or shelter. Women and children,

especially babies, would often die of exposure or starvation. Brown does not allow the reader to overlook the painful events. His history is told with impressive detail, down to the particulars of what individuals were doing on the mornings of battles, detailed statistics of the wounded and dead, and words spoken and written by participants on both sides. It is the expert use of details that reflects Brown's conviction of an historian seeking justice and truth, however belatedly. At the same time, Brown maintains an objective tone, despite the brutality he is recording, and this effectively allows the reader to absorb the implications and emotions of the injustices revealed.

Sympathetic to the spirituality of the Native Americans, Brown describes how their rich spiritual lives were often reviled or repressed. He recounts how white missionaries were often put in charge of the Native Americans living on the reservations and how they would ban non-Christian spirituality. The government banned the Ghost Dance, a powerful and healing spiritual ceremony. Brown details the murder of Sioux warrior chief Sitting Bull and the massacre of an unarmed camp of Ghost Dancers, finally putting an end to the dance.

Brown describes how the Native Americans watched as their land was ruined, the streams polluted, the trees cut down, and many animal species, such as the buffalo, almost completely destroyed. Several times, Brown quotes Native Americans, who, in addition to lamenting the destruction of their own way of life, were mystified and saddened by how the whites seemed to hate nature. Brown states, ''To the Indians it seemed that these Europeans hated everything in nature—the living forests and their birds and beasts, the grassy glades, the water, the soil, and the air itself.'' Brown also gives the reader glimpses into the Native Americans' connection with nature, when he refers to seasons as ''summer moon'' or the ''moon of strong cold'' rather than calendar time, for instance. This has the effect of creating more empathy in the reader for the lost culture.

Brown's history ends with the massacre at Wounded Knee, a devastating loss for Native America. The last lines of text remark, ironically, on a sign over a church: ''PEACE ON EARTH, GOOD WILL TO MEN,'' after the brutal killings. Then an eloquent quote by Black Elk, followed by an Indian song of longing, and a photograph and quote of Red Cloud are final reminders to the reader of the tragic history of the Native Americans.

Source: Douglas Dupler, Critical Essay on *Bury My Heart at Wounded Knee,* in *Nonfiction Classics for Students,* Gale, 2003.

Donald L. Fixico

In the following essay, Fixico places Bury My Heart at Wounded Knee *within the context of related works of its time, stressing its importance as the first work to humanize Native Americans for the general public.*

In 1971 Dee Brown wrote *Bury My Heart at Wounded Knee*—a book that stunned America, persuading a generation to listen to the voice of Native Americans. Society learned about the Indian as a victim in the American West.

The full impact involved the emergence of an academic Indian voice in the following years. Native Americans had always expressed their concerns and opinions about issues ranging from legal status, to living conditions, to past mistreatment at the hands of the United States government. But the Indian voice was not widely heard, at least by the dominant society, until the 1960s during the Civil Rights protests and the concurrent rise of American Indian activism. During the late 1960s and at the start of the next decade, *Bury My Heart at Wounded Knee* opened the door for the Native American voice and launched a generation of American Indian studies in academia.

At unexpected times, an important work comes along and jolts society, provoking a reaction—right time, right book. And Dee Brown's book has had a long life, perhaps because of its portrayal and inclusion of the Wounded Knee tragedy of 1890 with the slaughter of 350 Minneconjou Ghost Dancers (mostly women and children).

The book was copyrighted in 1970 and appeared in print in January 1971. During the remainder of 1971, Holt, Rinehart and Winston reprinted the book 13 times in 11 months, and it has sold five million copies! This is *impact,* even in the hard-edged world of capitalism! During these years of the so-called "Third World" movement, the book unveiled a story that Native Americans had always known.

While many enthralled readers turned the pages of *Bury My Heart*, their consciences acknowledged this mistreatment of the American Indian. Guilt seized them. Scholars, however, remained doubtful about Brown's work. The late historian Wilcomb Washburn noted:

Chief Sitting Bull

While Brown's work, from the scholarly point of view, leaves something to be desired, its impact has been phenomenal in raising the consciousness of the white Americans about the past history of Indians and whites in America.

The book capitalized on the liberal 1960s, offering something new and different as the decade closed.

Many of us recall those years, witnessing radical changes in America: bell bottoms, the peace sign, Jimi Hendrix, marijuana, Janis Joplin, the 1964 invasion of the Beatles, the Rolling Stones, the New Left, underground protest groups, Vietnam, the Civil Rights movement, the NAACP, John F. Kennedy, LBJ, and more that we wore, hated, believed in, smoked, and became immersed in.

For Native Americans, "Red Power" emerged as a philosophical outspokenness of politics and cultural renaissance, but it confirmed a national identity of "being Indian." The Chicago National Indian Conference and the rise of the National Indian Youth Council (NIYC) in 1961, Indian Fish-Ins in Washington in 1964, the founding of the American Indian Movement in 1968, Red Power, and the Alcatraz Take-over in 1969 witnessed a new era of Native American deconstruction and reaction for a generation of Native Americans who wanted to

> " The emotions that *Bury My Heart at Wounded Knee* brought forth in readers made for a precedent-setting work. Dee Brown described the feelings and emotions of Native Americans in such a way as no historians had successfully done—he humanized them."

study about themselves and their people's histories and cultures. It was a struggle.

But for Native Americans to succeed at higher education was not yet reality. In 1961, only 66 Indians graduated from four-year institutions. During that decade, the college dropout rate for Native Americans remained at 90 percent. By 1968, only 181 Native Americans had graduated from college. By 1970, Estelle Fuchs and Robert J. Havighurst estimated a 75 percent rate for Indian college dropouts. Twenty years later, in 1988 and 1989, 3,954 Indian students had received Bachelor's degrees, with 1,086 having received Master's degrees and 85 graduate students earning a Ph.D. However, Native Americans still believed that institutions of higher learning were a means for future betterment of Indian people.

Bury My Heart awakened scholars and writers, and especially Native Americans. Native scholars began writing about the feelings of Indian people and about their opinions. Indians felt the frustration of urban alienation and the influence of Red Power activists, and they began to put pen to paper.

In addition to Dee Brown's work, two other important books about Indians appeared during these years—Vine Deloria, Jr.'s *Custer Died for Your Sins: An Indian Manifesto* (1968) and N. Scott Momaday's *House Made of Dawn* (1966). The latter won the Pulitzer Prize, the only work written by a Native American to be recognized.

A part of this scholarly current to study American Indians derived especially from the political movements of Black Power, Brown Power, and Red Power. Civil Rights for minorities and equal rights

for women expressed during political protests and activism caused society and institutions of higher learning to reconsider the status and past written histories of ethnic groups and women. Thus, the 1960s represented pivotal changes in American society, as people contemplated their own lives and the values of the mainstream society and the dominant culture that had stressed the importance of education, economics, religion, and individualism.

Until the 1960s, mainstream society had refused to listen to, or to learn from, Native Americans. Naturally, this provoked the title of Vine Deloria, Jr.'s book, *We Talk; You Listen: New Tribes, New Turf.* From an Indian point of view, Deloria predicted in 1972:

> American society is unconsciously going Indian. Moods, attitudes, and values are changing. People are becoming more aware of their isolation even while they continue to worship the rugged individualist who needs no one. The self-sufficient man is casting about for a community to call his own. The glittering generalities and mythologies of American society no longer satisfy the need and desire to belong.

On the heels of *We Talk: You Listen* came Deloria's *God Is Red* (1974), in which he pointed out that Native Americans identify with place rather than time as do white men, and that Indians galvanize toward group identity rather than individuality. Undoubtedly, Americans were looking for security in various ways and forms, even looking to Native Americans because of their traditional values of communalism and environmental relationship with the earth. As a result of the self-examining society of the 1960s, people began to ask questions about their inner selves, wondering who they were, and they researched their roots. They needed something with which to identify, and to bring balance to their lives. Many looked toward history for answers, as the rugged individualist American began to break down.

Timing proved to be germane to the powerful influence of *Bury My Heart at Wounded Knee.* It was the link to the past, and a model by which people could re-examine that past. Although the revelation of America's mistreatment of Native Americans was shocking, it was not unique; 90 years earlier, Helen Hunt Jackson's *A Century of Dishonor* had been published—an exposé that had alerted the public to the plight of the American Indian. However, it was as a result of Dee Brown's book in 1971 that journalists, writers, and scholars began to offer new ideas and theories, and they introduced new ways to look at their subjects in a broader context with open minds.

Until the 1960s, the dominant society had maintained strict control over learning, forcing Western linear teaching into the minds of Indian students at boarding schools and missionary schools, while public schools berated the ways of Native Americans and presented them as inferior to white ways. The Native American perspective was ignored until the unleashing in the 1960s.

In his introduction to *Bury My Heart at Wounded Knee*, Dee Brown wrote:

> . . . I have tried to fashion a narrative of the conquest of the American West as the victims experienced it, using their own words whenever possible. Americans who have always looked westward when reading about this period should read this book facing eastward . . . This is not a cheerful book, but history has a way of intruding upon the present, and perhaps those who read it will have a clearer understanding of what the American Indian is, by knowing what he was.

The emotions that *Bury My Heart at Wounded Knee* brought forth in readers made for a precedent-setting work. Dee Brown described the feelings and emotions of Native Americans in such a way as no historians had successfully done—he humanized them.

As the decade of the 1970s began, numerous books continued to be published about Indians, resulting in some 13 books in print. In 1971, Hazel Hertzberg published *The Search for an American Indian Identity: Modern Pan-Indian Movements,* indicating that social, cultural, and political history of a minority was indeed important enough to write about, especially in the 20th century. Other noted works appeared as well, including Francis Paul Prucha, ed., *The Indian in American History* (1971); Joseph G. Jorgensen, *The Sun Dance Religion: Power for the Powerless* (1972); Richard Slotkin, *Regeneration Through Violence: The Mythology of the American Frontier, 1600–1860* (1973); Bernard Sheehan, *Seeds of Extinction: Jeffersonian Philanthropy and the American Indian* (1973); and *Memoirs of Chief Red Fox* (1972).

While these important works encouraged a growing interest in the American Indian, and as more books appeared on the horizon, *Bury My Heart at Wounded Knee* had articulated an Indian version of the history of the American West. Rediscovering the "Indian voice" had also occurred in 1971 with Virginia Irving Armstrong, *I Have Spoken: American History Through the Voices of the Indi-*

ans; W. C. Vanderwerth, *Indian Oratory: Famous Speeches Told by Noted Indian Chieftains* (1971); Joseph Cash and Herbert Hoover, eds., *To Be an Indian: an Oral History* (1971); and Joseph Epes Brown, ed., *The Sacred Pipe: Black Elk's Account of the Seven Rites of the Oglala Sioux* (1971). But though these works did not have the same success as *Bury My Heart at Wounded Knee*, the door had been opened for listening to the Indian point of view. Students and scholars in particular were keenly interested in what Indians thought about the history of Indian-white relations.

Meanwhile, the National Indian Youth Council and the American Indian Movement (AIM) expressed a contemporary Indian voice, albeit of multiple opinions, during the early 1970s. "The First Convocation of Indian Scholars," limited to 200 participants, convened in 1970 at Princeton University, and the "Second Convocation" occurred the following year at the Aspen Institute for Humanistic Studies in Colorado.

And as *Bury My Heart at Wounded Knee* was appearing in January 1971, other interests were developing simultaneously in Indian activism and Native American militancy. Indian activists protested that colleges and universities offered very little about American Indians—or incorrect information—in their college courses. Non-Indians, too, began to embrace the opportunity to study Native Americans to see the courses they had to offer. This interest in Indian curriculum was not new, but was rather a renaissance of Native American issues, which led to a genre of literature with increasing demands. Writings and scholarship was changing, and new sources and inspiration were pursued.

Because of the emergence of Native American studies programs, the momentum carried throughout the 1970s. Even history as an academic discipline began to re-examine its basic approach. In an article entitled "American Historians and the Idea of National Character: Some Problems and Prospects," David Stannard wrote about the American search for "National Character" as a means for writing history, and that historians were looking toward the behavioral sciences in their analyses. Yet, although new ideas about writing history entered the discipline, the old habit of disregarding Native Americans and other minorities still prevailed.

In the early 1970s, the discipline as practiced by mainstream historians refused to make Native Americans a true part of American history. Simultaneously, the Indian struggled for his place in other academic disciplines as well. In 1970, Jeanette Henry reprimanded the history profession and American society for denying Native Americans a proper place in the written history of this country:

> . . . Every dominant political class in any society attempts to control the ideology of the people most particularly through the learning process in the schools. It is not to be wondered at that ''this'' American society does the same. The school boards and curriculum commissions which control the adoption and purchase of textbooks usually adopt books to support the dominant political class. So too do the professors in universities, [*and*] departments of various disciplines.

During these times of Civil Rights protests, Indian activism, and AIM militancy, Indian academic warriors like Jeanette Henry and others took on the academic disciplines at academic conferences and in journals, books, and all forms of the printed word. The number of such warriors was small, drawing from a rank of less than 200 Native Americans holding a Ph.D. by the mid-1970s, and this group, which included outspoken Native Americans without doctorates, naturally polarized American academia and Native Americans.

The turf of battle of the American Indian Movement against the United States had been extended to academics, and leading this Indian attack was Vine Deloria, Jr.'s *Custer Died for Your Sins*; *We Talk, You Listen*; and *God Is Red,* as well as other related works. Deloria's chapter on ''Anthropologists and Other Friends'' in *Custer Died for Your Sins* became a volleying point for heated discussions, charging writers and scholars who exploited Indians for personal gains and misrepresenting Native Americans and their cultures. Deloria insulted anthropologists by writing in his inflammatory chapter that some people are cursed with plagues and bad luck, ''. . . but Indians have been cursed above all other people in history. Indians have anthropologists.''

In the middle of the battlefield, native scholars like the late Alfonso Ortiz challenged his own anthropology profession to re-examine Indians and treat them more appropriately. He realized in one of his writings that he had ''taken a position, fully mindful of the dangers of being shot at from both sides.'' Ortiz wrote:

> . . . Anthropology is a science born of imperialists and colonial powers and . . . , at best, all too many of its practitioners still approach their tribal and peasant subjects with a neo-colonist attitude.

He noted that there were too few Indian scholars to help turn the tide at that time in 1970. A stronger Indian academic voice was needed if, indeed, academia was to revise its paternalistic views of Native Americans.

Sensitive and open-minded non-Indian scholars began to include cultural studies in their writings about Native Americans. Hence, cross-cultural studies and cross-disciplinary works evolved. Attempting to understand Indian culture, environment, and community became essential in order to understand Native Americans. This approach, combined with academia's contemplation of new ideas and theories, urged a reconsideration of the previous means of examining history and the Indian and other minorities.

Then in 1970, the *Western Historical Quarterly* produced its first issue. The following year, the sixth president of the Western Historical Association, Robert Utley, assessed the field and changes in Western history amidst societal changes resulting from the 1960s. He wrote:

> Indeed, I shall be surprised if western studies do not gain new life from the intellectual and social ferment now troubling the nation. As attitudes, beliefs, assumptions, and traditions of American life come increasingly under scrutiny, stereotypes begin to disintegrate . . . Does not the current obsession with minority and ethnic studies suggest unplowed western fields? Scholars are already beginning to till these fields . . .

And in 1971, as an example of Utley's admonition, Doubleday published William Loren Katz's *The Black West,* a documentary and pictorial history; Seth M. Scheiner and Tilden G. Edelstein edited *The Black Americans: Interpretative Readings;* the third edition of Morris U. Schappes' edited work *A Documentary History of the Jews in the United States, 1654–1875,* reappeared in print; and Leonard Dinnerstein published his edited book, *Antisemitism in the United States.*

In November of 1969, *The Black Scholar* journal had produced its first issue, and other African American publications appeared, such as the *Journal of Black Studies* with its first issue published in 1970. Subsequently, the *Journal of Ethnic Studies* released its first issue in the spring of 1973. Other minority journals and publications followed throughout the decade and afterwards, such as the *Ethnic Forum* in the summer of 1981.

In 1971, Lawrence Towner, past president of Chicago's Newberry Library, and other key individuals, conceived of the idea to establish a center in the Library for studying the history of the American

Indian. Towner wanted Indian involvement, so he contacted D'Arcy McNickle, a Flathead Indian studying anthropology, who also studied at Oxford University. In September 1972, the Center for the History of the American Indian opened its doors for business with a supporting grant from the National Endowment for the Humanities, The Newberry Library, and 11 supporting universities. D'Arcy McNickle became the first director of the Center, with many scholars becoming research fellows who would study Native Americans over the years. In 1997, the McNickle Center celebrated its 25th year of researching and studying the American Indian.

In the 1970s, people learned that American Indians have always lived in their own way, in spite of federal policies designed to force them to assimilate into the dominant society. The current 547 federally recognized Native American tribes and other Indian communities exist according to their particular identity and heritage; and this need for freedom of expression involves culture, political concerns, religion, and intellectualism. Although American Indians have sought self-determination since the 1960s, a dominant control of the media, including textbook companies, the film industry, and a majority of publications, suppressed the advancement of Indian people and their communities throughout Indian country.

A "natural sovereignty" for Indian people has meant that all native communities possessed a heritage of freedom. A native identity is based on desired segregation from other peoples and their natural right to pursue their own way of life. This is done on reservations throughout Indian country and in urban Indian areas in most major cities where Native Americans survived the relocation program of the 1950s and 1960s. Currently, more than two-thirds of the total Indian population of just over two million live in urban areas; thus Indian country consists of reservations and urban Indian communities.

A history of struggle is common to all nations, and American Indian tribal nations have certainly had this experience. Their struggle has been one against European imperialism and the United States. The invasion of these foreign nations has defeated and suppressed the Native American, and, in some cases, annihilated Indian people.

Euroamerican colonization has a history of going beyond building homesteads and clearing the land for crops; this colonization experience has been one of deliberate destruction of Native Americans and their culture. Attempts at co-existence did not work out, and the Indian nations fell before the Euroamerican colonization after patriotic resistance in every region of the country.

Aside from attempts of genocide, the survival of Native Americans, even against overwhelming odds, compelled the United States to assimilate Indian people into the ideological "melting pot" of white values. Simultaneously, in order to accomplish this assimilation or desegregation, the United States government and its military sought to suppress the native intellectualism of Indian people. With biased scientific evidence in the late 1800s, and in an attempt to justify the American experience with Frederick Jackson Turner's "frontier thesis," America sought to subordinate Native Americans. An insecure American culture believed it necessary to deem Native American knowledge and native intellectualism to be inferior. Undoubtedly, this was intellectual racism on the part of America, which has not been fully addressed.

The conservativism of the Eisenhower era of the 1950s had caused a backlash against this kind of ideology, provoking an experimentation with liberalism during the next ten years and afterward. But as for Native Americans, they continued to look for themselves in textbooks and public forms of the media. The mainstream saw a "doomed" Indian in books and at the cinema. Perhaps, even worse, in the 20th century Native Americans had virtually disappeared, and simply were not needed by Turnerian historians to explain the history of this country.

In 1968, an Indian student (Shoshone and Bannock) enrolled at the University of California, Berkeley, expressed her frustration at finding her place in the white man's world:

> It's hard for me to go to college and eventually be assimilated and never be able to relate to the American Indian and their problems. I feel they're trying to make me into a white person ... There is little opportunity to learn anything about my own history; I've tried to take courses in history at the University. I can't find out anything about my people.

Until the late 1960s, post-modern America had continued to move forward with increasingly less interest in American Indians, leaving the issue up to Indians to fight for Indian education. But as American Indians were rarely in the path of the daily concerns of the federal government and the public in general, it was left to colleges and universities and Indian communities to advance the interests of America's original people. The American public and our nation's leaders needed to be educated about Indian people and their issues and concerns.

President Lyndon Johnson was sensitive and responded to the concerns of Native Americans and their problems when he gave his "Forgotten American" speech in 1968. In actuality, LBJ proved to be more understanding of Native Americans and their circumstances than his popular predecessor, John F. Kennedy.

Following Johnson's pro-Indian efforts, which included the Indian Civil Rights Act of 1968, Richard Nixon continued presidential support of Native Americans. In 1972, the Indian Education Act authorized educational programs for American Indian and Alaskan native children, college students and adults, with funding from the Department of Education. In addition, the Bureau of Indian Affairs also funded educational programs for Native Americans. The termination policy of the 1950s and 1960s came to a halt by Congress, and the Kennedy Study Report disclosed an increased need for Indian education. Furthermore, Indian action, especially the militancy of AIM, called for a new federal Indian policy during the early 1970s of the Nixon years.

In 1974, President Gerald Ford signed the Indian Self-Determination and Education Assistance Act, which took effect in 1975. This new federal Indian policy authorized the development of Indian education and other reform programs. In addition, organizations like the Ford Foundation and Donner Foundation saw it as their task to educate more Native Americans in graduate programs.

American Indian intellectualism has always existed, but it has not always been acknowledged. Unfortunately, the most brilliant Indian individuals were called to lead their people in war against the United States—those such as Tecumseh, Sitting Bull, and Chief Joseph in the 19th century. In postmodern America, Indian intellectualism should be allowed to be expressed; however, conservative academic attitudes have suppressed or ignored the opportunity for Native American thoughts and ideas. Should not American Indian intellectuals have the same right as others to offer their ideas, philosophies, and theories? Should not American Indian people have the same opportunities to obtain a college education and have the same opportunities to succeed as other Americans? Many years ago, before the first Native American Studies Program, the Lakota sage Luther Standing Bear challenged white society: "Why not a school of Indian thought,

built on the Indian pattern and conducted by Indian instructors?"

As teaching and discussing Native American studies became important in the late 1960s and in the 1970s, ethnic studies programs began to emerge on college campuses, and the study of American Indians experienced a renaissance.

Although in 1968 San Francisco State University became the first college to establish a Native American studies program, few people know that the first official Indian studies program had been attempted at the University of Oklahoma in 1914, when Senator Robert Owens of Oklahoma introduced a resolution in the United States Congress calling for an Indian Studies Department. However, nothing had resulted from Owens' efforts. Another effort was made in 1937, once again at the University of Oklahoma, but it too failed. The impetus for an American Indian studies program was premature until after World War II.

In 1968, American Indian studies programs also emerged at the University of Minnesota, the University of California, Berkeley, and later at the University of California, Los Angeles. In 1969, Trent University, Ontario, started the first native studies program in Canada. These early programs became the flagships of Indian studies in the United States.

Native American studies programs and departments began to develop during the 1970s, and they flourished. By 1985, 107 colleges and universities had either a program or department of American Indian studies. Many were a part of an ethnic studies program or a unit of an anthropology department. Eighteen Native American studies programs or departments offered majors, and 40 of these offered minors. (For example, a student could obtain a Ph.D. in the Ethnic Studies Department at the University of California, Berkeley, but Native American Studies was under the umbrella of Ethnic Studies.)

By 1995, six Native American studies units offered graduate programs, including the University of California-Berkeley, University of Arizona, University of California-Los Angeles, and Montana State University; and Harvard University continues to offer a graduate program in American Indian Education. During the mid-1990s, 13 research centers and institutions existed whose objectives focused on American Indians.

In 1976, an estimated 76,000 American Indian students attended accredited colleges and universities. By 1984, some 82,672 Native Americans were enrolled in colleges and universities. Another 60 percent of that number attended two-year community colleges. It was obvious that many Indian youth wished to pursue American Indian studies. By 1997, 124 Native American studies programs existed. Admittedly, most of these programs lack recognition and visibility; however, several have earned national distinction through the years for their activities such as the programs at Berkeley, UCLA, University of Minnesota, University of Oklahoma, and University of Arizona, Tucson.

In 1996, the American Indian studies program at the University of Arizona announced the end of a seven-year struggle to offer the first doctoral program in American Indian studies. With seven core Native American faculty, and with a total of 19 faculty participating in the program, American Indian studies at the University of Arizona have set an important new precedent.

The need for more visibility of Native American studies and other ways of academic advancement is imperative in educating other minorities and mainstream Americans about Native Americans and their many diverse cultures. Carter Blue Clark, a Muscogee Creek historian and executive vice president at Oklahoma City University, stated:

> American Indian Studies is trapped in . . . [a] cultural dilemma . . . American Indian Studies fits no standard academic mold. American Indian Studies is by its nature interdisciplinary . . . American Indians are unique, and so is their discipline. They stand alone among all of the other ethnic groups because of their history, which involves treaties, tribalism, and other aspects that set them apart.

The Native American presence in academia had emerged noticeably with the works of the first generation of Indian scholars in post-modern America—Vine Deloria, Jr., and N. Scott Momaday in the late 1960s, as well as Francis LaFlesche, John Milton Oskison, John Joseph Matthews, Luther Standing Bear, James Paytiamo, George Webb, John Tebble, John Rogers, and D'Arcy McNickle. Because the public and publishers seemed willing to entertain the writings of Native Americans, another group soon followed, consisting of Howard Adams, Robert Burnette, Harold Cardinal, Rupert Costo, Edward P. Dozier, Jack D. Forbes, Jeanette Henry, Bea Medicine, Alfonso Ortiz, and Robert K. Thomas. In the creative writing field, the list included Leslie Silko, Duane Niatum, Simon Ortiz, Gerald Vizenor, James Welch, Ray Young Bear, and many others.

American Indian intellectualism also has been expressed by publication of a dozen or more Native American journals, which were founded in the 1970s and 1980s. In the mid-1990s, articles about Native Americans were published in *Akwekon* (Cornell University, 1984), *American Indian Culture and Research Journal* (UCLA, 1974), *Journal of American Indian Education* (Arizona State University, 1961), *American Indian Law Journal* (Institute for the Development of Indian Law, Washington, D.C., 1975), *American Indian Law Review* (University of Oklahoma, 1973), *American Indian Quarterly* (now at University of Oklahoma, 1974), *Canadian Journal of Native Studies, Journal of Alaska Native Arts* (Institute of Alaska Native Arts, Fairbanks, Alaska, 1984), *Journal of Navajo Education* (Chinle, Arizona, 1983), *Native Studies Review* in Canada, *Tribal College Journal,* and *Wiscazo Sa Review* (Eastern Washington University, 1985). The majority of these journals are peer-judged and externally refereed. Because of the diversity of Native Americans and their multiple interests, more Indian journals are needed. Yet, human and financial resources are lacking, thus limiting American Indian and non-Indian scholars publishing their works.

American Indian identity in academia has required increased attention and action. In 1985, historian Carter Blue Clark stated:

> Interest in American Indians will continue as a result of the historic legacy of Manifest Destiny, yearning for family roots, and a lingering romantic attachment to the glories of a bygone era. The necessities of earning a living with marketable skills will not lessen the need to maintain Indian cultural ties and to learn more about one's Indianness through American Indian Studies. Even though some of the attributes of Indian studies will alter with changing demands from society and administrators, American Indian Studies will continue to offer insights into America's unique culture and heritage. The basic mission of American Indian Studies is to educate and enlighten all students about the diverse and rich cultures that make up American Indian life.

As Indian communities have continued to flourish—with much promise for this next century and the new millennium—academia has endeavored to keep pace. The number of tribally controlled colleges has increased. The first, the Navajo Community College, started as only an idea in the early 1960s. With funding from the Office of Economic Opportunity, the tribe, and the Donner Foundation, the Navajo Nation founded the Navajo Community College in 1968. Additional tribal colleges were soon established in California, North Dakota, and

South Dakota. As of this writing, there are 30 such colleges.

Tribal colleges received major support when the U.S. Congress passed the Tribally Controlled Community College Act in 1978, providing limited grants for starting these institutions in Indian country, including any Alaskan native village or village corporation approved by the Secretary of the Interior. At this pace, one college is being established each year. These community colleges base and develop their curriculum to meet the needs of their people, with practically oriented courses in business and administration.

The faculty for these 30 colleges are degreed Native Americans. It is now estimated that some 400 Native Americans in the United States have earned a Ph.D., and many others have earned a Master's degree. In the various academic fields for the professions, however, there are less than 25 Native Americans in each. And in each of the fields, the number of Native Americans, who are three-fourths or full-bloods are a fraction of the less than 25 in each field.

Institutions such as Arizona State University are extraordinary for having so many Native Americans holding doctorates; most colleges and universities have a couple, one, or none. Native American faculty and American Indian programs are vital to advancing the scholarship of Native American studies and to increasing the number of Indian college graduates. Unfortunately for American Indians, the colleges and universities that were founded to educate Native Americans, such as Dartmouth College, Harvard University, and the College of William and Mary, are not identified today as Indian schools.

Perhaps it is even more sad that the future of Native American studies—and the hope of graduating more American Indians—is in the hands of non-Indians who may not be able to give them the same attention that they commit to other minority groups and the mainstream. American Indian studies and Native Americans suffer from this virtual neglect, and this is reflected on college campuses across the country, where Indian students, faculty, and administrators are a mere fraction of the mainstream.

Yet, in spite of the suppression and neglect of American Indians on college campuses, the interest in them remains for many and complex reasons, including a curiosity of wanting to hear the Indian point of view. The late 1960s and early 1970s represented a drastic change in the study of Native

Americans, beginning with listening to the Indian voice of *Bury My Heart at Wounded Knee*—a voice that was varied, coming as it did from a myriad of Indian people who were outraged at the federal government, angry at the dominant society, and frustrated with their own people, or themselves. Dee Brown's work enabled this voice to be heard and gave it a sense of direction.

Source: Donald L. Fixico, "*Bury My Heart at Wounded Knee* and the Indian Voice in Native Studies," in *Journal of the West,* Vol. 39, No. 17, January 2000, pp. 7–15.

Sources

Brown, Dee, *Bury My Heart at Wounded Knee: An Indian History of the American West,* Holt, Rinehart and Winston, 1970, reprint, Owl Books, 2001.

Gilder, Joshua, "Who's on First," in *New York Magazine,* Vol. 13, No. 14, April 7, 1980, pp. 76–77.

McNeil, Helen, "Savages," in *New Statesman,* Vol. 82, No. 2115, October 1, 1971, pp. 444–45.

Momaday, N. Scott, "When the West Was Won and a Civilization Was Lost," in the *New York Times Book Review,* March 7, 1971, pp. 46–47.

Rechy, John, "The Flaws to Make a Fiction Shine," in the *Los Angeles Times Book Review,* April 3, 1983, pp. 2, 9.

Silko, Leslie Marmon, "They Were the Land's," in the *New York Times Book Review,* May 25, 1980, pp. 10, 22.

Further Reading

Ambrose, Stephen E., *Crazy Horse and Custer: The Parallel Lives of Two American Warriors,* Anchor, 1996.
    In this compelling set of profiles, Ambrose weaves a narrative that compares Crazy Horse to General George Armstrong Custer. As Ambrose shows, before the two leaders first met in battle at Little Big Horn in 1876, their lives were remarkably parallel.

Andrist, Ralph K., *The Long Death: The Last Days of the Plain Indians,* reprint, University of Oklahoma Press, 2001.
    This seminal work in Native-American studies, first published in 1964, describes how Native Americans were crowded into increasingly smaller areas by the massive westward expansion of white settlers.

Hirschfelder, Arlene, *Native Americans: A History in Pictures,* Dorling Kindersley, 2000.
    This book offers a detailed overview of Native-American history from ancestral times to the present day. It contains hundreds of photos, illustrations, maps, profiles of major Native-American leaders, famous quotations, and informative sidebars.

Nies, Judith, *Native American History: A Chronology of a Culture's Vast Achievements and Their Links to World Events,* Ballantine Books, 1996.

> Nies gives a thorough timeline of the major events in Native-American history, from prehistorical times until 1996. Using a two-column format, she places these events next to the other world events from the same year, giving readers a context within which to understand the Native-American events.

The Elements of Style

William Strunk, Jr.
E. B. White

1959

English professor William Strunk Jr. wrote *The Elements of Style* as a guide for his students at Cornell University and had it printed privately in 1918. In 1935, Strunk issued a revised edition, titled *The Elements and Practice of Composition*, with Edward A. Tenney as coauthor. Among Strunk's students was E. B. White, who many years later wrote an article about Strunk for the *New Yorker* magazine. The article led Macmillan publishers to ask White to revise Strunk's original book for general publication. (Strunk died in 1946.) This first published edition of *The Elements of Style* came out in 1959 and credited Strunk and White as coauthors. To supplement his other additions and revisions, White added a fifth chapter, "An Approach to Style." White's *New Yorker* article about Strunk was revised to serve as an introduction.

White made minor changes for a second edition published in 1972 and further additions and updates for the third edition, published in 1979. A fourth edition published in 1999 includes a new introduction written by White's stepson, Roger Angell.

Since publication of the 1959 edition, *The Elements of Style* has been widely considered a necessary reference for both academic and professional writers. Generations of students, teachers, writers, and editors have known it simply as "Strunk and White."

Author Biography

William Strunk, Jr., was born July 1, 1869, in Cincinnati, Ohio. After earning a bachelor's degree at the University of Cincinnati in 1890 and a Ph.D. at Cornell University in 1896, Strunk went on to have a long career as an educator. He taught English at Cornell for forty-six years.

Strunk wrote the first edition of *The Elements of Style* for the use of his students and had it privately printed in 1918. A revised edition titled *The Elements and Practice of Composition*, with Edward A. Tenney as coauthor, was printed in 1935. The only other book Strunk wrote was *English Metres*, published locally in 1922. Better known as an editor, Strunk edited works by important authors including William Shakespeare, John Dryden, and James Fenimore Cooper.

Strunk married Olivia Emilie Locke in 1900, and they had two sons and a daughter. Strunk died in Ithaca, New York, on September 26, 1946.

Elwyn Brooks White, who used the name E. B. White, was born July 11, 1899, in Mount Vernon, New York. White was Strunk's student at Cornell, from which he earned a bachelor's degree in 1921, and went on to become a well-known writer. In 1926, White went to work for *The New Yorker,* which had been founded a year earlier and would launch the careers of some of the most respected writers of the coming decades. White was widely appreciated as an essayist and humorist, but his best-known works today are his children's books, including *Stuart Little* (1945), *Charlotte's Web* (1952; the Newbery Honor Book for 1953 and winner of several other awards), and *The Trumpet of the Swan* (1970; nominated for a National Book Award in 1971 and winner of several awards including the Children's Book Award from the William Allen White Library at Emporia State University). In addition to many other awards and honorary degrees, White was honored in 1978 with a Pulitzer Prize special citation for his body of work.

In 1957, Macmillan hired White to revise Strunk's ''little book,'' as the professor had called it, for general publication. This edition of *The Elements of Style*, published in 1959, became the classic that generations of college students have known as ''Strunk and White.''

White married Katharine Sergeant Angell, an editor at *The New Yorker,* in 1929, and the two had a son together; Angell also had a son and daughter

E. B. White

from a previous marriage. White died in North Brooklin, Maine, on October 1, 1985, after suffering from Alzheimer's disease.

Plot Summary

Chapter 1: Elementary Rules of Usage

This chapter sets forth eleven rules of English usage dealing with the formation of possessives; correct use of commas, colons, and dashes; noun-verb agreement; pronoun cases; and participial phrases. Each rule is followed by a series of correct and incorrect examples with explanations. The chapter is not comprehensive (for example, it does not address all uses of commas); instead it addresses areas in which the authors felt errors were common at the time.

Chapter 2: Elementary Principles of Composition

Another set of eleven rules addresses structure in written work, moving from the overall structure of a piece (''Choose a suitable design and hold to it'') to sentence structure (''Place the emphatic words of a sentence at the end''). Again, each rule is followed by examples and amplification. The authors use excerpts from accomplished writers including Jean Stafford and E. M. Forster as models of effective composition.

Chapter 3: A Few Matters of Form

This very brief chapter covers details of the actual presentation of written work—what it should look like on the page. Issues addressed range from margins and headings to where to place punctuation marks in relation to parentheses.

Chapter 4: Words and Expressions Commonly Misused

This long chapter, the final section of Strunk's original manuscript, is a compendium of words and phrases that writers often misuse, again followed by explanations and examples. The list begins with the words ''aggravate'' and ''irritate,'' followed by an explanation that the two are not synonyms; ''irritate'' means ''to annoy,'' and ''aggravate'' means ''to add to an already annoying situation.'' The authors similarly clarify the meanings of ''alternate'' and ''alternative,'' ''among'' and ''between,'' and many other pairs.

Strunk and White consider a word misused if it has the wrong meaning for its use in the sentence or if it adds no meaning. For example, they point out that the word ''character'' is misused in the phrase ''acts of a hostile character,'' which they recommend shortening to ''hostile acts.''

Chapter 5: An Approach to Style (With a List of Reminders)

This chapter, White's addition to the original manuscript, begins by defining what White means by ''style'': ''Style is the sense of what is distinguished and distinguishing.'' White continues:

> Style is an increment in writing. When we speak of [F. Scott] Fitzgerald's style, we don't mean his command of the relative pronoun, we mean the sound his words make on paper. Every writer, by the way he uses the language, reveals something of his spirit, his habits, his capacities, his bias.

White uses examples from Thomas Paine (the famed ''These are the times that try men's souls'') and Thomas Wolfe to demonstrate that while meaning can be conveyed equally well by any number of constructions (''Times like these try men's souls''), one particular way of expressing an idea is often more pleasing, powerful, and memorable than any of the alternatives. The ability to express an idea in a

powerful way is a hallmark of style, White declares. He adds that some writers' styles are so distinctive that readers come to recognize their ''voices'' on paper as easily as they would learn to recognize their speaking voices. Quotations from William Faulkner, Ernest Hemingway, Robert Frost, and Walt Whitman illustrate this point.

Having shown what style is, White offers twenty-one suggestions designed to help novice writers develop their own styles. Some of these tips address technical matters, such as avoiding weak qualifiers (''rather,'' ''very,'' etc.) and using standard spelling (''through,'' not ''thru,'' for example). Other tips deal with more subjective issues: ''Do not explain too much''; ''Place yourself in the background.'' By the latter, White means that good writing ''draws the reader's attention to the sense and substance of the writing, rather than to the mood and temper of the author.''

Key Figures

William Faulkner

William Faulkner, the Nobel Prize-winning novelist who set his major novels in the fictional Yoknapatawpha County in Mississippi, is the only author whom Strunk and White use twice as a positive example. Faulkner is praised for the concrete details he uses to make his setting seem real and for an individual style that makes his writing immediately recognizable.

E. M. Forster

Strunk and White use an excerpt from the work of the English writer E. M. Forster as an example of laudable sentence structure. Primarily known as a novelist, Forster also wrote short stories and essays.

Robert Frost

American poet Robert Frost, who won four Pulitzer Prizes, is contrasted with Walt Whitman in a passage that discusses the importance of individual style.

Wolcott Gibbs

Wolcott Gibbs was an editor and a writer on the staff of the *New Yorker* from its early days. Gibbs is best remembered today for his short, humorous, and highly quotable comments on a variety of topics, and it is such a comment that Strunk and White quote in their book.

Ernest Hemingway

Strunk and White contrast the spare style of American author Ernest Hemingway with the detail-laden prose of William Faulkner to illustrate differences in individual style.

Abraham Lincoln

In a humorous paragraph, Strunk and White use the first line of Abraham Lincoln's famous Gettysburg Address to explore "the line between the fancy and the plain, between the atrocious and the felicitous." The authors declare that Lincoln "was flirting with disaster" with his opening line ("Four score and seven years ago") but that the president "achieved cadence while skirting the edge of fanciness." They offer several possible rephrasings of the line and explain why each is inferior to Lincoln's choice.

W. Somerset Maugham

Strunk and White use a paragraph from the English writer W. Somerset Maugham to support their argument that the pronouns "he" and "his" should be used when a writer is referring to both genders, avoiding what they consider the clumsy and unnecessary use of "he or she" and "his or her."

George Orwell

The English author George Orwell once "translated" a short passage from the King James Bible into flat, colorless contemporary prose as a way of ridiculing the latter kind of writing. Strunk and White reproduce Orwell's exercise for the same purpose.

Thomas Paine

Strunk and White take a famous line from American patriot Thomas Paine ("These are the times that try men's souls") and recast it in several ways to show why Paine's simple declarative sentence is the most powerful form in which to express his thought.

Herbert Spencer

In their only quotation from another volume on style, Strunk and White quote British philosopher Herbert Spencer in his *Philosophy of Style* on the difference between vague writing and vivid writing.

Jean Stafford

California-born writer Jean Stafford won the Pulitzer Prize in 1969 for *"The Short Stories of Jean Stafford."* Strunk and White quote her story "In the Zoo" as an example of writing made vivid through imagery.

Robert Louis Stevenson

Two lines from a poem by Scottish writer Robert Louis Stevenson provide the last example in the book of what Strunk and White consider good writing; Strunk and White credit Stevenson's "plainer style" for the enduring popularity of his poetry.

Walt Whitman

An excerpt from the work of American poet Walt Whitman is contrasted with one from Robert Frost to demonstrate the unique style of each writer.

Thomas Wolfe

Thomas Wolfe wrote four autobiographical novels of the American South before he died at an early age. Strunk and White use one sentence from Wolfe in discussing sentence structure. The authors praise Wolfe's sentence structure while hinting that he was nonetheless guilty of creating overblown prose.

Themes

Brevity

One principle that runs throughout *The Elements of Style* is that of brevity. To Strunk and White, good writing expresses thoughts economically. One of their "principles of composition" is to "omit needless words." The next rule advises to "avoid a succession of loose sentences." Later in the book, they instruct: "Do not explain too much." By way of examples, they shorten "in a hasty manner" to "hastily," "he is a man who" to "he," and so on. They make a special example of "the fact that," stating flatly, "It should be revised out of every sentence in which it occurs."

This theme of the book matched Strunk's personality and his teaching emphasis, as White remembers in his introduction to *The Elements of Style*:

"Omit needless words!" cries the author on page 23, and into that imperative Will Strunk really put his heart and soul. In the days when I was sitting in his

Topics for Further Study

- What do you think Professor Strunk would have to say about the writing that appears in today's newspapers, magazines, and books? Write a short essay, as if you were Strunk, critiquing the general state of written English in the United States today. As Strunk did, be sure to give examples to support your criticisms.

- Choose one of Strunk and White's rules or principles with which you disagree. Write a letter to the book's publisher in which you make a case for changing or deleting that rule or principle from the book.

- Research the history of *The New Yorker* from its founding to the present. Make a timeline showing the highlights of the magazine's history and the important writers who have worked there or contributed to the magazine.

- Read all or part of one of White's books for children. Consider to what extent the style White extols in *The Elements of Style* is reflected in his own work and how this style affects the quality of the work.

- Now that you have read *The Elements of Style*, reread a piece of your own writing. Revise the piece according to the dictates of Strunk and White, and then decide whether you think the revision has improved your writing.

---

class, he omitted so many needless words, and omitted them so forcibly and with such eagerness and obvious relish, that he often seemed in the position of having shortchanged himself—a man left with nothing more to say yet with time to fill, a radio prophet who had out-distanced the clock.

Strunk's original version of *The Elements of Style*, White writes, was ''his attempt to cut the vast tangle of English rhetoric down to size and write its rules and principles on the head of a pin.'' Strunk said it all in forty-three pages, and White reports that it was with wicked delight that the professor always referred to his work as ''the *little* book.''

Clarity

Along with urging writers to be brief, the authors admonish them to be clear. In his chapter on style, White makes his case for clarity in a way that is so serious it is almost shocking:

Muddiness is not merely a disturber of prose, it is also a destroyer of life, of hope: death on the highway caused by a badly worded road sign, heartbreak among lovers caused by a misplaced phrase in a well-intentioned letter, anguish of a traveler expecting to be met at a railroad station and not being met because of a slipshod telegram.

Having made his point, White goes on to acknowledge that there are humorous possibilities, too, in unclear writing. To prove it, he reports that the staid *New York Times* once informed its readers that Nelson Rockefeller was ''chairman of the Museum of Modern Art, which he entered in a fireman's raincoat during a recent fire, and founded the Museum of Primitive Art.'' White follows this with words that are slung together in his own distinctive style and that beg to be quoted. Referring to the quotation from the *Times,* he writes:

This we all love. But think of the tragedies that are rooted in ambiguity; think of that side, and be clear! When you say something, make sure you have said it. The chances of your having said it are only fair.

Clarity and its cousins, accuracy and precision, are the subtexts of rules presented throughout the book. ''Use definite, specific, concrete language,'' the authors write. ''Keep related words together.'' (The example given of a sentence that breaks this rule is, ''New York's first commercial human-sperm bank opened Friday with semen samples from eighteen men frozen in a stainless steel tank.'') The chapter on commonly misused words serves the cause of clarity by reminding writers not to use ''disinterested'' when they mean ''uninterested'' or ''enormity'' when they mean ''enormousness,'' pointing out that the word pairs are not synonymous.

Style

Authoritative Tone

Strunk wrote his original manuscript in the authoritative tone of the professor speaking from the lectern, and White, in his additions, followed Strunk's lead. While the authors acknowledge that some of their views are not universally held, they go on to present those views as representing the highest standards of written English. Virtually all of the book's rules and principles, and also much of the text that supports them, are presented in imperative sentences: ''Put statements in positive form''; ''express coordinate ideas in similar form'' (the principle of parallel construction); ''revise and rewrite.'' Following their own advice about not weakening sentences with vague qualifiers, Strunk and White never write ''try to . . .'' or ''it is a good idea to . . .'' or ''if possible . . .'' Their presentation can be summed up as follows: These are the rules. Good writers follow them. A reader of *The Elements of Style* is likely to conclude that Professor Strunk was not in the habit of asking his students, ''Are there any questions?'' His rules of written English are clear and neat and not open to discussion.

Humor

This authoritarian tone is made much more palatable by the abundant humor in the book. Without a heavy dose of humor, the authors would seem like cruel dictators. Their great sense of fun enlivens the text. They have a talent for making readers laugh at their own crimes against the language. Readers who know they are guilty of having written ''nauseous'' when they should have written ''nauseated'' feel corrected but not scolded when they read:

> *Nauseous. Nauseated.* The first means ''sickening to contemplate''; the second means ''sick at the stomach.'' Do not, therefore, say ''I feel nauseous,'' unless you are sure you have that effect on others.

Again, White's introduction credits Strunk's own sense of humor for the merry-prankster attitude that pervades the book. White reports that Strunk found the term ''student body'' gruesome and determined to do away with it; the professor visited the office of the *Alumni News* to suggest that the publication use ''studentry'' (which Strunk himself coined, after ''citizenry'') instead of ''student body.'' ''I am told,'' White writes, ''that the *News* editor was so charmed by the visit, if not by the word, that he ordered the student body buried, never to rise again.'' White goes on to register his opinion that ''studentry'' is ''not much of an improvement, but it does sound less cadaverous.'' Countless readers have been as charmed by the humor of Strunk and his coauthor as that collegiate editor was.

Scope

Reference books that become classics are often comprehensive, providing answers to every imaginable question on the topic it covers. But *The Elements of Style* is far from comprehensive. Though it is now a bigger book than the book Strunk wrote in the early 1900s, ''bigger'' is strictly relative, and the current edition has not outgrown Strunk's nickname for his version, ''the *little* book.'' The *New York Public Library Writer's Guide to Style and Usage,* at 838 pages, is comprehensive. *The Elements of Style*, at fewer than one hundred, is idiosyncratic. It became and remains a classic because it covers issues that trip up many writers and, even more so, because it speaks to those issues in a quirky but forceful way.

Historical Context

The New Yorker's *Golden Age*

As *The Elements of Style* has long been a classic style manual, *The New Yorker* has long been the standard-bearer of American magazine journalism. Harold Ross founded *The New Yorker* in 1925 and was its editor until his death in 1951. Ross envisioned the magazine as funny, literate, and sophisticated, and he famously said that it was not ''for the old lady in Dubuque.'' White began writing for the magazine in its first year and continued to do so until his death in 1985. He is widely credited

Compare & Contrast

- **1950s:** *The New Yorker* is a humorous, cosmopolitan magazine that publishes the work of literary stars, including humorists James Thurber and Ogden Nash and critic Dorothy Parker, known for her sharp wit. The magazine also is famous for its cartoons, contributed by Charles Addams and other well-known artists.

  Today: *The New Yorker* still publishes the work of highly respected writers (Calvin Trillin and John McPhee, for example) and cartoonists (Roz Chast and many others).

- **1950s:** Magazines are printed on paper, and consumers buy them at newstands or have them delivered by mail. Several months pass between the time an issue is written and the time it is delivered to readers.

  Today: Most magazines that publish paper editions also publish electronic editions on the Internet. Electronic publishing technology means that online editions can be updated constantly, and an article may be written, edited, and read by consumers all in the course of a single day. In addition to traditional magazines, there are thousands of e-zines, magazines that publish only electronic editions. Their quality varies widely, from highly professional journals to newsletters produced by hobbyists.

- **1950s:** The written word is the primary medium for the communication of news and information and is also an important entertainment medium. While television offers a limited number of news programs, most people depend on newspapers for in-depth and local news. While Americans love movies, they also look to books and magazines for humor and other forms of entertainment.

  Today: Visual media have overtaken text media in the realms of both news and entertainment. Hundreds of television channels exist, and some provide news coverage twenty-four hours a day. In addition, online news sources provide constantly updated news. Consumers can watch movies and other entertainment at home any time via videocassettes, DVDs, and cable and satellite movie channels, and, increasingly, on the Internet. All in all, Americans read less and watch more than they did in the past.

---

with creating the magazine's distinctive style. *The New Yorker* has been so influential that generations of aspiring writers have looked to it for guidance and inspiration, much as they have looked to Strunk and White's book.

The late 1950s, when *The Elements of Style* was first published, was something of a golden age in American magazine journalism. At the time, the editor of *The New Yorker* was William Shawn. The magazine had about 450,000 subscribers—a huge number for a magazine that was ostensibly written and edited for the residents of a single city—and enough advertising to make it solidly profitable. As has been true throughout its history, *The New Yorker* published some of the period's best writers, including John Updike, Jonathan Schell, and Calvin Trillin

in addition to White, who had a hand in every aspect of the magazine, from writing the famous "Talk of the Town" feature to creating a painting that appeared on the cover. The magazine featured a wide variety of articles, all well-written and well-edited, from satiric commentary to innovative short stories to tough investigative journalism. Edwin Emery, in his *The Press and America,* calls *The New Yorker* "possibly the most distinctive of American magazines" and writes that it "was more than cartoons, whimsy, and curiously plotless fiction; it had its penetrating 'Profiles,' its 'Reporter at Large,' and other incisive commentaries on public affairs."

The New Yorker of the late 1950s stood at the head of a distinguished class of American magazines. *Harper's* was more than one hundred years old, having begun as a literary journal and transformed itself into a public affairs magazine. *The Saturday Evening Post,* the magazine that *was* edited for the "old lady in Dubuque" and the rest of the heartland, had about six million subscribers nationwide who eagerly read its fiction, biographies, and current events reportage. *Esquire* was a literary magazine that published Ernest Hemingway, William Faulkner, John Steinbeck, Truman Capote, and many other stars in addition to new voices. *Reader's Digest* had been around since the 1920s, but began to reflect the conservative ideas and inspirational philosophies of its founder, DeWitt Wallace. It was the circulation king; between 1946 and 1970, its circulation doubled to nearly eighteen million in the United States plus ten million in sixty countries around the world. Political magazines also were having a heyday, with *National Review* in which William F. Buckley Jr. espoused the views of the right and the *Nation* and the *New Republic* which espoused views of the left.

Critical Overview

When it was first published, *The Elements of Style* was favorably reviewed in newspapers nationwide. P. F. Baum's 1960 review in the *Los Angeles Times Book Review* is representative. Baum writes:

> The world would be a better place if everybody read *The Elements of Style;* if it were read not just by writers and journalists but by all who write legal briefs, job applications, love letters, or notes to the teacher; read even by those who never write anything.

Baum praises the manual as "a monument to clear thinking cleanly voiced."

Edward C. Sampson, in his article on White for the *Twayne's United States Authors Series,* calls Strunk's original work "a short, precise guide to writing, free of jargon and written with a respect for the reader's intelligence and needs." Discussing White's chapter on style, Sampson writes, "Many of his examples . . . are felicitous, and he generally manages to be precise and helpful without being dogmatic." Sampson, however, finds White's own writing style lacking. He writes: "Curiously, this

chapter about style is not one of White's effective pieces. It is not always clear, it is sometimes inconsistent, and it is repetitious in a way rare for White." Sampson concludes that White "seems to be writing for himself or another artist, rather than for a freshman struggling with his weekly theme." Baum disagrees, writing, "The final chapter on writing style displays all White's own mastery of the essay form."

According to Sampson, White acknowledged that he had difficulty with his work on *The Elements of Style*, which undoubtedly came as a surprise to the many critics and readers who revered White as one of the finest essayists of his time. Sampson takes a quotation from White's book *The Points of My Compass,* in which he writes of *The Elements of Style,* "I felt uneasy posing as an expert on rhetoric, when the truth is I write by ear, always with difficulty and seldom with any exact notion of what is taking place under the hood."

The most scathing criticism of the book has come from a few feminist critics who find it a manual of misogyny rather than writing style. In a 1991 article for *Western Humanities Review,* Debra Fried objects not so much to Strunk and White's rules as to the examples they use to illustrate them. She objects to example sentences such as "Chloe smells good, as a pretty girl should," declaring that "What is most pernicious about [these] sentences is that they are advanced under the false colors of mere examples." They are not mere examples, Fried argues, but attempts to buttress male power and authority.

The Elements of Style has survived several decades of shifting theories about education, writing style, and gender politics. When it was published, it immediately became a popular text for college English and writing courses, and it is still widely used on college campuses today as well as in some high schools.

Criticism

Candyce Norvell

Norvell is an independent educational writer who specializes in English and literature and who

At the time of the 1959 edition of The Elements of Style, *the* New Yorker, *where E. B. White worked and wrote, was the standardbearer of literary journalism*

has done graduate work in religion. In this essay, Norvell defends The Elements of Style *against the arguments of feminist and other critics.*

In the past couple of decades, virtually every literary work bearing the label "classic" has been assailed as misogynistic, irrelevant, or both. Critics writing from a number of different perspectives, from postmodernist to feminist, have pointed out the myriad ways in which the writing of white males—whether they lived in ancient Greece or the twentieth-century United States—supposedly

denigrates everyone else. Some of these scholars, contradicting their own rhetoric about the importance of inclusion and diversity, have argued that the traditionally accepted canon of Western literature is so pernicious that it should be thrown onto the trash heap of history.

Anyone who supposes that a slim little manual of writing style like *The Elements of Style* is too apolitical and innocuous to attract the attention of such a mob would be underestimating the fury of the critics as well as their talent for tortured reasoning. How furious are they? How tortured is their reason-

What Do I Read Next?

- *Writings from "The New Yorker," 1925–1976* (1990), edited by Rebecca M. Dale, is a collection of some of White's contributions to the magazine.

- Gary Hoffman and Glynis Hoffman, authors of *Adiós, Strunk and White: A Handbook for the New Academic Essay* (1999), urge young writers to say goodbye to traditional grammar, organization, and objectivity. Their book provides a stark contrast to the style taught by Strunk and White.

- The *New York Public Library Writer's Guide to Style and Usage* (1994), edited by Andrea Sutcliffe, is as comprehensive (at 838 pages) as

The Elements of Style is brief. It delves into issues such as special characters used in foreign languages and gender bias in language.

- *On Writing: A Memoir of the Craft* (2000), by best-selling author Stephen King, is part autobiography and part writing textbook. King covers everything from paragraphs to plotting and even gives writing assignments. He recommends *The Elements of Style* to his readers.

- *Charlotte's Web* (1952), a moving story of friendship, is White's most famous and enduring children's book.

---

ing? A couple examples from an article that appeared in *Western Humanities Review* in 1991 provide a good answer. In this article, "Bewhiskered Examples in *The Elements of Style*," Debra Fried takes issue with Strunk and White for choosing Nehemiah 11:7 as their example of how to correctly use a colon to separate chapter from verse in a biblical citation. Ever alert for insidious attacks on nonwhite non-males, Fried suspected that Strunk and White must have been up to no good when they chose that particular example. She was outraged, but most likely not surprised, to find that Nehemiah 11:7 reads thus: "And these are the sons of Benjamin: Sallu the son of Meshullam, the son of Joed, the son of Pedaiah, the son of Kolaiah, the son of Maaseiah, the son of Ithiel, the son of Jesaiah." The choice of this verse to illustrate colon placement is an assault on womanhood, Fried reasons. Her sentences are not any easier to navigate than her reasoning, but only Fried's own words will do here. Therefore, here are Fried's own words:

> What do the sons of Benjamin have to do with the placement of the colon? Could it be that the Nehemiah text implies that genealogy is the originating instance of the colon . . . ? Do we have here a grammarian's just-so story . . . that teaches us that patriarchy . . . marked the beginning of the categorization that the colon authorizes and makes legible? Things of the

same type are those that a single patriarch has begotten; according to this logic, fathering becomes the reigning metaphor for categorizing, and the model for the relation of general to particular . . . is that of a father to his sons.

The text of the verse does not even appear in *The Elements of Style*, but Fried wants her readers to believe that Strunk and White planted the reference in hopes that theirs would look it up and thus be indoctrinated to believe (as far as this writer can figure out) that punctuation marks have gender, and colons are male, and that is bad.

Fried also objects to the sentence "As a mother of five, with another one on the way, my ironing board is always up." Strunk and White offer this as an example of a misplaced participial phrase, as the sentence, strictly read, states that the ironing board is a mother of five. Fried sees in the sentence the authors' disapproval of the woman who is speaking and, by extension, all women who have several children. Why is she sure that the authors feel this way? Well, she reasons, since Strunk and White advocate a "spare, crisp style" of writing, they obviously despise the woman for her "procreative productivity," which Fried claims is "incompatible" with concise writing and the economical use of words. Fried's thesis: If Strunk and White prefer

> **There is nothing wrong with writing down a string of words that make the writer feel that he or she is precocious, but the end result is not necessarily an essay.''**

fewer words to more words, then they must also prefer fewer children to more children. The ironing board in Strunk and White's sentence, writes Fried, is the woman's ''punishment for producing too many children.'' She further refers to these children as ''the ragged brood whose very number is a kind of raggedness no ironing will smooth.''

Of course, it is not possible to cross from Strunk and White's sentence to Fried's conclusion using the bridge of logic. A logical consideration of the two works—Strunk and White's book and Fried's article—reveals that only one of them uses judgmental language. Only Fried charges that the woman has ''too many'' children who comprise a ''ragged band.'' It is Fried, not Strunk and White, who denigrates the woman in the sentence and all women like her.

Fried's refrain is that the examples that Strunk and White use to illustrate their rules of usage and style consistently belittle women. A balanced reading of their book, however, finds that the examples are balanced in terms of gender. One example of proper use of the dash is ''His first thought on getting out of bed—if he had any thought at all—was to get back in again.'' If Strunk and White had used ''her'' and ''she'' in place of ''his'' and ''he,'' Fried no doubt would have lashed out at them for characterizing women as thoughtless and lazy. Since they did not use feminine pronouns, Fried seems to have disregarded the sentence. An example of subject-verb agreement is: ''His speech as well as his manner is objectionable.'' Again, imagine Fried's outrage if the sentence had been written about ''her'' speech and manner. ''The culprit, it turned out, was he'' clearly casts a male in the role of villain, and ''Will Jane or he be hired, do you think?'' puts Jane on an equal footing with a male in a job-related situation. All these examples appear within a few pages, but since they do not support Fried's argument, she ignores them.

Another recent argument for setting aside *The Elements of Style* has been that its insistence on standard rules of usage and grammar is archaic. Gary and Glynis Hoffman's book *Adiós, Strunk and White: A Handbook for the New Academic Essay,* is one purveyor of this argument. The Hoffmans disagree with Strunk and White on virtually every issue. Strunk and White discuss the importance of organization to good written work; the Hoffmans begin their first chapter with the subheading ''Style before Organization.'' While the idea that style takes precedence over structure would leave most writers (and writing teachers) scratching their heads, at least the phrase is comprehensible, which is more than can be said for what follows. The Hoffmans' highly idiosyncratic ''elements of style'' are listed as ''flow,'' ''pause,'' ''fusion,'' ''opt,'' and ''scrub.'' Of course, no matter how well a reader knows English, he or she will not be able to determine what the Hoffmans had in mind when they wrote these chapter headings or what activities or elements of the writing task the words refer to. The words as the Hoffmans use them do not communicate anything; they are just a list of words. Apparently, the authors felt free and creative when they wrote it, and freedom and creativity are what they preach and value. Putting ''Style before Organization'' means putting the writer's experience before the reader's understanding, and the Hoffmans' book provides a parade example.

There is nothing wrong with writing down a string of words that make the writer feel that he or she is precocious, but the end result is not necessarily an essay. It is not surprising, then, that one student who followed the Hoffmans' advice reported, in a customer review of their book on Amazon.com, ''The minute I applied this technique in my classes . . . i [sic] had teachers scrawling huge question marks on my papers.'' This student described the Hoffmans' guide as a ''right-in-your-face-conventional-inconventionalist [sic] book,'' so the professors' confusion is understandable.

The point is so elementary that one is almost embarrassed to have to make it: Whether the game in question is baseball or writing, rules are what make the game possible. Without rules, one or two people can toss a ball around and swing a bat at it and be entertained for a while. But they cannot really explore all the fascinating, amazing things that people can do with a ball and a bat unless they establish rules so that everybody understands what everybody else is doing, which allows the players to interact and the watchers to understand what they are watching. Rules make it possible to take a ball and a bat and a group of people and create a story—a story that, in athletic play, happens to be called a game—that all the players, and maybe millions of spectators, experience together as being exciting and enjoyable and meaningful. Just so, rules make it possible to put words on paper in such a way that they make a story that can excite and move and inspire millions of people. A series of words comprehensible only to the writers—flow, pause, fusion, opt, scrub—cannot do this.

The Hoffmans claim that the traditional rules of grammar and style are meaningless, but in fact these rules make meaning possible. Strunk and White offer no meaningless rules and no unnecessary ones. They offer just a small volume of rules, principles, and suggestions that provide a framework for clear written communication so that everybody can enjoy the game. Far from putting writers in stylistic straitjackets, they celebrate styles as diverse as those of Ernest Hemingway and William Faulkner, Robert Frost and Walt Whitman. Their sense of humor and creativity are on display on every page of *The Elements of Style*. They poke gentle fun at human beings of both genders and show disregard for none. For all these reasons, *The Elements of Style* will never go out of style.

Source: Candyce Norvell, Critical Essay on *The Elements of Style*, in *Nonfiction Classics for Students*, Gale, 2003.

Adrian Blevins

Blevins's is a poet and essayist who has taught at Hollins University, Sweet Briar College, and in the Virginia Community College system; Blevins' first full-length collection of poems, The Brass Girl Brouhaha, *is forthcoming from Ausable Press in September of 2003. In this essay, Blevins argues that* The Elements of Style *is potentially confusing because it sometimes confuses grammatical and mechanical competence with actual literary merit.*

The Elements of Style is, as E. B. White admits in its introduction, "a dusty rulebook." It governs everything from how to make possessive singular nouns plural to why the active voice is preferable to the passive. The majority of the book is Will Strunk's attempt, as E. B. White says in his introduction to the third edition, "to cut the vast tangle of English rhetoric down to size and write its rules and principles on the head of a pin." In so doing, *The Elements of Style* promotes a philosophy of composition whose first tenet is the idea that "good sense is the foundation of good writing," as Sir Winston Churchill has said. Because few writers

would disagree with this sentiment—and because it is among the first books to promote such a commonsense philosophy—*The Elements of Style* is an important book to anyone interested in English prose style. Nevertheless because Strunk and White sometimes confuse grammatical and mechanical competence with actual literary style, the book is also potentially confusing.

Most writing teachers urge students to become grammatically and mechanically proficient because students who understand and utilize Standard English will pass through their universities and colleges with less failure and frustration than students who do not. In other words, writers who do not write clear sentences risk more than just being misunderstood. Since careless mistakes are often thought to indicate a failure of character or a failure of intelligence, writers who do not take the necessary pains to be understood imply that they do not care about their readers, and in this way risk their reputations as persons. Writers who do not add the apostrophe after a plural possessive noun—just one example of the many mistakes novice writers make—imply, in other words, that they're either lazy or incompetent.

But because readers do evaluate a writer's character *and* intelligence based on the way she writes, any serious study of style cannot assume that mere grammatical and mechanical proficiency will, even eventually, generate the necessary tools for actual literary style. Style is not the result of a writer adhering to laws and edicts. Style is, instead, the very ways in which writers *violate* laws and edicts in order to distinguish themselves from other voices.

It is impossible to find writers who would dispute the idea that style is the result of distinguishing techniques and procedures, rather than the consequence of a devotion to usage rules and regulations. In *The Modern Stylists,* the American poet Donald Hall says, "the style is the man. Again and again, the modern stylists repeat this idea." Even E. B. White admits that style is a consequence of the individual techniques a specific writer has of distinguishing herself from other writers. He says, "When we speak of Fitzgerald's style, we don't mean his command of the relative pronoun, we mean the sound his words make on paper. Every writer, by the way he uses the language, reveals something of his spirit, his habits, his capacities, his bias."

Even a cursory investigation of the techniques of almost any significant writer in the Western literary tradition will also define literary style as the means and methods writers have of distinguishing

> " . . . because Strunk and White sometimes confuse grammatical and mechanical competence with actual literary style, the book is . . . potentially confusing."

their voices from others. Vladimir Nabokov's *Lolita* begins in this way:

> Lolita, light of my life, fire of my loins. My sin, my soul. Lo-lee-ta: the top of the tongue taking a trip of three steps down the palate to tap, at three, on the teeth. Lo. Lee. Ta.

This passage is composed of quick-moving, almost stream-of-consciousness sentence fragments, and is extremely "egocentric"—to use White's term—in the sense that it does nothing *but* express the narrator's opinion. Because of the repetition of the consonant "l" and "t" sounds—the "t" sound inaugurates eleven words and shows up in the middle of three in this passage, while the "l" sound kicks off seven and shows up in the middle of many more—it even risks seeming overwritten. Yet is not this paragraph *beyond* memorable? Although the three fragments and free-floating syllable sounds in this passage are anything but grammatically correct, the passage conveys urgency and obsession through its display of fleeting but focused thought. Nabokov is able, in other words, to convey with his style more than he would be able to convey with content alone. This passage also says as much about its writer as its topic, and reminds us how vivid and strange experience is by surprising us with its unprecedented technique.

In *On Beauty and Being Just,* the philosopher Elaine Scary says that beauty "is unprecedented," and that we all are drawn to the beautiful—in art and nature—because the beautiful "quickens . . . adrenalines . . . makes the heart beat faster . . . life more vivid, animated, living, worth living." In this way, Scary reinforces the idea that style, which is closely linked to beauty, cannot be the consequence of conventional linguistic behavior.

Two of White's suggestions in his "Approach to Style" are especially confusing to anyone seriously interested in actual prose style (rather than grammatical and mechanical proficiency). The first one, a suggestion for the writer to place herself "in the background" [so she might] "write in a way that draws the reader's attention to the sense and substance of the writing, rather than to the mood or temper of the author," undermines everything we know about style by advocating what for the lack of a better term can be called "voicelessness."

An additional suggestion of White's advises students not to inject their opinions into their texts because "opinions scattered indiscriminately about leave the mark of egotism on a work." By doing so, he completely avoids the fact that "the essence of all good style . . . is expressiveness," as the English writer Water Pater has said. In other words, White's suggestion for writers to keep themselves in the background of their texts and to avoid expressing opinions is not advice that will help writers develop style, but is rather a recipe for cultivating the lack of style that is one of the first marks of bad writing.

Perhaps the best evidence for the book's ambiguity is the *style* of *The Elements of Style* itself. That is, the main thing that distinguishes *The Elements of Style* from the multitude of composition handbooks available today is the *voice* Strunk and White generate in it. In the book's introduction, White says, in fact, that Strunk sounds sometimes like a "Sergeant . . . snapping orders to his platoon." White goes to great lengths to praise his old professor's "wisdom" and "attitude toward right and wrong." This attitude, which is sometimes military, but is also playful and humorous, comes about as a consequence of both White and Strunk's unwillingness to stay in the text's background. It is, in other words, a result of the authors' unwillingness to follow their own advice.

Speaking on how necessary it is to surround "parenthetical expressions" (these are sometimes called "non-restrictive clauses and phrases" or, in more liberal handbooks, "asides" and "interjections") with commas, Strunk tells us, "there is no defense for such punctuation as [in the sentence], 'Marjorie's husband, Colonel Nelson paid us a visit today.'" In his long treaties on diction or word choice, White advises writers "never to call a stomach a tummy without good reason." And, when he advises beginning writers to avoid overwriting, he says, "Rich, ornate prose is hard to digest, generally unwholesome, and sometimes nauseating." Such tidbits are interesting not because of the information they provide, but because of the attitude they take toward their subject matter and audience. This attitude constitutes the book's style, and also counters the idea that good writers should stay in the background of their texts.

One of the more popular handbooks used in colleges and universities today is Diana Hacker's *A Writer's Reference*. On the topic of the use of commas in parenthetical expressions, Hacker says, "Expressions that are distinctly parenthetical should be set off with commas. Providing supplemental comments or information, they interrupt the flow of a sentence or appear as afterthoughts." Hacker's chapter on diction or word choice is not so much a chapter as a list of words commonly misused. In comparison, White has a lot to say about diction in his "Approach to Style." He says, for just one example, to avoid "the elaborate, the pretentious, the coy, and the cute." Is not "the coy, and the cute" coy and cute? And is it therefore not only the violation of one of the rules laid out in *The Elements of Style*, but also, and more to the point, far more *interesting* than Hacker's sentence on parenthetical expressions?

In the final chapter of *The Elements of Style*, E. B. White admits to the futility of proposing that literary merit, which he calls "a high mystery," can be achieved by strict adherence to a set of rules. He asks, "Who can confidently say what ignites a certain combination of words, causing them to explode in the mind?" In his introduction to the third edition, White admits that even Will Strunk "was quick to acknowledge the fallacy of inflexibility and the danger of doctrine." Despite these caveats, neither Strunk nor White offers students useful suggestions for cultivating actual literary style, because they mistakenly assume that grammatical and mechanical proficiency is the same as style, which even the book itself proves to be nowhere near the case.

Source: Adrian Blevins, Critical Essay on *The Elements of Style,* in *Nonfiction Classics for Students,* Gale, 2003.

Allison DeFrees

DeFrees has a bachelor's degree in English from the University of Virginia and a law degree from the University of Texas and is a published writer and an editor. In the following essay, DeFrees discusses the practicality of using a timeworn guide to grammar and style in today's literary environment.

William Strunk, a professor at Cornell in the first part of the twentieth century, wrote and self-published a slim volume titled *The Elements of Style,* which was required reading for his students, and no one else. Four decades later, E. B. White, one of Professor Strunk's former students, edited the volume for Macmillan Publishing Company for the general public. Since then, "the little book," as Strunk referred to it, has sold millions of copies, and teachers everywhere rely on it to imbue their students with confidence and precision in writing. The rules of grammar and usage and the advice on style in the book are elemental—applicable to any style of writing, even in the present age, when adherence to form is ignored and even belittled as out of date.

With today's MTV generation bored and facing an embarrassment of choices, and who quake at the sight of a line of thought that runs longer than thirty seconds, it is more important than ever to write concisely, to get to one's point as quickly as possible. But what makes a writer strong and persuasive? Clarity of thought, cleanliness of form, confident statements are elements of good style. And, of course, an understanding of the subject matter is necessary. While the authors of *The Elements of Style* could not guarantee that a writer know his subject, they did provide a guide to remedy the abuses of sloppiness, ambiguity, and lack of confidence. What Strunk published in his textbook in 1918 for White and his other students at Cornell, and what White reiterated by editing and embellishing Strunk's little manual on writing for the general public, remains vital to the task of effective writing.

Strunk and White write for the reader. Their book teaches a writer how to do the same. What else is there, the book seems to assume, except the audience? If the purpose of a written work is to remain hidden from others, then it may well be that ascribing to rules of grammar is moot; but in fact, most people write so that others may read and comprehend. Because we live in a society that survives based on our ability to communicate our feelings and needs through words, languages have naturally evolved. Language developed as human mouths and brains became more complex. Thus, it is entirely natural that rules of usage also evolved through time, as a necessary means of allowing humans to better understand one another. Why, then, should the advent of email and faxes and cellular phone text-messaging obfuscate the need for a baseline set of rules? In each medium, the rules merge, shift, revamp themselves, resurfacing as a more or less complete set of dicta to explain how to communicate—via the Internet, pager, or cellphone. However, these methods of communication are all

> **The book does not profess to be biblical—it is effective because it displays with brevity and sincerity a way to write that is clear and steady, though not the only way.''**

exceptions; what remain are the rules. And those rules have seldom been more clearly set out than in Strunk and White's 5-ounce text, *The Elements of Style*. Grammatical rules and opinions exist, in abundance, that are not included in this text. But as a tiny whole, *The Elements of Style* provides a solid background from which any writer can confidently begin.

The book does not pretend to be more than it is; it is a manual on writing that one of E. B. White's college professors gave out to students, which White found useful, and which, years later, a publishing company asked White to edit for mass publication. White assented, and added a good bit of his personal luster to the task. In his introduction written for the 1979 edition of the book, White wrote that the textbook as written by Strunk ''seemed to me to contain rich deposits of gold.'' It is one man's ''attempt to cut the vast tangle of English rhetoric down to size and write its rules and principles on the head of a pin.'' That pin was a slim volume of forty-three pages, which remains intact but for the addition of new phrases and words and the updating of a few examples. To the slim volume, White added his valuable essay, ''An Approach to Style (With a List of Valuable Reminders),'' which he referred to as ''a mystery story, thinly disguised.'' He humbly allows that there is no single referendum on style, that there is ''no assurance that a person who thinks clearly will be able to write clearly, no key that unlocks the door, no inflexible rule by which writers may shape their course.''

In short, writing is a task that requires an enviable amount of skill. There is little or no time made for editing, and thus, knowing the rules is an ever more practical means of making a strong point. And in White's essay and Strunk's rules, a hopeful writer finds a welcome source of guidance. In the first chapters of the book are ''instructions drawn from established English usage''; the chapter on style, rather, ''contains advice drawn from a writer's experience of writing.''

In the book's language, the audience hears resolve thickening; from the left-hand examples on each page, to those on the right, Strunk proves the power of invigorated texts, trimming the fat of phrases and sentences and fine-tuning them to be read with thoroughbred speed. For example, an anonymous writer penned the following ambiguous sentence: ''Young and inexperienced, the task seemed easy to me.'' To whom do the adjectives ''young'' and ''inexperienced'' refer? It is not clear, but Strunk provides clarity with a rewritten sentence that lies adjacent to the unclear one: ''Young and inexperienced, I thought the task easy.'' Likewise, White, in his essay, provides ''gentle reminders'' about the very personal art of style, providing a gossamer of guidance after the strong hand of Strunk's grammatical whip. ''if you doubt that style is something of a mystery, try rewriting a familiar sentence and see what happens.'' Later in his essay, White states: ''[w]rite in a way that comes easily and naturally to you, using words and phrases that come readily to hand. But do not assume that because you have acted naturally your product is without flaw.'' And toward the end, he writes, ''[s]tyle takes its final shape more from attitudes of mind than from principles of composition, for, as an elderly practitioner once remarked, 'writing is an act of faith, not a trick of grammar.''' Through examples and fully argued points, Strunk and White impress upon their readers the vitality of good writing. In one of the book's most famous passages, Strunk writes:

> Vigorous writing is concise. A sentence should contain no unnecessary words, a paragraph no unnecessary sentences, for the same reason that a drawing should have no unnecessary parts. This requires not that the writer make all sentences short or avoid all detail and treat subjects only in outline, but that every word tell.

Strunk and White make their grammatical arguments vigorously. The authors are on their reader's side. The book is didactic, but also full of cheer, humor, and encouragement. In referring to how to write the date, the text declares that ''[t]he last form (''6 April 1988'') is an excellent way to write a date; the figures are separated by a word and are, for that reason, quickly grasped.'' In the section entitled ''Principles of Composition,'' the authors note: ''Many a tame sentence of description or exposition can be made lively and emphatic by substituting a transitive in the active voice for some such perfunctory expression as *there is* or *could be heard.*'' And the ever-clear: ''Prefer the specific to the general, the definite to the vague, the concrete to the abstract.'' The authors are determined to see their readers succeed, and if, for that reason, the tone of the writing is at times stern, the better for the reader. Life at the turn of this new century is pathetically forgiving of faults, doubts, and mistakes. As quickly as one may rise in western society, so may one also fall. To keep one's writing skills sharp decries laziness, and in the hubris of high-speed communication, provides a vital means of staying ahead of the game.

The Elements of Style remains as vital today as when it was first published within the confines of a single university. It has been attacked as out of date, as too brief, as narrow of mind. But critics who argue as much simply miss the point. The book does not profess to be biblical—it is effective because it displays with brevity and sincerity a way to write that is clear and steady, though not the only way. *The Elements of Style* provides a clear and succinct backdrop to English grammar, guiding the reader with verve and wit through the perils of poor punctuation and fatuous thought. In the end, what the reader arrives at is not a finishing point, but a beginning. And that is a gift, not only for those who call themselves writers, but for every man or woman who writes.

Source: Allison DeFrees, Critical Essay on *The Elements of Style,* in *Nonfiction Classics for Students,* Gale, 2003.

Arthur Plotnik

In the following essay, Plotnik traces both positive and negative critical response to The Elements of Style *since its initial publication.*

Elements of Style Author Knew Writing Rules Were Meant to be Bent

No American writing guide is more revered than the 5-ounce *Strunk & White,* a.k.a. *The Elements of Style* (Allyn & Bacon). ''Timeless,'' ''the best book of its kind we have,'' gush its idolaters. Yet, for all its glory, the tiny-shouldered book is also a magnet for bashers.

It is geriatric. First appearing in 1918, it underwent its fourth resuscitation in 2000. It is small and vulnerable—as pokable as the Pillsbury Doughboy for determined critics. And the coddling it enjoys from the writing establishment makes rebel blood boil. In a 1989 bashing, one alternative-press writer dubbed White ''a cranky old man.''

''Selective and quirky as it may be, *Strunk & White* has succored confused students and forgetful communicators for more than 40 years. As a guide to the 'plain English style,' the book may yet save America from choking on its jargon and obfuscations.''

Who is correct? For every basher who attacks *Elements* as a meager, authoritarian fossil, a corps of literati hails its grace, concision and moral sense. In a review of the fourth edition, conservative columnist Andrew Ferguson called it ''a book about life—about the value of custom, the necessity of roles, the corruptions of vanity, the primacy of good taste.''

The controversy, however, erupted long before the latest edition.

War Baby

In the late 1950s, a war flared between liberal and conservative language authorities. The liberals took a stand against ''elitist'' notions of ''correctness.'' They argued that actual widespread usage, not prescribed forms, determined the validity of language. This ''descriptive'' approach to standard English raised the hackles of ''prescriptivists,'' who believed in established roles and a hierarchy of expression.

One such prescriptivist was *New Yorker* writer and master essayist E. B. White. He condemned the descriptivist view of language as an ''Anything Goes'' school. Encouraged by a publisher, he entered the fray by updating the stem little handbook of William Strunk Jr., his 1919 English professor at Cornell. Strunk had called his privately printed book *The Elements of Style.*

White began the new *Elements* with a paean to Strunk and to the professor's belief in ''right and wrong.'' He added his touch to mundane points of grammar and form, then concluded with ''An Approach to Style,'' a classic of writing advice.

Here he showcased his own skills as he warned against excesses that tempt new and youthful writers.

Aside from this essay, the book treats only the most commonly violated fundamentals as the authors saw them: a few dozen issues in grammar and composition and a sampling of usage problems. Some entries support such fading niceties as the distinctions between "shall" and "will." Others simply reflect White's antiquated bugaboos—for example, the sin of using "fix" to mean "mend" in formal English.

Selective and quirky as it may be, *Strunk & White* has succored confused students and forgetful communicators for more than 40 years. As a guide to the "plain English style," the book may yet save America from choking on its jargon and obfuscations. And all writers must take seriously the perceptions of "correctness" in English. Readers sense "correct" and disciplined patterns, whether or not they favor or even understand them. Jarring this sense of order can do two things: It can lose readers by sidetracking them into concerns about wrongness. Or—as *Elements* fails to make clear—it can wake readers up and set them dancing.

Breaking the Rules

Both Strunk and White knew well that bending the rules—judiciously breaking them—can give writing its distinction, its edge, its very style. Bending them can spring writers from ruts, get them out of themselves, out of the ordinary, and into prose that comes alive, gets noticed, gets published.

"I felt uneasy at posing as an expert on rhetoric," White wrote in 1957, "when the truth is I write by ear, always with difficulty and seldom with any exact notion of what is taking place under the hood."

And Strunk himself affirmed that "the best writers sometimes disregard the rules of rhetoric. When they do so, however, the readers will usually find in the sentence some compensating merit, attained at the cost of the violation."

Writing is risk-taking. We bungee-jump from a sentence and pray the cord stops short of catastrophe. We day-trade in language, gambling that a hot image will hold up.

White described expression as "a living stream, shifting, changing, receiving new strength from a thousand tributaries," but advised "there is simply a better chance of doing well if the writer holds a steady course, enters the stream of English quietly, and does not thrash about."

Who, then, draws strength from those tributaries? Whose prose comes alive in the churning waters? Some writers who "thrash about" go under—but others make waves!

White's admonitions may apply in Composition 101, or for those with a riveting story that best tells itself. But what happens when quieted-down expression meets today's rock concert-like din of overloaded and under-stimulated brains?

White wrote in an era when the well-tempered essay found receptive minds, when readers willingly entered into quiet dialogue with an author. But the last few decades have brought New Journalism and rude, in-your-face communications media into the mainstream.

In this sometimes disparaging, sometimes liberating environment, expressiveness calls for break-a-leg performance; it wants aggressiveness, surprise, exuberance, responsiveness, intensity, rebelliousness—most of which White seems to disdain, except in his own prose.

In his essays and three unconventional children's classics, White went his own way as a writer. But in *Elements of Style*, he offered little encouragement for others to do so. Instead, he warned them against the "disinclination to submit to discipline." But how inclined to submission was White?

As a youth, he skimped through Cornell University with "anemic" interests in everything but writing. Shunning his native East Coast, he peddled roach powder in Minneapolis, reported for the *Seattle Times* and served as messboy aboard a ship cruising the Aleutian Islands before returning East as an advertising copywriter. He called himself disciplined, but he took risks in life and in writing, including the death-defying risk of telling others how to write.

White probably never meant to advise against taking chances, against drawing on all levels of language, against demolishing any rule to get attention.

It just comes out that way.

Source: Arthur Plotnik, "E. B. Whitewashed?," in the *Writer,* Vol. 114, No. 8, August 2001, pp. 10–12.

Sources

Baum, P. F., Review of *The Elements of Style,* in *Los Angeles Times Book Review,* 1960, reprint, August 22, 1982, p. 4.

Churchill, Winston, *My Early Life: A Roving Commission,* Scribner's, 1930, p. 218.

Emery, Edwin, *The Press and America,* 3d ed., Prentice-Hall, Inc., 1972, pp. 569–76.

Fried, Debra, ''Bewhiskered Examples in *The Elements of Style,*'' in *Western Humanities Review,* Vol. 45, No. 4, Winter 1991, pp. 304–11.

Hacker, Diane, *A Writer's Reference,* 5th ed., St. Martin's, 2002.

Hall, Donald, *The Modern Stylists,* Collier-Macmillan, 1968, p. 5.

Hoffman, Gary, and Glynis Hoffman, *Adiós, Strunk and White: A Handbook for the New Academic Essay,* 2d ed., Verve Press, 1999.

Nabokov, Vladimir, *Lolita,* G. P. Putnam's Sons, 1955, p. 11.

Pater, Walter, in *Contemporary Review,* February 1895, as quoted in Trimble, John, *Writing with Style,* Prentice Hall, 2000, p. 180.

Sampson, Edward C., ''Chapter Nine: *The Elements of Style,*'' in *E. B. White,* Twayne's United States Authors Series, 1974.

Scary, Elaine, *On Beauty and Being Just,* Princeton University Press, 1999, pp. 23–25.

Strunk, William, Jr., and E. B. White, *The Elements of Style,* 3d ed., Macmillan, 1979, p. 21.

White, E. B., *The Points of My Compass,* HarperCollins, 1979.

Further Reading

Elledge, Scott, *E. B. White: A Biography,* Norton, 1984.
This comprehensive biography by a Cornell University English professor covers White's personal and professional life.

Gill, Brendan, *Here at ''The New Yorker,''* Random House, 1975.
Brendan Gill was a staff writer at *The New Yorker* for more than forty years. His book provides an inside glimpse of life at the magazine and the famous writers and editors who worked there, including White.

McQuade, Donald, and Robert Atwan, eds., *Popular Writing in America: The Interaction of Style and Audience,* 5th ed., Oxford University Press, 1995.
This lengthy anthology explores style in every form of writing from advertising and newspapers to classic books. In addition to written examples, it includes numerous essays by authors as diverse as White, Frederick Douglass, Maxine Hong Kingston, and Annie Dillard.

Olmstead, Robert, *Elements of the Writing Craft,* Story Press, 1997.
Novelist and short story writer Robert Olmstead provides more than 150 focused writing lessons, each beginning with a sample from an accomplished writer that illustrates the technique. Olmstead then analyzes the sample and suggests exercises aspiring writers can do in order to practice the technique.

The Feminine Mystique

Betty Friedan

1963

When Betty Friedan's *The Feminine Mystique* was first published in the United States in 1963, it exploded into American consciousness. Since its first publication, critics and popular readers have been sharply divided on their assessment of the work. However, one fact is certain: *The Feminine Mystique* sparked a national debate about women's roles and in time was recognized as one of the central works of the modern women's movement. Friedan began writing the work after she attended her fifteen-year college reunion at Smith, a women's college. At this reunion, she gave a questionnaire to two hundred of her fellow classmates, and the results confirmed what she had already suspected—many American women were unhappy and did not know why. After three women's magazines refused to publish Friedan's results, because they contradicted the conventional assumptions about femininity, Friedan spent five years researching and writing *The Feminine Mystique*.

In the book, Friedan defines women's unhappiness as "the problem that has no name," then she launches into a detailed exploration of what she believes causes this problem. Through her research—which includes many theories, statistics, and first-person accounts—Friedan pins the blame on an idealized image of femininity that she calls the feminine mystique. According to Friedan, women have been encouraged to confine themselves to the narrow roles of housewife and mother, forsaking education and career aspirations in the process.

Friedan attempts to prove that the feminine mystique denies women the opportunity to develop their own identities, which can ultimately lead to problems for women and their families. Friedan sees the feminine mystique as a failed social experiment that World War II and the Cold War helped to create and which in turn contributed to postwar phenomena like the baby boom and the growth of suburbs. Although Friedan has written several more controversial works, *The Feminine Mystique* is the book that made her a household name, and it is still her best-known work.

Author Biography

Betty Friedan was born in Peoria, Illinois, on February 4, 1921. Friedan showed early writing talent, which she developed throughout high school and college. After graduating from Smith College, where she earned a psychology degree, she completed her master's degree in psychology at Berkeley. Friedan moved to New York, where she married Carl Friedan in 1947. She continued to use her writing talent in freelance articles, but ultimately she adhered to society's expectations and became a housewife in 1949.

During a fifteen-year reunion at Smith College, Friedan surveyed two hundred alumni and discovered that most were housewives who were unhappy with their lives. Friedan pursued the issue as her first book, which ultimately was published as *The Feminine Mystique* in 1963. The controversial book became an instant best-seller and inspired debates across the country. Following the success of the book, angry neighbors forced the Friedans to move out of their suburb and into the city. Friedan began writing and lecturing across the country on women's issues, then she realized that these separate acts were not enough to inspire change.

In 1966, she helped to found the National Organization for Women (NOW), where she served as president until 1970. That year, discouraged by the radical feminists who were beginning to gain influence in NOW, Friedan stepped down as president. However, she remained active in the women's movement. In fact, during her resignation speech, Friedan advocated a march on August 26, 1970, the

Betty Friedan

fiftieth anniversary of women's suffrage. The resulting Women's Strike for Equality, which took place in several U.S. cities, was one of the largest demonstrations for women's rights in American history.

In the 1970s, Friedan helped to found other women's organizations, including the National Women's Political Caucus (1971), which encouraged women to run for political office. However, Friedan grew increasingly more disillusioned with the radical direction that the women's movement was taking. In 1976, she published *It Changed My Life: Writings on the Women's Movement*, a collection of her writings from the 1960s and 1970s. The book, which included retrospective commentary, examined her personal experiences with the women's movement and portrayed radical feminists in a negative way. Likewise, in 1981's *The Second Stage*, Friedan argued that the radical direction of the women's movement had established a new stereotype of women and their abilities.

In 1993, Friedan shifted her focus with the publication of *The Fountain of Age*, which examined U.S. views and stereotypes of the elderly. Friedan's most recent works include a new examination of feminism, *Beyond Gender: The New Poli-*

tics of *Work and Family* (1997) and an autobiography, *Life So Far* (2000). She lives and works in New York.

Plot Summary

Chapter 1: The Problem That Has No Name

Friedan begins *The Feminine Mystique* with an introduction describing the problem that has no name—the widespread unhappiness of women. Using a practice that becomes common throughout the book, Friedan offers several case studies of unhappy women from around the United States, and she wonders whether this unhappiness is related to the female role of housewife.

Chapter 2: The Happy Housewife Heroine

Friedan examines women's magazines from before and after World War II. In 1930s magazines, stories feature confident and independent heroines, of whom many are involved in careers. However, in most women's magazines in the late 1940s, 1950s, and early 1960s, the Happy Housewife, whose only ambitions are marriage and motherhood, replaces the career-oriented New Woman. Friedan calls this homemaker ideal of femininity the feminine mystique.

Chapter 3: The Crisis in Woman's Identity

Friedan remembers her own decision to conform to society's expectations by giving up her promising career to raise children and finds that other young women still struggle with this decision. Many women drop out of school early to marry, afraid that if they wait too long or become too educated, they will not be able to attract a husband. Unfortunately, many women do not find fulfillment in the narrow roles of wife and mother and then fear something is wrong with them.

Chapter 4: The Passionate Journey

Friedan recalls the battles faced by nineteenth-century feminists in the United States. As in her own time, Friedan notes, nineteenth-century society attempted to restrict women to the roles of wife and

mother and slandered women who challenged this gentle image. However, despite harsh resistance, early feminists held their ground, and women were ultimately given many opportunities men enjoyed, including education, the right to pursue their own careers, and, most important, the right to vote. With this last major goal fulfilled, Friedan says, the early women's movement died.

Chapter 5: The Sexual Solipsism of Sigmund Freud

Friedan says that the feminine mystique derived much of its power from the psychological theories of Sigmund Freud, who attempted to redefine humanity in completely sexual terms. Many of his complex theories included labels like penis envy, which she says were used by proponents of the feminine mystique to explain why women were not happy in their roles as housewife and mother. Women found it hard to deny the flood of Freudian information that came from established academic and media sources.

Chapter 6: The Functional Freeze, the Feminine Protest, and Margaret Mead

Friedan discusses functionalism—a sociological discipline. By assigning each group a defined function in the social hierarchy, the functionalists believed that society would run smoothly. In this system, women were confined to their sexual biological roles as housewives and mothers and told that doing otherwise would upset the social balance. She also discusses the life and career of Margaret Mead, an eminent functionalist who helped promote but did not live according to the ideals of the feminine mystique.

Chapter 7: The Sex-Directed Educators

Friedan discusses the profound shift in women's education from the 1940s to the early 1960s. Sex-directed educators accused higher education of stealing women's femininity and capacity for sexual fulfillment. Many women's schools shifted to a sex-directed curriculum—non-challenging classes that focused mostly on marriage, family, and other subjects deemed suitable for women. Friedan says that sex-directed education arrests girls in their emotional development at a young age, because they never have to face the painful identity crisis and subsequent maturation that comes from dealing with many adult challenges.

Chapter 8: The Mistaken Choice

Women fulfilled many vital working roles while men were fighting World War II, but they faced dismissal, discrimination, or hostility when the men returned. Sex-directed educators blamed overeducated, career-focused mothers for the maladjustment of soldiers in World War II. For this reason women were encouraged to stay home and devote their attention completely to their children. However, Friedan cites later studies that show these overbearing mothers often raise maladjusted children. Friedan says that women mistakenly chose to become dependent housewives instead of the more painful route to identity and independence.

Chapter 9: The Sexual Sell

Friedan explores the strong commercial motivation that has helped to enforce the feminine mystique. She meets a man whom manufacturers hire to study and exploit women's unfulfilled desires. Through manipulative advertising, companies try to elevate the image of the housewife role. They encourage housewives to feel like worthy, intelligent, independent professionals who require many specialized products. However, as Friedan notes, it is a delicate balance, because these manufacturers do not want to inadvertently encourage housewives to be independent enough to become career women—who do not buy as many household products.

Chapter 10: Housewifery Expands to Fill the Time Available

Friedan interviews several full-time housewives and finds that they are not happy, but they are extremely busy with housework. Friedan realizes women unconsciously stretch their home duties to fill the time available, because the feminine mystique has taught women that this is their role, and if they ever complete their tasks they will become unneeded. Friedan says that the feminine mystique, which only works if women remain immature, prevents women from doing the work of which they are capable—a sign of maturity.

Chapter 11: The Sex-Seekers

While she is interviewing housewives for her book, Friedan notes that women often give explic-itly sexual answers to nonsexual questions. Since American housewives have been unable to find fulfillment and identity in housework alone, she says they have tried to seek it through sex. However, Friedan says that this depersonalizes sex and turns it into a game of control. Wives get frustrated if their husbands cannot fulfill their sexual desires, husbands resent their wives for being so dependent on them, and both seek release in extramarital affairs. Friedan also thinks that homosexuality is an abnormality that is associated with the feminine mystique.

Chapter 12: Progressive Dehumanization: The Comfortable Concentration Camp

Friedan discusses the fact that many children have lost interest in life or emotional growth. She attributes the change to the mother's lack of self, a side effect of the feminine mystique. When the mother lacks a self, she is dehumanized and tries to regain her human self through her husband and children. In the process, the children lose their own identities and become dehumanized. Friedan compares housewives to the dehumanized occupants of Hitler's concentration camps during World War II.

Chapter 13: The Forfeited Self

Friedan says that the problem that has no name is caused by trying to force American women to adhere to the feminine mystique—an ideal that goes against their natural, human need to grow. She discusses the human hierarchy of needs and notes that women have been trapped at the basic, physiological level, forced to find their identity through their sexual role alone. Friedan says that women need meaningful work just as men do to achieve self-actualization, the highest level on the hierarchy of needs.

Chapter 14: A New Life Plan for Women

Friedan discusses several case studies of women who have begun to go against the feminine mystique. She also advocates a new life plan for her women readers, including not viewing housework as a career; not trying to find total fulfillment through marriage and motherhood alone; and finding meaningful work that uses the woman's full mental capacity. She discusses the conflicts that many women will face in this journey to self-actualization, including their own fears and resistance from others. For each conflict, Friedan offers examples of women who have overcome it. Friedan promotes education as the ultimate method by which American women can avoid becoming trapped in the feminine mystique; calls for a drastic rethinking of what it means to be feminine; and offers several educational and occupational suggestions.

Key Figures

Sigmund Freud

Sigmund Freud was an Austrian psychologist who tried to define life in completely sexual terms. Friedan says that the basic ideas expressed in Freudian psychology—which emphasized freedom from a repressive morality—support women's attempts at emancipation. However, Friedan says that Freud's specific theories about women, which were equal parts chivalry and condescension, and which were largely a product of his observations of the repressed Victorian era in which he lived, helped to reinforce the repression of modern women. Freud called women's yearning for equality penis envy, a term that was seized upon by promoters of the feminine mystique. Friedan notes that the type of concrete scientific thinking that provided the basis for Freud's theories has since been replaced by a more complex system of scientific thought. Nevertheless, while many of Freud's theories were reinterpreted in this new light, Friedan says that the promoters of the feminine mystique did not reinterpret Freud's Victorian theory of femininity. Friedan believes that Freudian psychology was embraced so completely that it became almost like a religion.

A. C. Kinsey

Kinsey, a noted researcher, conducted many sex surveys. The early results from one of his major reports indicate that educated women have less-fulfilling sex lives. Various societal forces use these partial results as justification for encouraging women to become full-time housewives. When Kinsey's complete results were released nearly a decade later, they contradicted the early results, and now indi-

cated that women who marry early and become full-time housewives were less likely to achieve complete sexual fulfillment. Unfortunately, Friedan notes, the ranks of sexually frustrated housewives who followed Kinsey's advice find that it is difficult to break the pattern of the feminine mystique once they have subscribed to it. Through his surveys, Kinsey also studies the insatiable sexual desire of American wives, the increasing depersonalization of sex, extramarital affairs, and homosexuality. Friedan incorporates all of these studies in her argument against the feminine mystique.

The Manipulator

Manufacturers hire the man that Friedan refers to as the manipulator to show them how to exploit women's unfulfilled desires—to get them to buy more products.

A. H. Maslow

Maslow is a scientist who defined the human hierarchy of needs. Maslow noted that all humans strive to fulfill their basic, physiological needs first, but after that they desire to fulfill higher, mental functions. He stated that it is necessary for human beings to use their capacities and that if they do not they might weaken these capacities or develop problems. Maslow also studied the relationship between sexual fulfillment and self-esteem or dominance and found that women who have achieved dominance over their own identities have more fulfilling sex lives. Finally, Maslow noted that humans who have achieved self-actualization, the highest level of the hierarchy of needs, enjoy all of life more, even mundane daily tasks like housework. Friedan uses Maslow's findings to demonstrate that it is unhealthy to confine women to the basic, physiological level of the hierarchy, denying them the right to achieve their full human capacity.

Margaret Mead

Mead was an eminent sociologist who Friedan says subscribed to the functionalist discipline. Friedan calls Mead the most powerful negative influence on modern women. Mead promoted the necessity for confining women to their sexual biological roles as housewife and mother but did not live up to this ideal herself. Mead was an accomplished academic who published countless books and articles glorifying the feminine image and cautioning against trying to achieve masculine goals like higher education. Friedan cites Mead's *Male and Female* as the book that became the cornerstone of the feminine mystique. Friedan says that Mead betrayed Freudian tendencies in many of her writings. She also notes that Mead highlighted sociological examples of motherhood from primitive cultures as the ideal to be achieved in modern, civilized society. Friedan acknowledges Mead's feminist accomplishments—such as serving as an example of a respected, professional woman and humanizing sex—but criticizes Mead's role in helping to support the feminine mystique.

Themes

Social Roles

Before World War II, many women had the choice of becoming housewives or having careers, and many sources supported either choice. Friedan measures this public opinion of women by examining the images of women in women's magazines from before and after World War II. As she notes of the magazines before World War II: "The majority of heroines in the four major women's magazines . . . were career women—happily, proudly, adventurously, attractively career women—who loved and were loved by men." However, after World War II, Friedan notes that women were increasingly encouraged to become housewives and mothers alone, and to avoid becoming a "career-woman-devil." Many sources provided this encouragement, including psychologists who followed the teachings of Sigmund Freud. As Friedan notes, Freud believed that "It was woman's nature to be ruled by man, and her sickness to envy him." Freud called this concept, "penis envy," and Friedan says that the concept "was seized in this country in the 1940s as the literal explanation of all that was wrong with American women." Women's desire for equality was looked at as an abnormality, and women were encouraged to accept their roles as housewife and mother and leave the careers to men.

The functionalists took this idea one step further, saying that women should not compete with men in careers because it would upset the social order. As Friedan notes, the functionalist believed that "the status quo can be maintained only if the wife and mother is exclusively a homemaker or, at most, has a 'job' rather than a 'career.'" These and many other sources thought that confining women to their roles as housewife and mother would benefit children. However, as Friedan notes, mothers who devoted their lives entirely to their children ended up doing more harm than good. Says Friedan: "More and more of the new child pathologies seem to stem from that very symbiotic relationship with the mother, which has somehow kept children from becoming separate selves."

Identity

When society encouraged women to be full-time housewives and mothers, Friedan says that many women were not happy in these limited roles because the roles did not provide enough substance to form an identity. Friedan systematically examines the various outlets open to housewives, starting with housework. As her research indicates, many women who tried to base their identity on housework unconsciously took longer to do their housework than they needed to, because that was all that they had to do. Says Friedan, "no matter how much housework is expanded to fill the time available, it still presents little challenge to the adult mind." Women also tried to find their identities through sex. However, this did not work, either. Says Friedan, when a woman attempts to base her entire identity on sex, "she puts impossible demands on her own body, her 'femaleness,' as well as on her husband and his 'maleness.'" Ultimately, Friedan discovers that modern women, like men, are incapable of basing their identities on housework, sex, or family. She cites Maslow's hierarchy of needs, which illustrates the human need to grow. Women who subscribed to the feminine mystique were encouraged to restrict themselves to the basic, physiological level. However, as Friedan demonstrates, by doing this, these women were "not encouraged, or expected, to use their full capacities. In the name of femininity, they are encouraged to evade human growth."

Education

Friedan discusses education in many ways in *The Feminine Mystique*. As she notes at the begin-

Topics for Further Study

- Research recent female fertility studies and discuss how the findings may affect women who wish to have both a career and a family.

- Research the statistics regarding househusbands—fathers who choose to forgo a career to stay at home and take care of children. Compare the mental and physical effects on these fathers to the effects on mothers as noted in Friedan's *The Feminine Mystique* and discuss potential reasons for any similarities or differences that you find.

- In one column of a table, plot the major changes that Friedan advocated for women in the 1960s, as expressed by her in "A New Life Plan for Women," the final chapter of *The Feminine Mystique*. In the other column, fill in the current laws or other social changes that have fulfilled

Friedan's wishes. Discuss any of Friedan's suggested changes that have not happened yet, including any historical, economical, or social reasons that explain why.

- During the modern women's movement, the United States was also undergoing a Civil Rights movement. Research these two movements in the 1960s and discuss how they affected each other.

- Research the long history of women's struggle for equality in the United States. Create a timeline of major events in this struggle. Choose one major feminist from any point in this history, other than Friedan, and write a biography about her.

---

ning, the first wave of feminism had won women many rights, including the right to earn a higher education, just like men. However, as the feminine mystique was slowly formed, various academic and media sources seized on education as the culprit for women's widespread unhappiness, which they equated with lack of sexual fulfillment. Says Friedan, they accused educators "of defeminizing American women, of dooming them to frustration as housewives and mothers, or to celibate careers, to life without orgasm." Once this idea gained acceptance, many educational institutions, particularly women's colleges, felt the pressure to change to a sex-directed curriculum, one that focused on home and family, not on the outside world. As Friedan notes, studies eventually proved that women who pursued education and careers have a greater capacity for sexual fulfillment than those who restrict their educational and occupational opportunities. "Contrary to the feminine mystique, the Kinsey figures showed that the more educated the woman, the more likely she was to enjoy full sexual orgasm more often, and the less likely to be frigid." In fact, for Friedan, education is the solution to the feminine

mystique. "I think that education, and only education, has saved, and can continue to save, American women from the greater dangers of the feminine mystique."

Style

Manifesto

A manifesto is a written declaration, which defines the author's beliefs. In the beginning of *The Feminine Mystique* Friedan declares her belief that "the problem that has no name"—the widespread unhappiness of women—has a very definite cause. Says Friedan, "It is my thesis that the core of the problem for women today is not sexual but a problem of identity—a stunting or evasion of growth that is perpetuated by the feminine mystique." Manifestos are often political in nature, and Friedan's manifesto is no different. As she demonstrates in her book, powerful forces in education, media, and the corporate world benefited from restricting women to the narrow roles of housewife and mother. Says Friedan: "A great many people have, or think they have, a vested interest in 'Occupation: housewife.'" As a result, she notes that, if women follow her advice, they will need to deal with "the prejudices, mistaken fears, and unnecessary dilemmas" that will be offered as resistance to women's emancipation.

Point of View

Friedan narrates her book mainly from a first-person, or personal, point of view. Some of the time, this point of view is her own. Says Friedan, "Gradually I came to realize that the problem that has no name was shared by countless women in America." In other cases, Friedan includes first-person quotes from some of these countless women. Says one woman, "I ask myself why I'm so dissatisfied. I've got my health, fine children, a lovely new home, enough money." Friedan also includes first-person accounts from academics, professionals, and others to support her ideas. Even in the parts of the narration that do not use the characteristic "I" or "my" words, Friedan is narrating from a first-person point of view, because she is stating opinions that are based on her own experiences and observations. Says Friedan, "Judging from the women's magazines today, it would seem that the concrete details of women's lives are more interesting than their thoughts, their ideas, their dreams."

Tone

Friedan's tone, or attitude toward her subject matter, is assertive in *The Feminine Mystique*. Although she relies on an overwhelming variety of sources to back up her assertions, her word choice clearly conveys her anger at the various agents of the feminine mystique that have helped to oppress women. For example, when she is discussing the uninformed content of one of the women's magazines in the early 1960s, she notes that the "big, pretty magazine" is "fluffy and feminine," even though it is aimed at many college-educated women. Friedan also employs several sarcastic phrases. For example, she accuses Margaret Mead, an eminent sociologist, of being a hypocrite by promoting a lifestyle that Mead does not live herself. Says Friedan:

Mead's role "as the professional spokesman of femininity would have been less important if American women had taken the example of her own life, instead of listening to what she said in her books." Friedan also expresses her anger by placing emphasis on certain words. For example, at one point she discusses the sex-directed educators, who helped to reinforce the image that intellectual women had bad sex lives. As Friedan notes, with these kinds of messages, she can see why several generations of American girls "fled college and career to marry and have babies before they became so 'intellectual' that, heaven forbid, they wouldn't be able to enjoy sex 'in a feminine way.'"

Historical Context

World War II

World War II was such a monumental event that it is commonly used as a cultural divider for the twentieth century. Friedan also cites World War II as the main impetus for the development of the feminine mystique. Throughout the book, Friedan compares many prewar and postwar statistics and examples to support her points. For example, Friedan notes: "Fewer women in recent college graduating classes have gone on to distinguish themselves in a career or profession than those in the classes graduated before World War II, the Great Divide." World War II was a traumatic event for many Americans. Soldiers witnessed unspeakable horrors on the battlefields and in German concentration camps, which carried out the dehumanization and extermination of millions of Jews and others. For the wives and families of soldiers, the war was a time of loneliness and fear, as many wondered whether their loved ones would return home safely. At the end of the war, both soldiers and civilians were shocked by the U.S. decision to drop atomic bombs on Japan.

The Cold War

Several countries—including the communist Soviet Union—quickly followed suit by developing and testing their own atomic bombs. The 1947 Truman Doctrine, a policy that advocated having

Compare & Contrast

- **Mid 1940s–Early 1960s:** During the Cold War, Americans live in fear of nuclear war. Government sources do not give American citizens accurate or complete information about the potential effects of nuclear war and instead use propaganda to ease the minds of Americans.

  Today: Many Americans live in fear of terrorist attacks, especially biological and chemical warfare. President George W. Bush and other government representatives make frequent addresses to U.S. citizens, apprising them of the potential dangers of weapons of mass destruction.

- **Mid 1940s–Early 1960s:** Married women's happiness in the United States is equated mainly with sexual satisfaction, and many media sources print graphic and detailed descriptions of sex techniques and acts. However, premarital and extramarital sex is still viewed as taboo. In 1940, less than 4 percent of all births are to unmarried women.

  Today: Most research supports a balanced, healthy life—including work, nutrition, exercise, and sex—as the key to happiness for both men and women in the United States. Premarital and extramarital sex is common and does not register much shock except in conservative groups. In 1999, approximately one third of all births are to unmarried women.

- **Mid 1940s–Early 1960s:** Women are usually encouraged not to work in the same fields as men. Even when they do, they generally earn much less.

  Today: As the result of legislation from the last half of the twentieth century, many inequalities between men and women in the workforce have been eliminated, although in some areas, women still do not receive equal pay.

---

the United States back free countries against communist forces, ultimately helped increase the tension between the Soviet Union and the United States—and between communist states and democratic ones in general. This tension, which American citizens felt as the threat of nuclear war, was called the Cold War. This feeling increased as Congress approved the first peacetime draft in 1948, and as the United States fought in an undeclared war in Korea in the early 1950s.

The Postwar Baby Boom

The devastating experience of World War II and the fear of the Cold War caused many Americans to seek comfort by focusing on their homes and families. This is one of the many factors that attributed to a large baby boom—or large increase in birth rates—following the war. In fact, the United States was one of many industrialized countries that experienced a baby boom following World War II.

Four countries in particular—the United States, Canada, Australia, and New Zealand—experienced birth rates that far surpassed pre-war levels. In the 1950s, fertility rates in the United States reached their highest levels in decades. Says Friedan: ''By the end of the fifties, the United States birthrate was overtaking India's.''

The Growth of Suburbs

The huge postwar economic boom also helped the American baby boom. For World War II veterans, this economic boom often paid off in cheap home loans from the government. Seeking a better life and an escape from the Cold War, many ex-G.I.s chose to use these loans to move their families into suburban housing developments, commonly known as suburbs. Although the introduction of the automobile in the early twentieth century had helped to increase the number of suburbs in the United States, the growth of suburbs exploded in the 1950s when the federal government expanded the interstate highway system. Suburbs, at least in theory, provided a comfortable conformity where American families could pursue a stable life and attempt to escape the many horrors of recent years, including the Depression, World War II, and the Cold War.

Critical Overview

When *The Feminine Mystique* was first published in 1963, it exploded into American consciousness. Most critics were polarized in their views of the book. In the 1963 review for the *Times Literary Supplement,* the reviewer notes: "If, then, there is still a feminist fight to be fought it is for the right to work. And if they are to win it women must have all the ammunition they can of the calibre of this book." Likewise, in her 1963 review of the book for the *American Sociological Review,* Sylvia Fleis Fava applauds Friedan's solution to the problem that has no name. Says Fava: "Her answer, that we should take women seriously as individuals, not as women, resounds throughout the book; I heartily agree with it." However, some positive critics, including Fava, had reservations about the book. Says Fava: "Friedan tends to set up a counter-mystique; that all women must have creative interests outside the home to realize themselves. This can be just as confining and tension-producing as any other mold." Others gave mainly negative reviews, such as the 1963 reviewer for the *Yale Review,* who says of Friedan's ideas that "we have heard it before. But it is a long time since we have heard it in such strident and angry tones."

By the time the tenth anniversary edition of *The Feminine Mystique* was published, the modern women's movement was underway. In fact, many reviewers, such as Jane Howard in her 1974 review of the tenth-anniversary edition for the *New Republic,* noted the book's influence. Says Howard, Friedan's book, "more than any of the torrent of feminist documents that followed, set the women's movement in motion." Howard also notes that the book was written "with more passion than style, but her effect was and still is persuasive." Over the next decade, *The Feminine Mystique* also received critical attention upon the publication of Friedan's next

two books: *It Changed My Life: Writings on the Women's Movement* (1976) and *The Second Stage* (1981). Critics still had mixed views about Friedan's original book. In the *Saturday Review,* Sara Sanborn notes: "Every woman in America, whether she knows it or not, owes Betty Friedan a debt of gratitude." In regards to the modern women's movement, Sanborn says that "Friedan sounded the kickoff signal in 1963."

Others found fault with Friedan's research. In the *New York Times Book Review,* Herma Hill Kay says that the "suburban housewives" depicted in the book did not represent "large numbers of American women." Still others criticized the style. In her *Commonweal* article, Margaret O'Brien Steinfels says that the book had "endless yardage of popular prose laced with pseudo-psychology and sociology, chapter after chapter badly patched from old magazine articles." One of the most scathing reviews of *The Feminine Mystique,* and of Friedan herself, came from R. Emmett Tyrrell, Jr., who notes in the *American Spectator* that Friedan is an "invincibly stupid," "egregious pest," who has "spoken to an entire generation of young women and left them miserable, filling housewives with doubt and embarrassment while sending the professional gals out to scrimmage for their daily grub."

Today, critics are still largely divided in their views of *The Feminine Mystique,* which is still Friedan's best-known work. Some still consider Friedan's book as the main impetus for the modern women's movement, while others think that Friedan did more damage than good with her book. For example, in her 1995 *Commentary* article, Carol Iannone criticizes Friedan for introducing many negative aspects into feminism. These include making "the condition of the postwar American woman seem one of soul-strangling asphyxiation and spiritual death"; helping "initiate the now ever-expanding tendency to blame the most personal and complex of the ills of life on social or political conditions"; and helping "define that useful paradox so beloved by activist leaders, whereby unhappiness, anger, frustration can be seen as signs of health."

Regardless of whether a critic likes Friedan, few can deny the influence she has had on feminism. Says Mary Brewer in her 2001 entry on Friedan for the *Dictionary of Literary Biography:* "Despite its inconsistencies and drawbacks . . . Friedan's theory

Friedan's theory said that many American women were unhappy because they had no identities outside those of housewife and mother

of feminine identity as it is constructed by a male-dominated society has become seminal to feminist thought.''

Criticism

Ryan D. Poquette

Poquette has a bachelor's degree in English and specializes in writing about literature. In the

following essay, Poquette discusses the types of research that Friedan used in The Feminine Mystique *to support her argument that women have been repressed to the point of losing their identities and capacity for sexual fulfillment.*

In 1963, Betty Friedan made history when she published *The Feminine Mystique*. She knew that what she was writing was revolutionary, since the genesis of the book, the results from a questionnaire to her fellow alumni, had produced such a negative reaction from various women's magazines when

What Do I Read Next?

- In her controversial book *The Second Stage* (1981), Friedan defines a new mystique, the feminist mystique, which she says is supported by the superwoman stereotype—the woman who can do everything. Friedan advocates making the family the central focus in women's life and instituting separate standards for women and men, since women cannot be expected to perform at their highest levels at both work and home.

- In *The Masculine Mystique: The Politics of Masculinity* (1995), Andrew Kimbrell argues that American men are in crisis. As in Friedan's book, Kimbrell's manifesto examines men's history, discusses sociological factors that affect men, and offers a plan of action to combat the masculine mystique.

- In *The Difference: Growing Up Female in America* (1994), *Washington Post* columnist Judy Mann explores the difficulties of growing up as a female in the United States in the 1990s. Drawing on her own experiences, interviews with teenage girls, and a wealth of historical and cultural research, Mann discusses the various sociological forces that affect girls today and offers suggestions for new ways to raise boys and girls.

- Charlotte Perkins Gilman's novella *The Yellow Wallpaper* (1899), which is based on events in her own life, is one of the most powerful works by early feminists. In the story, a protagonist is locked into a third-floor room of a house by her husband and physician, who assumes that the woman's unhappiness can be cured by seclusion and lack of stimulation or movement. However, as the story progresses, the woman loses touch with reality, increasingly relating to a woman whom she envisions as living inside the room's yellow wallpaper.

- In the essay, *A Room of One's Own* (1929), Virginia Woolf argued that, in order for women to achieve the same greatness that male writers have, women need an income and privacy. In addition, Woolf discusses the fact that the idealistic and powerful portrayals of women in fiction have historically differed from the slave-like situations that many women faced in real life.

---

she tried to sell the results as an article in 1957. As Friedan notes in her introduction to the tenth anniversary edition of *The Feminine Mystique*, "the then male publisher of *McCall's* . . . turned the piece down in horror, despite underground efforts of female editors. The male *McCall's* editors said it couldn't be true." It was easy for these editors to turn down the results of one survey that did not uphold the conventional image of femininity. As Friedan notes in the same introduction, she told her agent: "I'll have to write a book to get this into print." However, as the resulting book indicates, Friedan learned something from her experience with the magazine editors. She realized that, in order to prove her point that women have been repressed by an idealized image, she would have to provide a wealth of research support, not just her own opinion.

When it comes to Friedan's research methods, the critics are as divided in their criticism as with all the other aspects of the work. Some critics believe that *The Feminine Mystique* is thoroughly researched and contains valid information. In her review of the book for the *American Sociological Review,* Sylvia Fleis Fava notes: "Friedan, by training a psychologist and by occupation a journalist, supports her thesis mainly with data from these fields." In her 1976 review of *It Changed My Life* for *Washington Post Book World,* Anne Bernays states: "A thoroughly researched analysis of what is wrong with us, Friedan's first book named and probed the 'nameless problem' that plagues women."

> "In the end, whether or not one thinks that Friedan succeeded in making her case, Friedan was right to assume that she had to provide overwhelming support for her controversial ideas."

However, not all critics think that Friedan's research was accurate or representative. In her review of *The Second Stage* for *Commonweal,* Margaret O'Brien Steinfels notes that *The Feminine Mystique* featured "endless yardage of popular prose laced with pseudo-psychology and sociology, chapter after chapter badly patched from old magazine articles." Likewise, in another review of *The Second Stage* for the *New York Times Book Review,* Herma Hill Kay notes: "Neither the suburban housewives described in *The Feminine Mystique* nor the radical feminists who, as portrayed in *The Second Stage,* perceived man as 'the enemy' represented large numbers of American women."

Friedan relied on three main types of examples to support her assertions—excerpts and paraphrases of academic theories, statistics, and first-person accounts. Friedan chose her academic theories very carefully, using them to serve one of two purposes. They either directly supported or contradicted her ideas. An example of the first is Maslow's hierarchy of needs. Friedan cites several selections from Maslow's work and ultimately uses it to support her assertion: "The transcendence of self, in sexual orgasm, as in creative experience, can only be attained by one who is himself, or herself, complete, by one who has realized his or her own identity." An example of the latter category is Friedan's discussion of Sigmund Freud, who is generally recognized as a brilliant Victorian psychologist whose ideas are somewhat dated. Friedan cites several selections from Freud that support the ideal of the feminine mystique, then notes that most of Freud's concepts were already being reinterpreted in the 1940s so that they better fit in with modern scientific theory and practice. However, Friedan points out that Freud's theory of femininity was not updated; it was applied literally to American women after World War II, so that "women today were considered no different than Victorian women."

Friedan also incorporates a number of statistics, numbers that are derived from a data sample. Statistics lend third-party credibility to arguments like Friedan's, because they are based on facts, not opinion. Friedan includes statistics on several topics, including marriage age, "By the end of the nineteen-fifties, the average marriage age of women in America dropped to 20, and was still dropping, into the teens"; higher education, "By the mid-fifties, 60 per cent dropped out of college to marry, or because they were afraid too much education would be a marriage bar"; and sex, "In American media there were more than 2 1/2 times as many references to sex in 1960 as in 1950, an increase from 509 to 1,341 'permissive' sex references in the 200 media studied."

Although academic theories and statistics help support an argument, they can also generalize the discussion and keep it at a distance from readers; it is hard for some readers to relate to a theory or number. As a result, Friedan also includes countless first-person accounts, which offer intimate examples from individual human lives—and thus tend to have a greater impact on readers. First-person accounts are credible because individuals speak for themselves. In fact, for some reviewers, this was the most important part of *The Feminine Mystique.* In her entry on Friedan for the *Dictionary of Literary Biography,* Mary F. Brewer notes that Friedan bases her arguments on "real American women's lives; she quotes profusely from the letters, interviews, and questionnaires she compiled from educated middle-class housewives and mothers who were struggling to find some meaning in their domestically bound lives."

As with the academic theories, Friedan employs two types of first-person accounts. In most of the cases, the personal quotes directly support Friedan's argument that women are unhappy in their role as housewives. For example, in the beginning of the book, Friedan includes several excerpts of interviews with depressed housewives. Says one desperate woman, "I begin to feel I have no personality. I'm a server of food and a putter-on of pants and a bedmaker, somebody who can be called on when you want something." Another woman notes: "The problem is always being the children's mommy, or the minister's wife and never being myself."

Friedan also quotes women who try to convince their readers that women should live up to the ideal image of femininity. For example, when Friedan is discussing the power that sex-directed educators had over society, she notes that many young women were led to believe that their emotional problems resulted from their traditional, career-focused, masculine education. Says one young woman: ''I have come to realize that I was educated to be a successful man and must now learn by myself to be a successful woman.'' However, after offering these first-person accounts, Friedan steadily dismantles them, using her various other kinds of research to try to prove that the women speaking these quotes were duped by the feminine mystique. As a response to the above quotation, for example, Friedan offers a study of college women that indicates ''those seniors who showed the greatest signs of growth were more 'masculine' in the sense of being less passive and conventional; but they were more 'feminine' in inner emotional life.''

Collectively, Friedan's academic theories, statistics, and first-person accounts provided various support for her argument that received a mixed reception from critics. No matter what any individual critic thought of Friedan's research, however, Friedan did achieve her ''call to awareness,'' as Cynthia Fuchs Epstein notes in her *Dissent* article. Says Epstein:

> The facts of history are lost to some critics. *The Feminine Mystique*, the work of a journalist with high exposure to the social sciences, laid out the problems women faced in post-World War II suburban ghettos or in the symbolic ghettos of sex-labeled jobs and subordinate roles in public life and in the family.

In the end, whether or not one thinks that Friedan succeeded in making her case, Friedan was right to assume that she had to provide overwhelming support for her controversial ideas. As she herself notes at one point about sex-directed education: ''It takes a very daring educator today to attack the sex-directed line, for he must challenge, in essence, the conventional image of femininity.'' Yet, this is exactly what Friedan was trying to do herself. She launched a daring attack against sex-directed educators, psychologists, sociologists, the media, the corporate world, and others whom she identified as agents of the feminine mystique. Says Sara Sanborn in the *Saturday Review,* ''she performed the writer's unique service by saying out loud what the rest of us had only nervously thought.''

Source: Ryan D. Poquette, Critical Essay on *The Feminine Mystique,* in *Nonfiction Classics for Students,* Gale, 2003.

Joyce Hart

Hart, with degrees in English literature and creative writing, focuses her published works on literary themes. In this essay, Hart intertwines a discussion of Friedan's work with the narrators and characters found in the short stories of Grace Paley.

Although there has been recent criticism of Betty Friedan's book *The Feminine Mystique*, there is no doubt, even in the minds of her harshest critics, that her book had such a profound impact on the female population during the 1960s that it has been credited with initiating the second wave of feminism in the United States. In order to better comprehend how *The Feminine Mystique* had such a profound impact on women of that era, it is important to understand who the mid-twentieth-century American woman was. Although it is impossible to gather information on every female and ask each of them to recall what it was like to be a woman in that turbulent era, it is feasible to look to one of the leading literary voices of that time to discern what her female characters were doing and thinking about.

With this objective in mind, the first author who comes to mind is Grace Paley, a contemporary of Friedan's, who made a point of writing strictly from a woman's perspective, discussing issues that were pertinent to the American female. She was one of the first American women writers to do so. She wrote during at time when female issues were considered worthy only of a kitchen-table discussion over coffee. She lived in a world that was completely dominated by men, in the home, in the workplace, and in the field of publishing. Yet, she had the confidence to compose her work with the highest literary skill that she was capable of and to write about what she knew best—women's daily lives and routines of the 1950s, the same topic that Friedan addresses.

Friedan interviewed many women in the course of her research for *The Feminine Mystique*, why add yet another voice to the mix? The answer is simple. It's one of interest. Friedan's examples support her thesis, but Paley's characters offer background color. Friedan's women respond to specific questions, while Paley's go about their business, offering readers brief glimpses into their lives. Friedan's writing dramatically changed the course of many women's lives, and it is the women as depicted in Paley's short stories that she most affected. Paley's characters, in her collection of short stories called *Enormous Changes at the Last Minute* (1960), were conceived before the publication of Friedan's 1963

> They might not have been able to put their finger on their misery, and they might have felt guilty about thinking about it, but women collectively knew that trying to define themselves through the feminine mystique was a life filled with 'crummy days.'"

classic. They consist of both formally educated women and those who are not formally educated. They are housewives and mothers who, at most, struggle with part time jobs. There is little mention of professional businesswomen. Paley's female characters therefore represent the epitome of Friedan's targeted audience. To listen to them is to hear the voices of the women who most often found themselves concealed under the veil of what Friedan refers to as the feminine mystique.

To begin with, readers should first understand what Friedan means when she writes about feminine mystique. For her it is the belief that was popular in the early part of the twentieth century that stated that the major source of women's frustrations was their own forgetfulness of what constituted femininity. Women, especially according to Sigmund Freud's basic tenet, were often found to be envious of men, so they tried to be like men. In attempting to do so, women denied their own natural instincts, which were "sexual passivity," submission to men, and their need to nurture. These traits, according to social propaganda at that time, were best developed in the role of wife and mother. Women should not worry about obtaining a college degree nor about the subsequent challenge of finding and advancing a professional career. Further education and involvement in the broader concept of society encompassed a man's world. For women to want to be involved outside of the home was testimony to their jealousy of men. "The new mystique makes the housewife-mothers, who never had a chance to be anything else, the model for all women," Friedan writes. This model confined women "to cooking, cleaning, washing, bearing children—into a religion, a pattern by

which all women must now live or deny their femininity."

In the first short story of Paley's collection, her female protagonist is sitting on the front steps of her local library when her ex-husband happens to stroll by. She says, "Hello, my life, I said. We had once been married for twenty-seven years, so I felt justified." With this simple statement, Paley acknowledges the feelings that women of her generation held in terms of defining themselves. They became so consumed with playing out their roles as wives that they were left with no concept of themselves. These were the women who bought the "new mystique," who modeled themselves on the 1950s definition of femininity. By turning their backs on their education and further exploration of self, their husband became their lives. They lived through their husbands' promotions, defeats, and challenges in the world outside their homes. In the same short story, the woman continues her brief dialogue with her ex-husband, who tells her that he is finally going to buy that sailboat he has always wanted. He still has dreams, he tells her. "But as for you, it's too late. You'll always want nothing," he says. This represents the problems and frustrations that the pre-Friedan women were suffering. They were caught in the middle of a paradox. They were being told that they needed nothing more than to take care of their husbands; but in doing so, their husbands often concluded that, since the women lived through them, they needed nothing for themselves. "But I do want *something*," Paley's character says. "I want, for instance, to be a different person." Paley's female might want to change; however, Paley concludes this story with the woman lamenting that although she is capable of taking action, especially when someone comes along and points out possible deficiencies, she is better known for her "hospitable remarks." In other words, she acquiesces. She does not want to upset the boat. She is, after all, the one who maintains the home, who keeps the balance. She seeks the perfect definition of femininity and remains lost in the feminine mystique.

The baby boom that occurred at the end of World War II was based on a number of factors, but Friedan believes that one of the major reasons was that "women who had once wanted careers were now making careers out of having babies." Motherhood was glorified by the feminine mystique, and therefore the more children a woman bore the more closely she matched the archetype of femininity. The feminine mystique promised self-fulfillment with each new baby, a promise that was seldom realized. As young wives, women sought recognition through their husbands. As mothers, women promoted themselves through their children. Their offspring's accomplishments were their own. It was one more excuse, Friedan states, for women to forego defining themselves.

Paley writes in her short story "Faith in the Afternoon," that her protagonist gave birth to two sons "to honor" her husband and "his way of loving." However, in a later story, "Faith in a Tree," when Faith's babies have matured to school age and she has realized several years of substituting her life for theirs, she states: "Just when I most needed important conversation, a sniff of the man-wide world, that is, at least one brainy companion who could translate my friendly language into his tongue of undying carnal love, I was forced to lounge in our neighborhood park, surrounded by children." With this characterization, Faith is beginning to discover the holes in the feminine mystique. Living through one's husband or one's children is not as gratifying as the women's magazine articles have portrayed. Faith is beginning to hunger for, as Friedan describes it, some undefined "something more." This thing that is missing in her life is not only difficult to define, it is almost impossible to think about. It goes against the essence of what a woman, what femininity, is. So Faith feels guilty for these thoughts. "I own two small boys," she reminds herself, "whose dependence on me takes up my lumpen time and my bourgeois feelings." She then goes on to state how much she loves them, how much she pampers them, how much her time and life is consumed by them. "I kiss those kids forty times a day." Although Faith may be craving intellectual stimulation, she wants to make sure that everyone knows that she is a good mother. The sacrifice of self is warranted. To be a wife and mother is all a woman needed, according to the feminine mystique. It is the educated career women who are really suffering.

Friedan states that when women, such as Paley's character Faith, felt most frustrated, they often turned to consumerism. They bought new things for the home. Manufacturers took note of this inclination and persuaded women into believing that they needed all the latest gadgets to keep their homes spotlessly clean. Paley's narrator in her story "Distance," misses her youth when she was free to define herself as only her own intuition demanded. However, her present situation is not so bad, she claims. She and her husband purchase new cars, and bought a television set "the minute it first came out," and have "everything grand for the kitchen." She says she has no complaints, but then goes on to state that reminiscing about her youth "is like a long hopeless homesickness." She lives with all the great conveniences, she says, but it is like living "in a foreign town." In spite of the joys of consumerism that are supposed to make her a better housewife, she does not feel at home in her dictated role. As a matter of fact, as Friedan has pointed out, Paley's female characters, like many of the frustrated housewives of the 1950s lost in the feminine mystique, are miserable. Things are falling apart. Life is not proving to be what the women thought it would be. Once, everything was "spotless, the kitchen was all inlay like broken-up bathroom tiles . . . . Formica on all surfaces, everything bright. The shine of the pots and pans was turned to stun the eyes of company," Paley writes in her story "Distance." Now, however, the female protagonist is lost in misery, and "she's always dirty. Crying crying crying." Some of Paley's women are lost in misery because their husbands have left them. Others have lost their husbands because they are depressed. Whatever the case, Paley's character Faith is confronted by her mother, who consoles her with the wisdom to better her life by cleaning up the house and cooking a special dinner. "Tell the children to be a little quiet. . . . He'll be home before you know it. . . . Do up your hair something special." It is the woman's fault that her marriage has fallen apart. She is unhappy because she has not been a good wife or a good mother.

"Life isn't that great," Paley's protagonist states in the short story "Living." "We've had nothing but crummy days and crummy guys and no money and broke all the time and cockroaches and nothing to do on Sunday but take the kids to Central Park and row on that lousy lake." It is an epiphany of sorts, albeit a depressing one. This is the life that many women played out based on the concept of feminine mystique, which, as Friedan points out, glorifies being a housewife as an end-all career. It is ironic, says Friedan, that at a time when doors were finally opened to women, thanks to the work and passion of the women involved in the first wave of feminism in the United States, when women could gain a college degree and find fulfilling professional careers, that the feminine mystique was born and promoted. Friedan states that this concept flourished under the psychological theories as well as the well-read women's magazine articles, both of which were male-dominated, that appeared to want to keep women from self-actualizing, keep them uneducated and housebound. It is a process of what Friedan refers to as the progressive dehumanization of women. As women on the cusp of the 1960s were beginning to realize, the life, as defined by the feminine mystique, was not that great. In fact, it was quite empty. They might not have been able to put their finger on their misery, and they might have felt guilty about thinking about it, but women collectively knew that trying to define themselves through the feminine mystique was a life filled with "crummy days." So when Friedan's book came out a few years later, they gobbled it up. Here was something that made sense of their lives. Here was someone who could see into their misery and name it. Here was a book that helped them understand why the feminine mystique was not working for them.

Source: Joyce Hart, Critical Essay on *The Feminine Mystique,* in *Nonfiction Classics for Students,* Gale, 2003.

Daniel Horowitz

In the following essay excerpt, Horowitz explores how events in Friedan's personal life and career in the 1950s and early 1960s influenced her completion of The Feminine Mystique.

It has become commonplace to see the publication of Betty Friedan's *The Feminine Mystique* in 1963 as a major turning point in the history of modern American feminism and, more generally, in the history of the postwar period. And with good reason, for her book was a key factor in the revival of the women's movement and in the transformation of the nation's awareness of the challenges middle-class suburban women faced. *The Feminine Mystique* helped millions of women comprehend, and then change, the conditions of their lives. The book took already familiar ideas, made them easily accessible, and gave them a forceful immediacy. It explored issues that others had articulated but failed to connect with women's experiences—the meaning of American history, the nature of alienated labor, the existence of the identity crisis, the threat of atomic warfare, the implications of Nazi anti-Semitism, the use of psychology as cultural criticism, and the dynamics of sexuality. By extending to women many of the ideas about the implications of affluence that widely read male authors had developed for white, middle-class men, Friedan's book not only stood as an important endpoint in the development of 1950s social criticism but also translated that tradition into feminist terms. In addition, the book raises questions about the trajectory of Friedan's ideology, specifically about the rela-

tionship between her labor radicalism of the 1940s and early 1950s and her feminism in the 1960s.

To connect a book to a life is no easy matter. Although Friedan herself has emphasized the importance of the questionnaires her Smith classmates filled out during the spring of 1957, when she was thirty-six years old, she also acknowledged in 1976 that in writing *The Feminine Mystique* "all the pieces of my own life came together for the first time." Here she was on the mark. It is impossible for someone to have come out of nowhere, and in so short a time, to the deep understanding of women's lives that Friedan offered in 1963. Experiences from her childhood in Peoria, her analysis of the Smith questionnaire, and all points in between, helped shape the 1963 book.

In Peoria Friedan began the journey so critical to the history of American feminism. There she first pondered the question of what hindered and fostered the aspirations of women. In addition, in that Illinois city anti-Semitism and labor's struggles first provided her with the material that would ignite her sense of social justice. At Smith College young Bettye Goldstein encountered social democratic and radical ideologies, as well as psychological perspectives, as she shifted the focus of her passion for progressive social change from anti-Semitism to anti-fascism, and then to the labor movement. From the defense of the maids in 1940 it was only a short step to her articulation in 1943 of a belief that working-class women were "fighters—that they refuse any longer to be paid or treated as some inferior species" by men. Labor union activity and participation in Popular Front feminism in the 1940s and early 1950s provided the bridge over which she moved from the working class to women as the repository of her hopes, as well as some of the material from which she would fashion her feminism in *The Feminine Mystique.*

Popular Front feminism—represented by the unionism of the CIO and the probing discussions around the Congress of American Women—deepened and broadened Friedan's commitments. Reading people like Elizabeth Hawes and writing for Federated Press and *UE News* gave Friedan sustained familiarity with issues such as protests over the impact of rising prices on households, the discontent of housewives with domestic work, the history of women in America, the dynamics of sex discrimination, the negative force of male chauvinism, and the possibility that the cultural apparatus of a capitalist society might suppress women's aspirations for better lives.

The discussions of women's issues in Old Left circles beginning in the 1940s and Friedan's 1963 book had a good deal in common. They both offered wide-ranging treatments of the forces arrayed against women—the media, education, and professional expertise. Progressive women in the 1940s and Friedan in 1963 explored the alienating nature of housework. They showed an awareness of male chauvinism but ultimately lay the blame at the door of capitalism. They saw *Modern Woman: The Lost Sex* as the text that helped launch the anti-feminist attack. They fought the fascist emphasis on Küche, Kinder, and Kirche.

Yet despite these similarities, the differences between Popular Front feminism and *The Feminine Mystique* were considerable. In articulating a middle-class, suburban feminism, Friedan both drew on and repudiated her Popular Front feminism. What happened in Friedan's life between 1953, when she last published an article on working women in the labor press, and 1963, when her book on suburban women appeared, fundamentally shaped *The Feminine Mystique*. Over time, a series of events undermined Friedan's hopes that male-led radical social movements would fight for women with the consistency and dedication she felt necessary. Disillusioned and chastened by the male chauvinism in unions but also by the Bomb, the Holocaust, the Cold War, and McCarthyism, she turned elsewhere. Her therapy in the mid-1950s enabled her to rethink her past and envision her future.

Always a writer who worked with the situations and material close at hand, in the early 1950s Friedan began to apply what she learned about working-class women in progressive feminist discussions of the 1940s to the situation that middle-class women faced in suburbs. Living in Parkway Village and Rockland County at the same time she was writing for the *Parkway Villager* and mass-circulation magazines, Friedan had begun to describe how middle-class and wealthy women worked against great odds to achieve and grow. What she wrote about democratic households and cooperative communities, as well as her long-held dream of the satisfactions that romance and marriage would provide, reflected her high hopes for what life in the suburbs might bring. Although she felt that in the mid-1950s she successfully broke through the strictures of the feminine mystique she would describe in her 1963 book, the problems with her

Anthropologist Margaret Mead, whose teachings Friedan believes helped support the idea of the feminine mystique

marriage and suburban life fostered in her a disillusionment different from but in many ways more profound than what she had experienced with the sexual politics of the Popular Front.

If all these experiences provided a general background out of which her 1963 book emerged, the more proximate origins of *The Feminine Mystique* lay in what she focused on during her career as a free-lance writer. She well understood the connection between the magazine articles she began to publish in the mid-1950s and her 1963 book. In addition, a critical impetus to her book was her response to McCarthyism. When she drew on her 1952 survey of her classmates to write "Was Their Education UnAmerican?" she first gave evidence of pondering the relationship between her Smith education, the struggle for civil liberties, and what it meant for women to thrive as thinkers and public figures in the suburbs. Then in her work on Intellectual Resources Pool, which began about the same time that she looked over those fateful questionnaires, Friedan paid sustained attention to the question of what it meant for middle-class women to develop an identity in American suburbs, including an identity as intellectuals. She asked these ques-

> To support her arguments, Friedan carried out wide-ranging research in women's magazines and the writings of social and behavioral scientists. She interviewed experts, professional women, and suburban housewives. She examined the short stories and human interest features in widely read women's magazines."

tions at a time when the whole culture, but especially anti-communists, seemed to be conspiring to suppress not only the vitality of intellectual life for which free speech was so important but also the aspirations of educated women to achieve a full sense of themselves. With her book, she reassured her own generation that their education mattered at the same time that she warned contemporary college students to take themselves more seriously.

The Feminine Mystique took Friedan an unexpected five plus years to complete. She was writing under conditions that were difficult at best and neither Carl nor her editor at W. W. Norton thought she would ever finish. The material was painful, and through her engagement with it, Friedan was rethinking her position on a range of issues. She was a wife with a commuting husband and a mother of three. By the end of 1957, Daniel was nine, Jonathan was five, and Emily was one. Her ten-year-old marriage to Carl was less than ideal, and in 1962 it took a turn for the worse. Carl complained to friends that when he came home at the end of the day, "that bitch" was busily writing her book on the dining-room table instead of preparing the meal in the kitchen. Carl often did not come home at night. Though his own career may not have been going well, he felt Betty was wasting her time. Her friends whispered that instead of ending the marriage she was writing about it. In addition, during almost the entire time she was working on the book she was also running the pool, and trying to publish articles in magazines. She had to travel for material— within the greater New York area for interviews, and to the New York Public Library where she took extensive notes on what she read. Without a secretary to type early drafts, let alone a photocopy machine or word processor, writing as many as a dozen drafts was laborious, tiring, and time consuming. In early 1961, having turned in half the manuscript to her publisher, she expected the book to be published before the year's end. But her agent, Marie Rodell, wrote back to an impatient Friedan that the manuscript was so long it would not have the impact Friedan desired. Not surprisingly, she was optimistic at some moments, discouraged at others.

To support her arguments, Friedan carried out wide-ranging research in women's magazines and the writings of social and behavioral scientists. She interviewed experts, professional women, and suburban housewives. She examined the short stories and human interest features in widely read women's magazines. Though Friedan made clear her reliance on such sources, there were some books that she read but acknowledged minimally or not at all. For example, she examined works by existentialists, and though their ideas influenced her writing, especially on the issue of how people could shape their identities, she did not fully make clear her indebtedness. Friedan also returned to Thorstein Veblen's *Theory of the Leisure Class* (1899), which she had read at Smith, now absorbing his iconoclastic social criticism, which demystified the dynamics of women's subjugation, especially the ways domestic ideology kept middle-class women from working outside the home.

She also carefully followed the arguments in Simone de Beauvoir's *Second Sex* (1953), but mentioned only its "insights into French women." Beauvoir had explored how class and patriarchy shaped women's lives. She provided what was, for the time, a sympathetic account of the situation lesbians faced. She fully recognized women's participation in the work force and the frustrations of domestic life. She offered a telling analysis of the power dynamics in marriage. Linking the personal and political, she discussed a "liberation" of women that would be "collective." Friedan's reading notes of Beauvoir's book reveal her great interest in Beauvoir's existentialism, including her linking of productivity and transcendence. In addition, she derived from Beauvoir a keen sense of how language, power, economic conditions, and sexuality divided men and women.

What she read in Beauvoir and Veblen, as well as what she understood from her own situation and her reading of American women's history, also found confirmation in Friedrich Engels's essay of 1884, "The Origin of the Family, Private Property and the State." Around 1959, she copied the following passage from a collection of the writings of Engels and Karl Marx:

> we see already that the emancipation of women and their equality with men are impossible and must remain so as long as women are excluded from socially productive work and restricted to housework, which is private. The emancipation of women becomes possible only when women are enabled to take part in production on a large, social scale, and when domestic duties require their attention only to a minor degree.

Here Friedan relied on Engels for support of the central thesis of her book, that women would achieve emancipation only when they entered the paid work force. Like feminists who preceded and followed her, she agreed with Engels's classic statement of women's condition. Her reliance on Engels strongly suggests that even in the late 1950s Marxism continued to inform her outlook. There is, however, one difference between what she read and what she wrote down. After Engels's words "when women are enabled to take part," Friedan added, in parentheses, her own words: "along with men." This was a significant addition, expressing both her experience as a Popular Front feminist and her hope for the cooperation of men in women's liberation.

The fact that she read Engels makes clear that Friedan and her editor had to make difficult decisions on what to leave out and include, a process that involved the questions of how much of her radical past to reveal, and how political and feminist the book would be. She also had to decide how to give it shock value and personal immediacy that would intensify its impact.

The magazine editors who in 1962 looked at articles derived from Friedan's book chapters raised questions about the scope, tone, and originality of her work. Some of their comments prefigured the anti-feminist diatribes that came with the book's publication in 1963. The editors at *Reporter* found Friedan's chapters "too shrill and humorless." A male editor from *Redbook* turned down one excerpt from the book, saying it was "heavy going," and another for expressing "a rather strident" perspective. "Put us down as a group of smug or evil males," remarked an editor of *Antioch Review,* who found that Friedan's chapter "The Sexual Sell" "contributes little to understanding or solution of the problems it raises." Friedan's article, he concluded, was "dubious sociology which attempts to answer too much with too little." Others questioned Friedan's originality. An editor at *American Scholar* found nothing especially new in what she had to say about Freud. A male editor of the journal of the National Education Association remarked that though an excerpt from the book pretended to present new material, in fact it had "the ring of past history." He illustrated his point by correctly noting that educators concerned about higher education for women had "already gone far beyond" what Friedan discussed. These responses gave Friedan a sense of the tough choices she had to make with the book, even as they intensified her sense of the importance of her message.

Friedan faced the problem of positioning her book in what she and her editors saw as an increasingly crowded field of writings on middle-class women. Although we tend to see *The Feminine Mystique* as a book that stands by itself, Friedan and her publisher were aware that others had already articulated many of the book's concerns. When a vice president of W. W. Norton wrote Pearl S. Buck to solicit a jacket blurb, he remarked that "one of our problems is that much is being written these days about the plight (or whatever it is) of the educated American woman; therefore, this one will have to fight its way out of a thicket." He may have been thinking of F. Ivan Nye and Lois W. Hoffman's *The Employed Mother in America* (1963), of Morton M. Hunt's *Her Infinite Variety: The American Woman as Lover, Mate or Rival* (1962), of Helen Gurley Brown's *Sex and the Single Girl* (1962), or of the abundant discussion by educators and social critics regarding the frustrations of suburban women to which Friedan herself was responding. Friedan also had to decide whether to emphasize the deliberations of the Presidential Commission on the Status of Women, whose work, underway in 1961, would result in a report that, like Friedan's book, appeared in 1963.

There were additional indications that Friedan was racing against the clock. While the book gave some the impression of a powerful and unshakable feminine mystique, Friedan herself acknowledged in the book that around 1960 the media began to pay attention to the discontents of middle-class American women. There is plenty of evidence that Friedan's readers, from professional women to housewives, found what she had to say either familiar or less than shocking. Some of those who reviewed the book found nothing particularly new or dramatic in it. Similarly, although some women who wrote Friedan indicated that they found an intense revelatory power in her words, others said they were tired of negative writings that, they believed, belabored the women's situation.

If what Friedan wrote was hardly new to so many, then why did the book have such an impact? We can begin to answer that question by examining the ways she reworked familiar themes to give them a special urgency, especially for middle-class white women. Nowhere was this clearer than on the issue of women's work. Especially striking is the contrast between her animus against the toil of housewives and volunteers and her strong preference for women entering the paid work force, a dichotomy a friend warned her not to fall back on. Here Friedan was advocating what she had learned from labor radicals who urged women to get paying jobs and to work cooperatively with men. Friedan recast the terms of a long-standing debate between men and women so that it would appeal to middle-class readers. In her discussion of housework, for example, she offered only scattered hints about the reluctance of husbands to help with household chores. At one moment, she mentioned ''the active resentment of husbands'' of career women, while elsewhere she praised cooperative husbands. Neither perspective enabled her to discuss openly or fully what she felt about her marriage, the sexual politics of marriage, and the attempts by women, herself included, to set things right. As a labor journalist she had talked of oppressive factory work for working-class women; in *The Feminine Mystique*, alienated labor involved the unrecompensed efforts by white, middle-class women to keep their suburban homes spotless. One reader picked up on what it might mean, in both trivial and profound ways, to apply a Marxist analysis to suburban women. In 1963, the woman wrote to Friedan that the book made her wish to rush into streets and cry ''To arms, sisters! You have nothing to lose but your vacuum cleaners.''

Friedan also cast her discussion of sexuality in terms that would appeal to conventional, middle-class, heterosexual suburban women. She promised that emancipation from the tensions of the feminine mystique would insure that women intensified their enjoyment of sex. Her statement that the ''dirty word *career* has too many celibate connotations'' underscored her preference for marriage. She hinted at the dangers of lesbianism when she discussed the sexual role models she had known in Peoria and at Smith. She contrasted ''old-maid'' teachers and women who cut their ''hair like a man'' with ''the

warm center of life'' she claimed she experienced in her parents' home. She was concerned that some mothers' misdirected sexual energies turned boys into homosexuals. She warned that for an increasing number of sons, the consequence of the feminine mystique was that ''parasitical'' mothers would cause homosexuality to spread ''like a murky smog over the American scene.'' Friedan's homophobia was standard for the period and reflects the antipathy to homosexuality widely shared in Popular Front circles. Her emphasis on feminized men and masculinized women echoed stereotypes widely held in the 1950s. What makes her perspective especially troubling is that it came at a time when reactionaries were hounding gays and lesbians out of government jobs on the assumption that ''sexual perversion'' had weakened their moral character, making them more likely to breach national security due to blackmail.

Friedan also made the history of women palatable to her audience. Although most scholars believe that 1960s feminism began without a sense of connection to the past, Friedan had long been aware of women's historic struggles, as many of her earlier writings make clear. Friedan not only talked of passion and ''revolution'' but connected women's struggles with those of African Americans and union members. Yet her version of the past highlighted women who were educated, physically attractive, and socially respectable. Friedan went to considerable lengths to connect historic feminism not with the stereotypical man-haters or ''neurotic victims of penis envy who wanted to be men'' but with married women who, she noted repeatedly, were ''dainty,'' ''pretty,'' and ''lovely.'' Unlike her writings for Federated Press and the *UE News*, which pointed out how millions of American women had to work hard in order to support a family economy under adverse situations, *The Feminine Mystique* described women's search for identity and personal growth, not the fight against discrimination or exploitation. While immigrant, African American, and union women were the subject of her 1953 *Women Fight For a Better Life! UE Picture Story of Women's Role in American History*, in *The Feminine Mystique* she remarked that female factory workers ''could not take the lead'' and that ''most of the leading feminists'' were from the middle class. In contrast, Eleanor Flexner's *Century of Struggle* (1959), on which Friedan relied in writing *The Feminine Mystique*, included extensive discussions of the social movements of African Americans, radicals, and union women.

Friedan also connected the conditions women faced with two of the great events that haunted her, as they did many members of her generation. At several points, she used the horrors of the Bomb to drive home her point. She contrasted domesticity with a world trembling ''on the brink of technological holocaust.'' She also chided women in the anti-nuclear Women's Strike for Peace who claimed that once the testing of atomic weapons ended, they would be glad to stay home and take care of their children. Yet for someone who exaggerated her own role as a housewife, it is ironic that Friedan criticized the professional artist who headed that movement for saying she was ''just a housewife.''

More problematic was Friedan's exploration of the parallels between the Nazi death camps and suburban homes as ''comfortable concentration camps,'' an analogy that exaggerated what suburban women faced and belittled the fate of victims of Naziism. This was the first time since 1946 that she had mentioned the Holocaust in print. Although in the end she acknowledged that such an analogy broke down, Friedan nonetheless spent several pages exploring the similarities. Just before her book appeared, two other Jewish writers, Stanley Elkins and Erving Goffman, had applied the Holocaust comparison to two institutions where a more compelling case could be made: slavery and a mental hospital. Similarly problematic was Friedan's omission of the anti-Semitism that drove the Nazis to murder millions of Jews. Like many Jews of her generation, Friedan hoped for a society in which anti-Semitism and race prejudice more generally would be wiped out. Therefore, in her book she strove for a race-neutral picture, in the process both trivializing and universalizing the experience of Jews.

While the concentration camp analogy grew out of her youthful antifascism, she gave no hint of how her early experiences with anti-Semitism had started her on the road to a passionate progressivism. There is a final reason that may explain why Friedan did not want to make explicit any connection between the situation Jews and women faced. Historically and in her own experience, there was a close connection between anti-Semitism and anti-radicalism. Yet despite the fact that feminist groups such as the Congress of American Women had a disproportionate share of Jews among their members and leaders, in public discussions anti-Semitism and anti-feminism had run along largely separate paths. On some level Friedan may have realized that it was best to use the discussion of the concentration camps to raise the consciousness of a wide range of readers without linking Naziism with anti-Semitism or feminism with Jews. Though the concentration camp analogy was careless and exaggerated, it nonetheless dramatically conveyed to Friedan's readers the horrible and dehumanized feeling of women who were trapped in their homes.

Another distinctive aspect of *The Feminine Mystique* was Friedan's use, and gendering, of contemporary psychology. She took what humanistic and ego psychologists had written about men, and occasionally about women, and turned it to feminist purposes. Drawing on studies by A. H. Maslow in the late 1930s, Friedan noted that the greater a woman's sense of dominance and self-esteem, the fuller her sexual satisfaction and ''the more her concern was directed outward to other people and to problems of the world.'' Despite this earlier research, by the 1950s the feminine mystique had influenced even Maslow, Friedan noted, encouraging him to believe women would achieve self-actualization primarily as wives and mothers. Maslow and others held such notions despite evidence from the Kinsey report that persuaded Friedan of a link between women's emancipation and their greater capacity for sexual fulfillment. However, Friedan hardly wished to rest her case for women's enhanced self-esteem on the likelihood of more and better orgasms. She rejected a narcissistic version of self-fulfillment. Drawing on the writings of David Riesman, Erik Erikson, and Olive Schreiner, and on the experience of frontier women, Friedan argued that people developed a healthy identity not through housekeeping, but through commitment to purposeful and sustained effort ''which reaches beyond biology, beyond the narrow walls of home, to help shape the future.''

Along with others, Friedan was exploring how to ground a cultural and social critique by rethinking the contributions of Sigmund Freud and Karl Marx, an enterprise that first captivated her in the early 1940s as an undergraduate. What Herbert Marcuse achieved in *Eros and Civilization: A Philosophical Inquiry into Freud* (1955), Friedan did almost a decade later, responding to the Cold War by minimizing her debt to Marx even as she relied on him. Central to her solutions to women's problems was her emphasis on personal growth, self-determination, and human potential. Here Friedan was participating in one of the major postwar cultural and intellectual movements, the application of psychological and therapeutic approaches to public policy and social issues. In the process, she recovered the lessons of her undergraduate and graduate studies, joining others such as Paul Goodman, Riesman, Margaret Mead, Erikson, Rollo May, Maslow, and Erich Fromm in using humanistic psychology and neo-Freudianism as the basis for a powerful cultural critique at a time when other formulations were politically discredited.

Like others, Friedan offered what the historian Ellen Herman has called a ''postmaterial agenda'' which employed psychological concepts to undergird feminism. Here Friedan was responding to the way writers—including Philip Wylie, Edward Strecker, Ferdinand Lundberg, and Marynia Farnham—used psychology to suggest that only the acceptance of domesticity would cure female frustrations. Friedan's contribution was to turn the argument around, asserting that women's misery came from the attempt to keep them in place. Psychology, rather than convincing women to adjust and conform, could be used to foster their personal growth and fuller embrace of non-domestic roles. Other observers suggested the troublesome nature of male identity in the 1950s; Friedan gave this theme a twist. She both recognized the problems posed by feminized men and masculinized women and went on to promise that the liberation of women would strengthen male and female identity alike. Friedan took from other writers an analysis that blamed the problems of diminished masculine identity on life in the suburbs, jobs in large organizations, and consumer culture; she then turned this explanation into an argument for women's liberation.

Source: Daniel Horowitz, ''The Development of *The Feminine Mystique,* 1957–63,'' in *Betty Friedan and the Making of ''The Feminine Mystique'': The American Left, The Cold War, and Modern Feminism,* University of Massachusetts Press, 1998, pp. 197–223.

Rachel Bowlby

In the following essay excerpt, Bowlby explores the link between femininity and consumerism that she finds in Friedan's The Feminine Mystique.

Published in 1963, *The Feminine Mystique* is commonly regarded both as a feminist classic and as a book which acted as a catalyst to the western feminist movement which began in the mid to late sixties. In the canon of post-war feminist works it sits somewhat isolated, and somewhat incongruously, midway between *The Second Sex* and the outpouring of texts and tracts later on. But the striking gap between 1948—the date of de Beauvoir's book—and 1963 in fact fits well with one of Friedan's principal contentions. The arguments of almost all

feminist social critics, before and after Friedan, involve the presupposition or demonstration that women's freedom either never existed or existed only in the remote past. Friedan, however, argues that women had freedom and lost it. And this peculiarity is perhaps a starting point for thinking about some of the echoes and overtones of the unidentified 'problem'. I want to explore some of the twists and turns of this unexpected structure of feminist narrative, and how it is related to Friedan's conceptions of subjectivity, femininity and the American nation. In particular, I am interested in the links that are made between femininity, in Friedan's sense, and the impact of consumerism, and in how these links impinge upon the form of Friedan's argument.

The genealogy of Friedan's particular 'problem' goes something like this. Not long ago, in the time of our grandmothers, strong 'pioneer' women got together to claim their rights to citizenship and equality on a par with men. They won access to higher education and the professions and all seemed set, thanks to their incomparable efforts, for a fair and sunny future for the now fully human second sex. But unfortunately there came World War Two, which brought young and old men flocking home to America with a craving for Mom and apple pie in the form of a wife and lots of children. To serve, or to reinforce, this need, the men of Madison Avenue stepped in. Lest there should be any women unwilling to comply with the scenario, advertising, magazines and the proliferation of domestic consumer goods saw to it that the 'image' of feminine fulfilment in the form of husband, babies and suburbia would be promoted to the exclusion of anything else. Other cultural forces came into play too. The evil prescriptions of a Freud who thought women's destiny was domestic and infantile entered and influenced every American mind. Higher education for women was dominated by a spurious use of sociology and anthropology to ensure girls got the message that their 'sex-role' as wives and mothers, and not their 'human' capacity to create and achieve in the working world, was the natural one. In any case, thanks to the bombardment of all these types of influence and suggestion, most of them left college halfway through to get married and reproduce. All the promise of a new generation of potentially free women, the daughters of the 'pioneers', has thus been knocked out of them, and it is now a matter of some urgency to expose the general fraud for what it is: to allow 'the problem with no name' to be spoken.

The dissatisfactions of suburbia centre, for Friedan, around an opposition between 'selfhood' and 'sex-role'—also glossed as 'humanity' and 'femininity'. The long-term planning arid 'creativity' involved in a worthy career are valorized by Friedan against the 'stunted' qualities of the woman who remains in a state of little-girl conformity, confined to her reproductive role and to fulfilment in the form of sex, by which Friedan means both reproduction and sexual pleasure. Motherhood, like that suburban wasteland, is a trap: Friedan has vivid metaphors of confinement to express this, including a chapter title of what now seems to be dubious taste—'Progressive Dehumanization: The Comfortable Concentration Camp'. A frequently repeated image of the apparently happy housewife with 'a stationwagon full of children' is itself used to epitomize 'this new image which insists she is not a person but a "woman."' Whereas the Victorians' problem was the repression of sexuality, that of the present is 'a stunting or evasion of growth.'

The account of socially induced 'femininity' as inhibited growth and as something which necessarily detracts from the achievement of full humanity can be placed in a tradition of feminist humanism which goes back to Mary Wollstonecraft. Friedan's narrative difficulty, however, is that she believes that the battles of Wollstonecraft and her successors, the 'pioneer' feminists, were fought and won, and she tries to explain what she now identifies as a relapse into a situation just as unsatisfactory as the one from which women freed themselves before.

Several culprits, of disparate provenance, are identified; I mentioned some of them at the beginning. One is the spread of psychoanalysis, taken as having reinforced conceptions of women as naturally inferior and naturally destined for merely domestic functions. An *ad hominem* attack on Freud himself, via his letters to his fiancée, is used as the basis for a reading of his account of femininity, and especially of penis envy, as both prescriptive and misogynistic. Freud is effectively likened to a salesman, purveying a false representation of women's nature: 'The fact is that to Freud, even more than to the magazine editor on Madison Avenue today, women were a strange, inferior, less-than-human species.'

Another set of culprits are 'the sex-directed educators', who have betrayed the high ideals of educational pioneers and who now offer courses which are intellectually unchallenging and whose explicit message, in courses with names like 'Ad-

> **The arguments of almost all feminist social critics, before and after Friedan, involve the presupposition or demonstration that women's freedom either never existed or existed only in the remote past. Friedan, however, argues that women had freedom and lost it."**

justment to Marriage' and 'Education for Family Living', is that of the feminine mystique—Mothers' Studies, perhaps. Such education is in reality 'an indoctrination of opinions and values through manipulation of the students' emotions; and in this manipulative disguise, it is no longer subject to the critical thinking demanded in other academic disciplines.' The identification of a conspiracy here does not, however, stop with the professors themselves: they too have been deceived, and Friedan goes on to describe 'the degree to which the feminine mystique has brainwashed American educators.'

Even the brainwashers are brainwashed, then: the plot continues to thicken. Closer to home, we find a rather familiar target for blame: the mother. Not, in this case, the current generation of mystified, over-young mothers, but *their* mothers. The nineteenth-century struggle for women's rights was not incomplete. Friedan states clearly: 'The ones who fought that battle won more than empty paper rights. They cast off the shadow of contempt and self-contempt that had degraded women for centuries.' But then something went wrong, and it is this which she is at a loss to explain:

> Why, with the removal of all the legal, political, economic and educational barriers that once kept woman from being man's equal, a person in her own right, an individual free to develop her own potential, should she accept this new image which insists she is not a person but a 'woman,' by definition barred from human existence and a voice in human destiny?

The next generation did not follow up the victory, but returned to the same domesticated forms of femininity from which their mothers had sought to free them. 'Did women really go home again as a reaction to feminism?' Friedan asks, with no little bewilderment. 'The fact is, that to women born after 1920, feminism was dead history.' This is like saying that emancipated slaves go back to their masters when the battle is forgotten, so Friedan adds more. Feminism was not only dead history, or not *dead* history at all, but 'a dirty word', evoking for 'mothers still trapped' and still raising daughters, 'the fiery, man-eating feminist, the career woman— loveless, alone.' And this was what they passed on to *their* daughters: 'These mothers were probably the real model for the man-eating myth.' After 'the passionate journey their grandmothers had begun' as pioneers of feminism, the subsequent generations were left with no positive image with which to identify. 'They had truly outgrown the old image; they were finally free to be what they chose to be. But what choice were they offered?'

The model of free choice brings us to the most often emphasized source of the feminine mystique: the media. Advertising, magazines and (to a lesser extent) popular novels and 'how-to' books from Spook to sausage rolls are treated as absolutely central to the propagation of the mystique. Friedan enters into the confessional mode in describing how she herself used to make her living writing articles to order on aspects of housewifery or mothering for magazines like *Good Housekeeping* or *Mademoiselle*. At this stage, significantly, it is tracked down as being primarily a male conspiracy; and in the height of her crime thriller mode, Friedan devotes a whole chapter to the results of her being given permission to delve into the secrets of an advertising agency's market research files. It is with all the force of a revelation that she points out the importance of advertising and consumption to the social control or the sociological description of American women:

> Properly manipulated . . . American housewives can be given the sense of identity, purpose, creativity, the self-realization, even the sexual joy they lack—by the buying of things. I suddenly realized the significance of the boast that women wield seventy-five per cent of the purchasing power in America. I suddenly saw American women as *victims* of that ghastly gift, that power at the point of purchase. The insights he shared with me so liberally revealed many things . . .

The image of femininity perpetrated by magazines is itself the first example brought forward by Friedan after her opening chapter on the barely articulated 'problem with no name'. She runs through typical articles and stories, showing how they share a common message and injunction to women, that they should seek their fulfilment in the form of marriage and homemaking. But, as with the history

of the feminist movement, this present, univocal image is contrasted sharply with a previous phase in magazine publishing when political stories could be part of the contents list, when there were more women writers than now, and when the housewife's role was not the be-all and end-all of the reader's presumed horizons. This earlier 'passionate search for truth and identity' is highlighted by a short story about a girl who secretly learns to fly. This, for Friedan, represents the heights of past achievement and serves as a measure of how far things have subsequently declined: 'It is like remembering a long forgotten dream, to recapture the memory of what a career meant to women before "career woman" became a dirty word in America.'

Given the recurrent rhetoric of manipulation and brainwashing, it is not surprising that the marketing case, around magazines and advertising, should be so crucial for Friedan. The fifties model of 'hidden persuaders' (the title of Vance Packard's 1957 book on the advertising industry)—of a barely discernible but thus all the more effective conspiracy—contributes to the mystery overtones of the diagnosis of the mystique and its origins. A distortion or 'blurring' of the image has occurred since the more open days of the flying story, so that false and fatuous models are being perpetrated throughout the land in every sphere of daily life. From education to therapy, to childcare, to journalism and advertising, women are being sold back down the river by the withholding of what ought to have been the fruits of their social emancipation. And crucially, whatever the relative priorities accorded to each of these agencies in perpetrating the mystique, it is the 'sell-out' metaphor of marketing which subsumes them all. The model of the marketing brainwash, of the insidious manipulation of advertising, is itself taken up as the model for a generalized social persuasion.

The harmful effects of the mystique are summed up by the repeated reference to 'waste'. Waste is what happens when the mystique takes over. The avoidance of waste represents the kind of emotional parsimony and efficient use of available human resources that fits with the paradigm of goal-setting and deferred gratification. The 'waste' is first of female 'human' potential that is going unused or untapped, owing to its deflection on to feminine channels falsely and misleadingly imaged as leading to authentic fulfilment. Friedan is in no doubt as to the relative valuation to be ascribed to domestic and other forms of work: the former can be summed up as 'trivia', to be kept to a functional—waste-free—minimum; the second is characterized by such heady pursuits as 'splitting atoms, penetrating outer space, creating art that illuminates human destiny, pioneering on the frontiers of society.'

This unquestioned valorization of high-flying, maximum-penetration activities over their 'feminine' alternatives is worth contrasting with its reversed form in a later feminist writer like Elaine Showalter. Writing in the late 1970s, Showalter blames what she identifies as the theoreticist excesses of literary criticism over the previous twenty years on a kind of masculinist emulation by male critics of their scientific rivals in the era of Sputnik. Friedan has human playing feminine as genuine plays trivial, artificial; Showalter makes the 'human achievement' pole explicitly masculine and the alternative an authentic femaleness.

Parallel to the idea of personal waste is that of national waste. Here Friedan introduces a full-scale narrative of imminent cultural decline precipitated by the menace of the marauding 'mystique'. This argument acquires an urgency distinct from the argument about women's individual waste. Friedan refers not only to 'the desperate need of this nation for the untapped reserves of women's intelligence', but also to a generalized domestication of all American people, men and women. After the war, she says, 'the whole nation stopped growing up' and it suffers now from 'a vacuum of larger purpose', from 'the lack of an ideology or national purpose.' So now the infantile and non-goal-oriented attributes of image-dominated women have been transferred to Americans in general. And here, instead of women being the victims, they are identified as the source. Friedan provides a whole gallery of monstrous females, chiefly in the form of the over-dominant mother who won't let her sons grow up and separate from her. An ideology of domestic 'togetherness' in marriage has made men so passive that even though their wives are at home all day with nothing better to do than get on with the chores, they still get drawn into the trivia of washing up, vacuuming and the rest in a way that their fathers did not.

There are indications in these sections of a nostalgia for a more authoritarian community and family structure, with mother and father each in his and her proper, traditional place and with the domestic sphere relegated to its rightful secondariness in relation to the public world of national achievement. It is interesting to note the difference here from arguments in the seventies about the desirability or imminent emergence of 'the sensitive man'

formed from a happy blend of 'feminine' and 'masculine' qualities—first, because clearly he figured a lot earlier, and secondly because at this stage in feminist argument he's represented as thoroughly feeble. It's not that Friedan wants to keep women in the home; rather, she thinks the home and its tasks should be reduced to a minimum so that both sexes can fulfil a genuinely 'human' function in the outside world.

More dramatically, Friedan sees 'frightening implications for the future of our nation in the parasitical softening that is being passed on to the new generation of children'. Specifically, she identifies 'a recent increase in the overt manifestations of male homosexuality', and comments:

> I do not think this is unrelated to the national embrace of the feminine mystique. For the feminine mystique has glorified and perpetuated the name of femininity and passive, childlike immaturity which is passed on from mother to son, as well as to daughters.

A little further on, this becomes 'the homosexuality that is spreading like a murky smog over the American scene'. What is striking here is not only the imagery of infection—the murky disease and the clean, almost Jamesian 'American scene'—but its manifest link to a process of cultural feminization. Male homosexuality as the end-point of the feminine mystique is not just artificial, a regrettable but accidental distortion of the reality it overlays: it is a sinister source of cultural contamination. This 'murky smog' is the final smut, the last 'dirty word' in the story of the mystique: that clean, feminine exterior is now found to hide a particularly nasty can of worms. Marketing and the mystique are together leading to 'bearded undisciplined beatnickery' and a 'deterioration of the human character.'

Male homosexual activity is further identified as 'hauntingly "feminine"' in its 'lack of lasting human satisfaction.' Friedan establishes a clear category of what she calls 'pseudo-sex', as engaged in by bored housewives, teenagers and male homosexuals. Again, it is interesting to note parallels with recent arguments seen as a backlash to the liberalization of sexual mores in the wake of the 1960s: here is Friedan making a case in 1963 for the return of real sex between real, whole people (of different sex) against a hypothetical backcloth of generalized promiscuity and a lowering of moral standards: 'For men, too, sex itself is taking on the unreal character of phantasy—depersonalized, dissatisfying, and finally inhuman.' The censure of 'the stunted world of sexual fantasy' is exactly parallel to the criticism of the stunted image of the feminine mystique. At the same time, the obsession with sex—or with pseudo-sex—is regarded as the focal point for the diversion of women from their true selfhood. Like a Victorian moralist, or a 1980s Victoria Gillick, Friedan asks: 'Why is it so difficult for these youngsters to postpone present pleasure for future long-term goals?'

And yet the argument about sexuality is not as straightforward as it appears. Friedan devotes some pages to the Kinsey reports on sexual behaviour which came out in the 1950s, and which in their revised form suggested a correlation between educational level and sexual fulfilment. She argues against pseudo-sex not on the grounds that it is immoral—though there is a didactic tone to the prose—but on the grounds that it isn't as good as it could be: 'Sex, for them [young girls] is not really sex at all. They have not even begun to experience a sexual response, much less "fulfilment."'

The further development of this occurs when Friedan suggests that real sexual fulfilment requires the other sort—'human' fulfilment—as a condition of possibility and therefore, implicitly, that if you want good sex you should see to your achievement in other areas first. Quoting the findings of 'Professor Maslow', Friedan concludes: 'It seemed as if fulfilment of personal capacity in this larger world opened new vistas of sexual ecstasy.' Friedan has not herself shifted the terms from those of the mystique itself. While she accuses it of diverting women, and perhaps men too, from full human achievement to merely sexual preoccupations, her own argument is effectively to say: 'That is pseudosex. Free yourself from the mystique and you can have the real thing.' So sex remains at the centre; it is not so much displaced as the excesses of a passion that detracts from rationality, but rather reinscribed as an even more fulfilling by-product of personal growth.

This brings us to another equivocation in Friedan's text. She describes, as we have seen, the various institutions and agencies which might be identified as responsible for the propagation or infliction of the mystique, whatever their motives or interests. She does not really explain why the mystique appeals, why it sticks, given the prior history of tough feminist values developed and put into action in the past. The only reason, ultimately, is a negative one: women obeyed, or adopted the mystique, because nothing better was on offer. Feminism was 'dead history' or even 'a dirty word', and a female member of the next generation was stuck 'for lack of an image that would help her to grow up as a woman true to herself.' Or in the passage quoted earlier: 'They had truly outgrown the old image. They were finally free to be what they chose to be. But what choice were they offered?'

Always there is the same humanist appeal to a pre-existing individual self, embryonically there from the start and available for a development which can be straight and true or may, by extraneous social influence, deviate from its natural course. A girl either grows—grows up, tall and strong—or else she is warped and stunted and remains in a state of immaturity or corruption. Friedan claims on the one hand that the 'lack of an image' of what she might be caused the fall-back into the error of false femininity: without the good model, there is no way for the girl to grow. On the other hand, because she conceives of the person as there all the time, she also appeals repeatedly to a 'basic' or 'hard core of self' which is called upon to resist its own feminization:

> By choosing femininity over the painful growth to full identity, by never achieving the hard core of self that comes not from fantasy but from mastering reality, these girls are doomed to suffer ultimately that bored, diffuse feeling of purposelessness, non-existence, non-involvement with the world that can be called *anomie,* or lack of identity, or merely felt as the problem that has no name.

Here, it is the girl's own active 'choosing' of the femininity which then makes her passively 'doomed to suffer'. She begins as a fully rational subject and condemns herself to the utter passivity of 'non-existence'. There is a hesitation as to victimization or agency in relation to which, in other cases, Friedan sometimes privileges one side and sometimes the other. To take another instance:

> In the last analysis, millions of able women in this free land chose, themselves, not to use the door education could have opened for them. The choice—and the responsibility—for the race back home was finally their own.

In this example, free choice is real: in 'this free land', women are ultimately free to choose 'themselves', and responsible for the mistakes they make. Home is the prison they preferred to the open, outside world of education and opportunity. In the earlier example—finally free, but what choice were they offered?'—choice is seen as limited by what is offered. No image available, therefore no possible identification with a self to match up to the free, or freed, 'New Woman'.

This oscillation recurs throughout the book. There is the 'inner voice' within that is the germ of an authentic protest; at the same time, there is the clear statement that the image conforms in a sense to what women want: 'This image . . . shapes women's lives today and mirrors their dreams.' In other words, the 'image' imprints itself in such a way as to be indistinguishable from those other dreams characterized as more primary and more true to the inner, human self. Friedan is constantly caught in this contradiction, which can be smoothed over only by accepting the arbitrary distinction between true and false dreams—between those that are from within and correspond to 'human' potential, and those that are from without and are imposed by the manipulators of the 'feminine' mystique.

Much of the difficulty stems from the fact that the language for each alternative is identical, having to do with wanting (or 'yearning'), choice and fulfilment. Friedan tells the story of the first feminist movement, whose emergence was prompted by a situation of confinement to the home and to a state of infantile underdevelopment similar to the one she identifies in the present. The problem for a woman then was that 'she could never grow up to ask the simply human question, "Who am I? What do I want?"' But what is wrong now is articulated in terms which seem to correspond to this acknowledgement of wanting, to a search for identity and fulfilment: 'Women who suffer this problem, in whom this voice is stirring, have lived their whole lives in the pursuit of feminine fulfilment.'

This double premise—first, that there is a basic 'core of self' which ought to develop according to its nature and to resist extraneous influence, and second, that without an external image there is no possibility of achieving a full identity—accounts, I think, for a final twist in the form of Friedan's argument. For it is as if the entire book is there to lay out the missing image of human selfhood excluded by the mystique, but that this can only be done by repeating exactly those forms of persuasion from outside which are identified as the insidious techniques of the mystique which is thereby displaced and excluded in its turn. Be a whole person, achieve your human potential, and you can have even more than is presently on offer.

This is not to dismiss the book of *The Feminine Mystique* as an advertisers' con on a par with that of the feminine mystique it takes as its object. It is rather to suggest that the denunciation of 'brainwashing' and 'manipulation' in the name of a sup-pressed authenticity may mean that the authenticity claimed instead is rhetorically just as suspect. Friedan counters the mystique's representation of the natural woman with her own, and lays her argument open to the same critique in the name of another feminine—or human—nature. (And this, as we shall see, is precisely what happens when she revises her own argument eighteen years later.) In the second chapter she cites as an example of the spuriousness of contemporary women's magazine journalism an editor who was heard to demand: 'Can't you dream up a new crisis for women?' Friedan's next chapter is entitled 'The Crisis in Women's Identity'.

In rereading—or reading—Friedan twenty or more years on, it is relatively easy to point out aspects which now seem anachronistic, either because they refer to demands which no longer seem pertinent or because they appear unacceptably narrow or biased. In the first category—demands no longer relevant—would appear, for example, the fact that western nations are not much worried by high birthrates any more, or the fact that in a time of high unemployment it is no longer feasible to marshal an argument that women are a wasted asset for the state.

In the second category—demands that now appear prejudiced—would be placed the heterosexist assumptions, not only in the representation of male homosexuality as a cultural symptom but also in the premise that the normal woman is heterosexual: Friedan refers, for example, to the 'perversion' of history by which nineteenth-century feminists are represented as 'man-hating, embittered, sex-starved spinsters' and proceeds to show, on the one hand, that many famous feminists 'loved, were loved, and married', and on the other that the cause was great enough to lead to a temporary abandonment of womanliness:

> Is it so hard to understand that emancipation, the right to full humanity, was important enough to generations of women, still alive or only recently dead, that some fought with their fists, and went to jail and even died for it? And for the right to human growth, some women denied their own sex, the desire to love and be loved by a man, and to bear children.

Here there is, clearly, a conception of natural sexual difference operating alongside the claim for recognition of women's humanity; and that difference consists in a heterosexual, childbearing destiny which would radically separate Friedan from many of her feminist successors. Her argument is that marriage and motherhood should be kept in their secondary, 'sexual' place, not that they are to be questioned in themselves as part of what she calls the 'life-plan' for women.

Also featuring in this category of now unacceptable assumptions would be the middle-class, professional focus which is implicit throughout and which occasionally shows another negative side. It is in the following terms that Friedan denounces the distorted evidence used to build statistical proof that working mothers are bad for children's development:

> How many women realize, even now, that the babies in these publicized cases, who withered away from lack of maternal affection, were not the children of educated, middle-class mothers who left them in others' care certain hours of the day to practice a profession or write a poem, or fight a political battle—but truly abandoned children: foundlings often deserted at birth by unwed mothers and drunken fathers, children who never had a home or tender loving care.

The asymmetry here between 'unwed' and 'drunken' is perhaps even more interesting than the vignette itself, with the two culpable parents stumbling around in their different states of post-natal incapacitation to throw out the baby 'at birth'. And interestingly, the 'home and tender loving care' which measure the extent of the foundling's deprivation figure here not as the false image of domestic happiness perpetrated by the feminine mystique, but as just what a baby deserves.

In academic circles, Friedan's humanist premises and triumphalist rhetoric of emancipation do now seem rather old-fashioned. The current emphasis on sexual difference as the starting point for questions, rather than as an ideological confusion masking women's full humanity, has the effect of relegating a perspective such as Friedan's to the status of being theoretically unsophisticated as well as historically outdated. But to fail to consider her on these grounds is to accept precisely those assumptions about concepts of progressive liberation and enlightenment, collective and individual, which the later models have put into question. The point is not to reject Friedan from some point of advanced knowledge either as simply 'of her time'—an argument for the early sixties of no interest now, or as benightedly prejudiced—good liberal as she was, we've come a long way since then. Rather, the very twists of her argument, with all the oddity of its details and contradictions, as seen from more than two decades later, may themselves suggest a different perspective on current feminist preoccupations and assumptions and current versions of feminist history and feminism's destination.

Friedan's basic theory of historical, as of individual, development is one of evolutionary maturation—from 'primitive' to civilized cultures, via the agency of pioneers, in the feminist movement as in American history. In this scheme, the present form of femininity is but a moderate deviation, to be ironed out—if the image is not too domestic—by a final mobilization of latent energy:

> In the light of women's long battle for emancipation, the recent sexual counterrevolution in America has been perhaps a final crisis, a strange breath-holding interval before the larva breaks out of the shell into maturity.

But elsewhere, Friedan half hints—and half despairingly—that there may be a structure more cyclical than progressive in the history of feminist argument. For instance:

> Encouraged by the mystique to evade their identity crisis, permitted to escape identity altogether in the name of sexual fulfilment, women once again are living with their feet bound in the old image of glorified femininity. And it is the same old image, despite its shiny new clothes, that trapped women for centuries and made the feminists rebel.

From femininity to feminism, to the forgetting of feminism to a return to femininity, to feminism again—and so on. Such would seem to be the sequence identified by this description, leaving no suggestion of a possible outcome of full feminist, or human, identity for women, since the story never ends.

This difficulty is highlighted by Friedan's own explicit shift of position since 1963. *The Second Stage* (1981) reads uncannily like a reversal of the terms of *The Feminine Mystique*. In place of the silently suffering, affluent housewife, we are here introduced to the secretly unfulfilled female executive who has taken on wholesale the offer of success in a man's world but is now experiencing the effects of the 'denial' of what turn out to have been valid feminine feelings. Where 'femininity' was the false image in the first book, its negative effects to be cured by feminist consciousness, 'feminist rhetoric' has now become the stale and stultifying demand, to be cured by the recovery of a measure of femininity. Rather than the feminine mystique, it is 'the *feminist* mystique' which is 'the problem'. Two halves assuredly make a whole, and balance will only be attained by acknowledging the importance of those traditionally female nurturing qualities and 'needs' which the first stage of feminism forced them to repudiate.

The role of the false, distorting image played by femininity in the earlier book is thus taken over in *The Second Stage* by the 'stunting' excesses of a feminism 'blind' to the caring, family values it had to reject in order to make its initial point. In arguing that the time has now come to 'transcend' the polarization of men and women, Friedan relies on the same types of double premises as in *The Feminine Mystique*. From one perspective, the new problems are generated by economic and national necessities (because of inflation and dwindling growth, women have to go out to work to balance the domestic budget; by the same token, macho masculinity *a la* John Wayne is no longer viable in post-Vietnam America). But at the same time, the solutions appeal to first principles: men are now able to put off what turn out to have been their own 'masks' of hyper-masculinity, to discover their underlying feelings; women, meanwhile, have got past the point of needing to assert themselves according to values now seen not as the 'human' norm but as excessively masculine. Femininity is now valorized as a buried potential, where previously it was regarded as a fabrication.

All this leaves open the whole question of what actually constitutes the difference between the sexes. Too much of either masculinity or femininity is bad for men and women, which suggests that they are not qualities tied to either sex: women must not get too much like men, any more than men should repress their feminine side. And yet, the whole aim of 'the transcendence of polarization' is that, in the words of the book's final sentence, we will all be 'spelling out own names, at last, as women and men'. The goal of feminism, having passed through all its 'evolutionary' stages, then, would be to make true men and women of us, while at the same time the attainment of such identities is predicated on a fusion of masculine and feminine qualities. Transcendence might be another impasse after all.

Source: Rachel Bowlby, "'The Problem with No Name': Rereading Friedan's *The Feminine Mystique*," in *Feminist Review,* No. 27, Autumn 1987, pp. 61–75.

Sources

Bernays, Anne, "Love Her or Leave Her," in *Washington Post Book World,* August 8, 1976, p. F7.

Brewer, Mary F., "Betty Friedan," in the *Dictionary of Literary Biography,* Vol. 246: *Twentieth-Century American Cultural Theorists,* Gale, 2001, pp. 128–39.

Epstein, Cynthia Fuchs, "The Major Myth of the Women's Movement," in *Dissent,* Vol. 46, No. 4, Fall 1999, pp. 83–86.

Fava, Sylvia Fleis, Review of *The Feminine Mystique,* in the *American Sociological Review,* Vol. 28, No. 6, December 1963, pp. 1053–54.

Friedan, Betty, *The Feminine Mystique,* W. W. Norton & Company, 2001.

———, "Introduction to the Tenth Anniversary Edition," in *The Feminine Mystique,* W. W. Norton & Company, 2001, pp. 3–7.

Howard, Jane, "Tenth Anniversary Edition," in *New Republic,* Vol. 170, No. 17, April 27, 1974, pp. 25–26.

Iannone, Carol, "What Moderate Feminists?" in *Commentary,* Vol. 99, June 1995, pp. 46–48.

Kay, Herma Hill, "Do We Suffer from a Feminist Mystique?" in the *New York Times Book Review,* November 22, 1981, pp. 3, 33.

Review of *The Feminine Mystique,* in the *Times Literary Supplement,* No. 3196, May 31, 1963, p. 391.

Review of *The Feminine Mystique,* in the *Yale Review,* Vol. 52, No. 3, Spring 1963, p. 12.

Sanborn, Sara, "Warm-Puppy Feminism," in *Saturday Review,* Vol. 3, No. 21, July 24, 1976, p. 26.

Steinfels, Margaret O'Brien, "All the World's a Stage," in *Commonweal,* Vol. 108, No. 23, December 18, 1981, pp. 726–28.

Tyrrell, R. Emmett, Jr., "The Worst Book of the Year," in the *American Spectator,* Vol. 15, No. 2, February 1982, pp. 4–5.

Further Reading

Crittenden, Ann, *The Price of Motherhood: Why the Most Important Job in the World Is Still the Least Valued,* Owl Books, 2002.

Crittenden, a noted economics journalist, asserts that mothers are penalized for their childbearing role. Crittenden uses studies and financial facts to show that all mothers, regardless of occupational or marital status, are at an economic disadvantage to others in society. Crittenden offers solutions to this problem based on working models found in such diverse areas as Sweden and the United States military.

Freedman, Estelle B., *No Turning Back: The History of Feminism and the Future of Women,* Ballantine Books, 2002.

In this engaging, narrative history of feminism, Freedman explores a wide range of issues, including race, politics, economics, and health, while providing her own critical interpretations of these topics.

Horowitz, Daniel, *Betty Friedan and the Making of "The Feminine Mystique": The American Left, the Cold War, and Modern Feminism,* University of Massachusetts Press, 2000.

In this noted biography of Friedan, Horowitz chronicles the development of Friedan's political and feminist ideas and challenges the popular assumption that Friedan was merely a suburban housewife when she wrote *The Feminine Mystique.* Horowitz examines the aspects of Friedan's life—such as her labor activism—that Friedan did not mention in her book, and explores the cultural and political climate that encouraged her to bury these facts about her life.

Schneir, Miriam, ed., *Feminism in Our Time: The Essential Writings, World War II to the Present,* Vintage Books, 1994.
Schneir's impressive anthology collects many contemporary feminist writings from the second half of the twentieth century, including several excerpts from longer works. Schneir also provides commentary on the writings.

The Golden Bough

James Frazer

1890

Ever since its first edition in 1890, *The Golden Bough* has been considered a major influence in the development of western thought. In this book, Sir James G. Frazer, a Cambridge researcher trained in classical literature, outlines ancient myths and folk legends, proposing that all civilizations go through three stages of development: belief in magic leads to organized religion, which eventually leads to faith in the powers of science. Frazer's literary style raised interest in the ideas of other world cultures at a time when western societies considered the peoples of Africa and Asia to be the products of ''primitive'' thought. In addition, his attempts to identify the basic story motifs to which all human beings respond was carried forth in the twentieth century by psychologists such as Carl Jung, who developed the idea of the collective unconscious, and by such literary masters as James Joyce and T. S. Eliot.

Frazer went on to expand the original book, first to a two-volume set and then to a total of thirteen volumes, before editing it down to one concise volume, which is the one that is most commonly read today. Over time, the book's reputation has changed. While it was once considered to be an important study in comparative anthropology, many social scientists later found fault with the methods that Frazer used in collecting materials: he never spoke directly to people of the cultures about which he wrote, but instead he relied on other researchers' findings and on questionnaires that he

gave to people who traveled to other lands. Frazer's conclusions are generally considered unreliable because he did not follow sound scientific procedures, but *The Golden Bough* is still revered as a well-written introduction to the subject of comparative religion.

Author Biography

James George Frazer was born on January 1, 1854, in Glasgow, Scotland. As he grew up he developed an interest in classical literature, which was his major when he enrolled in Glasgow University at age fifteen. After graduating Glasgow he received a scholarship to Trinity College at Cambridge, where he was given a teaching position in 1879. For the rest of his life, except for one unsatisfying year at Liverpool University in 1907, Frazer was associated with Trinity College.

In his early years at Trinity, Frazer formed a relationship with William Robertson Smith, who at that time was assembling the ninth edition of the *Encyclopaedia Britannica.* Smith asked Frazer, who had recently become interested in the cultures and stories of primitive people, to write an article about totemism for the encyclopedia. Frazer was a dedicated writer, spending twelve and fourteen hours a day researching in the library; when his finished entry proved too long to include in the encyclopedia, he published it as his first book, *Totemism,* in 1887.

Soon after that, Frazer started on what was to be the defining work of his lifetime, *The Golden Bough: A Study in Comparative Religion.* A two-volume edition was published in 1890; it was expanded to a three-volume edition that was published in 1900. Between 1911 and 1915 a thirteen-volume edition came out. In 1922, Frazer edited the twelve books down to one abridged edition. A revised abridged edition was released thirty-seven years later, in 1959, long after his death.

Most of Frazer's other writings revolved around anthropological themes that were introduced in *The Golden Bough.* These include *The Scope of Social Anthropology* (1908); *The Worship of Nature* (1926); and *Myths of the Origin of Fire* (1930). In 1914 he was knighted in recognition of his work.

Frazer died in 1941 in Cambridge, where he taught. He is credited by many with being one of the most influential writers of the twentieth century.

Plot Summary

Chapters 1–2

The entire line of inquiry of *The Golden Bough* is developed from one particular ritualistic practice that Frazer describes in the book's early pages. In Italy, he explains, there is a wooded area on the shore of Lake Nemi, which is dedicated to the memory of the Roman goddess Diana. By tradition, each priest of Diana who guards the forest, known as the King of the Wood, gained his position by murdering the priest who held the position before him. Tradition held that the King of the Wood must be killed by an escaped slave who would beat the king to death with a golden bough taken from a tree that grew in the grove. Frazer was curious about several elements in this tradition. He wondered why the priest is referred to as a king, a practice he learned was fairly common. Next, he wondered about the probability that the priest would spend much time worrying about would-be assassins ready to take his position from him. Finally, Frazer wondered why the golden bough was so important to the ritual and why there was an assumption that the branch of gold would always be available. Frazer's search for more information generates a long inquiry into myths and beliefs of various cultures.

Chapters 3–15

For an extended section near the beginning of his inquiry, Frazer looks at concepts associated with magic and how magic evolved into religion. He shows how kings were thought to have magical powers and how that idea translated throughout the ancient world into the idea of the king as a religious figure, sometimes equated with a god. At the same time, he also explores how trees, particularly oaks, came to hold special significance in agrarian societies.

Chapters 16–28

After establishing the connection between secular rulers and religion, Frazer looks at the ways in which this relationship endangered those important personages. He discusses taboos at length, drawing from a variety of cultures to establish that taboos occur both as primitive superstitions and as beliefs in modern, cultivated societies. Once he has described forbidden acts and how they fit into the established social order, Frazer brings in examples where the forbidden actions actually become part of the social code, focusing on the taboos that limited the actions of the king and/or priest. The discussion then leads to cultures that practice the killing of kings (so that their divine powers will not be left to wither with age) and the killing of sacred trees.

Chapters 29–49

Tying in myths that are related to the story of Diana, such as those involving Adonis, Attis, Osiris, and Demeter and Persephone, Frazer shows how various deities in world religions have been connected to the agricultural cycle of life and death. Each of these myths involves an important figure who is identified with the growth cycle, a figure who dies or is stolen away to the underworld but then is allowed to return to the earth for limited stretches of time, illustrating the idea that the deaths of gods are not catastrophic, but instead are considered to be part of the process of nature.

Chapters 50–61

Frazer explores a variety of methods of sacrifice throughout time and in different lands, including ritual killing of sacred animals in order to honor gods and killing animals as a way of symbolically killing evil. This discussion presents the concept of the scapegoat, which was originally an actual goat meant to represent evil but later came to be a human being who represented evil and was killed for the same purpose. Frazer draws connections between the idea of murdering kings in order to retain their divine power while it is still at its peak and the idea of killing people who can then take evil to the grave with them, and he speculates that the two practices became joined as one.

Chapters 62–67

In theorizing about why the golden bough is so important to the tradition of succession of the King of the Wood, Frazer connects gold, the sun, fire, and power. Trees that had been hit by lightning were, for example, often seen as especially significant because they were thought to have even more fire in them than ordinary trees that were burned for fuel. Frazer speculates that the golden bough may be an ancient name for mistletoe, which grows as a vine on oak trees, turns yellow or golden while the rest of the tree remains green, and is thought in several cultures to have mystical properties. Connecting the magical power of the kings with the magical powers ascribed to mistletoe, Frazer identifies the belief that the soul of a person could be put into some object for safekeeping and the belief that important persons could only be killed by something that was already a part of them: thus, if the power of the King of the Wood was already in the mistletoe, it would make sense that the bough would be the only thing needed to kill him.

Chapters 68–69

In the last two chapters, Frazer returns to the question of why the priest of Diana must be killed and why by the particular prescribed method. One conclusion to be reached from this inquiry, he says, is that the process of civilization leads from a primitive belief in magic to a more orderly belief in religion to, ultimately, a belief in science. Though confident that this is the natural progression for any society, he reminds readers that science is not necessarily the end of human growth and that there may be other systems of belief that will supplant it in the future.

Key Figures

Adonis

In addition to his story being a fixture of the Greek tradition, the legend of the Greek god Adonis, also known as Tammuz, has roots stretching back to Babylonia and Syria. As both Tammuz in Babylonia and Adonis in Greece, he was a god of vegetation and was seen as the embodiment of masculine beauty. He was loved by Aphrodite, the goddess of beauty, who hid him in a gold chest, which she gave to Persephone, the queen of the underworld, for safekeeping. When Persephone peeked in the chest and saw Adonis, she was captivated with his beauty and refused to give him back to Aphrodite. Zeus settled the dispute by giving him to each goddess for part of the year. The change of seasons was explained in connection to the place where Adonis was during each part of the year, since Aphrodite, lamenting when he was gone, refused to help plants or animals grow, marking winter in climates where it did not snow.

Aeneas

Aeneas is a central figure of Roman mythology. He is the title character of Virgil's masterpiece *The Aeneid,* which recounts his seven years of travels after the Greeks' siege of Troy. His journey ended when he landed in Italy and founded Rome. According to legend, Aeneas, before going to the underworld, was told that he must take with him a golden bough from an evergreen oak tree that grew in the grove of Diana, to give as a gift to the Queen of the Underworld.

Artemis
See Diana

Attis

Like Adonis, Attis was a god of vegetation, worshipped in Phrygia. He was a shepherd, famed for his good looks and beloved by Cybele, the goddess of fertility. His death is explained in different ways in different versions of his story, and he is said to have been turned into a pine tree, linking him to the tree mythology that drives the story of *The Golden Bough*. In a similar way to the story of Demeter and Persephone, Attis' death caused Cybele to grieve so much that the earth was thrown into a famine, and it is for this reason that annual rituals were performed in the fall to mourn the loss of Attis and in the spring to celebrate his return from the underworld.

Balder

In Scandinavian mythology, Balder the Beautiful could be harmed by nothing on heaven or earth except a bough of mistletoe. Frazer supposes that Balder was a personification of the mistletoe that grows on the oak tree, which was worshipped as sacred by the Scandinavians. This mistletoe is considered to be a possible source for the idea of the golden tree bough referred to in the book's title, thereby connecting the ancient Roman ritual practiced in Italy with the religious practices that developed in the countries of northern Europe.

Demeter

Demeter is the Greek goddess of the harvest. The story of Demeter and her daughter Persephone, one of the oldest Greek myths, has parallels in many ancient cultures. According to the myth, when Persephone was carried off by the lord of the underworld, Demeter refused to help the harvest, causing famine across the Earth. Zeus, the king of the gods, returned Persephone to her but ruled that she could only spend two-thirds of the year with Demeter and had to return to Hades for four months of the year. For the four months annually that she is gone, Demeter is said to mourn, accounting for the lack of vegetation in the wintertime. Frazer's analysis of the story centers on the poem *Hymn to Demeter,* by Homer. Elements of her story are found throughout the world, traced through the ''corn-mother'' goddess worshipped by Cretans during the Stone Age and similar stories about characters identified as corn spirits.

Diana

One of the most important figures in classical mythology, Diana is the Roman goddess of the hunt and of childbirth, associated with the Greek goddess Artemis. Her association with childbirth and fertility, as well as with hunting, led to the belief that she was also the goddess of wood, and in particular of oak, which is specified in the rituals that Frazer examines in *The Golden Bough*. The temple of Diana of the Wood, near the village of Nemi in Italy, is guarded by a priest who has earned his position by killing the previous priest, a ritual on which Frazer builds the book.

Dionysus

Dionysus is the god associated with the grape and, by extension, with wine and drunkenness. A religion was formed around the worship of him, celebrating the irrational over the rational, countering the focus on reason that characterized Greek culture. He is related to the book's focal story about the golden bough because, in addition to being god of grapes, he is considered god of all trees. Moreover, the practice of sacrificing goats in ceremonies to honor Dionysus resembles the ritual sacrifice of the King of the Forest in the golden bough tradition.

Egeria

Egeria is a water-nymph who is important in the sacred grove at Nemi because, like Diana, she can give ease to women in childbirth. Sometimes Egeria is considered to be another form of Diana.

Hippolytus
See Virbius

Isis

Sister and wife of Osiris in Egyptian mythology, Isis was given dozens of different personalities throughout the years. Frazer speculates that one of her original functions in mythology was that she was thought to be the goddess of corn and barley, having discovered them and given them to mankind. Over time, her image changed from that of the plain corn-mother (a function shared by the Roman goddess Diana) to a glamorous beauty, and as this transformation occurred she grew to be the most popular of all Egyptian deities.

King of the Wood

The King of the Wood is the traditional priest of the Arician grove. Frazer recounts how this position has been handed down, generation after generation, since antiquity. The book's title, *The Golden Bough*, refers to the tradition that states that the King of the Woods must be killed by an escaped slave, hit with a golden bough from a tree that grows there. The person who kills him then becomes the new King of the Wood. He is thought to represent a worldly husband to the goddess Diana. Throughout the course of the book, Frazer speculates about various theories explaining how the king's ritual murder came to be custom. The history of the position, as well as similar rituals in other cultures, is explored. Using this particularly significant ritual, Frazer examines the implications of hundreds of beliefs and their evolution over the centuries.

Numa

Numa was a wise king who was a husband or lover of Egeria. Since the legend of Egeria is closely associated with that of Diana, Frazer speculates that Numa has a place in the cult at Nemi that serves as a basis of the book. Numa is often thought to be another form of the King of the Wood.

Osiris

Osiris is an ancient Egyptian god whose death and resurrection were celebrated each year. Osiris was the most popular of Egyptian deities, and he was worshipped for centuries. As an Egyptian king, he is credited with having taught the Egyptians how to cultivate fruit from trees, while Isis, who was both his sister and his wife, taught the people how to plant and harvest grains. Osiris traveled the world, teaching people of foreign lands how to grow crops. When he returned to Egypt, though, he was ambushed by a cadre of forty-seven conspirators, led by one of his own brothers; they tricked him into a box and, sealing the lid, sent it floating off down the Nile. Isis found his body downstream and buried it, but Osiris lived on as the lord of the underworld.

Orestes

A very famous figure in Greek mythology, Orestes is thought, according to one legend, to have started the cult of Diana of the Woods. After killing the King of the Tauric Chersonese, Orestes is said to have fled to Nemi, the place where the golden bough ritual is followed, thereby introducing Diana to that part of Italy.

Persephone

Greek myth explains how Persephone, the daughter of Demeter, was playing in a field one day and was carried off by the Lord of the Underworld,

Pluto. When Demeter's grief threatened to destroy the world with famine, Zeus arranged for Persephone to return to the surface world for two-thirds of the year, but for the last third she always had to be Pluto's bride again in Hades. She also figures into the story of Adonis, with whom she fell in love and whom she tried to keep in the underworld with her, although Zeus allowed him to return to the earth's surface for several months each year to be with Aphrodite, who loved him first.

Tammuz

See Adonis

Virbius

Bearing the Roman name for the Greek hero Hippolytus, Virbius was Diana's lover and showed no interest in other women. When the goddess Aphrodite tried to take Virbius for herself he spurned her advances, and in her humiliation she persuaded his father to kill him, but Diana brought him back to life and hid him at Nemi. Among the rituals that make up the focus of *The Golden Bough*, Frazer includes the ban on horses at Nemi, which is thought to have started in recognition of the fact that Virbius was said to have been killed by being dragged behind horses. He is considered to be the founder of the sacred grove and the first king of Nemi.

Themes

Search for Knowledge

The central subject of this book, and the source of its title, is the ritual replacement of the priest of Diana at Aricia through murder. Frazer was so curious about this myth that he examined it with meticulous attention to detail. Hundreds of pages filled with thousands of examples from cultures throughout history are devoted to exploring myth. *The Golden Bough* contains sections that seem unrelated to Diana and the King of the Wood. Readers who do not follow the book from its beginning might wonder, for example, how it could possibly lead from Roman mythology to eighteenth-century Irish Christmas rituals or the custom of people of New Hebrides who throw their food leftovers into the sea.

Despite its strange and twisting side trips, though, this book returns to its main point often enough to assure readers that it is, in fact, about that one

Topics for Further Study

- Look for a behavior that is apparent in everyday life but that people seem to do for no other reason than tradition. Try to discover what that behavior might have developed from. Another way to go about this topic is to think about the mythical history of some object that did not exist when Frazer wrote, such as computers or cars.

- Make a chart or "family tree" of the mythical figures who are mentioned in *The Golden Bough*, showing their relationship to one another.

- George Lucas has said that he based much of his *Star Wars* film saga on mythological motifs. Research which mythic stories Lucas had in mind, and find where they fit into the argument Frazer presents in *The Golden Bough*.

- Choose one of the myths mentioned in the book and make your own picture of it, the way that Turner depicted the scene at the lake of Nemi.

---

specific myth. In addressing the question with such a tidal wave of information about a variety of cultures, Frazer illustrates something about knowledge and how it is acquired. The message that is embedded in his method is that knowledge is not simple or isolated but is instead only relevant when it is connected to related facts, which are themselves related to other facts.

Search for Self

In the course of discussing one academic question that leads him to a myriad of exotic, ancient cultural traditions, Frazer ends up showing how remote practices relate to modern times. With books about psychology or contemporary life, it is easy for readers to connect to their own lives, but *The Golden Bough* is burdened with the added responsibility of subject material that its author considers important precisely because it does not seem to directly affect his life or the lives of his readers. From the very beginning of the book, he does nothing to tell readers why they should care, leaving it to their own intelligence to deduce what the practices of dead civilizations have to do with the state of humanity today. Still, the personal relevance of everything in the book is hard to miss. The cold approach that Frazer takes toward the many cultures that he mentions in this book might be seen as a way for readers to distance themselves from his subjects, but then again, it is more likely to make readers see their own lives from the outside, through the objective eyes of the scientist.

The taboos of other cultures are different, but similar in structure, to modern cultural standards. The values of hunters and farmers, so strongly based in the cycles of the moon and the seasons, regulate modern life, from the holidays of the Judeo-Christian tradition (which coincide with pagan calendars) to the nine-month schedule of the U.S. school year. The tradition of sacrificing powerful priests and kings tells readers much about the otherwise contradictory ways celebrities are treated. In all of the traditions that Frazer has included in *The Golden Bough*, there is a common thread. He emphasizes this commonality by drawing his examples from as wide a pool as possible, in order to show that his ideas are not limited to just a few societies that happen to be similar. Frazer presents enough examples to make a convincing argument that what he says applies to the basic human situation.

Style

Archetype

An archetype is a model or type in literature that is considered to be universal, occurring in all cultures at all places and times. The story of the King of the Wood that Frazer focuses on in *The Golden Bough* has details that are specific to its context that do not appear in other circumstances, and so it cannot be considered archetypal. However, in trying to trace the source of this unique myth, Frazer finds that it derives from many other archetypes that gather together. Some examples of these are the stories of gods who bring on winter by descending to hell for several months a year; corn mother myths; ritual murder of scapegoats; and the reverence for the oak tree in societies where it grows. These archetypes are familiar, in some form, to all cultures. Some twentieth-century psychologists have speculated that archetypes are embedded in the genetic code of humans.

Folklore

The word "folklore" refers to the beliefs and traditions of groups of people. Usually, these cultural aspects are not formally recorded by the culture itself, which might be unaware of them; they are more likely to be recorded by an outside anthropologist. At the time that Frazer started to work on *The Golden Bough*, interest in the beliefs of the common people of a given culture was just starting to gain recognition: the word "folklore" was coined in 1846, just a few decades before Frazer's first edition.

Objectivity

One of the most notable aspects of Frazer's style is the dry, scientific tone of his writing. He never conveys an opinion or any feeling about the stories he relates. Given the volume of information that he presents, this objectivity can make it difficult for readers to absorb what he has to say: because the work shows no variance nor any emotional involvement of any kind, readers are left to determine the importance of each piece of information for themselves. Even though this characteristic makes the book less interesting to read, Frazer's objective tone is necessary. This book's main purpose is to be educational, not entertaining, and the objective tone assures that he is taking a properly neutral stance toward what he is reporting.

Historical Context

Frazer published the first edition of *The Golden Bough* in 1890, just eight years after the death of Charles Darwin. Darwin, a British naturalist, considered to be one of the greatest scientists of the nineteenth century, developed a theory of evolution, which he outlined in his 1859 book *On the Origins of Species.* This work popularized the phrase "survival of the fittest." According to Darwinian evolution, the species that were best fitted to their environments were the ones that were bound to survive, while the ones that were not well adapted tended to die off and become extinct. Within a species, genetic adaptations were achieved when those organisms that had the traits that were most important for their survival, such as speed or strength, were the ones that lived long enough to reproduce with other survivors, and the offspring of such unions inherited

advantageous traits, making each generation more likely to mature and reproduce than the previous one.

Darwin also argued that all organisms were descended from one single source and that they changed as they adapted to different situations. This idea, developed further in 1871 in *The Descent of Man,* met with much stronger opposition than the idea of natural selection and is contested to this day by some religious fundamentalists. Still, even his detractors would be forced to admit that Darwin was one of the most influential scientists of his day.

In *The Golden Bough*, readers can get a feel for the enthusiasm that Darwin's theories inspired in scientists of the late nineteenth century. Frazer's explanation of how cultures inevitably develop from primitive belief in magic to more complex belief in religion and then, finally, to a reliance on science shows an unwavering faith in the idea that, over time, entire systems of belief evolve from one form to another. It is a supposition, like Darwin's evolutionary scale, that would have seemed impossible to an earlier generation. By the end of the nineteenth century, however, sciences had shifted their focus from examining isolated events to studying events in respect to their relationship to similar events. Like Darwin, who had studied the different adaptations in similar species that had evolved in different climates, Frazer speculated about the ways that different story motifs appeared in altered but recognizable form in different cultures.

Frazer's belief in society's inevitable growth toward faith in science—which, today, is the theory of his that is most often rejected—can be seen mirrored in the works of the most well-known economic writer of his time, Karl Marx. In his 1848 tract *The Communist Manifesto,* Marx proposed that all world governments would pass through specific, predetermined periods of growth before ending up with Communist political structures. Like Frazer, Marx believed that there was just one logical outcome to the growth of society, and he believed that he could determine it scientifically.

While his theories about cultural progression were challenged from the very first publication of *The Golden Bough,* Frazer is still acknowledged as a highly influential anthropologist. His work generated a new interest in comparative anthropology, influencing a generation of late nineteenth-century psychologists, including Sigmund Freud (whose theories often alluded to stories from ancient myths)

Compare
&
Contrast

- **1890:** People in Europe and the United States know little about non-Western culture; they refer to Africa as ''The Dark Continent'' and Asia as ''The Mysterious Orient.''

    Today: Inexpensive travel and the Internet have made it possible for people all over the world to be aware of distant cultures.

- **1890:** Greek mythology is studied in almost all schools and is generally well-known.

    Today: More students know about the Greek gods from Disney movies than from studying them in class.

- **1890:** A scholar like Frazer can make an international reputation for his theories by making assumptions about the results of other anthropologists' work.

    Today: Leading scientists have research assistants who can assemble data under their supervision.

and Carl Jung (whose theory of the collective unconscious seems to explain Frazer's ideas of universal myths). *The Golden Bough* also influenced literature, particularly the work of James Joyce and T. S. Eliot. Within its own field of anthropology, however, Frazer's work has not been very influential, owing to the fact that he did not gather his information directly from the people about whom he wrote. All of his work is based on secondhand information rather than field work, and as a result the value of his writing is considered marginal.

Critical Overview

When it was first published, *The Golden Bough* was considered an insightful work that tied together the widely divergent canon of anthropology into one cohesive theory. The book was praised for its thoroughness and accepted as a major scientific accomplishment. A 1890 review in the *Journal of American Folklore,* for instance, proclaimed the anonymous reviewer ''grateful'' to Frazer ''for the exhibition of materials so rich, and for the literary skill with which he has made accessible observations so important to the central ideas of our modern thought.'' As time passed, however, questions arose about Frazer's methodology, which consisted of combining works that were gathered through non-scientific methods. His use of hearsay and third-person accounts of cultural practices made anthropologists doubt the value of his work as science.

Still the book's reputation as a work of literature grew. It was recognized as having influenced such important twentieth-century thinkers as Freud, Anatole France, Arnold Toynbee, Margaret Mead, and Oswald Spengler. In 1941, noted anthropologist Bronislaw Malinowski noted an inconsistency in Frazer's impact on the intellectual community when he stated that ''Frazer was and is one of the world's greatest teachers and masters'' but that, despite his enormous following, ''[h]is inability to convince seems to contradict his power to convert and to inspire.'' His point was that other writers followed Frazer for his vision and for the far-reaching thoroughness of his theories, even though they did not believe in the actual theories. By the second half of the century, critics found little sense in dwelling on shortcomings in *The Golden Bough* and instead accepted its impact. Stanley Edgar Hyman, for instance, wrote in 1962 that the book is ''not primarily anthropology, if it ever was, but a great imaginative vision of the human condition.'' He saw no problem with reading this book, which was meant to be a scientific work, as a work of literature, noting that the author was trained in literature and not in anthropology: ''It is in his original field of classical studies ... that Frazer may have produced his greatest effect.'' Since then, many critics have joined Hyman in accepting *The Golden Bough* as an important piece of literature, but not as an important scientific achievement.

Criticism

David Kelly

Kelly is an instructor of creative writing and literature at College of Lake County. In this essay, Kelly considers whether the reputation that Frazer's book has maintained since its first printing will carry on into the future.

There is every reason in the world to believe that Sir James Frazer's name will be remembered for many years, due to the resounding importance of his masterpiece, *The Golden Bough*. The book had a powerful impact when it was first published in 1890, reaching beyond the usual academic audience that reads such scholarly works and finding a place in the public consciousness. Between then and his death in 1941, Frazer kept the work in the public eye with subsequent additions and expansions. Since then, the book has never gone out of print.

On the other hand, it would be easy to believe that *The Golden Bough* has outlived its usefulness. Frazer's rich, airy, academic writing style, which once may have served to impress and attract non-academic readers, is now considered to be hard work for the average person. The book's vast, encyclopedic catalogue of cultural practices, gleaned from years and years of meticulous research, may have once been thought of as the best single source of facts on its subject, but now the Internet has made even more cultural information available in one location, much of it from primary sources. Modern readers, attracted to the ease of finding information and put off by Frazer's difficult, antiquated language, might bypass the experience of reading *The Golden Bough*, drawn instead to more accessible sources for the same ideas, so that in time the unthinkable might happen, and James Frazer, once considered among the most influential writers of the twentieth century, could drop from memory.

From the start, *The Golden Bough* was accepted as both a scientific and literary achievement. It was central in getting Frazer, who was trained in

> **Literary interpretation is not as concerned with whether the sources Frazer used are true as it is with how he explains the relationship between them. In that regard, no one can challenge his intellectual achievement.''**

classical literature, appointed a professorship for a year (in 1907) in social anthropology at Liverpool University. Such a casual crossing between the realms of science and art would be impossible today, when college education is more accessible. Today one could hardly be considered an expert in any field without at least having a degree in that area. At a time when demonstration of knowledge was more important than credentials, though, Frazer easily proved himself to be one of the most knowledgeable people in the world regarding social anthropology. Any reader of *The Golden Bough* can tell that Frazer weaves its fabric from such diverse strains of cultural practices because he is so entirely familiar and comfortable with such a wide variety of them. He has a point to make and thousands of examples to draw from in the course of making it.

It was his ability to weave a coherent tale that expanded Frazer's appeal beyond academics, making the book a success in the general population. There had been studies of folklore before, books and journals about obscure beliefs and practices. Studies of the myths of Greek and Roman mythologies had absorbed many academic careers. The greatest achievement of *The Golden Bough* was that it not only explained ideas from diverse areas of the globe but that it gave them meaning in relation to one another. The facts of, for example, a Scandinavian tradition, a Pakistani custom, and a pagan European ritual might be interesting to someone who has a background in such matters, who can put each piece of information into a context with others that one knows from experience. To an outsider, though, they are just unrelated facts. What Frazer did was, in effect, to make his readers feel like they are insiders. His narrative, starting with one fixed but somewhat arbitrary point, provides a context

What Do I Read Next?

- Joseph Campbell was arguably the most popular writer on myth in the late twentieth century. His most famous work is *The Power of Myth,* an overview of how mythology is relevant to contemporary life. The book was based on a six-part series that Campbell did for Public Television with Bill Moyers. It was published in 1991 by Anchor.

- Readers who are interested in Frazer's historical place as a student of myths can find out the state of the discipline before him in *The Rise of Modern Mythology, 1680–1860.* In this 1972 volume, authors Burton Feldman and Robert D. Richards give biographies of and samples from the great writers about myth, from Bernard Fontenelle (1657–1757) to Henry David Thoreau (1817–1862).

- In *Myth: Its Meaning and Function,* G. S. Kirk deals with weaknesses he found in works by Frazer and his followers: those of examining myths in relation to folktales and to rituals. This book was published by Cambridge University in 1970.

- *Schrödinger's Cat and "The Golden Bough"* (2000), by physicist Randy Bancroft, attempts to tie together science, magic, and mythology for the modern reader. It was published by University Press of America.

that all can absorb, which gave all his readers the chance to participate as if they are part of the panel of archeological experts.

One of the most important things that *The Golden Bough* illustrates is an attitude to take when comparing cultures. In its broad scope, the book recognized the diversity of cultural ideas. Reading it line by line, though, readers gain a sense of the sameness of all of cultural beliefs. Frazer provides a smooth ride through ages and across the globe, softened by his measured, objective tone. The book's authorial voice speaks with such firm confidence that it is difficult to disagree. Even in the 1800s, most of his readers would not have seen Joseph Mallord Turner's 1834 painting, which hung in London's National Gallery, but Frazer managed to draw them in, not alienate them, just as he has drawn in generations with his opening question, "Who does not know Turner's picture of the Golden Bough?" The discourse that follows the question could be considered a triumph of rhetoric, as he manages to hold the whole story of humanity together with sheer verbal dexterity. Now and then he brings the discussion back into focus with phrases such as "With these explanations and cautions I will now adduce some examples of gods" to remind readers of how one diversion or another fits into the larger picture. The persuasive power of using such a cultivated voice to address matters considered "primitive," such as magic and pagan religions, should not be underestimated either, as readers for more than a century have felt secure that *The Golden Bough*'s narrative would lead to the satisfactory conclusion that there is indeed order in the development of belief systems.

And, in fact, the book went on to become one of the most influential books of the twentieth century. T. S. Eliot acknowledged the influence of *The Golden Bough* on his 1922 poem *The Waste Land,* which is generally considered to be one of the most significant texts of the modernist movement. D. H. Lawrence is said to have studied the book's accounts of Aztec sacrifices when he was working on *Women in Love.* Joseph Conrad's Kurtz, who rules a remote jungle tribe in *Heart of Darkness* with a magical sort of charisma, shows the influence, if not directly of Frazer, then of someone who is familiar with his work. The poet Robert Graves was a follower. And, of course, all of the writers whom these writers influenced can be said to owe something to Frazer, whether they have read his work or not.

But with each generation, fewer and fewer read the book. The decline started within Frazer's lifetime, as questions were raised about his methods. When the book first came out during the Victorian era, it was an impressive enough feat for a writer to gather a broad sampling of information and string it together. The early twentieth century was an age of specialization, though. Industries, most notably automobile manufacturers, developed the system of division of labor that had each worker on the assembly line concentrate on one small aspect of the overall production. In the spirit of this division of labor, the scientific method of collecting information was brought under tighter scrutiny. Just as support for Sigmund Freud's far-reaching conclusions was dampened by his personal relationships with his patients, so Frazer's work came to be viewed with skepticism because of his way of gathering information. His research was done in the library, not the field: many of the customs he reported were not observed firsthand but were instead retellings of stories reported from travelers. The possibilities of error in this method are obvious and have been often reported. Because his findings were not based on observations from anthropologists trained to understand what they were seeing, scientific interest in his writing declined.

Still, it is as a work of literature that *The Golden Bough* has come to readers today. As such, it has been free of the strict rules of scientific data gathering. Literary interpretation is not as concerned with whether the sources Frazer used are true as it is with how he explains the relationship between them. In that regard, no one can challenge his intellectual achievement. The trouble is that, as a piece of literature, the book can be exceedingly boring.

There is no rule that says that good literature should not be boring, and the idea of boredom is entirely relative: usually, the things that fascinate people in adulthood are the things that most bored them when they were children. Still, there is also a good chance that a work written for an earlier age can lose interest for all but the most narrowly specialized. What *The Golden Bough* accomplished, in terms of information, worldview, and style, was what the world needed then. But with the information either discredited or available elsewhere more easily and his unified worldview so prevalent that it is taken for granted, all the modern reader is left with is an antiquated Victorian prose style. The book will always have its fans because every field has its fans of esoterica, but in all likelihood future readers of *The Golden Bough* will pride themselves

for having absorbed Frazer's story in the same way that collectors of such things take pride in the ownership of a rare old book.

Source: David Kelly, Critical Essay on *The Golden Bough,* in *Nonfiction Classics for Students,* Gale, 2003.

Bernard McKenna

In the following essay, McKenna shows how Frazer's assumed cultural superiority over and distance from his subjects in The Golden Bough *distinguish the work from a literary standpoint.*

Literary critics have traced the influence of Sir James Frazer's *The Golden Bough* through the works of authors as diverse as Scott Fitzgerald and Sigmund Freud. Almost no modern writer has escaped the scrutiny of comparison. However, only a few scholars have subjected *The Golden Bough* to the scrutiny of critical evaluation, and their studies are mostly responses to the "hostile scrutiny" of anthropologists and classical scholars who find fault with *The Golden Bough*'s theoretical framework and methodology. Their objections are twofold: On one level they find fault with Frazer's lack of field experience—he gathers his information only from secondary sources; on another level they object to Frazer's interpretation of this information— he can find no value for the myths and customs within their society. Yet, despite its failings as an anthropological text, *The Golden Bough* has considerable value precisely because of its sense of assumed superiority and consequent isolation, and no critic has adequately examined its structure based on these principles.

After reviewing the intricacies of Frazer's argument it becomes clear that he is schooled in the vocabulary of dominance and cannot escape its instruction. This does not simply mean his education at the University of Glasgow and Trinity College, Cambridge. It means that he approached his analysis from a position of superiority and refused to yield equality or even legitimacy to the objects of his study. The method of his examination can be discerned as a three-part process. First, there is an attempted contact. Unfortunately, the contact is often attempted through a medium that belies intimacy—the second part of the process. The medium could simply be the mistaken notion that human relations can be achieved solely through intellectual means, but it is more likely that some quality of his analysis made contact impossible. The result is limited communication—the method's final stage. This process manifests itself on many

> **The language implies a crude and simple culture populated by ignorant and brutal people whose form of worship is nothing more than a wasteland because it lacks a Christian framework. By today's standards Frazer's methodology for examining the subjects of his analysis seems absurd. . . ."**

levels of *The Golden Bough* beginning with Frazer's chosen sources, continuing through his method of examining those sources, and proceeding through the results of his analysis—the discovery of lost traditions harboring secret associations, the origins of the Nemi ritual, a cycle of death and regeneration modelled on the seasons, and a hierarchy of religious and societal progress.

On its most basic level, Frazer's analysis requires an association with the wider world; in order to report various traditions he must become intimate with a diversity of cultures. He seeks to prove that certain "motives have operated widely, perhaps universally, in human society, producing in varied circumstances a variety of institutions specifically different but generally alike." His study examines the ancient Greeks, Romans, and Egyptians; and various "barbarian" tribes—the Celts, Gauls, and Germanic people. In addition he bends his gaze towards corners of a world contemporary with his analysis—modern Europe, Africa, Asia, the Levant, the Americas, and Australia. The scope of his analysis succeeds in incorporating a diversity of cultures representing a global society throughout time.

Yet Frazer chooses incorporation through the distorted glass of imperialist perspective. His sources read like a canon of empire and dominance ranging from Julius Caesar to the Spanish Conquerors to the travellers and military expeditions contemporary with his study. His is the view of "Lieutenant Gamble" and "Colonel Dodge," "Captain Moseby" and "Captain Bourke." The survey begins and ends with the "Afghan Boundary Mission"; a "Jesuit" or other "Christian missionary"; and "the United States Polar Expedition"—all of whom saw non-Western peoples and lands as threatening, pagan, and hostile. The result is association simultaneous with disassociation.

He is able to see the alien society, able to gain some understanding of its practices, yet the understanding is distorted and facile. Quaint histories result with reports of "a sect in Orissa who worship the Queen of England as their chief divinity." Then there is

> a sect in the Punjab [who] worshipped a deity whom they called Nikkal Sen. This Nikkal Sen was no other than the redoubted General Nicholson, and nothing that the general could do or say damped the enthusiasm of his adorers. The more he punished them, the greater grew the religious awe with which they worshipped him.

Frazer and Nicholson present themselves as superior and stand amazed and contemptuous when their superiority mirrors itself in the behavior of the observed. There is affiliation—the contact of the adored or of the scientist hovering above his subjects—but the observer is distant and apart. He separates himself from the objects of his study and reports a people who are less than human, or at least less than English.

The canon of the uncivilized reads like a litany of Britain's late Victorian prejudices—prejudices that Frazer does not hesitate to carry through when he interprets his sources. It includes not only the obvious "barbarous" races—the "bush negroes of Surinam," the "heathen Syrians," the Jews, and the Catholic Irish. It also includes "the semi-barbarous nations of the New World" in addition to French, Swedish, and Austrian peasants. In short, anyone outside the British aristocratic and merchant classes is seen as a quaint storehouse of antiquated beliefs and traditions. It is the world of Kipling—characters from *Kim* and *The Jungle Book* who hold the secrets of the dark natural world, and it is the theater of Boucicault—the blacks of *Jessie Brown* or the stage Irishman happy in his drunken ignorance.

Frazer's vocabulary of association betrays the same type of prejudices and implies a systematic, if half-conscious, demeaning of non-English cultures. Images of "rude peoples all over the world" are paraded before a reader. We are shown examples of "primitive superstition and religion" taken from the "Old Heathen days." We see the representatives of the "savage hordes," and the "unfortunate beings" who are still taken by the "quaint superstition" and the "antique fancies" of "savage philosophers'' that are nothing more than "cobwebs of the brain." The language implies a crude and simple culture populated by ignorant and brutal people whose form of worship is nothing more than a wasteland because it lacks a Christian framework. By today's standards Frazer's methodology for examining the subjects of his analysis seems absurd, but this tendency characterized cultural studies in the late nineteenth century.

It distorts the objects of Frazer's study just as his choice of sources does. However, Frazer is aware of the possible harm of such an approach. He warns that "in reviewing the opinions and practices of ruder ages and races we shall do well to give them the benefit of that indulgence which we may one day stand in need of ourselves." Frazer begs indulgence for an inferiority he has conjured from the Victorian framework of analysis. He calls ceremonies rude if "no special class of persons is set aside for the performance of the rites," if "no special places are set apart" for the rituals, if "spirits not gods are recognized," and if "the rites are magical rather than propitiatory." It seems that difference implies inferiority and that these practices are only valued for their influence on civilized religion and have no import in and of themselves.

Yet there seems to be another value, produced as a consequence of the distortions and prejudices, only implicit in Frazer's analysis—the value of lost traditions harboring secret associations. He seems to relish "the days when Diana and Virbius still received the homage of their worshippers in the sacred grove." Even though "the temple of Diana . . . has disappeared, and the King of the Wood no longer stands sentinel over the Golden Bough," Frazer muses that "Nemi's woods are still green, and at evening you may hear the church bells of Albano, and perhaps, if the air be still, of Rome itself, ringing the Angelus." The old gods are still summoned, and Frazer's work is a type of summoning—an effort to conjure the sublime. It is as if the primitive and savage races can tap into a hidden power of the world, as if they can find a communion with nature that is beyond Frazer's grasp. He is like William Sharp who needed to conjure Fiona Macleod to contact the natural world, but, for both men, the posturings of assumed superiority distort the contact.

There is a sense of loss in Sharp and in Frazer, a sense of disconnectedness. Each wants to "partake of the new corn sacramentally" but can only do so through what they see as an inferior—a woman or a savage people. *Le roi est mort,* but there is no new king. There are only the delusions of the heathen—the "primitive man" who "fancies he can make the sun to shine, and can hasten or stay its going down," or "the savage" who "commonly explains the processes of inanimate nature by supposing that they are produced by living beings working in or behind the phenomena." The world is alive, is animate, for the uncivilized—for "the prettiest girl" in "the south-east of Ireland [who] on May Day . . . used to be chosen Queen of the district for twelve months. She was crowned with wild flowers; feasting, dancing, and rustic sports followed, and were closed by a grand procession in the evening." However, for Frazer, a world of emptiness and isolation dominates.

In 1909 he would write, in the preface to a volume of biblical passages selected for their literary interest, that

> though many of us can no longer, like our fathers, find in its pages the solution of the dark, the inscrutable riddle of human existence, yet the volume must be held sacred by all who reverence the high aspirations to which it gives utterance, and the pathetic associations with which the faith and piety of so many have invested the familiar words.

The words are seen as fragments of a lost tradition, of a lost contact. Frazer cannot see that it is his distortions, his assumed superiority, that has caused the separation and the consequent isolation.

There are other possible reasons for the sense of disconnectedness in his work. Among them is Frazer's method of examining his information. All of it is, somehow, made to support some aspect of the Nemi tradition. A world of customs and practices is laid out before him. His survey begins with "The King of the Wood." This does not necessarily mean the king of the Arician woods; any king or queen will do. Specifically, he mentions Diana and others. They have the attributes of a tree spirit or sylvan deity—they can control the weather or the state of wildlife and vegetation. Frazer then goes on to show that there is a sympathetic connection between the king and his kingdom. The ruler is subject to restrictions to help preserve it. If he should hurt himself the kingdom would suffer. Therefore, people would often subject their ruler to occasional trials, tests of wit and strength. If the king failed, his soul and the soul of the forest would be transferred to a successor; the king's soul would often be kept in some object for safekeeping until the trial was over. Numerous examples are cited, including Osiris and Dionysus. Their deaths and regenerations are supposed to be modelled on the pattern of the seasons. After superficial consideration, his study seems to develop fascinating relationships between a diversity of cultures.

However, each of these points simply develops a part of Frazer's Nemi thesis; they have limited value independently. Diana and the sylvan deities are mentioned because Aricia is a wooded area, and the King of the Wood is a manifestation of the tree spirit. The sympathetic connection between the king and his kingdom is important to the Nemi tradition because its king must survive occasional trials by combat to ensure his health and the consequent health of the woods. The notion of the external soul supports Nemi because the golden bough itself is the mistletoe where the king's soul is kept. These are the primary relationships between the plethora of cultural practices. All other connections are incidental to the Nemi tradition.

Consequently, on one level Frazer's study is simply a collection of fragments designed to serve Nemi. Certainly *The Golden Bough* represents much more than that; therein lies the danger of his approach. The various customs and individuals are dispossessed from their culture. Their relationship and unity must rely on the validity of Frazer's thesis because they cannot rely on the validity supplied by their respective societies. Obviously, a tradition cannot stand on its own merits if examined out of context. In subsequent editions of *The Golden Bough* Frazer downplays the role of Nemi and discredits his thesis, but his analysis retains the same structure. It continues to serve Nemi even after Nemi is removed. A collection of lost fragments remains to serve an invalid hypothesis.

The major component of this lost service is the cycle of death and rebirth modelled on the seasons:

> The annual death and revival of vegetation is a conception which readily presents itself to men in every stage of savagery and civilization; and the vastness of the scale on which this yearly decay and regeneration takes place, together with man's intimate dependence on it for subsistence, combine to render it the most striking annual phenomenon in nature, at least within the temperate zones. It is no wonder that a phenomenon so important, so striking, and so universal should, by suggesting similar ideas, have given rise to similar rites in many lands.

This motif rises again and again throughout Frazer's study. It appears in the Arician grove; in the persons of Attis, Adonis, and Osiris; in the corn spirit; and in the folk-tales and folk-customs of Europe.

However, Frazer destroys this continuity by classifying and ranking the various traditions. He feels that "the spring and harvest customs of our European peasantry deserve to rank as primitive," that "the writings even of these town-bred and cultured persons afford us an occasional glimpse of a Demeter as rude as the rudest that a remote German village can show," and that "the Indians of California, who, living in a fertile country under a serene and temperate sky, nevertheless rank near the bottom of the savage scale." Just as J. A. Cramb and the members of James Hunt's Anthropological Society distorted Darwin to create a human hierarchy, Frazer distorts an evolution in beliefs—a simple alteration of customs in response to environmental stimuli—to create an image of progress.

This classification results in Frazer's isolation. He stands on top of an evolutionary pyramid. Below him is the history of the world. Above him is an abyss of future uncertainty. Around him is the British Empire spread out in its imperial assurance. Specifically, Frazer outlines the progress from magic to religion to science. He sees magic "as the hope of directing the course of nature by his [mankind's] own unaided resources." Religion occurs when man "looks more and more to the gods as the sole repositories of those supernatural powers which he once claimed to share with them ... Therefore, prayer and sacrifice assume the leading place in religious ritual." "Still later, the conception of the elemental forces as personal agents" gives way "to the recognition of natural law." The former unity of worship of the death and regeneration of the seasons has given way to the rigidity of superiority.

Like a young Rajah, Frazer travels through the capitals of the world's major religious movements—the tribal villages of Africa, the primeval forests of Europe, the pastoral landscapes of ancient Egypt, the temples of classical Greece and Rome—classifying and organizing them into his complex framework and analysis. Darkest Africa and the Australian outback continue to function on the level of magic. Societies involved in totemism, like the Indians of the Americas, do have a "religion," but it is the most primitive type because it entails worshiping trees or wild animals. Communities that worship cattle or other domesticated creatures have "graduated" to a pastoral religion. The highest form of primitive worship is practiced by the agricultural societies, but even this final stage has two parts. On one level gods are seen as imminent spirits residing in cultivated plants, especially corn. On the second level, the Deists, spirits are transcendent like the gods of Greece and Rome. Christianity comes next. It retains some barbarous elements—the transubstantiation of the Catholic Mass, the sacrifice of the son of God—but is, for the most part, civilized. All these movements culminate in science and scientific reasoning. Frazer assembles and disseminates the world, tracing the origins of cultured society.

However, like the Germany of Carlyle's *Sartor Resartus,* Frazer keeps the world a "country of the mind." With rare exception he relies on the work and the stories of various scholars and colonial representatives. As he recognizes the danger of judging "rude and savage races," Frazer acknowledges the danger of not considering living testimony. He writes that "compared with the evidence afforded by living tradition, the testimony of ancient books on the subject of early religion is worth very little." However, just as his judgments on prejudice fail to permeate the depths of his analysis, Frazer's observations fail to escape "the course of" his "reading." He takes the field work of Mannhardt and Tyler, or Wilken and Gregor, and shapes it to his specifications for the history of religion and worship.

Consequently, his vast storehouse of information contains fragments of traditions that tend to support late Victorian conventions. Frazer assembles his catalogue of religious practices in such a way as to position the scientific and cultural achievements of the late nineteenth century as a point toward which all converges. Certainly, such notions of superiority are not limited to Frazer. In 1866 Luke Owen Pike posited the English at the top of an evolutionary hierarchy in *The English and Their Origin.* In 1870 Sir John Lubbock, in a book titled *The Origin of Civilization,* traced a progressive evolution similar to Frazer's. Victorian scientists and scholars accepted as fact the belief that man evolved from savagery to barbarism to civilization. Consequently, Frazer and his colleagues stand in self-imposed exile, isolated by the burdens of assumed superiority.

Obviously, both the method and the object of Frazer's inquiries find many models in the world he knew. The longing for a communion with a wider world, a world animate and alive, consumes vast portions of late Victorian society. Oscar Wilde asks to be taken from darkness—

> Come down, O Christ, and help me! reach thy hand,
> For I am drowning in a stormier sea
> Than Simon on thy lake of Galilee.

Gerard Manley Hopkins asks his God to notice

> banks and brakes
> Now, leaved how thick! laced they are again
> With fretty chervil, look, and fresh wind shakes
> Them; birds build—but not I build; no, but strain,
> Time's eunuch, and not breed one work that wakes.
> Mine, O thou lord of life, send my roots rain.

In addition, the rise of psychical research and a fascination with the occult are widespread, taking in both the uneducated and the highly educated. People are looking for lost gods, lost meanings, lost contacts. In a passage reminiscent of Frazer, Yeats writes that he

> planned a mystical Order which should buy or hire the castle, and keep it as a place where its members could retire for a while for contemplation, and where we might establish mysteries like those of Eleusis and Samo-thrace . . . I did not think this philosophy would be altogether pagan, for it was plain that its symbols must be selected from all those things that had moved men most during many, mainly Christian, centuries.

In many ways *The Golden Bough* is an altar prepared for the sacrifice waiting for its priest, and Frazer's worldwide inquiries are a searching or a summoning. However, as with Tristan, the cry comes back, *"oed' und leer das Meer."*

The origins of the lost connections lie deep in the Victorian consciousness. They can be discerned by examining the elements that keep Frazer at a distance from the objects of his inquiries—the assurance of empire, the certain superiority, the systematic demeaning of other cultures, and the manipulation of countless societies and traditions. There are Darwin and the industrial revolution making the old gods obsolete; there are Nicholson and Cardigan leading countless to a death for Queen and country, and for a peerage; and there is the Earl of Lucan insisting that "the population must be reduced" as skeletons and typhus grow in Ireland. Contact exists, but it is the contact of the master and the lash.

As a consequence, emptiness remains. As in Eliot's wasteland, there is talking but no communication. There is "A heap of broken images, where the sun beats, / And the dead trees give no shelter, the cricket no relief, / And the dry stone no sound of water." Only F. Scott Fitzgerald's "valley of ashes" is left—

> a fantastic farm where ashes grow like wheat into ridges and hills and grotesque gardens; where ashes take the forms of houses and chimneys and rising smoke and, finally, with a transcendent effort, of ash-gray men who move dimly and already crumbling through the powdery air.

The wastelands of the twenties were bred in the Arden and the Somme, but their tragedy was simply the final scene in the final act of the play of empire.

Source: Bernard McKenna, ''Isolation and the Sense of Assumed Superiority in Sir James Frazer's *The Golden Bough*,'' in *Nineteenth-Century Prose*, Vol. 19, No. 2, Summer 1992, pp. 49–59.

Marc Manganaro

In the following essay excerpt, Manganaro ''adopts current textual approaches to anthropology in an effort to understand the rhetorical power behind Frazer's masterwork.''

For well over half a century literary audiences have listened to modern artists and critics speak of Frazer's literariness and its salutary effects upon Modern art and criticism; Eliot found Frazer's literary ''vision'' and style an essential component of the emerging Modernist temperament, and by the early sixties Frye and Hyman brought to a culmination the literary usefulness of Frazer's graceful text for myth and ritual studies. Typical of interdisciplinary relations, however, was the lag between social scientific production and aesthetic appreciation and appropriation: Eliot's plaudits for Frazer in 1922 (in his Notes to *The Waste Land* as well as the famous review of Joyce's *Ulysses*) coincided with the publication of Bronislaw Malinowski's *Argonauts of the Western Pacific,* a model for the emerging functionalist monograph that would have little use for Frazer's self-confessed brand of literary social science. Malinowski's work, however, hardly constituted a radical break with a dominating Frazerian school; in fact, Frazer's method and ideas had been roundly attacked by leading anthropologists since the turn of the century. Leach's condemnation of Frazer in 1966, then, was anything but a novel statement in anthropological circles; in fact, the position required such a restatement only because a colleague had attempted a positive reappraisal of the author of *The Golden Bough.*

Though the sixties and seventies witnessed a thorough historical mapping of Frazer's literary influence (as seen primarily in studies by Stanley Edgar Hyman and John Vickery), the death of myth criticism in the 1960s signaled a waning of interest in Frazer on the part of literary theorists. Anthropological reality, it appeared, had finally arrested the literary world's fascination for *The Golden Bough.* However, Frazer's text, like the seasonal gods that populate it, will not stay in the ground. The defini-

tive critical biography of Frazer, by Robert Ackerman, has just appeared, a sure sign of increasing interest in Frazer studies. More broadly, recent theories arguing for the metaphorical nature of anthropological writing, made possible by literary criticism's questioning of the easy referentiality of language, encourage new readings of Frazer's already ''literary'' anthropological corpus.

This essay adopts current textual approaches to anthropology in an effort to understand the rhetorical power behind Frazer's masterwork. The anthropological authority operating in Frazer's text, I maintain, had significant repercussions in Modernist writing broadly conceived. That rhetorical authority, rooted in an alluring brand of literary comparativism, exerted a powerful influence upon the intricately linked poetics and politics of much Modernist writing. The analysis of *The Golden Bough*'s textual strategies, then, will not stop with Frazer's study, but will broaden to the ways in which its rhetorical tactics, and the ideologies underlying them, were duplicated in the texts of a major literary High Modernist—T. S. Eliot—and a prominent myth critic—Stanley Edgar Hyman.

The harshest anthropological attacks leveled at Frazer generally have centered on his reputation as the premier ''armchair anthropologist,'' the scholar who plundered the various travelers' reports that made their way into his study in order to draw gross evolutionary comparisons between the present-day ''savage'' and our Western ancestors. For anthropologists after Malinowski it was precisely the gap between Frazer the theorist and his ''man on the spot'' fieldworker that posed an insurmountable obstacle to ethnographic accuracy, to capturing the ''native'' in the pure state.

But as James Clifford and George Stocking have shown, modern ethnography closes this gap by creating the narrator-persona of the anthropologist fieldworker, a dominating figure whose ''field'' experience supposedly shapes the text. According to Clifford, the ''presence'' of the writer in the field creates in the reader a strong sense of the anthropologist-author's ''ethnographic authority,'' the rhetorical command that field-based anthropologists construct for themselves in the creation of ethnographic discourse. Primarily through the claim ''I was there'' (on the cultural ''spot''), the modern ethnographer becomes the voice of culture, effectively consolidating the power to represent cultures by shutting off other sources. Drawing his terms from Mikhail Bakhtin, Clifford describes how modern ethnographic discourse almost instantly becomes monologic, or single-voiced, since its single narrative point of view inevitably subsumes all "other" voices—most notably those of the native subjects. Clifford's description of the modern ethnographer's strategies emphasizes the Bakhtinian notion of the closing off of voices: "The tasks of textual transcription and translation along with the crucial dialogical role of interpreters and 'privileged informants' were relegated to a secondary, sometimes even despised, status."

Textualists of anthropology are attempting to shatter the illusion of post-Malinowskian ethnography as a transparent window to the anthropological subject, an illusion whose empowering metaphysics of presence has made orthodox the "realist" or representational fieldwork account known as the monograph. According to Clifford, the modern ethnographer's insistence on disregarding previous written accounts bolsters his authority by insisting upon a logocentric transformation of native "experience" into First Text: "The fieldworker, typically, starts from scratch, from a research *experience,* rather than from reading or transcribing. The field is not conceived of as already filled with texts."

The monographic denial of prior texts seems a deliberate reversal of what one could call the essential intertextuality of *The Golden Bough*, which is literally bursting with previous texts and points of view. Now this plurality of voices in *The Golden Bough* hardly means that Malinowski completely silences all other voices while Frazer permits total freedom of voice and self-representation to "native" and source. But the ethnographically unfortunate gap between Frazer and his informants does create a rhetorical situation in which the author *depends* upon other sources to an extent not usually found in a modern monograph. Indeed, for Frazer texts are his only "field." The result is anything but what Clifford calls the "integrated portrait" that the modern ethnographer wrests from "the research situation's ambiguities and diversities of meaning." Rather, *The Golden Bough*, published in various versions from 1890 to 1922, necessarily opens itself to other "voices" in ways that suggest the polyphonic in anthropology. And yet, as this essay hopes later to demonstrate, deeper analysis of Frazer's anthropological (as distinguished from "ethnographic") authority reveals a plurality that functions as ploy: indeed, the Frazerian text gains its power to appropriate and control cultural subject and reader from the illusion itself of openness, from

> " . . . a fundamental organizational oddity in *The Golden Bough* is the imbalance between the great multitude of legends, stories, songs and reports, and the theory on Arician priesthood that supposedly unites the whole work."

the pretense that the text functions as an objective, noninterpretive, polyphonic "arena of diversity."

In any ethnography, the controlling authors to some degree translate the voice of sources into their own words. But these voices, however much the ethnographic authoritarian tries to contain them, bleed out onto the margins of the page. The other voice always has its say if one listens. Clifford, alluding to Malinowski, states that "one may also read against the grain of the text's dominant voice, seeking out other, half-hidden authorities." But in Frazer's case the background noise is deafening, due to the sheer multitude and variety of cultural accounts that he draws, in encyclopedic manner, from historians, mythographers, missionaries, fieldworkers, translators and native informants, often quoting them at great length.

Frazer himself articulates those instances where polyvocality was most possible in *The Golden Bough* as moments of weakness. Whenever he gives in to the impulse to play tale-teller or ventriloquist, he then openly rationalizes and publicly defends his indulgence. For example, a fundamental organizational oddity in *The Golden Bough* is the imbalance between the great multitude of legends, stories, songs and reports, and the theory on Arician priesthood that supposedly unites the whole work. It is incredible to see Frazer proclaiming, in the opening of the first two-volume edition (1890), that he is providing these literally thousands of cultural accounts spanning the globe and the centuries for the purpose of answering two questions: "first, why had the priest [at Nemi] to slay his predecessor? And second, why, before he slew him, had he to pluck the Golden Bough?" Having stated his purpose, Frazer states that "it remains to try whether the survey of a wider field may not yield us the clues we seek''—and he tries, in ever-expanding editions, over the next quarter-century.

This imbalance did not go unnoticed. In 1901 a reviewer of the second edition of *The Golden Bough* quipped that the Golden Bough itself (that originary mistletoe, that Ur-branch of his fifteen-volume effort) was ''too slender a twig to sustain the weight of learning hung upon it.'' A generation ago Stanley Edgar Hyman, in *The Tangled Bank: Darwin, Marx, Frazer and Freud as Imaginative Writers,* commented on how Frazer ''tells myths, legends, folk tales, and similar stories on every occasion, whether or not they are relevant.'' And in his recent biography Ackerman consistently recounts Frazer's ''excessive use of examples that only tenuously exemplify.''

In one sense, Frazer simply could not maintain control over his line of argument, could not keep the myriad legends and fieldwork accounts tied to his thesis or in line with his method. This of course did not stop him from retelling those tales, but at least he felt some remorse over his compulsion. Ackerman documents Frazer's apologies and justifications in the correspondence with his publisher of fifty years, George Macmillan, concerning what Ackerman refers to as the ''pattern of uncontrollable swelling'' that ''became the rule in all his best-known works.'' Frazer's prefaces to the multiple editions of *The Golden Bough* well illustrate his varied attempts to justify the ever-increasing multitude of accounts. In the preface to the original edition, for example, he comments that ''a justification is perhaps needed of the length at which I have dwelt upon the popular festivals observed by European peasants,'' and rather lamely, he provides one: ''despite their fragmentary character'' they are ''the fullest and most trustworthy evidence we possess as to the primitive religion of the Aryans.''

The digressiveness that more fastidious critics castigated and Frazer himself felt compelled to excuse nonetheless had a powerful rhetorical effect upon Frazer's readership, a magnetizing pull that Frazer clearly was not willing to sacrifice for the sake of efficiency and concision. As Frazer spins out myth after myth, gradually the reader's attention shifts from whatever generalization ostensibly brought forth the need for illustration and onto the various stories themselves. Their intrinsic interest justifies their presence. Ackerman holds that the ''labyrinthine quality'' of Frazer's text is due to Frazer's ''unbridled willingness to digress'': the resultant ''profusion of data'' creates a rhetorical

context ''in which virtually any topic, as in a dream, may turn into any other.'' Indeed, Frazer's tellings can at times resemble a Lacanian fantasy: a mad jostling of signifiers, each linked by a thread to the one before and after, but often with no firm connection to the supposed purpose for the chain.

For example, in the opening section of *Taboo and the Perils of the Soul*, Part II of the twelve-volume third edition, Frazer's chronicle of ''Royal and Priestly Taboos'' leads him to consider ''taboos observed by African kings''; which leads him to discuss the prohibition upon the king ''to see the sea''; which leads to observations of how ''Egyptian priests loathed the sea''; which leads to sources commenting on how the Indians of the Peruvian Andes, ''sent by the Spaniards to work in the hot valleys of the coast,'' were horrified at the specter of the ocean opening before them; which leads to ''the inland people of Lampong in Sumatra,'' who ''are said to pay a kind of adoration to the sea, and to make it an offering of cakes and sweetmeats.'' In richly descriptive swells, Frazer has surged his way from taboos on kings to sea-worship. And crammed at the bottom of the page we find the sources for these (for Frazer) compelling narratives, including a Chief Native Commissioner for Mashonaland, the renowned van Gennep, a Father Porte from the *Missions Catholiques* and Plutarch.

Frazer's discontinuousness, however, cannot be attributed simply to bad organization. On the one hand, he was caught up in the stories he read, consumed by the voices he had heard, and he marched out justification, excuse and rationalization to legitimate his re-telling, or more accurately his re-writing. On the other hand, clearly Frazer realized the rhetorical effects of this at least seeming inability: the steady sale of his books, for one, clearly indicated that a reading public enjoyed participating in Frazer's obsessive, polyphonic discursiveness.

Clifford, in his effort to conceive the anthropologist as polyvocalist, cites Dickens' line ''He do the police in different voices'' to exemplify the novelist as Bakhtinian ''ventriloquist'' or ''polyphonist.'' Now Frazer is *not* the anthropological polyvocalist pure and simple, but in some respects Frazer's digressiveness historically has opened the door for ''other'' textual voices, for Clifford's ''more radical polyphony that would 'do the natives and the ethnographers in different voices.''' T. S. Eliot, for instance (whose use of *The Golden Bough* in *The Waste Land* helped lead an entire generation of starry-eyed literary critics into a profound misunderstanding of myth), publicly acknowledged and was grateful for the heterogeneity of Frazer's text. Two years after the publication of *The Waste Land,* Eliot gave recognition to the apparent openness and variety of Frazer's text, celebrating Frazer as the greatest of the anthropologists because he is essentially a non-interpretive reporter, having "withdrawn in more and more cautious abstention from the attempt to explain." Frazer's work is seen as having "perhaps greater permanence" than Freud's "because it is a statement of fact which is not involved in the maintenance or fall of any theory of the author's."

Indeed, Eliot here echoes Frazer's own defense against a number of attacks upon his theories of "primitive mentalities." His many prefaces to the various editions and volumes of *The Golden Bough* are filled with seemingly humble statements that downplay his own abilities and inclinations as "authority" by making the value of his work dependent upon the reliability and usefulness of his sources: "My contribution to the history of the human mind consists of little more than a rough and purely provisional classification of facts gathered almost entirely from printed sources." In fact, Frazer's defense often takes the form of a grandiloquent gesture of humility, such as the following, taken from the Preface to *Taboo and the Perils of the Soul:*

> The facts which I have put together in this volume . . . may perhaps serve as materials for a future science of Comparative Ethics. They are rough stones which await the master-builder, rude sketches which more cunning hands than mine may hereafter work up into a finished picture.

John Vickery acutely sees in Frazer's call for the "master-builder" the implication "that perhaps in some unforeseeable, miraculous fashion someone in the future will be able to master and utilize the quantities of data he has amassed"; but he does not discuss Frazer's minimizing of his own accomplishments as a stance that attempts to enshrine while it humbles, plotting the anthropologist-author a place in history by unassumingly constructing a history in which he himself would unquestionably have value (in which the "master" is, after all, a projection of himself). Similarly, Ackerman rightly points out how Frazer's "willingness to change his mind and his continual emphasis on the provisional nature of his findings combined to produce the most modest of professional personae," but the biographer does not make explicit how Frazer's rhetorical authority could be bolstered by professing flexibility and uncertainty; rather, he concludes that Frazer personally was "as far as possible from the dictator laying down the orthodoxy that must be followed at all costs . . . the opposite of prepossessing."

Frazer's "facts" are those observations culled, arranged and edited by the armchair anthropologist from "sources," primarily fieldworkers such as Spencer and Gillen. According to Frazer, what results is a compendium of facts, an open storehouse of cultural nuggets that is destined to stand the test of time well after the more contrived "theories" have fallen:

> In this as in other branches of study it is the fate of theories to be washed away like children's castles of sand by the rising tide of knowledge, and I am not so presumptuous as to expect or desire for mine an exemption from the common lot. I hold them all very lightly and have used them chiefly as convenient pegs on which to hang my collection of facts. For I believe that, while theories are transitory, a record of facts has a permanent value, and that as a chronicle of ancient customs and beliefs my book may retain its utility when my theories are as obsolete as the customs and beliefs deserve to be.

We can accept Ackerman's claim that Frazer the man "was genuinely humble before his facts and those who supplied them," but only if we appreciate the rhetorical advantage of that humbling gesture. We must remember that the master's bow of humility was accompanied by an insistence on the separation of fieldwork and theory, the latter of which, Frazer states, ought "regularly and rightly [to] be left to the comparative ethnologist." And there is no doubt that, despite his disclaimers to the value of theory, a theorist was what Frazer wanted to be. The reasoning Ackerman gives for Frazer's refusal to learn the language of the "natives" (he was a proficient linguist and classicist) sheds much light on Frazer's professional and discursive ambitions: "Knowledge of such a language would (or might) imply a specialization that he explicitly rejected. The role he assumed from the start was that of the generalist, one with the entire ethnographic world spread before him."

Frazer wanted it both ways: the status of the theorist, the controller, the author, but also the humble position of fact-collector. In his prefaces the pose is that of a student modestly accruing "facts"; but the result is a mammoth text brimming over with sources and voices, bearing the signature of the acclaimed author. The lesson was powerfully attractive to the literary Modernists. It is utterly significant that Clifford's choice as the epitome of polyphony, Dickens' line "He do the police in different voices,'' was the original subtitle of *The Waste Land.* And it is hardly fortuitous that in both Eliot's poem and *The Golden Bough* a virtual panoply of voices/sources emerges to complicate, at the very least, the notion of a controlling persona. That the ventriloqual is felt in the babble of voices in *The Waste Land* is indisputable, just as we can say that in Frazer's text the voices or script of ''others'' are heard both despite and because of the author's intentions.

Important recent criticism on *The Waste Land* revolves precisely around the issue of the freedom of its voices, with some extremely conflicting and useful responses. Calvin Bedient's recent book (entitled, not surprisingly, *He Do the Police in Different Voices*) sees *The Waste Land* as essentially polyphonic, but interprets the voices at work in the poem as babble that transcends signification and aspires toward the ineffable Absolute. Bedient opposes Terry Eagleton's view that the obstruction of meaning in the poem, the difficulty we have linking signifieds to signifiers, is actually a way to preserve surreptitiously the poem's ''meaning,'' which Eagleton sees as the paradoxical attempt to preserve and valorize ''Culture'' as conceived by Eliot. One view sees in the multiple voices an escape from cultural experience; the other insists upon an ideological, and ultimately monologic, underpinning.

The ''mad signifiers'' that refuse to connect in Frazer's rambling accounts may strike us as liberated from author-authoritarian, just as the babble in *The Waste Land* gives at least the illusion of freedom from controlling protagonist. At first glance, Eliot's praise of Frazer as reporter of ''facts'' is oddly juxtaposed against the verbal and cultural ''ruins'' of *The Waste Land.* But those ''facts'' make a certain sense as the ''fragments'' that the poem's persona, Tiresias, has ''shored against [his] ruins,'' nuggets of cultural verities representing the minimal stand of ''meaning'' against the onslaught of chaos.

Eliot, following Frazer, marched out the pure minimal authentic, the cultural ''facts'' (''despite their fragmentary character,'' Frazer reminds us) which apparently first emerged straight from the cultural fount, and at the affordable expense, so we are to believe, of the authoritative author. Frazer's valorization of the ''fact'' is hardly surprising, for he was a central figure in what Ackerman calls the attempts ''to raise [the social sciences] to the standards already achieved in the natural sciences.'' Eliot recognized the power of the ''scientific fact''

for a Modern literature that had few powerful literary predecessors and desperately needed to bolster the legitimacy of culture in general and literature in particular. And it was Eliot of all Modernists who was most concerned with establishing a highly respected cultural orthodoxy that had literary art at its center. As writers on a mission to salvage the wreck of Culture, however, the methods of Frazer and Eliot soon diverge. Eliot stands back from his text like a Joycean God, Ezra Pound paring his friend's poetry and fingernails; but as Frazer strains desperately, particularly in the later editions, to justify his work, he emerges as a kind of beleaguered Tiresias himself, amassing bits of cultural ''facts'' to ''shore against [*his*] ruins'' in a last-ditch attempt at salvaging the wreck of his gargantuan text.

And tentative though he was on theory, Frazer did hold his ''facts'' very tightly in his fist, not recognizing them, publicly anyway, as the highly skewed representations that they were. The generation of anthropologists after Frazer would roundly criticize him for failing to weigh the integrity of the various sources that reported his supposed ''facts.'' Quite typical of a modern anthropological perspective is Leach's criticism that in Frazer's text ''the most trivial observation of the most ignorant traveller is given the same weight as the most careful assessment of an experienced ethnographer.'' In the preface to the second edition of *The Golden Bough* Frazer admitted his cultural interpretations were ''light bridges'' that ''sooner or later break down,'' but he still had faith in the text as ''a repertory of facts''; he did *not* anticipate the criticism that the foundations of ''fact'' connected to those bridges had already been irrevocably weakened by contact. (Eliot did, doubting on several occasions whether social scientists *can* separate the ''description'' or ''fact'' of ''primitive experience'' from their own ''interpretations.'') Frazer's voice of authority, priding itself on its capacity to gain esteem by a calculated disavowal of its own authority, was in fact losing a critical defense: its sources.

Hyman writes that when Frazer decided in the culminating third edition of *The Golden Bough* that ''gods were not the embodiment of fertility rites but deified real men,'' he ''stopped taking any theory seriously'' and ''went back to being a literary man.'' That Frazer presented the third edition as a ''work of literature'' finds support in the preface to the first volume which, typically, promotes the work's ''artistic'' qualities while at the same time doggedly insisting upon its ''scientific'' integrity:

By discarding the austere form, without, I hope, sacrificing the solid substance, of a scientific treatise, I thought to cast my materials in a more artistic mould and so perhaps to attract readers, who might have been repelled by a more strictly logical and systematic arrangement of the facts.

That the third edition marks *the* moment at which Frazer transformed his persona from anthropologist to author is overstated, but the core of Hyman's point is well taken: as his work came increasingly under attack, Frazer did gradually shift his authorial perspective once more—from the gaze of the social scientist to the vision of the creative writer. Ackerman supports this notion of increasing literariness, citing "the increasing attention to the scenic element" in the third edition and in general claiming that "Frazer has now found a justification for enlisting his literary penchant in the service of the immensely enlarged third *Golden Bough*, his *magnum opus*." Typical of Frazer's strategies is his tactic, described by Ackerman, of claiming geography's relevance to religion "as a license for him to work up, out of his reading and imagination, the brilliant descriptive set pieces . . . that so characterize the third edition."

The relation between the move from anthropologist to author and Frazer's earlier shift from "theorist" to "collector of facts" is significant: both promote at least the illusion of greater latitude on the part of the writer. The move toward "fact collector" presumably lessens overt authorial control while allowing for the entry of more voices. And the shift to "author" inaugurates the notion that the work is henceforth excused of the need for scientific validation: as a "work of literature" *The Golden Bough* provides the author room to "play" with possibilities. The following statement is a disarmed and disarming example of Frazer's new attitude: "I put forward the hypothesis for no more than a web of conjectures woven from gossamer threads of popular superstition." Textual complexity and ambiguity is foregrounded; verification of theory is shuttled off to the background.

Frazer's tactic of posing his anthropological text as a beautiful, many sided literary artifact helps to explain the attraction that *The Golden Bough* had for midcentury myth critics. The literariness of Frazer, after all, was further illustration of how the rituals of culture did indeed ultimately weave Art, a mistaken notion passed on from Frazerian anthropology to the Cambridge Hellenists (such as Jane Harrison and Gilbert Murray) and then to critics such as Hyman, Lord Raglan, Phillip Wheelwright

and Richard Chase. The impact of Frazer's ideas upon ritual studies is fairly well documented; less discussed are the ways in which the stylistic and rhetorical features of Frazer's work have been replicated in those who espoused ritualist views. Hyman's *The Tangled Bank* is an ideal text for such discussion, since it is, first, written by a leading myth and ritual critic and, second, concerns Frazer himself as an imaginative writer.

Frazer's rhetorical figures, such as those "threads of popular superstition" that are part of his encompassing trope of the "web" of culture, were powerfully attractive to myth criticism as well as to the New Criticism, both of which solidified *The Golden Bough's* reputation as anthropological arche-text. A good example of the critical replication of Frazer's web-and-thread pattern can be found in *The Tangled Bank*, where Hyman alludes to his own title in his description of Frazer's web: "Frazer's common image for culture is of a great fabric, an orderly tangled bank. He writes of having touched only the fringe, having 'fingered only a few of the countless threads that compose the mighty web.'"

Hyman's figure for Frazer's design tells us as much about then-contemporary critical discussion as it does about an anthropological text of a half-century before. An "orderly tangled bank" is, after all, another variant of New Criticism's well-wrought urn: ornate, multifaceted, highly detailed, eminently ambiguous but ultimately encapsulated. The New Critical ideology of totalization that the orderly bank employs is explicitly pronounced in Hyman's introduction, where he states that "art" is "the work of the moral imagination, imposing order and form on disorderly and anarchic experience." (Hyman follows with a reference to Wallace Stevens' jar placed in Tennessee, an allusion that suggests the anthropologist-author making sense of the "primitive" wilderness.) Clearly, Frazer was being used to promote a critical ideology, but Hyman's appeal to Frazer's web is also testimony to the powerful duplicating effects of Frazer's own rhetorical strategies; it *is* the variability of Frazer's text, after all, that makes possible such a reading. . . .

Frazer's very inscribing of culture as woven "web," inscrutable as parts of that pattern might be, attempts to give "culture" a coherence. Frazer urges us to view his staking out of the term as a humble and hopelessly incomplete step toward knowing the unknowable. But reading against the grain of the text (as Clifford tells us we ought), we see not the humility and tentativeness of the anthropologist faced through a profusion of sources with his own overarching ignorance, but the rhetorical command of an author whose self-created network, those multiple threads of ''unreadable'' voices, sources and causes, derives from a principle of containment in which the anthropological subject (Frazer's frighteningly elusive ''savage'') must be safely (for us) enclosed, bracketed off within the text. Though we are told that the pattern cannot be deciphered, Frazer's forced figuration of ''black'' and ''red'' as ''magic'' and ''religion'' attempts to strangle the ''savage'' in the author's own ''orderly tangled bank,'' a carefully wrought textual jungle of positivist straight lines and right angles. In ''On Ethnographic Allegory'' Clifford speaks of modern ethnography's ''allegory of salvage,'' a ''rhetorical construct'' that perpetuates the value of the monograph by saying to its reader that ''the other [the 'native'] is lost, in disintegrating time and space, but saved in the text.'' Frazer's rhetoric of salvage is qualitatively different, for though he tells his readers that he collects the ''facts'' in order to help in the construction of a record, he admits to doing so precisely because the ''savage'' is still thriving within the city walls: Frazer is a salvager of Culture, not culture. His ''facts,'' if read aright, ultimately serve to banish the ''savage'' from the republic.

Source: Marc Manganaro, ''The Tangled Bank' Revisited: Anthropological Authority in Frazer's *The Golden Bough*,'' in *Yale Journal of Criticism,* Vol. 39, No. 17, Fall 1989, pp. 107–26.

Sabine MacCormack

In the following essay excerpt, MacCormack identifies consistency and coherency in the method and structure of The Golden Bough, *a strategy that reveals Frazer's points of interest.*

The Golden Bough is a work of many tensions and contradictions, not the least of which is one which the author himself repeatedly pointed to, that is the tension between fact and theory, objectivity and subjectivity. Thus, in the preface to *Aftermath*, published in 1936, twenty-three years after work on the *GB* itself was completed, Frazer says:

> Now as always, I hold all my theories very lightly and am ever ready to modify or abandon them in the light of new evidence. If my writings should survive the writer, they will do so, I believe, less for the theories which they propound than for the sake of the evidence which they record.

Elsewhere, Frazer describes his work as a repertory which may be used by subsequent scholars to sustain their own theories, and this was more than a polite disclaimer, since Frazer did not think that the discipline of anthropology had in his day reached a stage where it could maintain and prove any theory definitely. Thus, in 1905 he wrote, ''The Newtons and Darwins of anthropology will come after us,'' and, more gloomily in 1914:

> The longer I occupy myself with questions of ancient mythology, the more diffident I become of success in dealing with them, and I am apt to think that we who spend our years in searching for solutions of these insoluble problems are like Sisyphus perpetually rolling his stone uphill only to see it revolve again into the valley.

But at the same time, the *GB* does have a theoretical purpose, or rather, two interdependent theoretical purposes, the relation between which shifted in the course of the twenty-three years which elapsed between the publication of the first edition of the work in two volumes in 1890, and the publication of third edition in twelve volumes in 1913.

This shift is explained by Frazer himself in the prefaces to the three editions of this work. In 1890, he wrote:

> For some time, I have been preparing a general work on primitive superstition and religion. Among the problems which had attracted my attention was the hitherto unexplained rule of the Arician priesthood; and last spring . . . I came across some facts which . . . suggested an explanation of the rule in question. As the explanation, if correct, promised to throw light on some obscure features of primitive religion, I resolved to develop it fully, and . . . to issue it as a separate study. This book is the result.

According to the rule of the Roman priesthood of Aricia which Frazer here refers to, the aspirant priest had to kill the incumbent of the office, having first—as Frazer interpreted the rule—plucked a branch from a tree in the nearby sacred grove. This rule still preoccupied Frazer deeply in 1900, when in the preface to the second edition of the *GB*, in three volumes, he reiterated: ''this is not a general treatise on primitive superstition, but merely the investigation of one particular and narrowly limited problem, to wit, the rule of the Arician priesthood.'' By 1913, however, the position had changed. Frazer still begins and ends his work with the rule of the Arician priesthood, as he had done in 1890. But he viewed its role in his conclusions as marginal:

> Should my whole theory of this particular priesthood collapse—and I fully acknowledge the slenderness of the foundations on which it rests—its fall would hardly shake my general conclusions as to the evolution of primitive religion and society.

In the outcome, then, the *GB* became the treatise on primitive religion which initially Frazer had planned to issue separately from his researches on the Arician priesthood.

As might be expected, considering both its scope and the complexity of its aims, the *GB* has been widely criticized by classical scholars, anthropologists and others for errors of fact, theoretical framework and emphasis, so that almost no aspect of this very long and complex work has escaped hostile scrutiny. At the same time, however, the book has been, and arguably still is, extraordinarily influential. Thus, what reader of the *GB* will not find one of that work's principal themes, that of the Dying God, the victim sacrificed for the good of the crops, hauntingly evoked in T. S. Eliot's lines:

> That corpse you planted last year in your garden,
> has it begun to sprout? Will it bloom this year?

Another of the many authors who was deeply imbued with Frazerian ideas was Freud, who thought, as did Frazer, that "long-forgotten important happenings in the primeval history of the human family" are in fact not simply forgotten, but are ever re-enacted in new guises.

My purpose in the present study is to show that, despite its diverse themes, which, as we have seen, changed over time, the *GB* does have a fundamental methodological consistency and a coherent structure. This may help to explain the appeal which the work has exercised on its many readers. At the same time, it will be seen that the structure of the *GB* gives us an insight into Frazer's concept of the nature of human knowledge, and therefore into his aims in writing as he did.

To begin, then, with the structure of the *GB*. Throughout the book, Frazer expounds the rule of the priesthood of Aricia from two different points of view. Firstly, he examines evidence from ancient Greece and Rome in order to elucidate the workings of the rule, evidence, that is, which is *contiguous* in space and time. The parts of the *GB* which fall under this denominator are thus a historical exegesis—in the broadest sense of that term—of the rule of the priesthood. That is, they belong to the field of classical scholarship. Secondly, the rule of the priesthood is examined in the light of evidence drawn from all over the world and from all periods down to Frazer's own present. This second class of evidence is used because for various reasons it is *similar* to the functioning of the rule of the priesthood. These parts of the *GB* can be classified, in the nineteenth-century sense, as ethnography, a discipline which at

> **Expressed in Frazer's own terms, he applied to the solution of his chosen problem the two methods of human thought which he considered basic, that is, the association of ideas by contiguity, and the association of ideas by similarity."**

that time drew widely on cross-cultural comparisons to reach its results.

In terms of the scholarship of his own day, therefore, Frazer used the comparative method, which had been advocated as applicable to the study of human society by, among others, Lang and Tylor, in two respects, which converge on each other. That is, Frazer used the comparative method in the narrow sense by applying to the priesthood of Aricia *contiguous* evidence coming from the same civilization, that is, Rome, and from a geographical and culturally related one, that is, Greece. He then proceeded to apply the method to its fullest extent by bringing in materials from all periods and places on the ground that they were *similar* to the issue on which the *GB* revolves.

Expressed in Frazer's own terms, he applied to the solution of his chosen problem the two methods of human thought which he considered basic, that is, the association of ideas by contiguity, and the association of ideas by similarity. "The principles of association are . . . absolutely fundamental to the working of the human mind," he says. These two ways of association of ideas, according to Frazer, form the foundation of any advancement of human knowledge there can be, for it is by means of them that hypotheses and theories are formulated, so as to then be tested and accepted or rejected on the basis of "facts." There is a tension here in Frazer's thought between "facts" and hypotheses, to which we will return.

At present, we will examine Frazer's explanation of the rules of magic because he argues that they follow the same two basic laws of thought whereby ideas are associated with each other according to contiguity and similarity. The rules of magic are a fundamental theme in the *GB*, the theme which, along with the rule of the Arician priesthood, gives the work its continuity. Frazer classifies magic into two branches:

> If we analyze the principles of thought on which magic is based, they will . . . resolve themselves into two: first, that like produces like, or that an effect resembles its cause; and second, that things which have once been in contact with each other continue to act on each other at a distance. . . . The former principle may be called the law of similarity, and the latter the law of contact or contagion.

Now, magic, according to Frazer, is one of the ways in which man attempts to control his environment, and as such it is brought to bear on interpreting the rule of the priesthood of Aricia.

The priest of Aricia is viewed as, in origin, one of those ''departmental kings of nature'' whose professional knowledge of magic—for, Frazer holds, magicians were the first professionals in human society—enables him to cause the crops to grow, because, according to the citation above, an effect resembles its cause: the crops will be encouraged to grow by the rule of similarity, i.e., by imitative magic, whereby a rain-making ceremony produces rain. But, if similarity operates on the basis of cause and effect, so does contagion: that is, the priest-king must die when his strength fails lest his weakness—on the principle of contagion—contaminate the course of nature and cause the crops to fail. Hence the priest of Aricia must at some point be slain, the *GB* argues, by a stronger rival.

With this, it may be seen that the *GB* displays a coordinated pattern of meanings built up on three levels: first, it is stated that the human mind works by associations built up by means of the principles of contiguity (contagion) and similarity; second, the comparative method which Frazer uses to adduce his material is structured by the same principle, and third, magic, the *leitmotiv* of the work, is, by virtue of also being a product of the human mind, structured analogously. With this, I have of course said nothing about the truth or falsity of these propositions, or of the conclusions which arise from them. Rather, the purpose of raising the propositions was to show how the *GB*, despite its vast diversity, does have a coherent structure. On the one hand, it studies the workings of the human mind, and on the other, it is itself an exemplification of these workings. The argument of the *GB* thus revolves around two themes: there is, on the one hand, the story of the Arician priesthood, and on the other, there is the

human mind. And, as we have seen, the relationship between these two themes changed in the course of Frazer's researches.

But what of the essential truth or falsity, or even, simply the substantive content of a book which is constructed in this way? Are we dealing with a vicious circle, or with a work which does advance the enquiry it posits? I will argue that the *GB* does the latter.

Frazer began his literary career in 1879 by writing an essay entitled *The Growth of Plato's Ideal Theory*, which he published unaltered in 1930. In it, he was looking for a theory of knowledge. The reasons for which he rejected Plato's theory of knowledge and the theory of forms are crucial for an understanding of what is said, and how it is said in the *GB*. In *The Growth of Plato's Ideal Theory*, Frazer first argues that the ideal theory was derived from Socrates' theory of knowledge, and that Plato then turned it into a theory of being in such a way that knowing and being become the same thing. Frazer calls this ''the gigantic yet splendid error which converted a true theory of knowledge into a false theory of being . . . knowledge into ontology.'' Later in the book comes a statement which is crucial for our present purposes:

> [Plato] mistook the method and scope of physical enquiry. What a physical philosopher does is this: he puts himself in the most favourable position for watching the phenomena . . . ; then he registers the sequence . . . then, observing . . . he infers that this sequence is universal. . . . [The resulting] extended inferences are called laws of nature. They really are, however, nothing but inferences as to the sequence of our sensations. The philosophy of nature is after all the philosophy of mind.

In other words, Plato, according to Frazer, bestows objective existence on subjective abstractions.

Now, in the *GB*, Frazer repeatedly argues that savage philosophy, one product of which is magic, functions according to exactly the same error:

> Few men are sensible to the sharp line that divides the known from the unknown. To most it is a hazy borderland where perception and conception melt indissolubly into one.

> Men mistook the order of their ideas for the order of nature and hence imagined that the control which they have . . . over their thoughts permitted them to exercise a corresponding control over things.

In other words, being and knowing, perception and conception, are viewed by savage man as being one and the same thing.

Two points arise with respect to magic. Firstly, if being and knowing are the same thing, as, according to Frazer, they are in savage thought, because the savage makes no distinction between perception and conception, then what is known in the mind actually *is*. We may illustrate this state of affairs from Frazer's analysis of savage thought on death and immortality.

> At an early stage of his intellectual development man deems himself naturally immortal and imagines that were it not for the baleful arts of sorcerers . . . he would live for ever.

> Thus arguing . . . from his own sensations, he conceives of life as an indestructible kind of energy, which, when it disappears in one form, must necessarily reappear in another.

That is, for the savage, sensation expresses a permanent reality independent of the individual experiencing it. This reality, both in the mind and external to it, is ruled by the two laws of thought, similarity and contagion. Here we have the reason why a magical rite, when conceived and then performed, is, according to Frazer, considered by the savage to be efficacious in a predictable fashion, i.e., it is efficacious according to the laws of similarity and contagion.

In short, the magical rite is the cause of a specific effect. This relationship of cause and effect in magic as viewed by Frazer brings us to a further issue in his thought: his question why the "error" of magic turned out to be so durable:

> The answer seems to be that the fallacy was far from easy to detect . . . since in . . . most cases the desired event did actually follow at a longer or shorter interval, the performance of the rite which was designed to bring it about. . . . Hence the practical savage . . . might well turn a deaf ear to the theoretical doubter, the philosophical radical who presumed to hint that sunrise and spring must not after all be the direct consequence of the . . . performance of . . . certain ceremonies.

Frazer then transposes the argument to his own England, confronting a scientific innovator with "the man on the street," where the latter takes the former to task for being a "theorist, splitter of hairs and chopper of logic" and ignoring the evidence of facts which are "patent to everybody."

> If such reasonings could pass muster among ourselves, need we wonder that they long escaped detection by the savage?

In accordance with these ideas, Frazer, so as to distinguish magic from science, calls magic a pseudo-science. It is a science because by means of it, man seeks to control nature, but at the same time, it is a false science because it operates on the basis of an erroneous theory of cause and effect.

> The means by which [magical rites] were supposed to effect [their] end were imitation and sympathy. Led astray by his ignorance of the true causes of things, primitive man believed that in order to produce the great phenomena of nature on which his life depended, he had only to imitate them, and that immediately by a secret sympathy or mystic influence the little drama which he acted . . . would be taken up and repeated by mightier actors on a vaster scale.

In short, magic would be an unimpeachable body of knowledge—unimpeachable because coherent and systematic—were it not for the crucial flaw that it is built up on a false premise.

A difficulty arises here which runs throughout the *GB*. This is that on the one hand, Frazer rejects the possibility of absolute definitive knowledge, and on the other, he posits that a true explanation and understanding of phenomena of whatever kind can be reached through sustained observation and correlation of fact with theory. Perhaps, seeing that Frazer insists that he was studying nothing other than the human mind, what elsewhere he calls comparative ethics, one may argue that he should have renounced his insistence on "fact," that is, on objectivity external to and independent of the individual's mind.

We may at this point compare Frazer's analysis of human thought to Hume's. Hume also describes human thought as proceeding by association of ideas, but instead of Frazer's two categories of similarity and contiguity, he has three, resemblance, contiguity, and cause and effect. Thus where according to Hume cause and effect can figure as a mode of thought, according to Frazer they are an objective "scientific" reality, a reality independent of any observer. In other words, in locating cause and effect not in the human mind, but in an environment independent of the human mind, Frazer did posit a reality external to and independent of man and his perceptions.

This view of Frazer's affected his interpretation of magic, for thanks to it, he could conclude that the premiss of magic as he understood it was indeed false. At the same time, Frazer regarded magic and the mode of thought it exemplifies as resolving an impasse, and that not only among savages. Of the Plato of the middle period, when the ideas, according to Frazer, first emerged clearly, he says:

The cause why Socrates sat and talked . . . was that it seemed to him good to do so. . . . And if good is the cause of my actions, it must be the cause of all things, of material things as well as of human actions. Now, it is quite true that every voluntary action of every man is directed to . . . something that seems to him good. . . . But from the fact that all our voluntary actions are prompted by this mental perception of an object, were we to infer that every change in physical things is prompted by a striving after the good, we would be committing the same mistake into which savages fall when, from the analogy of their own acts, they ascribe the action of inanimate objects to a principle of life, thought and feeling inherent in these objects. However, we cannot suppose that Plato meant to suggest anything so extravagant.

Thus, according to Frazer, the predicament of explaining cause and effect is handled by Plato at this point in his thought in a fashion which is not altogether disconnected from how savages handle it. This is the "gigantic yet splendid error" we mentioned earlier.

The issue Frazer comments on in the above passage is how not only Plato (as he understands Plato) but also primitive man formulates a conceptual framework such as might render intelligible the reality which is external to man. This issue was carried over into the *GB*. Throughout the work, therefore, Frazer confronted the question of how effectively and durably a conceptual framework could be delineated by any one person or even, by any one generation of researchers and scholars. As in *Ideal Theory*, so in the *GB*, his estimate of the likelihood of success was cautious.

The task of the scientific discoverer is to trace the series of invariable antecedents and consequents, in other words, of physical, not final causes and effects.

Here also, cause and effect are realities independent of and outside the human mind. In principle, they may be definitively intelligible to human reason, but in actual fact, the advance of learning is at best exceedingly slow.

In reviewing the opinions and practices of ruder ages . . . we shall do well to look with leniency upon their errors as inevitable slips made in the search for truth, and to give them the benefit of that indulgence which we ourselves may one day stand in need of: cum excusatione itaque veteres audiendi sunt.

And at the end of the work we have a last image of the ancient quest for truth:

The advance of knowledge is an infinite progression toward a goal that forever recedes. We need not murmur at the endless pursuit:

Fatti non foste a viver come bruti,

Ma per seguir virtute e canoscenza.

Great things will come of that pursuit, though we may not enjoy them. Brighter stars will rise on some voyager of the future—some great Ulysses of the realms of thought—than shine on us. The dreams of magic may one day become the waking realities of science.

We have seen on what foundations the *GB* is constructed, and gone on to ask whether the work, in the light of its structure, can advance the enquiry it proposes, rather than merely create a vicious circle. To answer this question, we looked at how Frazer formulated his disagreement with Plato's theory of knowledge, and how he carried the results of the disagreement over into the *GB*. Put simply, Frazer concluded that in practice, knowledge is both finite and relative. But we also noted that Frazer very carefully stopped short of suggesting that the reality which according to him does exist outside the human mind must remain ultimately inexplicable.

Source: Sabine MacCormack, "Magic and the Human Mind: A Reconsideration of Frazer's *Golden Bough*," in *Arethusa*, Vol. 17, No. 2, Fall 1984, pp. 151–76.

Sources

Hyman, Stanley Edgar, "What Do You Dance?," in *The Tangled Bank: Darwin, Marx, Frazer, and Freud as Imaginative Writers*, Atheneum, 1962, pp. 212–32.

Malinowski, Bronislaw, "Sir James George Frazer," in *A Scientific Theory of Culture and Other Essays*, University of North Carolina Press, 1944, pp. 177–221.

Review of *The Golden Bough*, in the *Journal of American Folklore*, Vol. 3, No. 40, October–December 1890, pp. 316–9.

Further Reading

Bruner, Jerome S., "Myth and Identity," in *Myth and Mythmaking*, edited by Henry A. Murray, Beacon Press, 1960, pp. 276–87.
    Bruner examines the psychological reasons why humans are attracted to myths.

Downie, R. Angus, *Frazer and "The Golden Bough,"* Victor Gollancz Ltd., 1970.
    This study examines Frazer's entire career, including his influences, his methods, and his other writings.

Patai, Raphael, *Myth and Modern Man*, Prentice-Hall, Inc., 1972.
    Patai, whose early career interests overlapped with Frazer's, examines mythological aspects in contem-

porary America in such chapters as "Madison Avenue Myth and Magic," "The Myth of Oral Gratification: Coke and Smoke," and "The New Sex Myth."

Vickery, John B. *The Literary Impact of "The Golden Bough,"* Princeton University Press, 1973.

The focus here is on works by Yeats, D. H. Lawrence, T. S. Eliot, and James Joyce, all of which show Frazer's influence. Nearly a quarter of the book is about James Joyce.

The Liars' Club

Mary Karr

1995

Mary Karr's *The Liars' Club*, published in 1995 in New York is a memoir of Karr's turbulent childhood in the fictional eastern Texas town of Leechfield, and later in Colorado. Karr's immediate family consists of her sister Lecia, two years older than she; her father, Pete Karr, who works at an oil refinery; and her mother, who is emotionally unstable and hates living in Leechfield.

The memoir describes the sort of childhood that many people would wish to avoid. Mary's parents fight constantly and eventually divorce only to remarry later. Her mother's alcoholism and addiction to diet pills lead to many strange episodes, some of them frightening, as when she becomes unhinged and appears to be about to kill her children.

Mary's father is a rough-and-ready, quarrelsome native Texan with Native-American blood who excels as a teller of tall tales in his group of buddies who meet at the American Legion. This group is christened the Liars' Club.

Although the pages of *The Liars' Club* are chock full of arguments, fights, and unsavory incidents of all kinds, the memoir was hugely successful. This success is due to Karr's skills as a poet, her finely honed sense of humor, and her wonderful ear for the slang of eastern Texas. Readers probably also sense that underneath the surface turbulence, this dysfunctional family still loves each other.

Author Biography

Mary Karr was born in January 1955 in Texas, the daughter of J. P. Karr, an oil refinery worker, and Charlie Marie Karr, an artist and business owner. She had a difficult childhood which she describes in *The Liars' Club* and she left home when she was seventeen. Karr enrolled at Macalester College in St. Paul, Minnesota, but left after two years in order to travel. In 1978, she was admitted to Goddard College in Vermont where she met writers Tobias Wolff and Frank Conroy, both of whom encouraged her to write.

Karr found her calling as a poet. She has remarked that she wanted to be a poet from about age seven. Her first volume of poetry, *Abacus*, was published in 1987; her second volume, *The Devil's Tour*, appeared in 1993.

After *The Devil's Tour*, Karr wrote *The Liars' Club: A Memoir*, which brought her fame along with critical and commercial success. Published in 1995, *The Liars' Club* spent sixty weeks on the *New York Times* best-seller list. In 1996, the book won the PEN/Martha Albrand Award and the Texas Institute of Letters' Carr P. Collins Prize. It also won the New York Public Library Award.

Karr's third volume of poetry, *Viper Rum: With the afterword "Against Decoration,"* was published in 1998. This was followed in 2000 by *The Liars' Club* sequel, *Cherry: A Memoir*, in which Karr recalls her turbulent adolescence. *Cherry* was generally less well received than *The Liars' Club*.

Karr has been an assistant professor of English at various institutions, including Tufts University, Emerson College, Harvard University, and Sarah Lawrence College. She is currently the Peck Professor of English at Syracuse University in Syracuse, New York. She is a two-time winner of the Pushcart Prize in poetry and essay. In 1983, Karr married a fellow poet, whom she divorced in 1993. She has one son, Devereux Milburn.

Plot Summary

Part 1: Texas, 1961

The Liars' Club begins at a traumatic moment in Mary Karr's life, when she is seven. There has been a disturbance at her home in the town of Leechfield, Texas, as a result of which Mother is being taken from the house, having suffered a nervous breakdown. Mary and her nine-year-old sister Lecia are taken away by the sheriff and stay for a while elsewhere in the neighborhood.

Karr relates how her parents met and married and also tells of her father's childhood, explaining that she learned about these things by listening to the stories Daddy told to his drinking friends at the American Legion. This group of friends was known as the Liars' Club.

Mary's childhood is not easy. Her parents fight frequently, and although her mother threatens divorce, the couple stays together. Mary develops a sharp tongue, frequently using vulgar language she learned from her parents. She gets into fights at school.

Life for Mary becomes even more difficult when her grandmother, who has cancer, comes to live with her family. Grandma Moore is a bossy, critical, eccentric woman who carries a hacksaw around in a black doctor's bag and demands that Mary be spanked for misbehavior. Mary blames Grandma Moore for the worst times in her family, and Mary's own behavior deteriorates. She throws tantrums, bites her nails, walks in her sleep, and is suspended from second grade for attacking other children. To add to her misery, she is raped by an older boy in the neighborhood.

Grandma Moore dies a slow death. Her leg is amputated and the cancer spreads to her brain, making her, in Karr's words, crazy. She takes no pain medication but drinks beer all day. Since she dislikes Mary's father, he makes himself scarce while she is there, working double shifts and entertaining himself with hunting and fishing.

Grandma shows Mary a photo of a boy and girl, Tex and Belinda. She says they are Mary's half-brother and sister, but she does not explain what she means. She threatens that if Mary misbehaves, she will be sent away, like Tex and Belinda were. When Grandma Moore dies, shortly after the family returns home after fleeing a hurricane, Mary is relieved, although her sister Lecia is genuinely upset.

Another crisis erupts on a trip to the beach. Lecia is attacked by a man-of-war that leeches onto her leg, leaving bright red welts. Having wished many times for her sister to die, Mary now prays that she lives.

With Mother depressed and spending her time reading in bed, Mary is relieved when Daddy takes her to the Liars' Club once more, where she hears him spin a tall tale about how his father hung himself (his father is in fact still alive). Mother starts drinking to excess and this leads to even more vicious fights between her and her husband. On Mary's birthday, after a bitter quarrel, they all go out for the evening. But on their return, Mary's disturbed mother tries to grab the steering wheel and take the car over the edge of a bridge. Pete responds by knocking her unconscious. When she recovers she scratches his cheek bloody.

The situation gets worse. One night, Mother becomes unhinged, scrawling over all the mirrors with lipstick, smashing light bulbs, and burning the children's toys, furniture, and clothes. Then she advances on the children with a butcher's knife. She does not harm them and puts the knife down, but she calls the doctor and says she has just stabbed both children to death. This is the traumatic incident referred to at the beginning of the book. As a result, Mother is taken to a hospital for the mentally ill. Mary goes further out of control, shooting a BB gun at a boy who had been in a fight with her sister. The pellet hits the boy in the neck.

Part 2: Colorado, 1963

Having inherited money from Grandma Moore, the family is living in more comfortable circumstances. They move to Colorado Springs, where Mother buys a stone lodge on the side of a mountain. Mary is now eight years old. From the bedroom window, she and Lecia enjoy watching bears roaming around, and they learn to ride a horse. They spend an idyllic day fishing for trout with Daddy. Mother spends much of her time at the local bar. Soon Mary's parents announce they are to divorce, and they give the girls a choice as to with whom they wish to live. The girls choose Mother. Daddy returns to Texas the next day. A Mexican man named Hector moves in with Mother, and Mother calls him the girls' new daddy. The girls resist Hector's attempts to bond with them, and they miss their real father whom they unsuccessfully try to lure back.

They visit Antelope, the biggest city Mary has seen, but it is a disappointment to her. Mother rents a colonial house there, and the sisters each have their own bedroom for the first time. They attend a local school, where Mary still gets into fights. Mother's mental health continues to deteriorate. She becomes dependent on diet pills and spends most of her time drunk in bed. Her relationship with Hector sours, and she becomes moody and depressed, seeing no point in life. On one occasion she throws herself out of a moving car. In another traumatic incident, Mary is forced to perform oral sex on the man who is supposed to be baby-sitting her. She tells no one of how she was violated.

Life becomes so intolerable that Mother comes close to shooting Hector. Lecia and Mary, although they do not like Hector, try to protect him. That night, Lecia calls their father collect and tells him she and Mary are coming home. Daddy pays their airfare and is overjoyed to see them when they return. He prays their mother will soon join them. Mother returns soon after with Hector, intending only to pick up some clothes. However, Daddy beats up Hector, and Mother decides to stay and live with her family again.

Part 3: Texas Again, 1980

In 1980 Daddy has a stroke at the age of seventy and is incapacitated. Mother has stopped drinking but has become addicted to prescription drugs. She remains depressed. Mary, having left home permanently at seventeen, lives in Boston. She and her father have grown apart and no longer have much to say to each other. After Daddy's stroke, he loses the ability to speak coherently. Mary returns and helps her mother care for him.

One day, while searching the attic for old medical records, Mary comes upon a number of wedding rings. She asks her mother about them and Mother's anguished story comes out. Her first husband ran off with her two children, Belinda and Tex, and she saw them only once again. Each time she remarried, she expected her new husband to help her get her kids back, but the men quickly lost enthusiasm for the task. It was the strain of losing her children that led to Mother's mental instability over the years.

Key Figures

Ben Bederman

Ben Bederman is one of the members of the Liars' Club. He always listens carefully to Pete Karr's stories and is usually the first to ask a question. He visits Pete in the hospital after Pete has a stroke and is distressed at Pete's condition. Almost every night he sits for hours outside Pete's hospital room.

Cooter

Cooter is one of the members of the Liars' Club. He often picks on Shug and scolds him because he is bothered by the fact that Shug is black.

Daddy

See Pete Karr

Hector

Hector is a Mexican bartender who marries Mary's mother while they are living in Colorado. Mary and Lecia do not like him and refuse to accept him as their stepfather. Hector does not have a job and the couple lives off Charlie Marie's money. However, the marriage is not a success. Hector is frequently drunk. Charlie Marie criticizes him mercilessly and at one point she threatens him with a gun while he cowers in a chair and tells her to go ahead and shoot since his life is not worth anything. When Hector accompanies Charlie Marie to Texas to pick up some of her clothes, Pete overhears a derogatory remark that Hector makes to Charlie Marie. He drags Hector from his car, punches him to the ground, and then repeatedly hits him in the face. Then he kicks him, breaking one of Hector's ribs. Charlie Marie takes Hector to an emergency room and leaves him there. She then returns to live in Texas.

Charlie Marie Karr

Charlie Marie Karr is Mary's mother. She married seven times including twice to Pete Karr. Her fourth marriage, to an Italian sea captain named Paulo, was the one that first brought her to Leechfield, Texas, where she later met and married Pete Karr.

Unlike her husband, Charlie Marie is educated and intellectually curious. She spends a lot of her time reading widely in topics such as Russian history and French existentialism. She is also an artist, having studied art in New York's Greenwich Village, and has her own studio in the family home. She also listens to opera.

Charlie Marie's marriage to Pete Karr is happy at first, but they soon fall to fighting. She bitterly regrets leaving New York for the barren landscape of eastern Texas, and she threatens divorce many times. After her mother dies, Charlie Marie starts to drink, which has a bad effect on her already volatile temperament. In Texan parlance, she is considered ''nervous,'' a term that covers a wide range of mental problems. The fights with her husband become more frequent, and eventually she has a

Media Adaptations

- An audiocassette of Karr reading *The Liars' Club* was published in 1996 by Penguin Audiobooks.

---

mental breakdown. She smashes mirrors and light bulbs in the house, burns the children's clothes and furniture, and threatens them with a knife. As a result, she is taken away and spends a month at a hospital for the mentally ill.

When the family moves to Colorado, Charlie Marie's mental condition does not improve. She drinks to excess and becomes dependent on diet pills. Much of the time she just stays in bed, too depressed to get up. When she and Pete agree to divorce, the children elect to stay with their mother because they think that left alone she would get into serious trouble, whereas Pete could manage on his own. After Pete's departure, Charlie Marie marries Hector, but this marriage is no happier than her former one. When Charlie Marie almost shoots Hector, Mary and Lecia decide they will return to live with their father. However, it is not long before Charlie Marie leaves Hector and returns to live in Texas, eventually remarrying Pete.

At the end of the book, it transpires that the reason for Charlie Marie's chronic mental instability is that Tex and Belinda, her two children from her first marriage, were taken from her by her husband when he walked out on her. She saw these children only once again.

Lecia Karr

Lecia Karr is two years older than her sister Mary. Lecia is tough and frequently gets into fights, most of which she wins. She is able to beat boys several years older than she. She and Mary have a quarrelsome relationship, and on one occasion Lecia beats Mary in a fight. As the older of the two, Lecia often bosses Mary around, and she takes the lead in deciding what to do. It is she, for example, who decides that they will stay with their mother in

Colorado rather than go back to Texas with their father. Lecia's role in the family is to be the competent one while Mary is the cute one. Often, even at the age of ten or eleven, Lecia is more competent than her own mother. For example, she knows that when her mother has a crying fit after listening to opera music, it is time to put her to bed.

Lecia is also resourceful. Within two days of being viciously attacked by a man-of-war at the beach, she is charging the neighborhood kids money to see or touch her blisters. Mary's reaction at the moment the man-of-war wrapped its tentacles around Lecia's leg says a lot about the sisters' stormy relationship: having many times wished for Lecia to die, she at that moment prayed that Lecia would live.

Mary Karr

Mary Karr is the narrator of the memoir. She is a resourceful girl who has inherited her father's aggressive temperament and her mother's intelligence. She is dark-haired, unlike her blonde sister, and she looks vaguely Native American, like her father. As a young girl she adores her father and is enthralled by his storytelling at the Liars' Club, which she is allowed to attend. As a child, she cannot help but be influenced by her parents' quarrels, and she and Lecia fantasize about escaping and living somewhere else, such as a shack on the beach or the rest room of a convenience store.

Mary's life includes many traumatic incidents. She is raped by an older boy from the neighborhood when she is seven. She tells no one about it, because she is scared of the consequences of speaking out. In Colorado, when she is no more than nine, she is sexually abused by a babysitter. She also has to witness her parents' constant fighting; her mother's mental breakdown, during which her mother threatens her and Lecia with a knife; and her mother's threatening of Hector with a gun, during which incident Mary and Lecia throw themselves across Hector to protect him.

Not surprisingly, given her family background, Mary learns how to take care of herself physically. Feisty by nature, she acquires a reputation for herself as the worst little girl in the neighborhood. This reputation is sealed when she shoots a BB gun at a boy named Ricky Carter, hitting him in the neck. She has learned from her parents how to curse, and when she is challenged by the boy's father she retorts, "Eat me raw, mister." Mary frequently gets into fights with the neighborhood kids, and because she is small she never wins any. But she refuses to

give in, and prides herself on being able to take a beating.

In spite of all the traumas Mary suffers in her dysfunctional family, she still feels loved by her parents and she loves them in return. She shows her love by caring for her father after he has a stroke and by forgiving her mother for the wrongs she did to Mary.

Pete Karr

Pete Karr is Mary's father. A World War II veteran, he is a handsome, black-haired man with Native-American blood who works at the oil refinery. In forty-two years he never misses a day at work, even though he is a hard drinker. Pete is known for his storytelling abilities, and he holds his friends in the Liars' Club spellbound with his vivid tales of his childhood, although few of his stories are true. He is also known as a quarrelsome personality who is quick to get into fights, which he always wins. He even gives Mary, whom he affectionately calls Pokey, tips on how to fight, urging her to bite her opponents. His relationship with his children is warm, and he likes to indulge them, but he is also thrifty and does not like to waste money. He keeps scrupulous financial records and does not trust banks.

When Grandma Moore comes to live with the family, Pete stays out of the house as much as possible, and he is also absent for long periods during a strike at his workplace. A union man, he would hang around the union hall, waiting for news. During these periods, Mary would see little of her father.

Although his love for Charlie Marie is genuine, they quarrel frequently. After their divorce, Pete returns to live in Texas and makes little effort to stay in touch with his daughters. But he is delighted to see them when they return, and he is also eager for Charlie Marie to rejoin the family.

Pete has a stroke in 1980, seven years after his retirement at age sixty-three. After the stroke he cannot speak coherently and he is cared for by Charlie Marie and Mary.

Grandma Moore

Grandma Moore is Mary's grandmother on her mother's side. She is a bossy, critical woman who disapproves of Mary's marriage to Pete. When Grandma Moore gets cancer, she comes to live with the Karr family, and Pete makes himself scarce. Grandma immediately tries to impose her will on the way they all live. She has firm ideas about the proper way to do things. She tries to get Mary and Lecia to read the Bible every day, for example, and she never expresses a tender word to Mary. Instead, she is a disciplinarian and urges Charlie Marie to spank her daughter, even making a leather whip for the purpose. Grandma Moore is also eccentric; she carries a hacksaw around with her in a black doctor's bag.

When the cancer worsens, Grandma Moore's leg is amputated above the knee, and she wears an artificial leg. The cancer eventually spreads to her brain, making her even more cantankerous. Mary is not sorry when she dies. Grandma Moore leaves Charlie Marie a considerable amount of money in her will.

Mother

See Charlie Marie Karr

Shug

Shug is one of the members of the Liars' Club. He is the only black man that Mary ever sees in the American Legion, but he goes there only when the Liars' Club meets. He is openly skeptical when Pete Karr's stories get too incredible. He and Cooter are sometimes antagonistic towards one another.

Themes

Survival of Love

The Liars' Club is in many ways a grim story of the disruption of family life caused by a quarreling husband and wife, and a mother's alcoholism and mental instability. Although the devastating effect of this behavior on the children is apparent everywhere, especially in the aggressive behavior of Mary, it is not the main theme of the memoir. The main theme is the endurance of familial love in the worst of circumstances. The bonds generated by blood ties, even when put under tremendous strain, exercise a continual hold on the emotions and loyalties of the characters in the memoir.

It is noticeable that Karr, although writing as an adult, has preserved the nonjudgmental ways in which young children view their parents, even when the parents behave as badly as the Karrs do. Mary and Lecia never seem to blame their mother for her actions; they seem to be quite mature in their realization that it is simply the way Mother is and

sometimes they even take the initiative to look after her.

The love between father and daughter is never in question either, even though there are long periods when Mary sees little of her father. One of the most poignant moments in the memoir is when the two sisters return to Texas from Colorado to live with their father. He lies on the bed with the girls on either side of him and weeps tears of joy at their return. He prays that Charlie Marie will come back to him and sobs as he does so. As they do with their mother, the girls sense what their father needs, and they gently pat him until he quiets down.

The fact that Pete Karr prays for the return of the woman with whom he regularly had such vicious fights is also significant. There seems to be a bond between them that is hard to break, no matter what happens. In their own turbulent way, the couple continues to love each other.

The triumph of love is made most explicit in the last section of the book, set in 1980, when Karr was in her mid-twenties. It shows that the bonds of this thoroughly dysfunctional family remain tight. For example, there is a moment during the time Karr is caring for her father when she plays the audiotape she recorded of one of the stories he told to the Liars' Club. It takes her back to the days when by his storytelling gift her father could take her to times and places she had never known except through his voice. Just before playing the tape, she looks at her father's face, so shrunken and gaunt, and for a split second sees it as a death's head. At this point she wants nothing more than to hear him tell one of his stories. Playing the taped story while they both listen is a way of affirming life and the bond they share.

The endurance of love is also shown when Karr discovers the truth about why her mother went through such long periods of depression and mental instability (i.e., the loss of her children from her first marriage). This knowledge frees them both from feelings of guilt and allows more love to be present, even though it is a while before they both realize this.

A symbol of the endurance of love occurs on the last page of the memoir. As mother and daughter drive home from the Mexican café where all the secrets have been divulged, Mary notices small gatherings of fireflies in the flowers at the roadside: "How odd, I thought, that those bugs lived through the refinery poisons." She is referring to the toxic

Topics for Further Study

- Write your own one- to two-page memoir about an incident you remember from your childhood. Try to capture the child's way of seeing things. Write it in your own voice and style rather than trying to imitate Karr.

- Research the topic of alcoholism and the effects it has on families, particularly children. Why do some people become alcoholics while others who drink do not? Is there a cure for alcoholism?

- The Karr family is forced to flee Hurricane Carla in 1961 in Texas. Using the Internet, research Hurricane Carla and other major hurricanes along the Gulf Coast. What are the weather conditions that produce a hurricane? How has the technology of predicting the path of a hurricane changed since the 1960s? (Remember that in *The Liars' Club*, the storm unexpectedly hits a town in Louisiana rather than Leechfield, Texas, its predicted path.)

- Karr defines a dysfunctional family as "any family with more than one person in it." She means that every family is dysfunctional in one way or another. Do you agree? Why or why not? How would you define dysfunctional? Do you think that people can put bad childhood experiences behind them, or do those experiences mark people for life?

---

fumes that emanate from the oil refineries of Leechfield, but she also means for the reader to make the connection: the light of love, like a firefly in the night, continues to live in spite of the toxic atmosphere generated by a quarreling family.

Style

Imagery

Although Karr often uses vulgar expressions that are part and parcel of the way many of the local people speak, she also on many occasions uses highly poetic imagery. This creates quite a contrast for the reader. In one of the milder examples of local slang, for example, a girl emerging from a coma after contracting encephalitis is "half-a-bubble off plumb." But on the next page, Karr uses a more literary form of expression, a simile, to describe the effect of her father's voice on the neighborhood children: "the kids all startled a little the way a herd of antelope on one of those African documentaries will lift their heads from the water hole at the first scent of a lion." Examples of similes (figures of speech in which one thing is compared to something else in a way that brings out the resemblance between the two) might be found on almost every page. Karr's similes are often original and memorable. The oil storage tanks in Leechfield are "like the abandoned eggs of some terrible prehistoric insect." Mary's mother's eyes are like "the flawed green of cracked marbles." A large woman in a "flowered dress" looks "a lot like a sofa." When Mary and Lecia visit their post office mailbox in Colorado twice a day to see if there is a letter from their father, the box "always sat empty as a little coffin." This simile perfectly expresses the feeling of abandonment the girls feel when they do not hear from Daddy.

Setting

The fictional town of Leechfield, in eastern Texas, is important in creating the atmosphere of the memoir. Leechfield is in every way an oppressive place. Sitting in a semitropical latitude close to the Gulf of Mexico, it is three feet below sea level at its highest point and two rivers run through it. It is so damp and swamp-like that the homes are built without basements, since it would have been impossible to keep them dry. The many oil refineries and chemical plants give the whole town a smell like rotten eggs, a smell that gets worse the hotter the weather becomes. The night sky is an acid-green color because of the flames that rise from the oil refineries. According to Mary, the magazine *Business Week* voted it one of the ten ugliest towns on earth.

Leechfield was also the manufacturing site for Agent Orange, a herbicide used by the U.S. military during the Vietnam War to defoliate trees and shrubbery where the enemy could hide. Agent Orange is poisonous to humans, although this was not known at the time.

To add to Leechfield's hazards, the city is also afflicted by swarms of mosquitoes, which necessitates the spraying of DDT (a now-banned poison) from a huge hose on a mosquito truck. The neighborhood kids "slow race" their bicycles behind the truck, inhaling the fumes. The aim is to come in last, which means that the winners often vomit and faint from the poison they inhale.

This image of poison, as well as the whole unsavory atmosphere of Leechfield, is an apt metaphor for Mary's early life, lived in the poisonous arena of family discord. Yet when Daddy says the town is too ugly not to love, it also seems appropriate for the story that Mary tells, a story that is at times ugly, but also in its own way full of love.

Literary Techniques

Numerous additional literary devices are employed in the memoir, as noted in the critical essay. These devices include starting the memoir *in medias res;* the use of suspense; the technique of foreshadowing; and "genre blur," a writing trend Karr describes as blurring the boundaries between fiction and nonfiction.

Historical Context

Memoir Genre

A memoir differs from an autobiography in that it does not cover the writer's entire life, only selected portions. Traditionally, memoirs were written by public figures late in their lives, reflecting on great events in which they had played a part. Thus, politicians and statesmen have been noted memoirists. In a memoir, the focus was usually not on the writer, but on other well-known people the writer had known or encountered.

While there have always been literary memoirs as well as those by statesmen, in the 1990s the nature of the memoir genre began to change. Many of the new memoirs were written by relatively unknown writers with unusual experiences to relate rather than by well-known public figures. Susanna Kaysen's *Girl Interrupted* (1994), for example, was a bestselling memoir of Kaysen's life in a mental institution. Frequently, the new memoirs were about the author's childhood, with an emphasis placed on the honest, if painful, recall of unsavory details, including various forms of degradation, such as alcoholism, poverty, or sexual abuse.

In 1995 alone, approximately two hundred memoirs were published. *The Liars' Club* turned out to be the most popular of them all. It was followed in 1996 by Frank McCourt's bestselling memoir *Angela's Ashes,* about the author's impoverished upbringing in Ireland.

Commentators link the rapid growth of this kind of memoir to the popularity of confessional television and radio talk shows, in which people discuss the intimate details of their private lives. As James Atlas puts it in his *New York Times Magazine* article, "The Age of the Literary Memoir Is Now":

> In an era when "Oprah" reigns supreme and 12 step programs have been adopted as the new mantra, it's perhaps only natural for literary confession to join the parade. We live in a time when the very notion of privacy, of a zone beyond the reach of public probing, has become an alien concept.

Karr has her own explanation for the rise of the memoir genre. In an interview with Charlotte Innes in the *Los Angeles Times,* Karr says that it is due to "distrust of institutions; loss of faith in the moral authority of belief systems; and a corresponding turning inward and listening to one's own voice." She argues that because many families today break up, this leaves many people with a feeling of failure. They reach out to television and books in order to reestablish a sense of community, the feeling that they are not alone. In an essay in *New York Times Magazine,* Karr relates how hundreds of people came up to her after book readings she gave on nationwide tours and told her that her family reminded them of theirs. People felt encouraged and reassured by Karr's record of her personal experience. She concludes:

> Just as the novel form once took up experiences of urban, industrialized society that weren't being handled in epic poems or epistles, so memoir—with its single, intensely personal voice—wrestles subjects in a way readers of late find compelling.

Not all commentators see the growth of this type of memoir as a desirable trend. Novelist William Gass, writing in *Harper's* magazine a year before the publication of *The Liars' Club*, suggests that many writers of memoirs are too self-absorbed. They make the mistake of thinking every small thing that happened to them is important enough to be recorded. Gass also argues that it is almost impossible for a writer to convey a true account of his or her own past:

> Every moment a bit of the self slides away toward its station in the past, where it will be remembered partially, if at all; with distortions, if at all; and then rendered even more incompletely, with graver omissions.

Critical Overview

The Liars' Club remained almost sixty weeks on the *New York Times* best-seller list. Critical praise for the work has been unanimous, and critics have searched for the most glowing adjectives to describe it. Louis Ermelino, for example, in *People Weekly*, calls it ''an astonishing memoir'' and praises Karr's use of ''the rich cadence of the region and poetic images.'' In the *Nation*, Molly Ivins makes a similar point, commending Karr for her ''bilingualism,'' by which she means Karr's ability to switch freely from literate, educated prose to down-home Texan expressions. Ivins also praises Karr's observations about class, and she concludes her review in laudatory terms:

> This is a book that will stay gentle on your mind, stirring up memories of childhood and family. To have a poet's precision of language and a poet's gift for understanding emotion and a poet's insight into people applied to one of the roughest, toughest, ugliest places in America is an astounding event.

A *Publishers Weekly* critic notes that Karr ''views her parents with affection and an unusual understanding of their weaknesses.'' In *Time,* John Skow observes that there is probably a touch of exaggeration in some of Karr's more outlandish stories, such as when she finds the artificial leg of her dead grandmother while rummaging around in the attic, but Skow feels this exaggeration does not detract from the effectiveness of the book or its power to amuse: ''The choice in the book is between howling misery and howling laughter, and the reader veers toward laughter.''

Karen Schoemer in *Newsweek* notes Karr's ''captivating, anecdotal style,'' which ''meanders'' like a good story told by a member of the book's Liars' Club. The effect of Karr's style, says Schoemer, is that when she gets around to relating the story's most horrifying incidents, ''you're so completely in her corner that you feel just as trapped as she is. She's figured out a way to make every reader live through what no child should ever have to endure.''

Criticism

Bryan Aubrey

Aubrey holds a Ph.D. in English and has published many articles on twentieth-century literature. In this essay, Aubrey shows how Karr uses novelistic techniques in her memoir, and he also discusses how a memoirist may present a truthful account of her life even though she does not rely on a strictly literal, fact-by-fact approach.

Many readers of *The Liars' Club* have commented on Karr's acute memory of the intricate details of her early life. Some readers wondered whether the memoir was really true, since Karr's memory seemed so remarkable. After all, few people can remember their early childhood in such detail. This reaction on the part of some readers raises many interesting questions about how a memoir is written and what it means to say that something is ''true.''

The Liars' Club is as artfully arranged as any novel. It is not simply a chronological account of the events of Karr's life, like a diary would be. It begins, for example, *in medias res* (a Latin phrase which means, literally, ''in the middle of things''). The first incident Karr relates is the aftermath of Mother's demented rampage in which she burns the children's belongings and seems about to kill them. The incident is told in chapter 1 from the point of view of a child surrounded by large adults, a child who is bewildered at what is going on around her. But Karr is very careful not to let the reader in on the secret of what has led to this unsettling scene, even though Mary as the little girl is quite capable of explaining it, since she watched it all unfold. Karr's purpose in adopting this technique is to create interest and suspense for the reader. Readers continue on in the book because they want to know the full story of what happened in that incident. Karr keeps readers

What Do I Read Next?

- Karr's second memoir, *Cherry: A Memoir* (2000), describes her life as a rebellious adolescent. The memoir is written in the same style as *The Liars' Club:* by turns gritty, vulgar, and poetic. Karr goes through various adventures—many of them involving sex, romance, and drugs—in her quest to escape the confines of Leechfield, Texas. She turns a harsh light on her own follies as well as those of others.

- Frank McCourt's *Angela's Ashes* (1996) followed *The Liars' Club* onto bestseller lists. McCourt tells of his impoverished childhood and adolescence during the 1930s and 1940s in Limerick, Ireland. The story is a long catalog of deprivation and hardship, including his father's alcoholism and his mother's despair. McCourt describes the events without bitterness, anger, or blame, and many episodes are hilarious.

- James Salter's *Burning the Days: Recollection* (1998) is a highly acclaimed memoir. Unlike the authors of *The Liars' Club* and *Angela's Ashes,* Salter had an upper-middle-class upbringing, and in this memoir he describes his experiences as a fighter pilot in the Korean War and his subsequent life in the film business, traveling throughout the United States and Europe.

- Like *The Liars' Club,* Elizabeth Spencer's *Landscapes of the Heart: A Memoir* (1997) describes an upbringing in the American South, although in this case it is Mississippi rather than Texas. Spencer's narrative is more elegant and less rugged than Karr's, and she looks back at an earlier period (mostly the 1930s through the 1950s) with nostalgic affection.

- Tobias Wolff was one of Karr's writing mentors, and his *This Boy's Life: A Memoir* (1989) was exceptionally well received by reviewers. Like Karr, Wolff describes a difficult childhood in a dysfunctional family. However, as with Karr's memoir, his sense of humor and literary skill in telling his story alleviate the darkness of many of the events.

---

waiting until she explains the incident fully near the end of part I. In so doing, she accomplishes what every good novelist must do, which is to create suspense. Suspense means a state of uncertainty about what is going to happen.

Of course, the writer must also establish sympathy in the reader's mind for the character, so that readers are interested in her and concerned for her. Karr does this in masterly fashion by having the first incident revolve around the perceptions of a child who only half-understands what is happening around her. Like many children faced with disruption in the family, she feels that it is she who must have done something wrong. Karr also captures the child's irritation at being left out of whatever serious business is taking place because the grown-ups think the child would not understand: "When you're a kid and something big is going on, you might as well be furniture for all anybody says to you." It would be

hard for any reader not to be on Mary's side after comments like this one.

Creating a sense of mystery by the technique of foreshadowing is also part of Karr's array of novelistic techniques. The mystery is created when Grandma Moore shows Mary a photograph of two children, whom she calls Tex and Belinda. She tells Mary that they are Mary's brother and sister. Mary does not understand what she means, since she has never seen these children. Grandma says the children were sent away, and if Mary is bad, she will be sent away too. The full story does not emerge until the last few pages, when the adult Mary learns from her mother the circumstances under which Tex and Belinda, her mother's two children from her first marriage, were taken from her mother. The fact of that terrible loss explains Mother's history of mental problems. As in a good mystery novel, the author produces the solution only at the end, which also

> " . . . there are many ways of presenting truth, and it is possible for a writer to convey the essential emotional truth of a situation without necessarily sticking to a laborious account of the moment-by-moment facts of a person's life."

enables the memoir to end on a note of reconciliation and optimism.

Karr's artful way of telling her story, using techniques that fiction writers employ, resembles her father's technique in telling stories to the Liars' Club: "No matter how many tangents he took or how far the tale flew from its starting point before he reeled it back, he had this gift: he knew how to be believed." Like father, like daughter. Incidentally, Mary comments that most of Daddy's stories were not true. Not only this, but Karr has stated that she herself made up the stories told by her father in the memoir. The only exception to this was her father's one story that she recorded, which she played back for him after his stroke in 1980.

In spite of such acknowledged inventions, Karr has insisted that the events of the memoir really happened. In her acknowledgements in the front of the book, she states that she checked the veracity of what she had written with her sister. In interviews with journalists, she has indicated that many of the details came back to her during the long years she spent in psychotherapy, dealing with the legacy of such a disturbed family background.

However, there are many ways of presenting truth, and it is possible for a writer to convey the essential emotional truth of a situation without necessarily sticking to a laborious account of the moment-by-moment facts of a person's life. "Readers expect the truth," Karr told Charlotte Innes for the *Los Angeles Times,* "but nobody carries a tape recorder around with them all the time."

Karr points to a modern trend that she calls "genre blur," in which the usual boundaries between fiction and nonfiction have become less rigid. She explains, according to Innes, that the memoir "may offer its own aesthetic lies of compressed time, authorial bias and manipulated details."

By the phrase "compressed time," Karr means that events that were separated by perhaps days, weeks or months in real life can be condensed by the memoir writer for dramatic or other effect, so that they appear to have taken place over a much shorter period of time. This supplies the memoir with a much tighter structure and a consequent increase in narrative drive—the speed at which the story moves forward. This device makes it more interesting for the reader.

When Karr refers to "manipulated details," she means she has again used a storyteller's license. Most likely, she has on occasions taken several separate but similar incidents and condensed them into one, taking the most appropriate details from each incident. The result would be a composite that in the author's judgment tells the incident in the most powerful and effective way. At times also, Karr may not have adhered strictly to the real-life sequence of events. In other words, incidents in the memoir may not necessarily follow the order in which they occurred in real life. Karr reserves the right, as the creative author, to sequence the story in the way she thinks will produce the effect she wants. This is often how writers of fiction (and many contemporary memoirists too) work when drawing on incidents from real life. The point to bear in mind is that something can be true to the emotions and feelings involved in a situation, and to the relationships between the characters, without being strictly factual in all its details.

The last of the "aesthetic lies" that Karr identifies is "authorial bias." In writing about her own life, a writer may consciously or unconsciously shape her narrative to present herself the way she thinks she is or the way she wants to be perceived. All manner of things can be distorted in this way. It is almost impossible for a writer or anyone else to be objective about her own life. However hard a writer looks, there are things about herself that she simply cannot see. And even if she is sure of her own feelings and motivations, she cannot know for certain what others are thinking or how they view her. She cannot know their motivations with the same certainty that she thinks she knows her own.

There is also the problem of memory. Often people misremember past events, even as they are certain that they remember clearly. If two people are asked to remember an incident they shared, say, a decade ago, they are likely to come up with two very different sets of memories. But people usually make little allowance for these distortions that the passage of time imposes on them, confident that they remember things the way they "really" were, as if such a notion has an objective status, beyond the realm of one's fluctuating subjectivity.

Bearing all this in mind, perhaps the question of whether a memoir or an autobiography is true or false is irrelevant. A memoir is simply a viewpoint of one individual at a certain point in his or her life, and that individual will be conditioned by temperament, experience, desires, and beliefs to see her life in a certain way. Her viewpoint may change over time, rendering earlier judgments and beliefs obsolete. Karr tells us this in no uncertain manner on the last page of her memoir. After she learns the secrets of her mother's troubled life and has had some time to reflect on them, she realizes that the way she has habitually interpreted her life is not only a distorted view, but is altogether false:

> All the black crimes we believed ourselves guilty of were myths, stories we'd cobbled together out of fear. We expected no good news interspersed with the bad. Only the dark aspects of any story sank in. I never knew despair could lie.

In other words, Karr never realized that the interpretation she used to put on events, that at the time seemed so clear, certain, and obvious, could actually have been a false way of seeing things. It did not enter her head that there might be a completely different way of interpreting those very same events, a way much "truer" than the previous one.

What Karr reveals in the last few paragraphs of her memoir is that all personal judgments about one's life should be provisional only, subject to revision as later facts become known, as full stories are puzzled out, and as one gains more and more wisdom. There is no final truth, only successive revisionings, for today's truth may be tomorrow's lie.

Source: Bryan Aubrey, Critical Essay on *The Liars' Club,* in *Nonfiction Classics for Students,* Gale, 2003.

Adrian Blevins

Blevins's is a poet and essayist who has taught at Hollins University, Sweet Briar College, and in the Virginia Community College system; Blevins' first full-length collection of poems, The Brass Girl Brouhaha, *is forthcoming from Ausable Press in September of 2003. In this essay, Blevins argues that Mary Karr's penchant for concrete details undermines* The Liars' Club*'s believability.*

The English poet Samuel Taylor Coleridge uses the term 'the willing suspension of disbelief' to talk about how important it is for readers to *at least* pretend to believe that what they're reading is true. In fact, it is so common to assess the merits of literary fiction by evaluating its believability that even people who have never heard of Coleridge appraise the merits of texts and films on the basis of their willingness—or their lack of willingness—to suspend their disbelief. Bad actors can undermine good films by being "unconvincing" or by being scripted into too-unlikely situations and circumstances. Even unbelievable dialogue, which forces actors to speak in ways human beings do not and never have spoken, has the potential of limiting an audience's pleasure by reminding moviegoers that the narrative they're watching is an imaginative construct.

Although there are a multitude of ways fiction writers generate believability in their novels and stories, one of the most famous techniques is a reliance on concrete detail. In *The Art of Fiction,* John Gardner says that the fiction writer "gives us such details about the streets, stores, weather, politics, and concerns of Cleveland (or wherever the setting is) and such details about the looks, gestures, and experiences of his characters that we cannot help believing that the story he tells us is true." Even *The Elements of Style,* which is more of a rule book than a guide to writing fiction, promotes the importance of concrete detail. Strunk writes:

> If those who have studied the art of writing are in accord on any one point, it is on this: the surest way to arouse and hold the attention of the reader is by being specific, definite, and concrete. The greatest writers— Homer, Dante, Shakespeare—are effective largely because they deal in particulars and report the details that matter.

In this age of the memoir, however, it is a surprise that few critics have discussed the ways in which concrete detail, which is so necessary in fiction, might actually *damage* creative nonfiction. The most notable stylistic quality of *The Liars' Club* is the extremely specific detail with which Mary Karr records the generally horrific events of her childhood. Because this detail is *suspiciously* concrete or specific, it actually undermines the book's believability.

The Liars' Club begins when Karr is seven years old, after her mother has had the most violent and frightening of her many nervous breakdowns. The family doctor is kneeling before Karr, wearing "a yellow golf shirt unbuttoned so that sprouts of

> " . . . in *The Liars' Club*, Karr's penchant for detail, which presupposes that very small children . . . can, among other very specific details, remember the way a doctor's hair falls out of his shirt, destabilizes her reliability as a speaker."

hair showed in a V shape on his chest.'' Karr also tells us that the doctor had ''watery blue eyes behind thick glasses, and a mustache that looked like a caterpillar.'' She says she's wearing ''her favorite nightgown,'' which has ''a pattern of Texas bluebonnets bunched into nosegays tied with ribbon against a field of nappy white cotton,'' and that her sister is wearing ''pink pajamas.'' She describes ''a tallboy [that] was tipped over on its back like a stranded turtle, its drawers flung around,'' and ''the nutty smell [of coffee mixed with] the faint chemical stink from the gasoline fire in the back yard.'' Karr then tells us ''the volume on the night began to rise'':

> People with heavy boots stomped through the house. Somebody turned off the ambulance siren. The back screen opened and slammed. My daddy's dog, Nipper, was growling low and making his chain clank in the yard.

Although it's possible that a child whose mother may or may not have been trying to kill her would remember all these details—neurologists say that trauma slows down time and helps victims focus on details—Karr also remembers events that aren't as traumatic in *The Liars' Club*. She tells us, for example, that one night after she and her family moved to Colorado, they ordered ''meatloaf and mashed potatoes'' that Karr and her sister Lecia ''molded into volcanoes.''

The most tender parts of the memoir are the passages in which Karr goes fishing or to the Liars' Club with her father to listen to him and his friends— ''Cooter and Shug and Ben Bederman''—tell funny stories. The first such passage happens early in the book and here, too, Karr luxuriates in her obvious love affair with concrete detail. She tells us not only what each man says just exactly, but also, on one occasion, that the men and Karr ''each have a floatable Coca-Cola cushion to sit on'' and that Karr ''[jerks] the banana-yellow lure across the surface of the water so its tiny propellers whir and stop . . . ''

In other words, in *The Liars' Club*, Karr has completely abided by the rules governing the American creative writing workshop and associated texts and manuals. She's showing, rather than telling, by appealing to senses of sight, sound, touch, smell, and taste. Karr also takes great advantage of her experience with the image—the verbal picture—to evoke her memories in her readers' minds. Yet, since her acute memories of such details are sometimes impossible to believe, they make Karr suspect as a speaker.

As mentioned, fiction relies on details because readers have a difficult time enjoying anything they don't believe. Lyric poets also focus on details, which they're inclined to call images, not only because such details increase believability, but also because lyric poems use the particular as a kind of clay in order to still time and make individual experience seem more universal. The goal of personal essayists is to use concrete detail to expose their processes of mind and thought rather than to depict a series of narrative events. They are more inclined to admit to what they can't remember than to pretend to remember it. This technique increases the personal essayist's sincerity, which Phillip Lopate in ''The Art of Personal Essay'' says ''is meant to awaken the sympathy of the reader, who is apt to forgive the essayist's self-absorption in return for the warmth of his or her candor.'' In other words, in admitting what he doesn't know and can't remember, the personal essayist increases his credibility. Isn't a memoir more like a personal essay than a novel? Shouldn't it be?

One of the most explicit passages in *The Liars' Club* describes Karr's memory of her first rape, which happens when an ''evil boy'' from the neighborhood smells ''some kind of hurt or fear'' on her and takes her ''into somebody's garage'':

> He unbuttoned my white shirt and told me I was getting breasts [. . .] his grandparents had chipped in on braces for his snaggly teeth. They glinted in the half dark like a robot's grillwork. He pulled off my shoes and underwear and threw them in the corner in a ball, over where I knew there could be spiders. He pushed down his pants and put my head on his thing, which was unlike any of the boys' jokes about hot dogs and garden hoses.

This passage, like a later one in which one of Karr's babysitters forces her into a similar, if less complete sexual act, *should* inspire the reader's sympathy. But because of the book's almost obsessive reliance on concrete details, Karr does not always generate a sincere tone. The memoir seems at these times either overwritten or false.

In *The Situation of Poetry,* Robert Pinksy makes it clear that many modernist ideas, including those associated with the advantages of concrete details over abstractions and generalizations, have become too commonplace to continue to be interesting. Pinksy even criticizes certain images by the American poets Wallace Stevens and Marianne Moore, saying, ''the aggressive yoking of unlike things [can] sometimes amount to little more than showing off.''

Mary Karr is, of course, a poet, and her penchant for detail serves her intentions in her poetry. In the title poem of her collection *Viper Rum,* for example, she compares ''a tiny vine serpent'' to ''a single strand of luminous-green linguini.'' In so doing, Karr reminds us that one of the poet's primary tasks is to see the world so fully that we're reminded of its beauty and strangeness.

But in *The Liars' Club,* Karr's penchant for detail, which presupposes that very small children—even very small children who grow up to be writers—can, among other very specific details, remember the way a doctor's hair falls out of his shirt, destabilizes her reliability as a speaker. This lack of reliability undermines the entire book. In ''Such, Such Were the Joys,'' George Orwell, one of the best prose stylists ever to write in English, says, ''whoever writes about his childhood must beware of exaggeration and self-pity.'' Although Karr avoids self-pity by being absolutely merciless toward her parents' weaknesses, addictions, and collective lack of judgment, she commits the sin of exaggeration by claiming to remember such things as ''the odor that came out of [her father's] truck when [they had] crowbarred the padlock off and opened it.'' It would have been more profitable for her to more openly admit that, when it comes to recording memories, all writers must be lifelong members of the Liars' Club.

Source: Adrian Blevins, Critical Essay on *The Liars' Club,* in *Nonfiction Classics for Students,* Gale, 2003.

Josh Ozersky

Ozersky is a critic and historian. In this essay, Ozersky looks at the fine line between memoir and novel—a line nowhere finer, he contends, than in The Liars' Club.

As a book, *The Liars' Club* was so good that it transcended its genre; reading it today, it's easy to forget how influential it was when it was published in 1995. The literary memoir has a long and noble history, but the late 1990s saw what had been a fairly marginal genre move into the center of the publishing world as one memoir succeeded another at the top of the bestseller lists. Books like Frank McCourt's *Angela's Ashes,* Kathryn Harrison's *The Kiss,* Carolyn Knapp's *Drinking: A Love Story,* and David Sedaris's *Naked* sold like hotcakes, and their authors became major literary celebrities. But prior to the success of *The Liars' Club,* literary memoirs were much more of a specialized taste.

Mary Karr's childhood, though marked by domestic upheaval and an eccentric mother, wasn't really that unusual. Nor is the setting particularly exotic. Although she is molested by schoolboys twice in the book, she doesn't present this as a life-changing trauma. What makes *The Liars' Club* come alive is the force and art of her narration, which is so lively and expressive that it almost qualifies as a character itself.

Take, for example, the way she writes. In fact, it doesn't sound so much like writing as it does like talking, Karr is a very conscientious writer—a poet in fact—with a meticulous care for her choice of words. When she uses colloquial expressions, then, she's making a conscious decision. Why? Part of the reason is pure charm: *The Liars' Club* wasn't a phenomenal bestseller because it's hard to read. But a larger reason lies in her use of colloquial language to conjure up character, both her own and those she is writing about. For example, of her dying grandmother coming to live with her family, Karr writes, ''maybe it's wrong to blame Grandma Moore for much of the worst hurt in my family, but she was such a ring-tailed b—— that I do.'' That sentence begins with an adult, educated point of view—the language of therapeutic culture (''much of the worst hurt''), but it ends with a colloquial punchline, a funny Texas expression which serves to anticipate and dismiss an objection that might make Karr's character less than sympathetic. That mean, ornery, spunky little girl is the heroine of the book and has complete claim upon the reader by moving seamlessly between her adult character and the character of the child she was, Karr uses the best of both worlds. It's a calculating mixture of high-minded adult lan-

> ❝ . . . Karr is a very conscientious writer—a poet in fact—with a meticulous care for her choice of words. When she uses colloquial expressions, then, she's making a conscious decision. Why? Part of the reason is pure charm. . . .❞

guage and Texas sass, and it makes the book hard to put down.

Another payoff of Karr's skill is her ability to seem both within the action and also far away from it. When describing something especially vivid, like her experiences sitting in on a Liars' Club meeting or being molested by a neighborhood boy, she shifts to the present tense: "I am eye-level to the card table, sitting on an upended bait bucket, safe in my daddy's shadow, and yet in my head I'm finding my mother stretched out dead." Karr is simultaneously little Pokey, her father's favorite child, existing in a time and place so specific that she can tell you the tiniest physical detail of it and also outside herself, understanding her conflicted young mind better than she possibly could have at the time.

Besides creating her own presence, Karr's narrative strategies do something else too. They create for the reader the reality of her mother and father, the two most important other characters in the book. Unlike most memoir writers, Mary Karr doesn't really dwell on her own experiences and emotions. (Her molestation, for example, takes up less than two pages.) The book is really about her father and mother, their unique characters and the loving but rocky relationship between them. Mary Karr's mother Charlie is a bohemian, a romantic, irresponsible, impulsive, passionate, flighty, and given to bouts of insanity. Her father provides a grounded opposite; he is laconic, earthy, and unswerving in his devotion to his family. "With Mother," Karr writes, "I always felt on the edge of something new, something never before seen or read about or bought, something that would change us. . . . With Daddy and his friends, I always knew what would happen

and that left me feeling a sort of dreamy safety." The tension between the two is the engine which pushes the book forward. "Back then, heat still passed between my parents. You could practically warm your hands on it," Karr remembers.

The primary way readers get to know Charlie and Pete is through their language. Charlie's voice has little in it of Texas. But really, readers don't hear much of Charlie's voice. Karr describes what her mother does and says in her own language. She doesn't seem to talk much; in her most memorable scenes, such as her near-murderous car accident, she is singing "Mack the Knife." At other times, she is quoted in italics:

> We'd be driving past some guys in blue overalls selling watermelons off their truck bed and grinning like it was as good a way as any to pass an afternoon. She'd wag her head as if this were the most unbelievable spectacle, saying *God, to be that blissfully ignorant.*

The fact that readers so rarely hear Charlie's voice, and that it is so often stilted or cryptic when it is heard, contributes to her aura of mystery and menace. Who is this woman, readers ask. If the answer isn't clear, it's because it isn't clear to Mary Karr either, then or now. Charlie Marie comes through as a fascinating woman, whose bizarre behavior is only partially explained by the revelation Karr saves for the very end of the book.

Pete Karr, on the other hand, comes alive precisely because Mary Karr understands him so well. There may have been more to the real Pete Karr than his daughter Mary knew, but if so, it's not apparent in *The Liars' Club.* Mary Karr adores and admires her father in a way that illuminates her memoir from within, and the ultimate tribute is how frequently he dominates her narrative. The tall tales with which her father dominates *The Liars' Club* really don't have much to do with the book's action; the club itself only shows up a few times over the course of the book. But his language, with its expressiveness and Texas poetry, cuts through Mary Karr's narration. In a way, Pete Karr functions as a kind of masculine archetype in a book dominated by women.

> "I s— you not," Daddy said as he tore off a hunk of biscuit. "You touch a dead man sometime." He took a swallow of buttermilk. "Hard as that table. Got no more to do with being alive than that table does."

Mary Karr would no more be capable of speaking those lines than she would be able to knock out a romantic rival with one punch, any more than she could have her father's raspy chin, Lava soap and whiskey smell or superhuman virility. But she can, and does, use her father's colorful Texanisms to pepper her own language, which for the most part is like her mother's—vociferous but colorless, without regional flavor—an educated person's words. Like the fighting streak she is so proud of, this is a gift from her father that she cherishes.

In the end, *The Liars' Club* creates a space to live in Mary Karr's memories. Readers may not have anything in common with her or her family or with Texas or with the troubles she experienced. But by creating such a richly textured memoir in which language itself develops character so powerfully, we feel that we know the people at least as well as she does. Karr along with Frank McCourt, helped to change American letters by demonstrating how a novelist's eye for detail and ear for the way people talk could turn one person's memories into literature as moving and universal as any novel.

Source: Josh Ozersky, Critical Essay on *The Liars' Club,* in *Nonfiction Classics for Students,* Gale, 2003.

William Harmon

In the following essay excerpt, Harmon comments on Karr's move from poetry to prose in The Liars' Club *and praises how Karr captures certain elements of childhood including sound and scent.*

We may have financial straits to thank for Karr's decision to turn her family dramas into a memoir. It's certain that *The Liars' Club* has enjoyed much greater success and sales than her poetry; and criticism, God knows, makes money or friends for nobody. My review copy of *The Liars' Club* arrived in the custody of a thousand-word *blurbissimo* and a schedule of cities where Karr was to be available for publicity interviews: Philadelphia, Washington, New York, Boston, Syracuse, Seattle, Portland, San Francisco, Los Angeles, Minneapolis, Chicago—but nothing in the Southeast (where Viking may think we don't read) and nothing even near Texas (where Viking may think they read but are sensitive about stories of serial divorce, boozing, and worse excesses).

The Liars' Club, vulgar hoopla notwithstanding, is as good as anything of its kind that I know of. It includes much that I can still be amused but at the same time shocked by, in a kind of Tex-Mex-Cajun-Cherokee Gothic with some colorful reckless endangerment, like the conduct we find in the lower

> **"** *The Liars' Club,* **vulgar hoopla notwithstanding, is as good as anything of its kind that I know of. It includes much that I can still be amused but at the same time shocked by, in a kind of Tex-Mex-Cajun-Cherokee Gothic. . . ."**

precincts of Pat Conroy or the less grotesque passages of Harry Crews, with moments of narcosis from Jim Carroll or Kathy Acker, along with gestures toward intellectual respectability in the form of sizable epigraphs or quotations from R. D. Laing, Ezra Pound, W. B. Yeats, Cormac McCarthy, and Zbigniew Herbert.

The first-level Liar's Club is a group of East Texas workingmen who gather to drink and swap stories. At a second level, The Liars' Club is everybody in the book and, by a readily extended metaphor, everybody everywhere. The book focuses on the author's parents: a woman with a man's name and a man with no name but initials. Charlie was married seven times, twice to J. P., who fathered two of her children, Lecia (pronounced "Lisa") and Mary Marlene, who were born in the 1950s and went through an upbringing that veered from numbing poverty to million-dollar comfort, from warm familial love to malice hard to believe except as a symptom of madness. The book starts *in medias res,* with Charlie being taken away for committal after a hair-raising episode involving delusion, alcohol, fire, and a butcher knife. The rest of the memoir unfolds the circumstances of this focal nightmare and comes to a close with the family temporarily reunited in a moribund twilight of fatigue and mortal illness.

Someone who has read *Abacus* will encounter much familiar material in *The Liars' Club.* Late in the book, the father has suffered a stroke and is hard to feed. Mary tries to dislodge a bolus that may cause him to choke: "Then he bit me. Even before his eyes creaked open to thin slits, he clamped down with his slick gums hard enough to hold me by that finger. Like some terrier who'd caught me snitching his biscuit. We stood that way a minute—my finger in his mouth, his black eyes glaring out with no glimmer of recognition.'' Here, for comparison, is part of the poem ''Home During a Tropical Snowstorm I Feed My Father Lunch'':

> And when he choked
> I pried the leather jaw open,
> poked my finger past the slick gums
> to scoop an air passage
> till he bit down hard and glared,
> an animal dignity glowing
> in those bird-black eyes,
> which carried me past pity
> for once, for once
> all this terror twisting into joy.

The teacher who in a few years offers a seminar on Mary Karr's writing will find such moments a splendid way to illustrate the differences between prose and poetry.

Those quotations suggest another change when Karr moved from the poetry of *Abacus* to the prose of *The Liars' Club*. Readers do not handle poetry the way they handle prose or speech. If a poem says, ''And a small cabin build there, of clay and wattles made.'' I think, ''Poetic inversion.'' If a piece of prose said such a thing, I would think, ''Stupid: why not say, 'And build there a small cabin made of clay and wattles'?'' Or try this: to be poetry and peculiar is to be poetry; to be prose and peculiar is to be peculiar. With a definite narrator, such as Huckleberry Finn or Holden Caulfield or Ellen Foster, a reader takes the voice, with its idiosyncratic vocabulary and spelling, as just another functional fiction, something you read through or read past, murmuring to yourself, ''Well, I suppose some kids must talk like that.'' I don't think Karr has quite solved this problem, or (and this may be what Mark Twain and J. D. Salinger and Kaye Gibbons accomplished) has made her peace with it. If you try to put yourself into the person of a seven-year-old girl (as Mary Marlene is at the beginning of *The Liars' Club*), you may benefit from the colorful language of childhood, but you may forfeit some distance, perspective, and proportion. Writers employing a juvenile narrator or at least a narrator with access to a juvenile perspective seem to settle for a degree of compromise that allows for irony and travesty. Karr now and then seems stuck on the horns of a dilemma. She writes sentences like these: ''Tatting is an insane activity that involves an eensy shuttle, thin silk thread, and maniacal patience''; ''They're going to make their webs somewheres else, so you think for a minute that Wilbur's gonna sink back

into his porcine misery all over again.'' You have to work very hard indeed to make a reader believe you are justified in using *eensy, somewheres,* and *gonna* in sentences that also contain *maniacal* and *porcine*. The outcome for me is a defiant retention of disbelief. It comes down to a question of husbanding your resources. A poet can just steal and be done with it: poets repeat, quote, echo, refer, and allude all the time, so much so that it seems that poems are made of other poems. That's part of their defining peculiarity. But prose is something else. Consider this description: ''Gordon's being there embarrassed me. He had white girly hands. His skin was a mass of acne pits and scarring. Some poet wrote once about 'the young man carbuncular,' and that was Gordon.'' That's so wrong-sounding that I want to hit it with my rubber stamp that says DECORATIVE. Not even ''some poet'' is invoked in a passage about Charlie's ''very critical mother-in-law, whom we might describe metaphorically as a broomstick-wielding German housewife with a gaze merciless as the sun's.'' Weirdly, Mary Marlene had, many pages earlier, viewed her *other* grandmother through the lens of Yeats's ''The Second Coming'': ''And the worst being full of passionate intensity always put me in mind of Grandma, who was nothing if not intense''; but the earlier quotation is overtly identified as something from ''the famous Yeats poem about things falling apart.''

Style is also mismanaged here: ''Mother had a book of them, one portrait more gray-faced than the next,'' which I think ought to read ''more gray-faced than the one before.'' And there's the varmint *The New Yorker* used to call The Omnipotent Whom: ''The next time Hector and Mother traveled, we stayed with his sister Alicia, whom I'd have guessed was too old and fat to fight with her husband, Ralph.''

But these are mere blemishes. I want to testify that Karr captures one part of childhood sublimely: the world of artificial smells that is one of the first things we know about people and one of the last things to go away. Today a whiff of bay rum or Arrid can take me back fifty years and more, and Karr has a genius for specifying just what essence was in attendance when something important happened: Shalimar, Old Spice, Jergens, Burma Shave, Lava.

Source: William Harmon, ''Mary Karr, Mary Karr, Mary Karr, Mary Karr,'' in *Southern Review,* Vol. 33, No. 17, Winter 1997, pp. 150–55.

Sources

Atlas, James, ''The Age of the Literary Memoir Is Now,'' in *New York Times Magazine,* May 12, 1996, pp. 25–27.

Ermelino, Louis, Review of *The Liars' Club,* in *People Weekly,* Vol. 44, No. 3, July 17, 1995, p. 28.

Gardner, John, *The Art of Fiction,* Knopf, 1984, reprint, Vintage Books, 1985.

Gass, William, ''The Art of Self: Autobiography in an Age of Narcissism,'' in *Harper's Magazine,* May 1994, pp. 43–52.

Innes, Charlotte, ''In *The Liars' Club,* Mary Karr Uses Humor to Tell about Her Fractured Family,'' in *Los Angeles Times,* December 26, 1996, p. 5.

Ivins, Molly, Review of *The Liars' Club,* in the *Nation,* Vol. 261, No. 1, July 3, 1995, p. 21.

Karr, Mary, ''Dysfunctional Nation,'' in *New York Times Magazine,* May 12, 1996, p. 70.

———, *Viper Rum,* New Directions Publishing, 1998, p. 1.

Lopate, Phillip, *The Art of the Personal Essay,* Doubleday, 1994, p. xxxvii.

Orwell, George, *Such, Such Were the Joys,* Harcourt Brace and Company, 1952, p. 118.

Pinsky, Robert, *The Situation of Poetry,* Princeton University Press, 1976, p. 5.

Review of *The Liars' Club,* in *Publishers Weekly,* Vol. 242, No. 16, April 17, 1995, p. 45.

Schoemer, Karen, Review of *The Liars' Club,* in *Newsweek,* Vol. 126, No. 6, August 7, 1995, p. 61.

Skow, John, Review of *The Liars' Club,* in *Time,* Vol. 145, No. 26, June 26, 1995, p. 77.

Strunk, William, and E. B. White, *The Elements of Style,* 3d ed., Macmillan, 1979, p. 21.

Further Reading

Karr, Mary, and Frank McCourt, ''How We Met: Mary Karr & Frank McCourt,'' in *Independent Sunday* (London), July 8, 2001, p. 7.
    Karr and McCourt (McCourt is the author of *Angela's Ashes*), describe their personal relationship and offer comments on each other's work.

Karr, Mary, and Gabby Wood, ''The Books Interview: Mary Karr,'' in *Observer* (London), June 24, 2001, p. 17.
    In this interview, Karr talks about her life and her method of writing, saying that she discards large amounts of writing before settling on the final version.

Smith, Patrick, ''What Memoir Forgets,'' in the *Nation,* Vol. 267, No. 4, July 27, 1998, p. 30.
    Smith argues that the trend in autobiographical publishing is to share vivid emotional and personal details of individuals' lives. These books go beyond enlightenment in their relentless effort to entertain. What they lack (although Smith makes an exception of Karr's memoir) is insight into the impact of human relationships on the human condition.

Young, Elizabeth, Review of *The Liars' Club,* in *New Statesman & Society,* Vol. 8, No. 375, October 20, 1995, p. 39.
    This British review is as laudatory as most of the American ones. Young praises Karr's vivid, beautiful writing; the care with which it has been constructed; the mastery of East Texas slang; and Karr's sense of humor and emotional honesty.

The Lost Daughters of China

Karin Evans

2000

Karin Evans's *The Lost Daughters of China: Abandoned Girls, Their Journey to America, and the Search for a Missing Past* (New York, 2000) is an account of the experiences of Evans and her husband as they adopt a baby girl from an orphanage in China. The book interweaves Evans's personal story with information about Chinese culture and society. Of particular importance is the Chinese population policy that began in the 1980s, which restricted families to one child. This policy was established because China's leaders believed that the country, with one billion people, was overpopulated and would only be able to achieve economic prosperity with rigidly enforced population control. The result was that thousands of babies, almost all of them girls, were abandoned by their parents and had to be placed in orphanages. Many were adopted by American parents who, like Evans and her husband, had to go through a long bureaucratic process with many delays before they could connect with their new daughters in China.

In addition to providing a moving account of how two American parents bonded with a Chinese baby and brought her back to live in San Francisco, *The Lost Daughters of China* also raises many issues that Evans discusses in an accessible and interesting way: the challenges of raising a baby who has a different ethnicity than its parents; the place of women in Chinese society, both in history and today; and the origins and consequences of China's one-child policy.

Author Biography

Karin Evans is a journalist and author whose work has appeared in the *Los Angeles Times, Newsweek, San Francisco Examiner, Boston Globe,* and other publications. She was a founding editor of *Rocky Mountain Magazine,* was an editor at *Outside* magazine, and was a senior editor for the *San Francisco Examiner* Sunday magazine and for *Health* magazine. Evans spent two years working at the *Newsweek* Hong Kong bureau, where she became familiar with Chinese culture. She has commented that she felt drawn to that part of the world and felt at home there.

Evans lives in Berkeley, California, with her husband, attorney Mark Humbert, and their adopted daughter, Kelly Xiao Yu. The couple adopted Kelly in 1997 from Jiangmen, Guangdong, China. Evans's book *The Lost Daughters of China: Abandoned Girls, Their Journey to America, and the Search for a Missing Past* (2000) tells of her experience adopting a Chinese baby. Evans serves on the board of directors of the Half the Sky Foundation, which exists to help the orphaned children of China.

Plot Summary

Introduction

In the introduction to *The Lost Daughters of China*, Evans presents an overview of the topic of the large number of orphaned Chinese babies that have been adopted by American families. In 1997, Evans herself adopted her daughter, Kelly Xiao Yu, from an orphanage in southern China.

Chapter 1

Evans describes the long bureaucratic process that she and her husband Mark went through after they first decided in January 1996 to adopt a Chinese baby. They were both in their forties and had no children. Chinese baby girls were available for adoption because many were abandoned by their parents and ended up in state-run homes.

The process of adopting began at an international adoption agency in San Francisco, where Evans and her husband were informed that the total cost would be around fifteen thousand dollars and that the process would take about a year. In reality, it took nearly two years.

The couple had to apply to the Immigration and Naturalization Service for permission to adopt a foreign baby. This was the first step in what Evans describes as a sea of paperwork, confusing regulations, and bureaucratic delays. Finally, the U.S.-China liaison, a man she calls Max (which is apparently not his real name), calls to inform Karin and Mark they have a baby waiting for them in China. The baby is a year old and healthy.

Chapter 2

Evans describes the trip to China, which she and her husband make in company with several dozen other American adults who are also adopting Chinese babies. They arrive in Guangzhou, on the Pearl River Delta in southern China, eighty miles from Hong Kong. Evans describes the atmosphere of the city, which was hosting a business fair at the time, and notes the presence of twenty McDonalds restaurants. Guangzhou is rapidly growing, and many construction projects are underway.

Finally, along with the other American adopters, Evans and her husband receive their baby, whose name is Jiang Xiao Yu. She is healthy and appears to have been well cared for. The couple rechristens her Kelly Xiao Yu, after Evans's father, who died shortly before the adoption took place.

Chapter 3

Evans discusses the circumstances under which baby Chinese girls are abandoned and some of the cultural history of women in China. All that Evans knew about her new daughter was that she had been found abandoned at a local market when she was about three months old. Her birth parents and place of birth are unknown. This is typical of the Chinese baby girls put up for adoption. Evans points out that Chinese culture has a long history of discrimination in favor of male children. Girls are frequently regarded as just an extra mouth to feed.

Chapter 4

This chapter explains China's population control policy that has resulted in so many baby girls being abandoned or worse. The idea of slowing China's birthrate took root in the 1970s. China's population stood at one billion, and its leaders decided that the best way of producing economic growth was to instigate population control. The argument was that fewer people would lead to a rising standard of living and this in turn would produce political stability. In 1980, the policy became official. It was known as the one-child policy.

Families were restricted to one child, and this policy was enforced with some brutality, including forced abortions. Given the cultural preference for male children, baby girls were often abandoned, thus giving the family a chance to produce a son. The population policy created an imbalance in Chinese society: by 1990, five of China's thirty provinces had 120 boys for every 100 girls.

Chapter 5

Evans describes the ten days she and her husband spent with Kelly in Guangzhou before they returned to the United States. They bonded with the baby immediately, and Evans could hardly recall what life had been like without her, so perfect was the match. The new family spent their time sightseeing and wandering the streets of the city. Kelly and the other babies adopted by the American group were blessed in a Buddhist ceremony in a temple. On her arrival in San Francisco, Kelly quickly learned to adapt to her new environment.

Chapter 6

Evans's thoughts turn to the many Chinese babies that are orphaned but not adopted, noting that there may be as many as one million children in institutional care in China. She also comments that children with disabilities or major health problems, as well as older children, have only a slim chance of being adopted. Evans then discusses a television documentary, *The Dying Rooms,* which paints a grim picture of abuse in China's orphanages. She examines differing opinions about whether the documentary was an accurate portrayal of conditions in China's orphanages and points out that many problems are caused simply by poverty and lack of resources rather than intentional neglect.

Chapter 7

Evans describes the attempts of Americans who have adopted Chinese daughters to raise their children with an awareness of their Chinese heritage. Because of the large Chinese-American community in San Francisco, it is relatively easy for Evans to give Kelly some exposure to Chinese culture, and they celebrate the Chinese New Year and other occasions in the Chinese calendar. However, for people living in other parts of the country, such exposure may not be so easy. Evans describes some of the organizations that have been created to foster understanding of Chinese culture. She also explores the issue of ethnic identity and speculates about whether as they grow up the Chinese daughters will want to know more about their heritage or will regard themselves as completely American.

Chapter 8

Evans speculates about who Kelly's birth mother might have been and the circumstances that may have led her to give up her daughter. In general, few statistics exist to describe the families who abandon their babies. One study suggested that in half of all cases, the decision was made by the father; in 40 percent of cases, it was a joint decision. Only seldom did the mother make the decision on her own. The typical abandoned child was a healthy newborn girl who had one or more older sisters but no brothers.

Chapter 9

Evans considers the issue of whether it may be possible in the future for the adopted daughters from China to learn specific details about their birth families. There may, for example, be an increase in DNA testing, which could provide such information, although for that to occur the political situation in China would have to change.

Chapter 10

The author observes that as long as China's one-child policy continues, there will continue to be thousands more orphans, far more than can ever be adopted, since the pace of the adoption procedure is not likely to increase. But, she points out that the one-child policy is already being officially relaxed in some areas. Also, single children who marry other single children (as will increasingly be the case over the next decade) are allowed by the population policy to have two offspring.

Key Figures

Karin Evans

Karin Evans is a Caucasian woman from San Francisco. She is the author of the book and the person who adopts baby Kelly. Evans is in her late forties and has been previously married and divorced. She has no other children, her only son having died of a cerebral hemorrhage when he was three days old. She has thought of adopting ever since and has waited until the circumstances seemed right. She is certain she is pursuing the correct course as she navigates her way through the long adoption procedure, and she persists in her goal despite the delays and disappointments along the way. When she finally travels to China, meets Kelly, and takes her back to San Francisco, the bond she forms with the baby is immediate and profound. Evans is a thoughtful, resourceful woman who feels keenly her responsibilities as a new mother and accepts the challenge of raising Kelly with an awareness of her Chinese heritage.

Mark Humbert

Mark Humbert is Karin Evans's husband. He is a lawyer and, like his wife, he has long wanted children. He shares his wife's desire to adopt a baby girl from China. Also like Karin, he bonds immediately with the baby. He is overwhelmed by feelings of love and is surprised at the depth of those feelings and how quickly he is overtaken by them.

Max

Max is the liaison between U.S. and Chinese officials in charge of the adoption process. During the trip to China, Max acts as facilitator for the whole group of Americans. He is extremely efficient, seeming to be everywhere at once, smoothing the way with U.S. and Chinese officials, as well as with hotels, bus drivers, and waiters. Karin is extremely grateful for his help and calls him Uncle Max (and sometimes even Saint Max). She believes she owes as much to him as to anyone in her life.

Kelly Xiao Yu

Kelly Xiao Yu is the Chinese baby girl adopted by Karin and Mark. She is about a year old. The name given to her in the orphanage near Guangzhou is Jiang Xiao Yu. Jiang means ''river,'' Xiao means ''little,'' and Yu means ''education.'' Evans never discerns what the significance of ''little education'' might be as a name. One Chinese woman tells her that the word Yu, depending on the pronunciation and how it is written, may mean ''jade.'' Whatever the name means, Evans decides to retain it. However, she replaces the name Jiang with Kelly, in honor of Evans's late father. Evans and her husband soon discover that Kelly is affectionate and easy-tempered, with a full zest for life.

Topics for Further Study

- Research the issue of world population growth and write an essay about it. Do you feel it is desirable to reduce the world's population, and if so, by what methods?

- What might be some of the difficulties encountered by someone of Chinese ethnicity growing up in America? Should such a child be raised with an awareness of his or her Chinese cultural heritage, or is it more important for him or her to identify with mainstream American life and culture? Explain your answer.

- Should the state have any say in regulating reproductive practices, or should this be a private decision by the individual people concerned? Might a country like China have different needs than the United States in that respect? Explain your answer.

- Research the position of women in Chinese society today. How do their lives compare with the lives of women in the United States? Have Chinese women made progress in the last thirty years? What are some of the central issues they face today?

Themes

Love

The Lost Daughters of China is a love story. Although Evans discusses the larger issues of China's one-child policy, the book is primarily a human story rather than a political or sociological essay. The love story functions on several levels, and Evans takes care to emphasize all of them. Although she knows nothing at all of Kelly's birth mother, she feels confident in making certain deductions. She believes that the mother gave up her daughter only with great reluctance and grief and that she placed her in the market to ensure she would be quickly found. Evans believes without a doubt that Kelly's mother loved her. The baby's ready smile confirms it. Evans exonerates the mother from any blame for her actions and believes that she probably suffered in many ways because of them. The fact that the mother did not abort the baby is another sign that she loved her even before she was born, since abortions are easy to obtain and are even encouraged in China. Evans thinks of Kelly's birth mother as her Chinese soulmate.

The second level at which love occurs is in the orphanage. Although there have been reports of abuses taking place in China's orphanages, Evans is at pains to emphasize that Kelly received excellent care. She is well dressed, with brand new yellow corduroy shoes; she has been breast-fed (whether by the mother or the staff at the orphanage); and she trusts people and displays affection. The staff knows her as an individual, and the caregivers give Evans plenty of details about her: the baby can crawl and walk, she likes rice cereal and little pieces of apple and banana, and she can be mischievous. When Evans takes her away, one of the women waves to the baby, who responds by blowing a kiss and waving.

Finally, there is the love story between mother and daughter. For Evans, the experience is almost overwhelming. On their first full afternoon together, for example, ''We looked into each other's eyes and I covered her with kisses. It was a transcendent couple of hours, fixed in my memory now, both physical and mental.'' Shortly after they return to the United States, Evans has another realization. Holding Kelly in the kitchen, she knows suddenly and absolutely that she could not love the baby any more than she does at that moment: ''I loved her without condition, without reservation. There was simply no room left in my heart to love her more.'' Evans knows that even if she had given birth to Kelly herself, she could not love her more. She also knows that the difference in ethnicity means nothing; she and Kelly are mother and daughter in every sense of the word.

Loss

Alongside the love story is a story of loss. In the case of an adopted child from China, the two go hand in hand. Although Evans is understandably overwhelmed by her own experience of love for her new baby, she is also keenly aware of the other side of the coin. For her to have the chance to adopt the beautiful baby, many things must also be lost. First, there is the loss experienced by Kelly's birth mother, and Evans also spares some thoughts for the thousands of other Chinese women who give up their babies in similar circumstances. Their loss can never be calculated; the women themselves stay silent and anonymous. There are also many babies who are not so fortunate as Kelly and find no one to adopt them.

Evans wonders also whether, in spite of the joy Kelly shows, there may also be some lurking sadness, some sense of loss at what has happened to her. Evans herself feels great sadness when she leaves China, since that is all Kelly has ever known in her short life, and she may be leaving it behind forever. Kelly would never know for certain her origins or the way she had spent her first year of life.

Back in the United States, these thoughts continue to trouble Evans. When Kelly wakes at night and cries loudly, Evans wonders whether she is having a nightmare of being left in the market, of missing the orphanage, or about one of her early caregivers. Evans knows that that gap, that loss, in Kelly's life can never be filled. Kelly will never know her birth mother, who is untraceable, and her origins will always be shrouded in mystery.

Style

Figurative Language

Evans uses figurative language to explain the mysterious process of how and why adoptive parents get connected to their future daughters, who have been born on the other side of the world. She cites a Chinese story that describes how lovers are predestined to meet: a red thread connects them, no matter how far away they may be from each other. Evans explains that the Chinese-American adoptive community considers the expression to include parents and the children they adopt. The idea of the ''red thread'' gives expression to Evans's idea that there is an order and purpose in the universe. The way people become involved with each other is not random. It is part of a destiny that each person has to fulfill. This explains Evans's strong sense that it was absolutely right and inevitable that she and Kelly would become mother and daughter.

Evans notes that no one can prove one way or the other whether the thread—the hidden connection between two people that manifests itself at a certain time—really exists, or why, or how. She contents herself with this explanation: "Maybe the thread is woven partly from strands of destiny, partly from gratitude, partly from love. Maybe it's all a tribute to the openness of the human heart, both young and old."

On another occasion, Evans creates a symbol out of an everyday object. She is awakened one night by the prick of a needle that has been left in her hand-stitched, made-in-China quilt. She feels as if she has been poked by the anonymous seamstress, and in that small reminder of an absent craftswoman, the spirit of the seamstress comes through. Evans is able to imagine her at work. Evans moves from that thought to imagine the unknown, anonymous lives of the birth mothers of the adopted daughters. She realizes how closely connected these mothers still remain to their offspring, even though they gave them up for adoption, just as the needle connects the quilt to the seamstress. In the case of Evans's daughter, Kelly's ready smile is the clue that reveals the nature of her mother: even though she relinquished her baby, she loved her.

Creative Nonfiction

As a mixture of personal memoir, objective reporting, and historical analysis, with elements of travelogue thrown in as well, the book is not easily classified under traditional literary forms. This type of work, which has become popular over the last two decades, is referred to under a number of different names: creative nonfiction, personal journalism, the new journalism, or literary journalism. According to Theodore A. Rees Cheney, in *Writing Creative Nonfiction*, this new form combines "the skill of the storyteller and the research ability of the reporter." In this case, Evans tells a very personal story, of wanting a baby and of going through all the bureaucracy associated with adoption. She also tells the reader how she feels when she finally meets the baby and how she bonds with her. But Evans weaves into this personal memoir a wealth of factual information about the history of Chinese society, its attitudes toward women, and how China is changing today. The result of such an eclectic approach is usually a more interesting narrative, appealing to a wider group of readers, than a more scholarly approach that would exclude personal factors and confine itself to description and analysis of factual matters. It is not surprising, given that the author is a journalist rather than an academic, that she chose the livelier method. It presents history and current events with a human face.

Historical Context

China and Population Control

China is a huge country and has always had a large population. For much of its history, millions of Chinese peasants have lived in dire poverty. Floods and famine have frequently ravaged the land, and the death rate has always been high. During the 1930s, for example, in many rural areas the infant mortality rate was three hundred to every one thousand people, and average life expectancy was only twenty-four years.

The communist revolution in 1949 at first improved the fortunes of the country. Economic reform gave peasants greater security, and social welfare legislation in the cities gave many people retirement security. But as Evans points out, Chinese leader Mao Zedong's overambitious attempts at agricultural reform resulted in a huge famine. Between 1959 and 1962, famine claimed twenty million lives. It was the largest recorded famine in human history. The effects of famine and malnutrition were especially severe on children. In 1963, half of those people dying in China were under ten years old.

During the 1950s and 1960s, Mao Zedong did not believe that population control was necessary in China. He encouraged women to have more children. Like leaders in many developing countries, Chinese leaders regarded the population control movement as a Western idea designed to thwart their progress. In 1974, at the World Population Conference held in Bucharest, Romania, 136 countries attempted to reach a consensus on the need for population control. China, along with the Soviet Union, refused to support the movement.

But times were changing. When a new set of leaders came to power, especially Deng Xiaoping, limiting the population became Chinese government policy. The rationale was simple: fewer people would mean that China would be better able to feed its people and to make economic progress. The policy was reinforced by the findings of the 1982 census, which showed the population of China to be one billion. The aim of the one-child policy was to reduce the population to 700 million by 2050.

The policy had three main points. It advocated delayed marriage (at age twenty-two for men and twenty for women, although for women twenty-four was considered ideal). Childbearing was to be delayed, and there should be only one child per family. Ethnic minorities, however, were allowed to have two children.

The one-child policy announced in 1980 represented a drastic change, since at the time, as Evans points out, it was not uncommon for Chinese to have five or six children. The policy was often enforced cruelly, with millions of forced abortions and sterilizations. In cities, having a second child was punished with the loss of a job and a fine equivalent to three years' salary for each parent. Many families found ways of skirting the law, such as sending a pregnant woman to relatives and then failing to register the birth.

The policy also produced an increase in infanticide of girls. There were many reports of parents drowning or suffocating baby girls (as well as abandoning them) so that they could have another try at producing a boy. In one village alone, forty baby girls were drowned between 1980 and 1981.

In the late 1990s, there were signs that China's one-child policy might be easing. Laws that required parents to register for permits before having a child were abolished in some places, and it was no longer lawful to force women to undergo abortions and sterilization.

Critical Overview

The Lost Daughters of China received generally appreciative reviews. Eleanor J. Bader in *Library Journal* praises Evans's "riveting" examination of misogyny in China, pointing out that Evans does not "demonize" the Chinese people: "Instead, she eloquently assesses the conditions that force couples to abandon their offspring and chronicles the

emotional anguish that accompanies the decision to give up a child.''

For Vanessa Bush in *Booklist,* Evans "brings a mother's and a reporter's perspectives to this moving account of China's troubling [population] policy.'' The reviewer for *Publishers Weekly,* however, has mixed feelings. He or she finds the book strongest when Evans describes the way she and her new daughter quickly created a loving bond. But other sections of the book, in the reviewer's opinion, are not so strong. When Evans describes Chinese history and culture, her "lack of familiarity with China'' leads her to rely on secondary sources, resulting in a lack of "fresh insights.''

The most critical review of the book was written by Susan Greenhalgh in the journal *Population and Development Review.* Greenhalgh is herself a scholar of China's population policies. Although she acknowledged that *The Lost Daughters of China* is "finely crafted and deeply felt,'' she also feels that it presents a "romanticized portrait'' of the situation, "whisking from view the behind-the-scenes political dynamics that allowed the transfer of Chinese child to American parents to appear as a gesture of generosity and love.'' According to Greenhalgh, Evans ignores the fact that the adoption process was carefully stage-managed by Chinese officials who want to obscure the reality that the adoptions are the result of a population-control policy that depends on coercion.

Criticism

Bryan Aubrey

Aubrey holds a Ph.D. in English and has published many articles on twentieth-century literature. In this essay, Aubrey discusses the pressures that drove Chinese leaders to adopt the one-child policy in the early 1980s.

In her review of *The Lost Daughters of China*, Susan Greenhalgh, herself an expert in China population studies, criticized Evans for sugarcoating the story of Evans's adoption of Kelly. According to Greenhalgh, Evans too readily accepted the image

What Do I Read Next?

- Christine Hall's *Daughters of the Dragon: Women's Lives in Contemporary China* (1997) is a very readable account—much of it based on personal interviews—of all aspects of the lives of women in contemporary China. Hall examines topics including education, careers, sex and relationships, living conditions, fashion and beauty, leisure pursuits, religion, and politics.

- Adeline Yen Mah's bestselling memoir *Falling Leaves: The True Story of an Unwanted Chinese Daughter* (1997) describes her turbulent life, which began in an affluent family in the Chinese port city of Tianjin. She was emotionally abused by her stepmother but fought for her independence and went on to build a successful medical career in the United States. The memoir tells of her triumph over despair in a long search for love and understanding.

- *The Bonesetter's Daughter* (2001), by Amy Tan, explores the Chinese immigrant experience in America and the complex relationships between mothers and daughters. The novel weaves together two separate narratives: the story of LuLing, a young girl in 1930s China; and that of LuLing's daughter Ruth as a middle-aged woman in modern San Francisco.

- *Wild Swans: Three Daughters of China* (1992), by Jung Chang, is a dramatic and sometimes horrifying account of China as seen through the eyes of women of three different generations: the author, who left China in 1978; her mother, who married a communist revolutionary soldier; and her grandmother, who was sold as a concubine to Beijing's police chief.

- *Wuhu Diary: On Taking My Adopted Daughter Back to Her Hometown in China* (2001), by Emily Prager, is another story of adoption and China. Prager adopted an unwanted baby girl from Wuhu, a village in southern China. This mixture of memoir and travelogue is the story of her return to China with LuLu, her five-year-old daughter, to reintroduce the girl to her roots.

- The contents of *China Today: How Population Control, Human Rights, Government Repression, Hong Kong, and Democratic Reform Affect Life in China and Will Shape World Events into the New Century* (1995), by Donald Shanor and Constance Shanor, are clear from the title. The Shanors cover history, economics, foreign policy, and other fields as they examine the many different aspects of contemporary China.

---

that Chinese officials wished to project—that the orphans were being tenderly cared for and were handed over to their adoptive parents with love. In Greenhalgh's view, this obscured the political dynamics that operate behind the scenes in China. Rather than being lavished with love, the orphaned babies were in fact the victims of a deliberately coercive political policy that forced their abandonment and neglect.

In fairness to Evans, however, although she emphasizes the personal story of her adoption, she does not ignore the cruelties of the one-child policy. Indeed, it would be hard for the average reader not to feel indignant at her descriptions of some of the excesses of the policy, including forced, late-term abortions and compulsory sterilization.

People in the West have long known that such practices exist in China, ever since Steven W. Mosher revealed them in his 1983 book, *Broken Earth: The Rural Chinese*. The one-child policy has aroused fierce criticism in the West and has had repercussions on U.S.-Chinese relations. For example, during the Reagan administration of the 1980s, the United States withdrew its support for the United Nations Population Fund (UNFPA), which supports voluntary family planning and prenatal and maternal health care programs around the world, including China. The United States refused to support the

> "China's many well-wishers will hope that a move to voluntary family planning quickly makes coerced birth control a thing of the past."

fund because of domestic conservative opposition to birth control and abortion. The decision not to support UNFPA was reversed by the Clinton administration in 1993, but in 2002 President George W. Bush announced that the United States would withhold the $34 million voted by Congress for UNFPA. The official reason for this policy was that money given to the United Nations' agency would help the Chinese government to maintain its policy of forced abortion. Critics were swift to point out that the United Nations opposes forced abortions and sterilizations and that the money used by UNFPA in China is intended to show that voluntary family planning can be effective in tackling China's population crisis. However, the Bush administration declined to change its view.

Western distaste for the draconian nature of China's one-child policy is understandable, but what perhaps has been lacking is a full understanding of the pressures that drove Chinese leaders in the early 1980s to adopt the one-child policy in the first place. This is covered only very briefly in *The Lost Daughters of China*. A more detailed examination is contained in China scholar Jonathan D. Spence's book *The Search for Modern China*.

According to Spence, by 1981 it was clear to Chinese leaders that in the absence of population control, any economic gains China made through modernization would be cancelled out by the need to support a rising population. Such had been the case in other developing countries. Confirming these fears, the results of the 1982 census indicated that China's population had grown to over one billion, up from 694.6 million in 1964 (according to an earlier, and probably not entirely accurate, census).

The idea of instituting population control was not a new one. In the 1950s, some Chinese economists, as well as influential leaders such as Zhou Enlai, were advocating reductions in the birth rate.

But the triumph of political extremism during the 1960s, with its belief that the revolutionary will of the people, if properly organized, could ensure progress whatever the rise in population, ensured that the issue was not effectively addressed.

By the early 1980s, the population issue was no longer possible to ignore. Statistics showed that in 1981 in China, 6 million babies were born to couples who already had one child; 1.7 million babies were born to those who already had five or more children.

Spence explains that as they pondered their decisions, Chinese leaders had to bear five crucial factors in mind. First was the availability of suitable land for cultivation. Although its land area is larger than the United States, in the late 1970s China only had half as much cultivated land. In addition, China's larger population meant that the amount of cultivated land per capita was only .25 acres, compared to 2.10 acres for the United States. Not only this, the amount of available land was declining. In 1952, the per capita figure had been almost double, at .46 acres. Some of the decline was due to the construction of new homes, factories, and road and rail lines; much of the rest was due to badly planned government policies that produced industrial pollution and extensive deforestation.

The second factor, according to Spence, was the demographics of the population. In 1982 in China, there were many millions of women of childbearing age—over 81 million in their twenties and over 60 million in their thirties. There were also over 125 million girls aged ten to nineteen who were shortly to enter their childbearing years. This meant that unless measures were taken, there would soon be a sharp rise in the birth rate.

In addition to the youthful population, the number of old people was growing as well. This was due to improvements in diet and also in medical knowledge, which resulted in many dangerous infections and parasitic diseases being brought under control. Life expectancy in general rose by an average of eight or nine years over a period of only twenty-four years, from 1957 to 1981.

A third factor was the increasing urbanization of the population. This has implications for population size. In some rural areas, the death rate for infants under four was six times that in China's large cities, and life expectancy in China's cities was on average four years higher than in rural areas.

Therefore, increasing urbanization was sure to lead to a rise in overall population.

The fourth factor in Spence's list was the nature of the Chinese labor force. Compared with other industrialized countries, China's workforce started younger and retired earlier. Nearly one in five Chinese workers (18.09 percent) was between fifteen and nineteen, whereas in the United States the figure was less than half of that: 7.94 percent. These young workers did not have any opportunities for further education, and this reflected the fifth and final factor identified by Spence, the fact that the overall level of education of the population was low. Less than 1 percent of the workforce held college degrees, and nearly 74 percent of Chinese peasants had no education beyond elementary school level. Just over 28 percent of them were classified as illiterate or semi-illiterate. These low levels of education did not augur well for the modernization of Chinese society, which was the goal of the Chinese government.

Such were the factors that weighed upon the minds of the Chinese leaders when they made the decision that eventually led to Karin Evans and thousands of other American adoptive parents making their way to China to adopt an orphaned girl. Spence points out that China might have tried another approach than the one-child policy, that of encouraging women not to marry. This possibility was never seriously considered. Chinese women expected to marry. According to the 1982 census, over 94 percent were married by the time they were twenty-five, and over 99 percent by the age of twenty-nine.

Spence's list of five crucial factors in Chinese society makes it clear why Chinese leaders felt they had to take swift measures to curb population growth. Their actions can be further understood in the context of the world population control movement. China did not act in a vacuum; there had been efforts to curb world population since the 1950s. Experts warned of the dangers of overpopulation that would follow the decrease in infant and child mortality that had occurred since the end of World War II in 1945. In 1952, India became the first country to institute a government policy aimed at reducing the birth rate. However, many developing countries were slow to endorse the goals of the population control movement. It was not until the 1984 Second World Population Conference in Mexico City that the majority of developing nations, including China, gave their support to the movement. In 1994, at the United Nations Conference on Population in Cairo, the declared aim was to stabilize world population at 7.27 billion by 2015. Unless this is achieved, some experts warn that the population could reach 10.9 billion by 2050, a figure that many consider unsustainable, given the limits of the Earth's resources.

Seen in this light, it is clear that the concerns of the Chinese government about rising population, and its attempts to curb it, were entirely legitimate. Its coercive methods, most observers would agree, were not. The government was able to impose such methods because of a political system and ideology that are vastly different from those that operate in the West. The West prizes individual rights and freedoms, and has, especially in the United States, historically resisted any encroachment on those freedoms by the state. In China, however, traditionally the interests of the society and the family have taken precedence over the rights and interests of the individual. This has been even more apparent since the communist takeover of China in 1949, since communism is a totalitarian ideology in which the state assumes the power to regulate the lives of individuals.

As for the future, according to several reports, China's one-child policy was not being as rigidly enforced in the late 1990s as it had been earlier. If this also means a reduction in forced abortions and sterilization, it can only be welcomed. Another factor may provide some encouragement too. It has long been known that in countries where women are well educated and have economic independence and choices about how they will live, rates of childbirth are much lower than in countries (such as China) where women are poor, with low status and little education. It is because of this that in the 1980s and 1990s, the population control movement has emphasized, in addition to contraception and family planning, improvement in the status of women. This includes improvements in women's rights and their status in the family and the community. Another encouraging sign was the fact that China hosted the United Nations Fourth World Conference on Women in Beijing in September 1995. This drew national and international attention to the status of women in China.

China's many well-wishers will hope that a move to voluntary family planning quickly makes coerced birth control a thing of the past. They will also hope that a new emphasis on the rights of women will gradually reverse the historical bias in Chinese society in favor of men and male children—a bias that since 1980 has led to many cruelties against women and thousands of abandoned baby girls.

Source: Bryan Aubrey, Critical Essay on *The Lost Daughters of China: Abandoned Girls, Their Journey to America, and the Search for a Missing Past*, in *Nonfiction Classics for Students*, Gale, 2003.

Michelle Prebilic

Prebilic writes children's books, analytical essays, and technical publications and assists students in San Ramon, California, with language and reading skills. In this essay, Prebilic explores the book's obscure element—the violence towards, and belittlement of, women and children.

It may be tempting to read Karin Evans's book *The Lost Daughters of China: Abandoned Girls, Their Journey to America, and the Search for a Missing Past* in terms of the facts of her international adoption. Evans wonderfully articulates her adventures and trials in becoming the new mother of an adopted girl from China. As a journalist by profession, she has the ability to sculpt imagery to describe the places on her journey. Her vivid and moving descriptions of Guangzhou in southern China draw for readers a virtual paradise in their hearts and minds. She gives well-worded imagery that helps the reader ''taste'' and ''touch'' the landscape of China and its people.

Yet a deeper, more powerful meaning lies underneath the adoption journey itself. Much like a quilter uses stitched designs to hold together the two layers of cloth, Evans unfolds the myriad political and historical events that have created China as it is today. Evans did her homework; with 130 notes and an extensive bibliography, her book weaves together volumes of historical and political data with her personal adoption experience. These historical and political events, hidden within China's lush subtropical climate and rolling green fields, don't make headline news. ''Another baby abandoned'' has become a daily event like the weather. Perhaps the belittlement and violence towards women and children remains an obscure undercurrent amid the hustle and bustle of industrialized China. The good that arises out of these bad circumstances, suggests Evans, is the development of multicultural families. As people from the United States and other countries adopt Chinese girls, they make warm and loving homes for them. These lost daughters have a chance at life far better than they could find in China.

Evans's profound experience with adoption adds meaning to her journey towards motherhood. As she describes the Asian landscape, observes the Chinese people, or gazes down a river, she divulges her hopes and fears about her soon-to-be child. She uses the book as a way to divulge her personal experience. She selects her words artistically to present the full depth of her journey. Her words jump from the history of China's policies to her present adoption process, almost as if random thoughts develop her story. As her story unfolds, she imparts the wisdom that readers need to understand China's one-child policy, pointing out the less obvious yet troubling facts of China's human rights issues.

In this venue, Evans traces the history of China's one-child policy, accenting the culture's preference for males. She lists the tremendous pressures that led to stringent family planning: overpopulation, recurring natural disasters, and devastating poverty. These events put the country in crisis. At the same time, the belief that males take care of parents in old age and provide income fueled preference for male children. These factors coalesced to create a system of beliefs that allowed the Chinese government to implement a rigid family planning practice. The Chinese government meant well but failed in the implementation. Perhaps it failed because it tried to control the uncontrollable—women's fertility. Where did things go awry?

Perhaps, as Harry Wu speculates in *China's One-Child Policy Violates Human Rights,* it came from ''a top down system of control'' that emerged as the Chinese government mandated the practice of family planning. According to Wu, when the ''central government establishes general policy guidelines, and local governments institute and proscribe specific directives and regulations to meet these guidelines. . . . [they can take] remedial measures.'' Could it be that the dire need to reduce the population led to trying to enforce something—procreation—that cannot so easily be controlled? So although the idea may have been sound, even necessary, the crisis caused horrific actions. Evans grapples with these concepts as she presents the many facets of this one-child policy. She, like Wu and many other authors, indicates that the government goes to such extremes that it hunts women down and enforces sterilization or performs mandatory abortions at any stage of a pregnancy.

Why does the government choose to single out women? Some experts suggest that China still carries an archaic misogynistic view. According to a summary by the U.S. Department of State in *Human Rights Abuses in China Are Widespread,*

> [t]he People's Republic of China (PRC) is the paramount source of power. . . . Violence against women, including coercive family planning practices; . . . prostitution; discrimination against women; trafficking in women and children; abuse of children; and discrimination against the disabled and minorities are all problems. . . . Therefore, the PRC commit[s] widespread and well-documented human rights abuses in violation of internationally accepted norms.

With great respect for the Chinese people, Evans explores the violence against Chinese women. Using grace, she presents the facts in a respectful way that seeks improvement and compassion. Avoiding blatant criticism and condemnation, Evans explains that women in China have limited professional opportunities. If they work, they stay at the same job, accepting careers that usually don't pay well. Furthermore, the Chinese government controls women's reproductive lives—having a child requires permission. Not obtaining official permission can result in harassment, fines, and forced abortions. Although some of this control seems to be relaxing, experts believe that the damage caused by its procedures will be felt for many years.

Besides misogynistic views, Evans introduces readers to a deeper problem. Why are so many children, especially infants, abandoned? Perhaps, as Laura Sessions Stepp puts forth a universal truth in *Infants Now Murdered As Often As Teens,* "Infants are the most defenseless members of . . . society." Or as Stepp quotes Robert W. Block of the American Academy of Pediatrics child abuse committee, "stress . . . can trigger violent behavior. . . . Babies are easy targets." China's attitudes and policies have created intense stress on its families, similar to an earthquake that shakes a home's foundation.

Evans tackles infant desertion throughout her book. How could someone abandon her precious daughter in a marketplace among the melons? On one hand, Evans expresses deep gratitude for the opportunity to raise her Chinese child, saying that she could not love her daughter more if she were the biological mother. On the other hand, Evans questions the systems that have created an environment where a mother would purposefully get rid of her child. Evans's honest narrative does not turn the reader against China or its people but skillfully raises the question of human imperfection.

If babies are easy targets, then why don't all babies in China experience this demise? Evans

> **" China's attitudes and policies have created intense stress on its families, similar to an earthquake that shakes a home's foundation."**

voices the one question that reverberates throughout her masterpiece: "Why . . . were almost all the lost children in China girls?" Evans cannot provide a conclusive answer. Perhaps there is not one. However, she gives us insights that show readers how this might happen were they confronted with the same dilemma; a family could disown a woman for having a baby girl. The woman could lose her job and her home, and face a life of poverty.

Evans writes a passage where she places herself in the shoes of the biological mother. This helps readers appreciate the Chinese woman's plight. It gives honor to the courage and sorrow that the other human being must have felt in discarding her female infant. Evans interprets the action of abandonment to be an ultimate act of maternal love.

Is China alone in this belittlement of women and children? Certainly not! Other nations devalue women and children. Most recently the world has learned of the plight of Afghan women. Controlling governmental attitudes have prevented women from wearing what they wanted and from coming and going as they wished. According to Mavis Leno in an interview on the lives of Afghan women, the Taliban regime "punished if more than three unrelated women are found gathering together, if their windows are not painted dark so that no one can see in, or even if their shoes make a noise when they walk." Years of conflict and no investment in health care have contributed to some of the highest infant and maternal mortality rates in the world. Men have been affected too. As Leno continues in her interview, oppressive Taliban attitudes caused widespread poverty: "Men who depended on their wives' income as well as their own now are responsible for the total support of their family, and often had to help widowed family members." Belittling women hurts the entire population.

Perhaps even if the goals of such cultures have merit, oftentimes the execution of said goals fails. As Wu states in *China's One-Child Policy*

Violates Human Rights, China's population policy "should be based on volunteerism and education, not coercion and intimidation." As education and knowledge increase, prosperity rises. People understand their choices and feel safe. Choices lead to empowerment of every individual, which means people can work together to conquer complicated problems.

Evans started out to adopt a daughter so that she could raise a child with her husband. She displays courage in writing this bold and interesting book. Typical of a journalist who aims at communicating with a large audience, Evans states facts without judgment. It seems that she proposes more questions than answers as she successfully balances the Chinese weaknesses with positive aspects of its vibrant culture. In doing so, Evans refuses to limit herself to what one American university professor specializing in Chinese history tells her, "There's a limit to what people speak out about." To Evans, there is no limit.

In this way, she intricately pieces together the ideas as an intricate design on her quilt; Evans examines one idea at a time, developing her thoughts thoroughly. These ideas come together to encourage understanding and compassion for the Chinese struggles. With new knowledge, Evans gives readers a chance to support a healthier view of human rights in China. In asking the question why, Evans suggests that the problems and the answers are both in the unforeseen—what we cannot see "will always loom as an added obstacle" in the search for unity. The unforeseen in adoption is particularly troubling to Evans, for she will one day face this question of abandonment with daughter Kelly Xiao Yu. Nevertheless, just as Evans can present a difficult issue so admirably, she must have hope that only good will come. As Evans concludes, "May things improve for children everywhere."

Source: Michelle Prebilic, Critical Essay on *The Lost Daughters of China: Abandoned Girls, Their Journey to America, and the Search for a Missing Past,* in *Nonfiction Classics for Students,* Gale, 2003.

Allison DeFrees

DeFrees has a bachelor's degree in English from the University of Virginia and a law degree from the University of Texas and is a published writer and an editor. In the following essay, DeFrees discusses author Evans's use of personal experience to bring a more evocative understanding of,

and to make a more resonant argument in support of, female children adopted from China.

How does an author meld the contradiction of the vast sorrow of losing a child with the joy of gaining a new life? One effective method is through a careful distillation of fact and personal experience. In Karin Evans's history, *The Lost Daughters of China,* she writes a factual, nonfiction account of the adoption process for United States would-be parents to adopt female babies from orphanages in China. However, her account carries with it the weight of circumstance—Evans herself is an adoptive parent, and indeed, her inspiration for the book emanated from her own experience of going through the trials of the adoption process. Because Evans intersperses personal experience throughout the facts and secondary accounts, the reader observes both a personal and objective version of the adoption process and thus is able to glimpse life through the eyes of the anxious adopting family, the hopeless, anguished Chinese mothers and families, and the unassuming eyes of the children. It is a subtle and powerful method of persuasive writing, for in the end, Evans is trying to persuade herself, her husband, her adopted daughter, the government, and the Chinese mothers left with no choice but to give up their female babies that out of the horror of loss and abandonment there is hope, that for the barren there is new life, and that the circle of life can continue on a global scale.

In her introduction to the book, Evans claims three goals for the book, broad and far-reaching aims by anyone's standards. For herself, she wrote the book to begin to understand what life was likely to be like for her adopted Chinese daughter. For her daughter, she wrote the book to provide an opening for her to understand the world into which she was born. And for her reader, "the world at large," Evans claims that she wrote the book as "an attempt to fill in the blank spaces in a profound human exchange." How she knows it is profound, and how she can have the temerity to qualify the timbre of the experience, is because she has lived the experience. Thus, despite the enormousness of these desired aims, once the book reaches the hands of an anonymous reader, the goals are narrowed to a singular focus: to tell a story of what it means to love and to lose a child, with all of its ramifications. Again, Evans is in a unique position to relate this story. As she relates to her audience, several years before she and her husband embarked on the adoption process, she gave birth to a child who died a few hours after being born. In addition, Evans lived in Hong Kong for several years as a foreign correspondent for *Newsweek* and followed the political movement as China adopted a strict one-child-per-family law. Evans is a writer particularly attuned to loss, and again, her empathy provides a jarring vision of loss and fear and despondency among the Chinese women who are faced with the difficult position of deciding what to do with their ''unwanted'' daughters.

The bulk of the book is concerned with telling the stories of the men and women in China who gave up the thousands of babies that end up in Chinese orphanages each year. It is difficult to ferret out any specific information about the circumstances of each child's—for lack of a better word—abandonment, as the penalties by the Chinese government for abandoning a child are unforgiving, and mothers or families almost always do so with great secrecy, leaving their swaddled infants in the reeds of the river banks, on the doorsteps of orphanages, in marketplaces, anywhere the child might be found and rescued from infanticide or sex-selective abortion. Thus, it is difficult to trace the story of an adopted child from her roots to the cradle of her new, foreign parents, as the roots begin with the orphanage and, perhaps, a comment as to where the child was found: ''under a bridge,'' one couple was told; another told, ''beside a freeway''; and to the author and her husband, the adoption facilitator simply said, ''in a market.'' Which market? Which section of the market? By whom? Was she crying? How was she dressed? No answers? The anonymity of the situation and its similarity to so many other situations of abandoned girls threatens to meld each child into the fold of statistical data. However, it is here that Evans's personal vantage point enters to individualize things and to build a three-dimensional life of both the abandoned daughter and the lives she was entering and leaving:

> Like most other parents who've adopted children from China, we know nothing about the circumstances of our daughter's birth or about her birth parents. Once we were home, I asked a pediatrician whether her belly button would offer a clue as to whether she'd been born in a hospital or not. It didn't. Not that that particular information would have told us much—but I was straining to picture all the events in her life that I'd missed.

Evans's personal connection with her material becomes the vital component in her cache of storytelling techniques, because it offers an empathic, rather than a merely sympathetic, view. The

> ''Furthermore, by creating a fresh approach to the subject, Evans lends authenticity to the book, further engrossing the reader in the epic tale of an abandoned baby girl, a hopeful father and mother-to-be, a Chinese mother and family caught in the pendulum that swings between modernity and the arcane past.''

reader is one step closer to the realities of the experience, one step less removed from the confusion and horror and saving graces of the story of a child lost to her parents, through any variety of unfortunate circumstances, and bundled into the arms of a totally foreign culture. Evans writes about how she believed that her daughter—named Kelly Xiao Yu, a combination of her American name and her name given her at the orphanage (there is no trace of what name she might have had before she got to the orphanage)—must have been nursed, as she was prone to crawling on top of Evans and laying her cheek on Evans's breast. ''She sought out that warm spot as if she'd known it well, nestled, nudged me like a kitten.'' She seemed to have been treated with kindness and affection, but by whom? Who had bundled the child up for a last trip to the marketplace ''while [Evans] was at home in San Francisco, fretting about bureaucratic logjams?'' The question burned so brightly in her mind—and undoubtedly in the minds of thousands of adoptive parents enduring the same experience—that Evans often found herself ''trying to conjure the story from the few details [she] knew.''

Evans goes on to reenact the possible circumstances of that day in the market that her now-daughter was discovered, abandoned, and in doing so, paints a wrenching portrait of desperation and loss. The baby, stuffed in among fruits and vegetables and turtles and water beetles, would be discovered—by someone, a farmer, perhaps—cries would ring out, and then it would be announced that it was a baby girl. ''Enough said. Someone called the police and they came, as they'd done any number of places before, and took the child off to one of the nearby orphanages. . . .'' Evans again effectively intermingles her personal imagination with the plight of all the Chinese daughters being abandoned, bringing a face to so many faceless children.

In a later chapter, Evans discusses the persistence of the problem of abandoned female babies in China. She notes that the desperate measures resorted to by women and families faced with an additional female daughter will continue until the one-child policy is completely lifted, the Chinese economy improves dramatically, or ''some kind of pension is in place for rural poor people.'' She returns to Guangzhou, the city where she adopted her daughter, and pulls the reader back to burgeoning life in her daughter's would-be town. ''In Kelly's hometown at this time of year,'' she writes, ''the market would be busy as usual.'' Evans goes on to detail the bustle of the city, the shoppers, the motorbikes, the fisherman, all crowded into the marketplace, where women may be carrying vegetables, fish, or, perhaps, a baby. She then notes that over time, her image of the circumstances of her daughter's abandonment have altered. ''No longer does it seem fair or accurate to say that she was abandoned or left there. Rather, I think, she was 'delivered' to safety in that busy place—so clearly was it her mother's intention to save her.''

The Lost Daughters of China is a deeply moving factual account of the current state of affairs regarding abandoned children and adoption in China. The book depicts, through simple first-person accounting and straightforward factual and secondary accounts, true triumph over tragedy. But even more so, by telling the socio-political history of modern adoption in China—and of immigration policy in the United States—from a personal point of view, Evans universalizes her microcosmic experience. Rather than charting the thorough government censuses and facts and relying on the secondary accounts of professors, historians, adopted daughters, Chinese family members or villagers who might, in anonymity, talk, and American families who have successfully or unsuccessfully tried to adopt a Chinese baby daughter—all of which are valuable resources, and all of which provide vital information for Evans's book—and guessing down to the specifics of the experience, Evans begins with the specific, creating a powerful drama within the historical context of the Chinese adoption movement. Furthermore, by creating a fresh approach to the subject, Evans lends authenticity to the book, fur-

ther engrossing the reader in the epic tale of an abandoned baby girl, a hopeful father and mother-to-be, a Chinese mother and family caught in the pendulum that swings between modernity and the arcane past. Finally, *The Lost Daughters of China* is about human loss and longing and the inevitable global reach of the desire for family and community.

Source: Allison DeFrees, Critical Essay on *The Lost Daughters of China: Abandoned Girls, Their Journey to America, and the Search for a Missing Past,* in *Nonfiction Classics for Students,* Gale, 2003.

Sources

Bader, Eleanor J., Review of *The Lost Daughters of China,* in *Library Journal,* Vol. 125, No. 11, June 15, 2000, p. 101.

Bush, Vanessa, Review of *The Lost Daughters of China,* in *Booklist,* Vol. 96, No. 18, May 15, 2000, p. 1707.

Cheney, Theodore A. Rees, *Writing Creative Nonfiction,* Writer's Digest Books, 1987, p. 3.

Evans, Karin, *The Lost Daughters of China,* J. P. Tarcher, 2000.

Greenhalgh, Susan, Review of *The Lost Daughters of China,* in *Population and Development Review,* Vol. 26, No. 3, September 2000, p. 613.

Leno, Mavis, ''Lives of Afghan Women,'' Interview in the chat room via telephone, *cnn.com,* Los Angeles, CA, Friday, November 9, 2001 (2 p.m. EST).

Mosher, Steven W., *Broken Earth: The Rural Chinese,* The Free Press, 1983.

Muriel, Diana, ''Afghan Women Dying in Childbirth at Staggering Rates,'' *cnn.com,* December 6, 2002 (last accessed December 2002).

Review of *The Lost Daughters of China,* in *Publishers Weekly,* Vol. 247, No. 16, April 17, 2000, p. 67.

Spence, Jonathan D., *The Search for Modern China,* W. W. Norton, 1990, pp. 683–90.

Stepp, Laura Sessions, ''Infants Now Murdered as Often as Teens,'' in the *The Washington Post,* December 9, 2002.

U.S. Department of State, ''Human Rights Abuses in China Are Widespread,'' in *Opposing Viewpoints: China,* edited by James D. Torr, Greenhaven Press, 2001; excerpted from ''1999 Country Reports on Human Rights Practices,'' by the U.S. Department of State, February 25, 2000.

Wu, Harry, ''China's One-Child Policy Violates Human Rights,'' in *Opposing Viewpoints: China,* edited by James D. Torr, Greenhaven Press, 2001; excerpted from ''Forced Abortion and Sterilization: The View from the Inside,'' by Harry Wu, July 1998.

Further Reading

Croll, Elisabeth, *Changing Identities of Chinese Women: Rhetoric, Experience and Self-Perception in Twentieth-Century China,* Zed Books, 1995.

Croll discusses the successive revolutions attempted by Chinese women—within their society, communities, families, and themselves. The text is sometimes weighed down by scholarly jargon, but there is much useful information, including a discussion of female infanticide as a result of the one-child policy.

Faison, Seth, "Chinese Are Happily Breaking the 'One Child' Rule," in *New York Times,* August 17, 1997.

This article discusses how the one-child policy is currently being eased as China's economic growth has eroded the state's control over individual lives, creating many loopholes in the official enforcement of the policy.

Hartman, Betsy, *Reproductive Rights and Wrongs: The Global Politics of Population Control and Contraceptive Choice,* HarperCollins, 1987.

Hartman covers many topics, including the causes and consequences of population growth; the history of the population control movement; and the forces behind the development of contemporary contraceptive technologies. She also examines societies that have reduced population growth through social and economic development.

Reese, Lori, "Children's Palace: China Copes with the One-Child Policy," in *Time Asia,* Vol. 154, No. 12, September 27, 1999.

This article claims that Chinese parents in the cities are raising a generation of spoiled single kids. The parents, who had almost nothing in their youth, overcompensate now that times are more prosperous by indulging their child's every whim.

A Mathematician's Apology

G. H. Hardy

1940

Godfrey Harold (G. H.) Hardy's *A Mathematician's Apology*, first published in 1940 in England, is the memoir of the world-renowned mathematician, written in the last few years of his life while he was in failing health. The work is written in the form of an apology, which in literary terms means a defense. In this case, Hardy is defending his career as a theoretical mathematician. To make the defense comprehensible to the layperson, Hardy discards the language he would use in an academic paper and instead adopts a succinct and simple writing style aimed at a general audience. The book is not mathematical; rather, it is an affirmation of a career that happens to be mathematical and purely speculative.

It should be noted that Hardy speaks exclusively of men in his writing, which reflects the secondary role women of his era played in the British university system in general and in the field of mathematics in particular. Hardy does not mention or refer to a single woman intellectual or a work by a woman.

A Mathematician's Apology is a lasting testament to Hardy's passion for intellectual pursuits. Hardy likens mathematics to art and explains math in much the same way a critic explains art. He elaborates on the qualities of mathematical genius and the logical reasons for pursuing a career in mathematics, and he briefly outlines three of the most basic and timeless theorems in order to illustrate the inherent beauty of mathematics for the layperson. Many of the chapters also address the

differences between theoretical or "pure" mathematics—to which Hardy dedicated his life—and several types of "applied math," which he regards as largely inferior. The work also reveals the grave doubts Hardy harbored about the overall usefulness of his work and life. While *A Mathematician's Apology* has had an enormous influence on generations of mathematicians, it has also been viewed by many as a psychological document of a genius with depressive tendencies. As Hardy contemporary C. P. Snow acknowledges in the book's introduction, *A Mathematician's Apology* "is a book of haunting sadness."

Author Biography

Godfrey Harold (G. H.) Hardy was born on February 7, 1877, in Cranleigh, Surrey, England. Both his parents were educators and possessed mathematical skills. Even before learning to speak as a very young child, he demonstrated an extraordinary IQ and performed mathematical computations to amuse himself. After winning a scholarship to Winchester College in 1889, Hardy began the rigorous training of a mathematician.

In 1896, he entered Trinity College, Cambridge, where he trained under A. E. H. Love, who gave him his first serious conception of analysis by introducing him to Camille Jordan's *Cours d'analyse*. Thereafter, Hardy committed his life to mathematics, and by 1908 he had already made a significant contribution, with his greatest work in this early period being *A Course of Pure Mathematics*.

A watershed year for Hardy was 1911, as it marked the beginning of his thirty-five-year collaboration with fellow mathematician J. E. Littlewood. Two years later, in 1913, he received an unsolicited manuscript from Indian mathematician Srinivasa Ramanujan. Hardy immediately spotted Ramanujan's genius and brought him to Cambridge where, between 1914 and 1918, the men engaged in what would become one of mathematics' most remarkable collaborations.

It was during the years of World War I that Hardy also became known for his outspoken political views. Unlike most of his contemporaries and colleagues, Hardy held the Germans in high regard for their intellectual prowess and contributions to scientific thought. His ingrained distrust of British politicians contributed to his deep anger at Great Britain's participation in the war. He was particu-

larly upset over the interruption it caused in his various collaborations with colleagues outside England.

In 1919, Hardy left Cambridge for a position as the Savilian professor of geometry at Oxford, where he remained until 1931, at which time he returned to Cambridge, where he finished his professional career. An avid cricket fan and tennis player, Hardy remained physically active throughout his life until 1939 when, at the age of sixty-two, he had a heart attack. His remarkable mental powers quickly began to leave him and sports became impossible. He was also filled with anger that Europe had again entered into war. However, Hardy had one further gift to leave to the world, namely *A Mathematician's Apology*, published in 1940, which has inspired many people towards mathematics.

By the time World War II ended in 1945, Hardy's health was failing fast, as was his creativity. He gradually became depressed, and in early summer 1947, he unsuccessfully tried to take his own life by taking a large dose of barbiturates. He took so many, however, that he became sick before he died, and he was resuscitated and survived.

Hardy, who became almost as well known for his outspoken beliefs and rebellious spirit as for his mathematical skills, once listed among his most ardent wishes: 1) To prove the Riemann hypothesis (a famous unsolved mathematical problem); 2) to make a brilliant play in a crucial cricket match; 3) to prove the nonexistence of God; and 4) to murder Mussolini, the Italian fascist leader (Hoffman, *The Man Who Only Knew Numbers*).

Over the course of his lifetime, Hardy received many honors for his work. He was elected a fellow of the Royal Society in 1910, and he received the Royal Medal of the society in 1920 and the Sylvester Medal of the society in 1940. On December 1, 1947, shortly after hearing that he was to be given the Copley Medal, the highest honor of the Royal Society, Hardy passed away in Cambridge, Cambridgeshire, England.

Plot Summary

Chapters 1–2

Hardy opens his apology by asserting his belief that in the mere act of "writing about mathematics" he has lowered himself to a level below that of a pure mathematician. He equates himself in this position to that of an art critic—a profession he considers to be for "second-rate minds"—as opposed to the artist himself. Hardy describes a discussion he had on this subject with British poet A. E. Houseman. In chapter 2, Hardy introduces the questions he proposes to answer throughout the remainder of the book: Why is it worthwhile to make a career out of mathematics? And what is the proper justification of a mathematician's life?

Chapters 3–4

Hardy states that most people choose their career path because "it is the one and only thing that [they] can do at all well." Mathematics is a particularly specialized subject, and mathematicians themselves are not noted for their versatility. In chapter 4, he lists several mathematicians whom he considers immortal geniuses, and he points out that most of them reached their intellectual peaks or died before the age of forty. Those men who attempted new careers later in life were largely failures. Hardy uses these points to illustrate why he is now writing this memoir: simply put, he is too old to continue with theory, and he has no talent for any other career.

Chapters 5–9

Hardy concludes his responses to the questions he posed in chapter 3. As to why one would choose to become a mathematician, Hardy refers to a lecture he gave at Oxford twenty years earlier in which he posited that mathematics is chosen for three reasons. First, it is essentially a "harmless" profession; second, because the universe is so vast, if a few professors wasted their lives doing something at which they excelled, it would be "no overwhelming catastrophe"; and third, there is a "permanence" of mathematics that is "beyond the powers of the vast majority of men." It is here that Hardy adds what he believes are the three prime motivations that impel men to choose their professions: intellectual curiosity, professional pride, and ambition for reputation and the rewards it brings. To support these statements, Hardy lists several ancient civilizations that are long forgotten save for their mathematical discoveries. He concludes with a dream that mathematician and philosopher Bertrand Russell once related that expressed Russell's deep-seated fear that he would one day be forgotten by future generations.

Chapters 10–11

Hardy posits that mathematics has an aesthetic quality like that of art or poetry—a position for

which he and this book are best remembered. Hardy takes a swipe at one of his contemporaries, mathematician Lancelot Hogben, who was well-known for his opposition to Hardy's theories. Hardy uses the example of chess to refute Hogben. Because chess is revered by the masses and is an exercise in pure mathematics, though admittedly of a "lowly kind," when one appreciates the beauty of a particular chess move, one is in essence appreciating its mathematical beauty. However, since the best mathematics also demands "seriousness," or "importance," and since no chess player or problem "has ever affected the general development of scientific thought," chess is "trivial" compared to pure mathematics.

Chapters 12–14

Hardy uses the examples of proofs by Euclid and Pythagoras to illustrate the beauty of mathematics and then explains why they are significant in spite of the fact that they are not practical. These proofs are presented concisely and demand only a rudimentary background in mathematics to follow them. It is the only instance in the memoir in which Hardy attempts to explain mathematical concepts or logic.

Chapters 15–18

Hardy continues to refine his concept of mathematical beauty by further defining the idea of "seriousness." To do this, he introduces the concepts of "generality" and "depth." Generality can be loosely defined as "abstractness," while depth is comparable to "difficulty." He discusses mathematician and philosopher Alfred North Whitehead's assertions, which he quotes: "The certainty of mathematics rests entirely on abstract generality." Hardy partially accepts this argument from a logician's point of view but argues that theoreticians must look for the difference among generalities. With regard to "depth," Hardy employs a metaphor that equates theorems with geologic strata: the more difficult the theorem, the more layers it has, with each layer holding ideas that link to other ideas above and below it. He concludes this discussion in chapter 18 by explaining why chess can never be "beautiful." In short, the very nature of chess demands that any given move can be answered with multiple countermoves—what Hardy refers to as "proof by enumeration of cases," which is the antithesis of beauty in a mathematician's eye. Rather than being a beautiful collection of mathematical theorems competing with one another, a chess game is, at its heart, a psychological battle between two intelligent beings.

Chapters 19–21

Hardy returns to his Oxford lecture in order to address the question of the usefulness of mathematics. In short, Hardy states emphatically that although some "elementary" mathematics such as calculus have some utility, the "pure" mathematics with which he concerns himself cannot be justified on utilitarian grounds.

Chapters 22–24

Hardy returns to his comparison of "applied" and "theoretical" mathematics and states that it is a gross oversimplification to say that one has utility while the other does not. Hardy supports this statement by setting out to argue that pure mathematics is closer to "reality" than is applied mathematics. His assumption here is that there is a "mathematical reality" that exists that is no different from the "physical reality" to which most of us can relate. Mathematical reality is not a mental construct but rather an objective reality that exists in the world that can be discovered and described. Mathematicians who "create" proofs are actually doing little more than taking notes on their observations.

To illustrate this point, Hardy draws on the field of geology, which sets out to draw a "picture" of a part of mathematical reality. However, because geometry does not account for changes in spatiotemporal reality, such as those created by eclipses and earthquakes (since these are not mathematical concepts), the "drawing" a geometer creates in his theorems may suddenly have little to do with the physical reality surrounding him. However, the truths of the theorem remain unaffected. Or, to put it in even simpler terms, while spilling coffee on the pages of a Shakespeare play may make certain pages unreadable, the spill does not affect the play itself. By analogy, pure mathematicians concern themselves with the play, while applied mathematicians concern themselves with the pages on which the play is written.

In chapter 24, Hardy makes the seemingly paradoxical claim that despite these relationships, pure mathematicians are in fact the closer of the two to reality. Hardy's argument is as follows: an applied mathematician must work with a physical reality over which there is ample disagreement as to what comprises it. There is confusion as to what constitutes a chair, for instance: it may be a mass of whirling electrons, or it may be an "idea of God." The pure mathematician, however, works with a mathematical reality about which there is no ambiguity. No one disagrees as to what "2" or "317" is, and "317" is a prime number not because we "think it so" but rather because "it is so."

Chapter 25

Continuing the comparison of pure and applied mathematics, Hardy claims that pure mathematics is timeless, has a permanent aesthetic value, and its eternal qualities bring about a lasting sense of emotional satisfaction. The achievements of applied mathematicians, on the other hand, are more modern and temporal. Hardy leans towards calling the applied mathematical theories "useless."

Chapter 26

Hardy continues to delve into the idea of utility in mathematics, asking, "What part of mathematics are useful?" He goes on to list branches according to utility. He comes to the general conclusion that the more useful a type of mathematics is to an engineer or physicist, the less aesthetic value it has. Hardy prefers the world of imagination and art to the "humdrum" reality of applied mathematics. Hardy writes

> 'Imaginary' universes are so much more beautiful than this stupidly constructed 'real' one; and most of the finest productions of an applied mathematician's fancy must be rejected, as soon as they have been created, for the brutal but sufficient reason that they do not fit the facts.

Chapters 27–28

Hardy addresses some of the objections of his critics, especially applied mathematician Lancelot Hogben. Hardy's tone is snide and superior as he sums up his arguments regarding the differentiation between real and applied mathematics. He repeatedly uses the word "trivial" in reference to applied mathematics. According to Hardy, real mathematicians are artists. Hardy does not offer any justification of applied mathematics, saying only that it would appeal to Hogben. It is here that Hardy finally broaches the subject of utility and harm. Writing under the threat of an impending world war, Hardy feels that it is necessary to lead his discussion towards the relationship between mathematics and war. He comes to the conclusion that "real mathematics has no effects on war. No one has yet discovered any warlike purpose to be served by the theory of numbers or relativity, and it seems unlikely that anyone will do so for many years."

Hardy wrote these words only five years before the theories of relativity helped the United States develop the first atomic bomb.

Chapter 29

Hardy concludes his memoir by returning to a more personal narrative voice. This final chapter is far more autobiographical than the rest of the memoir. Having already stated his theories, Hardy feels justified in summing up his life. It is the summation of a man knowingly in his declining years. Although the tone is sad and melancholic, he seems to convince himself that his life has had meaning. In lines often quoted by critics of the work, Hardy writes, ''Well, I have done one thing *you* could never have done, and that is to have collaborated with both [mathematicians John Edensor] Littlewood and [Srinivasa] Ramanujan on something like equal terms.'' One quotes these lines so often because while so much of the work paints Hardy as pompous, this quotation is a clear illustration of his humility as well. He is able to recognize genius and also admit to his own limitations. In a work that carries a subtle sadness throughout it, these line spring forth as a positive affirmation of a genius' existence.

Key Figures

Niels Henrik Abel

Niels Henrik Abel was a Norwegian mathematician (1802–1829) known for the tremendous amount of brilliant work he completed in his brief, twenty-six-year life.

Francis Herbert Bradley

Metaphysician and philosopher F. H. Bradley (1846–1924) is most noted for his *Appearance and Reality* (1893), which was considered an important philosophical discussion of contemporary metaphysical thought at the time of its publication. He was also known by the influence his writing had on author T. S. Eliot.

Albert Einstein

German-born physicist Albert Einstein (1879–1955) is considered one of the most brilliant men who ever lived. His theory of relativity, which he introduced in 1915, was revolutionary. It related matter with energy and displaced Newtonian mechanics as the cornerstone of physics by introducing the concept of space-time. In 1921, he received the Nobel Prize. A Jewish pacifist, Einstein immigrated to the United States shortly after Hitler came to power.

Euclid

Euclid of Alexandria, Egypt (approximately 325–265 B.C.), is the most prominent mathematician of antiquity, best known for his treatise on mathematics titled *The Elements*. Euclid taught in Alexandria, but little else is known of his life. However, the timelessness of *The Elements* has made Euclid the leading mathematics teachers of all time.

John Burdon Sanderson Haldane

British geneticist, biologist, and writer John Burdon Sanderson (J. B. S.) Haldane (1892–1964) was one of the most influential scientists of the early twentieth century and was well known for his left-leaning politics. His numerous works include *Callinicus: A Defense of Chemical Warfare* (1925). Disillusioned with the state of Marxism after World War II, he eventually moved to India, where he continued to conduct scientific research.

Lancelot Hogben

Educated at Trinity College, Cambridge, Lancelot Hogben (1895–1975) is best known for his book *Mathematics for the Million,* which is considered a classic in its field. In the book, Hogben covers the entire spectrum of applied mathematics from simple math to advanced calculus. The work received positive reviews from the likes of H. G. Wells and Albert Einstein, though it achieved prominence due to the harsh criticism it received from G. H. Hardy.

Alfred Edward Houseman

British poet Alfred Edward (A. E.) Houseman (1859–1936) was known for the argument made in his 1933 lecture ''The Name and Nature of Poetry'' that poetry should appeal more to emotions than to intellect. He published several collections, including *Last Poems* (1922). His final collection, *More Poems,* was published shortly after his death in 1936.

Dr. Samuel Johnson

The leading literary scholar and critic of his time, Dr. Samuel Johnson (1709–1784) was equally celebrated for his brilliant and witty conversation. The work that firmly established Johnson's reputation was his *Dictionary of the English Language* (1755), the first comprehensive lexicographical work on English ever undertaken.

John Edensor Littlewood

For thirty-five years, John Edensor Littlewood (1885–1977) collaborated with G. H. Hardy, working on the theory of series, the Riemann zeta function, inequalities, and the theory of functions. The collaboration led to a series of papers, *Partito numerorum,* using the Hardy-Littlewood-Ramanujan analytical method. Among his many awards, Littlewood was elected a fellow of the Royal Society in 1915 and received the Royal Medal of the society in 1929. He received the Sylvester Medal of the society in 1943.

Sir Isaac Newton

Sir Isaac Newton (1642–1727) was one of history's most influential and famous scientists. His work as a mathematician, physicist, and astronomer brought him world renown. Newton rings, Newton's law, and the MKS unit of pressure (the Newton) are named after him.

Pythagoras

Greek philosopher and mathematician Pythagoras (c. 580–400 B.C.) lived most of his life in Crotona, in southern Italy. His doctrines "Kosmos," "Metempsychosis," and the "Music of the Spheres" are well known. The famous Pythagorean theorem, concerning right-angled triangles, holds that the square of the hypotenuse (i.e., the long line opposite the right angle) is equal to the sum of the squares of the other two sides. This idea was current for many centuries beforehand, but Pythagoras was the first to prove it to be true.

Srinivasa Ramanujan

Srinivasa Ramanujan (1887–1920) was a celebrated Indian mathematician. He is well known for his contributions to the analytical theory of numbers, elliptic functions, continued fractions, and infinite series. Despite a lack of formal higher education and a life of ill health and severe poverty, Ramanujan proved to be a preeminent mathematical genius of his time. In 1913, he sent a paper to G. H. Hardy, who immediately saw his genius and arranged to have him take a position at Trinity College, Cambridge, where for the next four years the two men collaborated on what are considered to be five of the most remarkable papers in their field. In 1918, an impressive list of mathematicians proposed his name for election as a fellow to the prestigious Royal Society of London, a rare honor that was immediately bestowed upon him. Even after his death at the young age of thirty-two, his notes continued to be a subject of research and a source of further mathematical theorems, formulas, and solutions.

Bertrand Arthur Williams Russell

Bertrand Arthur Williams Russell (1872–1970) is considered one of the founders of analytic philosophy. In 1900, following his education at Trinity College, Cambridge, Russell became acquainted with the work of Italian mathematician Giuseppe Peano. Peano's work inspired him to write *The Principles of Mathematics* (1903), which he subsequently expanded in collaboration with Alfred North Whitehead into the three volumes of *Principia Mathematica* (1910–1913). Russell's many essays, often in the form of short reflections or observations on moral or psychological topics, are written in a terse, vivid, and provocative style. Russell was also well known for his pacifist views, which cost him his job at Cambridge during World War I and also brought him a six-month jail sentence. His greatest literary achievement was *A History of Western Philosophy* (1945).

Charles Percy Snow

Charles Percy (C. P.) Snow (1905–1980) led a varied career that included scientific and civil service work, but he is best known as the author of the serialized fictional work entitled *Strangers and Brothers* (1940). His schooling was in chemistry and physics, and during World War II he served as director of technical personnel for Britain's Ministry of Labour. In 1957, he was knighted, and in 1964 he was named baron for his services to the Ministry of Labour. His 1959 Rede Lecture on "The Two Cultures and the Scientific Revolution," lamenting the increasing gulf between "literary intellectuals" and "scientists," provoked widespread and heated debate. In addition to his work in the sciences, Snow was the author of much short fiction published by London's *Sunday Times,* and over the course of his lifetime he published more than a dozen novels.

Themes

Aesthetics

One of Hardy's principal arguments is that theoretical mathematics, which he refers to as "real" or "pure" mathematics, has similar aesthetic qualities to those of art or poetry. Hardy invests much in his essay defending this position, explaining the

Topics for Further Study

- The ethical issues surrounding theoretical research are complex. Hardy called pure mathematics "gentle and clean." However, Einstein's theory of relativity played a direct influence in the development of the first atomic bomb. Research the role Einstein actually played in the development of the atomic bomb. Discuss the letter to President Franklin Delano Roosevelt that he signed urging the president to expedite its development in order to stop the spread of Nazism. How can you reconcile this act to Einstein's later pacifism?

- While people often read about the antiwar movement during the Vietnam War, one seldom hears about antiwar sentiment during World War I or World War II. In fact, Hardy and Bertrand Russell were among the few intellectuals of their day to speak out openly against the wars. Russell was, in fact, jailed briefly on account of his beliefs and activities. Research and write an essay about the antiwar movement during the First and Second World Wars, with an emphasis on the role intellectuals played. Include the roles Hardy and Russell played.

- Hardy believes that ancient mathematicians will be remembered for their influence long after their counterparts in the arts, literature, and philosophy are forgotten. He mentions Euclid and Pythagoras as two of the classical mathematicians who have achieved immortality. What other mathematicians from ancient civilizations have achieved similar status? Do you believe that their mathematical contributions exceed the contributions made by ancients of other disciplines, such as Plato, Socrates, and Homer? Why or why not?

- Among Hardy's proudest achievements, and what he is best remembered for, are his thiry-five-year collaboration with John Edensor Littlewood and his collaboration during World War I with Srinivasa Ramanujan. Outside of mathematics, there are numerous examples of famous collaborations. Research and write about one or two famous non-mathematical collaborations in the history of science or the arts.

- Hardy is clearly a product of Victorian England, particularly of its educational system. Research the aesthetic values and the social and cultural mores of Victorian society. What kind of influence do you believe they played in Hardy's development?

---

beauty of Pythagoras's and Euclid's theorems, and comparing the aesthetics of pure mathematics to the simplistic and vulgar exercises that make up applied mathematics.

Aging, Prime of Life, Depression, and Melancholy

A Mathematician's Apology was written during the final years of Hardy's life, shortly after a heart attack and a series of other physical ailments had rendered him mostly sedentary. This theme colors much of the text. Whereas in his prime he could devote his days to intense studies of concepts and vigorous games of cricket, those abilities were long lost to him as he was writing this memoir. Hardy firmly believed that mathematics is a young man's game. He uses several mathematicians—including Ramanujan, Newton, and others—as examples of geniuses who peaked in their twenties and thirties. By the time of the writing of this memoir, Hardy was in his sixties. This resulted in a melancholic tone that borders on depression. A few years following the publication of the book, Hardy unsuccessfully attempted suicide by taking an overdose of barbiturates.

Creative Process

Throughout *A Mathematician's Apology*, Hardy compares the "real" mathematician to the creative artist. He uses poetry and art to make this comparison. He believes there is an objective "mathematical reality" that exists in the world, which is no different from the "physical reality," and it is up to the mathematician to discover and describe that reality. The best of pure math can be held as the highest of all art forms.

Genius, Common Man/Everyman

At the expense of being criticized for elitism and snobbery, Hardy distinguishes between those who can perform a single task adequately—of which there are a small minority—and those who can perform a single task in their lives exceptionally, of which there are a significant few. These are the geniuses of the world, and Hardy is proud to have worked alongside those men he considered to be the most ingenious of all time, including Ramanujan and Littlewood.

Self-Doubt

Despite Hardy's elitist tendencies and tremendous confidence in his own intellectual abilities and importance, *A Mathematician's Apology* is imbued throughout with Hardy's severe self-doubts about his own worth as a human being and the worth of his contributions to mathematics and to the world. These self-doubts were, undoubtedly, caused in large part by his deteriorating physical state at the time of his writing and also in large part by the accumulation of years of criticism he received for so many of his views. The effects of years of being a "misunderstood genius" appear to have taken their toll, and one of the underlying purposes of writing this memoir is for Hardy to determine for himself if his life has been worthwhile.

Superiority, Egotism/Narcissism, Vanity, Conceit

Hardy admits that *A Mathematician's Apology* is an egotistical work. Men—and here Hardy includes himself—who choose to make a career out of mathematics do so in order to achieve a certain status of immortality. And if they sit down to write about their lives or their work, they do so because of their conviction that they have done something remarkable and should be remembered for it. Hardy does not hold back from stating his belief that he has made significant contributions to his field and that he is among the elite of the world in his field. Despite these views, however, his work embraces a certain amount of humility in that he recognizes greater geniuses than himself, and he feels proud to

have considered them to be among his colleagues and friends.

War

Hardy's famous collaboration with Ramanujan occurred during World War I, a war which Hardy adamantly opposed for both philosophical and practical reasons. Unlike most of his colleagues, Hardy held German society in high regard due to its advances in scientific thought, and he seriously mistrusted the British politicians. As a result, he was one of the few distinguished thinkers of his day, along with Bertrand Russell, who refused to support the war. On a practical level, Hardy thrived through his collaborations, many of which were with colleagues throughout Europe. The war had a tremendously disruptive influence on these efforts and hampered his professional development.

One of the great ironies of *A Mathematician's Apology*, written on the eve of World War II, is that Hardy defends the ethics of pure mathematics on the grounds that it is a "gentle and clean" field of study, unlike its counterpart, applied mathematics, which can make claim to its contributions, for instance, to the fields of ballistics. Hardy refuses to admit, or is unable to see, a causal relationship between theoretical math and warfare. He even goes so far as to predict that it would be years before Einstein's theory of relativity could be applied to any real-life situation.

Style

Apology

A Mathematician's Apology is, as the title implies, written in the form of an "apology," or defense. In this case, the author sets out to defend his chosen career: namely, theoretical, or what he calls "pure," mathematics. Although he was generally accepted for his brilliant theoretical insights, which resulted in many remarkable works and collaborations, Hardy's view that theoretical mathematics is an art form, while its counterpart, applied mathematics, is at best an application of trivial exercises, caused great disagreement among his contemporaries and thus spurred the need for this defense.

Tone

With this book, Hardy set out to address a general audience of both mathematicians and non-mathematicians alike, and as a result he employs a narrative style that could best explain in simple terms his profound and complex array of ideas. To that end, his tone, while often conveying a derogatory and elitist attitude toward his subject matter, never condescends to the reader with lofty diction; anyone with a rudimentary knowledge of mathematics would feel at home and comfortable with Hardy's style. At the same time, the ideas he expresses are of a depth that would satisfy his colleagues.

Hardy himself is an archetype of the misunderstood artist; a creative genius who was either far ahead of his times or hopelessly behind. As history has proven, he was a little of both. Hardy's own refusal to bow to the conventions of the time in regards to any subject matter, and his irrepressible need to offer his opinions and ideas regardless of the potential social or professional consequences, placed him in this lonely position. As a result, *A Mathematician's Apology* is anything but objective. While Hardy's argument is generally well defended, many of his subjective views, especially in regards to applied mathematics and chess, have been harshly criticized, and it is clear that as his life was drawing to a close, Hardly had achieved a melancholic acceptance of this position. Nevertheless, even to the end he refused to retreat on any of the views that defined his life and career.

Historical Context

Since Hardy elucidated a philosophy that stresses the timelessness and immortality of pure mathematics, it is very difficult to contextualize *A Mathematician's Apology* with respect to a single historical period. Viewed as an autobiographical memoir, *A Mathematician's Apology* is a product of a genius who came of age towards the end of the Victorian era and who died as the world entered the nuclear age. However, viewed as a philosophical treatise and justification of mathematics, the book begins with the ancient Greeks and extends to the eve of World War II.

Hardy was a product of the English educational system that retained intellectually mediocre clergymen as the main instructors until well into the nineteenth century. Although this system had been largely reformed by the turn of the century, mathematics was one of the last disciplines to be affected. Cambridge mathematician Norbert Wiener described the level of mathematics at Oxford as "contemptible." The training available at Cambridge was not much better, consisting of a severe exam system, the triposes, which relied on rote memorization rather than any degree of unique creativity; it was not a system that inspired a mathematical genius. The insufficiency of the English system meant that the English lagged behind other European countries in producing mathematicians and modern mathematical theories.

In his memoir, Hardy emphasizes that he became a mathematician in spite of this early training. Much of *A Mathematician's Apology* can be read as a subtle jab at the stifling environment of the English educational system. As Hardy's generation of mathematicians gained international recognition, they quickly instituted changes that treated mathematics more as a creative art than as an endless series of exercises in rote learning. Hardy himself, for instance, was instrumental in opposing the continuation of the rigid tripos exam system.

During the early part of the twentieth century, Britain was still very much an empire with territories spanning the globe, including India. The great Indian mathematician Srinivasa Ramanujan learned English as a result of the English colonial system. It was as a result of Britain's close relationship with India that Ramanujan and Hardy began a correspondence which was to result in one of the great collaborations in mathematics history. Hardy was able to procure a position for Ramanujan at Trinity College, Cambridge, which allowed the collaboration to flourish.

But Hardy's other collaborations at the time did not fare so well. By the time World War I broke out, Hardy was in his prime and had already begun working with several other mathematicians outside of England, who would ultimately have a lasting effect on both his own career and on mathematics as a whole. But with the outbreak of the war and the virulent nationalism that accompanied it, international collaboration proved exceedingly difficult, if not outright impossible.

Hardy became well known throughout his life for his outspoken views outside of the field of mathematics. The narrow-mindedness of many scientists within England, for instance, greatly concerned Hardy, and he let that be known. Unlike most intellects of his day, Hardy had a great reverence for

Compare & Contrast

- **1930s:** Technology still has limited, though powerful, uses in warfare; a war must be won largely from the strength of armed forces, with technology playing a secondary role.

  Today: The United States uses advanced technologies in its bombing campaigns against Iraq and Afghanistan, thus severely limiting the need for ground troops directly engaging in battle.

- **1930s:** The world has still not been exposed to the threat of nuclear annihilation. Nuclear fission is viewed as impractical, and Einstein's theory of relativity is still a concept remote from everyday life.

  Today: With the help of Einstein's theories, many nations have nuclear capabilities and can cause the destruction of mankind. Atomic testing in certain desert and ocean regions has had a lasting and adverse affect on the environment, and the threat of nuclear war between states continues to exist.

- **1930s:** Alexander Alekine, Mikhail Botvinnik,

and José Capablanca are celebrated for their mastery of chess. Chess is viewed as a game with an infinite number of continuations that can only be mastered by a particular kind of genius.

  Today: Chess computers have been developed that can beat some of the best players in the world. IBM has developed a computer that defeats the reigning champion grandmaster, Gary Kasparov. Computers are capable of calculating an immense number of various chess continuations.

- **1930s:** The profession of mathematics is an exclusive club, with a nearly all-male membership. In *A Mathematician's Apology,* Hardy does not mention a single female colleague or refer to a single female author.

  Today: Although less than one-fifth of all mathematicians and scientists are female, the Association of Women in Mathematics, founded in 1971, has over 4100 members, and there is wider recognition that gender disparities in the field are an issue to be addressed.

---

the German mathematical school and was greatly distressed by the anti-German sentiment that proliferated throughout England and particularly at Cambridge. His ability to separate German intellectual achievement from the exaggerated "inhuman" traits of the enemy which were spoken of throughout England made him somewhat of a pariah figure in this regard. He even went so far as to carry on an extensive correspondence with Swedish mathematician Gösta Mittag-Leffler, in which the two worked towards a reconciliation between German and Allied mathematicians with the war still raging.

Hardy wrote *A Mathematician's Apology* under the threat of another world war. Although he could not ignore the threat of that war, it is almost as if he includes the relationship between war and mathematics as an afterthought. He admits this in a brief note that follows the last chapter. Viewed with

the hindsight of today, his views concerning the improbability that a theory like relativity would have an effect on war in Hardy's lifetime appear to be grossly miscalculated and anachronistic. These views are the last gasp of an age of innocence and naiveté, ignoring or not fully recognizing the devastating effects that science—even the science of pure mathematics which Hardy considered to be "gentle and clean"—could have on humanity.

Critical Overview

In his review of *A Mathematician's Apology* in the *Spectator,* British author Graham Greene asserts that Hardy's philosophy is akin to the philosophy of an artist. "The real mathematician," according to Greene, "must justify himself as an artist." Indeed, Hardy's work is a very successful justification of the mathematician as artist, much in the literary tradition that includes *The Autobiography of Benvenuto Cellini;* Vincent Van Gogh's letters to his brother Theo; and, as Greene points out, the work of Henry James. Greene writes, "I know no writing—except perhaps Henry James's introductory essays—which conveys so clearly and with such an absence of fuss the excitement of the creative artist."

While the "uninitiated"—that is, non-mathematicians such as Greene—were apt to focus on the work as an artist's memoir, those with more rigorous mathematical training focused on the rift within the field of mathematics that *A Mathematician's Apology* brought to the fore. As the anonymous reviewer in the *Times Literary Supplement* observes, "'Real' mathematics deals only with the ultimate abstractions of number, and, if not in itself incapable of being put to 'use,' at least becomes only occasionally and accidentally useful." "Applied" mathematics, on the other hand, deals with numbers as useful scientific tools, which helps bring about innovation. Its definition implies utility, or usefulness, and is the opposite of the "math-as-art philosophy" Hardy espouses throughout the book. And true to Hardy's lifelong reputation for his candid opinions, Hardy did not hold back the scorn and derision he felt for the functional uses of mathematics. He refers to chess problems, for instance, as "trivial," regardless of their relative degrees of difficulty, and he similarly belittles applied mathematicians and their work throughout the book.

Hardy sums up this attitude at the beginning of chapter 28:

> There are then two mathematics. There is the real mathematics of the real mathematicians, and there is what I call the "trivial" mathematics, for want of a better word. The trivial mathematics may be justified by arguments that would appeal to [Lancelot] Hogben, or other writers of his school, but there is no such defense for the real mathematics, which must be justified as art if it can be justified at all.

Ironically, Hogben, the mathematician for whom Hardy reserved the word "trivial," appears to have been unaffected by the criticism. In fact, a late edition of Hogben's book, *Mathematics for the Million,* was reviewed in tandem with the reprint of *A Mathematician's Apology* in 1967 in the *Times Literary Supplement,* as a vivid illustration of the disagreement between the two views. As the re-

viewer notes, "For [Hardy] Hogben is 'admittedly not a mathematician' and 'real' mathematics is to Hogben 'merely an object of contemptuous pity.'" Despite the profound differences between the two works, the reviewer writes that they both "deserve the immortality they appear to have achieved."

Criticism

David Partikian

Partikian is a freelance writer, editor, and English instructor. In this essay, Partikian suggests that Hardy's text is a multifaceted work that should be appreciated primarily as an artistic treatise and memoir.

Mathematics is an exclusive club that opens its doors to a small number of gifted and often misunderstood individuals. Those who remain outside only have a vague perception of what it means to be a mathematician, and the perception that they do hold is more often than not hindered by an inability to understand exactly what it is that a mathematician does. Conversely, the expert mathematician is almost as ill-equipped as the layperson in trying to convey the beauty and joy of pure mathematics to non-mathematicians; the mathematician's reliance on abstractions and the specialized vocabulary that define him as a mathematician make him a poor choice to describe and verbalize his field to the layperson. One either grasps the inherent beauty of theorems and numbers, thereby earning entry into the club, or one cannot and remains a perplexed outsider unable to grasp the inscrutable formulas. At least this was the case until G. H. Hardy, one of the foremost mathematicians of the twentieth century, bridged the gap and allowed the non-mathematicians of the world a glimpse into the mind and values of a pure mathematician.

Past his intellectual prime and restricted physically by several years of failing health, Hardy decided to write *A Mathematician's Apology*, a book that can be appreciated by the mathematician and non-mathematician alike. The theorems that he outlines are among the most basic in the entire field. They are chosen so that the reader can both readily comprehend the explanations and easily perceive their aesthetic qualities. Hardy writes with the flavor and passion of an art lover about Euclid's proof of the existence of an infinity of prime numbers and

What Do I Read Next?

- *Copenhagen* (1998), a play by Michael Frayn, illustrates the moral issues faced by mathematicians and physicists during World War II. Hardy touches upon many similar subjects in his apology.

- *Mathematics for the Million,* by Hardy's contemporary Lancelot Hogben, was originally published in 1937 and republished in 1967. It is an influential work in the field of mathematics and offers a sharp contrast to Hardy's view of applied mathematics as trivial.

- Hardy's *Ramanujan: Twelve Lectures on Subjects Suggested by His Life and Work* (1940) is inspired by Hardy's working relationship with famed Indian mathematician Srinivasa Ramanujan. This book is only for those well-versed in mathematics.

- Harold Schonberg's *Grandmasters of Chess* (1973) provides brief biographical portraits of chess grandmasters as men of genius and artists, including Alexander Alekhine. These portraits contradict Hardy's assessment of chess and chess grandmasters as inartistic.

- The MacTutor History of Mathematics Archive, compiled by the University of St. Andrews, Scotland, and found on the World Wide Web at http://www-history.mcs.st-andrews.ac.uk/ (last accessed December 2002), contains, among other useful mathematics history, an archive of more than 1300 mathematicians' biographies. Information on Hardy includes a bibliography and several articles written by and about him, along with several obituaries.

- Sylvia Nasar's *A Beautiful Mind: The Life of Mathematical Genius and Nobel Laureate John Nash* (1998) is a biography of John Nash, Princeton professor and mathematician, whose primary work in Game Theory was already underpinning the economic system within his lifetime. Nasar's portrait of Nash's life includes sympathetic examinations of his work, his personal life, and his battle with schizophrenia.

Pythagoras's proof of the irrationality of the square root of two. The theorems he describes are representative of works of art precisely because they are so simple, which also makes them convenient as perfect examples for the general reader.

Since Hardy writes for an audience in large part comprising non-mathematicians, one must classify his essay with literary rather than mathematical headings. While the cold narrative voice of a mathematician does come forth at times in the prose, so do tones of elitism, disdain, and artistic snobbery, all of which do not normally belong in a mathematical essay. How then should we classify the essay if not as "mathematical"? *A Mathematician's Apology* is so multifaceted that it seems to transcend pigeonholing or categorizing. Restricting it to any single genre is an error that would cause a very restricted interpretation. For a thorough understanding of Hardy's intentions, one must read the work as a representative example of various literary genres including the apology, artistic manifesto, and memoir. In each of these genres, Hardy's elitist, value-laden tone invariably either demands unconditional acceptance or provokes severe disagreement.

A literary apology is a defense or justification for a particular way of life. Hardy, in calling his essay an apology, feels compelled to defend his chosen discipline. The urgency which he brings to the task leads one to believe that he is, at any given moment, trying to convince himself of the arguments. In order to present his belief that mathematics is an art, Hardy returns again and again to the concept of "utility" or "usefulness." Judging from the disproportionate amount of writing he dedicates to these definitions, the charge that real mathematics has no practical use must have truly bothered him over the years. The disdain Hardy reserves for the widely accepted notions of "utility" and "use-

> **Although Hardy's artistic philosophy has provoked widespread disagreement, his work remains extremely compelling as a personal memoir.''**

fulness'' is a further indication that the core of Hardy's philosophy resides in these definitions.

Hardy continually splits hairs in defining ''utility'' or ''usefulness'' in order to refine a definition that contradicts common sense. After Hardy has finished, the conventional conceptions of ''useful'' and ''useless'' have been inverted from what is generally accepted: what we commonly hold to be ''useful'' applications, such as engineering, geometry, and calculus, are ''trivial'' and useless to the real mathematician, according to Hardy. Conversely, the ''uselessness'' of real mathematics is precisely the reason why it is immortal and why one can consider it an art form. Hardy cannot contain his contempt and scorn for applied mathematics, calling it ''school'' mathematics and referring to its various worldly applications—such as engineering feats, ballistics, and aerodynamics—as ''repulsively ugly and intolerably dull.''

In belittling an entire subfield of mathematics, Hardy puts himself in a difficult position from which he can only extricate himself by twisting conventional definitions to justify his own field. His disdain for practical and useful applications forces him to redefine ''uselessness,'' a word that usually evokes negative images, in a manner that brings forth positive connotations. Herein lies the second stage of his definition and the beauty of the essay. Hardy may appear, to the careless reader, to have painted himself into a corner by proclaiming that it is ''not possible to justify the life of any genuine mathematician on the ground of the 'utility' of his work.'' According to Hardy's philosophy, ''applied'' mathematics is ''trivial'' because it is useful, while ''real'' mathematics is immortal and superior because it is useless. Furthermore, it is useless in the way that the highest art forms of humankind are useless. Much the way Taoist thought holds a certain type of uselessness as an outstanding character trait, Hardy compares the uselessness of ''real''

mathematics to the uselessness of art. In this sense, to be useless is the ultimate compliment, and ''real'' mathematics is the highest form of art. Hardy writes

> For mathematics is, of all the arts and sciences, the most austere, and the most remote, and a mathematician should be of all men the one who can most easily take refuge where, as Bertrand Russell says, ''one at least of our nobler impulses can best escape from the dreary exile of the actual world.'' . . . Mathematics is not a contemplative but a creative subject.

In setting down this philosophy and carefully describing its terms, Hardy creates a manifesto that describes real mathematics as an artistic movement, in much the same way the surrealist André Breton clarified an artistic movement in his *Manifesto of Surrealism.* Hardy puts forth the argument that real mathematicians have since time immemorial been artists of the highest caliber. This mathematician-as-artist motif was noticed immediately in early reviews of the work. In his 1941 review of *A Mathematician's Apology* in the *Spectator,* British author Graham Greene asserts that Hardy's philosophy is akin to the philosophy of an artist. ''The real mathematician . . . must justify himself as an artist,'' Greene writes.

Putting all accolades aside, there are those who remain unconvinced of the basic theories in Hardy's concept of mathematics as art and who take offense to his dismissive views of other artistic genres. Arthur Waley writes in an early review for the *New Statesman and Nation* that ''Dr. Hardy in this book is very definitely on the defensive, and his defense of mathematics consists in asserting that it is an art, like painting or poetry.'' However, a poet could easily take offense or pick apart the examples and arguments that Hardy puts forth in an attempt to show the inferiority of poetry as an art. Not only does Waley not buy into the logic, he writes, ''All this sounds like the comment of one whose contact with poetry is somewhat superficial.'' A similar argument can be proposed for many of the other disciplines and fields Hardy writes off as ''trivial.'' The most glaring example is chess. Chess grandmaster Alexander Alekhine is derisively described as a ''conjuror'' or ''ventriloquist,'' and chess is constantly belittled as ''trivial.'' Keeping Waley's objection in mind, it is clear that Hardy knows no more about chess than he does about poetry. His analysis and dismissals are superficial in that they do not take into account, for instance, the countless variations of set openings and the economy and aesthetic beauty of eliminating inefficient continuations in an attempt to bring about a ''winning'' position. In short, much as with poetry, Hardy writes off an entire field or artistic genre as inferior without having approached it with the same passion and knowledge he retains for theoretical mathematics; a chess grandmaster could easily argue that some of José Capablanca's games contain the same simplicity and beauty of a Euclidian theorem.

Hardy's derisive tone does not in any way imply final authority. The mathematician Lancelot Hogben (Hardy hesitates to even confer the title of mathematician on him), for whom Hardy reserves a flagrant contempt, has also achieved a significant and enduring reputation. A reprinted version of Hogben's book *Mathematics for the Million* was reviewed in tandem with the reprint of *A Mathematician's Apology* in 1967. The continuing popularity of both works indicates a particular rift within the field of mathematics and clearly shows that Hardy, though universally accepted as brilliant, is not necessarily considered the final authority he claims to be.

Although Hardy's artistic philosophy has provoked widespread disagreement, his work remains extremely compelling as a personal memoir. Snow, writing in his biographical portrait of Hardy that initially appeared in his *Variety of Men* and that is now included as the introduction in later editions of Hardy's essay, believes it to be a work of ''haunting sadness'' precisely because it is a ''passionate lament for creative powers that used to be and that will never come again.'' Viewed as a memoir, the work, particularly towards its conclusion, describes the trials and tribulations that a creative genius must undergo to excel in a field that does not appear to have the approval of the non-initiated. Both Snow's biographical portrait and Hardy's concluding chapters, for example, mention the insufficiency and stifling quality of the English educational system to which Hardy was subjected during his formative years. The mathematics departments at Cambridge relied on a contemptible and severe exam system, the triposes, which rewarded diligence rather than creativity. Hardy became a mathematician in spite of his education and was never truly appreciated by that system for the creative thinker that he was. The artistic genius is bound to remain misunderstood and held back by a callous society of Philistines; such a theme appears in numerous artistic memoirs and biographies of creative thinkers.

Although past the prime of his ability to contribute to the field of theoretical mathematics, Hardy retained the ability to describe to the layperson why the field of real mathematics is so lofty and noble. His eloquence and reluctant acceptance of his declining abilities allowed him to bridge the gap between genius and the common person, leaving a unique memoir to accompany his more creative artistic and mathematical endeavors. And although his derogatory statements and biased appraisal of real mathematics as the loftiest art form make him appear irrepressibly elitist, an undertone of humility caused by the realization of his declining physical and intellectual abilities balances Hardy's writing and has rendered *A Mathematician's Apology* an enduring classic.

Source: David Partikian, Critical Essay on *A Mathematician's Apology,* in *Nonfiction Classics for Students,* Gale, 2003.

Catherine Dybiec Holm

Holm is a freelance writer with speculative fiction and nonfiction publications. In this essay, Holm discusses the parallel Hardy draws between the pure mathematician and the artist.

Mathematics may not be the first pursuit that comes to mind when we speak of the creative process. The artist and the mathematician may seem to be on different ends of the spectrum. Storytelling, painting, literature, dance—these appear to be the realm of creative artists. Math, on the other hand, is an ''austere'' profession, little understood and sometimes feared. In *A Mathematician's Apology,* G. H. Hardy distinguishes between pure and applied mathematics and compares the pursuit of pure mathematics to the creative process. For the most part, the comparison works.

According to its definition, the word ''create'' means to bring into being, to make, or to make by giving a new character function or status. Creation is the formulation of the new. Writers create stories that have never been told or have never been told with that author's particular slant. Musical composers create original works or variations on existing works. Visual artists bring their visions into being using a number of media. And so, claims Hardy, pure mathematicians create new thought and new direction with their medium—numbers. In the introduction to *A Mathematician's Apology,* C. P. Snow refers to a review of Hardy's book by Graham Greene; Greene called *A Mathematician's Apology* one of the best accounts of ''what it was like to be a *creative artist.*''

Snow, who knew Hardy personally, claims that Hardy had little ''ego'' and thus had to make a great

> **Like a creative artist, Hardy is so sure of his passion for his subject that 'a defence of mathematics will be a defence of myself.' The artist and the art seem to be one and the same."**

effort in later life to assert his opinions. According to Snow, this aspect of Hardy's personality contributed to the "introspective insight and beautiful candour" of Hardy's thought process and writing. Throughout the book, Hardy clearly displays an artist's passion for his work, with candor that can be direct and unflinching. Hardy discusses the creative artist's potential to do something exceptional, and with characteristic bluntness and high standards claims that "if a man has any genuine talent, he should be ready to make almost any sacrifice in order to cultivate it to the full."

While Hardy promotes these standards for those with talent, he writes off much of the human population by claiming that "most people can do nothing well at all." For the reader who never knew Hardy personally, it is hard to tell whether this remark is indicative of excessive ego or of a creative person's high demands of himself and what he wishes to accomplish in life. To Snow, at least, Hardy's purpose in life and in the field of mathematics was "to bring rigour into English mathematical analysis." Hardy's purpose is so integral to his existence that he admits this and calls it "inevitable egotism." Good work, says Hardy, "is not done by 'humble' men." Like a creative artist, Hardy believes that for a human, "the noblest ambition is that of leaving behind one something of value."

Throughout *A Mathematician's Apology*, Hardy does not deny that he accomplished his life goal of bringing rigor into his field. However, he bemoans the fact (or the perception) that mathematicians do their best, most groundbreaking work at a relatively young age. The cause of Hardy's sadness is one aspect of a mathematician's life that seems to deviate from that of some creative artists. Hardy never tells the reader why older mathematicians do less than cutting-edge work. We might assume that as

mathematicians age, their mental faculties decrease. However, creative artists in certain other fields may paint, write, or perform well into old age. Given the creative artist's passion for creating, the reader might correctly assume that being unable to continue to create is akin to personal catastrophe or unbearable sadness.

It would be interesting to know how much satisfaction Hardy gleaned from continuing to work in mathematics into older age. Was his work truly inferior to what he had produced at a younger age? Was he able to feel as passionately about his later work in the field? In some creative endeavors such as literature, age, maturity, and experience may enrich the final product. An author's first novel published when she is twenty-five is likely to be vastly different than a novel the same author publishes when she is forty-five. Snow concurs with this view of literature, stating that "it is very rare for a writer to realize, with the finality of truth, that he is absolutely finished." But Snow, like Hardy, never explains why the work or the art of aging mathematicians diminishes.

Hardy's world of pure mathematics in this respect more resembles the career of an athlete or a dancer. Why is pure mathematics such an "all or nothing" proposition? Why does Hardy believe that when a creative man has lost the power or desire to create, "it is a pity but in that case he does not matter a great deal anyway, and it would be silly to bother about him?" Has Hardy really lost the ability to continue to create or is he feeling the pinch of competition from up-and-coming, younger mathematicians? While competition may enter into an artist's life, it does not need to affect the ability to continue to produce.

Regardless, it is Hardy's exposition of the mathematical process as a creative process that makes *A Mathematician's Apology* so accessible to the non-mathematical reader. Certainly, readers who are involved in some form of artistic creation or readers who have passionately and single-mindedly pursued the creation of something new in their lives are shown mathematics in a new light. And this is a good thing. Hardy admits that many people have an irrational fear of basic, applied mathematics. How could such people, therefore, be expected to understand the esoteric realms of pure mathematics, a field which Hardy calls "the most austere and most remote of all the arts and sciences"?

To Hardy, artists as well as mathematicians create patterns. Like the patterns that a poet or painter creates, the patterns that the mathematician creates must be beautiful. Hardy claims that the ideas in any of these forms need to flow well together; ''there is no permanent place in the world for ugly mathematics.'' On the other hand, Hardy readily admits to the difficulty of defining beauty, a dilemma shared by artists and mathematicians alike. Worthwhile mathematics, according to Hardy, should be ''serious as well as beautiful—'important.'''

One parallel between the creative process and the study of pure mathematics that Hardy does not elaborate upon is the role of the unknown. During the process of creativity, depending upon the particular artist and his or her style or mode of work, the end result may be completely unknown. For some creative artists, this is part of the thrill of creation. Hardy never alludes directly to any personal fascination, distaste, or indifference to this aspect of the creative process. We can probably assume that most mathematicians would be thrilled, in the course of their work, to discover something previously unknown; something so cutting-edge that it changed the direction of the field of mathematics and had profound implications. But the role of the unknown in the creative process can take on subtler aspects. In the area of novel writing, for example, some authors outline a novel completely before they start to write. Other novelists refuse to outline, writing the novel and figuring out the story, plot, and ending as they go. Many authors fall somewhere in between on this spectrum; outlining and preplanning to some degree but becoming fluid if needed to change course. While it may not be fair to compare pure mathematics research to novel writing, it might be interesting to know how comfortable or uncomfortable Hardy was with the unknown during his own research processes.

Hardy certainly has the purity of vision of a creative artist, or of anyone who knows what he wants to do and is doing what he loves. Immediately, he makes it clear that he prefers to do mathematics rather than engage in ''exposition, criticism, appreciation-work for second-rate minds.'' Critics, to Hardy, rank lower than scholars or poets, and he admits that it is a confession of weakness on his part to write about mathematics rather than actually writing mathematics. Like a creative artist, Hardy is so sure of his passion for his subject that ''a defence of mathematics will be a defence of myself.'' The artist and the art seem to be one and the same.

Finally, Hardy makes clear the difference between applied and pure (or real) mathematics, and it is clear that his heart and work are in the latter. To Hardy, the position of an applied mathematician is

> in some ways a little pathetic . . . he wants to be useful, he must work in a humdrum way, and he cannot give full play to his fancy, even when he wishes to rise to the heights. ''Imaginary'' universes are so much more beautiful than this stupidly constructed real one.''

As a creative artist might, Hardy sees value in transcending the ''real'' in pursuit of creativity, beauty, and significance. He can see no other way to justify real mathematics, other than justifying it as art, a view he claims is common among mathematicians.

Source: Catherine Dybiec Holm, Critical Essay on *A Mathematician's Apology,* in *Nonfiction Classics for Students,* Gale, 2003.

Sources

Dauben, Joseph W., ''Mathematics and World War I: The Internal Diplomacy of G. H. Hardy and Gösta Mittag-Leffler as Reflected in Their Personal Correspondence,'' in *Historia Mathematica,* Vol. 7, 1980, pp. 261–88.

Greene, Graham, ''The Austere Art,'' in *Spectator,* Vol. 165, December 20, 1940, p. 682.

''People Who Count,'' in *Times Literary Supplement,* December 28, 1967, p. 1266.

Snow, C. P., ''Foreword,'' in *A Mathematician's Apology,* by G. H. Hardy, Cambridge University Press, 1967, originally published in *Variety of Men,* by C. P. Snow, Scribner's, 1967.

Waley, Arthur, ''The Pattern of Mathematics,'' in *New Statesman and Nation,* Vol. 21, February 15, 1941, p. 169.

Wiener, Norbert, ''Obituary: Godfrey Harold Hardy (1877–1947),'' in *Bulletin of American Mathematics,* Vol. 55, 1949, pp. 72–77.

Further Reading

Berndt, Bruce C., and Robert A. Rankin, eds., *Ramanujan: Essays and Surveys,* American Mathematical Society, 2001.
 This collection of largely non-technical, highly accessible essays on the Indian mathematician, is the first of three books covering Srinivasa Ramanujan's life and includes several articles on his wife, his Indian colleagues, and his long illness.

Chan, L. H., ''Godfrey Harold Hardy (1877–1947)—the Man and the Mathematician,'' in *Menemui Matematik,* Vol. 1, 1979, pp. 1–13.

Chan provides a biographical portrait of Hardy that can be compared to that by C. P. Snow.

Golomb, Solomon W., "Mathematics after Forty Years of the Space Age," in *The Mathematical Intelligencer,* Fall 1999, p. 38.

Examining Hardy's assertion that pure mathematics has no relationship to issues of everyday life due to its inapplicability, Golomb argues that technological advances in the forty years since the publication of *A Mathematician's Apology* have largely proved his assertion to be false. Prime number theory, for instance, an area Hardy had a special claim to, has contributed to advances in cryptology. Golomb explains how several other mathematical fields that were also once considered "pure" are now clearly "applied," and he recounts his own experiences working in space programs during the fifties to further argue his case.

Hardy, G. H., *Bertrand Russell's Trinity,* Arno Press, 1977.

This book was originally published privately for Hardy by the University Press of Cambridge in 1942. In 1916, the philosopher Bertrand Russell was expelled from Trinity College, where he was lecturing, due to his objection to World War I. Hardy, who defended Russell and helped get him reinstated to the college after the war, sets out in this book to provide a full account of that incident and further helps to elucidate the lesser known history of conscientious objection during World War I.

Hoffman, Paul, *The Man Who Loved Only Numbers: The Story of Paul Erdös and the Search for Mathematical Truth,* Hyperion, 1998.

Hoffman provides a popular account of the life of the Hungarian mathematician Paul Erdös, who died in 1996 and was widely revered as one of the most prolific, if not the most bizarre, mathematicians who ever lived. He was known as much for his obsessive nature, nomadic existence, and boundless energy for the search for mathematical proofs as he was for his actual contributions to the science. Hoffman's book achieved widespread popular recognition at its publication and is accessible for the lay reader.

Kanigel, Robert, *The Man Who Knew Infinity: A Life of the Genius Ramanujan,* Scribner's, 1991.

Regarded as the definitive biography of Ramanujan, this book covers the mathematician's life from his early childhood to his death in 1920 with a strong emphasis on his years in England, where he collaborated with Hardy.

"A Professor's Ideals," in *Times Literary Supplement,* January 18, 1941, p. 33.

This article reiterates Hardy's philosophy that mathematics is a quest for beauty and truth.

Snow, C. P., *Variety of Men,* Scribner's, 1967.

C. P. Snow, a writer and a scientist who was a contemporary of Hardy, writes essays about several key early twentieth-century figures, including Hardy. The biographical sketch on Hardy has come to be included as the introduction in most modern editions of *A Mathematician's Apology.*

Wiener, Norbert, "Obituary: Godfrey Harold Hardy (1877–1947)," in *Bulletin of the American Mathematical Society,* Vol. 55, 1949, pp. 72–77.

This obituary gives an overview of Hardy's life and also details the problems he faced as a young man in the stifling English educational system.

Selected Essays, 1917–1932

T. S. Eliot

1932

In 1932, in London, T. S. Eliot published a selection of essays from among the prose he had written since 1917. By 1932, he was almost universally recognized as one of the most important living poets and critics of English literature, and *Selected Essays, 1917–1932* provided an in-depth overview of a theory that had fundamentally changed literary thinking.

Bound with a complex argument for a new theory and laced with allusions to almost every period of literary history, *Selected Essays, 1917–1932* may seem inaccessible or perhaps intended only for stuffy academics. But, it is important to remember two things while reading the book. First, Eliot was an American who had recently been baptized into the Church of England and who found it extremely important to sound civilized, learned, and authoritative in the grand role he had assigned himself. Second, since the success of Eliot's literary theory requires a vast knowledge and sweeping understanding of the whole of literature, the book needs to supply its reader with a broad variety of examples and parallels. After this is accomplished, the reader can go back and immerse him/herself in Eliot's idea of the classics of English literature.

Eliot revised and supplemented *Selected Essays, 1917–1932* in 1951, but this entry deals with the original version of the book. The earlier version presented then-vibrant and new material, which represented the beginnings of a shift in Eliot's thinking and which at times may seem contradic-

tory. It is important to treat the work as a whole, with examples supporting a grand and unified yet complex and subtle theory, to understand the book's profound influence and value.

Author Biography

Thomas Stearns (T. S.) Eliot was born into a large and prosperous family September 26, 1888, in St. Louis, Missouri. Eliot grew up with frequent visits to Massachusetts, where his father built a house overlooking Gloucester harbor, and entered Harvard as a philosophy student in 1906. His greatest influence there was "new humanist" philosopher Irving Babbitt, who helped Eliot form the basis for his philosophical theories.

In 1910, Eliot moved to Paris and then to Munich to study French and German literature, but he soon reenrolled at Harvard to study Eastern philosophy. With the outbreak of World War I, he began pursuing a doctoral thesis on F. H. Bradley while on a traveling fellowship to Merton College, Oxford. He stayed in Oxford until his marriage in 1915 to Vivien Haigh-Wood.

By this time, Eliot had written some of his most famous poetry, including "The Love Song of J. Alfred Prufrock." Ezra Pound, whom Eliot met in 1914 in Paris, was immediately struck by Eliot's talent and helped him publish his first collection of poetry by 1917. Pound and Eliot's lifelong friendship and collaboration on various journals eventually helped to establish them as the two main literary authorities of their generation. Upon completing his doctoral work, Eliot worked as a bank clerk and as the assistant editor of Pound's *Egoist,* a literary journal considered the major outlet for modernist thought.

Although his essays had already met with some critical success, Eliot's fame truly began in 1922 with the publication of his most influential poem, "The Waste Land." Appearing in a new quarterly called *Criterion,* of which Eliot was the founding editor, "The Waste Land" is a complex and multifaceted poem about, among other themes, the spiritual decay of Eliot's generation.

Eliot's religious thinking became increasingly important as his influence spread, and in 1927 he was officially baptized into the Church of England. The next year, in the title essay of *For Lancelot Andrewes: Essays on Style and Order*, he famously declared himself "classical in literature, royalist in politics, and Anglo-Catholic in religion."

By the 1930s, as noted by critics and writers such as E. M. Forster, Eliot was probably the most important literary figure in English. In 1932, he published *Selected Essays, 1917–1932*, which served to confirm his position in critical circles. He also began attempting to revive poetic drama in plays such as *The Family Reunion*, and in 1939 he wrote a classic book for children, *Old Possum's Book of Practical Cats*.

Eliot separated from his first wife in 1932, due to her physical and mental ill health; their marriage had made a painful and stressful impact on his life. In 1933, Eliot won the Nobel Prize for literature and was awarded the English Order of Merit. He remarried in 1957, ten years after his first wife died, and continued to write poetry, plays, and criticism until his own death in 1965 in London.

Plot Summary

Section 1

Selected Essays, 1917–1932 begins with an essay on the role of the "poet," or the author of a work of art written in English. A poet must understand his/her literary predecessors, Eliot argues, and carefully consider how his/her work of art will fit into the world of artistic tradition. Through "a continual extinction of personality" (or individual talent), a talented writer should become a translator of the emotions of his generation in a new way that adds to the poetic achievements of the past.

"The Function of Criticism" extends the theories of the previous essay to critical literature. Here too, writes Eliot, "the past should be altered by the present as much as the present is directed by the past." Critics should make a work of art clear to the reader and guide his taste.

Eliot states that John Middleton Murry provides an example of the difference between the "outside authority" of classicism and "inner voice" of romanticism. A critic must provide a useful explanation of the work of art with the important tools of "comparison and analysis" to help the reader understand it without prejudice. By following this method, Eliot writes, there is "the further possibility of arriving at something outside of ourselves, which may provisionally be called truth."

Section 2

In "Rhetoric and Poetic Drama," Eliot argues against the use of the term "rhetoric" (artificially argumentative or unnatural speech) to mean bad writing. Examples from Shakespeare and Renaissance dramatists demonstrate that rhetoric is sometimes a useful and appropriate authorial technique.

The next essay explores a number of tangents and often appears to stray from logical argument, although the subject is supposed to be "the possibility of poetic drama." The essay presents a discussion among seven voices, each named a letter from A to G. B begins with a speech ending in the statement that theater is essentially meant for amusement. A, C, D, and E question the place of morality in drama, and E points out that "form" (or aesthetic beauty, such as a Russian ballet) is the future of drama. Eventually the discussion comes closer to the original topic: whether poetic drama, or drama written in verse that is both poetically beautiful and dramatically compelling, is possible at the present time. G suggests that the seven of them form their own theater of poetic drama, "by ourselves and only for ourselves," but F and B maintain that this is not possible. E then states that plays simply need to be shorter, a solution A ridicules.

In "Euripides and Professor Murray," Eliot criticizes Professor Gilbert Murray, a popular Greek translator, and calls for translations that take into consideration the recent advances in aesthetic and scientific thought. "Seneca in Elizabethan Translation" begins with a discussion of the very influential Latin author and his plays, considering why he was so popular during both his time and the Renaissance, but became so unpopular afterwards. Seneca's characters are often unrealistic, Eliot argues, with long, contrived speeches, but the writer has great and consistent dramatic power. Seneca's ideas are a complex basis for Renaissance thought. Seneca is not responsible for the often bloody and violent nature of the period's plays, but his verse technique

T. S. Eliot

did serve as the foundation for the revolutionary literary forms of the Renaissance.

Section 3

Next comes a "preface to an unwritten book," titled "Four Elizabethan Dramatists." In this essay, Eliot emphasizes the need for a new "point of view toward the Elizabethan drama," because the two main critical approaches to it are both incorrect and indistinct. One approach assumes that plays should be read as literature, and the other "maintains the view that a play need not be literature at all"; but they are both wrong to separate drama and verse. Modern critics should understand that Elizabethan failures in dramatic unity and believability, and modern playwrights' failures in rhythmic verse, are both due to the lack of a firm dramatic convention (a consistent literary style among a community of writers).

An essay on Christopher Marlowe emphasizes that Marlowe's verse is an earlier version of the blank verse in Shakespeare but that it is (like that of all successful poets) a very unique application of the newly developing style. "Shakespeare and the Stoicism of Seneca" continues the discussion of Elizabethans and their influences. Critics are forever misinterpreting Shakespeare, says Eliot, and mistakenly assume he has a conscious and consistent ideology, although Senecan "stoicism" does underlie his work. Stoicism, a philosophical attitude popular in Roman times, stresses a passive response (a "join[ing one]self with the Universe") to a world seen as hostile to weak and insignificant humans. Shakespeare's tragic heroes consistently try to cheer themselves up with this fatalistic philosophy that ignores one's own mistakes and blames them on an evil world.

An essay on *Hamlet* argues that the play must not be, as is mostly the case, a study of the main character; it must examine the dramatics of the play itself. The play is an "artistic failure" because the primary emotion of the play is "inexpressible." Eliot notes that, since the events of the plot are not sufficient to drive the action, Shakespeare "tackled a problem that proved too much for him."

The next series of essays are evaluations of Elizabethan and Jacobean dramatists. To Eliot, Ben Jonson is a superb poet "of the surface." His characters do not have the "inner life" of Shakespeare's, but they sophisticatedly fit in with each other and with Jonson's unique dramatic world. Jonson's "fine sense of form" and his "deliberate" philosophy make him very worth the trouble that it takes to understand his work as a whole.

Thomas Middleton, on the other hand, "has no point of view" or "personality," according to Eliot, but he does have an excellent talent for depicting the "permanent human impulse" Eliot finds so important. Thomas Heywood has "no imaginative humor," writes Eliot. His success is in the "drama of common life" (Eliot thinks of his plays like soap operas); Heywood's work does not compare with the beauty of verse and drama that Eliot finds in Shakespeare.

Cyril Tourneur, who is typically thought to have written only two plays, is described as an excellent dramatist, like Middleton. A lengthy comparison of Tourneur's two plays reveal that *The Revenger's Tragedy,* although it is an "isolated masterpiece" of seemingly greater skill than *The Atheist's Tragedy,* actually was written first, a fact supported by what Eliot calls the "immaturity" of its horrific moral vision.

John Ford, meanwhile, despite having moments of great and unique style in blank verse, has

no "purpose" to his plays as a whole. Eliot believes he lacks the "soul of the poet" that Eliot considers vital to the great masters.

Finally, after emphasizing the importance of putting Elizabethan writers into a broad scholarly context, Eliot describes Philip Massinger as a poet of "exceptionally superior . . . literary talent," with an inclination towards the later style of the Restoration. However, Eliot notes that Massinger has a "paltry imagination" and no ability to capture human emotion like his predecessors.

Section 4

The *Divine Comedy* of medieval Italian poet Dante Alighieri is the subject of the next essay. The great poem has three sections, *Inferno* ("Hell"), *Purgatorio* ("Purgatory"), and *Paradiso* ("Heaven"), that describe Dante's descent through hell, his journey through purgatory, and his ascent through heaven until he reaches God. Eliot writes that Dante is the most "universal" of poets since the ancient Greeks and Romans, because of his visual imagination and his having lived in a time that was united under St. Thomas Aquinas's Christian philosophy.

Eliot discusses Dante's complex use of allegory, in which nearly everything is a symbol for something in the Christian philosophical universe. A reader can enjoy the poem without understanding these symbols but afterwards will probably want to explore their meaning and allegorical context. Eliot claims that Dante reaches the "complete scale of the depths and heights of human emotion" through allegory. He closes the essay by discussing Dante's early work, the *Vita Nuova* ("New Life"), which clarifies a major symbol in the *Divine Comedy,* that of Beatrice, the Florentine woman whom Dante loves first as a human and then as a divine virtue.

Section 5

In "The Metaphysical Poets," Eliot asserts that the poets in this group are too diverse and "permanently valuable" to be placed under the category of their title. Although these poets sometimes engage in "metaphysical conceits," or complex and long metaphors that are carried "to the furthest stage to which ingenuity can carry" them, so-called metaphysical poets wrote with more feeling than modern poets. They try "to find the verbal equivalent for states of mind and feeling,'' writes Eliot.

An essay on Andrew Marvell elaborates on Eliot's praise for the poetry of the seventeenth century (before the Restoration of Charles II). Marvell is not one of the greatest poets, but his generation's ''wit'' and balance between jest and seriousness come through in his best poems. The ''precious and needed and apparently extinct'' qualities that come through ''minor'' poets like Marvell reveal to Eliot the poetic superiority of an age.

In ''John Dryden,'' Eliot argues that appreciation for this eighteenth-century poet has dwindled because of the poor taste of the nineteenth century, which disfavored the material of Dryden's poetry. Although Eliot believes that Dryden lacks ''insight,'' he notes that Dryden's broad range, great wit, and lyrical genius make Dryden an extremely enjoyable, influential, and important poet.

William Blake, however, despite his own original genius and ''considerable understanding of human nature,'' lacked the ''framework of traditional ideas'' vital to Eliot's idea of a first-order poet. Eliot's essay on Blake describes Blake's ''visionary'' philosophy as too incomplete and ''remote from the world'' since it lacks an understanding of tradition.

''Swinburne As Poet'' briefly compares this writer with examples of poetry infused with more sense and meaning than Swinburne's works. Although Eliot finds him a superb linguist, Swinburne's meaning is ''merely the hallucination of meaning'' because it dwells entirely in language, as opposed to human feeling.

Section 6

''Lancelot Andrewes'' and ''John Bramhall'' discuss two influential seventeenth-century bishops of the Church of England. Eliot observes that Bishop Andrewes, although his writings are dense and not ''entertaining,'' wrote some of the ''finest prose'' in English. Andrewes is able to write with such excellent structure because he is unwaveringly committed to his theological subject.

Bishop Bramhall is, according to Eliot, not appreciated nearly enough for his ''mastery'' of logical argument. The essay on Bramhall contrasts

his writings with those of Thomas Hobbes to reveal that Bishop possesses the ''historical sense,'' ''philosophical basis,'' and vital ''middle way'' of argument that Hobbes lacks.

''Thoughts after Lambeth'' elaborates Eliot's views on the recent conflicts in the Church of England by examining the Lambeth Conference Report of 1930. The Lambeth Conference, which occurs once every ten years, is the major forum for the leaders of the Anglican Church. Despite some understandably poor ''verbiage'' of the report, writes Eliot, the conference marked ''an important stage'' towards the reunification of Christian religious sects. Overall, it was a successful effort to clarify the theological position of the Church of England at a time of particularly pronounced division and controversy.

Section 7

The final section of *Selected Essays, 1917–1932* concentrates on nineteenth-century artists, beginning with an essay on Baudelaire. In order to better understand one of the most important French poets of the nineteenth century, Eliot proposes to ''affirm the importance of Baudelaire's prose works.'' From these, it is clear that he has both a ''sense of his age'' and the ''inner disorder'' that is characteristic of his contemporaries. This comes out in his poetry, which has excellent ''superficial form'' but lacks inner unity.

The next two essays evaluate Walter Pater and Francis Herbert Bradley, two Victorian prose writers, in comparison with Matthew Arnold, the nineteenth-century critic famous for his views on literary and social culture. ''Arnold and Pater'' proposes that the ''art for art's sake'' aesthetic theory that Pater developed, a theory emphasizing that there are no grand outside principles for judging the merit of a work of art, is actually in direct line with Arnold's philosophy. Both theories represent to Eliot ''the degradation of philosophy and religion'' because they substitute cultural values for theological values.

Eliot writes in his next essay that Bradley's prose, like Pater's, has fundamental similarities in theme to Matthew Arnold's. But unlike Pater, Bradley is a careful and thorough philosophical thinker who is able to provide a unified basis for Arnold's unsuccessful attempts at philosophy.

A brief essay then praises popular actress Marie Lloyd because of her ''understanding of the people and sympathy with them." Next, "Wilkie Collins and Dickens" recognizes the importance of interesting and convincing drama (by which Eliot means sophisticated characterization) and good melodrama. Collins, although he could not create interesting and convincing characters like Dickens could, was a master of melodramatic novels.

The next two essays express Eliot's view on "humanism," a traditionalist philosophy stressing the importance of classic literature. As becomes clearer in "Second Thoughts About Humanism," Eliot affirms what he considers "pure humanism," which "makes for breadth, tolerance, equilibrium and sanity." But, he argues against the type of humanism that his former professor Irving Babbitt implies because to Eliot it unsuccessfully disregards religion.

In "Charles Whibley," Eliot praises his contemporary as a brilliant journalist with the ability to write with "life," as people normally speak. Whibley was also an important critic because of his vast literary knowledge and "personal gusto and curiosity."

Key Figures

Dante Alighieri

Alighieri (1265–1321) is one of the most revered poets of the Middle Ages. His *Divine Comedy,* written in the common language of Florence, Italy, is a masterpiece of Catholic philosophy and poetry. His earlier work, *Vita Nuova,* describes Dante's idealized youthful love for a Florentine woman named Beatrice. Eliot calls Dante the most "universal" of poets because his poetry has "peculiar lucidity" (a clear and transparent beauty) and his philosophy has the benefit of a united cultural belief (influenced by St. Thomas Aquinas). Born in 1265 and raised in Florence, Dante was exiled in 1301 because of fighting between political factions in the Guelph family.

Bishop Lancelot Andrewes

Andrewes (1555–1626) held a number of important positions in the Anglican Church between 1589 and 1626. Eliot revived an interest in this distinguished scholar and linguist—whose sermons are inaccessible to most people because of their dense classical allusions—by calling him "second to none in the history of the formation of the English Church."

St. Thomas Aquinas

St. Thomas Aquinas (1224–1274) was the most important religious philosopher of medieval Europe. By reconciling Aristotelian philosophy and Christian theology in *Summa theologica,* he created the extremely influential system of thought apparent in the work of Dante Alighieri.

William Archer

Archer (1856–1924) was an important critic who argued that modern plays were much more appropriate for the stage than earlier works and should be performed more often. Eliot argues with this view throughout section VII.

Matthew Arnold

Arnold (1822–1888) was one of the most important critics and advocates for "culture" (arts and humanities, particularly literature) in Victorian England. Champion of "disinterested criticism," he argued for a standard of critical taste that is not influenced by one's subjective perception of a work. He was not widely thought to be sacrilegious—in fact, he emphasized the importance of studying the Bible—but Eliot argues (particularly in section VII) that Arnold takes morality from culture when instead he should take it from religion. Arnold, like Eliot, wrote poetry in addition to criticism and was central in establishing the literary taste of his generation.

Irving Babbitt

Babbitt (1865–1933), who was Eliot's professor at Harvard, greatly influenced Eliot's philosophy. Babbitt is best known as the father of American "new humanism," which resisted the self-expressionist and romantic philosophies of the time. Instead, Babbitt advocated a return to classical modes of thought by studying traditional works of literature.

Charles-Pierre Baudelaire

A French poet, critic, and translator, Baudelaire (1821–1867) is mainly famous for his lyrical and truly felt (sometimes sordid) poetry. As a young man in Paris, he had affairs with prostitutes, went to prison, and contracted large debts. Eliot discusses Baudelaire's philosophy and tendency towards form in the first essay of section VII, implying that Baudelaire was a latent Christian despite the blasphemy in some of his poetry.

William Blake

Blake (1757–1827) was a poet and an artist of the romantic period. He never went to school but read widely and was taught by his mother until he became an engraver by trade. He crafted all of his poetic works into ornate plates of his own unique design. *Songs of Innocence and of Experience* is one of his earliest and perhaps best-known works, but he went on to create poems about mythological worlds and philosophical systems he invented.

Francis Herbert Bradley

An English philosopher about whom Eliot wrote his doctoral thesis, Bradley (1846–1924) was interested in ethics, logic, and metaphysics (a branch of philosophy that deals with the origins of the universe). In section VII, Eliot discusses Bradley's moral philosophy, its connection with religion, and its superiority to the philosophy of Matthew Arnold.

Bishop John Bramhall

Bramhall (1594–1663) was a British-Irish theologian who increased the revenue of the Irish church and wrote various Royalist and Anglican treatises.

Wilkie Collins

Collins (1824–1889) was an extremely popular Victorian novelist who, as Eliot points out in section VII, mastered the art of suspenseful storytelling. He co-wrote various plays and stories with Dickens but lost some of his influence when he began commenting on social issues. In the 1860s, Collins was thought to be the most skillful writer of "sensation fiction" (melodramatic and engaging novels that were often mysteries).

Charles Dickens

Dickens (1812–1870) was a vastly influential Victorian novelist, editor, and social critic. Like Wilkie Collins, though more permanently regarded as a profoundly talented novelist, he was a master of suspense and drama in his serialized novels. Almost all of his books take place in Victorian social contexts, often featuring desperately poor circumstances.

John Dryden

Poet, playwright, and critic of the English Restoration, Dryden (1631–1700) frequently changed his mode of expression and his opinion about historical or literary events, but nearly everything he wrote is considered important English literature. He formed a tradition of satirical verse and had an unsurpassed capacity for controlling language. Eliot discusses his recent unpopularity and explains that this is mainly due to the subject, as opposed to the quality, of his work.

Euripides

Ancient Greek dramatist Euripides (c. 480–406 B.C.) was one of the first pioneers in dramatic form. A master of surprise, he was famous for representing gods and heroes as real people in his tragedies. Eliot discusses the merits of various translations of Euripides, calling for new and better ones.

John Ford

Ford (c. 1586–1640) wrote plays and some poetry, mainly involving moral paradoxes. Eliot does not hold him in high esteem and writes that he has "an absence of purpose" despite his unique style.

Ben Jonson

Jonson (1572–1637) was a poet, critic, and playwright. Although some of his individual poems and plays are considered of the highest quality, Jonson is more famous for his influence on his contemporaries than for his own work. He led a group of writers called the "Sons of Ben," whose aims included getting closer to meaning through language. Eliot attempts to revive an interest in Jonson's plays, which, Eliot writes, are of the intellectual "surface" but nevertheless have a unique and engaging "form."

Marie Lloyd

Lloyd (1870–1922) was a popular actress and singer in London, known as "Our Marie" or "The Queen of the Music Hall" to her many fans.

Christopher Marlowe

Marlowe (1564–1593) was a playwright and poet. Possibly involved in the secret service of Elizabeth I, he is better known for the striking plays he wrote before his murder in a London pub. His uniquely defiant heroes and use of blank verse changed English drama and had a character all its own. Eliot provides a textual analysis of Marlowe in order to show the complex influence of his writing over later playwrights.

Andrew Marvell

Marvell (1621–1678) was a ''metaphysical poet,'' a term Ben Jonson used to describe seventeenth-century poets who used long, complex comparisons (a characterization Eliot discusses at length and argues is useless). As well as writing ambiguous and subtle poetry, Marvell was involved in various government positions before and after the Restoration of Charles II. Eliot praises his ''wit'' in section V, although he argues that Marvell lacks the individuality of a poet like Dryden.

Philip Massinger

There is much scholarly debate on which plays writer Massinger (1583–1640) actually wrote, as there is with many of his contemporaries. However, his talent with language and gift for satire are clear in the plays that are attributed to him.

Thomas Middleton

Middleton (1580–1627) was an unsentimental playwright who, Eliot notes, flatly depicted human relations without making judgements on them. Middleton collaborated on many of his plays and probably wrote passages in some of Shakespeare's plays, including *Macbeth*.

John Middleton Murry

John Middleton Murry (1889–1957) was a modernist critic. Eliot discusses him because of his dependence on the ''inner voice'' of criticism, which Eliot finds non-authoritative, insubstantial, and unreliable as a basis for critical thought.

Walter Pater

A Victorian critic, Pater (1839–1894) was the spokesperson for the aesthetic movement, best known for its creed ''art for art's sake.'' A master prose stylist, Pater argued that art can only be experienced by an individual on a subjective basis. Eliot writes that Pater's literary theory, which is the opposite of Eliot's own authoritative and classical theory, lacks a permanent moral and philosophical basis.

Lucius Annaeus Seneca

Seneca (c. 4–65 A.D.) was a Roman philosopher and dramatist born in Corduba, Spain (present-day Cordoba). Seneca's father was a teacher of rhetoric (the ancient Greek word for ''formal argument''). Seneca became a politician and, after an eight-year banishment, the tutor to Emperor Nero. He wrote nine tragedies that are generally considered to be intended for recitation, not performance; they contain no naturalistic or realistic speech but engage in rhetoric, about which Eliot has qualified reservations.

Eliot discusses Seneca's stoic philosophy at length, which he describes as a ''join[ing one]self with the Universe''). Stoicism was a philosophical attitude popular in Roman times, stressing a passive response to a world seen as hostile to weak and insignificant humans. Section III stresses that stoicism underlies Shakespeare as well as Renaissance writers; and since for Eliot it is an inferior philosophy to Christianity, it poses a problem for the moral and aesthetic quality of Renaissance plays. Seneca did not create stoicism, but he wrote about it and supposedly practiced it (although his pupil Nero was famous for excesses directly violating stoic belief).

William Shakespeare

Strikingly little is known about Shakespeare's life (1564–1616), given that he is probably the most famous English writer ever. Shakespeare was born in Stratford-upon-Avon, a town in the English midlands, and by 1592 had moved to London to act and write plays. He wrote poetry, including his famous sonnets, in addition to dramatic comedies, histories, and tragedies. His writing is revered for a variety of contradictory reasons. Many critics, like Eliot, praise him for his lyrical and poetical genius in addition to, in Eliot's words, the ''permanent human emotion'' displayed by his characters. No collected editions of Shakespeare's plays were published until 1623, when two members of his company collected the versions they considered authentic into the ''first folio.''

Algernon Charles Swinburne

Swinburne (1837–1909) was a prolific poet, playwright, novelist, and critic. He was known as a fierce opponent of mainstream Victorian morals, and his poems of 1866 made him both famous and hated because of their rebellious and even perverted themes. Swinburne had a superb capacity for imagination; he both experimented with old forms and created new ones, but Eliot points out that it is difficult to find ''meaning'' or consistency of thought in his works.

Cyril Tourneur

An Elizabethan playwright, Tourneur (c. 1575–1626) was probably involved in military and diplomatic work aside from writing at least two plays, but historians know very little about his life. Eliot praises his play *The Revenger's Tragedy* as a ''masterpiece'' but argues that it has a more ''immature moral vision'' than the other play attributed to Tourneur.

Themes

Tradition

Selected Essays, 1917–1932 begins with what is probably the most important theme of the collection: tradition. Eliot has a complex and personal idea of tradition, but mainly he refers to the vast canon of literature written by great authors of the past. He does not specifically mean literature written in English, but he does mean ''Western classical'' literature, from the ancient Greeks to Seneca, Dante, Chaucer, the Renaissance writers, Dryden, and Pope, through the romantics and the Victorians. In other words, tradition in *Selected Essays, 1917–1932* is literature that Eliot considers of the highest order, literature he deems important for modern English writers and critics to have read.

Eliot is one among many famous critics to have established such an idea of tradition; even in selecting and revising the list of important works, he heavily relies on such writers as Matthew Arnold, who is famous for identifying the classical literary canon in Victorian times. This seems somewhat ironic, since modernism, the literary movement of which Eliot is considered a great leader, is generally thought to break from the past. Eliot makes clear in his description of the importance of tradition, however, that writers of his time should only break with the very recent past, the age immediately before theirs, which Eliot considers to have gone astray in artistic principles. Indeed, Eliot finds art meaningless unless it is placed within the broad context of literary history. Literature finds its value in the way it communicates with the past. Eliot writes:

> Whoever has approved this idea of order, of the form of European, of English literature, will not find it preposterous that the past should be altered by the present as much as the present is directed by the past.

Although this sounds like a simple idea, it has very subtle and complicated results; it is the reason for Eliot's constant and difficult allusions and comparisons to so many different works, authors, and literary movements. Because of his concept of tradition, Eliot analyzes each single work only as a single part of the grand, shifting meaning of literature. In fact, it is difficult to appreciate Eliot's criticism of a single work without understanding his greater concept of the purpose of Western literature. Although it begins with the concept of ''a continual extinction of personality'' on the part of the poet in order to fit in with tradition, this concept changes and gradually develops *Selected Essays, 1917–1932*.

Dramatic Poetry

Eliot is interested throughout his essays in the merging of poetry and dramatics. He continually stresses the aesthetic ideal of beautiful verse and sophisticated use of language merged with realistic characters in compelling situations. The essays in section 2, especially, point out that a literary form, or convention, established by like-minded artists of a generation is necessary for great dramatic poetry to succeed. Often, Eliot judges writers almost entirely by how well they accomplish this feat; for Eliot, the two must coexist in all great pieces of literature. Essays on novelists like Dickens or poets like Marvell are few and tend not to place their subjects on the same level as a dramatic poet like Shakespeare.

Eliot's reasoning for the superiority of dramatic poetry had profound influence on the public taste of the day, including public opinion on his own

Topics for Further Study

- Listen to some classical music by Igor Stravinsky and others, written between 1917 and 1932. Describe its form using the criteria of *Selected Essays, 1917–1932.* How does Eliot's artistic theory apply to it? What do you think he would say about it? Then, listen to some music from the same time period by Louis Armstrong and Duke Ellington. Write a comparative review in Eliot's style, describing the artistic merits of the two types of music and how each fits into the tradition of Western music.

- Some critics (most notably Anthony Julius in his book *T. S. Eliot, Anti-Semitism, and Literary Form*) have accused Eliot of being anti-Semitic, and others have accused him of being a fascist. Research the history of this response to Eliot's work and his personal life and write an essay in which you discuss these theories and whether or not they are well founded. If these findings are true, do you think students should therefore not be reading Eliot's works?

- Read Eliot's *Collected Poems.* How does his critical theory relate to his poetry, and how would he fare under his own standards?

- Read one of the works that Eliot discusses at length in *Selected Essays, 1917–1932* and research other criticism on the work you choose. Does Eliot have a unique viewpoint? Do other critics follow a similar method of analysis? Do you agree with what Eliot says about the work?

- Eliot discusses philosophy and theology at length, and both are extremely important to his critical theory. Do some reading of early twentieth-century philosophers or theologians who discuss art at some point in their theories (F. H. Bradley, for example). What is the main philosophical trend of the time? How does Eliot fit into it?

---

creative writing. His plays, particularly *Murder in the Cathedral,* are meant to form the convention of dramatic poetry for which he argued in his essays.

Christianity

Christianity plays an increasingly important role in Eliot's critical thinking. Although section 1 provides an approach to literature that is not dependent on any religious belief, the philosophy underlying various authors and movements begins to be a criterion for judgment, especially in sections 4, 6, and 7. To Eliot, religion is absolutely vital to any discussion of philosophy or ethics: "If you remove the word 'human' and all that the belief in the supernatural has given to man, you can view him finally as no more than an extremely clever, adaptable, and mischievous little animal."

This quote emphasizes that Christianity is vital to Eliot's literary theory; his view of great writers is that they are "more" than animals and therefore require supernatural belief to create great literature. Eliot changes his idea, however, of whether a writer "thinks" and believes in a particular theology; he begins by denying this but later recognizes (as in the essay on William Blake) that theology is often a conscious effort that strongly influences the greatness of a work. Eventually, Christian thought is strongly present in Eliot's aesthetics as well as in his philosophy.

Style

Circuitous Argument

Selected Essays, 1917–1932 engages in a subtle and complex form of argument that can be called "circuitous," or roundabout and even indirect. Students of Eliot without a profound literary background in English literature are likely to find his essays very difficult reading material, not only because of the vast number of literary allusions but because of the complexity of the author's points that are subtly woven into the essays. Only after having read most or all of the *Selected Essays, 1917–1932* is Eliot's entire theory clear; the essays are a roundabout way of making a generalized, large-scale argument.

This does not mean that the argument is unspecific; as critic John Chalker writes in his essay "Authority and Personality in Eliot's Criticism": "Most of the *Selected Essays* were book reviews, yet, because of the precision with which he has established his theory, Eliot is able to present a continuing argument." Eliot's theory of literature often seems to contradict itself, and there are many places where it does so overtly (see "Christianity" above). Yet the entire collection, despite its indirect approach, is best seen as a thorough and subtle argument, using generalizations from nearly the entire history of literature as examples to support a theory.

The basis for Eliot's circuitous argument about the function and value of literature is in section I, but the brief and clear definition of art in the first two essays does not effectively sum up the gradually developing theory. "A Dialogue on Dramatic Poetry" is a more appropriate representation of the entire work's argumentative technique, since its tangents and varying unresolved opinions better represent the complex and shifting theory Eliot creates. Indeed, his circuitous argumentative technique is suited to the subtle, roundabout literary theory.

Rhetoric

When Eliot begins section 2 by arguing that "rhetoric" is not necessarily bad writing, he is subtly defending a characteristic of his own style. "Rhetoric" refers to a method of manipulating language, often with bombastic and artificial overtones, for the purposes of argument. Eliot's vast generalizations and obscure allusions are among his most effective stylistic methods; as Chalker writes, "What strikes one particularly about [the early essays] is their strongly rhetorical manner. The tone is immediately authoritative and magisterial."

In his role as a trendsetter, and, as critic Delmore Schwartz calls him in *T. S. Eliot, Critical Assessments,* a "literary dictator," Eliot develops an enormously influential theory of literature. And, although he tries to separate himself from Matthew Arnold, whose wide-ranging opinions determined the mainstream aesthetic views of his time, Eliot consciously places himself in a very similar role. His rhetorical style is very important to this process; by it, he ceases to sound like one critic with an opinion and moves into the role of an authority. The necessity of a conventional authority is vital to Eliot's theory (this is the "outer voice" of "the function of criticism"), and Eliot underscores his ability to provide exactly this with the rhetorical voice in his essays.

Historical Context

The Renaissance and English Writers

The Renaissance refers to the extremely broad European cultural movement characterized by a flowering of art and literature. Although it began in fourteenth-century Italy, the movement did not have much influence in English literature until the reign of Elizabeth I (1558 to 1603), which marked a new sophistication and sensibility in poetry and drama. Writers such as Edmund Spencer and Philip Sidney began this revolution in poetry, while Christopher Marlowe and Thomas Kyd were among the first pioneers in the new dramatic verse form that came to a height with the plays of William Shakespeare.

With the introduction of printing technology, lyric poetry became widely available to all classes for the first time, and this is one of the reasons that Elizabethan writing was not confined to the court. In the plays, which people of all types could see in the theaters in London's South Bank, graceful and innovative writing in iambic pentameter (a verse form in which each line has five iambs, or feet, of two syllables each) was combined with drama containing a broad range of realistic human emotions.

Poetry and drama—including Shakespeare's later tragedies—continued to develop rapidly after Elizabeth's death in 1603 and the ascension of James I of Scotland. Poets began to divide into two main new camps: the "Sons of Ben," who imitated

Compare & Contrast

- **1590s:** The British Empire is just beginning. With the defeat of the Spanish Armada in 1588, the seas are open to British trade and exploration, and British culture is showing the beginnings of racism towards future colonies.

  1920s: The British Empire is still strong, and Britain is still pervaded by imperialist thinking that emphasizes the superiority of British culture.

  Today: The British Empire has crumbled, and the British public is far more skeptical of notions of cultural superiority.

- **1590s:** Although Elizabeth I shows a greater degree of religious tolerance than the previous ruler, all British subjects are required to be members of the Church of England. In practice, a significant number of Puritans and Catholics retain their own beliefs. Atheism is taboo and very uncommon.

  1920s: The Church of England is building up to a crisis, with its authorities of very different minds about how to approach a developing lack of religious conviction in the British public.

  Today: Some bishops in the Church of England are acknowledged atheists. Although much of the British public remains devout, the general population has become significantly less religious in the past eighty years.

- **1590s:** English writing is flowering, but the respected literary canon is composed almost entirely of male, ancient Greek and Roman writers.

  1920s: Classical English literature has a fairly clear, firm, and ancient tradition. Feminist thought is beginning to be influential, but the general public does not often question the white-male-dominated literary canon.

  Today: English literature is pervaded by a multiplicity of viewpoints. Critics frequently condemn the white-male-oriented tradition and attempt to draw attention to undervalued minority writers.

- **1590s:** The most popular forms of art are plays, which anyone can attend, and lyric poetry, which is beginning to spread around England because of the invention of the printing press.

  1920s: Although poetry is becoming more important because of the revolution in style, popular forms of art are not so radically different from Victorian times, and it is the era of the novel.

  Today: Together with popular music, motion pictures (especially those from America) have exploded as one of the most popular art forms in England.

Ben Jonson's direct language intended to get closer to meaning, and the ''metaphysical poets'' (chiefly John Donne), who were characterized (unfairly, in Eliot's and others' views) by long and complex comparisons taken to the extreme. By the 1650s, Milton's technical genius to manipulate language marked the beginning of the Restoration period in 1660.

Victorian England

The other historical period of vital importance to *Selected Essays, 1917–1932* is the one immediately before Eliot's own. Chiefly important to Victorian literature are three main elements: the Industrial Revolution, the growth of the British Empire, and the fierce intellectual movement stressing moral self-consciousness. These combined to form a number of like-minded writers, particularly novelists, who wrote ''realist'' fiction attempting to display the actual social conditions of the time, often with moral judgments about social and political issues.

Victorian literature is also characterized, however, by the growing counterculture that exploded in the 1890s. Critics such as Walter Pater argued vehemently with eminent Victorian social and critical writers such as Matthew Arnold (although Eliot argues that Pater and Arnold are of the same philosophical disposition without knowing it). But Victorian values did not completely break down until the modernist movement of the early twentieth century.

Modernism

Modernism is generally considered to have coincided with World War I, which caused drastic changes to a variety of assumptions and ways of thinking. Many modernist writers, feeling that they could no longer express themselves in old forms, responded with experimental techniques that borrowed from a variety of other movements, most notably postimpressionism (which dealt with a simplification of form in the visual arts) and naturalism (which dealt with a deterministic universe involving a brutal struggle for individual survival). Most important to modernism in fiction was James Joyce's effort to deal with a multiplicity of viewpoints that lead to an "epiphany," or sudden moment of truth and understanding. In poetry, modernism was influenced by Eliot's own poetry, with modernist poems often reflecting the spiritual decadence of Eliot's "The Waste Land."

Eliot, with support from his friend Ezra Pound, was clearly the authoritative father figure of this movement. His theory, which guided the main current of modernist thought, desires both to experimentally break from the immediate past and to communicate closely with a dense tradition (creating a new but classical form). *Selected Essays, 1917–1932* is an effort to form a group of artists united around a common aesthetic goal. It was not entirely successful; despite Eliot's tone of voice throughout the essays that pretends he is speaking to a like-minded audience of critics and writers, modernism was not a single, united movement. Many authors were going in entirely different directions, trying different experimental forms that did not take the form of Eliot's somewhat classical and traditionalist approach. Nevertheless, everyone was influenced, one way or another, by Eliot's new aesthetic thinking.

Critical Overview

Although Ezra Pound and a few other radicals were supportive from the start, critics tended to resent or ignore the early essays anthologized in *Selected Essays, 1917–1932*. Arthur Waugh's "The New Poetry" called his poems "un-metrical, incoherent banalities" with "no steady current of ideas behind them." Waugh represents a group of critics who did not take Eliot's literary theory seriously.

But, by the time Eliot published *Selected Essays, 1917–1932* in 1932, he was already an extremely well-established critic. Some resented Eliot, as an American, telling the English what to think, and Delmore Schwartz points out in his essay "The Literary Dictatorship of T. S. Eliot" that many found Eliot far too overbearing and authoritative. All, however, found his thinking innovative and important. Richard Shusterman points out in his introduction to *T. S. Eliot and the Philosophy of Criticism:* "Whatever one thinks of the merit of Eliot's critical thought, its enormous influence on twentieth-century critical theory and practice cannot be denied."

Modern critical opinions on Eliot follow a similar formula. Recent critics, like Jean-Michel Rabaté in his essay "Tradition and T. S. Eliot," discuss some of the more innovative ways to approach Eliot's idea of a constantly changing literary past. Anthony Julius famously attacks Eliot's attitude towards Jews in his book, *T. S. Eliot, Anti-Semitism, and Literary Form:* "Of the many different kinds of anti-Semite, Eliot was the rarest kind: one who was able to place his anti-Semitism at the service of his art." But, as Shusterman goes on to argue, even such sharp attacks on Eliot's critical judgments are "powerful testimony to his lasting significance."

Criticism

Scott Trudell

Trudell is a freelance writer with a bachelor's degree in English literature. In the following essay, Trudell discusses the impact of religious belief on Eliot's theory of literature.

Eliot is a Christian critic, and his *Selected Essays, 1917–1932* develops a Christian view on literature. In an indirect, subtle way, his essays assume not only that the reader is extremely well-read in the classics of Western literature, but that he/she thinks as a Christian: "It is our business, as Christians, *as well as* readers of literature, to know what we ought

Medieval Italian poet Dante Alighieri, whose Divine Comedy *is discussed in one of Eliot's essays*

to like.'' But Eliot's theory of literature is valuable for all critical thinking, and its influence is much broader than one religious lens. In order to gauge the impact of *Selected Essays, 1917–1932*, it is important to understand where Eliot's literary philosophy requires a Christian viewpoint and where it is not confined to one.

First, it is necessary to briefly discuss what a Christian viewpoint on literature entails. On the simplest and most literal level, such a viewpoint would judge a work of art by two factors: how greatly its philosophy represents underlying Christian values and how greatly the author is talented to do this. Since a genuine knowledge and complete understanding of Christianity is required to criticize art on these terms, the viewpoint would maintain that a reader cannot fully appreciate or understand ''Christian art'' without believing in Christianity. And it would also maintain, therefore, that a reader cannot truly appreciate any work of art unless he/she believes in its religious or philosophical basis. This concept is not as simple as it sounds because it is unclear which art falls under which umbrella, and it is doubtful (even to Eliot) whether most art has this clear of a theological basis in the first place.

But, it is the necessary foundation of thought for any ''Christian critic.''

Samuel Hynes's essay ''The Trials of a Christian Critic'' discusses Eliot's contradictory affirmations that a critic can have an objective appreciation of a work regardless of his religion and that a critic's religious belief is necessary to his ''full understanding.'' Although Eliot entertains the idea that ''it must be possible to have full literary or poetic appreciation without sharing the beliefs of the poet,'' he later revises this to: ''It is possible, and sometimes necessary, to argue that full understanding must identify itself with full belief.'' Hynes writes that Eliot ''failed as a Christian critic'' because, ultimately, Eliot let religion take over his literary philosophy to the point where it was merely an extension of theology and as such had little value as a coherent theory of literature.

It is perhaps true, as Hynes proposes, that the subtle and carefully chosen literary theory Eliot developed, which makes every effort to find a complex universal criterion for judging the value of art irrespective of religion, ultimately fails in consistency and relies on a religious standpoint. Nevertheless, the bulk of Eliot's criticism is not strictly Christian, and his erection of a continuous English literary tradition that constantly changes with each new work of art is not fundamentally a Christian idea. For Eliot, the only complete and unified Christian art is the work of Dante; and however much he praises Dante in section IV as the most universal of poets, Eliot by no means judges all art simply by how close it comes to the achievements of *The Divine Comedy.*

Shakespeare, for example, whose underlying philosophy Eliot considers more ''Senecan'' than Christian, is clearly Eliot's choice for the greatest poet of all time: ''I believe that I have as high an estimate of the greatness of Shakespeare as a poet and dramatist as anyone living; I certainly believe that there is nothing greater.'' And, although Eliot qualifies this praise with the assertion that the philosophy behind Shakespeare is inferior to the theology behind Dante, it seems inappropriate to apply the Christian viewpoint to Eliot's judgment of the plays; it is hard to imagine Eliot arguing that he cannot ''fully appreciate'' Shakespeare's work because its Senecan moral foundation is not Christian enough for him. Even the attempt at subverting Shakespeare to Dante is suspicious given the amount of attention and importance given to the English Renaissance. If Eliot finds Renaissance philosophy

What Do I Read Next?

- *The Divine Comedy* (1321), by Dante Alighieri, describes the poet's descent into hell and eventual rise through purgatory to heaven. Although it is full of complex symbols and allusions, it is an extremely readable and exciting poem, not to mention its unequalled formal beauty.

- Eliot's *Collected Poems, 1909–1962* (1963) contains the definitive collection of the author's best poetry. It provides a superb overview of his long and varied poetic efforts, with some of the most important poems of the century.

- W. H. Auden's *The Dyer's Hand and Other Essays* (1962) contains a helpful alternative view to Eliot's literary philosophy. A collection of critical essays by a poet with a sophisticated critical eye, Auden's work combines a personal touch with a great breadth of observation.

- *The Riverside Shakespeare* (1974) is one of the best editions of Shakespeare's collected works. Alternatively, when beginning to explore Shakespeare's plays, it may be more economical to use the respected individual editions from Oxford University Press.

"inferior" to that of Dante, why do the Elizabethans excite him so much more?

One reason is that Eliot, while he does firmly believe in the superiority of Christian thinking, is very interested in the way a great poet operates in a literary world that is not unified in Christianity. Of course, Eliot (one of the most important poets of his century) sees himself in exactly this position. As Timothy Materer suggests in his essay "T. S. Eliot's Critical Program": "Eliot saw his literary criticism as a way of improving the appreciation of his own art."

This critical agenda underscores the importance of Eliot's commentary on his time and guides the reader to an appreciation of it. In "Tradition and the Individual Talent," Eliot argues that a poet should not (and cannot successfully) consciously formulate the philosophical or moral essence of his work; he must act as an unbiased "catalyst":

> The poet's mind is in fact a receptacle for seizing and storing up numberless feelings, phrases, images, which remain there until all particles which can unite to form a new compound are present together.

In this view, the poet's talent lies in what he makes of the conflicted ethos of his generation. Without this talent, few readers could successfully understand Eliot's poetry or plays, and Eliot considers himself quite an important receptacle to be understood.

But Eliot's criticism is more than a tool for understanding his creative writing. His revision of the English canon developed by Matthew Arnold is still very influential over what is thought to be classic literature today. And his "correction of taste" is not simply a move towards works that better represent Christian values. Indeed, Eliot's most important and lasting influence over critical thought is his subtle analysis of what he considers the highest form of literature: beautiful poetic language combined with compelling drama centered on "permanent human emotion."

His preference is the basis for a coherent and completely secular philosophy of art; it does not depend on a Christian philosophy at all, and it provides an objective criterion for judging literature. In fact, it is probably the most important non-Christian generalization to extract from Eliot's criticism. Such an extraction, which is consistent with the idea that a poet exists as a catalyst and not a conscious thinker about philosophical problems, has had visible effects on critical thought of all religious bases. Its emphasis on a balance between verse and drama—aimed at a high goal of beauty and truth, achieved through a specific convention of common thinking among a group of artists deeply

“If Eliot finds Renaissance philosophy 'inferior' to that of Dante, why do the Elizabethans excite him so much more?”

engaged with the past at the same time as they are breaking radically from it—is not a bad description of modernism, the complex literary movement for which Eliot was considered a great leader.

And this process by which Eliot analyzes the texts, regardless of his philosophical and moral judgments, is where a modern critical view finds value in his essays. Although it is difficult to define the specifics of this analysis, Eliot expresses its basis in his essay "The Function of Criticism" by describing the use of "a very highly developed sense of fact" and the employment of "comparison and analysis." It is more helpful to look at Eliot's essays themselves, however, to understand the sophisticated technique that allows Eliot to make his decisive judgments on the quality of so many authors; it is only clear when reading through Eliot's specific and intuitive reasoning about the language and meaning of his subject. This method of analyzing a piece of literature in its proper context creates a new standard for what should be considered beautiful art, an important suggested guideline for the thinking of a generation of artists (to which many adhered and against which many revolted).

Admittedly, this method of analysis does not fully represent Eliot's comprehensive aesthetic theory. For one thing, focusing only on the secular aspects of Eliot's theory vastly oversimplifies his literary taste; despite his assertion that great authors do not "think," he admits that much of artistic creation is a conscious process and makes no effort to separate fundamental philosophical belief and meaning from a judgment about what is a great piece of literature. Many authors succeed, for Eliot, by the conscious or unconscious philosophy in their work. Also, this extracting what is of secular value assumes that Eliot took a clear stance on the issue throughout his life; and as the long span of *Selected Essays, 1917–1932* shows, he changes his mind on even the most basic of his principles during the

fifteen-year period (during which time, notably, Eliot becomes increasingly religious).

Nevertheless, Eliot's method of textual analysis is his most lasting critical legacy in a multicultural, secular society. And it is the most important part of his careful, thorough overview of Western literature since the ancient Greeks. It is where his theory is the most "impersonal," and therefore applicable to other theorists, and it is the place where Eliot's poetic genius and intuitive understanding of language is most apparent. Indeed, it is an objective and almost scientific side of his analysis. Despite his assertion against the profusion of "individual talent" and personality, the more religious and moral judgments of his essays contain Eliot's most subjective (and therefore, by his own criteria, his most unhelpful) views on religion and literature. His comparison and analysis, meanwhile, masterfully place English writing into its appropriate tradition, just as they place Eliot's essays into the tradition of English critical theory.

Source: Scott Trudell, Critical Essay on *Selected Essays, 1917–1932,* in *Nonfiction Classics for Students,* Gale, 2003.

Alan Weinblatt

In the following essay excerpt, Weinblatt explores Eliot's efforts to "explore, to make sense out of and to illustrate the implications and consequences of his myth of failed adequation" in Selected Essays.

High theory and the evocation of intensely immediate experience as embodied, respectively, in Eliot's "essays of generalization (such as *Tradition and the Individual Talent*) and [his] appreciations of individual authors": the drama of Eliot's prose writings, especially of his *Selected Essays* is, at its most vital, to draw these poles together, to discover their mutuality, to declare them fully complementary facets of the same, common quest for adequation. At first this dramatic movement is not clearly evident. Dipping into *Selected Essays* at random, finding here the reassuringly familiar essay on "The Metaphysical Poets," there a relatively unknown, seemingly unrelated piece on the Church of England's Lambeth Conference of 1930 ("Thoughts after Lambeth"), the essays seem more independent, more self-contained—as befits their diverse publishing history as occasional essays, journalistic reviews or belletristic polemic. They do not at first reading appear implicated in the general meaning of each other. This deceptive impression of disconnection and autonomy is enhanced by Eliot's oft-rehearsed protest that he was no "systematic thinker," and that any search for system or architectonic in his work, erected on a structure of "sustained, exact, and closely knit argument and reasoning," must inevitably issue in failure or error.

What are we to think when at a certain moment, after sustained rereading, the argument of each essay, the conclusion, the summing up, the drawing forth of meaning from the subject at hand, begins to reveal a tell-tale similarity to each of the others? For, in almost every case, Eliot's method of procedure, his strategy of advance from premise to conclusion, is to invoke, to draw upon a highly limited repository of recurring words. These words echo and reecho themselves, catch up and pattern a multitude of disparate writers and situations into a common design, often amplifying each word's latent suggestivity in a variety of subject-matters (the comparative merit of specimens of poetry drawn from successive ages, or the contemporary dispute over humanism and religion, or disquisitions on education, sociology and the passing of the music hall era) until, almost without warning, each essay becomes but a particular, almost subordinate illustration of the more general, more critically important set of meanings, which it is Eliot's underlying aim to communicate.

The truth is, this technique of verbal refrain and reprise, this repertory of recurring words and phrases stems neither from genuine architectonic nor preconceived system but from an urgent, ongoing, underlying concern on Eliot's part to explore, to make sense out of and to illustrate the implications and consequences of his myth of failed adequation: the catastrophe of dissociated sensibility. Here "adequate objects" are repeatedly distinguished from "inadequate" ones, and "adequacy" unfailingly counterpoints "inadequacy." Here "intellect" struggles heroically to become adequate to "sensibility" and here "experience," "feeling," "emotion," "sensation," "enthusiasm," "passions," "emotional states," "emotional orgy," "emotional intensity and violence," and inexpressible "baffled emotion" surge over the bastion of "words," "language," "meaning," "receptacle," "gesture," "form," "expression," "clear purgation" and, of course, "objective correlative." Here the chiseled world of the "strong and simple outline," the "perfectly controlled" expression of emotion is set over against the unfocused world of that which is "inexpressible," the "incommunicable . . . vague and unformed," the world of "mistiness," "fluid haze," and shimmering "dream." Here swelling

> **" . . . the design of *Selected Essays* may be understood as a series of assays into the literary consequences of metaphysical pessimism, assays which depart from and return to this central myth."**

passion, unrelieved because undefined, is stymied from attaining to meaning in the form of "dogma," "revelation," "belief," and "religion."

Viewed from this perspective, the design of *Selected Essays* may be understood as a series of assays into the literary consequences of metaphysical pessimism, assays which depart from and return to this central myth. Taken in totality these assays chronicle the long, slow decline—in Eliot's eyes—of European literature from the time of Dante. Bearing directly on this point is a passage from Walter Jackson Bate's *The Burden of the Past and the English Poet:*

> A great deal of modern literature—and criticism—is haunted, as Stephen Spender says, by the thought of a "Second Fall of Man," and almost everything has been blamed: the Renaissance loss of the medieval unity of faith, Baconian science, British empiricism, Rousseau, the French Revolution, industrialism, nineteenth-century science, universities and academicism, the growing complexity of ordinary life, the spread of mass media.

At one time or another, Eliot touches upon almost all of these issues, but quickly propels each one into orbit around his own metaphysical sun. As catalogued by Eliot in the great majority of his "appreciations of individual authors," the effects of this haunting Second Fall, this cosmic universal dissociation of form and feeling, group themselves into two categories.

Into the first category fall those essays which treat of the overall inadequacy of *doctrinal thought*—be it as dogma, theology, ideology, theory or a developed, articulated point of view—to the underlying affections in which a particular doctrine is rooted and from which it draws emotional sustenance. Under the second category are grouped those essays which illustrate the inadequacy of particular *works of art*—work of art being used in the broadest sense to include any poem, play, narrative, essay, image, word or even gesture—as vehicles to convey the emotions from which they spring. Both categories bear striking witness to the inexorable crumbling of form into the ruin of meaninglessness which is Eliot's starkest poetic fear.

Language, Feeling, and Emotion

Of the four "appreciations of individual authors" in which the central argument is the failure of equilibration between some structure of doctrinal thought and the feelings and emotions it once successfully conveyed, perhaps the most graphic—and famous—illustration is "Arnold and Pater." Matthew Arnold, in his extensive writings on the unraveling of ties between Christianity and Culture, was engaged in waging, according to Eliot, a "religious campaign," and the upshot of this succession of field operations was to "affirm that the *emotions* of Christianity can and must be preserved without the *belief*," an affirmation whose inevitable consequence was the "divorce" of that special sensibility possessed by "religion," with its heights and depths of feeling and emotion, from its superstructure of doctrinal "thought." One outcome of this resulting imbalance—indeed severence—between emotions and belief where dogma no longer can function adequately to channel, shape and confer meaning on feeling, is "to leave Religion to be laid waste by the anarchy of feeling." With religion thus split, fragmented, open to the eddying currents of individual feeling, it becomes possible to install, in the place of dogma, either "Morals" or "Art." This substitution is accompanied by the need to translate everything either into morality—witness the "religious vapourings of Carlyle" or the "social fury of Ruskin"—or into the dangerous cult of "emotion and . . . sensation" which marks Pater's own "peculiar appropriation of religion." But for Eliot there exists also a third substitute for dogmatic religion, an outgrowth and later development of the foregoing, a substitute for which Arnold's campaign to elevate culture over dogma was incontrovertibly a "forerunner," and a substitute with which Eliot found himself, often to the exclusion of almost everything else, increasingly preoccupied and distressed: the substitute of Humanism. Dealt with at length over several years in a series of articles and heated rejoinders in the *Criterion* by such noteworthy controversialists as Herbert Read, G. K. Chesterton, and Allen Tate, the topic surfaces, in *Selected Essays*, in "The Humanism of Irving Babbitt." The focal difficulty with Humanism, unlike dogma, is that, although it offered itself as an "*alternative* to religion," it could provide no clear definition of itself, no unchallengeable intellectual edifice, no anatomy of belief open to inspection and deliberative consideration. A loose amalgam of overlapping and often contradictory tenets, some drawn from religion, others from the classical tradition, and still others from the confluence of both, the generally accepted premises of Humanism—order, discipline, tradition, continuity, proportion, restraint, reason, authority, privilege, and aristocracy—might provide temporary solace for those "unable to take the religious view—that is to say . . . dogma or revelation" but would fail to provide "a view of life . . . durable beyond one or two generations." The reasons for this failure are not far to seek. In terms of actual operation, the Humanism of Eliot's day split irreparably into morality in the form of what Babbitt, no doubt thinking of Matthew Arnold's "best self," called the "inner check," a doctrine of self-control by moral restraint, and simultaneously into an attempt, equally vital if futile, to provide, in Babbitt's words, "an enthusiasm"—an infusing or eliciting of feeling and emotion which "man" naturally "craves"—"that will lift him out of his merely rational self." But between an influx of amorphous "enthusiasm" and an ideally defined "inner check" there is neither connection nor commerce: enthusiasm and inner check appear as mindless adversaries engaged in an endless tug of war, the former to inflate the ego with sporadic doses of a heady intoxicant, the latter to prick it back into place. Enthusiasm and inner check are shards of a broken whole, the fragmentary remains of Christian "theology in its last agonies." Isolated "morality" must come to appear "hideous" because it loses all touch with the "personal and real emotions . . . this morality [once] supported and into which it introduced a kind of order." Religion is always "in danger of petrifaction into mere ritual and habit," but lacking a central, articulated, and living framework of belief, it can never be "renewed and refreshed by" a mere "awakening of feeling" or by the unbiased scrutiny of "critical reason." Humanism is a sham because it denies the supernatural, because its elevation of reason denies the dispossession of the intellect, because it denies the primacy of the emotive, and because it denies the quest for adequation.

This same decay of dogma is apparent, not surprisingly, in "Baudelaire," but the reaction of Baudelaire's self is strikingly different: it engages in a drama of positive, if agonizing, search to overcome this dogmatic vacuum. Although Baudelaire experiences a growing recognition of the "fact that no human relations are adequate to human desires," there is an accompanying battle to transcend this obstacle, to overcome, as Eliot sees it, the typical nineteenth-century "disbelief in any further [supernatural] object for human desires than that which, being human, fails to satisfy them." With the swelling "content of [religious] feeling . . . constantly bursting the receptacle" of available dogma, Baudelaire's answer was neither to suppress such feelings, deal with them in isolation, or limit their importance through a rejection of belief, but rather to accept them, to welcome them, to crave them in the form of "Satanism": for such rejoicing in the emotion of evil, stripped of its inevitable trappings of flamboyance and theatricalism, "amounts to a dim intuition of a part . . . of Christianity," an abandonment of "theological innocence" and religious ignorance by "discovering Christianity for himself." And the part of Christianity which he investigated was the reality and meaning of "suffering," the reality of Original Sin that implies, even if always beyond the farthest hope of being reached, "the possibility of a positive state of beatitude." Recognizing, however imperfectly, the vast latitude of the religious sensibility, Baudelaire explored one small segment of that scale, but explored it with unmatched ferocity. Impressive for his thoroughgoing rejection of both the "naturalist" and "humanist" positions, Baudelaire is even more so for his positive recognition that his "business was not to practise Christianity"—that he could never bring himself to do—"but . . . what was much more important for his time . . . to assert its *necessity.*" Beginning with a self-intuited emotional reality, Baudelaire finds his way, if just barely, to the threshold of an intellectual reality, to the assertion of a supernatural, adequate reality.

Finding an Adequate Object

This same logic, writ large, informs the spiritual allegory that Eliot traces in "The *Pensées* of Pascal." Pascal begins in "despair," a pocket of despair so deep and dark, a clear-cut emotion that "corresponds [so] exactly to the facts" of an unillumined, spiritually sere world, that it "cannot be dismissed as mental disease." Because Pascal was "a man of strong passions," his passions threatened, terrified, tyrannized so long as no "spiritual explanation"—no intellectual explanation adequate to his felt demon—"could be found." But then, by a process of logic that fills Eliot with awe,

Pascal comes to recognize that "if certain emotional states . . . are inherently and by inspection known to be good, then the satisfactory explanation of the world"—the adequate explanation—"must be an explanation which will admit the 'reality' of these values." It follows, therefore, that if the "emotional" state of "what in the highest sense can be called 'saintliness' . . . [is] inherently and by inspection known to be good, then the satisfactory"—the adequate—"explanation of the world" must accommodate and give lucid expression to the existence of this value. The result of this spiritual conversion was the plan of the *Pensées,* a book which "was to have been a carefully constructed defence of Christianity, a true Apology and a kind of Grammar of Assent, setting forth the *reasons* which will *convince the intellect.*" To the right mind, Christianity is attractive precisely because of the difficulty it poses "to the disorderly mind and to the unruly passions"—the mind turning over in an agony of doubt, the passions bottled up in unending turbulence. In healthy religion we find, as Eliot would argue over and again, not merely emotion and belief twined in ideal concord. We find, in the first place, a means of attaining that "*intellectual* satisfaction" we crave and without which we "do not want [religion] at all." We find, in the second, a means of "disciplin[ing] and training . . . emotion" by making it significant, a means "only attainable through dogmatic religion." We find, finally, an object worthy of pursuit, even if unattainable, because of a permanence—a permanence of adequation—that answers to the heart's need:

> I should say that it was at any rate essential for Religion that we should have the conception of an immutable object or Reality the knowledge of which shall be the final object of that will; and there can be no permanent reality if there is no permanent truth. I am of course quite ready to admit that human apprehension of truth varies, changes and perhaps develops, but that is a property of human imperfection rather than of truth. You cannot conceive of truth at all, the word has no meaning, except by conceiving of it as something permanent. And that is really assumed even by those who deny it. For you cannot even say it changes except in reference to something which does not change; the idea of change is impossible without the idea of permanence.

Composed roughly of thirteen essays, the second of the two broad categories into which Eliot's "appreciations of individual authors" comes to enclose themselves, focuses on individual works of art whose expressive powers, either through authorial perplexity or linguistic debility, are flawed by a practical, operative inability to transmute feeling into form. This category is itself, of necessity, divisible into two groups, depending on whether our momentary perspective or vantage point directs attention to objects large or small: those essays which explore at length the failure of language, of individual words—the smallest building block of literature—either singly or collectively, to attach themselves to reality; and those essays, dealing with complete works of art, which center on what Eliot came to call the dilemma of "baffled emotion," works whose overall shortcoming Eliot described using the notion of the "objective correlative." On the topic of verbal insufficiency Eliot's most important commentary is to be located in "Swinburne as Poet." Eliot begins by cataloguing Swinburne's highly idiosyncratic style and peculiar verbal habits—the "adjectives [which] are practically blanks," the "slightly veiled and resonant abstractions" which are embedded in the large poem to no visible purpose, and become therefore "destitute of meaning," the words chosen "merely for the tinkle," the general absence of lines so singular and unique that they "can never be recaptured in other words," the penchant for "diffuseness" in place of "concentration," the sense of being seduced by "the most general word . . . because his [underlying] emotion . . . [is] never particular." Finding here a distinct pathology of language, Eliot is driven to set forth the theoretical premise that "language in a healthy state," an ideal condition unlike that to be found in Swinburne, "presents the object, is so close to the object that the two are identified." Ideally, words and their objects are inseparable; to exchange one word for another is, unwittingly, to transform reality, to alter it, to dismantle it. Swinburne scants objects, relishing the word in decadent isolation.

For Eliot, words never constitute a mere aperture onto an independent reality set over against them. Eliot assumes that "the name" of an object—be it physical, emotional, or a tangled complex of both—is never "merely a convenient means for denoting something which exists in complete independence of the name." For Eliot words cannot be merely *signs* for an independent, preexisting reality. On the contrary, words are *symbols* which cannot "be . . . arbitrarily amputated from the object . . . [they] symbolize," for "[n]o symbol . . . is ever a mere symbol, but is continuous with that which it symbolizes." Eliot goes further by stating that an "explicit recognition of an object as such" cannot actually occur "without the beginnings of speech," and as speech develops and evolves, growing in achieved nuance and complexity, an equal and corresponding evolution of reality takes place. In more drastic terms: "without words, no objects." One might successfully argue, as both Eliot and Merleau-Ponty appear to, that language is a higher form of experience, continuous with it while nurturing it into adequate form.

Language and Reality

"Language," adds Eliot, is always "a development of reality as well," and whenever "language shows a richness of content and intricacy of connections," these "are as well an enrichment of the reality grasped. For if a symbol were to be plucked from the soil of experience, it would become "a symbol that symbolize[s] nothing"—ceasing to "be a symbol at all" and becoming instead "another reality . . . [consisting of] certain [idle] marks on paper."

Granting that "Swinburne was . . . a master of words," for Eliot this particular mastery consists not in a finely honed skill which renders the object more precise, more concrete, more palpable, but rather in a massive talent for obscurantism—for shrouding the object in an impenetrable verbal haze. The distinctive quality possessed by Swinburne's words is the ability to radiate "suggestions" which scatter endlessly in all directions while pinpointing nothing with "denotation." "If," as a result, "they suggest nothing, it is because they suggest too much;" Swinburne fell prey to the illegitimate—because autonomous—blandishments of suggestive language, its associative richness leading to irresponsibility, its profusion of possible meanings which collectively mean nothing; it was "the word that [gave] him the thrill," laments Eliot, "not the object. When you take to pieces any verse of Swinburne, you find always that the object was not there—only the word."

Eliot's judgment of Swinburne comes from his conviction that Swinburne has abandoned pursuit of experience for escape to an aerie from which the real world has been banished: "human feelings . . . in Swinburne's case do not exist." His "morbidity" is not of feeling—these are nowhere to be found—but of "language." For Swinburne the "object"—the felt object toward which adequation proceeds—"has ceased to exist," with the consequence that "meaning is merely the hallucination of meaning," and "language, uprooted, had adapted itself to an independent life of atmospheric nourishment." Only a "man of genius"—though the context transforms the term into a blatant misnomer—"could dwell so exclusively and consistently among words as Swinburne." This genius manifests itself in that extraordinary ability of "so little material" to "release such an amazing number of words," all of which attempt to amplify and increase "the vague associations" they are capable of eliciting, without ever becoming anchored in a real "emotion" that is "particular," without ever being "focused." Like the dream that fails to sustain its reality upon awakening, Swinburne's work possesses an air of dreamlike deception; like a dream, his work seems to hover tantalizingly on the brink of important meaning without ever attaining it, without ever trembling into adequate form. This is Eliot's meaning when he says that Swinburne's statements seem to counterfeit "tremendous statement[s], like statements made in our dreams." In Swinburne's work the quest for adequation becomes irrelevant, since his world "does not depend upon some other world which it simulates; it has the necessary completeness and self-sufficiency for justification and permanence." Perfection for Swinburne is the perfection of irrelevance, for ultimately the kind of "language which is . . . important" is language which has embarked on the task of adequation, language that finds itself "struggling to digest and express new objects, new groups of objects, new feelings, new aspects" of the real.

With some slight variation the same charge is made in such essays as "Philip Massinger," "Seneca in Elizabethan Translation," "Euripedes and Professor Murray," and, in more extreme form, in "Four Elizabethan Dramatists." Massinger, for example, is viewed as a poet whose "feeling for language," whose sheer lust for things verbal, has "outstripped his feeling for things; . . . his eye and his vocabulary were not in co-operation." In Senecan drama, "the drama is all in the word, and the word has no further reality behind it," unlike the Greek drama or the drama of Shakespeare, where "[b]ehind the drama of words is the drama of action . . . and the particular emotion." In them, "[t]he phrase, beautiful as it may be, stands for a greater beauty still." In his acid, frontal attack on John Gilbert Murray's translation of Euripides' *Medea* from the Greek, Eliot accuses Murray of a fundamental disregard for language which betrays him into the sloppiness of employing "two words where the Greek language requires one, and where the English language will provide him with one," and of "stretch[ing] . . . Greek brevity to fit the loose frame of William Morris, and . . . the fluid haze of Swinburne." The problem also imbues "Four Elizabethan Dramatists," where the devaluation of words is com-

pounded and exacerbated by a parallel loss of artistic conventions—convention defined as any "selection or structure or distortion in subject matter or technique" which results in "form or rhythm [being] imposed upon the world of action." The outcome is a loss of conventional "form[s]" capable of "arrest[ing] . . . the flow of spirit at any particular point before it expands and ends its course in the desert of exact likeness to . . . reality. . ." Here the desert of reality refers to the impoverished, circumscribed territory of the individual ego, cut off from the depths and heights of the emotional reality which lies outside its own narrow pale; since a lack of conventions or forms exists to describe this alien richness, this other existence becomes a reproach to the artist, taunting him with his own impotence. When conventions do exist, an impoverishment of language may render literature improbable; but when the conventions themselves are lost, literature becomes impossible, since conventions are the norms of reality which mediate our existence and make possible art in the first place.

In only two essays, "Marie Lloyd" and "Wilkie Collins and Dickens," does Eliot discern some slight grounds for optimism. Of Marie Lloyd, the renowned music hall artist, Eliot writes that there resided in "her smallest gesture"—her singular, theatrical vocabulary—a "perfect expressiveness" for what she felt; in consequence, "no other comedian succeeded so well in giving expression to the [emotive] life of . . . [her] audience . . . the soul of the people." In the other case, that of Wilkie Collins and Dickens, Eliot seeks to draw a distinction between "pure melodrama," that form of art where we "accept an improbability"—a situation incapable of affording intellectual satisfaction—"for the sake of seeing the thrilling situation"—a climactic surge of raw emotion untethered to intellectual meaning—as opposed to a higher art where, instead of accepting melodramatic "coincidence, set without shame or pretence," we find "fate . . . which merges into character," and "the melodramatic—the accidental—becomes . . . the dramatic—the fatal." After the momentary thrill of the melodramatic we demand a return to a higher art based on a harmonious intellectual scheme adequate not simply to the eliciting of emotions but to rendering them significant in an integrated, organic whole.

Eliot and the Objective Correlative
But Eliot's most compelling attention, as manifested in the turns, twists, and responses of his argument, is paid to that group of essays dealing

with whole works of art in which the quest for adequation is mysteriously blocked, in which the endeavor to express "emotion" is "baffled." No "correlative" in the "objective" world of language and form can be found for the unarticulated feelings which underlie such works. In several of these essays, Eliot turns to a mode of argument that hinges on comparison and contrast, on mulling over the latent assets and hidden defects of two works set in juxtaposition or in weighing the comparative merits of two figures placed side by side, and watching as the scale balances, first this way, then that, on the point of an imaginary fulcrum.

Of those essays where a single figure alone is scrutinized, the case of Tennyson is both instructive and typical. Despite Tennyson's undisputed diversity of lyric form, Eliot delivers himself of a virtually formulaic summary of Tennyson's plight. His tragedy resides in the fact that his "real feelings . . . profound and tumultuous as they are, never arrive at expression," because of a paradoxical failure, despite their powerful intensity and Tennyson's own insistent poetic experimentation, to find a form adequate to their pent-up force, a form that would transform melancholia into meaning. Tennyson's long-harbored and long-submerged "emotional intensity and violence . . . emotion so deeply suppressed, even from himself, as to tend rather towards the blackest melancholia than towards dramatic action" could ultimately achieve "no . . . clear purgation." Tennyson committed errors which were grave to the degree that they thwarted adequation—"fundamental error[s in the choice] of form." A closely parallel case is Cyril Tourneur. The emotions which rise to the surface in *The Revenger's Tragedy*—"cynicism," "loathing and disgust of humanity" are held by Eliot to be "immature in the respect that they exceed the [dramatic] object," they overwhelm the confines of the play because in the end the play proves a fundamentally inadequate vehicle for their full expression. Indeed, Eliot concludes that any "objective equivalents" for such emotions could be found only in "characters practising the grossest vices; characters which seem merely to be specters projected from the poet's inner world of nightmare, some horror beyond words."

The four essays which pivot on comparison and contrast—"Francis Herbert Bradley" (to whom John Ruskin is unfavorably compared); "Lancelot Andrewes" (who is applauded at the expense of John Donne); and "Hamlet and His Problems" which must be read in immediate conjunction with

the essay on "Ben Jonson"—widen this circle of argument but scarcely alter the relentless flow of Eliot's thought. They comprise a brilliant triad whose purpose is to advance, augment, and amplify Eliot's argument. Bradley and Ruskin furnish a useful point of departure. The prose flights of Bradley, in which intellectual toil "is perfectly welded with the matter" to produce his "great gift of style," are the issue of a man whose "pleasure was the singular one of thinking." It is a poignant irony that Bradley's own underlying philosophic pessimism toward adequation is couched in a style which proves supremely adequate to its embodied matter. In the case of Ruskin, on the other hand, "[o]ne feels that the emotional . . . intensity . . . is partly a deflection of something that was *baffled* in life, whereas Bradley, like Newman, is directly and wholly that which he is." And this terse analysis points back to the comparison of Donne with Andrewes in the previous year to which, though less volubly expansive, it is the logical successor. The "emotion" found in Andrewes's sermons "is purely contemplative" because it issues solely from a self-absorbing contemplation of an adequate object—the careful elucidation of the essential dogma of the Incarnation.

Having found an adequate object allows both for the harmonious absorption of feeling into object, and for the triumphant denotation of feeling by object, a reciprocal, self-enhancing process in which form renders feeling adequate and feeling renders form meaningful. The entirety of Andrewes's prose sermons is made "adequate"—and here Eliot is at pains to underscore his point—only by means of "his emotions [being] wholly contained in and explained by the object. But with Donne, there is always the something else, the 'baffling'" swarm of feelings which remains isolate, objectless. Donne is perpetually engaged in searching for "an object which shall be adequate to his feelings," whereas "Andrewes is wholly absorbed in the object and therefore responds with the adequate emotion." In Donne there is discoverable a little of the nervous ascent and descent of "the religious spellbinder, the flesh-creeper, the sorcerer of emotional orgy," ready to play to a rapt audience, to whip up and indulge quivering and taut emotions. But this theatrical bent, this rhetorical ability is purchased at the price of "spiritual discipline," in that it prevents and is itself the offspring of some obstacle that hinders his "experience [from being] . . . perfectly controlled," perfectly ordered, made perfectly meaningful by the attainment of a satisfactory object. In consequence, there hovers about the edges of Donne's poetry and sermons some taint of the ''incommunicable,'' feeling which is at once ''the vague and unformed,'' and ''experience'' which, because imperfectly realized and therefore imperfectly understood, ''is not perfectly controlled.'' No such taint darkens the pages of Andrewes, whose overspreading mastery is everywhere grounded in an achieved harmony of ''[i]ntellect and sensibility,'' a harmonious perfection, unshadowed by tenuity or hesitation, of adequation. Indeed, the reader becomes the witness to this unfolding drama. He follows ''the movement of . . . [Andrewes's] thought'' as he ''takes a word and derives the world from it: squeezing and squeezing the word until it yields a full juice of meaning,'' until this ''examination of words'' and meanings which can be wrung from them terminates ''in the ecstasy of [intellectual and emotional] assent.''

By the time we reach Eliot's famous dyad of essays about ''baffled emotion''—''Hamlet and His Problems'' and ''Ben Jonson''—we are fully habituated to his speculative and generalizing terms, to the origins and central concerns of his argument. Perhaps this allows us better to perceive the imperfections beneath this dyad's notoriety, its failure to formulate an all-embracing statement whose hard-surfaced, intellectual, abstract tone would suffice to stand alone, a formula whose a priori, scientific elegance and inescapable determinism would, once and for all, interpose itself between Eliot and the dilemma of adequation.

Eliot begins his discussion of *Hamlet* by noting that in a wholly successful work of art,

> The artistic ''inevitability'' lies in this complete adequacy of the external to the emotion; and this is precisely what is deficient in *Hamlet.* Hamlet (the man) is dominated by an emotion which is inexpressible, because it is in *excess* of the facts as they appear. . . *Hamlet* . . . is full of some stuff that the writer could not drag to light, contemplate, or manipulate into art.

To the extent that *Hamlet* remains a play about an unrecoverable, unfathomable emotion, unlike the lucidly defined emotional motivations animating Shakespeare's other tragedies—''the *suspicion* of Othello, the *infatuation* of Antony, or the *pride* of Coriolanus''—our inspection of its shortcomings must commence with the ''disgust . . . occasioned [in Hamlet] by his mother,'' while recognizing at the same time ''that his mother is not an adequate equivalent for it; his disgust envelopes and exceeds her. It is thus a feeling which he cannot understand; he cannot objectify it, and it therefore remains to

poison life and obstruct action.'' There is recognizable here an insidious overlapping of art and artist in which the dilemma of Hamlet and that of his creator are seen to join and become one: ''Hamlet's bafflement at the absence of objective equivalent to his feelings is a prolongation of the bafflement of his creator in the face of his artistic problem.'' Shakespeare himself had sounded the theme of the scourge of baffled emotion as early as *Titus Andronicus,* his first tragedy: ''Sorrow concealed, like an oven stopp'd,/ Doth burn the heart to cinders where it is.'' Thus far Eliot's analysis is beyond reproach; but then, in the face of this dilemma of baffled emotion, Eliot, with a striking lack of elaboration in an essay of barely six pages, proceeds to erect a massive theory.

''The only way of expressing emotion in the form of art,'' says Eliot, ''is by finding an 'objective correlative'; in other words, a set of objects, a situation, a chain of events which shall be the formula of that *particular* emotion; such that when the external facts, which must terminate in sensory experience, are given, the emotion is immediately evoked.'' The first clause of this ill-begotten formulation merely repeats that emotion must attain to the nobility of form to find expression and achieve meaning. Eliot then engrafts a second formula, bedecked with scientific ostentation, that is both contradictory to the sense of his initial premise and erroneous in its own right. He posits nothing less than the existence of a fixed hierarchy of emotions whose existence would be reflected and confirmed by a corresponding hierarchy of ''formula[s] . . . for [each] . . . *particular* emotion,'' such that when a particular formula—a word, a phrase, a situation, a chain of events, an adequate vehicle of whatever description—is supplied, the emotion is automatically elicited. This latter formulation rings with automatism, and is steeped in the logic of stimulus and response. It comes across as wholly invalid in a universe of process, and untrue to the underlying drift of Eliot's thought as we have followed it thus far.

Pessimism Inherent in the Quest for Adequation

For if such a project of fitting together hierarchies of emotion and adequate vehicles of form could be undertaken and achieved once and for all, adequation would cease to be a dilemma and the very task and endeavor of art—''the fight to recover what has been lost/And found and lost again and again'' would at a stroke be subverted, indeed disappear forever. In the midst of a cosmos in process, as Eliot sadly concludes elsewhere, the attainment of such final certitude, either in life or art, is impossible. . .

Source: Alan Weinblatt, ''Adequation as Myth in the Design of *Selected Essays*,'' in *T. S. Eliot and the Myth of Adequation*, UMI Research Press, 1984, pp. 15–36.

Peter Quennel

In the following review, Quennel comments on Eliot's lack of ornamentation in Selected Essays *and asserts that ''the austerity of his professional attitude commands respect.''*

Mr. Eliot's volume of *Selected Essays*, just now published as he leaves us for America, represents in four hundred and fifty pages fifteen successive years of work. Here are essays from the early *Sacred Wood*, which first made its appearance in 1920; here, too, is a large part of *For Lancelot Andrewes*. The brilliant trilogy, entitled *Homage to John Dryden*, re-emerges next to the little book on Dante. *Thoughts after Lambeth* also recur. Two essays reproving Professor Babbitt, and generally setting about the neo-Humanists, are neighboured by a brief encomium on Marie Lloyd. A sympathetic portrait of Charles Whibley brings this various procession to a close.

The last choice was particularly apt. Mr. Eliot ends the survey of his own criticism by a study of a very different type of critic, precisely—even dramatically—opposed to himself. All that Whibley was not, Eliot is. All the qualities that the older critic possessed—and the modern writer is not behind-hand in appreciation; he pays a generous tribute to Whibley's talents—are qualities he himself has never displayed. How far this abstention has been deliberate is a problem both fascinating and hard to solve. Whibley was a 'man of the world' in literature. I do not suggest that Mr. Eliot's critical work shows any lack of worldly knowledge, but his knowledge is of a specialised and rarified kind, accumulated by a special sort of experience. He is analytical rather than discursive. It is the peculiar strength of such critics as Charles Whibley that the enthusiasm they have derived from their private reading should be reflected on the surface of their critical style, and that they should charm us by a warmth of reflected enjoyment. Pleasure is made the basis of understanding, while analysis provides a subsidiary means of approach.

Enjoy, begs the critic, as I enjoy! True, every critic worth the title must have appreciated before he can expound; but then appreciation may assume

conflicting guises. Whibley's appreciation of English literature was that of a cultivated and scholarly man of the world, an epicurean in the purest and oldest sense, *honnête homme,* like Saint Evremond or Sir William Temple. His prose has a Cyrenaic smoothness; and Mr. Eliot practises literature as a form of asceticism. Though we read his critical work for our own pleasure, we can't help feeling that it was often written from a sense of duty.

Not that he seems to toil against the grain. No reader of *Homage to John Dryden* and the Elizabethan essays in *The Sacred Wood* can doubt that he is capable of deep enjoyment and thinks pedagogy a poor substitute for true delight. He has said as much himself in the former study. My point is that, since puritan and epicure are both preoccupied in the last resort by the pursuit of happiness, Mr. Eliot has chosen the puritanical method. He analyses in order that we may enjoy; he sacrifices immediate charm to ultimate clarity.

And so one feature distinguishes all his criticism—an avoidance, carried to strict lengths, of what he considers vain and superfluous ornament. Let the critic, he implies, remain a critic. He has expressed his distrust of the common type of writer whose critical efforts are a secondary form of creation, a consolation-prize in the race he has failed to win. Hence a marked absence of phrases and redundant imagery. He never starts a campaign with a display of fireworks, never marches around a citadel to the blast of trumpets. It has become, one feels, a rigid code of honour to observe the courtesy of a scientific siege.

These preferences must be accepted by his readers: few phrases, no brilliant and lively discursions, a prose style intentionally cold and colourless which throws his subject into clear if chilly relief—a style, in short, consistently self-effacing. It is an impersonal style, and when prejudice emerges—as it is apt to do, even here, from time to time—and he speaks of the Arch-Fiend in *Paradise Lost* as 'Milton's curly-headed Byronic hero.' the effect is not infrequently a trifle awkward. Whether his rare phrases are awkward through want of interest, or whether he eschews them from lack of facility, we can only conjecture.

I mean facility of the pyrotechnic kind. At all events, they are unimportant in his critical essays where words for the sake of words seldom figure. Some writers begin by blindfolding us with verbal eloquence, lead us up a steep and difficult path, snatch off the bandage and show us the view. Eliot starts by removing the scales from our eyes. An operation for cataract is always painful; and many fellow critics confronted by an opening paragraph which states—oh, so simply and oh, so coldly! albeit with a certain underlying benevolence—that if they admire *this* they are not likely to admire *that* and had much better return to their false gods, have been known to snort indignantly in the surgeon's face and argue that they prefer their original dimness.

Mr. F.L. Lucas is one of these. Unfortunately, whereas critics of the type of Whibley are as uncommon as critics of the type of Eliot, Mr. Lucas belongs to a large school. He is the literary, or pseudo, 'man of the world,' who enjoys tremendously writing about literature—we men of the world know what is good!—but, although his cheerful enthusiasm is sometimes infectious, it never crystallises in a distinct point of view.

And a distinct point of view Eliot has. Mr. Lucas once arrayed against the critic some of his more startling literary judgments—that *Hamlet* is unsuccessful as a work of art, that Crashaw is a finer poet than Shelley—and asked us to draw our own conclusions. Well, we don't go to a critic for absolute truth; that is to say, we can't measure a critic's usefulness by totting up a balance-sheet of right and wrong. Literary excellence is comparative at the best of times; and, whatever may be our opinion of Crashaw's merits—and he had some merits which to Shelley were quite unknown—there is little doubt that, as expressed by Mr. Eliot, the contrast was provocative and stimulating.

The opinion was at least consistent with his attitude. To appreciate Mr. Eliot at his critical worth, it is not necessary to accept his every paragraph or regard him as the Rhadamanthus of Russell Square. One may regret, for example, his sponsorship of Lancelot Andrewes and consider that the Bishop's quaintly allusive pietism is inferior to the baroque eloquence of John Donne. One may even hold aloof from Mother Church. . . . The fact remains that, granted his point of view, Mr. Eliot cannot be charged with inconsistency. A cenobite in the waterless landscape of *The Waste Land*, he has now adapted himself to a more regular monastic life.

Objections, of course, can be raised. We are accustomed to envisage the perfect critic as being suspended in the void—preferably in the void of mild agnosticism—who surveys the world with disabused detachment. We are offended by any touch of *parti pris*. True, all criticism enshrines

French poet, critic, and translator Charles-Pierre Baudelaire, the subject of an essay in the collection

some prejudice; but we hate to think that such prejudice as we may encounter is imposed on us by an orthodox religious system. Mr. Eliot is now essentially orthodox. As long as the point of view, to which I have referred, continues to assimilate these beliefs—they are foreshadowed even in *The Waste Land* it seems impertinent to quarrel with private convictions. Puritanism is a dominant mode in English literature, and Mr. Eliot is a puritan of American ancestry.

It is a Puritan intelligence he brings to bear. Critics naturally less ascetic have proved less sensitive to the beauties of language and added less to our understanding of its spell. Mr. Eliot writes as a poet but not poetically. Looking through this volume of *Selected Essays*, it is very hard to find a chapter or a single line in which the desire to make an effect or round a paragraph predominates over a Spartan sense of fitness. No metaphor, flown with syllabic intoxication, breaks into the strenuous hush of the critic's dissecting-room.

There he labours, and on subjects very diverse. Mr. Eliot is not temperamentally expansive, but his interests are sympathetic and range wide. He treats of Swinburne as sensibly as of Andrew Marvell, of

> " These preferences must be accepted by his readers: few phrases, no brilliant and lively discursions, a prose style intentionally cold and colourless which throws his subject into clear if chilly relief—a style, in short, consistently self-effacing."

Blake, Jonson, Baudelaire and many others, always with an experienced and odd touch like an artist investigating a foreign studio. It is perhaps one of his greatest critical virtues that he should have done his best to redeem modern criticism from its tendency to slovenly picturesqueness. We may agree with him, or violently disagree. The austerity of his professional attitude commands respect.

Source: Peter Quennel, ''T. S. Eliot the Critic,'' in *New Statesman*, No. 4, October 1, 1932, pp. 377–78.

Waldo Frank

In the following review, Frank recommends reading Selected Essays *as a means of seeing Eliot ''as a whole.''*

The collected essays of Mr. Eliot provide a portrait of a mind that for the past twelve years has prominently played on the American literary scene. The volume contains theoretical chapters from *The Sacred Wood* eleven papers on the Elizabethan dramatists, the entire brochure on Dante, essays on the Metaphysical Poets and on Dryden, Blake, Baudelaire, Swinburne. It represents Mr. Eliot's social and theological position in the studies of Lancelot Andrewes, in *Thoughts After Lambeth*, and in the two essays on Babbitt et al., which did so much more to discomfit the new humanists than the lunges of their foes. And finally, it reveals the more casual man—delightfully—on topics like poetry in drama, Wilkie Collins, Dickens and Marie Lloyd. The book portrays a sensitive, finely endowed person. Itself an accumulation of comments on many matters, it suggests a review of like nature: one is tempted to pass from page to page detailing, comparing, dissenting. But the place of Mr. Eliot as a

literary influence in our time, and the cultural crisis of our time, make this method inadvisable. It is important to employ the book as a means for seeing the man whole; and, having done so, to deduce a measure of his values as a leader and thereby a measure of the time which took him as a leader.

The first revelation is of a man with an exquisite, almost infallible, taste for the stuffs of literary art. Whether he touches a line of Dante or of Swinburne, a melodrama of Cyril Tourneur or of Wilkie Collins, the prosody of Baudelaire or of Blake, Mr. Eliot evinces an esthetic delight which implies true contact with his subject. This first trait is particularly distinguished in an age in which the field of literary discussion has been almost monopolized by writers who may know something of baseball or economics but who ignore the nature of literary art. The second trait of Mr. Eliot, not less pervasive but more subtly entextured in his book, his moral sense; and this, coupled with his first, is even more rare. We have had plenty of moralists—More, Mencken, Lewisohn, are examples—writing on literature and totally insensitive to literary esthetics; we have had a few 'estheticians' disclaiming the moral sense (as if esthetic form were some kind of insubstantial absolute and not an organic configuration of ordinary human experience and motive), and therefore writing with even worse futility on books. When Mr. Eliot compares lines in Massinger and Shakespeare, contrasts tropes in Dryden and Milton, draws a prosodic sequence from Donne to Shelley, he reveals, in his taste and judgement, the moral integer: he knows the *human nature* of esthetics. This moral sense is organic in the man; it is no mere acceptance of rules, it is not moralistic. Being the permeation, within his specific literary experience, of his general view of life, the moral quality in Mr. Eliot is religious. Everywhere, although he may be discussing merely a choice of verbs in Middleton. he reveals a general and definite attitude toward existence taken as a whole: and this attitude, when logically formed, becomes religion.

T.S. Eliot, then, is portrayed by this book as a man with a sense of the whole, with a conviction of his place in the whole, as a man engaged in an activity (literature) for which he is fitted and to which he gives his entire equipment. Such a crystallization comes close to what Nietzsche meant by a cultural act; and in an epoch whose literary critics have been insensitive and incompetent men, it makes Mr. Eliot an exceedingly welcome figure. If, however, we turn from those contemporaries in contrast with whose nullity he looms, and measure him rather by his own subjects and by the literary exigencies of our epoch, Mr. Eliot dwindles. No single major essay in this book, for instance, can be said to be organic either as a presentation of its subject or as a literary essay. Consider the 'Dante' in whose study he is at his best: every observation is exact, many a phrase stands forth a luminous gem; but the observations merely mount arithmetically into so many pages of running comment. Dante and his work are never objectified, never dimensionally re-created either in the world of Dante or in the world of T.S. Eliot. Or consider the justly admired pages on the Elizabethans: they contain glimpses both precise and profound into the art of the theatre, into the poets and their world. But none of the plays, none of the dramatists, is made to stand whole, either in the epoch, in the drama, or in some total conception of the critic.

If, then, as I have stated, there is wholeness in Mr. Eliot, we are led to question what kind of wholeness it must be that can focus so superbly on details in a dozen poets and a dozen epochs, and yet fail to envelop any one of them. It is true that this failure is not always complete. In the 'Baudelaire,' for instance, or the 'Swinburne,' we obtain a kind of two-dimensional cross section, built from the prosodic study, which we can place for ourselves in the organic milieu of the nineteenth century. But in the essays on the more cosmic men there are no dimensions beyond mere points of light. And in the studies of dynamic but little-discussed figures, the failure is disastrous. The pages on Bradley, for example, proceed without the faintest evocation of the two ideological worlds—Hegelianism and English individualism—which Bradley sought to synthesize. The chapter on Lancelot Andrewes is a mere ringing of personal responses to the old priest's music, which become sentimental and pretentious, since there is no effort to place this music in the symphony of Roman Catholic, Jewish and Arabic exegesis, from which it was never truly independent.

T.S. Eliot, it becomes plain, is a man of integrity in the real sense of the word; but his vision is such that it can never hold more than details; and his energy is too weak to give organic form either to his subjects or to his essays. Unlike most of his fellows, who suffer in chaos, he lives in a 'universe.' But this 'universe' of Mr. Eliot's is evidently small and minor. It is achieved by huge and deliberate exclusions. It scarcely contacts with the modern world—the world whose radical transformations in physics, psychology and economics have dissolved all the old formal values. Nor does it really embrace the

> **The first revelation is of a man with an exquisite, almost infallible, taste for the stuffs of literary art. . . . Mr. Eliot evinces an esthetic delight which implies true contact with his subject."**

past worlds with which Mr. Eliot is so sympathetic: Dantean Europe or Jacobean England. This failure of mastery even on Mr. Eliot's chosen ground is revealing. No one can understand a living past who is not actively engaged in the living present. For any past age is an integer in the creating of today, and only by conscious sharing of this creation can the past, as part of it, be understood. Fundamentally, Mr. Eliot's subjective love of the Anglo-Catholic tradition leaves him as remote from what England really was as his distaste for modern problems leaves him remote from us—and for the same reason.

That reason brings us to the heart of our portrait. Any living world, whether it be Seneca's or Shakespeare's or our own, in so far as it lives, is dynamic; and Mr. Eliot's world is static. Wherefore, in confrontation with a chaos of dynamic forces like our modern era, a chaos which our dynamic will must meet, grapple with, and mold, Mr. Eliot can only ignore; and in confrontation with dynamic worlds of the past, he can only rather sentimentally adore. His own static vision picks out details, reflects them and variates them into a kind of series, like the stills of a cinema, whose total effect may be sensitive and delightful, but cannot be organic.

This same static quality explains Mr. Eliot's loyalty to a class and a class creed. A static universe does not evolve, cannot believe in evolving. It does, however, accumulate, and its 'additions' make a quantitative change—the one kind of change and of cultural contribution which Mr. Eliot admits (see his essays on 'Tradition,' 'Individual Talent' and 'The Function of Criticism'). In a static universe, transfiguration and revelation, and the capacity for these, are all stratified in the past. And this is another way of saying that Mr. Eliot's spiritual experiences, from which issue his moral and esthetic taste, although they are real, have the form not of life, but of an inherited convention. Thus Mr. Eliot, with a religious sense, conceives of no religion except the orthodox Christian; with a tragic sense, conceives of man's struggle exclusively in the cant meanings of Original Sin; with a sense of the spirit's need of discipline and order—both in society and in the person—dreams of no method but that of a mon-eyed class ruling through church and state.

Are such views valid, in the sense of having a relationship with reality? Is there a position from which the universe is static; in which transfiguration and revelation are past; in which Good, Evil, and the given political and economic forms are absolute? The answer is Yes, in the sense that death, being real, is valid. The living world of the mind is as dynamic as the material world (they are one); there, too, the individual life must partake of the dynamism of the whole, and when it is severed from that dynamism we call it dead. The only difference is that in the world of the mind we do not commonly employ the term 'death'; we prefer to say conventional, dogmatic, static. Mr. Eliot's position is that of a man who has withdrawn from growth—in our meaning, withdrawn from life. *He* is static, his soul's transfiguration is past, whatever progress he conceives must be a mere consolidation of himself into forms already uttered. His intellectual, spiritual and poetic 'life' is a rationalization of this death deep within him.

We hold now, I believe, the key to T.S. Eliot. He is a man who has abdicated; but since he has been deeply sensitized to life, the articulation of his experience remains an exquisite, lingering echo. Such abdicated men have always existed, and have never been vital: even in periods of cultural stability (like that of Dante, for example), the cultural whole had constantly to be recreated by dynamic men. But in our age, where stability has foundered into chaos, and where the need for spiritual growth has become absolutely identified with the bare struggle for survival, the discrepancy between a man like Mr. Eliot and adequate leadership becomes enormous.

What we have really defined in our portrait of T.S. Eliot is a type of minor poet. He is in the tradition, neither of our major poets—Poe, Whitman, Melville—nor of the great Victorians. He is close to a cultivated and popular figure like Thomas Gray; and his 'Waste Land' is a poem as good, and of the same nature, as the 'Elegy.' Gray also was a technical innovator with an immense appeal because he foreshadowed, unconsciously, what was to become the dominant appetite of Europe: closeness to na-ture. From the energy of this appetite, Titans were to evolve the method for absorbing and controlling nature. But in Gray, the motion took a reactionary form: a sentimental harking back to the values of Puritanism (and to the language of Milton). The analogy with *The Waste Land* is complete. Here, too, is technical innovation together with a vague foreshadowing of what is *now* the dominant need of the world: the need of an organic, a livable Whole in which all men and all man may function. This foreshadowed need gives to the poem its pathos, its unity and its importance. But, as in Gray, it is negatively stated by an evocation of a sentimental memory and by the use of old materials—in Mr. Eliot's case, more diffused and catholic, since no strong Milton stands immediately behind him.

The questions remain: why has Mr. Eliot been a leader and what does his leadership reveal about our literary generation? The questions are swiftly answered. Even in an age of confused standards, there is recognition of literary merit. Mr. Eliot's clarity, it is true, is achieved not by integrating the chaos that has bewildered us, but by withdrawal. Yet to the men whom the cultural dissolution has frightened and weakened (the majority of men), these limitations make him only more acceptable. A long time ago, I wrote of what I called 'the comfort of limit,' and explained its appeal to many types of mind lost in our modern chaos. Only athletic souls can face a world that has become, perhaps more than any other era, an overwhelmingly open and darkened future. The temptation to limit this world, either by rationalistically charting its future (a disguised reactionism) or by merely advocating its reform in an image of the past, is great and manifold.

All the dogmatisms of our day are really such 'limits'—such simplifications of the real. There is the dogmatism of science (the comfort of limiting reality and its mastery to problems of mechanics and addition); there is the dogmatism of cynical despair (the comfort of giving up hope and therefore struggle); there is the dogmatism of a pseudo-Marxian dialectic (the comfort of explaining the human tragedy in terms solely of a simple, solvable class struggle). And, for the weakly poetic, there is the haven of an elegiac past, like Mr. Eliot's, in which great poets still sing and sure priests thunder.

The one way of life that has no limit and affords no comfort is the way ahead—into the bitter and dark and bloody dawn of a new world, wherein mankind shall integrate without loss the stormy elements that make the chaos of our day, and its promise.

Source: Waldo Frank, "The 'Universe' of T. S. Eliot," in *New Republic,* No. 72, October 1932, pp. 294–95.

Shusterman, Richard, ed., *T. S. Eliot and the Philosophy of Criticism,* Gerald Duckworth & Co. Ltd., 1988.

Waugh, Arthur, "The New Poetry," in *T. S. Eliot, The Critical Heritage,* edited by Michael Grant, Routledge, 1997, pp. 67–68.

Sources

Chalker, John, "Authority and Personality in Eliot's Criticism," in *T. S. Eliot and the Philosophy of Criticism,* edited by Richard Shusterman, Gerald Duckworth & Co. Ltd., 1988, pp. 195–208.

Eliot, T. S., *For Lancelot Andrewes: Essays on Style and Order,* Haskell House, 1965.

Hynes, Samuel, "The Trials of a Christian Critic," in *The Literary Criticism of T. S. Eliot,* edited by David Newton-de Molina, Athlone Press, 1977, pp. 64–65, 71, 87.

Julius, Anthony, *T. S. Eliot, Anti-Semitism, and Literary Form,* Cambridge University Press, 1995.

Materer, Timothy, "T. S. Eliot's Critical Program," in *The Cambridge Companion to T. S. Eliot,* edited by A. David Moody, Cambridge University Press, 1994, pp. 48–59.

Rabaté, Jean-Michel, "Tradition and T. S. Eliot," in *The Cambridge Companion to T. S. Eliot,* edited by A. David Moody, Cambridge University Press, 1994, pp. 210–11.

Schwartz, Delmore, "The Literary Dictatorship of T. S. Eliot," in *T. S. Eliot: Critical Assessments,* edited by Graham Clarke, Christopher Helm, 1990, pp. 178–79.

Further Reading

Bradbury, Malcolm, and James McFarlane, *Modernism: 1890–1930,* Viking Press, 1991.
> Bradbury and McFarlane provide an insightful overview of the modernist period, and their book is a clear and readable way to begin understanding Eliot's era.

Gordon, Lyndall, *T. S. Eliot: An Imperfect Life,* Vintage, 1998.
> Gordon provides an interesting and comprehensive biography of Eliot that includes a way to think about his poetry and prose.

Martin, Graham, *Eliot in Perspective,* Macmillan and Co., 1970.
> This collection of essays represents an important anthology of views about Eliot from a symposium shortly after his death. It provides a useful overview of the author's impact as perceived after his illustrious career came to an end.

Moody, David A., ed., *The Cambridge Companion to T. S. Eliot,* Cambridge University Press, 1994.
> The variety of essays in this book provide a good overview of modern critical stances on Eliot's works. It is a good place to begin an in-depth analysis of various themes in *Selected Essays.*

Shame

Annie Ernaux

1997

When she was twelve years old, Annie Ernaux witnessed her father threatening to kill her mother. This dramatic childhood experience changed Ernaux in ways that she could not fully comprehend. So she committed herself to fully analyzing all the circumstances of her life at the time of the incident, and the results of that examination is Ernaux's eighth published work, the memoir *La Honte* (1997, Paris), translated into English as *Shame* (1998, New York). *Shame* was selected by *Publishers Weekly* as a best book of 1998.

In this book, Ernaux does not attempt to draw any conclusions. She simply gathers as many memories as she can about her town and her school, her extended family and their social standing in the community, her parents' cafe and grocery store, and her mother and father. By searching through news stories and staring at old photographs, she recalls as closely as possible the emotions she experienced in the summer of 1952, when her father lifted a scythe in his hand and threatened her mother. Who she was before that incident and who she became after it are the driving forces behind this story.

However, the memoir is not just about the author. It is also about the small Normandy town in which she grew up and the social structure that was in place there. Ernaux explores the awkwardness of puberty, the inflexibility of the Roman Catholic Church, and the narrow-mindedness of the small-town sentiment that decreed that everyone should strive to be like everyone else. Ernaux's shame is

that she felt she had to keep a secret. She believed that she must never reveal what she witnessed between her father and mother for fear of being ostracized. She must never reveal that she, or her family, was in any way different.

Author Biography

Annie Ernaux plays a dominant role in contemporary French literature. Her minimalist style of writing and her presentation of women and people of the working class have endeared her to French readers for many years. The manner in which she blurs the lines between fiction and autobiography have earned her credit as one of France's avant-garde contemporary authors who is changing the face of literature. In the past decade, Ernaux's work has won readership in countries outside of France, as her books are being translated into English. The topics of all of her books somewhat resemble one another as Ernaux returns to her childhood and early adult memories to search for the most honest and objective observation of the events that have molded her life.

Ernaux was born September 1, 1940, in Lillebonne, France, the daughter of Alphonse and Blanche Duchesne. Her parents were simple country folk who worked their way up the social ladder through their success as small business owners. Ernaux's parents, intent on giving her a better education than they themselves had received, saved their money so they could afford to send their daughter to private schools, a privilege usually reserved for the upper-class citizens of their small town. Ironically, it was her education that would eventually create a wedge between Ernaux and her parents, creating a gap that Ernaux would later try to understand through her writing.

When Ernaux graduated from high school, she enrolled at Rouen University, outside of Paris, an area where she has remained ever since. Upon earning her college degree in teaching literature, she became a high school teacher and then a professor at the Centre National d'Enseignement par Correspondence. In addition, she has worked as a visiting instructor at U.S. colleges, where she taught French literature, conducting her classes in her native tongue.

Ernaux has published fourteen books, with eight of them translated into English. Her most critically acclaimed works include her first novel *Les armoires vides* (1974), translated in 1990 as *Cleaned Out*, which recounts an illegal abortion that

Annie Ernaux

her protagonist undergoes while a college student. Two memoirs that she wrote, *La place* (1984), translated as *A Man's Place* and *Une femme* (1987), translated as *A Woman's Story*, focus on her relationship with her father and, in the second book, on her memories of her mother. In 1984 *A Man's Place* won the Prix Renaudot, one of France's most important literary awards. The publication of these books solidified her success, winning her much critical attention and a wider readership. Ernaux's book *La Honte* (1997), translated as *Shame* (1998), reviews Ernaux's relationship with her parents through very specific childhood memories that took place one day in the summer of 1952. Two more recent books return to the theme of her mother and Ernaux's abortion.

Ernaux was married to Philippe Ernaux in 1964 but divorced him in 1985. She has two sons, Eric and David, and currently lives outside Paris.

Plot Summary

Part 1

Ernaux opens her memoir *Shame* with the sentence "My father tried to kill my mother one

Sunday in June, in the early afternoon.'' She then proceeds to recall the incidents around that particular day. She had just recently come home from church; her parents had an argument; her father threatened her mother with a scythe.

She next explains how she has often related the opening sentence from the book to several men in her life but later realized that was a mistake. This was her way of showing she was ''crazy about them,'' but her declaration only made them shy away from her.

After writing the memoir, Ernaux states that she realized her father's threat was probably not so unique. These things happen, maybe in all families. However, before she fully explored the incident in words, she tells her readers, ''that Sunday was like a veil that came between me and everything I did.''

Ernaux has two photographs of herself that were taken around that same time period, one before the incident and one shortly after it. She looks at them as objectively as she can and describes what she sees. She states that if she had never seen the photographs before, she would ''never believe that the little girl is me.'' The first photograph was taken after she received her First Holy Communion, a time of innocent childhood. The second was taken with her father on their trip to Lourdes, a time, she states, that marked an era ''when I shall never cease to feel ashamed.'' To further stir her memories, she describes some mementoes she has saved, each imbued with fragments of her experiences as a young girl.

She visits the archives in Rouen, a small city outside Paris, to study old newspapers of 1952, and although the events are familiar, she knows them only as an adult who has read history, not as a child of that day, except for a cartoon she recognizes. She has subconsciously been searching for details of her own story, she confesses, for that is the only event of the day that is real to her.

Part 2

In the beginning of part two, Ernaux describes the area around her hometown, a place from which in 1952 she had never ventured. She lived in northern France, which is referred to as Normandy, in a small town ''squeezed in between Le Havre and Rouen.'' Most of the year is spent in her hometown, but on occasion, her mother takes her to one of the larger cities to buy things they need. She discusses how the inhabitants of her hometown refer to the larger cities, how they dress when they go there, and

how differently they feel about themselves when they are surrounded by people who are better educated and more sophisticated.

Ernaux contrasts city life with the general feeling of comfort of being in her small town, where everyone knows her. Then she more carefully describes her town, the city center, and the various neighborhoods—how they differ from one another and how they change as she walks further away from the heart of the city. The movement from the heart of the city to the outskirts implies a ''social hierarchy'' from rich to poor. Next she focuses on her specific house, which includes the grocery-haberdashery-cafe that her parents own. The family's living quarters are contained somewhere within the business quarters, offering little privacy.

From here, Ernaux becomes more detailed in her description of her parents' work, stating when the store is open, who the customers are, what her parents do all day. She also includes stories about some members of her extended family, where they live, where they work, and how she and her cousins pass the time of day. Once again, she focuses on the social hierarchy of her town, only this time she refers to it in terms of language. At the heart of the city, proper French is spoken, but by the time one travels into her neighborhood, people speak a different dialect. She then lists familiar gestures that her family knew well, such as how to clean oneself without wasting water and how to ''express silent contempt: shrugging one's shoulders, turning round and vigorously slapping one's a—.'' Conversation amongst adults mostly concerns memories, Ernaux writes. ''People are forever remembering,'' she says. The major topic is World War II, with dialogues describing what life was like before the war, during the war, or after the war. The war is the epic event around which everything else is measured.

Children are considered to be naturally ''malicious,'' Ernaux relates. Corporal punishment is not only the norm, but according to Ernaux, parents talked about the spankings with a sense of pride in how hard they hit their children. If parents were not disciplining their children, they sat around and gossiped. In order to gather information on one another, the adults resorted to spying.

Ernaux concludes this section with more commentary about the socialization process in her community. She tells about how people are judged by their ability to be social, which involves more than just the talent for communicating. One must also know all the local customs, such as never asking another villager about his or her personal life; reciprocating gifts; and being aware of when it is proper to greet one another on the street and when it is not. She also lists a set of rules that she had to follow when she welcomed customers in the cafe.

Part 3

In part three, Ernaux describes her life at school. She attended a private boarding school, although she did not sleep there as many of the children did. She was the only child in her extended family and the only child in her neighborhood who did not attend public school. The private school was run by the Roman Catholic Church, and a long list of rules that governed behavior was strictly enforced. Ernaux lists some of the more mundane rules: children were never allowed to touch the handrail on the stairways; they must always line up for five minutes, in complete silence, before reentering the building after lunch; they were not allowed to make eye contact with their teachers; and no one was allowed to leave the classroom to go to the bathroom. Being a religious school, prayer and other rituals such as confession, were intertwined in the all school lessons. As a matter of fact, Ernaux states, ''The observance of religious practices . . . appears to take precedence over the acquisition of knowledge.''

In 1952 Ernaux was in fifth grade. She had not yet begun puberty but was fascinated with the older girls who had. She lamented the fact that they had blouses that ''billow out,'' and she did not. She felt inferior to these girls, resenting the fact that they were progressing toward adulthood, in her opinion, quicker than she was. She studied fashion magazines and tried to look older, but between her mother's strict disciplines and the rules of her school, her choices were limited.

Part 4

Ernaux ends her memoir by discussing how her father's attempt to murder her mother changed her life. When she felt as if she did not fit in society, or within any special youth group of her own, she blamed it on that event. ''I feel that all the events of that summer served only to confirm our state of disgrace,'' she says of her family. She then lists some of the sadder moments of that summer: her grandmother died; her uncle beat his wife in public; Ernaux contracted a bad cold and cough that lasted most of the summer; and in another fit of anger, her father pulled her glasses from her head and threw them to the ground, shattering them. She also discusses a trip that she and her father took to Lourdes.

While on the Lourdes trip, Ernaux realized her family's lack of social status outside of her village. Her father was constantly suspicious about everything; Ernaux's clothes did not match up to those of the only other young girl on the trip; and Ernaux recognized her father's lack of knowledge of more sophisticated social customs. Her father's complaints about the city food (the more refined presentation was distasteful to him) made Ernaux feel as if she and her family lived in a separate world, one that was below the sophistication of city life. She also believed, at that time, that she was destined to live out her life in that lesser capacity, in which she would never enjoy the luxuries of indoor plumbing, fresh sheets on the bed, more than one pair of good shoes, and the other extravagances she experienced on the Lourdes trip.

Ernaux ends her book with the comment, ''There is no point in going on. My shame was followed by more shame, only to be followed by more shame.''

Key Figures

Father

The focus on this work is on Ernaux, the narrator, as she examines her past. However, it is her father who has created the one event that stirs her memories. In a fit of anger, her father threatened to kill her mother. It was the kind of anger that Ernaux witnessed only once, but once was enough. Her father's attempted (or threatened) murder of her mother went against the major morals of the church, of her society, of her family. No one outside the family would ever know about it (as far as Ernaux knows), and no one inside the family would ever talk about it. Because of her father's assault, Ernaux felt isolated.

Ernaux's father was a hardworking man who was gentle with his daughter. One of the few photographs that Ernaux has saved, and from which she tries to remember her childhood, is of herself with her father on a trip to Lourdes. Her father was an uneducated and unworldly man who embarrassed Ernaux outside of their familiar neighborhood. He did not understand city culture. He did not have the means to treat his daughter cosmopolitan wares. Back home, however, her father was sociable and commanded respect because of his small-town prosperity, where he indulged his daughter by providing a private-school education.

Mother

Ernaux speaks less of her mother than of her father. In some ways, she sees her mother as victim. In other ways, she understands that her mother provoked some of the hardships (and her father's murderous threat). She knew that her mother had a bad temper and was often the source of her parents' arguments. Her mother was also the disciplinarian in the family, demanding that Ernaux finish her chores and keep up her studies. It is also her mother who takes her on annual trips to the city to purchase the extra comforts of life that cannot be found in their hometown. Although the trips are exciting, Ernaux senses her mother's uneasiness, because in the city her mother knows no one, unlike in her own community in which everyone knows everyone else's business, from childhood through old age.

Her mother is also religious. However, Ernaux points out that her mother practices religion for other reasons than spiritual insights. She goes to church and prays as a way to ensure material and social success, and as a way to gain personal perfection.

Narrator

It can be assumed that the narrator of this book is Ernaux, as she recounts the details of the day in 1952 when her father threatened to kill her mother. The narrator recounts that event as honestly as she can, looking back some forty years to her childhood. In an attempt to understand her father's anger and how her mother provoked it, as well as to understand her own role in the event, the narrator tries to recreate all the surrounding circumstances that led up to that moment and all the consequential feelings that came after it.

The narrator, in the process of trying to understand her childhood, offers a sociological view of her small town in provincial France, almost a decade after the destruction and trauma of World War II. It was a time of reconstruction, but through the narrator's rendering, it is her generation that most wants to build a new future, escaping the old, rigid forms of social status and the confines of patriarchy and religious rule.

Ernaux uses old photographs, microfiche newspapers, and souvenirs from childhood to help her recollect that tumultuous year. She is often disappointed when she does not find direct connections between these objects and her memories, wondering (through a child's eyes) why there was no account in the newspapers, for instance, about her father's threat. This single event was so upsetting, and yet she does not find a glimpse of the emotions she remembers, not even in the photographs of herself. The goal of everyone in her small town, Ernaux explains, is to be like everyone else. The traumatic incident between her parents has made this impossible, in Ernaux's mind. Therefore, the event brought shame to her, a shame that continues to plague her in her adult life; and in the end, she can find no way out of it, no way to explain or relieve it.

Themes

Shame

The title of the book delineates the main topic of Ernaux's work. In the small village in which she grows up, to be different is to be shameful. Success is determined as much by fitting in as by accruing wealth. The disreputable secret that the narrator of this work must keep to herself is not so much that her father attempted to kill her mother but that by his actions he has marked the family as being different. Shame begins from this event and grows as Ernaux notices the lack of education that is prevalent in her extended family, demonstrated by their colloquial language, their small-town customs, and their disregard of sophistication. She is also shamed by her late arrival into puberty, far behind other girls her own age. Her flat chest, her scanty wardrobe, her private education, and her living on the outskirts of town all make her feel set apart from one group of people or another. When she is at school, she is shamed by her body and clothes. When she must leave school, which is in the heart of the small town, and walk home to the more rustic part of the village where she lives, she is shamed by her heritage. When she uses the knowledge that she has gained from her private schooling, she is shamed by her parents and family, whose minds are clouded by uneducated misconceptions. Everywhere she turns, she finds that she does not fit in and is therefore constantly reminded that by the traditional assessment of her village, she is shamefully regarded as a failure.

Topics for Further Study

- Although the major focus of this book is the author's relationship with her mother and father, there is an undercurrent of class relationships. Explore some of these elements. Write a paper about how Ernaux represents the various class structures in her hometown and where she places her family in that social hierarchy.

- Ernaux mentions her trip with her father to Lourdes. Research this city. What is the significance of this place? Find related sites in other parts of the world and present your findings to your class, explaining where the sites are located; why they are considered sacred; what religion, if any, they are related to; and how popular they are today.

- Read Ernaux's *A Man's Place*, a book about her father. Then write a one-act play representing a dialogue between father and daughter. Use the scene of their bus trip to Lourdes. Demonstrate the gap between them through a discussion of a particular event that both of them experience.

- Research the economic structure of your town (or if you live in a large city, restrict your research to a specific community within the city). What percentage of the population is living in poverty? What percentage is considered middle class? Upper class? Find a map of the area and color code the neighborhoods that are considered the poorest and those considered the richest. Visit at least one representative section from each group. What are the differences you find?

- Research the area of France in which Ernaux grew up. Describe the geography, history, and culture. How was it affected by World War II? How has it changed since then?

Social Hierarchy

The town in which Ernaux spent her childhood was laid out in such a way that the richest structures were built within the center of town, and as one walked toward the outskirts, the houses and buildings slowly declined in value. If one were wealthy, one lived in the heart of town. Anyone who lived along the outskirts was not only poor but belonged on the lowest rung of the social ladder. Traveling from a small town to the larger cities also marked a transition. People in the larger cities dressed differently, talked differently, and ate different kinds of foods. When someone from a smaller town went into the larger cities, a change in attitude and dress was imperative in order not to make a fool of oneself.

Likewise, within the small town, anyone who did not talk the local dialect, whether they were from another country or from a city that was too far away to be known, was labeled a foreigner and was not to be trusted. People were judged either good or bad by their actions. For example, women who drank, had abortions, or lived together with a man without being married were considered bad, as were divorces, communists, and women who did not keep their houses clean.

Childhood Memories

Ernaux writes this book from a vantage point of at least three decades removed from the events she writes about. She tries to remember as objectively as she can what happened on a day in the summer of 1952. It is this day that not only robbed her of her childhood but affected the rest of her life. The event was her father's attempted murder of her mother, or at least that is how Ernaux remembers it.

In order to envision this day and its circumstances, Ernaux tries to remember everything about that time of her life. She recalls her experiences in school: how she felt about her teachers, her classmates, and her own body and clothes; how she regarded her education; how she felt about walking to school and studying at home; and how her family reacted to the knowledge she was gaining. She describes the building in which she lived, relating where she spent most of her time, how she greeted customers who came to her parents' store, where she went to the bathroom, and how little privacy she had. She recounts the various relationships in her family. She tells of trips that she made with her mother and with her father, and she describes souvenirs that she has retained.

In order to jog her memory, Ernaux examines two photographs taken of her during that summer, trying to recall who she was at that time. She wonders what she was thinking, what she was feeling, and how she saw the world. She also tries to see the difference in stance or attitude between the two images, one having been taken before her father's angry outburst and one taken later. She is surprised to find that when she goes to the library and studies copies of newspapers of that specific year, there is no mention of her own personal events. The stories in the papers are of things that she slightly recalls but are of no significance to her personal drama.

Religion

Catholicism is prevalent in Ernaux's book. She attends a Catholic school, which incorporates Catholic philosophy and religion throughout all school lessons. Catholic ceremonies are also part of her education. Of her two parents, her mother is the more religious, but Ernaux states that in her mind, her mother's religion was practiced not for spiritual but for practical reasons. Religion was a hedge for her mother, Ernaux believes, against poverty and hunger, and toward social acceptance. An important aspect of that year was Ernaux's trip with her father to Lourdes, a place sacred to Catholics. A miracle reportedly had happened at Lourdes, and annual visits to the place were supposed to guarantee good health.

Style

Point of View

Shame is written in the first-person point of view, which is a natural form for the memoir. The narrator is an adult, looking back to her childhood

and attempting to understand through a re-creation of the summer of 1952 who she was and what she was feeling. Although Ernaux uses a first-person narrator, she insists that she is retelling the events with the cold objectivity of a reporter. She accomplishes this by offering no analysis of her feelings or the events that stirred them. Rather, she describes things, makes lists of things, and breaks down things into their most elementary parts. It is as if she is writing what she sees, not what she feels.

Journal Writing

Shame is written as if Ernaux were keeping a journal. It is a form of writing that Ernaux often uses, whether she is writing fiction or nonfiction. In this way, she pulls her reader into her story as if offering a secret glance of her most private thoughts. The book also reads as if the author were writing only for herself; as if she were on a journey through her memories, trying to make sense of them. She is not writing to tell a story; although in the end a story is told, however unconventional it may be. It is bits and pieces strung together on a fine cord that Ernaux cleverly ties together in the process of examining the contents of her mind.

Lists

In the midst of her narrative, Ernaux often breaks away and offers her readers lists of things. At one point, she lists the contents of a box she has saved from childhood, a box in which she finds souvenirs. In another section, she describes the provincial customs of her village through a long list of what so-called proper members do. She also offers a list of definitions that describe when a child matures into adulthood. Through the use of lists, Ernaux simplifies her narrative. She does not have to make up stories that explain the phrases contained in the lists. She merely introduces them with a few words such as ''it is good form to,'' and then she makes a list of characteristics that apply. Readers draw their own conclusions and fill in the gaps.

Memories Invoked through Photographs

Throughout Ernaux's memoir, she refers to two photographs she has in her possession, taken within a few months of each other during the summer of 1952. One photograph was taken before her father assaulted her mother; the other was taken shortly after. By looking at the photographs, Ernaux accomplishes many different things. First, she provides the reader an image of her adult self looking at herself as a child, which reminds the reader that Ernaux is examining memories from an adult point of view, reflecting on a time that happened long ago. It also emphasizes her personal mandate to remain as objective as possible. When she looks at the pictures, she relates that she hardly knows the little girl in them. She remembers the incident of the picture-taking but not what the young girl was feeling.

Another thing that the photographs achieve is a launching point for Ernaux. One of the pictures was taken after her First Holy Communion, an important religious ceremony in the Catholic Church in which young children participate. The ceremony is significant, so the picture jars memories, opening up pathways to other connected events. The same is true of the second photo, which was taken when she and her father traveled to Lourdes, another important event in her life.

The photographs are also symbolic of the kind of writing that Ernaux attempts. She presents the entire memoir as if she were taking pictures. She describes her town, her parents, her school, her extended family, her parents' store, and her trips with her mother and father. *Shame* is like a scrapbook of collected photos that Ernaux presents through words.

Historical Context

Modern French Literature

In the 1950s, while Annie Ernaux was still a teenager, the theater of the absurd was created, through which playwrights attempted to emulate their sentiment of the meaninglessness of life. This same concept was present in literature and was espoused through a philosophy called existentialism, of which writers Jean-Paul Sartre and Albert Camus were two strong proponents. There was also the birth of the so-called New Novel in which writers attempted to distance themselves from the traditional storytelling techniques and focus their writing on merely describing events as seen by their invented characters. Time sequences were not always chronological and settings were often surreal. Some of the better-known writers of the New Novel

included Alain Robbe-Grillet and Michel Butor. Younger writers such as novelist Nathalie Sarraute searched for new ways to express themselves and did not bother to use identifiable characters or plots in their stories, while author Marguerite Duras emphasized the importance of creating a mood.

By the 1970s the feminist movement began to affect French literature. Simone De Beauvoir had written *The Second Sex* (1953), which initiated books on feminist thinking. It was during this time that literary critics began analyzing the writings of women of this decade as well as female authors of the past. By the 1990s Helene Cixous and Marguerite Duras were considered the two main feminist writers in French literature. Language was often a main focus of feminist writers, many of whom tried to break away from what they referred to as a masculine vocabulary and attempted to create a language of their own. Ernaux has been cited as a writer who examines language and social conventions, as she uses her work to explore the differences between lower- and middle-class populations and the lives of women.

Normandy

Ernaux was born in Lillebonne, France, which is located in northern France in a territory referred to as Normandy. Celtic tribes inhabited this area in ancient times, and it was later conquered by the Romans. Most of the people of Normandy were Christianized during the third and fourth centuries, with Catholicism remaining the primary church in modern times. Although Roman Catholicism is the major religion, there are Protestant enclaves closely associated with the cities of Rouen, Caen, and the village of Luneray. The dominance of the Catholic Church, however, is seen in the grand cathedrals, the art, the traditions, and many of the festivals.

The long and accessible Normandy coastline brought much of Normandy's wealth, as well as much of its warfare, beginning with the Vikings and continuing with the Allied Forces in 1944, in their attempts to take back France from the German stronghold. Allied Forces landed in Normandy on June 6, 1944. The region experienced heavy bombing during the war, causing the destruction of many lives and many historical buildings.

The capital of Normandy is Rouen, with Cherbourg and Le Havre being the major port cities. In past times, most of the population was concentrated in large villages amidst farmlands, but in contemporary times mass migration to the cities occurred. Much of Normandy's geography is flat grasslands and farmland, explaining its economic dependency on agriculture.

Normandy's provincial language reflects Nordic, Anglo-Saxon, and Frankish influences. However, as the younger generations received higher educations, a more standardized form of French was spoken, and the Norman dialect is quickly declining.

In terms of modern politics, Normandy, like the rest of France immediately following World War II, was ruled by General Charles de Gaulle, who formed a provisional government after the Germans were ousted in 1944. He became the president a year later. In October 1945 there was a vote to create a new constitution, which eventually created the Fourth Republic. This marked the first time that French women had the right to vote. In ensuing years, the United States offered aid to France to rebuild its cities and industries, but this did not end France's financial or political difficulties. The Communist Party remained strong in France after the war, controlling most of the labor unions. Costly strikes often interrupted production. During the late 1940s and into the 1950s, France also witnessed revolutions in many of its colonies, first in Indochina. There was also a war in Algeria that lasted into the early 1960s, a war that was heavily supported by many French, especially after the Algerians turned to terrorism tactics when they became disenfranchised with the declaration of peace. President de Gaulle remained in power until 1969, when he resigned after the people of France turned down his bid to reform the constitution.

Critical Overview

Critics often preface their remarks about particular works by Ernaux by first stating that her writing reads like a confessional of personal experience and of the emotions that were derived from it, and that it is difficult to distinguish between her novels and her memoir, as she blurs the lines between fiction and nonfiction. Her ability to bare her soul and the language that she uses to do so are usually highly complimented. For instance, Donna Seaman, writing for *Booklist,* calls *Shame* "a terse and powerful memoir." Seaman compares Ernaux's ability to

investigate her emotions to the "precision of a scientist." She commends the author's "beautifully crafted and unsettling narrative" for its descriptions of the intimate details of living in a small town in France in the 1950s.

Ernaux's writing follows a minimalist style, which on a grammatical level eliminates most adjectives and adverbs and on a meaningful level strips away redundancy and gets right to the point of her topic. Phoebe-Lou Adams in *Atlantic Monthly* praises Ernaux's style for its precision, its detachment, and its lack of "ornament." She describes *Shame* as a "cool, factual, ironic study of life . . ."

In a review for *Publishers Weekly,* Jeff Zaleski also commends Ernaux's simplistic style. He states that other writers might brood "endlessly over the personal significance" of the focal event of Ernaux's memoir—her father's assault on her mother—but "Ernaux is much too cool-headed for that." Zaleski then points out details of Ernaux's style, noting the various lists she employs in the book, thus stripping "herself and her memories of any comforting myth." Due to this objective view of her childhood, Zaleski finds that Ernaux's essay makes the reader "face the jarring facts of being human."

Ernaux's writing tends to read like journal entries, whether it is based on truth or on her imagination. Robert Buckeye praises this technique in the *Review of Contemporary Fiction.* "It has been the particular strength and virtue of her writing," Buckeye writes, "to refuse to make this story a story; to make it literature would be to falsify it, distance ourselves from it, give it a drama it does not have." Claire Messud in the *New York Times* also focuses on Ernaux's refusal to tell her story in conventional form. She "defies the contemporary demands of her genre," Messud observes, refusing to satisfy the "desire for melodramatic intimate revelation and the smoothness of fictional taletelling." The results of Ernaux's diary-like writing gives *Shame* "a searing authenticity and reveals the slipperiness of much that we call memoir," Messud states.

Ernaux, in her attempt to remain objective, offers little analysis of her experiences. She presents the events much as a reporter might, with only the facts of her experience offered. However, most critics approve of this style. As E. Nicole Meyer notes in *World Literature Today,* "Ernaux's talent lies in her distinctive style, characterized by its

Shame *takes place in a village like this one on France's Normandy coast*

simplicity. . . . In the space of a few pages, she captures the reader, who is seduced by the economy of her prose.'' Or as Julia Abramson, also writing for *World Literature Today,* states, Ernaux's simplistic and honest style represents her ''yearning toward perfection.''

Criticism

Joyce Hart

Hart, with degrees in English literature and creative writing, focuses her published works on literary themes. In this essay, Hart concentrates on the theme of alienation that weaves its way through Ernaux's memoir, looking for clues to define its cause.

In the memoir *Shame,* Annie Ernaux examines what she remembers of her childhood, the social customs of her village, and her overall feelings of shame. Over and over again in her recollections, whether she writes of her family's social status and the customs of her immediate and extended family or of the village in which she lives, she demonstrates her

sense of not fitting in. Her description of the scene of her father threatening her mother with a scythe expresses another form of alienation because, she concluded, that this event would forever mark her family as being different from every other family in her small town. As a matter of fact, almost everything that Ernaux describes in her memoir is done so with an overtone of alienation.

In writing her book, Ernaux exposes more than just the details about her father's anger and her mother's role as victim, and she relates more than just a historic record of her village life. The book also brings to light details about the author's personality, things which are bared not just in what she writes but also in what she does not write. Underneath the details is a story about a young girl who lives in isolation in almost every facet of her life. Although Ernaux attempts to blame her father's actions for her loneliness, it is dubious that all her feelings of alienation have their foundation in the one focal event that has caused her the most shame.

Ernaux begins her memoir with a description of the scene between her father and mother. Her father is filled with rage. Her mother does not seem to realize that her nagging is pushing him to the edge. He suddenly erupts. A struggle ensues, and Ernaux's father drags her mother to the basement and threat-

What Do I Read Next?

- Ernaux wrote *A Woman's Story* (1991, translated edition) after witnessing her mother's death. In it she weaves a tale between fact and fiction about her mother's experiences before, during, and after World War II in France. The book was named a *New York Times* Notable Book.

- In *A Man's Place* (1992, translated edition), Ernaux reveals the disparities that existed between her father and herself. He was raised in the country and knew only of country ways. Ernaux ran to the city and an urban existence as soon as she was old enough to do so. Ernaux was as eager to get away from the country life as her father was to cling to it.

- For a male perspective on growing up in Europe both during and after World War II, *All Rivers Run to the Sea: Memoirs* (1996), by Elie Wiesel, relates the story of his youth in Romania, his imprisonment at Auschwitz during the war, and his discovery of his writer's voice while living in France. Wiesel subsequently became an American citizen. He was appointed chair of the President's Commission on the Holocaust and is the recipient of the Congressional Gold Medal of Achievement and the 1995 Nobel Peace Prize.

- Emmanuele Bernheim, a French contemporary of Ernaux whose style of writing is often compared to Ernaux's, wrote *Sa Femme: Or the Other Woman* (1995), a story about a doctor who becomes obsessed with the man with whom she is having a clandestine sexual relationship. Bernheim's novel is similar to Ernaux's *Simple Passion* (1993), which is also about a woman obsessed with her relationship with a married man.

- Ian McEwan won the Booker Prize in 1998 and narrowly missed the same prize for his novel *Atonement* (2002), in which he tells the story of Briony Tallis, a thirteen-year-old girl who will eventually grow up to be a writer. As a child in the summer of 1935, Briony accuses a young boy of assault, which causes him to spend time in prison. Through this story, McEwan explores the psychological stress of untold secrets.

- W. G. Sebald's *Austerlitz* (2002), winner of the Berlin Literature Prize and a *Los Angeles Times* book award, recounts the story of Jacques Austerlitz, a melancholy youth who believes that due to some great error in his past he is being forced to live out a life that is not his. The story is told through conversations between Austerlitz and an unnamed narrator over a thirty-year period of coincidental meetings.

---

ens to cut her throat with a scythe. At least, this is how the youthful Ernaux remembers it. The scene is a moment, a terrible moment from which Ernaux has trouble releasing herself. She becomes stuck there, she believes, unable to develop any further, at least on a psychological level. There is no one to release her from the painful secret that she feels compelled to keep. Her parents will not discuss it; so for them, it is as if it never occurred. If she mentions it to anyone in her extended family, she fears she will disgrace her parents and therefore herself. She would never dream of mentioning it to anyone at school. Later in life she does tell certain men whom she dates that her father tried to kill her mother. This statement is offered to them as a gift, as a way of showing them that she is willing to open her heart to them. Her present, however, is often misunderstood and rejected.

Basing her memoir on this incident when her father threatened her mother, Ernaux implies that the alienation that subsequently defined her life was the result of her father's act. The fact that she felt forced to maintain this secret could explain a certain distraction that she experienced that summer. For example, her performance at school took a turn for the worse after the incident. While she once prided herself for her quick intelligence, she later all but failed a national exam. This is easy enough to link to the traumatic event, but can she rightfully connect all her other lonely feelings to this too?

Blaming everything on this incident seems to be pushing the matter a bit too far. The event was traumatic, for sure. It was so disturbing that when Ernaux studies photographs of herself taken during the summer of 1952, she barely recognizes the young girl who is pictured there. The emotional energy that it must have taken to try to understand her mother and father's relationship, as well as to suppress the horrific scene between them, could explain the sense of alienation that she believes exists between her adult self and the twelve-year-old girl she once was. That young girl was burdened with an event that scared her. When Ernaux searches through old newspapers, she half expects the story of her parents to be written in bold headlines. Because it was such an important part of her life, she cannot imagine how the newspapers could have ignored it. As an adult, of course, Ernaux realizes that other families experience similar, or even worse, tragedies. That is the difference between Ernaux, the adult, and Ernaux, the twelve-year-old child. That is also why it is hard for the adult Ernaux to fully recognize the child in the photograph. It is too difficult to relive those childhood memories, not only because they were complicated but also because the adult Ernaux understands so much more about life. Her father's threat could explain Ernaux's alienation from her parents and maybe even from her extended family. However, it does not completely explain other gaps she experienced between herself and her classmates and her community.

For instance, Ernaux devotes a large section of her book to her relationship with children her own age. She states that she felt secluded from them because she was a late bloomer. While other girls showed signs of puberty, Ernaux remained flat-chested. Although she desperately wanted to cultivate a friendship with the girls whose blouses were ''billowing out'' or who were wearing stockings on Sundays, signs that they were going through ''the gradual metamorphosis'' from youth to adolescence, she did not gain access to them. She desired to befriend these girls because she felt left out and wanted to learn more about sexual matters, about things that the adults in her life would never tell her. She believed that the girls held the answers to the secrets she most anxiously sought to understand.

In an attempt to appeal to the older girls, Ernaux dreamed about wearing makeup to give

> **She desired to befriend these girls because she felt left out and wanted to learn more about sexual matters, about things that the adults in her life would never tell her.''**

herself a more mature look. She begged her mother, to no avail, to buy her a wide elastic belt, a summer fashion that emphasized the maturing figures of the girls who wore them. No matter how hard she tried, or how hard she fantasized, she could not find a way to impress these girls, to demonstrate that she was ready to learn the mysterious facts of life that only they could convey. Her body did not follow her dictates—her desires to be a woman—and this made her feel ashamed. Worse yet, when she was forced to make a presentation in class, in front of the senior students, she expected them to laugh at her, to make fun of her. Instead, they barely noticed her, an even worse shame.

Failing to earn the attention of the girls who were showing signs of puberty, Ernaux then focused on a classmate more like her, in an attempt to make a friend. The girl was an outsider like Ernaux, coming from the outer edges of the village, from the farmlands rather than from the inner, more sophisticated heart of the small town where most of the other girls lived. When Ernaux describes this young girl, however, she does so in unflattering terms. She portrays the girl in this way: ''She worked desperately hard to achieve mediocre results.'' However, this girl was the best that Ernaux could find; the one girl who would talk to her, although most of their conversations centered on food. Their relationship did not go very deep. They walked to and from school together but never invited one another inside their respective homes.

The shame Ernaux cultivated from her father's attack on her mother surely could have influenced Ernaux's shyness. She might have felt that she could not open up her thoughts to anyone for fear she might tell them things that would impact her family's social standing. She could have feared that she would give away the big secret she felt compelled to hold onto. However, it does not seem fair to blame her father's act for the pubescent awkwardness and introverted personality that seemed to haunt her. Her alienation from children of her own age was a powerful force of its own, possibly based on a lack of self-confidence or fear of rejection. Although it seems to have thwarted her, in many ways it is no different from many other teenagers' reactions to the strange and mysterious changes and challenges that occur in puberty.

Ernaux's education was, in general, another source of alienation. She was the only child in her extended family and the only child in her neighborhood who attended private school. So she finds herself isolated during school because of her shyness and after school because she does not share the same experiences with the neighborhood children. It is also her education that, at times, separates her from her father. Although he has made a special effort to send her to the Catholic school because he appreciates the fact that this will allow her opportunities that he never had, he also makes fun of her when she attempts to use the skills she has learned. For example, he does not understand her need to use so-called proper French, while he is more comfortable speaking in his local dialect.

"To be like everyone else was people's universal ambition, the ultimate dream," Ernaux writes. It was a dream that Ernaux could never attain. In the privacy of her own home, she was constantly reminded of her parents and their strange connection to, and revulsion toward, one another. She believed at the time that her parents were different from all other parents in her town. Since her town was her world, she felt as if her difference marked her and would continue to set her apart for the rest of her life. At school, she was undeveloped, unsophisticated, and unsupported financially in the ways that the other girls enjoyed. This again made her stand out as a unique person, which in her mind was exactly the opposite of what she wanted to be. In her neighborhood, she was again the odd person out, the only child whose parents took her education seriously enough to send her to private school. When she traveled outside her small town to Rouen, a nearby larger city, she was the outsider there too. She talked and dressed differently from the people she saw on the street. When she and her father visited Lourdes, they were the only ones without enough money to spend on expensive souvenirs. Everywhere she went, Ernaux felt isolated.

Her stated reason for writing this memoir is to better understand her childhood, especially the event of her father's assaulting her mother; but even in her attempt to do this, she realizes the huge gap between the incident and the words with which she tries to remember it. In her effort to comprehend this most memorable scene of her childhood, she declares, "The words which I have used to describe it seem strange, almost incongruous. It has become a scene destined for other people." In other words, the more she explores the circumstances of her childhood, the more distant they become, so removed from her that it is as if the event happened to someone else. The result is that in the end, she even feels alienated from herself. The irony here, however, is that as much as she would like to distance herself from her past, she cannot do so. It is a part of her. So she does the next best thing. She writes about it.

Source: Joyce Hart, Critical Essay on *Shame,* in *Nonfiction Classics for Students,* Gale, 2003.

Catherine Dybiec Holm

Holm is a freelance writer with speculative fiction and nonfiction publications. In this essay, Holm notes the elliptical and subtle ways that Ernaux touches on the topic of shame.

A reader picking up Annie Ernaux's memoir would expect the content to reflect the title. Such a reader might think that the book dealt directly with the shame that the twelve-year-old narrator experienced on a day in June 1952 when her father tried to kill her mother. But Ernaux is too skilled and unusual a writer to hit the reader over the head with a straight-on examination of shame. Instead, Ernaux examines shame by coming at it through a number of interesting angles: class, the dynamics of a small town, memory, and the context of the processes she uses to capture her feelings about the event. Ernaux is a strategic writer who accomplishes much with her sparse and unusual approach. The haunting, precise, and often distant tone of the language gives the memoir an emotional punch that works more effectively than talking directly about the topic of shame.

Ernaux dives in, right on the first page. Following the unflinching first sentence—"My father tried to kill my mother one Sunday in June, in the early afternoon"—Ernaux proceeds to follow this with a recitation of the day's events leading to the incident. The cool, matter-of-fact prose contrasts nicely with the horror of the event at home and makes it doubly effective for the reader, rather than an overly emotional presentation.

Ernaux continues to use this technique—the juxtaposition of the horrid with the everyday, and all of it presented in cool, casual language—immediately after the incident.

> My father wasn't his normal self; his hands were still trembling and he had that unfamiliar voice. He kept on repeating, ''Why are you crying? I didn't do anything to you.'' . . . My mother was saying, ''Come on, it's over.'' Afterward the three of us went for a bicycle ride in the countryside nearby . . . That was the end of it.

It's a typical denial of a dysfunctional incident that should be recognized as important. After it occurs, the family acts as if the threat to kill never occurred. The little girl takes her cue from her parents. It makes sense that she'd have a difficult time dealing with the incident later in life; denial has been modeled for her at an early age.

Ernaux admits that the process of writing about the incident may help her achieve some necessary distance from it. It almost sounds as if she is trying to convince herself that the incident was less momentous than it should be.

> In fact, now that I have finally committed it to paper, I feel that it is an ordinary incident, far more common among families than I had originally thought. It may be that narrative, any kind of narrative, lends normality to people's deeds, including the most dramatic ones . . . It has become a scene destined for other people.

In the narrative that follows, Ernaux describes her way of coping with everyday life after her father's attack on her mother. Again, the author doesn't come straight out and say that she purposefully distanced herself to protect her emotions, but she gives readers enough hints so that they suspect that this is likely. For Ernaux, the existence of this event in her personal history creates a barrier that she perceives the rest of her life through. She refers to that infamous Sunday as an impermeable ''veil.'' The author continued to go through the motions of life: ''I would play, I would read, I would behave normally but somehow I wasn't there. Everything had become artificial.''

A psychologist might describe this behavior as dissociation, but it's much more effective, for us, the reader, to experience the echoes of Ernaux's dissociation through her cool concise language use and the honest look at what was actually going on inside her mind as a child. The author continues in the same vein, to try and examine the event objectively, without attaching emotion, when she says, ''it was no one's fault, no one was to blame.''

> **" Because Ernaux so aptly captures these almost unconscious thought processes, she is able to talk about shame in unusual and elliptical ways, and avoid getting caught in the trap of overdone or over-obvious sentimentality."**

Only occasionally, and very sparingly, Ernaux admits to the reader the full impact of that Sunday incident. At one point, she refers to ''the indescribable terror'' that she will always associate with the date.

The ''shame'' of the title refers not only to the horrendous, surreal incident that pierced Ernaux's life on a Sunday afternoon. Other aspects of the author's life conspire to create a sense of shame for the young girl of the memoir. Ernaux lives in a world of spoken and unspoken rules. The unspoken rules encompass a knowing she has about her social class in life; she and her family are poorer than some, and are aware of it. There is shame associated with this, but again, Ernaux shows us this with effective anecdotes, rather than subjecting the reader to an overly obviously ''telling'' of the fact. In one case she describes a photo of her and her father:

> I imagine I kept this snapshot because it was different from the others, portraying us as chic people, holiday-makers, which of course we weren't. In both photographs I am smiling with my lips closed because of my decayed, uneven teeth.

Decayed teeth likely imply that a family is unable to afford dental care, but Ernaux lets us figure this out for ourselves and infer the origins of shame, which is rewarding and interesting for the reader.

Ernaux examines her father's attack on her mother in subtle, unusual ways that could be called elliptical or tangential. Not content to tell us directly of the incident, she relates how it continued to affect her over time, even many years later. The results are interesting, unexpected, and completely human, but they reveal an author who truly understands the workings of her own mind. Many people probably have thoughts like the following, but they are so fleeting and subtle that if not captured at once, they are quickly overpowered by more obvious and basic mental processes. For example, Ernaux looks at the incident using the context of two photos, one taken at her First Communion (a Catholic celebration), the other taken in the summer of the year her father tried to kill her mother. Of the photos, Ernaux notes, ''one shows me in my Communion dress, closing off my childhood days; the other one introduces the era when I shall never cease to feel ashamed.'' With very few words, Ernaux effectively shows the reader how these photos represent two milestones in her life. We can all relate to the memories—good or bad—that a photo may invoke, though it's difficult to capture the essence, or impact, in words, as has Ernaux.

In another unusual look at the incident, Ernaux examines the use of the simple phrase ''that summer.'' Says Ernaux,

> to write about ''that summer'' or ''the summer of my twelfth year'' is to romanticize events that could never feature in a novel . . . I cannot imagine any of these days ever belonging to the magical world conveyed by the expression ''that summer.''

This is an interesting and unexpected look at the incident. Ernaux tells us, with the skilled use of few words, that the words ''that summer'' will never conjure for her the typical events of a childhood summer. We can fill in the blanks, imagine the happy times she never experienced, even though she's given us nothing but a cool reference to an idea—what a child's ideal summer should be like.

Ernaux admits that she's used the event between her parents as a kind of milestone; a way to measure the impact of other experiences. No other event has come close to having the impact that the 1952 attack has had: ''I have never ceased to compare the other events in my life in order to assess their degree of painfulness, without finding anything that could measure up to it.'' This is an example of something that we commonly do—compare events against one defining event—but it's something that we may not even think about doing. Because Ernaux so aptly captures these almost unconscious thought processes, she is able to talk about shame in unusual and elliptical ways, and avoid getting caught in the trap of overdone or over-obvious sentimentality.

Ernaux, in her musings, seems to have transcended the obvious. This is illustrated when she expresses a complete disinterest in psychotherapy to help her describe the incident. She has a more concise, effective description:

> I expect nothing from psychotherapy or therapy, whose rudimentary conclusions became clear to me a long time ago—a domineering mother, a father whose submissiveness shattered by a murderous gesture. . . . To state ''it's a childhood trauma'' or ''that day the idols were knocked off their pedestal'' does nothing to explain a scene which could only be conveyed by the expression that came to me at the time: to *breathe disaster*. Here abstract speech fails to reach me.

We, as readers, believe that the explanations of therapists fail to capture the event for Ernaux. But cleverly, she's slipped the information in for us, since her simpler expression is not enough for those of us who need to be told of the intricacies of her family relationships. We've now been given alternate descriptions and explanations for the incident. And we can also infer a sense of the narrator's personality—a possible impatience with simple, too-obvious explanations. Ernaux has accomplished a lot in one short paragraph.

Again, the author tries to approach the problem from a new angle—she looks at newspapers to try to get a sense for that day. She expects to ''breathe disaster'' again, and when readers hear that loaded phrase, they are plunged into the horrific, not-quite-definable but effective mood that Ernaux created with those two words. What she realizes, with her newspaper perusal, is that she expected to find coverage of her father's attack on her mother. Ernaux realizes that ''not one of the billion events that had happened somewhere in the world that Sunday afternoon could stand the comparison without producing the same feelings of dismay.'' Yet again, with very few words, the reader has been treated to her feelings of dread as she goes through each dated newspaper in 1952, fearing to reach the date in June. We feel the impact the event still has on her life in the 1990s, even though she refers back to it in the most elliptical ways possible.

Ernaux's world is shaped by rules, and an astute reader can conclude that these rules could only have exacerbated the shame that she felt as a child. For example, the author grew up in a small town, with a small town's typical lack of anonymity and unwritten, complex social norms. Ernaux is well aware of how her town measures up, or doesn't measure up, to the nearest larger city, Rouen. Says the author, ''In Rouen, one always feels slightly 'at a disadvantage'—less sophisticated, less intelligent, and generally speaking, less gracious with one's body and speech.''

A small town, on the other hand, has intense relationships and all the interconnectedness that this implies. Ernaux notes, when at home, that ''in the street I pass men and women whom my mother and father almost married before they met.'' The impact of such a place can be powerful. Ernaux notes that when she returns to her hometown, she succumbs to a ''state of lethargy that prevents me from thinking or even remembering, as if the place were going to swallow me up once again.'' The author leaves it to the reader to discern whether these feelings have to do with the 1952 incident, or the invisible constraints of a small town, or both. Ernaux's eye misses nothing: the intricacies of small town communication, the rituals at home, enforced politeness, conformity, required ways to act in the family store or at school. Though these aspects might initially seem disparate and unrelated, Ernaux succeeds in showing how they played a part in the shame she felt as a child, and how all these aspects conspired to give the incident between her parents its lasting power.

A *Publishers Weekly* reviewer notes that ''with unsparing lucidity,'' Ernaux strips herself and her memories of any comforting myth, and in the process, she forces us to face the jarring facts of being human.'' Because of the approach Ernaux uses, she provides a subtle and satisfying read, giving the reader endless new ways to examine the topic of one person's shame.

Source: Catherine Dybiec Holm, Critical Essay on *Shame*, in *Nonfiction Classics for Students,* Gale, 2003.

Allison DeFrees

DeFrees has a bachelor's degree in English from the University of Virginia and a law degree from the University of Texas and is a published writer and an editor. In the following essay, DeFrees discusses author Ernaux's use of time to show how a single, seminal event in a person's life can shade and contour the way that individual looks at life.

What is shame? What does it mean to be ashamed? Shame can be clearly labeled and worn on the sleeve or it can be internal, like a shameful secret, invisible but for the ways it leaks into a person's responses to other people and events. Both are fraught with sorrow and regret, but it is the insidious nature of private shame that may be the more devastating, for there is no release, and thus, no escape. In Annie Ernaux's memoir *Shame*, the author deals with her hidden shame through the genre of memoir, allowing furtive glimpses into the mind of a young girl facing the often brutal transition from adolescence

to adulthood. Ernaux manipulates time to inspire her refracted memory; by careening back and forth between three specific sets of events, she allows the reader to follow the jarring experience of trying to relive events that are difficult, and sometimes impossible, to comprehend. Ernaux uses the present tense to recall a specific period of her adolescence, distilling her past into discrete memories that provide the reader with an objective skeleton of Ernaux's life, upon which the author subtly and devastatingly expounds.

There is shock value to the memoir's commencement: ''My father tried to kill my mother one Sunday in June, in the early afternoon.'' Ernaux drains the suspense from the story in the very first sentence, giving away the climax as the narration begins. However, by taking away the seminal suspense, she actually infuses the book with a renewed vigor. Having learned of this big, shocking event, the reader is compelled to know more. Human beings are, in fact, in a constant state of assessment, running over the particulars of our quotidian lives, adjudging the effects that some or another act on our parts might have on ourselves or others, reassessing the past in order to better understand our present actions, as well as to avoid pain or mistakes in the future. Life is a fractured whole, full of pieces that refuse to fit neatly together and reveal a clear, whole reflection of a person's existence and its larger meaning. Instead, the pieces meet jaggedly—and sometimes not at all. In the end, what is left is a partially realized portrait, full of questions, misunderstandings, mysteries, and gorgeous, intermittent moments of clarity. Ernaux's *Shame* is a pristine rendering of the jagged picture.

Shame is laid out as a triptych. The story begins with Ernaux's description of her father attacking her mother with a scythe, which introduces Ernaux's descriptions of the summer of 1952, when the attack took place. The second story line describes a series of events in the author's life, both at school and at home, that led up to that climactic summer. Finally, Ernaux describes memories from a bus trip she took to Lourdes, France, with her father in the year following the attack. A beginning, a middle, and an end—a seeming adherence to conventionality. But the storytelling is anything but conventional. Ernaux weaves the three sets of memories intricately and seamlessly through one another with a sense of stream-of-consciousness writing, similar to the way in which individuals recall the past, wherein memories simply flow in rapid, random succession. But here again, Ernaux fools the reader with seeming

> **"Life is a fractured whole, full of pieces that refuse to fit neatly together and reveal a clear, whole reflection of a person's existence and its larger meaning. . . . In the end, what is left is a partially realized portrait, full of questions, misunderstandings, mysteries, and gorgeous, intermittent moments of clarity."**

simplicity, for although the story weaves in and out of memories, the order is carefully planned and presented; there are no extraneous or gratuitous thoughts falling across the pages of this spare text: ''Naturally I shall not opt for narrative, . . . [n]either shall I content myself with merely picking out and transcribing the images I remember; I shall process them like documents, examining them from different angles to give them meaning.''

Throughout the story, Ernaux recognizes that it is impossible to tell a history unstoried by the bias of time and personal reflections on the events. Thus, Ernaux interjects her current opinions in parenthetical statements, freely allowing herself a judicial voice of reflection. Outside the parentheticals, she mainly keeps to the facts (though she sometimes recalls her childhood opinion on how she may have felt at the time an event occurred), sparing the reader from didactic interpretation and thus allowing the reader to form his own opinion of the story being told. Ernaux's innovative style of interjecting commentary through parenthetical statements stems from necessity. She tells the story as a series of recollections shorn of explication because she cannot explain the events—because, finally, she cannot explain what she does not understand:

> (After evoking the images I have of that summer, I feel inclined to write ''then I discovered that'' or ''then I realized that,'' words implying a clear perception of the events one has lived through. But in my case there is no understanding, only this feeling of shame that has fossilized the images and stripped them of meaning. The fact that I experience such

inertia and nothingness is something that cannot be denied. It is the ultimate truth.)

Ernaux's writing style is loose yet vigorous, casual yet exact. In only 111 double-spaced pages, she pours forth a vivid sampling of an adolescent girl whose mind is being concretized by the events happening in her life. It is fairly obvious that adolescents are impressionable and that the events and emotions that they experience during those impressionable years will affect the way that they look at and live their lives. But it is rare to get a first-hand look at the events themselves, as opposed to commentary on how the events shaped the person. By providing lists of events and keepsakes, Ernaux allows the reader to draw his own conclusions as to how the events leading up to and following that summer day when Ernaux's father attacked her mother affected Ernaux's life. She lists a litany of actions condemned by the nuns who ran her school; she relays lists of items she has saved or salvaged from 1952; and she lists a series of violent or shameful events that occurred to her or her family in the immediate aftermath of her father's attack on her mother. She writes to the point of exhaustion; her list-making ends when a redolent redundancy sets in, seemingly enveloping her in shame. ''There is no point in going on. My shame was followed by more shame, only to be followed by more shame.'' By the end of the book, Ernaux is almost apologetic for the seeming shortcomings of a book that cannot answer its own questions. In writing *Shame*, she had hoped to write ''the sort of book that makes it impossible for me to withstand the gaze of others.'' Her goal proved unattainable—what degree of shame could possibly be conveyed by the writing of a book which seeks to measure up to the events experienced in my twelfth year''—but the book remained. Herein lies the book's greatest strength: by attempting to examine a part of her life and ''get to the bottom of things,'' and then failing to come to any conclusion, Ernaux reveals an unerring, universal truth: that life holds no hard and fast answers, that events occur, and that there is no certainty that we can ever truly know why or how they affect us, but only that they do.

Shame is a shockingly bare tale; it tells not by telling but rather by transposing scattered events of her life and re-ordering them in a list-like fashion. However, Ernaux's simplicity of style is, in fact, anything but. It is a depiction of family ties, desperation, and the intangible relics of memory that grow and change, haunting a life. In Catholic, small-town France in the 1950s, little was left to chance, and little was kept secret, and it is therefore all the more astonishing that the seminal, shocking event in Ernaux's life would, even after dissection through time, remain such a little-understood event. It speaks volumes about the unspeakable nature of tragedy. And it leads people in myriad directions: toward recovery, toward penitence, toward anger, toward shame. Ernaux's experience of watching her father try to choke her mother, and her memories that preceded and followed it, are select for the very reason that all of our memories are select: we remember what we can, what time allows, and what our heart is able to bear. Sometimes, the whole truth is too much, or else too little. The reader cannot know what transpired between mother and father before and after the fight that altered Ernaux's perception of her place in society and solidified her sense of shame, and in the end, it is immaterial, for it is one's perception, and not objective truth, that ultimately matters.

Source: Allison DeFrees, Critical Essay on *Shame*, in *Nonfiction Classics for Students*, Gale, 2003.

Sources

Abramson, Julia, Review of *Se perdre*, in *World Literature Today*, Vol. 76, No. 1, January 1, 2002, p. 171.

Adams, Phoebe-Lou, Review of *Shame*, in *Atlantic Monthly*, Vol. 282, No. 4, October 1998, p. 118.

Buckeye, Robert, Review of *Shame*, in *Review of Contemporary Fiction*, Vol. 19, No. 1, Spring 1999, pp. 175–76.

Messud, Claire, ''A Family Apart,'' in the *New York Times*, September 13, 1998, p. 16.

Meyer, E. Nicole, Review of *La vie exterieure: 1993–1999*, in *World Literature Today*, Vol. 76, No. 1, January 1, 2002, p. 179.

Seaman, Donna, Review of *Shame*, in *Booklist*, Vol. 94, No. 21, July 1998, p. 1850.

Zaleski, Jeff, Review of *Shame*, in *Publishers Weekly*, Vol. 245, No. 24, June 15, 1998, p. 50.

Further Reading

Gavronsky, Serge, *Toward a New Poetics: Contemporary Writing in France*, University of California Press, 1994.
Avant-garde French poetry and prose have been changing quite liberally in the late twentieth century. Gavronsky's collection of twelve interviews with some of France's most important writers explores these developments. The interviews include writers discussing their own creative processes as well as an overview of current literary theory.

Hollier, Denis, and R. Howard Bloch, eds., *A New History of French Literature*, Harvard University Press, 1994.
A recent collection of essays by both American and European literary scholars, this book discusses various movements, genres, and circumstances of French literature from the ninth century through the twentieth century.

McIlvanney, Siobhan, *Annie Ernaux: The Return to Origins*, Liverpool University Press, 2001.
This book is literary criticism of Ernaux's extensive body of work.

Solomon, Andrew, *The Noonday Demon: An Atlas of Depression*, Scribner's, 2001.
Solomon, an award-winning novelist, began suffering from depression as a senior in college. His condition worsened after his mother's death, a time when he considered suicide. In an attempt to understand his condition and its treatment, he researched various worldwide practices. He also examined depression as it affected other literary figures such as Virginia Woolf, George Eliot, John Keats, John Milton, and Samuel Beckett. His book has been credited with providing an illuminating view on this topic.

Thomas, Lyn, *Annie Ernaux: An Introduction to the Writer and Her Audience*, Berg Publishing, Ltd., 1999.
Thomas's depth of understanding of Ernaux's work is very visible in this study. It includes a survey of Ernaux's books as well as a prediction of how future critics will view her life's work.

Steal This Book

Abbie Hoffman

1971

In the introduction to *Steal This Book*, famous 1960s protest organizer Abbie Hoffman describes the work as ''a manual for survival in the prison that is Amerika,'' spelling the country's name incorrectly to show disrespect for the law. First published in 1971, it was rejected by over thirty publishers and then went on to become a best-seller when Hoffman published it himself. The book is a compendium of methods that individuals can use to live freely, without participating in the social order. These tips range in levels of legality from addresses of free health clinics and inexpensive restaurants to ways of cheating pay phones and methods for making explosive devices.

Even in its day, Hoffman's advice was of questionable practicality. Some of his tips, the more complicated ones, involve multiple identities and underworld connections; others, such as switching price labels while shopping, are so obvious that they seem hardly worth writing. As time has passed, most of the loopholes Hoffman exploits in this book have been closed, due in part to the attention this book brought to them. Still, *Steal This Book* is an important historical document, a lively example of a time when America's youth felt at war with the status quo, and petty crime was considered a justifiable way to stand up against the corruption of the system.

Author Biography

Abbott "Abbie" Hoffman was born November 30, 1936, in Worcester, Massachusetts. His family was solidly American middle class: his father John worked as a pharmacist before opening a successful medical supply distribution company, and his mother Florence was a homemaker. For the early part of Hoffman's life, he followed the social mainstream. He graduated from Brandeis University in 1959 with a degree in psychology and then earned a master's degree at Berkeley. In 1960, at the age of twenty-three, he married his first wife Sheila, with whom he had two children. He and Sheila divorced in 1966.

The social changes that swept through America profoundly changed his perspective. He became involved in the civil rights movement in the early 1960s, first volunteering to go to segregated southern states and stand beside blacks who were challenging racist practices and later organizing a cooperative in New York City to distribute crafts made by southern blacks who had been fired for their activism. By the mid-1960s, he shifted his attention to fighting the growing Vietnam conflict. As a leader of the antiwar movement, Hoffman gained a reputation around New York for his organizational skills and his skill at getting the attention of the media. In 1967 he married Anita Kushner, who became his partner in many antiwar activities. He and Anita had one son and divorced in 1980.

In 1968, along with Jerry Rubin and other like-minded activists, Hoffman created the Youth International Party or Yippie Party. The Yippies held several high-profile, antiestablishment protests, including showering the floor of the New York Stock Exchange with money and a mock attempt to "levitate" the Pentagon. They gained international attention as protest leaders at the 1968 Democratic National Convention in Chicago. The convention became a violent spectacle of demonstrators facing off against the police, National Guard, and Army. News footage of Chicago police in riot gear beating teenagers with nightsticks shocked the world. Because of the violence in Chicago, Hoffman and six other organizers became defendants in the infamous Chicago Seven trial. Hoffman mocked the court proceeding as a circus by showing up in

Abbie Hoffman

costumes and doing handstands, showing a disdain for the establishment shared by many youths of the time.

By the end of the 1960s, Hoffman had receded from public attention. In 1973 he was arrested for taking part in a cocaine deal. Faced with jail time, he instead went underground, traveling under an assumed name. He continued to publish books and magazine articles and took up with Johanna Lawrenson, who would be his companion for the rest of his life. In 1980 Hoffman surrendered to the authorities. The world found out that under the false identity "Barry Freed," Hoffman had been instrumental in working for environmental causes in upstate New York. In light of the community work he had done as Barry Freed, he was given a light sentence.

Throughout the 1980s Hoffman served as an organizer for social causes and supported himself by giving lectures on college campuses. Few of his friends knew he suffered from severe bipolar disorder. In 1989, in the throes of an acute bout of depression, he committed suicide with a barbiturate overdose.

Plot Summary

Survive!

The first section of *Steal This Book* offers advice on how to live cheaply or freely in America. Doing so is explained as a political statement, a way of showing resistance to the exploitation that Hoffman says is inherent in a capitalist society. This section starts out with tips about "Free Food," covering such diverse methods as crashing a bon voyage party on a steamship, putting a bug on a restaurant plate to avoid paying the meal, shoplifting, and inexpensive recipes. Other parts of this section include advice on "Free Clothing and Furniture," "Free Housing," "Free Education," "Free Money," and "Free Dope."

Some of the methods Hoffman suggests for obtaining free goods and services are presented in the form of lists of social organizations in the business of helping impoverished people, such as community health clinics and food pantries. Other advice comes in the form of suggestions for how to use commonly available objects around the house. Most of Hoffman's tips reflect the book's revolutionary spirit, showing readers techniques for using established services such as busses, phones, hotels, and electricity, without having to pay for them. The details offered in the book range from advice for growing marijuana to lists of which foreign coins will work in vending machines in place of higher-priced American currency.

Fight!

In the second section of the book, Hoffman addresses issues related to the area with which he is most often associated: that of violent and nonviolent social protests. This section includes methods of spreading one's political message, such as operating printing presses and underground radio stations and cutting into the broadcast frequencies of television stations in order to broadcast one's own programming.

A large part of this section is devoted to survival tips to be used during street demonstration. Hoffman suggests when and where to plan demonstrations to get the most media attention, as well as such minute details as sensible ways to dress and what kind of shoes to wear. Much of his advice assumes that protests will turn into violent confrontations; therefore, his advice is geared toward clothes that cannot be grabbed by police officers and strong shoes with which to kick. Gas masks and helmets are also recommended.

This section of the book also deals with weapons radicals can use to defend themselves against the police and, in general, to destroy businesses. Hoffman gives tips about street fighting and knife fighting and reviews which kinds of guns are useful for which situations. He also explains several methods for making crude bombs. There is also information about dealing with the results of demonstrations, including first aid tips and advice for finding free legal counsel. This section ends with some advice about living underground under an assumed name in order to avoid the law.

Liberate!

In the last section of the book, Hoffman gives specific advice for living inexpensively in four U.S. cities: New York, Chicago, Los Angeles, and San Francisco. In each, he tells readers where to go for free housing, food, medical care, and legal aid. He also recommends diversions such as theaters, movie houses, and places that hold poetry readings. Restaurants that have free food available or that offer large portions at small prices are also recommended. Each city has some area of advice specific to it alone. The New York section, for instance, tells about sneaking onto the subway for free; in Chicago, Hoffman praises the availability of cheap food; Los Angeles has a section rating the beaches; and his writing about San Francisco emphasizes the city's parks.

Key Figures

Bert Cohen

The title page of *Steal This Book* lists Cohen as "accessory after the fact." He was the person who did the book's graphic design, giving it the look of an "underground newspaper" of the type published for little money by revolutionaries in the 1960s.

Lisa Fithian

Fithian wrote the foreword to the 2002 edition of the book. A long-time community activist, she is a member of the Direct Action Network and is involved in political issues. She has recently been in the news for her part in organizing protestors at the 2000 Democratic National Convention in Los Angeles, an act she shares in common with Hoffman's activities to mobilize the Yippie movement at the 1968 Chicago Democratic National Convention. In 2001 she was arrested and held for several days while preparing to protest at the G-20 summit in Ottawa, Canada. After being detained for two days, she was released for lack of evidence.

Al Giordano

Giordano is an activist who worked with Abbie Hoffman. He wrote "Still a Steal," the introduction to the 2001 edition of *Steal This Book*. Giordano worked with Hoffman on social and environmental causes from 1980, when he was twenty, to the time of Hoffman's death in 1989. During the 1990s, he worked as a journalist for the *Boston Phoenix*. As a result of investigations into Latin American drug policies, he began a Web site dedicated to reporting on the United States' war against drugs. For several years Giordano was a defendant in a libel suit brought against him by the Bank of Mexico in response to an article about major narcotics trafficking on the property of the bank's owner.

Izak Haber

On the book's title page, Haber is listed as "co-conspirator," a term used in law to imply that someone is guilty of working with another guilty party. In fact, it was Haber who first approached Hoffman with the idea of *Steal This Book*. Much of the material he presented to Hoffman as his research was actually copied verbatim from other published sources. After five weeks of working together, Hoffman fired him, paying him a small amount for the twenty pages of original material he had produced. Haber later published an article in *Rolling Stone* saying his research had been stolen by Hoffman.

Abbie Hoffman

At the time when he wrote *Steal This Book*, Abbie Hoffman was internationally famous as a leader of a 1960s youth movement. He was active in various organizations that existed to oppose the Vietnam War and came to media prominence as one of the most visible protesters involved in organizing antiwar demonstrations during the Democratic National Convention in Chicago in 1968. The convention became a violent spectacle of demonstrators facing off against the police, National Guard, and Army. After it was over, Hoffman and other demon-

Media Adaptations

- The 2000 motion picture *Steal This Movie* is not an adaptation of this book, as is commonly assumed; actually it is a biography of Hoffman. It was directed by Robert Greenwald and stars Vincent D'Onofrio, Janeane Garofalo, and Jeanne Tripplehorn. It is available from Trimark Home Video.

stration leaders were charged in federal court with having encouraged demonstrators to cross state lines to go to Chicago and for encouraging resistance when police wanted to move protesters away from the convention hall. The trial of the Chicago Seven became a media circus, in part due to Hoffman's irreverent attitude. In the end, five defendants were found guilty, but the convictions were later overturned. A few of the defendants, however, including Hoffman, did spend a few weeks in jail in 1971 for contempt of court. Hoffman wrote the introduction for *Steal This Book* while in jail.

Hoffman assembled the tips that he offers in *Steal This Book* from a variety of sources. Most of them are from anecdotal evidence given to him from people he met while working for various protest movements. Others were mailed to him in response to advertisements he placed in underground newspapers across the country. In most cases, Hoffman researched the tips he had been given to assure that the suggested techniques would work and that the services and organizations recommended in the book were legitimate.

Throughout the book, Hoffman gives a running commentary on the "survival techniques" about which he writes, telling readers which techniques work well, which do not, and which he is not familiar enough to judge. He is as honest as he can be about the usefulness of each technique and is not at all hesitant to point out myths and misconceptions when he finds them. Although this book is a collaborative effort, Hoffman's is the only name on the cover. Because of this, he takes responsibility for the usefulness of the information it contains. As a result, the information about organizing protest movements and publicizing rallies, which were his areas of expertise, tend to be more fully detailed than segments about such matters as collecting multiple welfare checks or shoplifting.

One area that appears to have been developed imaginatively is the subject of bomb-making. Hoffman never was involved in violent confrontation against the authorities, and no one ever accused him of being involved in violent struggles. Still, the information about building bombs and using guns against the police is richly detailed. The information and techniques outlined in these sections may or may not have come from people who had true experience, but the chance that Hoffman himself verified these experiences is small. To this extent, *Steal This Book* is not the survival guide it claims to be, but is instead an idealized version of a radical lifestyle.

Anita Hoffman

Abbie Hoffman's second wife was his constant companion at the time that *Steal This Book* was written, working with him on many of his social activities in the late 1970s until he dropped out of public life in 1973. She was instrumental in the writing and research of this book, and is the woman in many of the book's photographs. Although Hoffman only mentions Anita in the book's introduction, the tips contained in the book reflect the lifestyle they lived together throughout the late 1960s and early 1970s.

Themes

Class Conflict

One basic premise behind the ideas expressed in *Steal This Book* is that there is a war between different classes of American society. It is this war that justifies the use of criminal measures. Hoffman recognizes moral social responsibilities. As he says in the book's introduction, "Our moral dictionary says no heisting from each other. To steal from a brother or sister is evil. To *not* steal from the institutions that are the pillars of the Pig Empire is equally immoral."

With the phrase "Pig Empire," he refers to those who have economic power. In defining them

as the enemy and claiming the right to use any means to combat the enemy, Hoffman permits all sorts of antisocial behaviors. Stealing is a natural way to weaken an economically powerful enemy, and the book advises many methods to take advantage of international business conglomerates such as the telephone and airline industries. But the book does not discriminate among different levels of economic ownership; small shopkeepers are targeted as often as large corporations, having been defined in the class struggle as "them" versus "us."

In addition to advocating stealing from economic entities, the book also gives advice about destroying property without personal gain in the section titled "Trashing," which leads into advice on hand-to-hand combat against the police and using explosives and firearms. Since the privileged classes have the benefit of police protection, and the police have superior weapons and training, Hoffman suggests using any means available, no matter how violent. All of the book's destructive techniques are discussed in terms of the struggle against those with wealth.

Freedom

The identifying characteristic of the target audience of this book is a desire for freedom from social constraints. In the late 1960s and early 1970s rallying cry "freedom" was popular. In the name of freedom, people—usually young people, who had not yet invested much into the social order—dropped out of society, living off what they could gather from handouts and sharing, and stealing when they could. In the drive for economic independence, many young people practiced the tips Hoffman offers in his book long before these tips were gathered together and published. To those who wanted to escape from the "slavery" of the social order, this book offered a promise of freedom.

The tips in the book offer financial freedom by showing readers places they can stay and eat for nothing or close to nothing. There are long lists of social service institutions, especially in the section titled "Liberate!" which focuses on four American cities as case studies. Hoffman covers the basic essentials of survival and other necessities—such as entertainment and education—that can be obtained at no cost. Overall, the book is designed to make life easier for people who desire to be free from the economic mainstream, who do not want to pledge their minds and hearts to employers just to gather enough money to live comfortable lives.

Safety

This book represents an honest acknowledgement that the young people of the sixties were bound to participate in the illegal activities that are mentioned. Rather than assuming they would follow the law or that they deserved to suffer whatever fate might befall them if they did not, Hoffman compiled a guide for those who chose to follow the illegal path, with the hope of guiding them safely through the dangers of outlaw life. The book was shocking to readers and reviewers of the establishment, who saw its primary purpose as being to encourage illegal activities. But a good case can be made that it is meant to look after the safety of young American citizens who would be engaging in illegal activities anyway.

The safety tips in *Steal This Book* include honest explanations of different types of venereal diseases and places readers can go for treatment; tips about which recreational drugs are harmful and to what degrees; self-defense tips; first-aid tips for those hurt in fights and demonstrations; and nutrition advice for those preparing food on a budget. Because most of the practices described in the book were socially shunned at best and illegal at worst, information about them was difficult to come by in 1971, and therefore the safety of the thousands of youths who had dropped out of society was left at risk.

Topics for Further Study

- Interview people at your school and in your community about tips that can be used to gain free goods and services legally and compile a list.

- Find a Web site run by organizers of political demonstrations, and see if the tips they give for self-protection are different than the ones Hoffman gave in the 1970s. Research and explain how modern demonstrations are different than those in the 1960s and 1970s.

- Prepare a tape of an hour-long broadcast your class would make if you started your own underground radio station.

- Hold a mock trial for someone arrested using the tips for stealing suggested in this book. Have the prosecution make the case for social order and the defense make the case, as Hoffman puts it in the book's introduction, that ''corporate feudalism [is] the only robbery worthy of being called 'crime,' for it is committed against the people as a whole.''

Style

Zeitgeist

The German term *zeitgeist* means ''the spirit of the time.'' It is often possible to relate the time in which an author was working to the moral and intellectual trends that prevailed when she or he was writing. For instance, the wealth and hedonism of the jazz age are important clues to understanding *The Great Gatsby*. In the case of *Steal This Book*, it would be almost impossible to separate the zeitgeist of 1960s America from Hoffman's writing style. The book is disorganized, repeating some advice and straying off its stated mission at what appears to be the author's whim. For instance, the section on ''knife fighting'' has little to do with the political subject of fighting off police oppression, assuming that no police anywhere use knives to attack criminal suspects; it is more likely a subject Hoffman had experienced and felt like including in this guide, despite the irrelevance. Because the spirit of the time gravitated toward freedom and rebellion, the book is free to drift toward the sort of irrelevancies that would be considered distractions if included in books written for a different audience.

Tone

Almost as important as the advice given in *Steal This Book* is the tone that Hoffman takes throughout the work. It is his tone that conveys his attitude. Though the practicality of many of his tips might be questioned, what is clear is that he takes a consistent attitude throughout. This book offered some useful tips and many ideas that were not even realistic when it was first published. Over time, many of the corporate interests Hoffman encourages readers to ''rip off'' have refined their security measures in order to avoid being victimized by the kinds of malicious crimes he describes. Still, this is a useful document because it conveys through its tone a way of looking at the world that was prevalent in the 1960s and 1970s.

The book's tone is set by the use of the word ''pig.'' Though the word later came to be used mainly as an insult toward police, Hoffman uses it here to describe anyone who is greedy, lazy, and small-minded. His assumption is that these are the attributes shared by those in power, making anyone who is part of the economic system a ''pig,'' and thereby a fair victim of robbery, ''trashing,'' and violence. The word is frequently used to refer to members of the police force, but that is because they are the members of the establishment with which readers would most likely come into contact if they followed the book's guidelines. In general though, the police, corporate employees, politicians, and business owners are all workers for what Hoffman refers to as the ''Pig Empire.''

Historical Context

Opposition to War

The organized resistance to the Vietnam War in the 1960s grew directly out of the civil rights movement of the 1950s. Up until the 1950s, America was still a segregated country, in spite of the fact slavery had formally ended in 1865. Southern states had laws, informally referred to as ''Jim Crow'' laws, that refused blacks equal access to the same public services that whites used, including transportation, housing, and schools. In 1957 the Southern Christian Leadership Conference (SCLC), an organization of black churches and ministers, was formed under the leadership of Reverend Martin Luther King Jr. to organize protests against racism. The organization welcomed the participation of northern whites, usually college-aged students who volunteered to fight injustice, risking their lives by attending marches and voter registration drives with southern blacks.

Starting in 1965, the SCLC changed its focus to fighting poverty in the North. White participants, including Abbie Hoffman, felt themselves being forced out by the group's new agenda. With the skills they had learned organizing protests, they focused on the growing dissatisfaction over the war in Vietnam.

The struggle between North Vietnam and South Vietnam had gone on mostly unnoticed by Americans since 1949. Americans had given financial and tactical aid to South Vietnam, fearful that a victory by the communist government of the North would lead to a spread of communism all across the continent. President John F. Kennedy sent the first U.S. troops into the region in 1961; in 1964 President Lyndon Johnson used a report of North Vietnamese ships attacking an American ship to have Congress pass the Gulf of Tonkin Resolution, allowing the president to escalate the war. By the end of 1965, 200,000 American soldiers were committed to the region. Years passed and American warplanes bombed Vietnamese villages, American soldiers died in battle, and an increasing number of American citizens quit believing that the abstract idea of stopping communism was a sensible explanation for the destruction. On college campuses, outrage against the war expanded to a distrust and hatred of the government in general. The outrage of the nation's young people was channeled into political action by activists like Hoffman who had participated in the civil rights movement.

The Chicago Seven Trial

In 1968 various antiwar organizations called their members to attend the Democratic National Convention in Chicago to show their opposition to President Johnson, a Democrat, and to Hubert Humphrey, his vice president. Humphrey supported the war and was expected to be the Democratic presidential nominee. The protesters were opposed by overwhelming resistance from the government. Standing up against 5,000 protestors were 12,000 police, 6,000 army troops, and 5,000 National Guardsmen. From August 25 to 29, the streets near the convention center were scenes of violence, as the police, under orders from Chicago Mayor Richard Daley, attacked unarmed protesters with clubs, tear gas, and guns. The protesters' chant that ''The whole world is watching!'' turned out to be true. Watching on television, Americans were in general more sympathetic to the bloodied protestors than the police and their strong-arm tactics. A government report commissioned later to investigate what happened in Chicago coined the term ''police riot.''

After Richard Nixon was elected on a law-and-order ticket, the Justice Department went about prosecuting the organizers who had encouraged people to come to Chicago to attend the protest. They were charged with conspiring to cross state lines to commit a felony, even though several of the defendants had never met one another or talked to each other before arriving in Chicago. Abbie Hoff-

Compare
&
Contrast

- **1971:** Angered at the U.S. involvement in the Vietnam War, many American citizens feel the need to resist the prevailing social order, sometimes violently.

  Today: Frightened by the prospect of terrorist attacks, many citizens look to the American government for protection.

- **1971:** One of the longest periods of economic growth in the country's history makes it possible for young people to take financial security for granted, turning their backs on the morally unsatisfying pursuit of money.

  Today: The unstable economy makes money harder to come by, which in turn makes it harder to survive off sharing or handouts.

- **1971:** *Steal This Book* takes a position that large, faceless corporations are inhumane and deserve to be robbed.

  Today: Advances in transportation and telecommunication have made corporations multinational and therefore even more impersonal. Nineteen-sixties-like protests are aimed against the G-20 Conference and the World Trade Organization, groups that coordinate world-dominating corporations.

- **1971:** Abbie Hoffman writes a guidebook so that readers who are not part of the hippie movement but are interested in participating, can benefit from the informal tips usually passed from one person to another by word of mouth.

  Today: Informal tips like these can generally be found on the Internet.

- **1971:** There are two major world superpowers: America, with a capitalist economy that supports private ownership, and the Soviet Union, with a communist economy that is based on government ownership.

  Today: Since the fall of the Soviet Union in 1989, the American form of capitalism is the main economic influence in the world.

---

man and Jerry Rubin had been the founders of the Youth International Party, or Yippie which focused on promoting change through raising public awareness with shocking and humorous stunts, such as backing their own nominee for the presidency—a pig from a local farm. Others came from the Black Panther Party, the Students for a Democratic Society, and the National Mobilization to End the War.

Throughout the trial in autumn 1969, Hoffman and Rubin brought media attention to what they saw as the ridiculousness of the government's charges. They arrived in court in costumes, dressed as revolutionary war soldiers and as Chicago police officers, and addressed Judge Julius Hoffman as ''Julie.'' These antics made Hoffman a hero to those who saw the whole trial as a political farce.

In the end, the defendants were found guilty of inciting a riot, with all convictions overturned on appeal. Hoffman was one of the defendants who had to spend a few weeks in jail for contempt of court. It was during this relatively light sentence that he wrote the introduction to *Steal This Book*, a fact that he alludes to in the book's opening pages.

Steal This Book carried the Yippie attitude of resistance into the 1970s, even as the antiestablishment fervor was fading. Throughout the decades, it has been considered with almost mythical reverence by those who support the cultural revolution of the sixties, even though the advice it gives is seldom practiced.

Critical Overview

Hoffman had trouble finding a publisher for *Steal This Book*. He insisted the three-word phrase, which had appeared in small print on the back jacket of his earlier book *Woodstock Nation*, must be the title, even though some publishers would have been glad to print it in spite of its advice for illegal activity, if only it did not tell consumers to steal from *them*. In all, over thirty publishers rejected it before Hoffman paid to have it published by Grove Press. Even then, many bookstores refused to carry the book, and major distribution chains refused to handle it. Libraries refused to put it on their shelves. In several cases where people committing crimes were found to have *Steal This Book* among their possessions, prosecutors tried to indict Hoffman as a criminal conspirator.

After a glowing review by Dotson Rader in the *New York Times Book Review,* sales of the book began to pick up. According to Jack Hoffman, Abbie Hoffman's brother, Rader's review was that the book was most useful when perceived as a way of getting to know its author. In his book *Run Run Run: The Lives of Abbie Hoffman,* Jack Hoffman quotes Rader's position as saying, "It reads as if Hoffman decided it was time to sit down and advise his children on what to avoid and what was worth having in America. He says that if you want to be free, then America might kill you. You must know certain things if you are to survive." Presenting the book as a source of insight into America's most famous and interesting hippie made the book itself interesting and famous. Hoffman toured the country, appearing on local talk shows to stir up interest.

It was not long after the publication of *Steal This Book* that the public began to turn against Hoffman. Rumors circulated that he was living a luxurious lifestyle from the book's proceeds, living in a penthouse apartment and socializing with celebrities. Most of the money from the book in fact was donated to the Black Panthers Defense Fund. Though the rumors were unfounded, they cast a pall of hypocrisy over the project. In 1973 Hoffman was arrested for selling cocaine and he went underground to avoid a jail sentence. The arrest seemed to confirm the rumors of an extravagant lifestyle and living in hiding, he was unable to support his book.

Since its publication, *Steal This Book* has continuously stayed in print. No reviewers have recommended the advice it gives and except for Rader, none has seriously thought of it as way of understanding its complex author. Still, it captures the antiestablishment mood of the 1960s, an era that, even by the time of the book's publication in 1971, was fading into nostalgia.

Criticism

David Kelly

Kelly is an instructor of creative writing and literature at College of Lake County. In this essay, Kelly considers whether Steal This Book *is still relevant for readers in the twenty-first century.*

Abbie Hoffman's best-known piece of writing, *Steal This Book*, has one of the most recognized and often copied titles in publishing history. Newspaper articles and books about Hoffman often use some variation on this phrase, such as *Steal This Dream* and *Live This Book*. A 2000 film about Hoffman's life was called *Steal This Movie,* leading many into the mistaken assumption that it was an adaptation of this random crazy-quilt of a book. Hoffman himself, knowing how much of a catchphrase the title had become, cannibalized his own work when he titled his 1987 book about America's anti-drug hysteria *Steal This Urine Test.*

The title is familiar all over the world, but like Thomas Wolfe's *You Can't Go Home Again* and Ernest Hemingway's *Death in the Afternoon,* it may have more power as a slogan than as an entry point into the book itself. Some critics would have no problem if the book were never read again; it was never written "well," by anybody's standards, and a good case can be made that once the novelty has worn off, the book has outlived any minimal value it had. Others hold onto it, though, as a magic totem that keeps the spirit of its time alive, and they fear its loss would represent yet another blow against free thought and individualism. To them, this is a work that purposely set out to defy all of the rules, and so it would be foolish to judge it by any other book's standards.

The problem with treating *Steal This Book* as a sacred object and declaring it off limits to criticism is that, though it makes the book less vulnerable, it also renders it less interesting. To say this book sets its own standards is the same thing as saying that we cannot talk about it as a book, and with that kind of restriction people are bound to wander away from it. What is needed is to find a standard by which to measure the book and talk about it.

One of Hoffman's stated goals was to parody the kinds of travel books that commonly show people how to take in an exotic land on a budget. As such, his last section, titled ''Liberate,'' was just right for its time. It gives specific names, addresses, prices, and preferred menu items. Best of all, the world to which it introduced its readers was one of soup kitchens, public libraries, and throwaways, all of the things urban dwellers usually do not notice in their environment and that tourists, far from being directed toward them, are usually advised to avoid. As a satire of the establishment, the book was highly successful, showing the positive side of things the social mainstream feared and disdained, such as poverty and crime. Adding advice about system abuse and drugs to the travel tips, one can see that the book's agenda was to shine a positive light onto anything the straight society tried to suppress. Any objections on moral grounds, then, just fed the satire, making it grow stronger even after the book was already finished.

The problem with reading it like this is that the book becomes a throwaway, as dated and as doomed to obsolescence as the travel guides it parodies. Frankly, there is no big market for travel books ten years old or older: their prices are out of date, they talk about places that have gone out of business, and they almost always have been replaced by newer models with more relevant information. So it is with *Steal This Book*. Not only are most of the great bargains gone, but also faded from the American culture is that need to point out the establishment's hypocrisy. We live in an ironic age, in which the order of the day, from entertainment to advertising to political rhetoric, is to point out one's own internal contradictions with a wink. True, a good case can be made that the current level of irony might never have been reached without Abbie Hoffman, but being a creator of it does not excuse him from its effects. There is something a little too naive about pointing out that the mainstream culture is hypocritical, as if only the talented few can see it. We are all aware of the hypocrisy. These days, satire needs to be more subtle than portraying the enemy as violent and clueless. For some, this kind of obviousness might be considered a reminder of simpler times, when satire moved at an easier pace. Accepting the book in that spirit, though, puts Abbie

Abbie Hoffman, a week before going on trial for the Chicago Seven incident, holding a toy bomb to be used in a demonstration related to the trial

Hoffman's revolutionary tribute to youth culture in the same category of nostalgia as silent movies and radio dramas. It is not really satire; if it is about a world from which the reader is comfortably removed, it then becomes camp.

Another way to look at *Steal This Book* today would be to forget about the humor, which depended on the circumstances of the sixties and seventies, and to concentrate on its value as a guide to orchestrating a successful urban revolution. True, America is less interested in revolution today than it was then, but the general lack of interest does not in itself make Hoffman's advice any less practical. Bombs are still bombs, demonstrations are still public displays of opposition and when the bombing and demonstrations are done, medical and legal aid is still required. Some of his advice has lost its relevance over time—for instance, it is now cheaper and easier for a struggling radical group to post its ideas on a Web site than to print an underground newspaper—but the staleness of those cases is offset by his masterful sense of how to draw media attention even to a small event. Even today's Web sites lack the insight into social protest that Hoff-

What Do I Read Next?

- *The Autobiography of Abbie Hoffman* was originally published in 1980 under the title *Soon to Be a Major Motion Picture.* It captures the story of his public and private life from his birth through the time he lived as an outlaw. The current edition, published in 2000 by Four Walls Eight Windows, has new pictures that were not in the original publication.

- In *Abbie Hoffman: American Rebel* (1992), Marty Jeter, who knew him from covering Yippie events for an underground newspaper, tells the story of Hoffman's life. Jeter's work is sympathetic and thorough with frequent references to Hoffman's own writings.

- *The Whole Earth Catalog,* edited by Stewart Brand and Peter Warshall, did what Hoffman attempted to do, but in a nonviolent and anti-confrontational way: it offered the wisdom of the alternative lifestyle to readers who wished to participate. First published in 1968, it has been frequently updated, including *The Millennium Whole Earth Catalog,* published by HarperCollins in 1995.

- While Hoffman was living underground to avoid arrest for his 1973 cocaine charge, he exchanged letters with his wife Anita. They published their correspondences in 1976 as *To America with Love: Letters from the Underground.* Covered in the book are such matters as Hoffman's fear of being killed by the government, his work on his autobiography, and his growing love for another woman, Joanna Lawrenson.

- Tom Hayden, a codefendant with Hoffman in the infamous Chicago Seven trial, went on to become a state senator in California. He gave his version of the 1960s in his book *Reunion* (1989), published by Crowell-Collier Press.

- Edward H. Romney is a political conservative who has been financially independent since 1969. His political views are the opposite of Hoffman's, but the advice he gives in *Living Well on Practically Nothing* is similar to that in *Steal This Book.* A revised version of Romney's book was published in 2001 by Paladin Press.

---

man had, if only because protest today is such a rare occasion, while for him it was an everyday event.

Unfortunately, revolution is serious business, and the book's satirical element works against this. It would be nice to say that satire and revolution, when mixed together, yield a well-rounded, healthy worldview that is smart enough to distrust and yet sincere enough to fight for a cause. The actual result of the merger though can be frightening. The chapters of *Steal This Book* that deal with guns and street fighting, for instance, fall somewhere in the middle of the book's possible uses. They are too much a product of Hoffman's romantic imagination to be useful as battle training, but also seem counterproductive to social revolution certain to attract the sort of violent response from the government that spells the end for any gang of protesters, however well

armed. On the other hand, this is a violent world, and it is hard to take advice about fighting with weapons as a joke, especially as a joke on the dominant culture. Perhaps at the time Hoffman actually believed that guns and knives could be used to overthrow the government, though the knife fighting passages of the book make it pretty clear that he, at least some of the time, used the idea of revolution to play out some 1950s street gang fantasy from his youth. As sound as the book's advice for protestors is, it blurs the line of reality with its glib treatment of weapons. Groups that took up arms against the government did not fare well even before the world became vigilant against terrorist attacks, and they seem particularly delusional now.

Of all of the tips passed along in *Steal This Book*, perhaps the most telling is the one about getting free buffalo from the government. In that one small episode, Hoffman captured the whole essence of the book and the significance it will have for coming generations. Hoffman advised readers to write to the Department of the Interior, Washington, D.C., 20420, claiming that the government had some program to give away buffalo to anyone who wrote and agreed to pay their buffalo's freight charge. As a tip, it was not a very practical one; the program had already been discontinued by the time the book was written. A true guide book would have dropped it right there. It was included in the book anyway, as a sort of advertisement for Hoffman and his methods. "So many people have written them recently demanding their Free Buffalo," he wrote, "that they called a press conference to publicly attack the Yippies for creating chaos in the government." Presumably, no matter how many letters the Department of the Interior received asking for free buffaloes, the government was never really in danger of falling into chaos. Telling it this way though, poses a minor bureaucratic situation as a major battle between the government and the Yippies, with the government backing down, defeated by its own rules, reduced to babbling and to publicly acknowledging the power of the Yippies' information sharing.

Hoffman goes on to tell his readers, "Don't take any buffalo s—- from these petty bureaucrats, demand the real thing. Demand your Free Buffalo." He could not have picked a better symbol for his own book. The word "buffalo" was once a slang term for intimidation or deception. Currently, the most common association with the word is of the animal that once roamed the plains until government-sponsored massacres pushed them near extinction. Now it is the Yippies who are nearly extinct, and readers are still left to wonder just how much Abbie Hoffman was trying to buffalo them.

The book's relevance comes down to this: a little bit of a reminder of a dying breed, a little bit of a riddle about the mind of the man who wrote it, and a little bit of the rebellious attitude that we all suppress. It is up to each reader to decide if these add up to something they feel is worth reading, but one thing that seems pretty clear is that there is enough here to make the book worth it for some people, and there will be for a long time to come.

Source: David Kelly, Critical Essay on *Steal This Book*, in *Nonfiction Classics for Students*, Gale, 2003.

> " True, a good case can be made that the current level of irony might never have been reached without Abbie Hoffman, but being a creator of it does not excuse him from its effects."

Josh Ozersky

Ozersky is a critic and historian. In this essay, Ozersky looks at Steal This Book *as a product of the late 1960s and its author, Abbie Hoffman, as a romantic icon of the time.*

Students coming to *Steal This Book* for the first time may find themselves a little perplexed. The current edition of the book begins with three separate introductions, each testifying to Abbie Hoffman's inspirational courage as a revolutionary. *Steal This Book* is said to be "his most widely read" and "his most notorious." In Hoffman's introduction, he speaks of *Steal This Book* as "a manual of survival in the prison that is Amerika." What follows is a breezy guide to shoplifting, freeloading, and milking the system, peppered with cartoons. There are sections on building bombs, guerrilla broadcasting, and street fighting, but these are short and not particularly useful. (Hoffman's advises would-be knife fighters to "work out with the jabbing method in front of a mirror and in a few days you'll get it down pretty well.")

More puzzling still is Hoffman's general tone. Despite his subversive rhetoric, Hoffman sounds like nothing so much as a boastful, mouthy teenager, the kid who wears an anarchist symbol on his denim jacket and bores everybody with his self-serving rhetoric. It's impossible to imagine anybody taking this person seriously as a record store cashier, let alone a revolutionary leader. And yet Hoffman's reputation has only grown since his death in 1989. *Steal This Movie,* a major Hollywood release, came out in 2000.

But understanding Abbie Hoffman, his book and the man himself is difficult without a solid understanding of the 1960s and his role in them. Despite the fact that he is associated with the baby

> **Steal This Book isn't really about how to steal food, build a sterno bomb, or start a commune. It's about how to be Abbie Hoffman."**

boom (it was Hoffman who coined the phrase "Woodstock Nation") and figured so prominently in many of the signal events of the counterculture, Hoffman was not a baby boomer himself. Abbie Hoffman was born in 1936, which means that he became conscious of public life in the years immediately after World War II. Those years were ones marked by an unusual brew of anxiety, conformity, and a generalized feeling of moral superiority in America that rankled many. In fact, the conservatism of the Truman and Eisenhower years was highly exceptional, a result of having won the greatest war ever fought and the worst depression in American history simultaneously. Many adults felt that America had the high moral ground in the struggle against Soviet communism, and the moral imperatives of the 1960s, such as civil rights and women's liberation, were not yet on the horizon.

As a result, to many young people of Hoffman's generation, America seemed smug and oppressive, its citizens brainwashed by material goods and government propaganda. They dismissed all dissent as "pink" and were satisfied with women, minorities, and the poor kept low. Hoffman's generation was born too late to know the privations of the depression, so America's glee at things like row houses, new cars, and the security of suburbs and corporate jobs seemed merely greedy to them. And it so happened that when the great causes of the early 1960s came along, they were just coming into their early adulthood.

Some, like Tom Hayden of the University of Michigan, applied all the seriousness of cold war civics to creating a "new left," which would oppose the political status quo from a radical but serious-minded and deeply moralistic perspective. At the same time, an apolitical "counterculture" was being formed in places like San Francisco's Haight-Ashbury district. This movement could hardly have been less political. Although given over to

sloganeering and a sometimes-justified paranoia about "the straight world," most hippies sought pleasure in their own lives and had little use for political debate and organization.

Abbie Hoffman was among the first to become well known for fusing both camps, and that is what *Steal This Book* is all about. Hoffman came to prominence in 1968, when he and several other antiwar activists came upon the idea of organizing an outrageous "festival of life" at the 1968 Democratic National Convention in Chicago. Calling themselves the Youth International Party or "Yippies," they proposed to substitute outrage, street theater, and "cultural revolution" for the tiresome programs offered by the New Left. Hoffman was the most visible of the provocateurs who clowned for the cameras in Lincoln Park, and when Mayor Richard Daley unleashed an army of policemen to attack the protesters, Hoffman was cast into the national spotlight.

It was a place that suited him well. As *Steal This Book* suggests, Hoffman had no real political program and little in the way even of political rhetoric. What he was good at was playing the gadfly, spouting incendiary rhetoric, and mugging for the camera. (He tried to seize the stage at Woodstock for a Yippie rant, but the crowd booed loudly and guitarist Pete Townshend of The Who knocked him off the stage by bashing his head with a guitar. The "Woodstock Nation" cheered loudly, many going so far as to call it Townshend's greatest solo.) Hoffman was not easily gotten rid of, however, and he became a major media star in those years. In 1969, Hoffman and several other Yippies, along with Black Panther leader Bobby Seale, were defendants in a much-publicized trial of the Chicago Seven. With Hoffman's newfound celebrity to emulate, many New Left activists took to the streets, doing whatever was necessary to get media exposure. "The whole world is watching" was their motto, and the spectacle so repelled most Americans that the New Left was extinguished as soon as the spectacle grew tiresome, which it soon did. Hoffman kept publishing books and his name remained one to conjure with, but he was a walking anachronism after the early 1970s and disappeared from public view for most of the decade.

Steal This Book was published in 1970, at the very acme of Hoffman's fame. *Steal This Book* isn't really about how to steal food, build a sterno bomb, or start a commune. It's about how to be Abbie Hoffman. Not the real Abbie Hoffman, of course, but the mythologized Abbie Hoffman, the clown prince of the New Left, the archetypal radical insurgent. Hoffman's entire public career consisted of the creation of this myth, and in fact *Steal This Book* was one of the crowning achievements in that career.

Notice that Hoffman seldom talks about himself in *Steal This Book*. And yet, on nearly every page, his presence is the primary message. Hoffman's other books are written with a similar strategy, but where they relied on political rhetoric and grand sociological themes ("We are the Woodstock Nation"), here Hoffman presents his would-be emulators with an encyclopedia guide for outwitting "Amerika." Seen from without, this is just a faulty manual for petty criminals, written by an incompetent. But from within, *Steal This Book* is a celebration of the trickster myth, with Abbie Hoffman as the B'rer Rabbit / Bugs Bunny hero who constantly outwits those bigger than him. By making the techniques seem so easily heroic ("Communicating to masses of people . . . is very important. It drives the MAN berserk and gives hope to comrades in the struggle"), Hoffman invites his readers to identify with his own fantasy of rebellion. Thus, practicing with a knife in a mirror isn't just fantasizing; it actually trains you to become an effective knife fighter.

There is surely something laughable in the transparency of all this. But it doesn't take away from *Steal This Book*'s value as the romantic literature of a distant time and place. As a manual for insurgents, *Steal This Book* isn't worth the paper it's written on; but as a document of a unique episode in American history, it can hardly be surpassed.

Source: Josh Ozersky, Critical Essay on *Steal This Book,* in *Nonfiction Classics for Students,* Gale, 2003.

Chris Semansky

Semansky is an instructor of literature and writes on literature and culture for various publications. In this essay, Semansky considers the idea of counterculture in Hoffman's book.

Abbie Hoffman's how-to guide for beating the system, *Steal This Book*, embodies many of the values of the 1960s counterculture, a counterculture that has survived into the twenty-first century, albeit greatly transformed. However, many of the actions that Hoffman advocates in the book, actions that have helped to define the counterculture itself, are no longer possible because of legal and cultural changes in the last thirty years. An exploration of some of these actions will give readers a sense of how much America has changed during this time.

An activist who protested Americans' selfishness and acquisitiveness, Hoffman sought to shape the counterculture movement while providing its sympathizers with the tools to survive. One of Hoffman's recommendations for how to survive in America was to hitchhike. By hitchhiking people could share rides and they did not contribute to polluting the country's air or to furthering America's dependence on foreign oil. Hitchhiking costs nothing and in the 1960s and early 1970s, was legal in most states. It also carried with it a certain allure linked to the image of the free spirit, someone not bogged down by the demands of work, family, and home ownership. During the 1950s, Beat writers like Jack Kerouac in novels such as *On the Road* helped to popularize hitchhiking with romantic descriptions of road life. During the 1960s and much of the 1970s, it was common to see hitchhikers along highways, thumb up and heading for their next adventure. In the twenty-first century, however, hitchhiking is highly regulated, if not illegal, in most states and on almost every interstate highway, and hitchhiker sightings are decreasing. In the last twenty-some years, the image of the hitchhiker has changed from that of a carefree hippie looking for a free ride to that of a deranged killer looking for his next victim. This change, in part, is a result of the media's demonization of hitchhiking and of the increasing fear many Americans have of strangers, a fear fed by popular culture's representation of hitchhikers in movies and on television as psychotic killers.

The change in attitude towards hitchhikers also reflects the public's suspicion of anyone they perceive as trying to obtain something for free. The image of the hippie as a benign and spaced-out freeloader was already well formed in the public imagination by the end of the 1970s. However, during the Reagan administration of the 1980s, the hippie became a joke, a symbol of national shame, product of a troubled era with impossible ideals based on the sharing, rather than the hoarding, of resources.

If hitchhiking has fallen out of practice because the political climate of the country has changed, then trying to "get one over" on corporate America has changed because of increasing corporate vigilance and technological change. Many of Hoffman's recommendations on how to extract free services such as telephone calls are now untenable.

The Chicago Seven defendants

For example, spinning two pennies counterclockwise into the nickel slot of a pay phone to mimic the action of two nickels does not work because local calls are no longer ten cents, and because the mechanism for pay phones has been digitized. Likewise, shoplifting, a practice to which Hoffman dedicates a number of pages, is now considerably more difficult due to the proliferation of surveillance cameras and store use of electronic data tags.

The American public's attitude towards corporations has also changed. In 2002, almost half of all Americans own stock either directly or through their pension funds. Cheating the telephone company or shoplifting from a major department store then is not simply stealing from the rich, but also stealing from oneself. America is more corporate now than it was in 1970, and more Americans, whether they like it or not, are part of the corporate fabric of the country. The link between large corporations and the average citizen has been made abundantly clear in the last two years, when millions of people saw their retirement funds collapse after the bubble in Internet stocks burst, and multi-billion dollar corporations such as World Com and Enron went bankrupt.

Many of Hoffman's recommendations on how to fight the government and corporations, though arguably more important now than ever before as corporations continue to expand, are also becoming increasingly untenable. Protesters can still print underground newspapers and start up low-powered pirate radio stations, as he recommends, but the advent of the Internet has made these strategies relatively insignificant. Anyone with a gripe and an Internet connection can now put up a Web site for less money than it would cost to print a broadsheet. The primary task that faces protesters trying to get their word out via the world wide web is marketing. With literally billions of websites online and tens of thousands of new ones being created each day, attracting the attention of already message-saturated readers is a formidable task.

The advice that does remain relevant today is Hoffman's description of how to plan and stage a street demonstration. His suggestions on how to secure permits and how to dress for a demonstration and prepare for possible responses from authorities are still useful, and many of them were implemented during demonstrations in Seattle against the policies of the World Trade Organization in 1999. However, Hoffman's recommendations for using flash guns, tear gas, mace, and Molotov cocktails, while foolhardy in 1970, are almost suicidal today, as law enforcement officials are ready to pounce on the perpetrators of any act of public violence in the wake of the terrorist attacks of September 11, 2001.

Indeed, September 11 has radically changed the shape of America's counterculture, which is literally built on the freedom of speech guaranteed by the First Amendment. Arguing that the United States is at war with terrorists, the current administration is developing a system, the Total Information Awareness (TIA) program, that would collect data from private companies and public agencies on every living American, making it easier for the government to profile and track the actions of its citizens, and—it claims—to identify foreign terrorists. Similarly, the Federal Bureau of Investigation compiled a massive file on Hoffman during his life, tracking his activities as an environmental activist and free speech advocate. This file, most of which has been released under the Freedom of Information Act, is available on the World Wide Web, as is the complete text of Hoffman's book.

Although much of the information in *Steal This Book* is outdated, its spirit of protest against the status quo remains strong; so strong in fact, that most libraries do not carry copies of the book (selling 250,000 copies in its first six months), even though it was a bestseller when it was first published and remains a classic of counterculture literature. Many of the bookstores that do carry it keep the book locked behind a glass case, so that enterprising ''shoppers'' do not heed the title's command. The book's many tips on how to survive a culture that is more focused on individual rather than community gain were sent in to Hoffman after the publication of his book *Woodstock Nation*. *Steal This Book* was written while he was in Cook County Jail awaiting charges stemming from his protests at the Democratic National Convention in Chicago in 1968. As such, *Steal This Book* is as much an encyclopedia as it is a how-to book, and Hoffman's voice is the voice of a generation determined to change business as usual.

Source: Chris Semansky, Critical Essay on *Steal This Book,* in *Nonfiction Classics for Students,* Gale, 2003.

Sources

Hoffman, Abbie, *Steal This Book,* Four Walls Eight Windows, 2002.

❝ Arguing that the United States is at war with terrorists, the current administration is developing . . . the . . . (TIA) program, that would collect data from private companies and public agencies on every living American, making it easier for the government to profile and track the actions of its citizens, and—it claims—to identify foreign terrorists.❞

Hoffman, Jack, and Daniel Simon, *Run Run Run: The Lives of Abbie Hoffman,* G. P. Putnam's Sons, 1994, p. 179.

Rader, Dotson, Review of *Steal This Book,* in the *New York Times Sunday Book Review,* July 15, 1971.

Further Reading

Becker, Theodore L., and Anthony L. Donaldson, *Live This Book: Abbie Hoffman's Philosophy for a Free and Green America,* The Noble Press, Inc., 1991.
    This is one of the few sources that seriously considers the philosophical and spiritual bases for Hoffman's brand of media manipulation. Written after his death, the book takes into account his whole life, including his post-sixties political organizing under an assumed name.

Farber, David, *Chicago '68,* University of Chicago Press, 1995.
    The events in Chicago of 1968 were important in American history and in understanding the full significance of Abbie Hoffman's place in it. This book is a scholarly explanation of the dynamic forces involved, including a detailed explanation of Hoffman's Yippie philosophy.

Isserman, Maurice, and Michael Kazin, *America Divided: The Civil War of the 1960s,* Oxford University Press, 2000.
    The authors take a balanced, scholarly look at the political turmoil of the decade, careful to avoid common mistakes of romanticizing the hippie movement or unfairly blaming it for society's ills.

Sloman, Larry, *Steal This Dream: Abbie Hoffman and the Counterculture Revolution in America,* Doubleday, 1998.
    This oral history compiles hundreds of interviews from people who knew Hoffman and presents their impressions of him in their own words.

The Varieties of Religious Experience

William James

1902

In *The Varieties of Religious Experience: A Study in Human Nature* (1902), William James offers a sense of validity to the formerly abstract idea of spiritual experience. With an understanding of physiology, psychology, and philosophy, James studied cases of religious inspiration and concluded there were specific aspects of human consciousness that contained energies that could come to a person's assistance in time of great need. The result is what he refers to as the religious experience.

Trained in chemistry and medicine, James looked at religious experience as a scientist might, by researching many case studies. However, his theories about religious experience were also heavily influenced by his philosophical interests, which drew him to conclude that an unseen reality does exist and is available to everyone for exploration. His sentiments were somewhat aligned with the beliefs of the transcendentalists, with his work honoring the individual rather than the institutions of religion.

The Varieties of Religious Experience is actually a collection of lectures James delivered in Edinburgh, Scotland. The lectures were sponsored by Adam Gifford, who was interested in promoting a series of studies of what he referred to as a natural theology. James's lectures became by far the most popular in the series. James also received international attention and praise as one of the first American philosophers to have his ideas welcomed and respected in Europe. Although not cited as James's

best book, *The Varieties of Religious Experience* continues to be referred to as one of the best books on religion. In his day, intellectuals tended to categorize religious experiences as no more than a nervous condition or a reaction caused by indigestion. *The Varieties of Religious Experience* portrays the need for a sense of the spiritual as a natural and healthy psychological function.

The Varieties of Religious Experience has been so successful that it has been reprinted thirty-six times. It is lauded as being as influential and as significant in the twentieth century as it was when first published. To emphasize this point, the board of the Modern Library established that James's book is the second-best nonfiction book of the twentieth century.

Author Biography

William James is referred to as the father of American psychology. He is known for his two-volume work, *The Principles of Psychology*, which summarizes his theories in a field that in the early twentieth century was considered a relatively new science. These volumes took James twelve years to write. However, by the time he completed this work, his interests began leaning more toward philosophy.

James was born January 11, 1842, in New York City, to Mary and Henry James, Sr., an independently wealthy man who associated with transcendentalists Ralph Waldo Emerson and Henry David Thoreau. James's father believed in unorthodox education and sent his children to a variety of schools. James's education included attending schools in London, Geneva, Paris, Dresden, and Boston. By the time James entered Harvard's Lawrence Scientific School, he was fluent in five different languages. Upon receiving his undergraduate degree, James entered medical school at Harvard, but he dropped out in 1865 and instead took a long trip down the Amazon River with Louis Agassiz, a prominent Harvard biologist. Eventually James returned to school, earning a medical degree in 1869. Afterward, he spent a few years in Europe, where he became fascinated with the study of physiology and the New Psychology.

For the next several years, James remained jobless, living off his parents' wealth. Then in 1872 he was offered a chance to teach a newly created course in physiology and anatomy at Harvard. Three years later, James changed the name of this course to "The Relations Between Physiology and Psychology," later refining his material to include only the topic of psychology. At this point, there were no other American college professors teaching courses in psychology. Toward the end of his teaching career, his course underwent another transformation as James's interests switched from psychology to philosophy. However, for all of his interests, it was his studies and experiments in psychology that most influenced international scientific thought.

In 1890 James's *The Principles of Psychology* was published. James had written it to be used as a college guide, and it quickly became a bestselling textbook. Some of the concepts included in the book include stream of consciousness, pain, sensations of motion, the self, imagination, perception, the emotions, and will.

The Varieties of Religious Experience: A Study in Human Nature was the result of the Gifford Lecture Series, which James delivered at the University of Edinburgh in Scotland. The lectures explored the relationship between religious experience and what was then termed abnormal psychology. His interest was not in religious institutions and their rituals but rather the individual experience in relationship to whatever that person considered sacred or divine. Along with *The Principles of Psychology*, *The Varieties of Religious Experience* is considered James's seminal work. Some of his other books include *The Will to Believe and Other Essays in Popular Philosophy* (1897), *Pragmatism: A New Name for Some Old Ways of Thinking* (1907), *A Pluralistic Universe* (1909), and *Some Problems of Philosophy* (1911). James received several honorary degrees in his lifetime, including doctor of law degrees from three different universities: Princeton University in 1896, the University of Edinburgh in 1902, and Harvard University in 1903.

In 1878 James married Alice Howe Gibbens, a Boston schoolteacher and pianist, who remained James's closest friend and intellectual confidant throughout their marriage. James, who suffered greatly from depression throughout his life, often credited his wife for helping him maintain his psychological balance. The couple had five children. Among James's own siblings was his famous brother, novelist Henry James.

On August 26, 1910, at the age of sixty-eight, James died of heart disease at his summer home in New Hampshire, nine years after presenting his Gifford lectures in Edinburgh. In his *New York Times* obituary, James is called "America's foremost philosophical writer, virtual founder of the modern school of psychology and exponent of pragmatism.'' He was survived by his wife and four of his children.

Plot Summary

Lectures 1–3

In the first two lectures, James sets the ground rules or parameters of the topic he will be discussing. He begins with definitions and establishes the fact that his lectures are not based on anthropological evidence or studies but rather on personal documents that relay personal experience. He states that as he is neither a theologian nor a scholar in the history of religion, his talks are based on ''a descriptive survey'' of religious tendencies that exhibit themselves through the examples he offers.

James also discusses how he defines religious experience through the emotion of excitement, which offers immediate delight and dispenses enough good feeling to affect a good portion of the individual's life. Unlike the scientific dialogue of his time in regards to religious experience, he does not judge an individual as mentally deranged merely because that person has an unexplainable incident. Rather, he looks at religious experience by its results.

James emphasizes that his lectures are in no way directed at institutionalized religion but rather at individual experience, or what one person might experience in solitude. He then notes there are two different ways of accepting the universe: a passive, stoic stance, in which one agrees to the circumstances whether one likes them or not; or a passionate happy stance, in which one agrees with the circumstances. The emotional mood of the individual makes the difference.

In lecture three, James writes that most people have a sense of the presence of evil as well as that of good. Mystical experiences are those rare, brief experiences in which a person senses the presence of God. The opposite sensation—that of evil—presents itself in the form of something unpleasant. These feelings often cannot be explained and therefore cannot be proven. This lies in conflict with philosophical rationalism, which discounts mysticism. However, James believes that rationalism provides a superficial account of life.

William James

Lectures 4–10

James states that one of the primary goals in life is to find and maintain happiness. If this is true, then it is easy to conclude that ''any persistent enjoyment may *produce* the sort of religion which consists in a grateful admiration of the gift of so happy an existence.'' This is not to be confused with a hedonistic outlook on life but rather understood in terms of a deeper, inner happiness. From this thought, it can easily be taken that the proof of a religion might be based on how happy it makes someone feel. Some people appear to have been born with a propensity to see life as entirely good. James refers to a statement by Francis W. Newman in which the concepts of the ''once-born'' and the ''twice-born'' are defined. The once-born rarely considers evil, or even imperfections within the self. An individual is innocent and childlike. James later discusses the twice-born.

Healthy-mindedness is the term James applies to the once-born, who have a way of seeing everything as good. This optimism has led to what James calls the ''mind-cure movement,'' with Ralph Waldo Emerson being one of its strongest influences. The basic belief with this movement is that healthy-minded attitudes can conquer all feelings of doubt, misery, worry, and ''all precautionary states of mind.'' In its extreme, this religious philosophy can lead to faith healing. Whereas the mind-cure movement believes that the mind controls and creates reality, scientists often believe that reality is independent of the mind.

The sick soul is discussed in lectures six and seven. The sick soul, in contrast to the healthy-minded, maximizes evil, believing that the underlying essence of life is evil. James finds a problem with this way of thought, but he also finds difficulty accepting that everything in life is good. Some people believe in a God that is all good, James writes. But that leaves one to wonder how evil fits in. Where did it come from? People who believe in a benevolent God state that this spiritual head is only responsible for making sure that evil will eventually be overcome. The difficulty of placing evil somewhere on the shoulders of God is one of the basic paradoxes of philosophy, James states.

There are different levels of being a sick soul. For some, evil is just a minor setback or a maladjustment that will eventually be corrected. For others, evil is so deeply rooted that it causes the individual to become neurotic, to the point the person cannot experience joy. The sick soul must be twice-born in order to find happiness.

Lecture eight covers the concept of the divided self and its reunification. The twice-born are said to have inner conflict that must be resolved. They tend to see the other, more positive side of life but tend to believe it is deceptive. James covers different types of conversions of well-known, twice-born individuals, such as John Bunyan, whose conversion was gradual, and St. Paul, whose conversion was very sudden.

In the next two lectures, James discusses various types of conversions. There are some that cause ordinary changes of a person's character. Other types may change the deeper patterns of the habits of a person's life. Some come about of one's own effort and will, while a second type seems to come from an external source. Sudden conversions, which some religions actually demand, may cause a decrease in carnal appetite and crude bodily pleasures. James states that some sudden conversions are similar to neurotic symptoms. Feelings associated with conversions include a sense of control by a supreme power outside of oneself and a sense of assurance, which rids one of worry and in its place instills a sense of perceiving truths never before known.

Lectures 11–13

The topic of all three lectures is saintliness, which contains the attributes of charity, devotion, trust, patience, and bravery. In this state, one feels that life has a deeper meaning and there is a pronounced belief in an Ideal Power, to which one is willing to surrender. This brings about a feeling of immense elation and freedom, and one's emotions focus on love and ''harmonious affections.'' There appears to be a sense of inner tranquility that resides in an individual with these qualities. In a somber personality, the form of saintliness takes on the essence of submission; whereas in a more cheerful personality, it takes on a sense of joyous consent.

In extreme cases, there is a tendency to want to withdraw from the world, which contains too many distractions of corruption. Examples include the ascetic person and people who resign themselves to monasteries to practice a contemplative life.

James then defines various psychological levels of asceticism, a practice of self-denial. In asceticism, there is a tendency toward simplicity in life, ridding oneself of excessive pleasures and comforts. Pain is tolerated without complaint. These sacrifices tend to make the ascetic person happy. Taken to extremes, this tendency can become a neurosis and may be caused by a pessimistic sense of self or by a perversion of ''bodily sensibility.'' James then explains different levels of asceticism, some of them extreme, such as that displayed by St. John of the Cross, who ate only what he disliked; did only what disgusted him; aspired not to what he considered the highest but what he considered the lowest and most contemptible; and despised himself and wished that others would too. St. John of the Cross was considered a mystic.

Lectures 14–15

The value of saintliness follows in lectures fourteen and fifteen. James writes that extravagance of saintliness often leads to fanaticism in aggressive personalities, and it can motivate the invention of legends around honored persons who are revered. There are also the saintly personalities who take on what James refers to as ''theopathic saintliness,'' wherein a person becomes so absorbed in the love of God that human love is useless. This type of saintliness usually exists in gentle people. James then refers to German philosopher Friedrich Nietzsche, who was a critic of saintly personalities, finding them to be weak. James disagrees, calling many saintly people the visionaries of the future.

Lectures 16–20

Lectures sixteen and seventeen deal with mysticism, to which James ascribes the following characteristics: it cannot be defined but only directly experienced; has a noetic quality, leaving one with a feeling of insight or knowledge; is a transient experience; and has a sense of passivity, as if another personality has taken over. Examples of mystic experience include a sense of deep understanding of a particular maxim; an experience of déjà vu; a sense of being completely stripped of all essence of self; and chemical intoxication. There are different practices that can induce a mystical state, or at least discontinue the sense of ordinary consciousness. This sense can be brought on by nature, by a sense of immortality, or by methods practiced, for instance, in yoga, Sufism, and Buddhism.

In lecture eighteen, James discusses philosophy and its inability to come to terms with the religious experience. Philosophy attempts to construct arguments for God's existence, without success. James believes that the religious feeling is beyond verbal expression and rational assessment.

In lecture nineteen, James returns to organized religions, discussing aspects of religious worship. In lecture twenty, he draws his conclusions, which include the inability to create a science of religion because most scientists are biased against religions. He also concludes that religion should respect individual experiences, in which feeling pervades and fact is in the making.

Key Figures

Marcus Aurelius

Marcus Aurelius (121–180 A.D.) was a Roman emperor and renown stoic who wrote a famous book on how to live. James quotes from Aurelius's writing to demonstrate his stoic nature, which agrees *to* the circumstances of life but not necessarily *with* them.

Jonathan Edwards

Theologian and metaphysician Jonathan Edwards (1703–1758) was born in Connecticut, the only son of eleven children. He graduated from Yale at the age of seventeen and became a minister, as his father and grandfather were before him. James quotes Edwards throughout his lectures but in particular in his first lecture: "by their fruits ye shall

Media Adaptations

- An audiotape of James's *The Varieties of Religious Experience,* narrated by Flo Gibson and published in 2001, is available from Audio Book Contractors. A 1994 audio version narrated by Erik Bauersfeld is available from Knowledge Tapes.

know them, not by their roots.'' Man's roots, James expounds, are inaccessible. Only by the empirical evidence of the fruit is something known. This is one of James's basic tenets. Only by the results of a practice does one know if it is true.

George Fox

Founder of the Society of Friends (Quakers), George Fox (1624–1691) was born in England and traveled around Europe and the New World promoting his religious views. James often uses Fox as an example of a person using his or her pathological features (such as ''nervous instability'') to help give him or her ''religious authority and influence.'' James states that no one of any reputation would state that Fox's mind was unsound, despite the fact that his published journal abounds in entries that make Fox sound like a ''psychopath.'' Fox often had visions that would direct him to do strange things, such as pulling off his shoes and walking barefoot in winter and crying out that people he met should repent.

Georg Wilhelm Friedrich Hegel

Born in Stuttgart, Germany, Georg Hegel (1770–1831) was the central philosophical influence on Karl Marx and Fredrick Engels. James refers to Hegel's theories in his lecture on philosophy. He mentions two Hegelian school principles. The first is that ''the fullness of life can be construed to thought only by recognizing that every object which our thought may propose to itself involves the notion of some other object which seems at first to negate the first one.'' The second principle states that if a person is conscious of a negation, that person is "virtually to be beyond it." In other words, the concept of the finite, James writes, somehow already acknowledges the infinite.

Immanuel Kant

German philosopher Immanuel Kant (1724–1804) had a strong influence on the study of metaphysics and ethics, and spent most of his life attempting to answer the question, "What do we know?" In his lecture "The Reality of the Unseen," James calls upon some of Kant's thoughts about the nature of God and soul. James paraphrases Kant, who believed that since these concepts "cover no distinctive sense-content," theoretically they are "devoid of any significance." However, Kant did concede that the concept of God and soul hold meaning in practice of life and that people have the right to act *as if* they held substance. In other words, people can live their lives *as if* there is a God.

Martin Luther

James refers to Martin Luther (1483–1546), whose philosophy was to become the foundation of the Lutheran Church, in his lecture about the sick soul, and in later lectures, because of Luther's rather melancholic disposition. The quotes that James uses display Luther's sense of almost desperate need for a belief in a god.

Frederic W. H. Myers

Frederic W. H. Myers (1843–1901) was a member of the Society for Psychical Research. During his lifetime, he published several essays on subliminal consciousness, a concept that James addresses in his lectures on conversion. James writes, "this discovery of a consciousness existing beyond the field . . . casts light on many phenomena of religious biography." Myers coined the word *automatism*, to which James refers. It is a reference to unaccountable impulses such as automatic writing, by which an individual writes things of which he or she claims not to understand the meaning. Later, James quotes from a letter from Myers in which Myers discusses prayer.

John Henry Newman

John Henry Newman (1801–1890) was a cardinal in the Roman Catholic Church, and James quotes him in his lecture on philosophy that states that theology is "a science in the strictest sense of the word." Newman claimed that truths about God could be (and were) known and could be claimed as fact "just as we have a science of the stars and call it astronomy." James uses Newman to point out the dogmatic nature of institutionalized religion, in which feeling is valid only for the individual and "is pitted against reason," which is considered universally valid.

Friedrich Nietzsche

Born in Prussia, Friedrich Nietzsche (1844–1900) has greatly influenced the philosophical world. James refers to Nietzsche's comments on saintliness, of which James states, "The most inimical critic of the saintly impulses whom I know is Nietzsche." Nietzsche contrasts saintliness to the aggressive nature of the military type, with emphasis and advantage on the latter. In other words, according to Nietzsche saintliness was a weakness.

Saint John of the Cross

Cofounder of the Roman Catholic order of Carmelites and doctor of mystic theology, Saint John of the Cross (1542–1591) provides James in his lecture on saintliness with an extreme type of ascetic personality. James quotes St. John at length in a list of all the ways in which St. John finds to humiliate and humble himself. For example, St. John believed that people should not seek what is best in life but rather they should seek what is worst "so that you may enter for the love of Christ into a complete destitution."

Edwin Diller Starbuck

Throughout the lecture on conversion, James often refers to the studies of E. D. Starbuck (1866–1947), a Stanford University professor who along with James was considered one of the pioneers in the study of the psychology of religion. In particular, James mentions Starbuck's statistical research on conversion among adolescents. Starbuck published several books after James's death, two of which are *The Psychology of Religion* (1911) and *Religion in Transition* (1937).

Leo Tolstoy

James uses the story about Russian author Leo Tolstoy's long bout with melancholia and his subsequent recovery as an example of a conversion over a long period of time. Tolstoy (1828–1910) published an account of his depression and religious experience in his book *My Confession* (1887). He suffered from what James calls anhedonia, the ''passive loss of appetite for all life's values.'' During this time, Tolstoy could find no reason to continue with life since everything he accomplished would end with his death. He could find no meaning in life, despite the fact that he was happily married, was a success, and received praise for his work from an international community. He often contemplated suicide during this period, although he states he never actually thought he would do it. Over the course of a year, he slowly began to realize that all humankind was put on this Earth to live for some reason. The concept of an infinite God broadened his scope and made him stop thinking about his own finite parameters.

Walt Whitman

James uses American poet Walt Whitman (1819–1892) as his prime example of the healthy-minded individual. James quotes one of Whitman's students, who states that Whitman could find supreme happiness just strolling outside and looking at the grass, the trees, and the sky. According to James, everything in life pleased Whitman, and he enjoyed a wide readership in his time (a readership that continues in the twenty-first century) because of his ''systematic expulsion from his writing of all contractile elements.'' Whitman wrote in the first person not as an egotist, James writes, but as Universal Man. His poetry reassures his readers that everything in life is good. James also quotes Whitman in his lecture on mysticism, claiming that Whitman's poetry contains a ''classical expression of this sporadic type of mystical experience.''

Themes

Religion

In order to talk about religious experience, James must first define the term *religion*. He quickly points out that the main theme of his lectures is not the institution of religion but rather the personal experience of it. His focus is on the psychological aspects of religion, and to do this, he must deal with the individual. Following the same premise, he also states that it is not the rules and rituals of religious experience in which he is interested but the religious feelings and the emotions of the individual. To this end, he relies on stories about people he has known and works of literature and autobiography he has read. He writes that he does not want to use examples from religious people who follow ''the conventional observances'' of their country. In other words, he does not want to use examples of people who comply with the dictates of their church. Rather, he wants to use only people who have what he calls original experiences. The religion he refers to is that which ''exists not as a dull habit, but as an acute fever.'' Having established this definition, James then tackles all aspects of the personal religious experiences.

Belief

There is a sense of an unknown reality or power that exists in religious experiences. This sense is the basis of belief. Whatever this feeling is, it cannot be seen and yet it gives the believer the idea that there is some mystical order in life. As James writes, religious experience imparts the desire to align oneself with this power, as it is the source of supreme good in which all things are harmonious. This belief, James states, is the ''religious attitude of the soul.'' Belief in general, James writes, is like stating ''as if.'' Taking the concept from philosopher Immanuel Kant, James offers the conclusion that belief consists of accepting various concepts as if they exist, even though they cannot be proven. It is this belief that underlies all religious experience.

In all the examples that James offers in this book, his subjects believe that they have had religious or spiritual experiences that make little rational sense, and each the occurrence is very real for the person who has it. Without belief, there would be no religion.

Happiness and Depression

Having suffered through several years of depression and having come out of this with what he describes as a spiritual experience, James writes about this devastating state of mind as well as its contrasting emotion, happiness. He uses the poet Walt Whitman as the perfect example of healthy-mindedness, a state of acceptance of life that can

Topics for Further Study

- James did not put a lot of faith in organized religion, but rather in the personal experience of religious inspiration. Focus on his arguments against institutionalized religion, then research the philosophical ideas of Martin Luther. How do the two mens' ideas clash? Write your conclusions and explain where you stand in this debate.

- Research the basic tenets of the transcendentalists, and read Emerson's lecture "Self Reliance." Create a dialogue between James and Emerson on the topic of religion based on your comparison.

- Choose one of James's contemporaries (such as Carl Jung, Alfred Adler, or Wilhelm Wundt) and compare his theory of people's need for religion to James's. In what areas are they of like minds? How do they differ? In your opinion, are their theories compatible with modern times? Why or why not?

- Interview two clerical leaders of two very different local churches, synagogues, and/or mosques. Prepare yourself for the meetings with a list of at least fifteen to twenty questions. These questions should reflect the ideas that James has put forth in his book. Some of the questions might reflect some of your own considerations after reading the book. Write a paper of your findings, comparing the thoughts of the clerics with James's theories.

- One of the concluding chapters of James's book deals with mysticism. Research three major organized religions (such as Buddhism, Taoism, Christianity, Islam, or Judaism). How does each define mysticism? Who are the primary mystics of each religion? How does the subject of mysticism differ from one religion to another?

---

lead to happiness. James believes that this state does not just mean the ability to laugh or to indulge oneself in pleasures but to maintain a persistent, enjoyable existence. It is more an inner happiness than an outer one, the kind of happiness that Whitman was able to portray in his poetry—a love of life. According to James, Whitman was able to write his poems in such a way that "a passionate and mystic ontological emotion suffuses" it and in the end persuades "the reader that men and women, life and death, and all things are divinely good."

However, there is a problem, according to James, if that healthy-minded person refuses to accept the existence of evil. In this case, the positive attitude has taken that person too far, refusing to accept reality. People who are so optimistic as to ignore the evil in life decline to even think about evil as that thinking, in and of itself, is also evil.

At the opposite end of the spectrum is what James refers to as the sick soul, an individual who maximizes evil. James writes that the question of

evil and the resultant unhappiness that it brings is hard to ignore, for even in the life of a most purely happy individual, death still awaits. Then there is also the question of the source of evil. Is God, the all-good creator, also responsible for evil and unhappiness? Does evil exist as part of the whole, never to be destroyed? Or is it a separate entity that humankind can work toward erasing from reality? A healthy-minded person, James reports, would have to believe in the latter, that is, that evil can be rid from the system, that it is not part of the whole.

For people who believe that evil is a part of the whole, there are different degrees to how it affects them. "There are people for whom evil means only a mal-adjustment with *things*," James writes, "a wrong correspondence of one's life with the environment." This is a more curable type of evil. However, for other individuals, the problem goes much deeper. There is "a wrongness or vice in his essential nature, which no alteration of the environment, or any superficial rearrangement of the inner self, can cure, and which requires a supernatural remedy.''

Spiritual Enthusiasm

There is a sense of happiness or excitement, James declares, in religious experiences. This excitement empowers the individual. It makes depression and melancholy fall away. Meaning is restored to life. There is created a deeper piety and desire to be charitable. Confidence and compassion for fellow beings is high. One becomes focused and earnest about one's goals, ridding one of inhibitions. Temptations that might formerly have deterred one from the path of saintliness are extinguished, and feelings of great happiness and freedom are immense. It is through the feelings, or rather through the observation of the one who experiences these feelings, that James measures religious experience. According to James, it is not the words of the individual claiming to have found religion, but rather through his or her being, empowered by strong emotions, that qualifies it as a truly religious experience.

Pragmatism

The term pragmatism in everyday use implies practicality and common sense. However, the pragmatism to which James refers is actually a word he himself coined in regards to a particular element in the study of philosophy. It was through pragmatism that James attempted to apply scientific inquiry to the process of thinking. In an article for *American Heritage,* Louis Menand states that James suggested that all one had to do ''was to ask what practical effects our choosing one view rather than another might have.'' James's intention in pragmatism, according to Menand, ''was to open a window, in what he regarded as an excessively materialistic and scientific age, for faith in God.''

In *The Varieties of Religious Experience*, James applies pragmatism to the concept of God, relating his own comfort in doing so because he can eliminate many of the philosophical attributes of the concept of God and maintain only those that have an effect on him. For example, James could not fathom any reason for God to have attributes of indivisibility, simplicity, superiority, and self-felicity in Himself, as these had no practical applications for James. He states that since they have no connections to an

individual's life, ''what vital difference can it possibly make to a man's religion whether they be true or false?''

Style

Since *The Varieties of Religious Experience* was originally delivered in the form of spoken lectures, the style of writing is dictated more by the rules of oration than by those of composition. A series of twenty separate lectures were given by James in 1901. In these lectures, James first presents his ideas, then defines their terms and provides examples to demonstrate the significance of his findings.

James talks directly to the audience in the first-person point of view. His arguments follow a logical path, sometimes using questions to lead his discussion forward and next providing the responses as he interprets them. Since his lectures offer extensive material that must be slowly assimilated, he breaks down his information into easily digestible portions. His use of examples not only adds significance to his theories but also offers a break in the intellectual discourse. The examples put a face on the concepts James is trying to convey and are like stories within stories, often encompassing extraordinary events.

The structure of James's lectures follows a pattern that begins with the basic understanding of religion and neurology and then slowly rises from the more practical to the highest elevations of the spiritual, concluding with lectures on saintliness, mysticism, and philosophy. In so doing, James builds a strong foundation of understanding. He provides a language for all who are listening to him, so they will completely understand his meaning. For example, he makes it very clear that in his talks, he is in no way referring to any specific religious practice or belief. His motive is not to discuss specific established religions and their beliefs. His goal is only to expound on the psychological and philosophical role of religious belief in the individual experience. By carefully defining his terms, he relaxes the audience and helps it more carefully focus on his development as he moves away from definition and begins discourse of more abstract concepts.

Historical Context

James's Contemporaries

Alfred Adler (1870–1937), an Austrian psychiatrist, began his studies with Sigmund Freud but eventually disagreed with Freud's emphasis on sexual trauma as the main source of mental disorders and parted ways with him. Adler's main theory was that people should be studied as a whole, as beings who spend their lives reacting to the environment, rather than as a summation of their drives and emotions. In respect to religion, he contended that human belief in a God was one way of aspiring toward perfection. His theories were expounded in his book *Neurotic Constitution* (1912).

Sigmund Freud (1856–1939), also an Austrian psychiatrist, is often called the father of psychoanalysis. His research on the unconscious still affects the study of psychology in the twenty-first century. His basic tenet was that people experience conflicts between what they desire and what are the confines of their societal customs. The development of religion, Freud contended, began with a child's need for a relationship with the father. Later in life, Freud published the book *The Future of Illusion* (1927), in which he debunked theories of religion on scientific grounds.

Carl Jung (1875–1961) was at one time a pupil of Freud, but like Adler, Jung also disagreed with Freud's emphasis on sexuality. Jung's interest was in the connection between the conscious and unconscious minds. One of his main theories stated there were two different properties of the unconscious; one was personal and the other was universal. Jung believed that humans have a natural religious function, and their psychic health depends on expressing it. His religious concepts can be found in his *Modern Man in Search of a Soul* (1933) and *Psychology and Religion* (1938).

Wilhelm Wundt (1832–1920) was born in Germany, the son of a Lutheran pastor. Like James, Wundt was interested in both psychology and philosophy. He did research at the University of Leipzig on sensation and perception—similar to what James was doing at the same time at Harvard, with both men being credited with beginning what eventually was referred to as experimental psychology. Later in his life, Wundt focused on cultural psychology by studying the mythologies, cultural practices, literature, and art of various societies. In *Elements of Folk Psychology: Outlines of a Psychological History of the Development of Mankind* (1916), Wundt develops his concepts of religion.

Political and Social Developments at the Turn of the Century

During the early 1900s, turmoil spread around the world. In the United States, great monopolies continued despite the passage in 1890 of the Sherman Antitrust Act. Unsafe working conditions at factories often resulted in death, and there were no protective laws in place to keep children out of the workplace. There were no mandatory laws to provide guaranteed education, and only 10 percent of the population graduated from high school. Civil rights for minorities did not exist, and lynchings were on the rise in the South. A woman's right to vote was not written into an amendment until 1919. Internationally, World War I was waiting on the horizon.

On the positive side, the Wright brothers were perfecting their flying machines and Henry Ford established the Ford Motor Company, which would produce the first affordable automobiles, greatly influencing the overall wealth of the United States, and dramatically changing American culture. American pop culture, fashion, and fads spread quickly overseas. The first electric typewriter was invented, as was the hamburger, ice cream cone, comic book, jukebox, and telephone Yellow Pages. New York City put its first taxis on the streets, and the first Rose Bowl and first World Series were played.

In 1901 Theodore Roosevelt became the twenty-sixth American president. He pursued an aggressive thrust to make the United States one of the world powers in order to protect national security. When he took office, U.S. naval power was only the fifth strongest in the world, but he increased U.S. military strength so that a few years later only Britain exceeded the size and capabilities of the U.S. Navy. The Roosevelt Corollary to the Monroe Doctrine, which Roosevelt wrote, began the United

Compare & Contrast

- **1910s:** Buddhism becomes popular in the West. Zen Buddhism is spread through the presentations of Japanese Zen leader D. T. Suzuki.

  1950s: June 30, 1956, the phrase "In God We Trust" is adopted as the U.S. national motto. In the following year it begins to appear on U.S. paper currency. It was already in use on certain coins since 1864.

  Today: Cardinal Francis Arinze, a Nigerian who is on the short list for candidates to succeed Pope John Paul II, travels around the world promoting inter-religious dialogue. He is the president of the Vatican's Pontifical Council for Interreligious Dialogue.

- **1910s:** Sigmund Freud publishes his book *The Interpretation of Dreams* in English in 1913, and the first journal devoted to psychology, *Journal of Applied Psychology,* begins publishing in 1917.

  1950s: In 1950, Alan M. Turing publishes his article "Computing Machinery and Intelligence" in the quarterly *Mind,* and the American Association of Psychology publishes the first *Code of Ethics of Psychologists* in 1953.

  Today: The 27th International Congress of Psychology is held in Stockholm, Sweden, in July 2000. A U.S. Labor Department census for the year 2000 reports that there are approximately 200,000 psychologists employed in the United States.

States' role as a so-called peacekeeper or policeman in the world.

Literature and the Arts in the Early 1900s

In 1900 Theodore Dreiser's novel *Sister Carrie* shocked the American public with its portrayal of a woman who uses her body and sexuality to attain success. In France, Auguste Rodin completed his sculpture *The Thinker,* while in Britain, Joseph Conrad published his novel *Lord Jim.* Also in Europe, Anton Checkhov produced his play *Uncle Vanya,* and Henri Matisse began the fauvist movement in painting, a form that integrated loud colors, primitive elements, and eccentric ideas on the canvas. A year later, another painter, Pablo Picasso, began his so-called blue period. Also in 1901, the first Nobel Prize in literature was awarded.

In 1903 the movie *The Great Train Robbery* excited audiences, who then demanded more fiction films. In the same year, Jack London wrote *The Call of the Wild.* Isadora Duncan opened the first school of modern dance in 1905 in Berlin. Audiences initially had a hard time understanding this dance form. In London, Richard Strauss presented his opera *Salome,* which included the shocking "Dance of the Seven Veils," a dance that ironically kept people filling the theater despite its so-called lewd expression. Several imitative versions of the opera and dance were performed throughout the United States and Europe in the years to come.

Joel Chandler Harris published *Uncle Remus and Br'er Rabbit* in 1906. Three years later, in 1909, Tchaikovsky's *Nutcracker Suite* was recorded and packaged, becoming the first commercial "album" produced. That same year, the *New York Times* published the first-ever movie review.

Critical Overview

When the world celebrated the one-hundredth anniversary of the publication of James's *The Varieties of Religious Experience,* it seemed upon rereading that James had written the book not only for the turn of the twentieth century but also for the turn of the twenty-first century. Listed as one of the most read books of the twentieth century, *The Varieties of Religious Experience* is experiencing a rebirth and new understanding. This reawakening to James's work has been so strong that it is described by Erin Leib in an article for the *New Republic* as a ''recent blizzard.'' In her article, Leib describes James as an ''obsessively religious man, who was committed to devising a philosophy that would provide a foundation for spiritual experience, and to opening up room for faith in an increasingly secular world.'' In mentioning James's book in particular, Leib comments that *The Varieties of Religious Experience* ''became one of the most widely read and most highly influential treatises on religion by an American.'' It did so, Leib notes, by ''inaugurat[ing] a Copernican turn in religious studies away from the objective terms of religion—God, the cosmos— toward the subjective human experience of religion.''

Charles Taylor—a professor of philosophy who, like James, has delivered the Gifford Lectures at the University of Edinburgh—has written a book on James titled *The Varieties of Religious Experience Today: William James Revisited* (2002). In an article for *Commonweal,* Taylor explains:

> It is almost a hundred years since William James delivered his celebrated Gifford Lectures in Edinburgh on *The Varieties of Religious Experience*. I want to look again at this remarkable book, reflecting on what it has to say to us at the turn of a new century.

Taylor continues, ''In fact it turns out to have a lot to say. It is astonishing how little dated it is. You can even find yourself forgetting that these lectures were delivered a hundred years ago.''

In the same article, Taylor states, ''James is our great philosopher of the cusp,'' referring to the space between the definition of religion as created by institutionalized religious practice and the ''gut feeling'' of the individual. The reason James's work remains so vibrant today, Taylor claims, ''is because James stands so nakedly and so volubly in this exposed spot.'' The book, says Taylor, has ''resonated'' for over a century and ''will go on doing so for many years to come.''

Carol Zaleski, a professor at Smith College, wrote an article about *The Varieties of Religious Experience* for *First Things: A Monthly Journal of Religion and Public Life.* In this article Zaleski states that *The Varieties of Religious Experience*

may not be James's best book, ''but it is our best book about religious experience, our best defense against skeptics, and our surest incitement to a genuine public dialogue about the significance of personal religious experience for our common life.'' Although Zaleski is a little disappointed that James does not find spiritual comfort in any organized religion, she nonetheless claims that James's ''great contribution is to make religion a live option for those estranged from traditional faith.''

Zaleski wrote another article for the *Christian Century,* in the form of a letter to James. In the beginning of her letter, she acknowledges that *The Varieties of Religious Experience* is ''the greatest modern book on personal religion.'' One of the reasons for this, she writes to James, is that ''You remain the unsurpassed defender of religious experience against theories that reduce it to the product of this or that implacable force.''

Criticism

Joyce Hart

Hart, with degrees in English literature and creative writing, focuses her published works on literary themes. In this essay, Hart reflects on James's discussions on sublime happiness and on his reference to Tolstoy's experience with melancholia to better illuminate James's definition of a religious state of mind.

William James begins his fourth lecture in *The Varieties of Religious Experience* with the question, ''What is human life's chief concern?'' Shortly thereafter he provides the answer, which is ''happiness.'' Happiness, James tells his readers, is the source behind everything that an individual does, so much so that the overall goal of life is to gain, keep, or recover happiness. It is not mere laughter of which James speaks. It is something that goes much deeper. It goes so deep that this kind of happiness might even be referred to as a religious experience. James clarifies that happiness itself is not religion, but ''we must admit that any persistent enjoyment may *produce* the sort of religion which consists in a grateful admiration of the gift of so happy an existence.'' Although happiness is not a religion, the ''more complex ways of experiencing religion'' are ways of ''producing happiness.'' But to what kind of happiness is James referring?

To better understand happiness, it might be a good idea to uncover first what James refers to as unhappiness. One of the best examples of this emotional state, or what James calls a ''religious melancholy,'' is provided through an excerpt from *My Confession* (1887) by famed Russian author Leo Tolstoy. Before offering Tolstoy's words, James, who defines Tolstoy's mental condition as anhedonia, or the ''passive loss of appetite for all life's values,'' expounds on Tolstoy's state of mind by describing how the world might have appeared to Tolstoy when he was in the midst of his depression. In this state, familiar things that used to inspire him suddenly lost all value. In such a world of no meaning, emotions are drained from the objects and experiences that surround the person involved. For example, where once the sunset might have stirred the emotions of someone, with its beauty or overwhelming sense of romance, it no longer holds significance. In its place is only the fact that the sun is setting; a rainbow of colors tints the sky; and night falls. That is it. It is an event that does not elicit any feelings. There is no importance in one event over another. James compares the ability of an object to stir emotions to the power of love. A woman can stand in front of a man whom she does not love and no matter what that man does in her favor, if love is not there, it will never be there. It cannot be rationalized into existence. Conversely, if a woman loves a man, no matter what he does, he arouses her emotions. In other words, mental states come involuntarily. However, when certain emotions take over a person's mind, they change that person's life. The emotions, or passions of life, are gifts, James writes. They are also ''non-logical.'' They cannot be explained by the intellect.

Tolstoy seems to agree with James, as he relates that his depression made no sense to him at all. There were no elements in his life on which the melancholy could be blamed. It came over him at a time in his life when he was enjoying tremendous success. He was also very much in love with his wife; his children were healthy; and the family lived in a beautiful home. However, for some reason the value of these things was totally withdrawn from him, to the point that Tolstoy considered suicide. What did it matter that he had all these things,

St. John of the Cross, a sixteenth-century cleric and mystic theologian discussed by James in his lectures on saintliness

Tolstoy began to wonder, when in the end he would die and all these things would fade away? No matter how hard Tolstoy tried to reason with his despair, the only concept that came to him was, as quoted in James, ''the meaningless absurdity of life.'' So why continue it?

Tolstoy had lost the gift, the abstraction that gives value to life, and no matter what he did with his rational mind, he could not find it. His passageway out of his depression came to him gradually, in what he refers to as a thirst for God, a feeling that rose out of his heart, not his intellect.

So there are now two aspects that help to define this feeling of happiness that motivates all beings. First it is not something that can be thought up. It has nothing to do with the intellect. Rather, it comes from the heart and it comes as a gift. James also relates that this gift—which physiologists of his day stated came from the personal organism, while theologians said it came from the grace of God—will give the lucky person who receives it ''a new sphere of power.'' When all else fails in the outward world, the person on whom this gift is bestowed will have an inward ''enthusiastic temper of espousal''

What Do I Read Next?

- A reading of Bruce Kuklick's collection *William James: Writings 1902–1910* (1988) offers a comprehensive understanding of the range of James's views. This work also includes addresses on Emerson and James's famous essay "The Moral Equivalent of War."

- James's *Essays in Religion and Morality* (1982) extends the concepts covered in *The Varieties of Religious Experience. Essays in Religion and Morality* was published by James's *alma mater,* Harvard University, and includes an introduction by John J. McDermott, a Jamesian scholar.

- *The Meaning of Truth: A Sequel to "Pragmatism"* (1909) was one of the last books by James to be published before his death. This book delves into the most important of James's philosophical discourses.

- James's most significant study, *The Principles of Psychology* (1905), was one of the first comprehensive textbooks about the study of psychology, leading to James earning the title of "father of psychology."

- James was close to his brother Henry, a novelist who spent most of his life living in Europe. The brothers' correspondence is collected in *William and Henry James: Selected Letters* (1997), which offers an insider's look at their relationship and shared concepts.

- To gain a further understanding of the development of religious experience in the United States, read *The Republic of Many Mansions: Foundations of American Religious Thought* (1990) by Denise Lardner Carmody and John Tully Carmody. The book contains a study of Thomas Jefferson's religious thoughts as well as those of James and the Puritans, and other general readings on the topic of pragmatism.

- In *The Unity of William James's Thought* (2002), Wesley Cooper, a professor of philosophy, argues against the dismissal of James's philosophical discourse by traditional philosophers who claim that James's background in philosophy does not go deep enough to be considered legitimate. Cooper finds evidence to the contrary, demonstrating that James writes on different levels at different times, incorporating his doctrine of pure experience into his theories of psychology and pragmatism.

---

that will redeem and vivify him or her. While those without the gift of happiness will be totally destroyed, the gifted person will triumph.

James adds more information about this emotion that colors and fills life with value by giving it the attribute of solemnity. The concept of solemnity, James admits, is hard to define, but nonetheless, he attempts to shine a little light on the topic. "It is never crude," he writes. It is also never simple. He states that ironically "it seems to contain a certain measure of its own opposite in solution." In other words, within this state of solemn happiness is also the state of sadness, as if the two define one another. This gives the reader a better grasp on the depth of happiness to which James refers. It is

now easier to understand how this happiness is not the simple laughter at some joke. Solemn happiness is not caused by what James refers to as any of the animal pleasures of life, those of the body. It is something more sublime and sustaining. "This sort of happiness in the absolute and everlasting," James writes, "is what we find nowhere but in religion."

Only as a religious experience does happiness penetrate a person so deeply. This religious happiness is not a momentary escape from a person's hardships or fears. Again James states that it is hard to explain this kind of happiness; that a person will only understand it if she or he experiences it first-hand. However, he does say that solemn happiness is so great that it causes a person to not even consider escape, because somewhere deep inside, this person knows that whatever is presently considered a challenge has already, on some other level, been overcome. It gives the individual a sense that ''a higher happiness holds a lower unhappiness in check.'' An individual who experiences this kind of happiness is also not afraid of challenges and in many instances welcomes them. Along with the gift of solemn happiness also comes the willingness for self-sacrifice and surrender. Without the gift, a person might be willing to sacrifice and might even do so without complaint; but the person who has this form of sublime happiness will go out of his or her way to seek such challenges, believing that in doing so his or her happiness will increase.

Returning to Tolstoy's story, readers will find that in his healing process, Tolstoy rekindled his sense of faith. ''Faith is the sense of life,'' he writes. ''It is the force by which we live.'' Taking Tolstoy's comment and adding it to James's concept that happiness underlies everything that people do, readers have to conclude that faith and happiness are related. James actually insinuates this in his narrative on Tolstoy when he writes that Tolstoy struggled with his depression because he was only considering the finite objects of life. This was all that his rational mind could do. It was not until Tolstoy freed his thinking to include the emotions, or irrational sentiments, that he was able to allow faith to enter his consciousness. Not until Tolstoy recognized that the emptiness he was feeling was due to his concentration to please only his ''animal needs'' was he able to release himself. By changing his focus to his higher, more sacred needs, Tolstoy was able to restore his faith. James writes, ''therein lay happiness again.''

The infinite, as represented by the concept of an everlasting God, allowed Tolstoy to broaden his ideas about life. Once he concentrated on the feeling of God's presence, ''glad aspirations towards life'' arose inside of him. After this, Tolstoy simplified his life. He dropped out of the society of intellectuals whose main purpose was to understand living only in context of the rational. He was then able to better understand and appreciate the life of the ''peasants, and has felt right and happy . . . ever since.''

James claims that Tolstoy's change in life was based on an inner conflict. His soul craved more than the surface happiness of the intellectual society of which he was a major member. He needed a period of deeper inner reflection in order to fully

> ❝ **If happiness is a gift that one cannot find merely in a rational exploration, maybe James is implying that through deep introspection, a person might, in the least, prepare the way for that gift to appear and thus create his or her own variety of religious experience.** ❞

comprehend how shallow his happiness was. He needed to discover his soul's ''genuine habitat and vocation,'' as James puts it. He had to find the truth of his soul. With this statement, James seems to be inferring that it is in finding the truth of one's soul that one finds happiness—the deep, spiritual, and sublime form of this emotion. If happiness is a gift that one cannot find merely in a rational exploration, maybe James is implying that through deep introspection, a person might, in the least, prepare the way for that gift to appear and thus create his or her own variety of religious experience.

Source: Joyce Hart, Critical Essay on *The Varieties of Religious Experience,* in *Nonfiction Classics for Students,* Gale, 2003.

Candyce Norvell

Norvell is an independent educational writer who specializes in English and literature and who has done graduate work in religion. In this essay, Norvell outlines five key, recurring issues in debate over religious experience and how James's discussion of these issues is relevant to today's readers.

No book becomes a classic unless it has something to say to generations of readers. One of the remarkable things about *The Varieties of Religious Experience* is how much of it is still timely one hundred years after its first publication, in spite of massive changes in society, culture, and science.

An important reason for the book's lasting relevance is that it deals with many of the polarities that perennially characterize debate about religious experience: psychology versus spirituality, naturalism versus supernaturalism, and so on. Even more

> **In recent years, Americans have seen some of their most respected religious authorities arrested for horrific crimes and humiliated in the media for immoral behavior. Understandably, this causes some people to conclude that religion has no power to improve people."**

important, though, is *how* James deals with these issues. His rational, detached approach sets him apart from a large majority of commentators both in his own time and today, making his book a useful tool for thoughtful readers seeking to make sense of religious arguments that are often fueled more by emotions than facts.

The defining characteristic of discussions of religious matters is that they tend to be extremely polarized. The people who bother to debate religion at all are people who have strong feelings about it. As well, most of them have entrenched positions that they are committed to defending. For example, many commentators are members of the clergy. Whatever opinions they hold have been taught to them by authority figures at least from their school days and possibly from their childhoods. Their careers, their paychecks, their acceptance in their social circles and even within their families are all dependent upon their continued embrace and energetic defense of whatever religious ideas they profess. If they were to admit uncertainty or error on any substantive issue, all the structures of their lives would crumble. This is why religious debate is so often highly emotional and even vicious. The participants have everything to lose, and therefore they defend their long-held beliefs at all cost. Too often, facts and realities that seem to contradict their beliefs are suppressed, denied, or twisted beyond recognition; objective reality is sacrificed to subjective beliefs.

Of course, the same phenomenon occurs on the side of anti-religionists. Psychologists, for example—whose careers and social networks often also depend upon their loyalties to certain beliefs—may set themselves up against religious interpretations of life (more about this below), refuse to confront facts that do not fit their dearly held theories, and label religious experience as "disease."

This makes James a rarity. He is an objective, emotionally detached commentator. He was a man who, by his own account, did not experience the supernatural and ecstatic states he writes about, yet he had no desire to deem them invalid or pathological just because they were foreign to him. He was a psychologist who was more interested in an accurate understanding of human experience than he was in elevating his own discipline above the claims of religion. He comes to the discussion not as someone with a position to defend but as someone seeking to understand a particular dimension of human experience. This makes James a valuable mediator of ideas that are often spoken of as being irreconcilable. He subjects the polarities of religious debate to logic and observation. In some cases, he finds that what had seemed to be opposing ideas can be reconciled. In others, he makes a clearly reasoned case for one idea over another.

The remainder of this essay will briefly examine five issues that are as divisive today as they were when James wrote, and James's position on each one.

In James's day, psychology and religion regarded each other as irrelevant at best and as destructive at worst. The leading voices of the two disciplines saw themselves as being engaged in a battle for the same turf, which psychologists called the psyche and religionists called the soul. Each side claimed to have the authoritative truth about the nature of the psyche/soul. To give one important example, conversion experiences sprang from the individual's own mind and were often pathological according to psychology, but had a divine source and a supremely beneficial purpose according to religion.

Although James was a psychologist (among other professions), his conclusions are that there is no real, inevitable polarity between psychology and religion and that religion has things to teach psychology. James reiterates throughout his book that psychology, like other sciences, is incomplete; it does not yet understand all human phenomena. Therefore, he reasons, it is inappropriate for psychology to diagnose and label religious experiences; and it is highly inappropriate to label as pathological a phenomenon such as conversion that has beneficial results. (James's definition of a conversion experience is limited, and he is well aware that not every emotional experience is in fact a spiritual experience that bears the expected fruit.)

Readers who are familiar with the tenor of modern psychology know that it still is often in conflict with religion. In his introduction to a collection of essays on *The Varieties of Religious Experience* that appeared in the *Journal of Consciousness Studies,* editor Michel Ferrari writes that one of the essayists "notes that *Varieties* promotes the radical idea that religious experience has something important to contribute to psychology and wonders why we are no closer to implementing this idea one hundred years after the publication of *Varieties.*"

James's efforts at peacemaking may have been ignored by psychology and religion as institutions, but they have no doubt been helpful to countless individuals seeking to make sense of the institutions' competing claims.

The debate between naturalism and supernaturalism raged in James's times and rages on today. Some people believe in supernatural forces and events; some do not. James patiently explains that if an idea or hypothesis cannot be proven, it does not logically follow that the idea is false. It may be that the available methods of seeking proof are inadequate. The history of the humble aspirin tablet is often used to explain this idea. Unlike today's new medications, aspirin was widely used for about a century before it was subjected to any controlled testing, because such tests simply had not yet been developed. During this time, some physicians and others claimed that aspirin had no efficacy beyond that of a placebo; no one could prove that it worked, they reasoned, and therefore it did not work. When more sophisticated tests were finally available, researchers were able to discover exactly how aspirin worked to alleviate pain and to understand why it was so effective, as millions of "faithful" users had long known. James makes a similar case for the possibility of supernatural forces and experiences; the fact that science cannot (yet) apprehend them is not proof that they are not there.

The medical scientists and intellectuals of James's day generally thought that so-called supernatural experiences were actually side effects of physical disturbances such as fever or trauma. In addition to being a psychologist, James was also an expert in anatomy, and so the medical scientists were part of his intellectual community. Once again, however, he was willing to part ways with them when logic and facts led him to do so. He took the view that science should not call invalid what its methods were incapable of measuring, and based on his own observations and research (and against his own lack of experience of the supernatural) he concluded that the supernatural does exist apart from natural causes such as illness.

Having set himself against his own professional and intellectual communities by making a case for spirituality apart from psychology and for the supernatural, James goes on to set himself against the mainstream religious authorities of his time by endorsing religious pluralism over the exclusive truth-claims of any one religion.

James's research showed him that adherents of many different religions—Christianity, Buddhism, Hinduism, and others—have remarkably similar religious experiences with virtually identical results in the lives of the affected individuals. Therefore, he concluded that it is not logical that one of these religions is true and the others are false.

On this issue, the passage of time has brought a shift toward James's point of view. But the issue is still a divisive one in an American culture that is home to many religions, some of which make competing claims to exclusive truth. Here, too, James's voice is one of calm reason amid a sea of shouts.

Positive thinking, then called "mind-cure," was all the rage in James's day. In the simplest terms, the idea of mind-cure is that evil does not really exist except as an idea in people's minds and that to banish thoughts of evil from one's mind is to be free of all evil. The definition of evil is broad, including physical injury and illness as well as acts of violence. According to mind-cure, any person who never thinks of such things will never fall victim to them.

This issue remains relevant and much debated today because a strain of mind-cure thinking runs through many ideas and philosophies that come under the broad heading "New Age." In the last half of the twentieth century, much of American society embraced, or at least flirted with the idea that all morality is relative and nothing is good or evil in an absolute sense. Often bundled with this philosophy was the concept that individuals were the creators of their own destinies and had the power, through positive thinking and other similar methods, to determine what would happen to them.

As he often does, James takes a middle course. He acknowledges that the many firsthand reports of success with these methods are evidence that there is some truth in the philosophies underlying them. But he concludes that these philosophies give only a partially accurate view of reality; evil does have objective existence, he argues, and cannot always be escaped under any circumstances. His brief discussion of evil is a valuable contribution to humankind's efforts to answer what may be the most difficult questions of all: Does evil exist, and if so, why?

Finally, there is one further often-debated issue that James addresses in a way that can provide guidance to today's readers. It was true in his time as it is now that people who are trying to evaluate the claims of religion are often faced with a stark contrast between what a religion teaches and how its members behave. Religious seekers who have been assured that adopting a religion will make them better people are more than occasionally disappointed to find that long-time adherents of that very same religion are no better than they themselves are, and perhaps worse. In recent years, Americans have seen some of their most respected religious authorities arrested for horrific crimes and humiliated in the media for immoral behavior. Understandably, this causes some people to conclude that religion has no power to improve people.

James confronts this issue in its particularly American form. American Christianity, more than that of other countries, has focused on the conversion experience as the culmination of spiritual life. So James tackles the question of why people who claim to have had such experiences sometimes behave no differently than they did in the past. The painful spectacle, for example, of baseball player Daryl Strawberry's serial conversions and alternating periods of drug abuse and criminal activity leave many sincere seekers either deeply confused or completely skeptical about the reality and meaning of religious experience.

James's discussions of the nature of the conversion experience and its place in the larger context of spiritual life, and of the broader issue of emotional experience and its relation to moral and behavioral reform, help readers grapple with these issues in a thoughtful, sophisticated way.

Religion and religious experience are difficult subjects to come to terms with, as even James acknowledges. Yet the urge to come to terms with them is virtually universal. A large majority of individuals, at some time in their lives, find themselves engaged with these issues. James's book is a true classic in that it provides valuable help in thinking about complex issues that, in various guises, face every generation of readers.

Source: Candyce Norvell, Critical Essay on *The Varieties of Religious Experience,* in *Nonfiction Classics for Students,* Gale, 2003.

Charles Taylor

In the following essay, Taylor explores the continued relevance of The Varieties of Religious Experience, *finding its ideas concerning the need for spiritual belief in an age of science fitting for today's world.*

It is almost a hundred years since William James delivered his celebrated Gifford Lectures in Edinburgh on *The Varieties of Religious Experience.* I want to look again at this remarkable book, reflecting on what it has to say to us at the turn of a new century.

In fact it turns out to have a lot to say. It is astonishing how little dated it is. You can even find yourself forgetting that these lectures were delivered a hundred years ago.

What was James's take on religion? What was the wider agenda of which it was part? Like any sensitive intellectual of his time and place, James had to argue against the voices, within and without, that held that religion was a thing of the past, that one could no longer in conscience believe in this kind of thing in an age of science. A passage in *Varieties* gives a sense of what is at stake in this inner debate. James is speaking of those who are for one reason or another incapable of religious conversion. He refers to some whose ''inaptitude'' is intellectual in origin:

> Their religious faculties may be checked in their natural tendency to expand, by beliefs about the world that are inhibitive, the pessimistic and materialistic beliefs, for example, within which so many good souls, who in former times would have freely indulged their religious propensities, find themselves nowadays, as it were, frozen; or the agnostic vetoes upon faith as something weak and shameful, under which so many of us today lie cowering, afraid to use our instincts.

A fuller discussion of these ''agnostic vetoes,'' and the answer to them, occurs in James's essay ''The Will to Believe.'' Here it is plain that the main source of the vetoes is a kind of ethics of belief illustrated, James contends, in the work of English mathematician and philosopher William Clifford (1845–79). Clifford's *The Ethics of Belief* starts from a notion of what proper scientific procedure is: Never turn your hypotheses into accepted theories until the evidence is adequate. It then promotes this into a moral precept for life in general.

The underlying picture of our condition, according to Clifford, is that we find certain hypotheses more pleasing, more flattering, more comforting, and are thus tempted to believe them. It is the path of manliness, courage, and integrity to turn our backs on these facile comforts, and face the universe as it really is. But so strong are the temptations to deviate from this path that we must make it an unbreakable precept never to give our assent unless the evidence compels it. James quotes Clifford: "It is wrong always, and everywhere, and for anyone, to believe anything upon insufficient evidence."

James opposes to this his own counterprinciple:

Our passional nature not only lawfully may, but must, decide an option between propositions, whenever it is a genuine option that cannot by its nature be decided on intellectual grounds; for to say, under such circumstances, "Do not decide, but leave the question open," is itself a passional decision—just like deciding yes or no—and is attended with the same risk of losing the truth.

Backing this principle is James's own view of the human predicament. Clifford assumes that there is only one road to truth: We put the hypotheses that appeal to us under severe tests, and those that survive are worthy of adoption—the kind of procedure whose spirit was recaptured in our time by Karl Popper's method of conjectures and refutation. To put it dramatically, we can win the right to believe a hypothesis only by first treating it with maximum suspicion and hostility. James holds, on the contrary, that there are some domains in which truths will be hidden from us unless we go at least halfway toward them. Do you like me or not? If I am determined to test this by adopting a stance of maximum distance and suspicion, the chances are that I will forfeit the chance of a positive answer. An analogous phenomenon on the scale of the whole society is social trust; doubt it root and branch, and you will destroy it.

But can the same kind of logic apply to religion, that is, to a belief in something that by hypothesis is way beyond our power to create? James thinks it can.

What is created is not God or the eternal, but there is a certain grasp of these, and a certain succor from these that can never be ours unless we open

Jonathan Edwards, whose teachings James draws on throughout his lectures

ourselves to them in faith. James is, in a sense, building on the Augustinian insight that in certain domains love and self-opening enable us to understand what we would never grasp otherwise.

What does that tell us about what the path of rationality consists in for someone who stands on the threshold, deciding whether he should permit himself to believe in God? On one side is the fear of believing something false if he follows his instincts here. But on the other there is the hope of opening out what are now inaccessible truths through the prior step of faith. Faced with this double possibility it is no longer so clear that Clifford's ethic is the appropriate one, because it was taking account of only the first possibility. As James notes,

I, therefore, cannot see my way to accepting the agnostic rules for truth-seeking, or willfully agree to keep my willing nature out of the game. I cannot do so for the plain reason, that *a rule of thinking which would absolutely prevent me from acknowledging certain kinds of truth if those kinds of truth were really there, would be an irrational rule.*

The minimal form of James's argument is, then, that the supposed superior rationality of the "agnostic veto" on belief—don't believe in God until you have overwhelming evidence—disappears

> **James has in a sense opened up to view an important part of the struggle between belief and unbelief in modern culture."**

once you see that there is an option between two risks of loss of truth.

Everybody should be free to choose his own kind of risk. But this minimal form easily flips into a stronger variant, which is captured by the italicized clause I have just quoted. Taking the agnostic stance could here be taxed as the less rational one.

This is similar grounds to those laid out in Pascal's famous wager. James evokes this early in *Varieties* and treats it rather caustically. But on reflection, this may be because the Pascalian form is specially directed to converting the interlocutor to Catholicism, to "Masses and holy water." But if one takes the general form of Pascal's argument here—that you should weight two risks not only by their probabilities but also by their prospective "payoffs"—then James himself seems to entertain something of the sort. Religion is not only a "forced option," that is, one in which there is no third way, no way of avoiding choice, but it is also a "momentous option. We are supposed to gain, even now, by our belief, and to lose by our nonbelief, a certain vital good." The likeness increases when we reflect that Pascal never thought of his wager argument as standing alone, appealing as it were purely to the betting side of our nature, to the instincts that take over when we enter the casinos at Las Vegas. He, too, holds the Augustinian view that in matters divine we need to love before we know.

But the issue could be put in other terms again. The single-risk view of the agnostics seems more plausible than James's double-risk thesis because they take for granted that our desires can only be an obstacle to our finding the truth. The crucial issue is thus the place of "our volitional nature" in the theoretical realm. The very idea that things will go better in the search for truth if you keep out passion, desire, and willing seems utterly implausible to James—not just for the reason he thinks he has demonstrated, that certain truths only open to us as a

result of our commitment, but also because it seems so clear to him that we never operate this way.

So one way he frames the issue is that the agnostic vetoers are asking that he "willfully agree to keep my willing nature out of the game." But from another standpoint, neither side is really doing this. Agnosticism "is not intellect against all passions, then; it is only intellect with one passion laying down its law." To put it in the harsh language of a later politics, those who claim to be keeping passion out are suffering from false consciousness. This is not the way the mind works at all. Rationalism gives an account of only a part of our mental life, and one that is "relatively superficial."

> It is the part which has the prestige undoubtedly, for it has the loquacity, it can challenge you for proofs, and chop logic, and put you down with words. But it will fail to convince or convert you all the same, if your dumb intuitions are opposed to its conclusions. If you have intuitions at all, they come from a deeper level of your nature than the loquacious level which rationalism inhabits. Your whole subconscious life, your impulses, your faiths, your needs, your divinations, have prepared the premises, of which your consciousness now feels the weight of the result; and something in you absolutely knows that that result must be truer than any logic-chopping rationalistic talk, however clever, that may contradict it.

James has in a sense opened up to view an important part of the struggle between belief and unbelief in modern culture. We can see it, after a fashion, from both sides of the fence: even though James has himself come down on one side, we can still feel the force of the other side. Of course, the objections to belief are not only on epistemological grounds. There are also those who feel that the God of theism has utterly failed the challenge of theodicy: how we can believe in a good and omnipotent God, given the state of the world?

But if we keep to the epistemological-moral issue of the ethics of belief, James clarifies why it always seems to end in a standoff. (1) Each side is drawing on very different sources, and (2) our culture as a whole cannot seem to get to a point where one of these no longer speaks to us. And yet (3) we cannot seem to function at all unless we relate to one or the other.

The reason the argument is so difficult, and so hard to join, is that each side stands within its own view of the human moral predicament. The various facets of each stance support each other, so that there seems nowhere you can justifiably stand outside. The agnostic view propounds some picture (or range of pictures) of the universe and human nature. This has going for it that it can claim to result from "science," with all the prestige that this carries with it. It can even look from the inside as though this was all you need to say. But from the outside it isn't at all clear that what everyone could agree are the undoubted findings of modern natural science quite add up to a proof of, say, materialism, or whatever the religion-excluding view is.

From the inside the "proof" seems solid, because certain interpretations are ruled out on the grounds that they seem "speculative" or "metaphysical." From the outside, this looks like a classical *petitio principii*. But from the inside the move seems unavoidable, because it is powered by certain ethical views. These are the ones that James laid bare: It is wrong, uncourageous, unmanly, a kind of self-indulgent cheating, to have recourse to this kind of interpretation, which we know appeals to something in us, offers comfort, or meaning, and which we therefore should fend off, unless absolutely driven to them by the evidence, which is manifestly not the case. The position holds firm because it locks together a scientific-epistemological view and a moral one.

From the other side, the same basic phenomena show up, but in an entirely different shape. One of the crucial features that justifies aversion to certain interpretations from the agnostic standpoint, namely that they in some way attract us, shows up from the believer's standpoint as what justifies our interest. And that very much for the reasons which James explores, namely that this attraction is the hint that there is something important here which we need to explore further, that this exploration can lead us to something of vital significance, which would otherwise remain closed to us. Epistemology and ethics (in the sense of intuitions about what is of crucial importance) combine here.

From this standpoint, the agnostic's closure is self-inflicted, the claim that there is nothing here which ought to interest us a kind of self-fulfilling prophecy. A similar accusation of circularity is hurled in the other direction. The believer is thought to have invented the delusion that beguiles him.

As we saw, the attraction of certain feelings and intuitions has a totally different significance in the two stances. This totality forces a choice; one cannot accord the two rival meanings to these crucial features at the same time. You can't really sit on the fence, because you need some reading of these features to get on with life.

And yet both these stances remain possible to many people in our world. Secularists once hoped that with the advance of science and enlightenment, and the articulation of a new, humanist ethic, the illusory nature of religion would be more and more apparent, and its attractions would fade, indeed, give way to repulsion. Many believers thought that unbelief was so clearly a willed blindness that people would one day wake up and see through it once and for all. But this is not how it has worked out, not even perhaps how it could work out. People go on feeling a sense of unease at the world of unbelief: some sense that something big, something important has been left out, some level of profound desire has been ignored, some greater reality outside us has been closed off. The articulations given to this unease are very varied, but it persists, and they recur in ever more ramified forms. But at the same time, the sense of dignity, control, adulthood, autonomy, connected to unbelief go on attracting people, and seem set to do so into an indefinite future.

What is more, a close attention to the debate seems to indicate that most people feel both pulls. They have to go one way, but they never fully shake off the call of the other. So the faith of believers is fragilized, not just by the fact that other people, equally intelligent, often equally good and dedicated, disagree with them, but also by the fact that they can still see themselves as reflected in the other perspective, that is, as drawn by a too-indulgent view of things. For what believer doesn't have the sense that her view of God is too simple, too anthropocentric, too indulgent? We all lie to some extent "cowering" under "the agnostic vetoes upon faith as something weak and shameful."

On the other side, the call to faith is still there as an understood temptation. Even if we think that it no longer applies to us, we see it as drawing others. Part of the great continuing interest of James's century-old work is that it lays out the dynamics of this battle so well and clearly. He is on one side, but he helps you imagine what it's like to be on either. In one way, we might interpret him as having wanted to show that you ought to come down on one side, the stronger thesis I offered above; but the weaker reading is just that he wanted to rebut the idea that reason forces you to the agnostic choice. As Edward Madden puts it in his introduction to *The Will to Believe,* James might be seen as arguing really for a "right to believe"; the right to follow one's own gut instinct in this domain, free of an intimidation grounded in invalid arguments.

What is especially striking about this account is that it brings out the bare issue so starkly, uncomplicated by further questions. It gives a stripped-down version of the debate; and this in two ways, both of which connect centrally to James's take on religion as experience. First, precisely because he abandons so much of the traditional ground of religion, because he has no use for collective connections through sacraments or ways of life, because the intellectual articulations are made secondary, the key point—what to make of the gut instinct that there is something more?—stands out very clearly.

And this allows us to see the second way in which James focuses the debate. It is after all to do with religious experience, albeit in a sense somewhat more generic than James's. As one stands on the cusp between the two great options, it is all a matter of the sense you have that there is something more, bigger, outside you. Now whether, granted you take the faith branch, this remains "religious experience" in James's special sense, steering clear of collective connections and over-theorization, is a question yet to be determined. But as you stand on the cusp, all you have to go on is a (very likely poorly articulated) gut feeling.

James is our great philosopher of the cusp. He tells us more than anyone else about what it's like to stand in that open space and feel the winds pulling you now here, now there. He describes a crucial site of modernity and articulates the decisive drama enacted there. It took very exceptional qualities to do this. Very likely it needed someone who had been through a searing experience of "morbidity" as James had been, and had come out the other side. But it also needed someone of wide sympathy and extraordinary powers of phenomenological description; further, it needed someone who could feel and articulate the continuing ambivalence in himself. It probably also needed someone who had ultimately come down, with whatever inner tremors, on the faith side; but this may be a bit of believers' chauvinism that I am adding to the equation.

In any event, it is because James stands so nakedly and so volubly in this exposed spot that his work has resonated for a hundred years, and will go on doing so for many years to come.

Source: Charles Taylor, "Risking Belief: Why William James Still Matters," in *Commonweal*, Vol. 129, No. 5, March 8, 2002, pp. 14–17.

John E. Smith

In the following excerpt, Smith discusses James's psychological approach to religion.

I. The Experimental Approach and the Generic Meaning of Religion

Whatever philosophical conclusions were to result from his inquiry, James was convinced that a psychological approach was necessary because of the intimate connection religion bears to individual, personal experience. It was for this reason that he turned to works of piety, autobiographies, confessions, and diaries for his primary material. He made clear at the outset that the question as to what the religious propensities are and what their philosophical significance may be represent two distinct and different orders of question. This distinction in turn translates itself into the difference between determining the origin and nature of something and seeking for its meaning or importance. The former he called an existential proposition and the latter a judgment of value. James held that neither "can be deduced immediately from the other," but that the two can be connected through a theory specifying what peculiarities a feeling, state of mind, or belief taken as fact would have to possess in order to have value for some purpose.

As is well known, James rejected "medical materialism," by which he meant the attempt to "explain" states of mind and their significance for the one who has them through the individual's physical constitution. The conversion experience of Saint Paul, for example, would, on this approach, be understood through his epileptic symptoms. In opposition to this type of analysis, James insisted that causes and origins do not furnish the key to the meaning and value of experience; we must look instead to the fruits of our experience, not excluding the immediate delight we take in it. James's three criteria for judging these fruits—immediate luminousness, philosophical reasonableness, and moral helpfulness—owe much to what he had learned from such works as Edwards' *Treatise Concerning Religious Affections* and the writings of Saint Teresa. James was under no illusion about the difficulty of applying these criteria. These tests, as Perry has pointed out, have roots in James's own philosophy, but it would be a mistake to suppose that he imposed them solely on his own initiative, for they reflect as well the criteria he saw being used by those engaged in assessing the validity of their own religious experience.

In marking out the topic, James made it clear that his central concern would be religion as it appears in the life and experience of the individual, in contrast to institutional and theological concerns. This emphasis is most evident in the well-known working definition of "religion" proposed for the purpose of the lectures—"*the feelings, acts, and experiences of individual men in their solitude, so far as they apprehend themselves to stand in relation to whatever they may consider the divine.*" In a way that is reminiscent of Tillich's characterization of religion as "ultimate concern," James supplemented his definition by calling religion "a man's total reaction upon life," but with the understanding that it must be "solemn" as opposed to a trifling or cynical type of response. In his contrast of religion with morality, James, seeking to lay hold of what is distinctive of religion, set forth one of his deepest insights into the religious dimension.

For James the moral personality is one motivated by objective ends and not merely by personal considerations; dedication to these ends he saw as heroic because it calls for energy and may bring hardship and pain. James saw morality as a kind of cosmic patriotism always in need of *volunteers*. He chose that term advisedly because it focuses on the distinctive feature of the moral hero—"the effort of volition." "The moralist," writes James, "must hold his breath and keep his muscles tense" in a stance toward life which is akin to an "athletic attitude." This attitude, in James's view, has its own value and is sufficient if all goes well, but it seemed to him that the moral personality lacks something that the religious man enjoys. James believed that the insufficiency of morality becomes manifest when the athletic attitude breaks down in the face of the decay of our bodies, or when a morbid fear arises from a sense of powerlessness and the failure of our purposes. To sustain life under these circumstances we need consolation in our weakness and a feeling that there is a spirit in the universe that recognizes and secures our life despite our shortcomings. James saw at this point what many have come to recognize as the absolutely distinctive feature of the religious: "There is a state of mind known to religious men, but to no other, in which the will to assert ourselves and hold our own has been displaced by a willingness to close our mouths and be as nothing in the floods and water-spouts of God. . . . Fear is not held in abeyance as it is by mere morality, it is positively expunged and washed away." This religious feeling, the "gift of grace" which cannot be commanded at will, James

> **As James rightly saw, religion is not something that can be understood by attending only to the individual self. . . . There he refers to the individual standing in *relation* to whatever is taken to be 'the divine,' and this means a response to a reality *standing beyond the self*—the unseen order."**

regarded as an addition to the person's life in the form of a special happiness that goes beyond finite escapes, reliefs, and liberations. As James correctly saw, those who think of religion largely in terms of an "escape" miss the essential point; from the religious standpoint there is no need for escape because of the firm conviction that the evil of the world has been *permanently* overcome. How religion annuls annihilation is said to be "religion's secret," and to understand it one must be a religious person of "the extreme type."

We shall, of course, have more dealings with surrender in connection with the sick soul and regeneration. It is sufficient now to emphasize James's concern to grasp what belongs, to religion as such, in contrast to those states of mind which "fall short" of that mark. James was well aware that morality requires a surrender of petty and egotistical concerns, but he regarded the *form* of the surrender in religion as unique. In religion, he claimed, surrender is "positively espoused" in an attitude of joy; in other frames of mind surrender may be accepted as a necessity and sacrifice endured without complaint, but the surplus of joy is missing. It is remarkable indeed and a testimony to James's willingness to follow the facts that, despite his strong commitment to the moral and strenuous life, he nevertheless recognized the limits of moral endeavor and had a genuine appreciation for the religious insight that tells us there are goods in human life only to be attained by surrender or "letting go."

As James rightly saw, religion is not something that can be understood by attending only to the individual self, a fact underlined in his working definition. There he refers to the individual standing in *relation* to whatever is taken to be "the divine," and this means a response to a reality *standing beyond the self*—the unseen order. Religion in the broadest terms involves the belief that there is, an unseen order and that our supreme good is found in harmoniously adjusting ourselves to it. Here he was echoing the view, well established among philosophers and historians of religion, that the most ancient and pervasive conception of the divine is to be found in the idea of a *sacred order* embracing justice and truth and presiding over human destiny. James repeatedly insisted that whatever other beliefs religion may include, the conviction that reality is not exhausted by the visible world is absolutely essential.

Belief in the unseen world has special significance for James because it shows our capacity to respond to what is in consciousness as an object not of the senses but of thought alone, and he was interested in determining how the sentiment of reality gradually adheres to what comes before us in the form of pure ideas for which there is no corresponding model in any past experience. In passages that may indeed sound strange coming frown an "empiricist," James argued that not only in religion but in our knowledge of nature abstract ideas "form the background for all our facts" and that through them we are able to understand and to deal with the world. That our minds can be so determined by abstractions he took to be one of the cardinal "facts in our human constitution." In the realm of religion this background shows itself in the form of an object of belief—the unseen world—calling forth such a powerful sentiment of reality that a person's entire life is affected by it, even though that "object" is not present to our mind in the sense that we could give it a definite description. In support of his claim, James perceptively pointed out that there are "ethical societies" or "churches without a God" where the moral law is regarded as more real than the objects of ordinary experience and that many scientists look upon the "laws of nature" with a reverence that borders on the religious. We shall have occasion later to see the significant role that the idea of the cosmic order came to play in James's development of his hypothesis about the "More" and the individual's relation to it.

James had his ambivalences and ambiguities; he could, for example, denounce rationalism and the *a priori* while commending an experiential approach and yet at the same time side with the a priorists in their account of basic categories and necessary truths, concluding that in this matter "the so-called Experience philosophy has failed to prove its point." Therefore we must not be misled by the emphasis he placed on the role of pure ideas in support of his claim about the unseen world. For we are also told that the feeling of reality is more like a sensation than an intellectual function and that feelings of this sort are more convincing than the results of reasoning. It would appear, then, that reason is not the source of the sense of reality nor can it help buttress that sense. According to James, the convictions about what is real that determine the course of lives derive from a level deeper than argument. He was quite confident that we *know* that those premises prepared in our subconscious life which now impinge on our consciousness are *truer* than any arguments to the contrary. Bradley once remarked that metaphysics consists in finding bad reasons for what we all believe on instinct; similarly, James maintained that in religion and metaphysics, rational articulation has its force only when feelings of reality "have already been impressed in favor of the same conclusion." This would certainly suggest that, despite James's talk about our intuitions and reason working together, the relation between the two is more akin to that of master and slave; "Our impulsive belief," James writes, "is here always what sets up the original body of truth, and our philosophy is but its showy verbalized translation."

To consider the issue posed here at any length would take us too far afield; one point, however, must be noted in an effort to avoid confusion. James could have retained his view that the sense of reality attaching to belief in the unseen is not the product of coercive argument and even retained his claim that religious experience has no intellectual content of its own, *without* also assigning a status to concepts and arguments which *ipso facto* excludes them from making any positive contribution to the interpretation and appraisal of religious experience. This point is crucial, and it stems entirely from James's failure to develop a consistent theory of the nature and role of concepts; at times he held a positive view according to which concepts perform the valid function of articulating meaning implicit in direct experience, while at others he saw concepts as mere surrogates for such experience, second-hand and derivative forms of expression to be set, as dead formulas, against the individual's living encounters with reality. The latter view, if pushed consistently, would militate against James's own analyses in

Varieties itself. It is most likely that he did not feel the need to consider the matter further because, as he said, his claim is not that it is *better* for the subconscious and nonrational to hold primacy in religion, but rather "that they do so hold it as a matter of fact." Fact, it would seem, is as capable of ending an argument as it is of supporting one.

II. The Sick Soul, the Divided Self, and the Process of Regeneration

The key to understanding what James meant by the sick soul has two aspects: first, the idea is intimately related to his distinction between the "once-born" and the "twice-born," and, second, the predicament of the sick soul stands in marked contrast to what James called "the religion of healthy-mindedness." The onceborn dwell on the cheer, the goodness, the light, the beneficence, and the kindness in the world and envisage no obstacles that cannot be overcome by holding fast to the attitude of optimism. The twiceborn are acutely aware of the darker aspects of the universe, the evil it contains, and the human propensities that contribute to sorrow, suffering, sin, and corruption; they, moreover, find no resolution for this situation either in the denial of the reality of these facts or in the belief that they can be overcome by human resources alone. *The sick soul obviously falls within the second category and finds the world's meaning not in any turning away from or denial of evil, but rather in coming to terms with it in the fear and anguish of personal life.* The once-born, on the contrary, look upon the expressed concerns of the sick soul as "morbid" and self-defeating, ills that are easily vanquished by firmly adhering to the optimistic frame of mind so well exhibited by Walt Whitman, whom James described as a "paradigm" of this outlook on life.

Here James made everything depend on the two basically different ways in which we regard evil. There are those, James wrote, for whom *evil* means "only a mal-adjustment with *things*" and hence is something that is curable though change and readjustment. At the other pole are those who do not envisage evil as primarily a relation between the self and particular external things, but as "something more radical and general, a wrongness or vice in [one's] essential nature," not to be cured by rearranging the environment or even the inner self because it "requires a supernatural remedy." Ever sensitive to the nuances, James laid hold here of an important and often neglected distinction: those who regard evil as ills and sins in the *plural,* he said, invariably see them as "removable in detail," while those for whom sin is *singular,* something ineradicably ingrained in our natural subjectivity, see no resolution in terms of "superficial piecemeal operations."

From his study of the profound experiences of Tolstoy and Bunyan, James was convinced that our entire emotional state, by which he meant a person's total to the world, basically affects the sort of world we encounter. If we were to strip ourselves of all the emotion the world inspires in us and try to experience the world as it exists purely in itself, the deadness that would result would be unimaginable—there would be no significance, no character, no perspective, no concern. The world would just be "there"—a medley of many colorless things. Tolstoy's temporary *anhedonia,* his experience of the world as remote, sinister, strange, and dull, had, in James's view, the powerful effect of changing his experience of reality because this negative perception induced him to seek a resolution beyond the estrangement that had thrown him into despair. James's chief complaint against the healthy-minded attitude is that it prevents us from ever seeing the force of this predicament. When failure, the awareness of the transiency of things and goods, the disappearance of youth, and the specter of death press upon us, the healthy-minded, sustaining their happy-go-lucky attitude, can say no more than "Cheer up, old fellow," and James regarded that as no answer at all. Unlike Tolstoy, who confronted his disenchantment with life by posing questions—Why should I live? Why should I do anything? Is there in life any purpose?—and who, through the very concern manifest in these candid questions, sought for and found a resolution overcoming melancholy, the healthyminded can but resign and settle for an Epicurean refinement or a Stoic moral purity, the highest level possible for the once-born. James declared this way of confronting the negative aspects of life as totally inadequate because it leaves the world in "the shape of an unreconciled contradiction" and seeks "no higher unity."

James's appraisal of the impasse that exists between the healthyminded and those who take the experience of evil seriously throws further light on the criteria of judgment he employed. After concluding that "morbid-mindedness ranges over the wider scale of experience," James went on to say that, regardless of the extent to which healthy-mindedness "works" or fulfills a psychologically important function (and he admitted that for certain purposes it does), it nevertheless breaks down and shows its impotence when melancholy settles upon us. In addition, and this is the important point, James declared healthy-mindedness to be wanting as a ''philosophical doctrine'' because the evil it refuses to account for or even acknowledge is a genuine part of reality. Since, he argued, the reality of evil cannot be denied, there is a philosophical presumption that it should have some rational significance, and hence those who disregard evil adopt an outlook less comprehensive than one finds in systems that try to include the negative elements in human life. This shows that, for all his criticism of abstract rationality, James had not abandoned it altogether in order to assess beliefs solely in terms of their satisfying certain human needs. There is, in fact, a most interesting mixture of the psychological, the philosophical, and the religious in this part of the argument. Healthy-mindedness has been acknowledged to have a certain legitimacy in meeting *psychological* needs, but it falls short *philosophically* in its failure to come to terms with the reality of evil. Finally, the optimistic attitude is subject to *religious* criticism as well. For in James's view the most complete religions ''are those in which the pessimistic elements are best developed,'' and he cited Buddhism and Christianity as meeting the standard because both are religions of deliverance wherein one must die to an unreal life in order to enter into the real existence. For the once-born there is nothing insurmountable to be delivered from, no unreal life in the first place.

A reader of *Varieties* wonder whether James thought of the sick soul and the divided self as the same. The answer is that he did, but there is some difference of emphasis in his discussion of them. To begin with, both conceptions refer to the twice-born, but in considering the sick soul James paid more attention to the actual variety of psychological states and moods involved, whereas in his account of the divided self the focus is on a more abstract feature—the fundamental nature of the discordance in the self and on the ways in which the self may be unified in conversion. The point becomes clear when one considers James's choice of a passage from Saint Augustine's *Confessions* as a cardinal example of the divided self. Reflecting on his vivid awareness of the conflict within him between two wills, the carnal will (well established through habit) and the spiritual will (which should have mastery but proves to be too weak), Augustine wrote, ''It was myself indeed in both the wills, yet more myself in that which approved in myself than in that which I disapproved in myself.'' What more candid

acknowledgment of this predicament could there be? Augustine was, as he confessed, convinced that he should surrender to divine love, but he was unable to give up the self that pleased him more, and hence he remained in bondage. His anguish stemmed from the shame he felt in the face of his ambivalence; he knew that the spiritual self should triumph, but he also knew that he was unable to will the victory. This experience served to focus the central concern manifest in James's account of conversion: How is the divided self to be unified and the inner discord overcome so that the higher self may emerge in the process?

As a prelude to considering this question, James made two observations based on the cases he studied. The first is that the unification of the divided self may occur in more than one way: gradually or abruptly, through alterations in our feelings or powers to act, through new intellectual insights, or through mystical experience. In short, there are varieties in the forms of conversion and no single standard pattern. Second, and more important, James conceived the problem of reaching unity out of discord in such general terms that the religious solution is made to appear as but one type among others. New birth may even take the form of a move away from religion, into an attitude of disbelief, or newness of life may be found in abandoning a rigorous morality for a life of liberty and license. Nor are these all the possibilities he envisaged. Firmness and stability in life, he claimed, may result from any number of stimuli—love, ambition, revenge, or patriotic devotion—because we are dealing with the ''same psychological form of event,'' an equilibrium following a turmoil of conflict and inconsistency. Having conceived the situation in such broad terms, James then faced the new problem of distinguishing the specifically *religious* form of conversion from other types.

By ''conversion'' James meant a regeneration or renewal of life whereby the person acquires assurance that the divided self has been overcome. Transformation of the self means essentially the establishing of a *dominant aim* that expels all rivals and becomes the habitual center of a person s energies. Religious conversion means that religious beliefs previously dormant or merely peripheral now become central and dominant. It is noteworthy that James described the mind of the candidate for conversion in much the same terms he would later employ in his summary statement about the nature of all religion. The individual, he wrote, starts with an awareness of incompleteness, wrongness, and sin, and sin, and from this consciousness springs the desire to escape; the transformation is effected when the "positive ideal" for which the person longs becomes the center of life. We have here nothing other than the "uneasiness" and the "resolution" formula that James held to be the "uniform deliverance in which religions all appear to meet." We shall return to this contention; at this juncture, however, we should note that the "uniform deliverance" helps us to understand the nature of specifically religious conversion. As James repeatedly emphasized, the type of defect in man envisaged by such religions as Buddhism, Judaism, and Christianity is not to be abolished by an act of will stemming from the same self that is in need, and this clearly suggests that religious conversion is essentially of the involuntary type. As James's many examples show, the emergence of the regenerated self cannot be conceived as a wholly volitional affair.

One of the most instructive parts of James's psychological account of self-surrender has to do with the new light that it throws on the limits of the will to believe. When we find a man who is inconsolable, caught in a web of sin and want, James wrote, it is simply absurd to tell him that all is well and that there is no reason for worry. For the only consciousness he has tells him that *all is not well*; such advice is not only inappropriate but simply false. "The will to believe," James freely acknowledged, "cannot be stretched as far as that." We may strengthen our faith in an incipient belief already possessed, but "we cannot create a belief out of whole cloth," especially when our experience tells us the opposite. The reason that the voluntary solution cannot work is that the better attitude proposed for overcoming the predicament is a negation of the only mind we have and, as James maintained, "we cannot actively will a pure negation." This should help to dispose of the widely held belief that James had an extravagant conception of the scope within which the will to believe can be effective. He was here making the same point he had made at the beginning of his essay "The Will to Believe." As regards a present fact, the mind is bound down, and the will cannot force belief to the contrary. As he wrote, a man with a high fever may *say* that he is well, but he is *powerless* to *believe* it. Similarly, the person in despair is unable to believe that his despair is illusory and that he lives in a world of hope.

James's concern to persuade his audience expressed itself repeatedly in attempts to anticipate objections. In this instance he considered the possibility that the whole phenomenon of regeneration might be a strictly "natural" process, divine in its fruits, but neither more nor less so in its *causation* and mechanism than any other process of man's inner life. Although he referred to "the whole phenomenon of regeneration," the basic question he raised was prompted by a consideration of "instantaneous conversion" accompanied by the belief that a special miraculous visitation from the divine is in evidence. Here the "field" theory of consciousness, according to which a complex mental episode replaces the singular "idea" that was the focus of associationist psychology, provided him with a means of clarifying what might be involved in supposed sudden transformations of the self. Since this field is not determinate, there is in addition to the ordinary field of consciousness an extramarginal one that remains related to the primary consciousness and makes its presence felt. This extramarginal consciousness is what James called the "subconscious self." His main contention with regard to sudden conversion is that the subject must have a well-developed subconscious self congenial to influences from beyond it and that when this essential condition is fulfilled there may come a critical point at which the subconscious takes command and the new self is born. James, however, speaking as a psychologist, did not claim that describing the process in these terms precludes the presence of the divine. On the contrary, he saw the subliminal as a door that might remain "ajar or open" to higher spiritual influences, but he insisted that without that door these powers would be lost in the "hubbub of the waking life."

Now, we may ask, what contribution does this excursion into the matter of sudden conversion make to answering the question of whether the process of regeneration is a "natural" one or not? The answer is that the psychologically acceptable theory of the subliminal self provided James with the mechanism for describing the process of conversion in terms consistent with "natural" explanation, but he clearly understood that the subconscious does not of itself generate the powers that may impinge on it from without. This "supernatural" dimension was to enter the picture later on when James dealt with the idea of the "More" in reality, especially on its "far" side. At this point, however, it needs to be stressed that, despite what James said about Jonathan Edwards' failure to show that any chasm exists between a supernatural state of grace and an "exceptionally high degree of natural goodness," he did not deny that the "perception of external control," the sense of being related to a transcendent reality beyond our will, is an essential element in any account of regeneration. For after all, James never gave up his contention that the divided self, understood in the religious sense, is unable to unify itself from its own resources.

Source: John E. Smith, ''Introduction by John E. Smith,'' in *The Varieties of Religious Experience,* Harvard University Press, 1985, pp. xi–li.

Sources

Ferrari, Michel, Introduction, in *Journal of Consciousness Studies,* Vol. 9, No. 9–10, 2002, pp. 1–10.

Leib, Erin, ''God's Pragmatist,'' in *New Republic,* June 24, 2002, p. 38.

Menand, Louis, ''The Return of Pragmatism,'' in *American Heritage,* Vol. 48, No. 6, October 1997, pp. 48–57.

Taylor, Charles, ''Risking Belief: Why William James Still Matters,'' in *Commonweal,* Vol. 129, No. 5, March 8, 2002, p. 14.

Turing, Alan M., ''Computing Machinery and Intelligence,'' in *Mind,* Vol. 59, No. 236, October 1950, pp. 433–60.

''William James Dies: Great Psychologist,'' in the *New York Times,* August 27, 1910.

Zaleski, Carol, ''A Letter to William James,'' in *Christian Century,* Vol. 1, No. 2, January 16, 2002, p. 32.

———, ''William James, *The Varieties of Religious Experience* (1902),'' in *First Things: A Monthly Journal of Religion and Public Life,* March 2000, p. 60.

Further Reading

Feinstein, Howard M., *Becoming William James,* Cornell University Press, 1999.
  This biography of James was originally published in 1982. This edition offers a new introduction.

Grattan, C. Hartley, *The Three Jameses; A Family of Minds,* Longmans, Green, and Company, 1932.
  Grattan presents the lives of father Henry and his most famous sons, William and Henry.

James, Alice, *Alice James, Her Brothers—Her Journal,* edited by Anna Robeson Burr, Milford House, 1972.
  Originally published in 1934, this book presents the lives of the men in the James family (William, Henry, Garth, and Robertson) through the writings of their sister Alice.

Johnson, Michael G., and Tracy B. Henley, eds., *Reflections on ''The Principles of Psychology'': William James after a Century,* L. Erlbaum Associates, 1990.
  This book is comprehensive study of the history of psychology with a special emphasis on James's work.

Olin, Doris, ed., *William James: ''Pragmatism'' in Focus,* Routledge, 1992.
  This is a collection of essays by twentieth-century thinkers such as Bertrand Russell, reflecting on James's concepts of truth, meaning, metaphysics, and pragmatism.

Perry, Ralph Barton, ed., *Collected Essays and Reviews,* by William James, Longmans, Green, and Company, 1920.
  James's essays on psychology, philosophy, and psychical research are presented and reviewed by his contemporaries.

Rowe, Stephen C., ed., *The Vision of James,* Element Books, 1996.
  Stephen C. Rowe, a professor of philosophy, offers a focused collection of James's philosophical views.

Simon, Linda, ed., *William James Remembered,* University of Nebraska Press, 1996.
  There are twenty-five different memoirs in this collection, written by faculty and family members, students, and other friends of James, allowing the reader to see many facets of James. At the beginning of each memoir, Simon explains who the writer is, putting his or her writing in context.

Skrupskelis, Ignas K., and Elizabeth M. Berkeley, eds., *The Correspondence of William James,* University Press of Virginia, 1992.
  This ten-volume collection of letters offers a more personal glimpse of James. Each volume corresponds to a specific time period in James's life.

Glossary of Literary Terms

A

Abstract: Used as a noun, the term refers to a short summary or outline of a longer work. As an adjective applied to writing or literary works, abstract refers to words or phrases that name things not knowable through the five senses. Examples of abstracts include the *Cliffs Notes* summaries of major literary works. Examples of abstract terms or concepts include ''idea,'' ''guilt'' ''honesty,'' and ''loyalty.''

Absurd, Theater of the: See *Theater of the Absurd*

Absurdism: See *Theater of the Absurd*

Act: A major section of a play. Acts are divided into varying numbers of shorter scenes. From ancient times to the nineteenth century plays were generally constructed of five acts, but modern works typically consist of one, two, or three acts. Examples of five-act plays include the works of Sophocles and Shakespeare, while the plays of Arthur Miller commonly have a three-act structure.

Acto: A one-act Chicano theater piece developed out of collective improvisation. *Actos* were performed by members of Luis Valdez's Teatro Campesino in California during the mid-1960s.

Aestheticism: A literary and artistic movement of the nineteenth century. Followers of the movement believed that art should not be mixed with social, political, or moral teaching. The statement ''art for art's sake'' is a good summary of aestheticism. The movement had its roots in France, but it gained widespread importance in England in the last half of the nineteenth century, where it helped change the Victorian practice of including moral lessons in literature. Oscar Wilde is one of the best-known ''aesthetes'' of the late nineteenth century.

Age of Johnson: The period in English literature between 1750 and 1798, named after the most prominent literary figure of the age, Samuel Johnson. Works written during this time are noted for their emphasis on ''sensibility,'' or emotional quality. These works formed a transition between the rational works of the Age of Reason, or Neoclassical period, and the emphasis on individual feelings and responses of the Romantic period. Significant writers during the Age of Johnson included the novelists Ann Radcliffe and Henry Mackenzie, dramatists Richard Sheridan and Oliver Goldsmith, and poets William Collins and Thomas Gray. Also known as Age of Sensibility

Age of Reason: See *Neoclassicism*

Age of Sensibility: See *Age of Johnson*

Alexandrine Meter: See *Meter*

Allegory: A narrative technique in which characters representing things or abstract ideas are used to convey a message or teach a lesson. Allegory is typically used to teach moral, ethical, or religious lessons but is sometimes used for satiric or political purposes. Examples of allegorical works include

Edmund Spenser's *The Faerie Queene* and John Bunyan's *The Pilgrim's Progress.*

Allusion: A reference to a familiar literary or historical person or event, used to make an idea more easily understood. For example, describing someone as a "Romeo" makes an allusion to William Shakespeare's famous young lover in *Romeo and Juliet.*

Amerind Literature: The writing and oral traditions of Native Americans. Native American literature was originally passed on by word of mouth, so it consisted largely of stories and events that were easily memorized. Amerind prose is often rhythmic like poetry because it was recited to the beat of a ceremonial drum. Examples of Amerind literature include the autobiographical *Black Elk Speaks,* the works of N. Scott Momaday, James Welch, and Craig Lee Strete, and the poetry of Luci Tapahonso.

Analogy: A comparison of two things made to explain something unfamiliar through its similarities to something familiar, or to prove one point based on the acceptedness of another. Similes and metaphors are types of analogies. Analogies often take the form of an extended simile, as in William Blake's aphorism: "As the caterpillar chooses the fairest leaves to lay her eggs on, so the priest lays his curse on the fairest joys."

Angry Young Men: A group of British writers of the 1950s whose work expressed bitterness and disillusionment with society. Common to their work is an anti-hero who rebels against a corrupt social order and strives for personal integrity. The term has been used to describe Kingsley Amis, John Osborne, Colin Wilson, John Wain, and others.

Antagonist: The major character in a narrative or drama who works against the hero or protagonist. An example of an evil antagonist is Richard Lovelace in Samuel Richardson's *Clarissa,* while a virtuous antagonist is Macduff in William Shakespeare's *Macbeth.*

Anthropomorphism: The presentation of animals or objects in human shape or with human characteristics. The term is derived from the Greek word for "human form." The fables of Aesop, the animated films of Walt Disney, and Richard Adams's *Watership Down* feature anthropomorphic characters.

Anti-hero: A central character in a work of literature who lacks traditional heroic qualities such as courage, physical prowess, and fortitude. Anti-heros typically distrust conventional values and are unable to commit themselves to any ideals. They generally feel helpless in a world over which they have no control. Anti-heroes usually accept, and often celebrate, their positions as social outcasts. A well-known anti-hero is Yossarian in Joseph Heller's novel *Catch-22.*

Antimasque: See *Masque*

Antithesis: The antithesis of something is its direct opposite. In literature, the use of antithesis as a figure of speech results in two statements that show a contrast through the balancing of two opposite ideas. Technically, it is the second portion of the statement that is defined as the "antithesis"; the first portion is the "thesis." An example of antithesis is found in the following portion of Abraham Lincoln's "Gettysburg Address"; notice the opposition between the verbs "remember" and "forget" and the phrases "what we say" and "what they did": "The world will little note nor long remember what we say here, but it can never forget what they did here."

Apocrypha: Writings tentatively attributed to an author but not proven or universally accepted to be their works. The term was originally applied to certain books of the Bible that were not considered inspired and so were not included in the "sacred canon." Geoffrey Chaucer, William Shakespeare, Thomas Kyd, Thomas Middleton, and John Marston all have apocrypha. Apocryphal books of the Bible include the Old Testament's Book of Enoch and New Testament's Gospel of Peter.

Apollonian and Dionysian: The two impulses believed to guide authors of dramatic tragedy. The Apollonian impulse is named after Apollo, the Greek god of light and beauty and the symbol of intellectual order. The Dionysian impulse is named after Dionysus, the Greek god of wine and the symbol of the unrestrained forces of nature. The Apollonian impulse is to create a rational, harmonious world, while the Dionysian is to express the irrational forces of personality. Friedrich Nietzche uses these terms in *The Birth of Tragedy* to designate contrasting elements in Greek tragedy.

Apostrophe: A statement, question, or request addressed to an inanimate object or concept or to a nonexistent or absent person. Requests for inspiration from the muses in poetry are examples of apostrophe, as is Marc Antony's address to Caesar's corpse in William Shakespeare's *Julius Caesar:* "O, pardon me, thou bleeding piece of earth, That I am meek and gentle with these butchers!. . . Woe to the hand that shed this costly blood!. . . ''

Archetype: The word archetype is commonly used to describe an original pattern or model from which all other things of the same kind are made. This term was introduced to literary criticism from the psychology of Carl Jung. It expresses Jung's theory that behind every person's ''unconscious,'' or repressed memories of the past, lies the ''collective unconscious'' of the human race: memories of the countless typical experiences of our ancestors. These memories are said to prompt illogical associations that trigger powerful emotions in the reader. Often, the emotional process is primitive, even primordial. Archetypes are the literary images that grow out of the ''collective unconscious.'' They appear in literature as incidents and plots that repeat basic patterns of life. They may also appear as stereotyped characters. Examples of literary archetypes include themes such as birth and death and characters such as the Earth Mother.

Argument: The argument of a work is the author's subject matter or principal idea. Examples of defined ''argument'' portions of works include John Milton's *Arguments* to each of the books of *Paradise Lost* and the ''Argument'' to Robert Herrick's *Hesperides.*

Aristotelian Criticism: Specifically, the method of evaluating and analyzing tragedy formulated by the Greek philosopher Aristotle in his *Poetics.* More generally, the term indicates any form of criticism that follows Aristotle's views. Aristotelian criticism focuses on the form and logical structure of a work, apart from its historical or social context, in contrast to ''Platonic Criticism,'' which stresses the usefulness of art. Adherents of New Criticism including John Crowe Ransom and Cleanth Brooks utilize and value the basic ideas of Aristotelian criticism for textual analysis.

Art for Art's Sake: See *Aestheticism*

Aside: A comment made by a stage performer that is intended to be heard by the audience but supposedly not by other characters. Eugene O'Neill's *Strange Interlude* is an extended use of the aside in modern theater.

Audience: The people for whom a piece of literature is written. Authors usually write with a certain audience in mind, for example, children, members of a religious or ethnic group, or colleagues in a professional field. The term ''audience'' also applies to the people who gather to see or hear any performance, including plays, poetry readings, speeches, and concerts. Jane Austen's parody of the gothic novel, *Northanger Abbey,* was originally intended for (and also pokes fun at) an audience of young and avid female gothic novel readers.

Avant-garde: A French term meaning ''vanguard.'' It is used in literary criticism to describe new writing that rejects traditional approaches to literature in favor of innovations in style or content. Twentieth-century examples of the literary *avant-garde* include the Black Mountain School of poets, the Bloomsbury Group, and the Beat Movement.

B

Ballad: A short poem that tells a simple story and has a repeated refrain. Ballads were originally intended to be sung. Early ballads, known as folk ballads, were passed down through generations, so their authors are often unknown. Later ballads composed by known authors are called literary ballads. An example of an anonymous folk ballad is ''Edward,'' which dates from the Middle Ages. Samuel Taylor Coleridge's ''The Rime of the Ancient Mariner'' and John Keats's ''La Belle Dame sans Merci'' are examples of literary ballads.

Baroque: A term used in literary criticism to describe literature that is complex or ornate in style or diction. Baroque works typically express tension, anxiety, and violent emotion. The term ''Baroque Age'' designates a period in Western European literature beginning in the late sixteenth century and ending about one hundred years later. Works of this period often mirror the qualities of works more generally associated with the label ''baroque'' and sometimes feature elaborate conceits. Examples of Baroque works include John Lyly's *Euphues: The Anatomy of Wit,* Luis de Gongora's *Soledads,* and William Shakespeare's *As You Like It.*

Baroque Age: See *Baroque*

Baroque Period: See *Baroque*

Beat Generation: See *Beat Movement*

Beat Movement: A period featuring a group of American poets and novelists of the 1950s and 1960s—including Jack Kerouac, Allen Ginsberg, Gregory Corso, William S. Burroughs, and Lawrence Ferlinghetti—who rejected established social and literary values. Using such techniques as stream of consciousness writing and jazz-influenced free verse and focusing on unusual or abnormal states of mind—generated by religious ecstasy or the use of drugs—the Beat writers aimed to create works that were unconventional in both form and subject matter. Kerouac's *On the Road* is perhaps the best-known example of a Beat Generation novel, and Ginsberg's *Howl* is a famous collection of Beat poetry.

Black Aesthetic Movement: A period of artistic and literary development among African Americans in the 1960s and early 1970s. This was the first major African-American artistic movement since the Harlem Renaissance and was closely paralleled by the civil rights and black power movements. The black aesthetic writers attempted to produce works of art that would be meaningful to the black masses. Key figures in black aesthetics included one of its founders, poet and playwright Amiri Baraka, formerly known as LeRoi Jones; poet and essayist Haki R. Madhubuti, formerly Don L. Lee; poet and playwright Sonia Sanchez; and dramatist Ed Bullins. Works representative of the Black Aesthetic Movement include Amiri Baraka's play *Dutchman,* a 1964 Obie award-winner; *Black Fire: An Anthology of Afro-American Writing,* edited by Baraka and playwright Larry Neal and published in 1968; and Sonia Sanchez's poetry collection *We a BaddDDD People,* published in 1970. Also known as Black Arts Movement.

Black Arts Movement: See *Black Aesthetic Movement*

Black Comedy: See *Black Humor*

Black Humor: Writing that places grotesque elements side by side with humorous ones in an attempt to shock the reader, forcing him or her to laugh at the horrifying reality of a disordered world. Joseph Heller's novel *Catch-22* is considered a superb example of the use of black humor. Other well-known authors who use black humor include Kurt Vonnegut, Edward Albee, Eugene Ionesco, and Harold Pinter. Also known as Black Comedy.

Blank Verse: Loosely, any unrhymed poetry, but more generally, unrhymed iambic pentameter verse (composed of lines of five two-syllable feet with the first syllable accented, the second unaccented). Blank verse has been used by poets since the Renaissance for its flexibility and its graceful, dignified tone. John Milton's *Paradise Lost* is in blank verse, as are most of William Shakespeare's plays.

Bloomsbury Group: A group of English writers, artists, and intellectuals who held informal artistic and philosophical discussions in Bloomsbury, a district of London, from around 1907 to the early 1930s. The Bloomsbury Group held no uniform philosophical beliefs but did commonly express an aversion to moral prudery and a desire for greater social tolerance. At various times the circle included Virginia Woolf, E. M. Forster, Clive Bell, Lytton Strachey, and John Maynard Keynes.

Bon Mot: A French term meaning "good word." A *bon mot* is a witty remark or clever observation. Charles Lamb and Oscar Wilde are celebrated for their witty *bon mots.* Two examples by Oscar Wilde stand out: (1) "All women become their mothers. That is their tragedy. No man does. That's his." (2) "A man cannot be too careful in the choice of his enemies."

Breath Verse: See *Projective Verse*

Burlesque: Any literary work that uses exaggeration to make its subject appear ridiculous, either by treating a trivial subject with profound seriousness or by treating a dignified subject frivolously. The word "burlesque" may also be used as an adjective, as in "burlesque show," to mean "striptease act." Examples of literary burlesque include the comedies of Aristophanes, Miguel de Cervantes's *Don Quixote,*, Samuel Butler's poem "Hudibras," and John Gay's play *The Beggar's Opera.*

C

Cadence: The natural rhythm of language caused by the alternation of accented and unaccented syllables. Much modern poetry—notably free verse—deliberately manipulates cadence to create complex rhythmic effects. James Macpherson's "Ossian poems" are richly cadenced, as is the poetry of the Symbolists, Walt Whitman, and Amy Lowell.

Caesura: A pause in a line of poetry, usually occurring near the middle. It typically corresponds to a break in the natural rhythm or sense of the line but is sometimes shifted to create special meanings or rhythmic effects. The opening line of Edgar Allan Poe's "The Raven" contains a caesura following "dreary": "Once upon a midnight dreary, while I pondered weak and weary. . . ."

Canzone: A short Italian or Provencal lyric poem, commonly about love and often set to music. The *canzone* has no set form but typically contains five or six stanzas made up of seven to twenty lines of eleven syllables each. A shorter, five- to ten-line "envoy," or concluding stanza, completes the poem.

Masters of the *canzone* form include Petrarch, Dante Alighieri, Torquato Tasso, and Guido Cavalcanti.

Carpe Diem: A Latin term meaning "seize the day." This is a traditional theme of poetry, especially lyrics. A *carpe diem* poem advises the reader or the person it addresses to live for today and enjoy the pleasures of the moment. Two celebrated *carpe diem* poems are Andrew Marvell's "To His Coy Mistress" and Robert Herrick's poem beginning "Gather ye rosebuds while ye may. . . ."

Catharsis: The release or purging of unwanted emotions— specifically fear and pity—brought about by exposure to art. The term was first used by the Greek philosopher Aristotle in his *Poetics* to refer to the desired effect of tragedy on spectators. A famous example of catharsis is realized in Sophocles' *Oedipus Rex,* when Oedipus discovers that his wife, Jacosta, is his own mother and that the stranger he killed on the road was his own father.

Celtic Renaissance: A period of Irish literary and cultural history at the end of the nineteenth century. Followers of the movement aimed to create a romantic vision of Celtic myth and legend. The most significant works of the Celtic Renaissance typically present a dreamy, unreal world, usually in reaction against the reality of contemporary problems. William Butler Yeats's *The Wanderings of Oisin* is among the most significant works of the Celtic Renaissance. Also known as Celtic Twilight.

Celtic Twilight: See *Celtic Renaissance*

Character: Broadly speaking, a person in a literary work. The actions of characters are what constitute the plot of a story, novel, or poem. There are numerous types of characters, ranging from simple, stereotypical figures to intricate, multifaceted ones. In the techniques of anthropomorphism and personification, animals—and even places or things—can assume aspects of character. "Characterization" is the process by which an author creates vivid, believable characters in a work of art. This may be done in a variety of ways, including (1) direct description of the character by the narrator; (2) the direct presentation of the speech, thoughts, or actions of the character; and (3) the responses of other characters to the character. The term "character" also refers to a form originated by the ancient Greek writer Theophrastus that later became popular in the seventeenth and eighteenth centuries. It is a short essay or sketch of a person who prominently displays a specific attribute or quality, such as miserliness or ambition. Notable characters in literature include Oedipus Rex, Don Quixote de la Mancha, Macbeth, Candide, Hester Prynne, Ebenezer Scrooge, Huckleberry Finn, Jay Gatsby, Scarlett O'Hara, James Bond, and Kunta Kinte.

Characterization: See *Character*

Chorus: In ancient Greek drama, a group of actors who commented on and interpreted the unfolding action on the stage. Initially the chorus was a major component of the presentation, but over time it became less significant, with its numbers reduced and its role eventually limited to commentary between acts. By the sixteenth century the chorus—if employed at all—was typically a single person who provided a prologue and an epilogue and occasionally appeared between acts to introduce or underscore an important event. The chorus in William Shakespeare's *Henry V* functions in this way. Modern dramas rarely feature a chorus, but T. S. Eliot's *Murder in the Cathedral* and Arthur Miller's *A View from the Bridge* are notable exceptions. The Stage Manager in Thornton Wilder's *Our Town* performs a role similar to that of the chorus.

Chronicle: A record of events presented in chronological order. Although the scope and level of detail provided varies greatly among the chronicles surviving from ancient times, some, such as the *Anglo-Saxon Chronicle,* feature vivid descriptions and a lively recounting of events. During the Elizabethan Age, many dramas— appropriately called "chronicle plays"—were based on material from chronicles. Many of William Shakespeare's dramas of English history as well as Christopher Marlowe's *Edward II* are based in part on Raphael Holinshead's *Chronicles of England, Scotland, and Ireland.*

Classical: In its strictest definition in literary criticism, classicism refers to works of ancient Greek or Roman literature. The term may also be used to describe a literary work of recognized importance (a "classic") from any time period or literature that exhibits the traits of classicism. Classical authors from ancient Greek and Roman times include Juvenal and Homer. Examples of later works and authors now described as classical include French literature of the seventeenth century, Western novels of the nineteenth century, and American fiction of the mid-nineteenth century such as that written by James Fenimore Cooper and Mark Twain.

Classicism: A term used in literary criticism to describe critical doctrines that have their roots in ancient Greek and Roman literature, philosophy, and art. Works associated with classicism typically exhibit restraint on the part of the author, unity of design and purpose, clarity, simplicity, logical organization, and respect for tradition. Examples of literary classicism include Cicero's prose, the dramas of Pierre Corneille and Jean Racine, the poetry of John Dryden and Alexander Pope, and the writings of J. W. von Goethe, G. E. Lessing, and T. S. Eliot.

Climax: The turning point in a narrative, the moment when the conflict is at its most intense. Typically, the structure of stories, novels, and plays is one of rising action, in which tension builds to the climax, followed by falling action, in which tension lessens as the story moves to its conclusion. The climax in James Fenimore Cooper's *The Last of the Mohicans* occurs when Magua and his captive Cora are pursued to the edge of a cliff by Uncas. Magua kills Uncas but is subsequently killed by Hawkeye.

Colloquialism: A word, phrase, or form of pronunciation that is acceptable in casual conversation but not in formal, written communication. It is considered more acceptable than slang. An example of colloquialism can be found in Rudyard Kipling's *Barrack-room Ballads:* When 'Omer smote 'is bloomin' lyre He'd 'eard men sing by land and sea; An' what he thought 'e might require 'E went an' took—the same as me!

Comedy: One of two major types of drama, the other being tragedy. Its aim is to amuse, and it typically ends happily. Comedy assumes many forms, such as farce and burlesque, and uses a variety of techniques, from parody to satire. In a restricted sense the term comedy refers only to dramatic presentations, but in general usage it is commonly applied to nondramatic works as well. Examples of comedies range from the plays of Aristophanes, Terrence, and Plautus, Dante Alighieri's *The Divine Comedy,* Francois Rabelais's *Pantagruel* and *Gargantua,* and some of Geoffrey Chaucer's tales and William Shakespeare's plays to Noel Coward's play *Private Lives* and James Thurber's short story "The Secret Life of Walter Mitty."

Comedy of Manners: A play about the manners and conventions of an aristocratic, highly sophisticated society. The characters are usually types rather than individualized personalities, and plot is less important than atmosphere. Such plays were an important aspect of late seventeenth-century English comedy. The comedy of manners was revived in the eighteenth century by Oliver Goldsmith and Richard Brinsley Sheridan, enjoyed a second revival in the late nineteenth century, and has endured into the twentieth century. Examples of comedies of manners include William Congreve's *The Way of the World* in the late seventeenth century, Oliver Goldsmith's *She Stoops to Conquer* and Richard Brinsley Sheridan's *The School for Scandal* in the eighteenth century, Oscar Wilde's *The Importance of Being Earnest* in the nineteenth century, and W. Somerset Maugham's *The Circle* in the twentieth century.

Comic Relief: The use of humor to lighten the mood of a serious or tragic story, especially in plays. The technique is very common in Elizabethan works, and can be an integral part of the plot or simply a brief event designed to break the tension of the scene. The Gravediggers' scene in William Shakespeare's *Hamlet* is a frequently cited example of comic relief.

Commedia dell'arte: An Italian term meaning "the comedy of guilds" or "the comedy of professional actors." This form of dramatic comedy was popular in Italy during the sixteenth century. Actors were assigned stock roles (such as Pulcinella, the stupid servant, or Pantalone, the old merchant) and given a basic plot to follow, but all dialogue was improvised. The roles were rigidly typed and the plots were formulaic, usually revolving around young lovers who thwarted their elders and attained wealth and happiness. A rigid convention of the *commedia dell'arte* is the periodic intrusion of Harlequin, who interrupts the play with low buffoonery. Peppino de Filippo's *Metamorphoses of a Wandering Minstrel* gave modern audiences an idea of what *commedia dell'arte* may have been like. Various scenarios for *commedia dell'arte* were compiled in Petraccone's *La commedia dell'arte, storia, technica, scenari,* published in 1927.

Complaint: A lyric poem, popular in the Renaissance, in which the speaker expresses sorrow about his or her condition. Typically, the speaker's sadness is caused by an unresponsive lover, but some complaints cite other sources of unhappiness, such as poverty or fate. A commonly cited example is "A Complaint by Night of the Lover Not Beloved" by Henry Howard, Earl of Surrey. Thomas Sackville's "Complaint of Henry, Duke of Buckingham" traces the duke's unhappiness to his ruthless ambition.

Conceit: A clever and fanciful metaphor, usually expressed through elaborate and extended comparison, that presents a striking parallel between two seemingly dissimilar things—for example, elaborately comparing a beautiful woman to an object like a garden or the sun. The conceit was a popular device throughout the Elizabethan Age and Baroque Age and was the principal technique of the seventeenth-century English metaphysical poets. This usage of the word conceit is unrelated to the best-known definition of conceit as an arrogant attitude or behavior. The conceit figures prominently in the works of John Donne, Emily Dickinson, and T. S. Eliot.

Concrete: Concrete is the opposite of abstract, and refers to a thing that actually exists or a description that allows the reader to experience an object or concept with the senses. Henry David Thoreau's *Walden* contains much concrete description of nature and wildlife.

Concrete Poetry: Poetry in which visual elements play a large part in the poetic effect. Punctuation marks, letters, or words are arranged on a page to form a visual design: a cross, for example, or a bumblebee. Max Bill and Eugene Gomringer were among the early practitioners of concrete poetry; Haroldo de Campos and Augusto de Campos are among contemporary authors of concrete poetry.

Confessional Poetry: A form of poetry in which the poet reveals very personal, intimate, sometimes shocking information about himself or herself. Anne Sexton, Sylvia Plath, Robert Lowell, and John Berryman wrote poetry in the confessional vein.

Conflict: The conflict in a work of fiction is the issue to be resolved in the story. It usually occurs between two characters, the protagonist and the antagonist, or between the protagonist and society or the protagonist and himself or herself. Conflict in Theodore Dreiser's novel *Sister Carrie* comes as a result of urban society, while Jack London's short story "To Build a Fire" concerns the protagonist's battle against the cold and himself.

Connotation: The impression that a word gives beyond its defined meaning. Connotations may be universally understood or may be significant only to a certain group. Both "horse" and "steed" denote the same animal, but "steed" has a different connotation, deriving from the chivalrous or romantic narratives in which the word was once often used.

Consonance: Consonance occurs in poetry when words appearing at the ends of two or more verses have similar final consonant sounds but have final vowel sounds that differ, as with "stuff" and "off." Consonance is found in "The curfew tolls the knells of parting day" from Thomas Grey's "An Elegy Written in a Country Church Yard." Also known as Half Rhyme or Slant Rhyme.

Convention: Any widely accepted literary device, style, or form. A soliloquy, in which a character reveals to the audience his or her private thoughts, is an example of a dramatic convention.

Corrido: A Mexican ballad. Examples of *corridos* include "Muerte del afamado Bilito," "La voz de mi conciencia," "Lucio Perez," "La juida," and "Los presos."

Couplet: Two lines of poetry with the same rhyme and meter, often expressing a complete and self-contained thought. The following couplet is from Alexander Pope's "Elegy to the Memory of an Unfortunate Lady": 'Tis Use alone that sanctifies Expense, And Splendour borrows all her rays from Sense.

Criticism: The systematic study and evaluation of literary works, usually based on a specific method or set of principles. An important part of literary studies since ancient times, the practice of criticism has given rise to numerous theories, methods, and "schools," sometimes producing conflicting, even contradictory, interpretations of literature in general as well as of individual works. Even such basic issues as what constitutes a poem or a novel have been the subject of much criticism over the centuries. Seminal texts of literary criticism include Plato's *Republic,* Aristotle's *Poetics,* Sir Philip Sidney's *The Defence of Poesie,* John Dryden's *Of Dramatic Poesie,* and William Wordsworth's "Preface" to the second edition of his *Lyrical Ballads.* Contemporary schools of criticism include deconstruction, feminist, psychoanalytic, poststructuralist, new historicist, postcolonialist, and reader- response.

D

Dactyl: See *Foot*

Dadaism: A protest movement in art and literature founded by Tristan Tzara in 1916. Followers of the movement expressed their outrage at the destruction brought about by World War I by revolting against numerous forms of social convention. The Dadaists presented works marked by calculated madness and flamboyant nonsense. They stressed total freedom of expression, commonly through primitive displays of emotion and illogical, often senseless, poetry. The movement ended shortly after the war, when it was replaced by surrealism. Proponents of Dadaism include Andre Breton, Louis Aragon, Philippe Soupault, and Paul Eluard.

Decadent: See *Decadents*

Decadents: The followers of a nineteenth-century literary movement that had its beginnings in French aestheticism. Decadent literature displays a fascination with perverse and morbid states; a search for novelty and sensation—the ''new thrill''; a preoccupation with mysticism; and a belief in the senselessness of human existence. The movement is closely associated with the doctrine Art for Art's Sake. The term ''decadence'' is sometimes used to denote a decline in the quality of art or literature following a period of greatness. Major French decadents are Charles Baudelaire and Arthur Rimbaud. English decadents include Oscar Wilde, Ernest Dowson, and Frank Harris.

Deconstruction: A method of literary criticism developed by Jacques Derrida and characterized by multiple conflicting interpretations of a given work. Deconstructionists consider the impact of the language of a work and suggest that the true meaning of the work is not necessarily the meaning that the author intended. Jacques Derrida's *De la grammatologie* is the seminal text on deconstructive strategies; among American practitioners of this method of criticism are Paul de Man and J. Hillis Miller.

Deduction: The process of reaching a conclusion through reasoning from general premises to a specific premise. An example of deduction is present in the following syllogism: Premise: All mammals are animals. Premise: All whales are mammals. Conclusion: Therefore, all whales are animals.

Denotation: The definition of a word, apart from the impressions or feelings it creates in the reader. The word ''apartheid'' denotes a political and economic policy of segregation by race, but its connotations— oppression, slavery, inequality—are numerous.

Denouement: A French word meaning ''the unknotting.'' In literary criticism, it denotes the resolution of conflict in fiction or drama. The *denouement* follows the climax and provides an outcome to the primary plot situation as well as an explanation of secondary plot complications. The *denouement* often involves a character's recognition of his or her state of mind or moral condition. A well-known example of *denouement* is the last scene of the play *As You Like It* by William Shakespeare, in which couples are married, an evildoer repents, the identities of two disguised characters are revealed, and a ruler is restored to power. Also known as Falling Action.

Description: Descriptive writing is intended to allow a reader to picture the scene or setting in which the action of a story takes place. The form this description takes often evokes an intended emotional response—a dark, spooky graveyard will evoke fear, and a peaceful, sunny meadow will evoke calmness. An example of a descriptive story is Edgar Allan Poe's *Landor's Cottage,* which offers a detailed depiction of a New York country estate.

Detective Story: A narrative about the solution of a mystery or the identification of a criminal. The conventions of the detective story include the detective's scrupulous use of logic in solving the mystery; incompetent or ineffectual police; a suspect who appears guilty at first but is later proved innocent; and the detective's friend or confidant— often the narrator—whose slowness in interpreting clues emphasizes by contrast the detective's brilliance. Edgar Allan Poe's ''Murders in the Rue Morgue'' is commonly regarded as the earliest example of this type of story. With this work, Poe established many of the conventions of the detective story genre, which are still in practice. Other practitioners of this vast and extremely popular genre include Arthur Conan Doyle, Dashiell Hammett, and Agatha Christie.

Deus ex machina: A Latin term meaning ''god out of a machine.'' In Greek drama, a god was often lowered onto the stage by a mechanism of some kind to rescue the hero or untangle the plot. By extension, the term refers to any artificial device or coincidence used to bring about a convenient and simple solution to a plot. This is a common device in melodramas and includes such fortunate circumstances as the sudden receipt of a legacy to save the family farm or a last-minute stay of execution. The *deus ex machina* invariably rewards the virtuous and punishes evildoers. Examples of *deus ex machina* include King Louis XIV in Jean-Baptiste Moliere's *Tartuffe* and Queen Victoria in *The Pirates of Penzance* by William Gilbert and Arthur Sullivan. Bertolt Brecht parodies the abuse of such devices in the conclusion of his *Threepenny Opera.*

Dialogue: In its widest sense, dialogue is simply conversation between people in a literary work; in its most restricted sense, it refers specifically to the speech of characters in a drama. As a specific literary genre, a ''dialogue'' is a composition in which characters debate an issue or idea. The Greek philosopher Plato frequently expounded his theories in the form of dialogues.

Diction: The selection and arrangement of words in a literary work. Either or both may vary depending on the desired effect. There are four general types of diction: ''formal,'' used in scholarly or lofty writing; ''informal,'' used in relaxed but educated conversation; ''colloquial,'' used in everyday speech; and ''slang,'' containing newly coined words and other terms not accepted in formal usage.

Didactic: A term used to describe works of literature that aim to teach some moral, religious, political, or practical lesson. Although didactic elements are often found in artistically pleasing works, the term ''didactic'' usually refers to literature in which the message is more important than the form. The term may also be used to criticize a work that the critic finds ''overly didactic,'' that is, heavy-handed in its delivery of a lesson. Examples of didactic literature include John Bunyan's *Pilgrim's Progress,* Alexander Pope's *Essay on Criticism,* Jean-Jacques Rousseau's *Emile,* and Elizabeth Inchbald's *Simple Story.*

Dimeter: See *Meter*

Dionysian: See *Apollonian and Dionysian*

Discordia concours: A Latin phrase meaning ''discord in harmony.'' The term was coined by the eighteenth-century English writer Samuel Johnson to describe ''a combination of dissimilar images or discovery of occult resemblances in things apparently unlike.'' Johnson created the expression by reversing a phrase by the Latin poet Horace. The metaphysical poetry of John Donne, Richard Crashaw, Abraham Cowley, George Herbert, and Edward Taylor among others, contains many examples of *discordia concours.* In Donne's ''A Valediction: Forbidding Mourning,'' the poet compares the union of himself with his lover to a draftsman's compass: If they be two, they are two so, As stiff twin compasses are two: Thy soul, the fixed foot, makes no show To move, but doth, if the other do; And though it in the center sit, Yet when the other far doth roam, It leans, and hearkens after it, And grows erect, as that comes home.

Dissonance: A combination of harsh or jarring sounds, especially in poetry. Although such combinations may be accidental, poets sometimes intentionally make them to achieve particular effects. Dissonance is also sometimes used to refer to close but not identical rhymes. When this is the case, the word functions as a synonym for consonance. Robert Browning, Gerard Manley Hopkins, and many other poets have made deliberate use of dissonance.

Doppelganger: A literary technique by which a character is duplicated (usually in the form of an alter ego, though sometimes as a ghostly counterpart) or divided into two distinct, usually opposite personalities. The use of this character device is widespread in nineteenth- and twentieth- century literature, and indicates a growing awareness among authors that the ''self'' is really a composite of many ''selves.'' A well-known story containing a *doppelganger* character is Robert Louis Stevenson's *Dr. Jekyll and Mr. Hyde,* which dramatizes an internal struggle between good and evil. Also known as The Double.

Double Entendre: A corruption of a French phrase meaning ''double meaning.'' The term is used to indicate a word or phrase that is deliberately ambiguous, especially when one of the meanings is risque or improper. An example of a *double entendre* is the Elizabethan usage of the verb ''die,'' which refers both to death and to orgasm.

Double, The: See *Doppelganger*

Draft: Any preliminary version of a written work. An author may write dozens of drafts which are revised to form the final work, or he or she may write only one, with few or no revisions. Dorothy Parker's observation that ''I can't write five words but that I change seven'' humorously indicates the purpose of the draft.

Drama: In its widest sense, a drama is any work designed to be presented by actors on a stage. Similarly, ''drama'' denotes a broad literary genre that includes a variety of forms, from pageant and spectacle to tragedy and comedy, as well as countless types and subtypes. More commonly in modern usage, however, a drama is a work that treats serious subjects and themes but does not aim at the grandeur of tragedy. This use of the term originated with the eighteenth-century French writer Denis Diderot, who used the word *drame* to designate his plays about middle- class life; thus ''drama'' typically features characters of a less exalted stature than those of tragedy. Examples of classical dramas include Menander's comedy *Dyscolus* and Sophocles' tragedy *Oedipus Rex.* Contemporary dramas include Eugene O'Neill's *The Iceman Cometh,* Lillian Hellman's *Little Foxes,* and August Wilson's *Ma Rainey's Black Bottom.*

Dramatic Irony: Occurs when the audience of a play or the reader of a work of literature knows something that a character in the work itself does not know. The irony is in the contrast between the intended meaning of the statements or actions of a character and the additional information understood by the audience. A celebrated example of dramatic irony is in Act V of William Shakespeare's *Romeo and Juliet,* where two young lovers meet their end as a result of a tragic misunderstanding. Here, the audience has full knowledge that Juliet's apparent ''death'' is merely temporary; she will regain her senses when the mysterious ''sleeping potion'' she has taken wears off. But Romeo, mistaking Juliet's drug-induced trance for true death, kills himself in grief. Upon awakening, Juliet discovers Romeo's corpse and, in despair, slays herself.

Dramatic Monologue: See *Monologue*

Dramatic Poetry: Any lyric work that employs elements of drama such as dialogue, conflict, or characterization, but excluding works that are intended for stage presentation. A monologue is a form of dramatic poetry.

Dramatis Personae: The characters in a work of literature, particularly a drama. The list of characters printed before the main text of a play or in the program is the *dramatis personae.*

Dream Allegory: See *Dream Vision*

Dream Vision: A literary convention, chiefly of the Middle Ages. In a dream vision a story is presented as a literal dream of the narrator. This device was commonly used to teach moral and religious lessons. Important works of this type are *The Divine Comedy* by Dante Alighieri, *Piers Plowman* by William Langland, and *The Pilgrim's Progress* by John Bunyan. Also known as Dream Allegory.

Dystopia: An imaginary place in a work of fiction where the characters lead dehumanized, fearful lives. Jack London's *The Iron Heel,* Yevgeny Zamyatin's *My,* Aldous Huxley's *Brave New World,* George Orwell's *Nineteen Eighty-four,* and Margaret Atwood's *Handmaid's Tale* portray versions of dystopia.

E

Eclogue: In classical literature, a poem featuring rural themes and structured as a dialogue among shepherds. Eclogues often took specific poetic forms, such as elegies or love poems. Some were written as the soliloquy of a shepherd. In later centuries, ''eclogue'' came to refer to any poem that was in the pastoral tradition or that had a dialogue or monologue structure. A classical example of an eclogue is Virgil's *Eclogues,* also known as *Bucolics.* Giovanni

Boccaccio, Edmund Spenser, Andrew Marvell, Jonathan Swift, and Louis MacNeice also wrote eclogues.

Edwardian: Describes cultural conventions identified with the period of the reign of Edward VII of England (1901–1910). Writers of the Edwardian Age typically displayed a strong reaction against the propriety and conservatism of the Victorian Age. Their work often exhibits distrust of authority in religion, politics, and art and expresses strong doubts about the soundness of conventional values. Writers of this era include George Bernard Shaw, H. G. Wells, and Joseph Conrad.

Edwardian Age: See *Edwardian*

Electra Complex: A daughter's amorous obsession with her father. The term Electra complex comes from the plays of Euripides and Sophocles entitled *Electra,* in which the character Electra drives her brother Orestes to kill their mother and her lover in revenge for the murder of their father.

Elegy: A lyric poem that laments the death of a person or the eventual death of all people. In a conventional elegy, set in a classical world, the poet and subject are spoken of as shepherds. In modern criticism, the word elegy is often used to refer to a poem that is melancholy or mournfully contemplative. John Milton's ''Lycidas'' and Percy Bysshe Shelley's ''Adonais'' are two examples of this form.

Elizabethan Age: A period of great economic growth, religious controversy, and nationalism closely associated with the reign of Elizabeth I of England (1558–1603). The Elizabethan Age is considered a part of the general renaissance—that is, the flowering of arts and literature—that took place in Europe during the fourteenth through sixteenth centuries. The era is considered the golden age of English literature. The most important dramas in English and a great deal of lyric poetry were produced during this period, and modern English criticism began around this time. The notable authors of the period—Philip Sidney, Edmund Spenser, Christopher Marlowe, William Shakespeare, Ben Jonson, Francis Bacon, and John Donne—are among the best in all of English literature.

Elizabethan Drama: English comic and tragic plays produced during the Renaissance, or more narrowly, those plays written during the last years of and few years after Queen Elizabeth's reign. William Shakespeare is considered an Elizabethan dramatist in the broader sense, although most of his work was produced during the reign of James I. Examples of Elizabethan comedies include John

Lyly's *The Woman in the Moone,* Thomas Dekker's *The Roaring Girl, or, Moll Cut Purse,* and William Shakespeare's *Twelfth Night.* Examples of Elizabethan tragedies include William Shakespeare's *Antony and Cleopatra,* Thomas Kyd's *The Spanish Tragedy,* and John Webster's *The Tragedy of the Duchess of Malfi.*

Empathy: A sense of shared experience, including emotional and physical feelings, with someone or something other than oneself. Empathy is often used to describe the response of a reader to a literary character. An example of an empathic passage is William Shakespeare's description in his narrative poem *Venus and Adonis* of: the snail, whose tender horns being hit, Shrinks backward in his shelly cave with pain. Readers of Gerard Manley Hopkins's *The Windhover* may experience some of the physical sensations evoked in the description of the movement of the falcon.

English Sonnet: See *Sonnet*

Enjambment: The running over of the sense and structure of a line of verse or a couplet into the following verse or couplet. Andrew Marvell's "To His Coy Mistress" is structured as a series of enjambments, as in lines 11–12: "My vegetable love should grow/Vaster than empires and more slow."

Enlightenment, The: An eighteenth-century philosophical movement. It began in France but had a wide impact throughout Europe and America. Thinkers of the Enlightenment valued reason and believed that both the individual and society could achieve a state of perfection. Corresponding to this essentially humanist vision was a resistance to religious authority. Important figures of the Enlightenment were Denis Diderot and Voltaire in France, Edward Gibbon and David Hume in England, and Thomas Paine and Thomas Jefferson in the United States.

Epic: A long narrative poem about the adventures of a hero of great historic or legendary importance. The setting is vast and the action is often given cosmic significance through the intervention of supernatural forces such as gods, angels, or demons. Epics are typically written in a classical style of grand simplicity with elaborate metaphors and allusions that enhance the symbolic importance of a hero's adventures. Some well-known epics are Homer's *Iliad* and *Odyssey,* Virgil's *Aeneid,* and John Milton's *Paradise Lost.*

Epic Simile: See *Homeric Simile*

Epic Theater: A theory of theatrical presentation developed by twentieth-century German playwright Bertolt Brecht. Brecht created a type of drama that the audience could view with complete detachment. He used what he termed "alienation effects" to create an emotional distance between the audience and the action on stage. Among these effects are: short, self-contained scenes that keep the play from building to a cathartic climax; songs that comment on the action; and techniques of acting that prevent the actor from developing an emotional identity with his role. Besides the plays of Bertolt Brecht, other plays that utilize epic theater conventions include those of Georg Buchner, Frank Wedekind, Erwin Piscator, and Leopold Jessner.

Epigram: A saying that makes the speaker's point quickly and concisely. Samuel Taylor Coleridge wrote an epigram that neatly sums up the form: What is an Epigram? A Dwarfish whole, Its body brevity, and wit its soul.

Epilogue: A concluding statement or section of a literary work. In dramas, particularly those of the seventeenth and eighteenth centuries, the epilogue is a closing speech, often in verse, delivered by an actor at the end of a play and spoken directly to the audience. A famous epilogue is Puck's speech at the end of William Shakespeare's *A Midsummer Night's Dream.*

Epiphany: A sudden revelation of truth inspired by a seemingly trivial incident. The term was widely used by James Joyce in his critical writings, and the stories in Joyce's *Dubliners* are commonly called "epiphanies."

Episode: An incident that forms part of a story and is significantly related to it. Episodes may be either self-contained narratives or events that depend on a larger context for their sense and importance. Examples of episodes include the founding of Wilmington, Delaware in Charles Reade's *The Disinherited Heir* and the individual events comprising the picaresque novels and medieval romances.

Episodic Plot: See *Plot*

Epitaph: An inscription on a tomb or tombstone, or a verse written on the occasion of a person's death. Epitaphs may be serious or humorous. Dorothy Parker's epitaph reads, "I told you I was sick."

Epithalamion: A song or poem written to honor and commemorate a marriage ceremony. Famous examples include Edmund Spenser's "Epithalamion'' and e. e. cummings's ''Epithalamion.'' Also spelled Epithalamium.

Epithalamium: See *Epithalamion*

Epithet: A word or phrase, often disparaging or abusive, that expresses a character trait of someone or something. ''The Napoleon of crime'' is an epithet applied to Professor Moriarty, arch-rival of Sherlock Holmes in Arthur Conan Doyle's series of detective stories.

Exempla: See *Exemplum*

Exemplum: A tale with a moral message. This form of literary sermonizing flourished during the Middle Ages, when *exempla* appeared in collections known as ''example-books.'' The works of Geoffrey Chaucer are full of *exempla*.

Existentialism: A predominantly twentieth-century philosophy concerned with the nature and perception of human existence. There are two major strains of existentialist thought: atheistic and Christian. Followers of atheistic existentialism believe that the individual is alone in a godless universe and that the basic human condition is one of suffering and loneliness. Nevertheless, because there are no fixed values, individuals can create their own characters— indeed, they can shape themselves—through the exercise of free will. The atheistic strain culminates in and is popularly associated with the works of Jean-Paul Sartre. The Christian existentialists, on the other hand, believe that only in God may people find freedom from life's anguish. The two strains hold certain beliefs in common: that existence cannot be fully understood or described through empirical effort; that anguish is a universal element of life; that individuals must bear responsibility for their actions; and that there is no common standard of behavior or perception for religious and ethical matters. Existentialist thought figures prominently in the works of such authors as Eugene Ionesco, Franz Kafka, Fyodor Dostoyevsky, Simone de Beauvoir, Samuel Beckett, and Albert Camus.

Expatriates: See *Expatriatism*

Expatriatism: The practice of leaving one's country to live for an extended period in another country. Literary expatriates include English poets Percy Bysshe Shelley and John Keats in Italy, Polish novelist Joseph Conrad in England, American writers Richard Wright, James Baldwin, Gertrude Stein, and Ernest Hemingway in France, and Trinidadian author Neil Bissondath in Canada.

Exposition: Writing intended to explain the nature of an idea, thing, or theme. Expository writing is often combined with description, narration, or argument. In dramatic writing, the exposition is the introductory material which presents the characters, setting, and tone of the play. An example of dramatic exposition occurs in many nineteenth-century drawing-room comedies in which the butler and the maid open the play with relevant talk about their master and mistress; in composition, exposition relays factual information, as in encyclopedia entries.

Expressionism: An indistinct literary term, originally used to describe an early twentieth-century school of German painting. The term applies to almost any mode of unconventional, highly subjective writing that distorts reality in some way. Advocates of Expressionism include dramatists George Kaiser, Ernst Toller, Luigi Pirandello, Federico Garcia Lorca, Eugene O'Neill, and Elmer Rice; poets George Heym, Ernst Stadler, August Stramm, Gottfried Benn, and Georg Trakl; and novelists Franz Kafka and James Joyce.

Extended Monologue: See *Monologue*

F

Fable: A prose or verse narrative intended to convey a moral. Animals or inanimate objects with human characteristics often serve as characters in fables. A famous fable is Aesop's ''The Tortoise and the Hare.''

Fairy Tales: Short narratives featuring mythical beings such as fairies, elves, and sprites. These tales originally belonged to the folklore of a particular nation or region, such as those collected in Germany by Jacob and Wilhelm Grimm. Two other celebrated writers of fairy tales are Hans Christian Andersen and Rudyard Kipling.

Falling Action: See *Denouement*

Fantasy: A literary form related to mythology and folklore. Fantasy literature is typically set in non-existent realms and features supernatural beings. Notable examples of fantasy literature are *The Lord of the Rings* by J. R. R. Tolkien and the Gormenghast trilogy by Mervyn Peake.

Farce: A type of comedy characterized by broad humor, outlandish incidents, and often vulgar subject matter. Much of the ''comedy'' in film and television could more accurately be described as farce.

Feet: See *Foot*

Feminine Rhyme: See *Rhyme*

Femme fatale: A French phrase with the literal translation "fatal woman." A *femme fatale* is a sensuous, alluring woman who often leads men into danger or trouble. A classic example of the *femme fatale* is the nameless character in Billy Wilder's *The Seven Year Itch,* portrayed by Marilyn Monroe in the film adaptation.

Fiction: Any story that is the product of imagination rather than a documentation of fact. characters and events in such narratives may be based in real life but their ultimate form and configuration is a creation of the author. Geoffrey Chaucer's *The Canterbury Tales,* Laurence Sterne's *Tristram Shandy,* and Margaret Mitchell's *Gone with the Wind* are examples of fiction.

Figurative Language: A technique in writing in which the author temporarily interrupts the order, construction, or meaning of the writing for a particular effect. This interruption takes the form of one or more figures of speech such as hyperbole, irony, or simile. Figurative language is the opposite of literal language, in which every word is truthful, accurate, and free of exaggeration or embellishment. Examples of figurative language are tropes such as metaphor and rhetorical figures such as apostrophe.

Figures of Speech: Writing that differs from customary conventions for construction, meaning, order, or significance for the purpose of a special meaning or effect. There are two major types of figures of speech: rhetorical figures, which do not make changes in the meaning of the words, and tropes, which do. Types of figures of speech include simile, hyperbole, alliteration, and pun, among many others.

Fin de siecle: A French term meaning "end of the century." The term is used to denote the last decade of the nineteenth century, a transition period when writers and other artists abandoned old conventions and looked for new techniques and objectives. Two writers commonly associated with the *fin de siecle* mindset are Oscar Wilde and George Bernard Shaw.

First Person: See *Point of View*

Flashback: A device used in literature to present action that occurred before the beginning of the story. Flashbacks are often introduced as the dreams or recollections of one or more characters. Flashback techniques are often used in films, where they are typically set off by a gradual changing of one picture to another.

Foil: A character in a work of literature whose physical or psychological qualities contrast strongly with, and therefore highlight, the corresponding qualities of another character. In his Sherlock Holmes stories, Arthur Conan Doyle portrayed Dr. Watson as a man of normal habits and intelligence, making him a foil for the eccentric and wonderfully perceptive Sherlock Holmes.

Folk Ballad: See *Ballad*

Folklore: Traditions and myths preserved in a culture or group of people. Typically, these are passed on by word of mouth in various forms—such as legends, songs, and proverbs— or preserved in customs and ceremonies. This term was first used by W. J. Thoms in 1846. Sir James Frazer's *The Golden Bough* is the record of English folklore; myths about the frontier and the Old South exemplify American folklore.

Folktale: A story originating in oral tradition. Folktales fall into a variety of categories, including legends, ghost stories, fairy tales, fables, and anecdotes based on historical figures and events. Examples of folktales include Giambattista Basile's *The Pentamerone,* which contains the tales of Puss in Boots, Rapunzel, Cinderella, and Beauty and the Beast, and Joel Chandler Harris's Uncle Remus stories, which represent transplanted African folktales and American tales about the characters Mike Fink, Johnny Appleseed, Paul Bunyan, and Pecos Bill.

Foot: The smallest unit of rhythm in a line of poetry. In English-language poetry, a foot is typically one accented syllable combined with one or two unaccented syllables. There are many different types of feet. When the accent is on the second syllable of a two syllable word (con- *tort*), the foot is an "iamb"; the reverse accentual pattern (*tor* -ture) is a "trochee." Other feet that commonly occur in poetry in English are "anapest", two unaccented syllables followed by an accented syllable as in inter-*cept,* and "dactyl", an accented syllable followed by two unaccented syllables as in *su*-i- cide.

Foreshadowing: A device used in literature to create expectation or to set up an explanation of later developments. In Charles Dickens's *Great Expectations,* the graveyard encounter at the beginning of the novel between Pip and the escaped convict Magwitch foreshadows the baleful atmosphere and events that comprise much of the narrative.

Form: The pattern or construction of a work which identifies its genre and distinguishes it from other genres. Examples of forms include the different genres, such as the lyric form or the short story form, and various patterns for poetry, such as the verse form or the stanza form.

Formalism: In literary criticism, the belief that literature should follow prescribed rules of construction, such as those that govern the sonnet form. Examples of formalism are found in the work of the New Critics and structuralists.

Fourteener Meter: See *Meter*

Free Verse: Poetry that lacks regular metrical and rhyme patterns but that tries to capture the cadences of everyday speech. The form allows a poet to exploit a variety of rhythmical effects within a single poem. Free-verse techniques have been widely used in the twentieth century by such writers as Ezra Pound, T. S. Eliot, Carl Sandburg, and William Carlos Williams. Also known as *Vers libre.*

Futurism: A flamboyant literary and artistic movement that developed in France, Italy, and Russia from 1908 through the 1920s. Futurist theater and poetry abandoned traditional literary forms. In their place, followers of the movement attempted to achieve total freedom of expression through bizarre imagery and deformed or newly invented words. The Futurists were self-consciously modern artists who attempted to incorporate the appearances and sounds of modern life into their work. Futurist writers include Filippo Tommaso Marinetti, Wyndham Lewis, Guillaume Apollinaire, Velimir Khlebnikov, and Vladimir Mayakovsky.

G

Genre: A category of literary work. In critical theory, genre may refer to both the content of a given work—tragedy, comedy, pastoral—and to its form, such as poetry, novel, or drama. This term also refers to types of popular literature, as in the genres of science fiction or the detective story.

Genteel Tradition: A term coined by critic George Santayana to describe the literary practice of certain late nineteenth- century American writers, especially New Englanders. Followers of the Genteel Tradition emphasized conventionality in social, religious, moral, and literary standards. Some of the best-known writers of the Genteel Tradition are R. H. Stoddard and Bayard Taylor.

Gilded Age: A period in American history during the 1870s characterized by political corruption and materialism. A number of important novels of social and political criticism were written during this time. Examples of Gilded Age literature include Henry Adams's *Democracy* and F. Marion Crawford's *An American Politician.*

Gothic: See *Gothicism*

Gothicism: In literary criticism, works characterized by a taste for the medieval or morbidly attractive. A gothic novel prominently features elements of horror, the supernatural, gloom, and violence: clanking chains, terror, charnel houses, ghosts, medieval castles, and mysteriously slamming doors. The term ''gothic novel'' is also applied to novels that lack elements of the traditional Gothic setting but that create a similar atmosphere of terror or dread. Mary Shelley's *Frankenstein* is perhaps the best-known English work of this kind.

Gothic Novel: See *Gothicism*

Great Chain of Being: The belief that all things and creatures in nature are organized in a hierarchy from inanimate objects at the bottom to God at the top. This system of belief was popular in the seventeenth and eighteenth centuries. A summary of the concept of the great chain of being can be found in the first epistle of Alexander Pope's *An Essay on Man,* and more recently in Arthur O. Lovejoy's *The Great Chain of Being: A Study of the History of an Idea.*

Grotesque: In literary criticism, the subject matter of a work or a style of expression characterized by exaggeration, deformity, freakishness, and disorder. The grotesque often includes an element of comic absurdity. Early examples of literary grotesque include Francois Rabelais's *Pantagruel* and *Gargantua* and Thomas Nashe's *The Unfortunate Traveller,* while more recent examples can be found in the works of Edgar Allan Poe, Evelyn Waugh, Eudora Welty, Flannery O'Connor, Eugene Ionesco, Gunter Grass, Thomas Mann, Mervyn Peake, and Joseph Heller, among many others.

H

Haiku: The shortest form of Japanese poetry, constructed in three lines of five, seven, and five syllables respectively. The message of a *haiku* poem usually centers on some aspect of spirituality and provokes an emotional response in the reader. Early masters of *haiku* include Basho, Buson, Kobayashi

Issa, and Masaoka Shiki. English writers of *haiku* include the Imagists, notably Ezra Pound, H. D., Amy Lowell, Carl Sandburg, and William Carlos Williams. Also known as *Hokku.*

Half Rhyme: See *Consonance*

Hamartia: In tragedy, the event or act that leads to the hero's or heroine's downfall. This term is often incorrectly used as a synonym for tragic flaw. In Richard Wright's *Native Son,* the act that seals Bigger Thomas's fate is his first impulsive murder.

Harlem Renaissance: The Harlem Renaissance of the 1920s is generally considered the first significant movement of black writers and artists in the United States. During this period, new and established black writers published more fiction and poetry than ever before, the first influential black literary journals were established, and black authors and artists received their first widespread recognition and serious critical appraisal. Among the major writers associated with this period are Claude McKay, Jean Toomer, Countee Cullen, Langston Hughes, Arna Bontemps, Nella Larsen, and Zora Neale Hurston. Works representative of the Harlem Renaissance include Arna Bontemps's poems ''The Return'' and ''Golgotha Is a Mountain,'' Claude McKay's novel *Home to Harlem,* Nella Larsen's novel *Passing,* Langston Hughes's poem ''The Negro Speaks of Rivers,'' and the journals *Crisis* and *Opportunity,* both founded during this period. Also known as Negro Renaissance and New Negro Movement.

Harlequin: A stock character of the *commedia dell'arte* who occasionally interrupted the action with silly antics. Harlequin first appeared on the English stage in John Day's *The Travailes of the Three English Brothers.* The San Francisco Mime Troupe is one of the few modern groups to adapt Harlequin to the needs of contemporary satire.

Hellenism: Imitation of ancient Greek thought or styles. Also, an approach to life that focuses on the growth and development of the intellect. ''Hellenism'' is sometimes used to refer to the belief that reason can be applied to examine all human experience. A cogent discussion of Hellenism can be found in Matthew Arnold's *Culture and Anarchy.*

Heptameter: See *Meter*

Hero/Heroine: The principal sympathetic character (male or female) in a literary work. Heroes and heroines typically exhibit admirable traits: idealism, courage, and integrity, for example. Famous heroes and heroines include Pip in Charles Dickens's *Great Expectations,* the anonymous narrator in Ralph Ellison's *Invisible Man,* and Sethe in Toni Morrison's *Beloved.*

Heroic Couplet: A rhyming couplet written in iambic pentameter (a verse with five iambic feet). The following lines by Alexander Pope are an example: ''Truth guards the Poet, sanctifies the line,/ And makes Immortal, Verse as mean as mine.''

Heroic Line: The meter and length of a line of verse in epic or heroic poetry. This varies by language and time period. For example, in English poetry, the heroic line is iambic pentameter (a verse with five iambic feet); in French, the alexandrine (a verse with six iambic feet); in classical literature, dactylic hexameter (a verse with six dactylic feet).

Heroine: See *Hero/Heroine*

Hexameter: See *Meter*

Historical Criticism: The study of a work based on its impact on the world of the time period in which it was written. Examples of postmodern historical criticism can be found in the work of Michel Foucault, Hayden White, Stephen Greenblatt, and Jonathan Goldberg.

Hokku: See *Haiku*

Holocaust: See *Holocaust Literature*

Holocaust Literature: Literature influenced by or written about the Holocaust of World War II. Such literature includes true stories of survival in concentration camps, escape, and life after the war, as well as fictional works and poetry. Representative works of Holocaust literature include Saul Bellow's *Mr. Sammler's Planet,* Anne Frank's *The Diary of a Young Girl,* Jerzy Kosinski's *The Painted Bird,* Arthur Miller's *Incident at Vichy,* Czeslaw Milosz's *Collected Poems,* William Styron's *Sophie's Choice,* and Art Spiegelman's *Maus.*

Homeric Simile: An elaborate, detailed comparison written as a simile many lines in length. An example of an epic simile from John Milton's *Paradise Lost* follows: Angel Forms, who lay entranced Thick as autumnal leaves that strow the brooks In Vallombrosa, where the Etrurian shades High over-arched embower; or scattered sedge Afloat, when with fierce winds Orion armed Hath vexed the Red-Sea coast, whose waves o'erthrew Busiris and his Memphian chivalry, While with perfidious hatred they pursued The sojourners of

Goshen, who beheld From the safe shore their floating carcasses And broken chariot-wheels. Also known as Epic Simile.

Horatian Satire: See *Satire*

Humanism: A philosophy that places faith in the dignity of humankind and rejects the medieval perception of the individual as a weak, fallen creature. "Humanists" typically believe in the perfectibility of human nature and view reason and education as the means to that end. Humanist thought is represented in the works of Marsilio Ficino, Ludovico Castelvetro, Edmund Spenser, John Milton, Dean John Colet, Desiderius Erasmus, John Dryden, Alexander Pope, Matthew Arnold, and Irving Babbitt.

Humors: Mentions of the humors refer to the ancient Greek theory that a person's health and personality were determined by the balance of four basic fluids in the body: blood, phlegm, yellow bile, and black bile. A dominance of any fluid would cause extremes in behavior. An excess of blood created a sanguine person who was joyful, aggressive, and passionate; a phlegmatic person was shy, fearful, and sluggish; too much yellow bile led to a choleric temperament characterized by impatience, anger, bitterness, and stubbornness; and excessive black bile created melancholy, a state of laziness, gluttony, and lack of motivation. Literary treatment of the humors is exemplified by several characters in Ben Jonson's plays *Every Man in His Humour* and *Every Man out of His Humour*. Also spelled Humours.

Humours: See *Humors*

Hyperbole: In literary criticism, deliberate exaggeration used to achieve an effect. In William Shakespeare's *Macbeth*, Lady Macbeth hyperbolizes when she says, "All the perfumes of Arabia could not sweeten this little hand."

I

Iamb: See *Foot*

Idiom: A word construction or verbal expression closely associated with a given language. For example, in colloquial English the construction "how come" can be used instead of "why" to introduce a question. Similarly, "a piece of cake" is sometimes used to describe a task that is easily done.

Image: A concrete representation of an object or sensory experience. Typically, such a representation helps evoke the feelings associated with the object or experience itself. Images are either "literal" or "figurative." Literal images are especially concrete and involve little or no extension of the obvious meaning of the words used to express them. Figurative images do not follow the literal meaning of the words exactly. Images in literature are usually visual, but the term "image" can also refer to the representation of any sensory experience. In his poem "The Shepherd's Hour," Paul Verlaine presents the following image: "The Moon is red through horizon's fog;/ In a dancing mist the hazy meadow sleeps." The first line is broadly literal, while the second line involves turns of meaning associated with dancing and sleeping.

Imagery: The array of images in a literary work. Also, figurative language. William Butler Yeats's "The Second Coming" offers a powerful image of encroaching anarchy: Turning and turning in the widening gyre The falcon cannot hear the falconer; Things fall apart. . . .

Imagism: An English and American poetry movement that flourished between 1908 and 1917. The Imagists used precise, clearly presented images in their works. They also used common, everyday speech and aimed for conciseness, concrete imagery, and the creation of new rhythms. Participants in the Imagist movement included Ezra Pound, H. D. (Hilda Doolittle), and Amy Lowell, among others.

In medias res: A Latin term meaning "in the middle of things." It refers to the technique of beginning a story at its midpoint and then using various flashback devices to reveal previous action. This technique originated in such epics as Virgil's *Aeneid*.

Induction: The process of reaching a conclusion by reasoning from specific premises to form a general premise. Also, an introductory portion of a work of literature, especially a play. Geoffrey Chaucer's "Prologue" to the *Canterbury Tales,* Thomas Sackville's "Induction" to *The Mirror of Magistrates,* and the opening scene in William Shakespeare's *The Taming of the Shrew* are examples of inductions to literary works.

Intentional Fallacy: The belief that judgments of a literary work based solely on an author's stated or implied intentions are false and misleading. Critics who believe in the concept of the intentional fallacy typically argue that the work itself is sufficient matter for interpretation, even though they may concede that an author's statement of purpose can be useful. Analysis of William Wordsworth's *Lyrical Ballads* based on the observations about poetry he makes in his "Preface" to the second edition of that work is an example of the intentional fallacy.

Interior Monologue: A narrative technique in which characters' thoughts are revealed in a way that appears to be uncontrolled by the author. The interior monologue typically aims to reveal the inner self of a character. It portrays emotional experiences as they occur at both a conscious and unconscious level. images are often used to represent sensations or emotions. One of the best-known interior monologues in English is the Molly Bloom section at the close of James Joyce's *Ulysses.* The interior monologue is also common in the works of Virginia Woolf.

Internal Rhyme: Rhyme that occurs within a single line of verse. An example is in the opening line of Edgar Allan Poe's "The Raven": "Once upon a midnight dreary, while I pondered weak and weary." Here, "dreary" and "weary" make an internal rhyme.

Irish Literary Renaissance: A late nineteenth- and early twentieth-century movement in Irish literature. Members of the movement aimed to reduce the influence of British culture in Ireland and create an Irish national literature. William Butler Yeats, George Moore, and Sean O'Casey are three of the best-known figures of the movement.

Irony: In literary criticism, the effect of language in which the intended meaning is the opposite of what is stated. The title of Jonathan Swift's "A Modest Proposal" is ironic because what Swift proposes in this essay is cannibalism—hardly "modest."

Italian Sonnet: See *Sonnet*

J

Jacobean Age: The period of the reign of James I of England (1603–1625). The early literature of this period reflected the worldview of the Elizabethan Age, but a darker, more cynical attitude steadily grew in the art and literature of the Jacobean Age. This was an important time for English drama and poetry. Milestones include William Shakespeare's tragedies, tragi-comedies, and sonnets; Ben Jonson's various dramas; and John Donne's metaphysical poetry.

Jargon: Language that is used or understood only by a select group of people. Jargon may refer to terminology used in a certain profession, such as

computer jargon, or it may refer to any nonsensical language that is not understood by most people. Literary examples of jargon are Francois Villon's *Ballades en jargon,* which is composed in the secret language of the *coquillards,* and Anthony Burgess's *A Clockwork Orange,* narrated in the fictional characters' language of "Nadsat."

Juvenalian Satire: See *Satire*

K

Knickerbocker Group: A somewhat indistinct group of New York writers of the first half of the nineteenth century. Members of the group were linked only by location and a common theme: New York life. Two famous members of the Knickerbocker Group were Washington Irving and William Cullen Bryant. The group's name derives from Irving's *Knickerbocker's History of New York.*

L

Lais: See *Lay*

Lay: A song or simple narrative poem. The form originated in medieval France. Early French *lais* were often based on the Celtic legends and other tales sung by Breton minstrels—thus the name of the "Breton lay." In fourteenth-century England, the term "lay" was used to describe short narratives written in imitation of the Breton lays. The most notable of these is Geoffrey Chaucer's "The Minstrel's Tale."

Leitmotiv: See *Motif*

Literal Language: An author uses literal language when he or she writes without exaggerating or embellishing the subject matter and without any tools of figurative language. To say "He ran very quickly down the street" is to use literal language, whereas to say "He ran like a hare down the street" would be using figurative language.

Literary Ballad: See *Ballad*

Literature: Literature is broadly defined as any written or spoken material, but the term most often refers to creative works. Literature includes poetry, drama, fiction, and many kinds of nonfiction writing, as well as oral, dramatic, and broadcast compositions not necessarily preserved in a written format, such as films and television programs.

Lost Generation: A term first used by Gertrude Stein to describe the post-World War I generation of

American writers: men and women haunted by a sense of betrayal and emptiness brought about by the destructiveness of the war. The term is commonly applied to Hart Crane, Ernest Hemingway, F. Scott Fitzgerald, and others.

Lyric Poetry: A poem expressing the subjective feelings and personal emotions of the poet. Such poetry is melodic, since it was originally accompanied by a lyre in recitals. Most Western poetry in the twentieth century may be classified as lyrical. Examples of lyric poetry include A. E. Housman's elegy "To an Athlete Dying Young," the odes of Pindar and Horace, Thomas Gray and William Collins, the sonnets of Sir Thomas Wyatt and Sir Philip Sidney, Elizabeth Barrett Browning and Rainer Maria Rilke, and a host of other forms in the poetry of William Blake and Christina Rossetti, among many others.

M

Mannerism: Exaggerated, artificial adherence to a literary manner or style. Also, a popular style of the visual arts of late sixteenth-century Europe that was marked by elongation of the human form and by intentional spatial distortion. Literary works that are self-consciously high-toned and artistic are often said to be "mannered." Authors of such works include Henry James and Gertrude Stein.

Masculine Rhyme: See *Rhyme*

Masque: A lavish and elaborate form of entertainment, often performed in royal courts, that emphasizes song, dance, and costumery. The Renaissance form of the masque grew out of the spectacles of masked figures common in medieval England and Europe. The masque reached its peak of popularity and development in seventeenth-century England, during the reigns of James I and, especially, of Charles I. Ben Jonson, the most significant masque writer, also created the "antimasque," which incorporates elements of humor and the grotesque into the traditional masque and achieved greater dramatic quality. Masque-like interludes appear in Edmund Spenser's *The Faerie Queene* and in William Shakespeare's *The Tempest.* One of the best-known English masques is John Milton's *Comus.*

Measure: The foot, verse, or time sequence used in a literary work, especially a poem. Measure is often used somewhat incorrectly as a synonym for meter.

Melodrama: A play in which the typical plot is a conflict between characters who personify extreme good and evil. Melodramas usually end happily and emphasize sensationalism. Other literary forms that use the same techniques are often labeled "melodramatic." The term was formerly used to describe a combination of drama and music; as such, it was synonymous with "opera." Augustin Daly's *Under the Gaslight* and Dion Boucicault's *The Octoroon, The Colleen Bawn,* and *The Poor of New York* are examples of melodramas. The most popular media for twentieth-century melodramas are motion pictures and television.

Metaphor: A figure of speech that expresses an idea through the image of another object. Metaphors suggest the essence of the first object by identifying it with certain qualities of the second object. An example is "But soft, what light through yonder window breaks?/ It is the east, and Juliet is the sun" in William Shakespeare's *Romeo and Juliet.* Here, Juliet, the first object, is identified with qualities of the second object, the sun.

Metaphysical Conceit: See *Conceit*

Metaphysical Poetry: The body of poetry produced by a group of seventeenth-century English writers called the "Metaphysical Poets." The group includes John Donne and Andrew Marvell. The Metaphysical Poets made use of everyday speech, intellectual analysis, and unique imagery. They aimed to portray the ordinary conflicts and contradictions of life. Their poems often took the form of an argument, and many of them emphasize physical and religious love as well as the fleeting nature of life. Elaborate conceits are typical in metaphysical poetry. Marvell's "To His Coy Mistress" is a well-known example of a metaphysical poem.

Metaphysical Poets: See *Metaphysical Poetry*

Meter: In literary criticism, the repetition of sound patterns that creates a rhythm in poetry. The patterns are based on the number of syllables and the presence and absence of accents. The unit of rhythm in a line is called a foot. Types of meter are classified according to the number of feet in a line. These are the standard English lines: Monometer, one foot; Dimeter, two feet; Trimeter, three feet; Tetrameter, four feet; Pentameter, five feet; Hexameter, six feet (also called the Alexandrine); Heptameter, seven feet (also called the "Fourteener" when the feet are iambic). The most common English meter is the iambic pentameter, in which each line contains ten syllables, or five iambic feet, which individually are composed of an unstressed syllable followed by an accented syllable. Both of the following lines from Alfred, Lord Tennyson's

''Ulysses'' are written in iambic pentameter: Made weak by time and fate, but strong in will To strive, to seek, to find, and not to yield.

Mise en scene: The costumes, scenery, and other properties of a drama. Herbert Beerbohm Tree was renowned for the elaborate *mises en scene* of his lavish Shakespearean productions at His Majesty's Theatre between 1897 and 1915.

Modernism: Modern literary practices. Also, the principles of a literary school that lasted from roughly the beginning of the twentieth century until the end of World War II. Modernism is defined by its rejection of the literary conventions of the nineteenth century and by its opposition to conventional morality, taste, traditions, and economic values. Many writers are associated with the concepts of Modernism, including Albert Camus, Marcel Proust, D. H. Lawrence, W. H. Auden, Ernest Hemingway, William Faulkner, William Butler Yeats, Thomas Mann, Tennessee Williams, Eugene O'Neill, and James Joyce.

Monologue: A composition, written or oral, by a single individual. More specifically, a speech given by a single individual in a drama or other public entertainment. It has no set length, although it is usually several or more lines long. An example of an ''extended monologue''—that is, a monologue of great length and seriousness—occurs in the one-act, one-character play *The Stronger* by August Strindberg.

Monometer: See *Meter*

Mood: The prevailing emotions of a work or of the author in his or her creation of the work. The mood of a work is not always what might be expected based on its subject matter. The poem ''Dover Beach'' by Matthew Arnold offers examples of two different moods originating from the same experience: watching the ocean at night. The mood of the first three lines— The sea is calm tonight The tide is full, the moon lies fair Upon the straights. . . . is in sharp contrast to the mood of the last three lines— And we are here as on a darkling plain Swept with confused alarms of struggle and flight, Where ignorant armies clash by night.

Motif: A theme, character type, image, metaphor, or other verbal element that recurs throughout a single work of literature or occurs in a number of different works over a period of time. For example, the various manifestations of the color white in Herman Melville's *Moby Dick* is a ''specific'' *motif*, while the trials of star-crossed lovers is a ''conventional''

motif from the literature of all periods. Also known as *Motiv* or *Leitmotiv*.

Motiv: See *Motif*

Muckrakers: An early twentieth-century group of American writers. Typically, their works exposed the wrongdoings of big business and government in the United States. Upton Sinclair's *The Jungle* exemplifies the muckraking novel.

Muses: Nine Greek mythological goddesses, the daughters of Zeus and Mnemosyne (Memory). Each muse patronized a specific area of the liberal arts and sciences. Calliope presided over epic poetry, Clio over history, Erato over love poetry, Euterpe over music or lyric poetry, Melpomene over tragedy, Polyhymnia over hymns to the gods, Terpsichore over dance, Thalia over comedy, and Urania over astronomy. Poets and writers traditionally made appeals to the Muses for inspiration in their work. John Milton invokes the aid of a muse at the beginning of the first book of his *Paradise Lost:* Of Man's First disobedience, and the Fruit of the Forbidden Tree, whose mortal taste Brought Death into the World, and all our woe, With loss of Eden, till one greater Man Restore us, and regain the blissful Seat, Sing Heav'nly Muse, that on the secret top of Oreb, or of Sinai, didst inspire That Shepherd, who first taught the chosen Seed, In the Beginning how the Heav'ns and Earth Rose out of Chaos. . . .

Mystery: See *Suspense*

Myth: An anonymous tale emerging from the traditional beliefs of a culture or social unit. Myths use supernatural explanations for natural phenomena. They may also explain cosmic issues like creation and death. Collections of myths, known as mythologies, are common to all cultures and nations, but the best-known myths belong to the Norse, Roman, and Greek mythologies. A famous myth is the story of Arachne, an arrogant young girl who challenged a goddess, Athena, to a weaving contest; when the girl won, Athena was enraged and turned Arachne into a spider, thus explaining the existence of spiders.

N

Narration: The telling of a series of events, real or invented. A narration may be either a simple narrative, in which the events are recounted chronologically, or a narrative with a plot, in which the account is given in a style reflecting the author's artistic concept of the story. Narration is sometimes used as a synonym for "storyline." The recounting of scary stories around a campfire is a form of narration.

Narrative: A verse or prose accounting of an event or sequence of events, real or invented. The term is also used as an adjective in the sense "method of narration." For example, in literary criticism, the expression "narrative technique" usually refers to the way the author structures and presents his or her story. Narratives range from the shortest accounts of events, as in Julius Caesar's remark, "I came, I saw, I conquered," to the longest historical or biographical works, as in Edward Gibbon's *The Decline and Fall of the Roman Empire,* as well as diaries, travelogues, novels, ballads, epics, short stories, and other fictional forms.

Narrative Poetry: A nondramatic poem in which the author tells a story. Such poems may be of any length or level of complexity. Epics such as *Beowulf* and ballads are forms of narrative poetry.

Narrator: The teller of a story. The narrator may be the author or a character in the story through whom the author speaks. Huckleberry Finn is the narrator of Mark Twain's *The Adventures of Huckleberry Finn.*

Naturalism: A literary movement of the late nineteenth and early twentieth centuries. The movement's major theorist, French novelist Emile Zola, envisioned a type of fiction that would examine human life with the objectivity of scientific inquiry. The Naturalists typically viewed human beings as either the products of "biological determinism," ruled by hereditary instincts and engaged in an endless struggle for survival, or as the products of "socioeconomic determinism," ruled by social and economic forces beyond their control. In their works, the Naturalists generally ignored the highest levels of society and focused on degradation: poverty, alcoholism, prostitution, insanity, and disease. Naturalism influenced authors throughout the world, including Henrik Ibsen and Thomas Hardy. In the United States, in particular, Naturalism had a profound impact. Among the authors who embraced its principles are Theodore Dreiser, Eugene O'Neill, Stephen Crane, Jack London, and Frank Norris.

Negritude: A literary movement based on the concept of a shared cultural bond on the part of black Africans, wherever they may be in the world. It traces its origins to the former French colonies of Africa and the Caribbean. Negritude poets, novelists, and essayists generally stress four points in their writings: One, black alienation from tradi-

tional African culture can lead to feelings of inferiority. Two, European colonialism and Western education should be resisted. Three, black Africans should seek to affirm and define their own identity. Four, African culture can and should be reclaimed. Many Negritude writers also claim that blacks can make unique contributions to the world, based on a heightened appreciation of nature, rhythm, and human emotions—aspects of life they say are not so highly valued in the materialistic and rationalistic West. Examples of Negritude literature include the poetry of both Senegalese Leopold Senghor in *Hosties noires* and Martiniquais Aime-Fernand Cesaire in *Return to My Native Land.*

Negro Renaissance: See *Harlem Renaissance*

Neoclassical Period: See *Neoclassicism*

Neoclassicism: In literary criticism, this term refers to the revival of the attitudes and styles of expression of classical literature. It is generally used to describe a period in European history beginning in the late seventeenth century and lasting until about 1800. In its purest form, Neoclassicism marked a return to order, proportion, restraint, logic, accuracy, and decorum. In England, where Neoclassicism perhaps was most popular, it reflected the influence of seventeenth- century French writers, especially dramatists. Neoclassical writers typically reacted against the intensity and enthusiasm of the Renaissance period. They wrote works that appealed to the intellect, using elevated language and classical literary forms such as satire and the ode. Neoclassical works were often governed by the classical goal of instruction. English neoclassicists included Alexander Pope, Jonathan Swift, Joseph Addison, Sir Richard Steele, John Gay, and Matthew Prior; French neoclassicists included Pierre Corneille and Jean-Baptiste Moliere. Also known as Age of Reason.

Neoclassicists: See *Neoclassicism*

New Criticism: A movement in literary criticism, dating from the late 1920s, that stressed close textual analysis in the interpretation of works of literature. The New Critics saw little merit in historical and biographical analysis. Rather, they aimed to examine the text alone, free from the question of how external events—biographical or otherwise—may have helped shape it. This predominantly American school was named "New Criticism" by one of its practitioners, John Crowe Ransom. Other important New Critics included Allen Tate, R. P. Blackmur, Robert Penn Warren, and Cleanth Brooks.

New Negro Movement: See *Harlem Renaissance*

Noble Savage: The idea that primitive man is noble and good but becomes evil and corrupted as he becomes civilized. The concept of the noble savage originated in the Renaissance period but is more closely identified with such later writers as Jean-Jacques Rousseau and Aphra Behn. First described in John Dryden's play *The Conquest of Granada,* the noble savage is portrayed by the various Native Americans in James Fenimore Cooper's "Leatherstocking Tales," by Queequeg, Daggoo, and Tashtego in Herman Melville's *Moby Dick,* and by John the Savage in Aldous Huxley's *Brave New World.*

O

Objective Correlative: An outward set of objects, a situation, or a chain of events corresponding to an inward experience and evoking this experience in the reader. The term frequently appears in modern criticism in discussions of authors' intended effects on the emotional responses of readers. This term was originally used by T. S. Eliot in his 1919 essay "Hamlet."

Objectivity: A quality in writing characterized by the absence of the author's opinion or feeling about the subject matter. Objectivity is an important factor in criticism. The novels of Henry James and, to a certain extent, the poems of John Larkin demonstrate objectivity, and it is central to John Keats's concept of "negative capability." Critical and journalistic writing usually are or attempt to be objective.

Occasional Verse: poetry written on the occasion of a significant historical or personal event. *Vers de societe* is sometimes called occasional verse although it is of a less serious nature. Famous examples of occasional verse include Andrew Marvell's "Horatian Ode upon Cromwell's Return from England," Walt Whitman's "When Lilacs Last in the Dooryard Bloom'd"— written upon the death of Abraham Lincoln—and Edmund Spenser's commemoration of his wedding, "Epithalamion."

Octave: A poem or stanza composed of eight lines. The term octave most often represents the first eight lines of a Petrarchan sonnet. An example of an octave is taken from a translation of a Petrarchan sonnet by Sir Thomas Wyatt: The pillar perisht is whereto I leant, The strongest stay of mine unquiet mind; The like of it no man again can find, From East to West Still seeking though he went. To mind unhap! for hap away hath rent Of all my joy the very

bark and rind; And I, alas, by chance am thus assigned Daily to mourn till death do it relent.

Ode: Name given to an extended lyric poem characterized by exalted emotion and dignified style. An ode usually concerns a single, serious theme. Most odes, but not all, are addressed to an object or individual. Odes are distinguished from other lyric poetic forms by their complex rhythmic and stanzaic patterns. An example of this form is John Keats's "Ode to a Nightingale."

Oedipus Complex: A son's amorous obsession with his mother. The phrase is derived from the story of the ancient Theban hero Oedipus, who unknowingly killed his father and married his mother. Literary occurrences of the Oedipus complex include Andre Gide's *Oedipe* and Jean Cocteau's *La Machine infernale,* as well as the most famous, Sophocles' *Oedipus Rex.*

Omniscience: See *Point of View*

Onomatopoeia: The use of words whose sounds express or suggest their meaning. In its simplest sense, onomatopoeia may be represented by words that mimic the sounds they denote such as "hiss" or "meow." At a more subtle level, the pattern and rhythm of sounds and rhymes of a line or poem may be onomatopoeic. A celebrated example of onomatopoeia is the repetition of the word "bells" in Edgar Allan Poe's poem "The Bells."

Opera: A type of stage performance, usually a drama, in which the dialogue is sung. Classic examples of opera include Giuseppi Verdi's *La traviata,* Giacomo Puccini's *La Boheme,* and Richard Wagner's *Tristan und Isolde.* Major twentieth- century contributors to the form include Richard Strauss and Alban Berg.

Operetta: A usually romantic comic opera. John Gay's *The Beggar's Opera,* Richard Sheridan's *The Duenna,* and numerous works by William Gilbert and Arthur Sullivan are examples of operettas.

Oral Tradition: See *Oral Transmission*

Oral Transmission: A process by which songs, ballads, folklore, and other material are transmitted by word of mouth. The tradition of oral transmission predates the written record systems of literate society. Oral transmission preserves material sometimes over generations, although often with variations. Memory plays a large part in the recitation and preservation of orally transmitted material. Breton lays, French *fabliaux,* national epics (including the Anglo- Saxon *Beowulf,* the Spanish *El Cid,* and the Finnish *Kalevala*), Native American myths and legends, and African folktales told by plantation slaves are examples of orally transmitted literature.

Oration: Formal speaking intended to motivate the listeners to some action or feeling. Such public speaking was much more common before the development of timely printed communication such as newspapers. Famous examples of oration include Abraham Lincoln's "Gettysburg Address" and Dr. Martin Luther King Jr.'s "I Have a Dream" speech.

Ottava Rima: An eight-line stanza of poetry composed in iambic pentameter (a five-foot line in which each foot consists of an unaccented syllable followed by an accented syllable), following the abababcc rhyme scheme. This form has been prominently used by such important English writers as Lord Byron, Henry Wadsworth Longfellow, and W. B. Yeats.

Oxymoron: A phrase combining two contradictory terms. Oxymorons may be intentional or unintentional. The following speech from William Shakespeare's *Romeo and Juliet* uses several oxymorons: Why, then, O brawling love! O loving hate! O anything, of nothing first create! O heavy lightness! serious vanity! Mis-shapen chaos of well-seeming forms! Feather of lead, bright smoke, cold fire, sick health! This love feel I, that feel no love in this.

P

Pantheism: The idea that all things are both a manifestation or revelation of God and a part of God at the same time. Pantheism was a common attitude in the early societies of Egypt, India, and Greece—the term derives from the Greek *pan* meaning "all" and *theos* meaning "deity." It later became a significant part of the Christian faith. William Wordsworth and Ralph Waldo Emerson are among the many writers who have expressed the pantheistic attitude in their works.

Parable: A story intended to teach a moral lesson or answer an ethical question. In the West, the best examples of parables are those of Jesus Christ in the New Testament, notably "The Prodigal Son," but parables also are used in Sufism, rabbinic literature, Hasidism, and Zen Buddhism.

Paradox: A statement that appears illogical or contradictory at first, but may actually point to an underlying truth. "Less is more" is an example of a paradox. Literary examples include Francis Bacon's statement, "The most corrected copies are commonly the least correct," and "All animals are equal, but some animals are more equal than others" from George Orwell's *Animal Farm*.

Parallelism: A method of comparison of two ideas in which each is developed in the same grammatical structure. Ralph Waldo Emerson's "Civilization" contains this example of parallelism: Raphael paints wisdom; Handel sings it, Phidias carves it, Shakespeare writes it, Wren builds it, Columbus sails it, Luther preaches it, Washington arms it, Watt mechanizes it.

Parnassianism: A mid nineteenth-century movement in French literature. Followers of the movement stressed adherence to well-defined artistic forms as a reaction against the often chaotic expression of the artist's ego that dominated the work of the Romantics. The Parnassians also rejected the moral, ethical, and social themes exhibited in the works of French Romantics such as Victor Hugo. The aesthetic doctrines of the Parnassians strongly influenced the later symbolist and decadent movements. Members of the Parnassian school include Leconte de Lisle, Sully Prudhomme, Albert Glatigny, Francois Coppee, and Theodore de Banville.

Parody: In literary criticism, this term refers to an imitation of a serious literary work or the signature style of a particular author in a ridiculous manner. A typical parody adopts the style of the original and applies it to an inappropriate subject for humorous effect. Parody is a form of satire and could be considered the literary equivalent of a caricature or cartoon. Henry Fielding's *Shamela* is a parody of Samuel Richardson's *Pamela*.

Pastoral: A term derived from the Latin word "pastor," meaning shepherd. A pastoral is a literary composition on a rural theme. The conventions of the pastoral were originated by the third-century Greek poet Theocritus, who wrote about the experiences, love affairs, and pastimes of Sicilian shepherds. In a pastoral, characters and language of a courtly nature are often placed in a simple setting. The term pastoral is also used to classify dramas, elegies, and lyrics that exhibit the use of country settings and shepherd characters. Percy Bysshe Shelley's "Adonais" and John Milton's "Lycidas" are two famous examples of pastorals.

Pastorela: The Spanish name for the shepherds play, a folk drama reenacted during the Christmas season. Examples of *pastorelas* include Gomez

Manrique's *Representacion del nacimiento* and the dramas of Lucas Fernandez and Juan del Encina.

Pathetic Fallacy: A term coined by English critic John Ruskin to identify writing that falsely endows nonhuman things with human intentions and feelings, such as "angry clouds" and "sad trees." The pathetic fallacy is a required convention in the classical poetic form of the pastoral elegy, and it is used in the modern poetry of T. S. Eliot, Ezra Pound, and the Imagists. Also known as Poetic Fallacy.

Pelado: Literally the "skinned one" or shirtless one, he was the stock underdog, sharp-witted picaresque character of Mexican vaudeville and tent shows. The *pelado* is found in such works as Don Catarino's *Los effectos de la crisis* and *Regreso a mi tierra.*

Pen Name: See *Pseudonym*

Pentameter: See *Meter*

Persona: A Latin term meaning "mask." *Personae* are the characters in a fictional work of literature. The *persona* generally functions as a mask through which the author tells a story in a voice other than his or her own. A *persona* is usually either a character in a story who acts as a narrator or an "implied author," a voice created by the author to act as the narrator for himself or herself. *Personae* include the narrator of Geoffrey Chaucer's *Canterbury Tales* and Marlow in Joseph Conrad's *Heart of Darkness.*

Personae: See *Persona*

Personal Point of View: See *Point of View*

Personification: A figure of speech that gives human qualities to abstract ideas, animals, and inanimate objects. William Shakespeare used personification in *Romeo and Juliet* in the lines "Arise, fair sun, and kill the envious moon,/ Who is already sick and pale with grief." Here, the moon is portrayed as being envious, sick, and pale with grief—all markedly human qualities. Also known as *Prosopopoeia.*

Petrarchan Sonnet: See *Sonnet*

Phenomenology: A method of literary criticism based on the belief that things have no existence outside of human consciousness or awareness. Proponents of this theory believe that art is a process that takes place in the mind of the observer as he or she contemplates an object rather than a quality of the object itself. Among phenomenological critics

are Edmund Husserl, George Poulet, Marcel Raymond, and Roman Ingarden.

Picaresque Novel: Episodic fiction depicting the adventures of a roguish central character ("picaro" is Spanish for "rogue"). The picaresque hero is commonly a low-born but clever individual who wanders into and out of various affairs of love, danger, and farcical intrigue. These involvements may take place at all social levels and typically present a humorous and wide-ranging satire of a given society. Prominent examples of the picaresque novel are *Don Quixote* by Miguel de Cervantes, *Tom Jones* by Henry Fielding, and *Moll Flanders* by Daniel Defoe.

Plagiarism: Claiming another person's written material as one's own. Plagiarism can take the form of direct, word-for- word copying or the theft of the substance or idea of the work. A student who copies an encyclopedia entry and turns it in as a report for school is guilty of plagiarism.

Platonic Criticism: A form of criticism that stresses an artistic work's usefulness as an agent of social engineering rather than any quality or value of the work itself. Platonic criticism takes as its starting point the ancient Greek philosopher Plato's comments on art in his *Republic.*

Platonism: The embracing of the doctrines of the philosopher Plato, popular among the poets of the Renaissance and the Romantic period. Platonism is more flexible than Aristotelian Criticism and places more emphasis on the supernatural and unknown aspects of life. Platonism is expressed in the love poetry of the Renaissance, the fourth book of Baldassare Castiglione's *The Book of the Courtier,* and the poetry of William Blake, William Wordsworth, Percy Bysshe Shelley, Friedrich Holderlin, William Butler Yeats, and Wallace Stevens.

Play: See *Drama*

Plot: In literary criticism, this term refers to the pattern of events in a narrative or drama. In its simplest sense, the plot guides the author in composing the work and helps the reader follow the work. Typically, plots exhibit causality and unity and have a beginning, a middle, and an end. Sometimes, however, a plot may consist of a series of disconnected events, in which case it is known as an "episodic plot." In his *Aspects of the Novel,* E. M. Forster distinguishes between a story, defined as a "narrative of events arranged in their time- sequence," and plot, which organizes the events to a "sense of causality." This definition closely mirrors Aristotle's discussion of plot in his *Poetics.*

Poem: In its broadest sense, a composition utilizing rhyme, meter, concrete detail, and expressive language to create a literary experience with emotional and aesthetic appeal. Typical poems include sonnets, odes, elegies, *haiku,* ballads, and free verse.

Poet: An author who writes poetry or verse. The term is also used to refer to an artist or writer who has an exceptional gift for expression, imagination, and energy in the making of art in any form. Well-known poets include Horace, Basho, Sir Philip Sidney, Sir Edmund Spenser, John Donne, Andrew Marvell, Alexander Pope, Jonathan Swift, George Gordon, Lord Byron, John Keats, Christina Rossetti, W. H. Auden, Stevie Smith, and Sylvia Plath.

Poetic Fallacy: See *Pathetic Fallacy*

Poetic Justice: An outcome in a literary work, not necessarily a poem, in which the good are rewarded and the evil are punished, especially in ways that particularly fit their virtues or crimes. For example, a murderer may himself be murdered, or a thief will find himself penniless.

Poetic License: Distortions of fact and literary convention made by a writer—not always a poet—for the sake of the effect gained. Poetic license is closely related to the concept of "artistic freedom." An author exercises poetic license by saying that a pile of money "reaches as high as a mountain" when the pile is actually only a foot or two high.

Poetics: This term has two closely related meanings. It denotes (1) an aesthetic theory in literary criticism about the essence of poetry or (2) rules prescribing the proper methods, content, style, or diction of poetry. The term poetics may also refer to theories about literature in general, not just poetry.

Poetry: In its broadest sense, writing that aims to present ideas and evoke an emotional experience in the reader through the use of meter, imagery, connotative and concrete words, and a carefully constructed structure based on rhythmic patterns. Poetry typically relies on words and expressions that have several layers of meaning. It also makes use of the effects of regular rhythm on the ear and may make a strong appeal to the senses through the use of imagery. Edgar Allan Poe's "Annabel Lee" and Walt Whitman's *Leaves of Grass* are famous examples of poetry.

Point of View: The narrative perspective from which a literary work is presented to the reader.

There are four traditional points of view. The "third person omniscient" gives the reader a "godlike" perspective, unrestricted by time or place, from which to see actions and look into the minds of characters. This allows the author to comment openly on characters and events in the work. The "third person" point of view presents the events of the story from outside of any single character's perception, much like the omniscient point of view, but the reader must understand the action as it takes place and without any special insight into characters' minds or motivations. The "first person" or "personal" point of view relates events as they are perceived by a single character. The main character "tells" the story and may offer opinions about the action and characters which differ from those of the author. Much less common than omniscient, third person, and first person is the "second person" point of view, wherein the author tells the story as if it is happening to the reader. James Thurber employs the omniscient point of view in his short story "The Secret Life of Walter Mitty." Ernest Hemingway's "A Clean, Well-Lighted Place" is a short story told from the third person point of view. Mark Twain's novel *Huck Finn* is presented from the first person viewpoint. Jay McInerney's *Bright Lights, Big City* is an example of a novel which uses the second person point of view.

Polemic: A work in which the author takes a stand on a controversial subject, such as abortion or religion. Such works are often extremely argumentative or provocative. Classic examples of polemics include John Milton's *Aeropagitica* and Thomas Paine's *The American Crisis.*

Pornography: Writing intended to provoke feelings of lust in the reader. Such works are often condemned by critics and teachers, but those which can be shown to have literary value are viewed less harshly. Literary works that have been described as pornographic include Ovid's *The Art of Love,* Margaret of Angouleme's *Heptameron,* John Cleland's *Memoirs of a Woman of Pleasure; or, the Life of Fanny Hill,* the anonymous *My Secret Life,* D. H. Lawrence's *Lady Chatterley's Lover,* and Vladimir Nabokov's *Lolita.*

Post-Aesthetic Movement: An artistic response made by African Americans to the black aesthetic movement of the 1960s and early '70s. Writers since that time have adopted a somewhat different tone in their work, with less emphasis placed on the disparity between black and white in the United States. In the words of post-aesthetic authors such as Toni Morrison, John Edgar Wideman, and Kristin Hunter, African Americans are portrayed as looking inward for answers to their own questions, rather than always looking to the outside world. Two well-known examples of works produced as part of the post-aesthetic movement are the Pulitzer Prize-winning novels *The Color Purple* by Alice Walker and *Beloved* by Toni Morrison.

Postmodernism: Writing from the 1960s forward characterized by experimentation and continuing to apply some of the fundamentals of modernism, which included existentialism and alienation. Postmodernists have gone a step further in the rejection of tradition begun with the modernists by also rejecting traditional forms, preferring the anti-novel over the novel and the anti-hero over the hero. Postmodern writers include Alain Robbe-Grillet, Thomas Pynchon, Margaret Drabble, John Fowles, Adolfo Bioy-Casares, and Gabriel Garcia Marquez.

Pre-Raphaelites: A circle of writers and artists in mid nineteenth-century England. Valuing the pre-Renaissance artistic qualities of religious symbolism, lavish pictorialism, and natural sensuousness, the Pre-Raphaelites cultivated a sense of mystery and melancholy that influenced later writers associated with the Symbolist and Decadent movements. The major members of the group include Dante Gabriel Rossetti, Christina Rossetti, Algernon Swinburne, and Walter Pater.

Primitivism: The belief that primitive peoples were nobler and less flawed than civilized peoples because they had not been subjected to the tainting influence of society. Examples of literature espousing primitivism include Aphra Behn's *Oroonoko: Or, The History of the Royal Slave,* Jean-Jacques Rousseau's *Julie ou la Nouvelle Heloise,* Oliver Goldsmith's *The Deserted Village,* the poems of Robert Burns, Herman Melville's stories *Typee, Omoo,* and *Mardi,* many poems of William Butler Yeats and Robert Frost, and William Golding's novel *Lord of the Flies.*

Projective Verse: A form of free verse in which the poet's breathing pattern determines the lines of the poem. Poets who advocate projective verse are against all formal structures in writing, including meter and form. Besides its creators, Robert Creeley, Robert Duncan, and Charles Olson, two other well-known projective verse poets are Denise Levertov and LeRoi Jones (Amiri Baraka). Also known as Breath Verse.

Prologue: An introductory section of a literary work. It often contains information establishing the situation of the characters or presents information about the setting, time period, or action. In drama, the prologue is spoken by a chorus or by one of the principal characters. In the ''General Prologue'' of *The Canterbury Tales,* Geoffrey Chaucer describes the main characters and establishes the setting and purpose of the work.

Prose: A literary medium that attempts to mirror the language of everyday speech. It is distinguished from poetry by its use of unmetered, unrhymed language consisting of logically related sentences. Prose is usually grouped into paragraphs that form a cohesive whole such as an essay or a novel. Recognized masters of English prose writing include Sir Thomas Malory, William Caxton, Raphael Holinshed, Joseph Addison, Mark Twain, and Ernest Hemingway.

Prosopopoeia: See *Personification*

Protagonist: The central character of a story who serves as a focus for its themes and incidents and as the principal rationale for its development. The protagonist is sometimes referred to in discussions of modern literature as the hero or anti-hero. Well-known protagonists are Hamlet in William Shakespeare's *Hamlet* and Jay Gatsby in F. Scott Fitzgerald's *The Great Gatsby.*

Protest Fiction: Protest fiction has as its primary purpose the protesting of some social injustice, such as racism or discrimination. One example of protest fiction is a series of five novels by Chester Himes, beginning in 1945 with *If He Hollers Let Him Go* and ending in 1955 with *The Primitive.* These works depict the destructive effects of race and gender stereotyping in the context of interracial relationships. Another African American author whose works often revolve around themes of social protest is John Oliver Killens. James Baldwin's essay ''Everybody's Protest Novel'' generated controversy by attacking the authors of protest fiction.

Proverb: A brief, sage saying that expresses a truth about life in a striking manner. ''They are not all cooks who carry long knives'' is an example of a proverb.

Pseudonym: A name assumed by a writer, most often intended to prevent his or her identification as the author of a work. Two or more authors may work together under one pseudonym, or an author may use a different name for each genre he or she publishes in. Some publishing companies maintain ''house pseudonyms,'' under which any number of authors may write installations in a series. Some authors also choose a pseudonym over their real names the way an actor may use a stage name. Examples of pseudonyms (with the author's real name in parentheses) include Voltaire (Francois-Marie Arouet), Novalis (Friedrich von Hardenberg), Currer Bell (Charlotte Bronte), Ellis Bell (Emily Bronte), George Eliot (Maryann Evans), Honorio Bustos Donmecq (Adolfo Bioy-Casares and Jorge Luis Borges), and Richard Bachman (Stephen King).

Pun: A play on words that have similar sounds but different meanings. A serious example of the pun is from John Donne's ''A Hymne to God the Father'': Sweare by thyself, that at my death thy sonne Shall shine as he shines now, and hereto fore; And, having done that, Thou haste done; I fear no more.

Pure Poetry: poetry written without instructional intent or moral purpose that aims only to please a reader by its imagery or musical flow. The term pure poetry is used as the antonym of the term ''didacticism.'' The poetry of Edgar Allan Poe, Stephane Mallarme, Paul Verlaine, Paul Valery, Juan Ramoz Jimenez, and Jorge Guillen offer examples of pure poetry.

Q

Quatrain: A four-line stanza of a poem or an entire poem consisting of four lines. The following quatrain is from Robert Herrick's ''To Live Merrily, and to Trust to Good Verses'': Round, round, the root do's run; And being ravisht thus, Come, I will drink a Tun To my *Propertius*.

R

Raisonneur: A character in a drama who functions as a spokesperson for the dramatist's views. The *raisonneur* typically observes the play without becoming central to its action. *Raisonneurs* were very common in plays of the nineteenth century.

Realism: A nineteenth-century European literary movement that sought to portray familiar characters, situations, and settings in a realistic manner. This was done primarily by using an objective narrative point of view and through the buildup of accurate detail. The standard for success of any realistic work depends on how faithfully it transfers common experience into fictional forms. The realistic method may be altered or extended, as in stream of consciousness writing, to record highly subjec-

tive experience. Seminal authors in the tradition of Realism include Honore de Balzac, Gustave Flaubert, and Henry James.

Refrain: A phrase repeated at intervals throughout a poem. A refrain may appear at the end of each stanza or at less regular intervals. It may be altered slightly at each appearance. Some refrains are non-sense expressions—as with ''Nevermore'' in Edgar Allan Poe's ''The Raven''—that seem to take on a different significance with each use.

Renaissance: The period in European history that marked the end of the Middle Ages. It began in Italy in the late fourteenth century. In broad terms, it is usually seen as spanning the fourteenth, fifteenth, and sixteenth centuries, although it did not reach Great Britain, for example, until the 1480s or so. The Renaissance saw an awakening in almost every sphere of human activity, especially science, philosophy, and the arts. The period is best defined by the emergence of a general philosophy that emphasized the importance of the intellect, the individual, and world affairs. It contrasts strongly with the medieval worldview, characterized by the dominant concerns of faith, the social collective, and spiritual salvation. Prominent writers during the Renaissance include Niccolo Machiavelli and Baldassare Castiglione in Italy, Miguel de Cervantes and Lope de Vega in Spain, Jean Froissart and Francois Rabelais in France, Sir Thomas More and Sir Philip Sidney in England, and Desiderius Erasmus in Holland.

Repartee: Conversation featuring snappy retorts and witticisms. Masters of *repartee* include Sydney Smith, Charles Lamb, and Oscar Wilde. An example is recorded in the meeting of ''Beau'' Nash and John Wesley: Nash said, ''I never make way for a fool,'' to which Wesley responded, ''Don't you? I always do,'' and stepped aside.

Resolution: The portion of a story following the climax, in which the conflict is resolved. The resolution of Jane Austen's *Northanger Abbey* is neatly summed up in the following sentence: ''Henry and Catherine were married, the bells rang and every body smiled.''

Restoration: See *Restoration Age*

Restoration Age: A period in English literature beginning with the crowning of Charles II in 1660 and running to about 1700. The era, which was characterized by a reaction against Puritanism, was the first great age of the comedy of manners. The finest literature of the era is typically witty and urbane, and often lewd. Prominent Restoration Age writers include William Congreve, Samuel Pepys, John Dryden, and John Milton.

Revenge Tragedy: A dramatic form popular during the Elizabethan Age, in which the protagonist, directed by the ghost of his murdered father or son, inflicts retaliation upon a powerful villain. Notable features of the revenge tragedy include violence, bizarre criminal acts, intrigue, insanity, a hesitant protagonist, and the use of soliloquy. Thomas Kyd's *Spanish Tragedy* is the first example of revenge tragedy in English, and William Shakespeare's *Hamlet* is perhaps the best. Extreme examples of revenge tragedy, such as John Webster's *The Duchess of Malfi,* are labeled "tragedies of blood." Also known as Tragedy of Blood.

Revista: The Spanish term for a vaudeville musical revue. Examples of *revistas* include Antonio Guzman Aguilera's *Mexico para los mexicanos,* Daniel Vanegas's *Maldito jazz,* and Don Catarino's *Whiskey, morfina y marihuana* and *El desterrado.*

Rhetoric: In literary criticism, this term denotes the art of ethical persuasion. In its strictest sense, rhetoric adheres to various principles developed since classical times for arranging facts and ideas in a clear, persuasive, appealing manner. The term is also used to refer to effective prose in general and theories of or methods for composing effective prose. Classical examples of rhetorics include *The Rhetoric of Aristotle,* Quintillian's *Institutio Oratoria,* and Cicero's *Ad Herennium.*

Rhetorical Question: A question intended to provoke thought, but not an expressed answer, in the reader. It is most commonly used in oratory and other persuasive genres. The following lines from Thomas Gray's "Elegy Written in a Country Churchyard" ask rhetorical questions: Can storied urn or animated bust Back to its mansion call the fleeting breath? Can Honour's voice provoke the silent dust, Or Flattery soothe the dull cold ear of Death?

Rhyme: When used as a noun in literary criticism, this term generally refers to a poem in which words sound identical or very similar and appear in parallel positions in two or more lines. Rhymes are classified into different types according to where they fall in a line or stanza or according to the degree of similarity they exhibit in their spellings and sounds. Some major types of rhyme are "masculine" rhyme, "feminine" rhyme, and "triple" rhyme. In a masculine rhyme, the rhyming sound falls in a single accented syllable, as with "heat"

and "eat." Feminine rhyme is a rhyme of two syllables, one stressed and one unstressed, as with "merry" and "tarry." Triple rhyme matches the sound of the accented syllable and the two unaccented syllables that follow: "narrative" and "declarative." Robert Browning alternates feminine and masculine rhymes in his "Soliloquy of the Spanish Cloister": Gr-r-r—there go, my heart's abhorrence! Water your damned flower-pots, do! If hate killed men, Brother Lawrence, God's blood, would not mine kill you! What? Your myrtle-bush wants trimming? Oh, that rose has prior claims— Needs its leaden vase filled brimming? Hell dry you up with flames! Triple rhymes can be found in Thomas Hood's "Bridge of Sighs," George Gordon Byron's satirical verse, and Ogden Nash's comic poems.

Rhyme Royal: A stanza of seven lines composed in iambic pentameter and rhymed *ababbcc.* The name is said to be a tribute to King James I of Scotland, who made much use of the form in his poetry. Examples of rhyme royal include Geoffrey Chaucer's *The Parlement of Foules,* William Shakespeare's *The Rape of Lucrece,* William Morris's *The Early Paradise,* and John Masefield's *The Widow in the Bye Street.*

Rhyme Scheme: See *Rhyme*

Rhythm: A regular pattern of sound, time intervals, or events occurring in writing, most often and most discernably in poetry. Regular, reliable rhythm is known to be soothing to humans, while interrupted, unpredictable, or rapidly changing rhythm is disturbing. These effects are known to authors, who use them to produce a desired reaction in the reader. An example of a form of irregular rhythm is sprung rhythm poetry; quantitative verse, on the other hand, is very regular in its rhythm.

Rising Action: The part of a drama where the plot becomes increasingly complicated. Rising action leads up to the climax, or turning point, of a drama. The final "chase scene" of an action film is generally the rising action which culminates in the film's climax.

Rococo: A style of European architecture that flourished in the eighteenth century, especially in France. The most notable features of *rococo* are its extensive use of ornamentation and its themes of lightness, gaiety, and intimacy. In literary criticism, the term is often used disparagingly to refer to a decadent or over-ornamental style. Alexander Pope's "The Rape of the Lock" is an example of literary *rococo.*

Roman a clef: A French phrase meaning "novel with a key." It refers to a narrative in which real persons are portrayed under fictitious names. Jack Kerouac, for example, portrayed various real-life beat generation figures under fictitious names in his *On the Road.*

Romance: A broad term, usually denoting a narrative with exotic, exaggerated, often idealized characters, scenes, and themes. Nathaniel Hawthorne called his *The House of the Seven Gables* and *The Marble Faun* romances in order to distinguish them from clearly realistic works.

Romantic Age: See *Romanticism*

Romanticism: This term has two widely accepted meanings. In historical criticism, it refers to a European intellectual and artistic movement of the late eighteenth and early nineteenth centuries that sought greater freedom of personal expression than that allowed by the strict rules of literary form and logic of the eighteenth-century neoclassicists. The Romantics preferred emotional and imaginative expression to rational analysis. They considered the individual to be at the center of all experience and so placed him or her at the center of their art. The Romantics believed that the creative imagination reveals nobler truths—unique feelings and attitudes—than those that could be discovered by logic or by scientific examination. Both the natural world and the state of childhood were important sources for revelations of "eternal truths." "Romanticism" is also used as a general term to refer to a type of sensibility found in all periods of literary history and usually considered to be in opposition to the principles of classicism. In this sense, Romanticism signifies any work or philosophy in which the exotic or dreamlike figure strongly, or that is devoted to individualistic expression, self-analysis, or a pursuit of a higher realm of knowledge than can be discovered by human reason. Prominent Romantics include Jean-Jacques Rousseau, William Wordsworth, John Keats, Lord Byron, and Johann Wolfgang von Goethe.

Romantics: See *Romanticism*

Russian Symbolism: A Russian poetic movement, derived from French symbolism, that flourished between 1894 and 1910. While some Russian Symbolists continued in the French tradition, stressing aestheticism and the importance of suggestion above didactic intent, others saw their craft as a form of mystical worship, and themselves as mediators between the supernatural and the mundane. Russian symbolists include Aleksandr Blok, Vyacheslav Ivanovich Ivanov, Fyodor Sologub, Andrey Bely, Nikolay Gumilyov, and Vladimir Sergeyevich Solovyov.

S

Satire: A work that uses ridicule, humor, and wit to criticize and provoke change in human nature and institutions. There are two major types of satire: "formal" or "direct" satire speaks directly to the reader or to a character in the work; "indirect" satire relies upon the ridiculous behavior of its characters to make its point. Formal satire is further divided into two manners: the "Horatian," which ridicules gently, and the "Juvenalian," which derides its subjects harshly and bitterly. Voltaire's novella *Candide* is an indirect satire. Jonathan Swift's essay "A Modest Proposal" is a Juvenalian satire.

Scansion: The analysis or "scanning" of a poem to determine its meter and often its rhyme scheme. The most common system of scansion uses accents (slanted lines drawn above syllables) to show stressed syllables, breves (curved lines drawn above syllables) to show unstressed syllables, and vertical lines to separate each foot. In the first line of John Keats's *Endymion,* "A thing of beauty is a joy forever:" the word "thing," the first syllable of "beauty," the word "joy," and the second syllable of "forever" are stressed, while the words "A" and "of," the second syllable of "beauty," the word "a," and the first and third syllables of "forever" are unstressed. In the second line: "Its loveliness increases; it will never" a pair of vertical lines separate the foot ending with "increases" and the one beginning with "it."

Scene: A subdivision of an act of a drama, consisting of continuous action taking place at a single time and in a single location. The beginnings and endings of scenes may be indicated by clearing the stage of actors and props or by the entrances and exits of important characters. The first act of William Shakespeare's *Winter's Tale* is comprised of two scenes.

Science Fiction: A type of narrative about or based upon real or imagined scientific theories and technology. Science fiction is often peopled with alien creatures and set on other planets or in different dimensions. Karel Capek's *R.U.R.* is a major work of science fiction.

Second Person: See *Point of View*

Semiotics: The study of how literary forms and conventions affect the meaning of language. Semioticians include Ferdinand de Saussure, Charles Sanders Pierce, Claude Levi-Strauss, Jacques Lacan, Michel Foucault, Jacques Derrida, Roland Barthes, and Julia Kristeva.

Sestet: Any six-line poem or stanza. Examples of the sestet include the last six lines of the Petrarchan sonnet form, the stanza form of Robert Burns's "A Poet's Welcome to his love-begotten Daughter," and the sestina form in W. H. Auden's "Paysage Moralise."

Setting: The time, place, and culture in which the action of a narrative takes place. The elements of setting may include geographic location, characters' physical and mental environments, prevailing cultural attitudes, or the historical time in which the action takes place. Examples of settings include the romanticized Scotland in Sir Walter Scott's "Waverley" novels, the French provincial setting in Gustave Flaubert's *Madame Bovary,* the fictional Wessex country of Thomas Hardy's novels, and the small towns of southern Ontario in Alice Munro's short stories.

Shakespearean Sonnet: See *Sonnet*

Signifying Monkey: A popular trickster figure in black folklore, with hundreds of tales about this character documented since the 19th century. Henry Louis Gates Jr. examines the history of the signifying monkey in *The Signifying Monkey: Towards a Theory of Afro-American Literary Criticism,* published in 1988.

Simile: A comparison, usually using "like" or "as", of two essentially dissimilar things, as in "coffee as cold as ice" or "He sounded like a broken record." The title of Ernest Hemingway's "Hills Like White Elephants" contains a simile.

Slang: A type of informal verbal communication that is generally unacceptable for formal writing. Slang words and phrases are often colorful exaggerations used to emphasize the speaker's point; they may also be shortened versions of an often-used word or phrase. Examples of American slang from the 1990s include "yuppie" (an acronym for Young Urban Professional), "awesome" (for "excellent"), wired (for "nervous" or "excited"), and "chill out" (for relax).

Slant Rhyme: See *Consonance*

Slave Narrative: Autobiographical accounts of American slave life as told by escaped slaves. These works first appeared during the abolition movement of the 1830s through the 1850s. Olaudah Equiano's *The Interesting Narrative of Olaudah Equiano, or Gustavus Vassa, The African* and Harriet Ann Jacobs's *Incidents in the Life of a Slave Girl* are examples of the slave narrative.

Social Realism: See *Socialist Realism*

Socialist Realism: The Socialist Realism school of literary theory was proposed by Maxim Gorky and established as a dogma by the first Soviet Congress of Writers. It demanded adherence to a communist worldview in works of literature. Its doctrines required an objective viewpoint comprehensible to the working classes and themes of social struggle featuring strong proletarian heroes. A successful work of socialist realism is Nikolay Ostrovsky's *Kak zakalyalas stal* (*How the Steel Was Tempered*). Also known as Social Realism.

Soliloquy: A monologue in a drama used to give the audience information and to develop the speaker's character. It is typically a projection of the speaker's innermost thoughts. Usually delivered while the speaker is alone on stage, a soliloquy is intended to present an illusion of unspoken reflection. A celebrated soliloquy is Hamlet's "To be or not to be" speech in William Shakespeare's *Hamlet.*

Sonnet: A fourteen-line poem, usually composed in iambic pentameter, employing one of several rhyme schemes. There are three major types of sonnets, upon which all other variations of the form are based: the "Petrarchan" or "Italian" sonnet, the "Shakespearean" or "English" sonnet, and the "Spenserian" sonnet. A Petrarchan sonnet consists of an octave rhymed *abbaabba* and a "sestet" rhymed either *cdecde, cdccdc,* or *cdedce.* The octave poses a question or problem, relates a narrative, or puts forth a proposition; the sestet presents a solution to the problem, comments upon the narrative, or applies the proposition put forth in the octave. The Shakespearean sonnet is divided into three quatrains and a couplet rhymed *abab cdcd efef gg.* The couplet provides an epigrammatic comment on the narrative or problem put forth in the quatrains. The Spenserian sonnet uses three quatrains and a couplet like the Shakespearean, but links their three rhyme schemes in this way: *abab bcbc cdcd ee.* The Spenserian sonnet develops its theme in two parts like the Petrarchan, its final six lines resolving a problem, analyzing a narrative, or applying a proposition put forth in its first eight lines. Examples of sonnets can be found in Petrarch's *Canzoniere,* Edmund Spenser's *Amoretti,* Elizabeth Barrett

Browning's *Sonnets from the Portuguese,* Rainer Maria Rilke's *Sonnets to Orpheus,* and Adrienne Rich's poem "The Insusceptibles."

Spenserian Sonnet: See *Sonnet*

Spenserian Stanza: A nine-line stanza having eight verses in iambic pentameter, its ninth verse in iambic hexameter, and the rhyme scheme ababbcbcc. This stanza form was first used by Edmund Spenser in his allegorical poem *The Faerie Queene.*

Spondee: In poetry meter, a foot consisting of two long or stressed syllables occurring together. This form is quite rare in English verse, and is usually composed of two monosyllabic words. The first foot in the following line from Robert Burns's "Green Grow the Rashes" is an example of a spondee: Green grow the rashes, O

Sprung Rhythm: Versification using a specific number of accented syllables per line but disregarding the number of unaccented syllables that fall in each line, producing an irregular rhythm in the poem. Gerard Manley Hopkins, who coined the term "sprung rhythm," is the most notable practitioner of this technique.

Stanza: A subdivision of a poem consisting of lines grouped together, often in recurring patterns of rhyme, line length, and meter. Stanzas may also serve as units of thought in a poem much like paragraphs in prose. Examples of stanza forms include the quatrain, *terza rima, ottava rima,* Spenserian, and the so-called *In Memoriam* stanza from Alfred, Lord Tennyson's poem by that title. The following is an example of the latter form: Love is and was my lord and king, And in his presence I attend To hear the tidings of my friend, Which every hour his couriers bring.

Stereotype: A stereotype was originally the name for a duplication made during the printing process; this led to its modern definition as a person or thing that is (or is assumed to be) the same as all others of its type. Common stereotypical characters include the absent- minded professor, the nagging wife, the troublemaking teenager, and the kindhearted grandmother.

Stream of Consciousness: A narrative technique for rendering the inward experience of a character. This technique is designed to give the impression of an ever-changing series of thoughts, emotions, images, and memories in the spontaneous and seemingly illogical order that they occur in life. The

textbook example of stream of consciousness is the last section of James Joyce's *Ulysses.*

Structuralism: A twentieth-century movement in literary criticism that examines how literary texts arrive at their meanings, rather than the meanings themselves. There are two major types of structuralist analysis: one examines the way patterns of linguistic structures unify a specific text and emphasize certain elements of that text, and the other interprets the way literary forms and conventions affect the meaning of language itself. Prominent structuralists include Michel Foucault, Roman Jakobson, and Roland Barthes.

Structure: The form taken by a piece of literature. The structure may be made obvious for ease of understanding, as in nonfiction works, or may obscured for artistic purposes, as in some poetry or seemingly "unstructured" prose. Examples of common literary structures include the plot of a narrative, the acts and scenes of a drama, and such poetic forms as the Shakespearean sonnet and the Pindaric ode.

Sturm und Drang: A German term meaning "storm and stress." It refers to a German literary movement of the 1770s and 1780s that reacted against the order and rationalism of the enlightenment, focusing instead on the intense experience of extraordinary individuals. Highly romantic, works of this movement, such as Johann Wolfgang von Goethe's *Gotz von Berlichingen,* are typified by realism, rebelliousness, and intense emotionalism.

Style: A writer's distinctive manner of arranging words to suit his or her ideas and purpose in writing. The unique imprint of the author's personality upon his or her writing, style is the product of an author's way of arranging ideas and his or her use of diction, different sentence structures, rhythm, figures of speech, rhetorical principles, and other elements of composition. Styles may be classified according to period (Metaphysical, Augustan, Georgian), individual authors (Chaucerian, Miltonic, Jamesian), level (grand, middle, low, plain), or language (scientific, expository, poetic, journalistic).

Subject: The person, event, or theme at the center of a work of literature. A work may have one or more subjects of each type, with shorter works tending to have fewer and longer works tending to have more. The subjects of James Baldwin's novel *Go Tell It on the Mountain* include the themes of father-son relationships, religious conversion, black life, and sexuality. The subjects of Anne Frank's

Diary of a Young Girl include Anne and her family members as well as World War II, the Holocaust, and the themes of war, isolation, injustice, and racism.

Subjectivity: Writing that expresses the author's personal feelings about his subject, and which may or may not include factual information about the subject. Subjectivity is demonstrated in James Joyce's *Portrait of the Artist as a Young Man,* Samuel Butler's *The Way of All Flesh,* and Thomas Wolfe's *Look Homeward, Angel.*

Subplot: A secondary story in a narrative. A subplot may serve as a motivating or complicating force for the main plot of the work, or it may provide emphasis for, or relief from, the main plot. The conflict between the Capulets and the Montagues in William Shakespeare's *Romeo and Juliet* is an example of a subplot.

Surrealism: A term introduced to criticism by Guillaume Apollinaire and later adopted by Andre Breton. It refers to a French literary and artistic movement founded in the 1920s. The Surrealists sought to express unconscious thoughts and feelings in their works. The best-known technique used for achieving this aim was automatic writing—transcriptions of spontaneous outpourings from the unconscious. The Surrealists proposed to unify the contrary levels of conscious and unconscious, dream and reality, objectivity and subjectivity into a new level of ''super-realism.'' Surrealism can be found in the poetry of Paul Eluard, Pierre Reverdy, and Louis Aragon, among others.

Suspense: A literary device in which the author maintains the audience's attention through the buildup of events, the outcome of which will soon be revealed. Suspense in William Shakespeare's *Hamlet* is sustained throughout by the question of whether or not the Prince will achieve what he has been instructed to do and of what he intends to do.

Syllogism: A method of presenting a logical argument. In its most basic form, the syllogism consists of a major premise, a minor premise, and a conclusion. An example of a syllogism is: Major premise: When it snows, the streets get wet. Minor premise: It is snowing. Conclusion: The streets are wet.

Symbol: Something that suggests or stands for something else without losing its original identity. In literature, symbols combine their literal meaning with the suggestion of an abstract concept. Literary symbols are of two types: those that carry complex associations of meaning no matter what their con-

texts, and those that derive their suggestive meaning from their functions in specific literary works. Examples of symbols are sunshine suggesting happiness, rain suggesting sorrow, and storm clouds suggesting despair.

Symbolism: This term has two widely accepted meanings. In historical criticism, it denotes an early modernist literary movement initiated in France during the nineteenth century that reacted against the prevailing standards of realism. Writers in this movement aimed to evoke, indirectly and symbolically, an order of being beyond the material world of the five senses. Poetic expression of personal emotion figured strongly in the movement, typically by means of a private set of symbols uniquely identifiable with the individual poet. The principal aim of the Symbolists was to express in words the highly complex feelings that grew out of everyday contact with the world. In a broader sense, the term ''symbolism'' refers to the use of one object to represent another. Early members of the Symbolist movement included the French authors Charles Baudelaire and Arthur Rimbaud; William Butler Yeats, James Joyce, and T. S. Eliot were influenced as the movement moved to Ireland, England, and the United States. Examples of the concept of symbolism include a flag that stands for a nation or movement, or an empty cupboard used to suggest hopelessness, poverty, and despair.

Symbolist: See *Symbolism*

Symbolist Movement: See *Symbolism*

Sympathetic Fallacy: See *Affective Fallacy*

T

Tale: A story told by a narrator with a simple plot and little character development. Tales are usually relatively short and often carry a simple message. Examples of tales can be found in the work of Rudyard Kipling, Somerset Maugham, Saki, Anton Chekhov, Guy de Maupassant, and Armistead Maupin.

Tall Tale: A humorous tale told in a straightforward, credible tone but relating absolutely impossible events or feats of the characters. Such tales were commonly told of frontier adventures during the settlement of the west in the United States. Tall tales have been spun around such legendary heroes as Mike Fink, Paul Bunyan, Davy Crockett, Johnny Appleseed, and Captain Stormalong as well as the real-life William F. Cody and Annie Oakley. Literary use of tall tales can be found in Washington Irving's *History of New York,* Mark Twain's *Life on the Mississippi,* and in the German R. F. Raspe's *Baron Munchausen's Narratives of His Marvellous Travels and Campaigns in Russia.*

Tanka: A form of Japanese poetry similar to *haiku.* A *tanka* is five lines long, with the lines containing five, seven, five, seven, and seven syllables respectively. Skilled *tanka* authors include Ishikawa Takuboku, Masaoka Shiki, Amy Lowell, and Adelaide Crapsey.

Teatro Grottesco: See *Theater of the Grotesque*

Terza Rima: A three-line stanza form in poetry in which the rhymes are made on the last word of each line in the following manner: the first and third lines of the first stanza, then the second line of the first stanza and the first and third lines of the second stanza, and so on with the middle line of any stanza rhyming with the first and third lines of the following stanza. An example of *terza rima* is Percy Bysshe Shelley's ''The Triumph of Love'': As in that trance of wondrous thought I lay This was the tenour of my waking dream. Methought I sate beside a public way Thick strewn with summer dust, and a great stream Of people there was hurrying to and fro Numerous as gnats upon the evening gleam,. . .

Tetrameter: See *Meter*

Textual Criticism: A branch of literary criticism that seeks to establish the authoritative text of a literary work. Textual critics typically compare all known manuscripts or printings of a single work in order to assess the meanings of differences and revisions. This procedure allows them to arrive at a definitive version that (supposedly) corresponds to the author's original intention. Textual criticism was applied during the Renaissance to salvage the classical texts of Greece and Rome, and modern works have been studied, for instance, to undo deliberate correction or censorship, as in the case of novels by Stephen Crane and Theodore Dreiser.

Theater of Cruelty: Term used to denote a group of theatrical techniques designed to eliminate the psychological and emotional distance between actors and audience. This concept, introduced in the 1930s in France, was intended to inspire a more intense theatrical experience than conventional theater allowed. The ''cruelty'' of this dramatic theory signified not sadism but heightened actor/audience involvement in the dramatic event. The theater of cruelty was theorized by Antonin Artaud in his *Le Theatre et son double (The Theatre and Its Double),* and also appears in the work of Jerzy Grotowski, Jean Genet, Jean Vilar, and Arthur Adamov, among others.

Theater of the Absurd: A post-World War II dramatic trend characterized by radical theatrical innovations. In works influenced by the Theater of the absurd, nontraditional, sometimes grotesque characterizations, plots, and stage sets reveal a meaningless universe in which human values are irrelevant. Existentialist themes of estrangement, absurdity, and futility link many of the works of this movement. The principal writers of the Theater of the Absurd are Samuel Beckett, Eugene Ionesco, Jean Genet, and Harold Pinter.

Theater of the Grotesque: An Italian theatrical movement characterized by plays written around the ironic and macabre aspects of daily life in the World War I era. Theater of the Grotesque was named after the play *The Mask and the Face* by Luigi Chiarelli, which was described as ''a grotesque in three acts.'' The movement influenced the work of Italian dramatist Luigi Pirandello, author of *Right You Are, If You Think You Are.* Also known as *Teatro Grottesco.*

Theme: The main point of a work of literature. The term is used interchangeably with thesis. The theme of William Shakespeare's *Othello*—jealousy—is a common one.

Thesis: A thesis is both an essay and the point argued in the essay. Thesis novels and thesis plays share the quality of containing a thesis which is supported through the action of the story. A master's thesis and a doctoral dissertation are two theses required of graduate students.

Thesis Play: See *Thesis*

Three Unities: See *Unities*

Tone: The author's attitude toward his or her audience may be deduced from the tone of the work. A formal tone may create distance or convey politeness, while an informal tone may encourage a friendly, intimate, or intrusive feeling in the reader. The author's attitude toward his or her subject matter may also be deduced from the tone of the words he or she uses in discussing it. The tone of John F. Kennedy's speech which included the appeal to ''ask not what your country can do for you'' was intended to instill feelings of camaraderie and national pride in listeners.

Tragedy: A drama in prose or poetry about a noble, courageous hero of excellent character who, because of some tragic character flaw or *hamartia*, brings ruin upon him- or herself. Tragedy treats its subjects in a dignified and serious manner, using poetic language to help evoke pity and fear and bring about catharsis, a purging of these emotions. The tragic form was practiced extensively by the ancient Greeks. In the Middle Ages, when classical works were virtually unknown, tragedy came to denote any works about the fall of persons from exalted to low conditions due to any reason: fate, vice, weakness, etc. According to the classical definition of tragedy, such works present the ''pathetic''—that which evokes pity—rather than the tragic. The classical form of tragedy was revived in the sixteenth century; it flourished especially on the Elizabethan stage. In modern times, dramatists have attempted to adapt the form to the needs of modern society by drawing their heroes from the ranks of ordinary men and women and defining the nobility of these heroes in terms of spirit rather than exalted social standing. The greatest classical example of tragedy is Sophocles' *Oedipus Rex*. The ''pathetic'' derivation is exemplified in ''The Monk's Tale'' in Geoffrey Chaucer's *Canterbury Tales.* Notable works produced during the sixteenth century revival include William Shakespeare's *Hamlet, Othello,* and *King Lear.* Modern dramatists working in the tragic tradition include Henrik Ibsen, Arthur Miller, and Eugene O'Neill.

Tragedy of Blood: See *Revenge Tragedy*

Tragic Flaw: In a tragedy, the quality within the hero or heroine which leads to his or her downfall. Examples of the tragic flaw include Othello's jealousy and Hamlet's indecisiveness, although most great tragedies defy such simple interpretation.

Transcendentalism: An American philosophical and religious movement, based in New England from around 1835 until the Civil War. Transcendentalism was a form of American romanticism that had its roots abroad in the works of Thomas Carlyle, Samuel Coleridge, and Johann Wolfgang von Goethe. The Transcendentalists stressed the importance of intuition and subjective experience in communication with God. They rejected religious dogma and texts in favor of mysticism and scientific naturalism. They pursued truths that lie beyond the ''colorless'' realms perceived by reason and the senses and were active social reformers in public education, women's rights, and the abolition of slavery. Promi-

nent members of the group include Ralph Waldo Emerson and Henry David Thoreau.

Trickster: A character or figure common in Native American and African literature who uses his ingenuity to defeat enemies and escape difficult situations. Tricksters are most often animals, such as the spider, hare, or coyote, although they may take the form of humans as well. Examples of trickster tales include Thomas King's *A Coyote Columbus Story,* Ashley F. Bryan's *The Dancing Granny* and Ishmael Reed's *The Last Days of Louisiana Red.*

Trimeter: See *Meter*

Triple Rhyme: See *Rhyme*

Trochee: See *Foot*

U

Understatement: See *Irony*

Unities: Strict rules of dramatic structure, formulated by Italian and French critics of the Renaissance and based loosely on the principles of drama discussed by Aristotle in his *Poetics.* Foremost among these rules were the three unities of action, time, and place that compelled a dramatist to: (1) construct a single plot with a beginning, middle, and end that details the causal relationships of action and character; (2) restrict the action to the events of a single day; and (3) limit the scene to a single place or city. The unities were observed faithfully by continental European writers until the Romantic Age, but they were never regularly observed in English drama. Modern dramatists are typically more concerned with a unity of impression or emotional effect than with any of the classical unities. The unities are observed in Pierre Corneille's tragedy *Polyeuctes* and Jean-Baptiste Racine's *Phedre.* Also known as Three Unities.

Urban Realism: A branch of realist writing that attempts to accurately reflect the often harsh facts of modern urban existence. Some works by Stephen Crane, Theodore Dreiser, Charles Dickens, Fyodor Dostoyevsky, Emile Zola, Abraham Cahan, and Henry Fuller feature urban realism. Modern examples include Claude Brown's *Manchild in the Promised Land* and Ron Milner's *What the Wine Sellers Buy.*

Utopia: A fictional perfect place, such as ''paradise'' or ''heaven.'' Early literary utopias were included in Plato's *Republic* and Sir Thomas More's *Utopia,* while more modern utopias can be found in

Samuel Butler's *Erewhon,* Theodor Herzka's *A Visit to Freeland,* and H. G. Wells' *A Modern Utopia.*

Utopian: See *Utopia*

Utopianism: See *Utopia*

V

Verisimilitude: Literally, the appearance of truth. In literary criticism, the term refers to aspects of a work of literature that seem true to the reader. Verisimilitude is achieved in the work of Honore de Balzac, Gustave Flaubert, and Henry James, among other late nineteenth-century realist writers.

Vers de societe: See *Occasional Verse*

Vers libre: See *Free Verse*

Verse: A line of metered language, a line of a poem, or any work written in verse. The following line of verse is from the epic poem *Don Juan* by Lord Byron: "My way is to begin with the beginning."

Versification: The writing of verse. Versification may also refer to the meter, rhyme, and other mechanical components of a poem. Composition of a "Roses are red, violets are blue" poem to suit an occasion is a common form of versification practiced by students.

Victorian: Refers broadly to the reign of Queen Victoria of England (1837–1901) and to anything with qualities typical of that era. For example, the qualities of smug narrowmindedness, bourgeois materialism, faith in social progress, and priggish morality are often considered Victorian. This stereotype is contradicted by such dramatic intellectual developments as the theories of Charles Darwin, Karl Marx, and Sigmund Freud (which stirred strong debates in England) and the critical attitudes of serious Victorian writers like Charles Dickens and George Eliot. In literature, the Victorian Period was the great age of the English novel, and the latter part of the era saw the rise of movements such as decadence and symbolism. Works of Victorian lit-

erature include the poetry of Robert Browning and Alfred, Lord Tennyson, the criticism of Matthew Arnold and John Ruskin, and the novels of Emily Bronte, William Makepeace Thackeray, and Thomas Hardy. Also known as Victorian Age and Victorian Period.

Victorian Age: See *Victorian*

Victorian Period: See *Victorian*

W

Weltanschauung: A German term referring to a person's worldview or philosophy. Examples of *weltanschauung* include Thomas Hardy's view of the human being as the victim of fate, destiny, or impersonal forces and circumstances, and the disillusioned and laconic cynicism expressed by such poets of the 1930s as W. H. Auden, Sir Stephen Spender, and Sir William Empson.

Weltschmerz: A German term meaning "world pain." It describes a sense of anguish about the nature of existence, usually associated with a melancholy, pessimistic attitude. *Weltschmerz* was expressed in England by George Gordon, Lord Byron in his *Manfred* and *Childe Harold's Pilgrimage,* in France by Viscount de Chateaubriand, Alfred de Vigny, and Alfred de Musset, in Russia by Aleksandr Pushkin and Mikhail Lermontov, in Poland by Juliusz Slowacki, and in America by Nathaniel Hawthorne.

Z

Zarzuela: A type of Spanish operetta. Writers of *zarzuelas* include Lope de Vega and Pedro Calderon.

Zeitgeist: A German term meaning "spirit of the time." It refers to the moral and intellectual trends of a given era. Examples of *zeitgeist* include the preoccupation with the more morbid aspects of dying and death in some Jacobean literature, especially in the works of dramatists Cyril Tourneur and John Webster, and the decadence of the French Symbolists.

Cumulative
Author/Title Index

Nationality/Ethnicity Index

Subject/Theme Index